Economics: An Analytical Introduction

To my parents Asher and Regina,
My wife Daphna,
My son Alon,
My daughter Tamar.

Economics: An Analytical Introduction

Amos Witztum

OXFORD
UNIVERSITY PRESS

OXFORD

UNIVERSITY PRESS

Great Clarendon Street, Oxford OX2 6DP

Oxford University Press is a department of the University of Oxford.
It furthers the University's objective of excellence in research, scholarship,
and education by publishing worldwide in

Oxford New York

Auckland Cape Town Dar es Salaam Hong Kong Karachi
Kuala Lumpur Madrid Melbourne Mexico City Nairobi
New Delhi Shanghai Taipei Toronto

With offices in

Argentina Austria Brazil Chile Czech Republic France Greece
Guatemala Hungary Italy Japan Poland Portugal Singapore
South Korea Switzerland Thailand Turkey Ukraine Vietnam

Oxford is a registered trade mark of Oxford University Press
in the UK and in certain other countries

Published in the United States
by Oxford University Press Inc., New York

British Library Cataloguing in Publication Data
(Data available)

Library of Congress Cataloging in Publication Data
(Data available)

ISBN 978–0–19–927163–4

Typeset by Newgen Imaging Systems (P) Ltd., Chennai, India
Printed in Great Britain
on acid-free paper by
CPI Group (UK) Ltd, Croydon, CR0 4YY

■ BRIEF CONTENTS

■ CONTENTS

▪ PREFACE AND ACKNOWLEDGEMENTS

This book had been long in the making. Since I became responsible for the introductory course of the University of London's programme for External Students, I felt a need to design a course that would teach the core of economic analysis for what it really is: a sophisticated and powerful language with which to deal with social issues. Over the years I had written a considerable amount of material for the UOL programme for External Students which culminated in an extensive *Subject Guide* upon which this book has been based.

The experience at the UOL-programme for External Students was crucial to the production of this book. Against the trend of lowering expectations I have had the opportunity to experiment the effects on students of an increase in expectations. Instead of concentrating on trying to persuade students that economics actually describes the world out there and feed them with endless boxes which purport to demonstrate it, I felt that there was a greater need to better develop their critical faculties. This means both to recognize some of the difficulties with setting up the models as well as some of the difficulties in their application. This is by no means an easy task and sometimes one may lose sight of the main objective when one engages in gaining command over complex concepts. But perhaps the best way of achieving this is by concentrating on a better understanding of the internal logic of the various tools of analysis and their correspondence with daily language rather than by relying on their descriptive powers.

The results were very encouraging. In spite of the great diversity in the intake of the programme for External Students, students rose to the challenge. By following the *Subject Guide* students were able to achieve quite remarkable abilities in dealing with new problems and new challenges. I am therefore grateful to the University of London Programme for External Students, for both supporting my attempts to raise standards as well as producing the material in the *Subject Guide*. In particular, I am grateful to the team at Mrs Gosling's office at the London School of Economics who worked hard on producing the original *Subject Guide*. In particular I wish to thank Sam Carpenter and Mark Baltovic for their invaluable technical support in the process. I am also grateful to Rosie Gosling and Alan Marin who gave an overall support to my activities within the External Programme.

I also wish to thank Joe Pearlman from London Metropolitan University, Saul Estrin from London Business School, Oren Sussman from Oxford University, Richard Jackman, John Lane and Diane Reynier from the London School of Economics, Aditya Goenka from Essex University, Andrei Tolstopiatenko and Simon Commander from the World Bank, Oleg Zamkov and Natalia Frolova from the International College of Economics and Finance in Moscow whose continuous enthusiasm and support has kept my faith in this project.

A special thank is due to Oxford University Press and in particular, Tim Page, for their confidence, support and perseverance. I am also in debt to their wonderful production team.

Most of all, naturally, I am in debt to my parents, Asher and Regina and grateful to my family who had to suffer the slings and arrows of someone who wanted to be. The love of my wife, Daphna and my two children, Alon and Tamar, has been an immeasurable source of strength, comfort and inspiration. They are, perhaps, the most important means in the production of this book.

GENERAL INTRODUCTION

You are about to embark on the study of *economic analysis*. The motivation for studying economics can vary considerably, but once the decision to study has been made, it makes sense to use the opportunity to get the most out of the subject. Economics as a discipline deals with the broad issue of resource allocation. Within it, an ongoing debate is raging over the question of how best to organize economic activities such that the allocation of resources will achieve what society desires. The developments within this debate feed continuously into political discussions and thus expose all members of society to the consequences of economic investigation. The academic side of economics provides the concepts, tools of analysis, and reasoning upon which such a debate is based. To be able to understand the logic of an existing system or the motivation behind the drive for its change, one must necessarily understand economics. Besides the obvious benefits to society from having better informed citizens, such an understanding can provide you with the ability to take advantage of the system—an ability and drive which are naturally taken into account in economic analysis.

The purpose of this book is to assist you in your endeavour and to guide you through the labyrinth of material. There are, of course, many textbooks around, and I would like to explain how this one is different from the others. There are two main underlying themes which distinguish this text from others. One is substantive and the other, pedagogical.

Let me begin with the substantive difference. Economics is a broad subject. A quick glance at some of the major textbooks is sufficient to make even the bravest of students faint. Apart from the scary geometrical and algebraic expositions, there is the issue of quantity. The subject matter of economics appears to be so enormous that one begins to wonder whether studying it is not just another form of Sisyphean work.[1]

Although it is true that the subject matter of economics is broad, it does not follow that the study of it should become so laborious. To see this, one must ask what exactly economics is. There are many possible answers to this question. Some would tend towards arguing that economics is a science which is capable of accurately *describing* the social-economic environment and able both to explain and predict changes in it. From this point of view, the author of a textbook would wish to persuade the reader of the success of his economics by demonstrating its success in describing the world around us.

Another approach is based on the understanding that economics is really *a way of thinking: a language*. In the narrow sense of the word, it is a way of thinking about those things which are defined as economic activities. In a broader sense, it is a method of thinking about all questions concerning the organization of society. The scope of the subject (its *semantics*) can, therefore, sometimes appear to be almost unlimited. However, the subject itself—the principles of analysis (its *grammar*)—is very well defined and well under control.

In other words, unlike most other textbooks, I will not make an implicit assumption that economics is a successful science. This means that I will not try to persuade you through boxes and case studies that economics has a good record of successful predictions or useful explanations. Nor will I try to show you that the success of economics is a reason to apply it—as it is—in all other areas of the social sciences. By saying this I am not trying to imply that economics has not been successful. If it had not, why would I want you to study it? Instead, my underlying assumption is that economics has been very successful, but as a *language* rather than as a hard science. Obviously, these are very contentious statements and perhaps not the right way of starting a textbook in the subject. Nevertheless, it is this understanding of economics as an academic discipline which lies behind the structure of this textbook.

The purpose of this book is to introduce the student to the fundamentals of economic *analysis*. This means that what we are concerned with is the study of the way economists think rather than the extent of what they have said.

So the good news about this perception of the subject is that a great deal of what appears in some other books is of less interest to us. The bad news is that, as we are dealing with a language and a method of analysis, logic (hence mathematics) is an important component of our subject. Still, before you panic, let me qualify this and say that most logical arguments can also be presented in a less formal way. Therefore, although mathematics lies at the heart of the subject by virtue of being a form of logic, mathematical expositions are not an essential part of learning the language of economics.

The pedagogical element that distinguishes this book is, of course, not unrelated to the substantive issue. In contrast to the breadth of some introductory textbooks, this book is much more focused. This means that instead of becoming acquainted with a little bit about a lot of things, I would like you to gain a real command over fewer things. The key difference here is between 'becoming acquainted' and 'gaining command'. For the former, one would normally need to know about concepts in economics. To 'gain command', however, one needs to know the concepts. Evidently, there is a profound difference between studying for these two kinds of purpose.

To *know about* economics, it is indeed sufficient to read about the various economic concepts. Then, whenever you encounter them, you will understand what is meant by these concepts. This is almost the same as being able to recognize the meaning of words in a foreign language. But this, as I am sure you will agree, is far from being sufficient to be able to *speak* a foreign language. To achieve this, one has to learn some grammar too. Most textbooks tend to emphasize the 'words' which are used in economics. I, on the other hand, wish to emphasize its 'grammar'.

To *know what* concepts are, one must not only acquaint oneself with their meaning; one must also be able to use them. This means that, after learning about the concept, one must do as many *application exercises* as possible. Exercises can, however, sometimes be misleading. A question such as 'explain the meaning of concept A' is *not* an exercise question. An exercise is a *problem*, normally described in daily language, where the student is expected to

1. choose the right framework of analysis with which to deal with the problem;
2. translate the real-life situation (described in real-life language) into the language of the model;
3. use the model, or the concept, to derive a solution to the problem.

In this book you will find a great deal of this. You will find that after setting up the concepts and basic tools of analysis—sometimes in a critical manner—the book takes you through a set of such exercises trying to ensure that you both understand the tools of analysis (and their limitation) and are capable of relating them to the real world around us.

How to Study

To make full use of this book in learning the language of economics, it is recommended that before you examine my solution to a problem, you try to solve it yourself and then compare your own solution to the one which is provided in the book. If they do not match, it is not sufficient for you to say, 'Oh, *now* I understand the answer'. When you understand the answer provided it means only that you understand how *I do it*. This does not mean that you can do it yourself. In other words, you probably have obtained only what may be called *passive understanding*. To reach the level of *active understanding* you must go over your own solution and try to understand what it is that led you to answer the way you did. Only by clearing away embedded misconceptions will the route to learning the new language be clear.

Whether or not you have access to any teaching institute, the key to a good learning process is group work. Of course, one can learn on one's own, but having someone else with whom one can communicate is very important. If there are not enough people around you who study the same course, it would still be useful if you could persuade someone to work with you. What you should then do is to try to explain to them what you have been learning. If you succeed in teaching economics to your neighbour's cousin, you have done very well.

There are two reasons why it is important to study with others. First, you are exposed to alternative ways of thinking, which is almost universally an enriching experience. Second, by having to articulate your own arguments you are raising the level of economics in your cognition. Thus, your understanding becomes part of the way you think and your ability to *speak* economics will be considerably enhanced.

Some Basic Tools

Many students find the use of mathematics in economics intimidating. There are no sound reasons for this fear. Although there is some use of mathematical *notation*, the level of mathematical analysis which is required is very low indeed. Still, to ensure that technical problems do not create unnecessary obstacles, I recommend that before you do anything else you focus on clarifying such basic concepts as what is meant by a point in a plane, a function, a graph, a slope, a derivative, and tangency. In particular, you must have a good understanding of slopes as these are very important tools in understanding the geometrical expositions of the subject. To assist in this endeavour I would like to direct you to the short Technical Notes in which I introduce students to the most basic notions of mathematics and geometry.

Do not start work before these basic tools are properly understood.

NOTES

1. Sisyphus, king of Corinth, is a figure from Greek mythology who was doomed, for his tyranny and wickedness, to endless labour in the Underworld. He had to push uphill a heavy rock which would always slip from his arms to roll down to the bottom.

1 **Introduction**

■ **MAJOR POINTS IN SUMMARY**

In this chapter we examine some general principles associated with human inquiry and examine the origin of the two central concepts in modern economics: efficiency and price. We shall see that these concepts are the immediate derivatives of the way in which we perceive an economic problem.

1.1 Economics as a theory

1.1.1 What is economics all about?

Perhaps the most general definition of the subject can be given in the following way: economics is the discipline which studies the organization of economic activities in society. You may, at first, think that this is too much of an abstraction. After all, how do questions such as 'how much to produce?' or 'for whom to produce?' or 'at what price to produce?' or, perhaps a more immediate question, 'how can I make money?' relate to the general problem of the social organization of economic activities?

The response to these questions is fairly straightforward. The institutions created by society to resolve what is perceived to be the economic problem will have detrimental effects on the answers to any of the above questions. Thus, issues such as 'how much to produce?' (or what can be more broadly framed as 'how to produce?') or 'how to make money?' will inevitably depend on whether society adopts, say, competitive institutions as opposed to cooperative ones. It will also depend on the degree to which the system is decentralized. Naturally, the system that will emerge will be a manifestation of the solution to what is commonly perceived as the 'economic problem'.

From daily encounters with economic analysis I am sure that the two terms which are probably most closely associated with the subject in your mind are **efficiency** and **opportunity cost**. As you will see in Section 1.2, the economic problem underlying modern economic analysis is that of reconciling unlimited (or unsatiated) wants with universal scarcity. These two fundamental concepts (of efficiency and opportunity costs) in modern economic analysis are derived directly from this problem, that is, we measure economic performance in terms of efficiency, and opportunity costs constitute the modern conception of price. Remove this definition of the economic problem and efficiency may no longer be the criterion of economic performance. Nor would opportunity cost be the benchmark of price. As these two concepts are so important, so is the perception of the economic problem from which they have been derived.

There are two questions which immediately come to mind regarding both the economic problem and its proposed solutions. First, is there an economic problem which is universal both in time and space? Namely, is what we nowadays consider as the economic problem also perceived as such by every culture on the globe at any particular point in time (*space*) and, has it always been perceived as such (*time*)? Second, does a particular perception of the economic problem dictate a single type of institutional solution?

Clearly these are very complex questions and answering them is not easy. My short version of the answer to both questions is negative. Namely, the perception of the economic problem underlying modern economics is by no means universal in either time or space. And, any particular perception of the economic problem does not necessitate a single type of institutional solution.

Consider, for instance, the Greeks: both Plato (*c*.427–347 BC) and Aristotle (*c*.384–322 BC) wrote extensively on social organization. While it is true that neither of them wrote a treatise on economics, some elements of economic organization are present in the writings of both scholars. Moreover, the fact that they did not write about economics separately is in itself significant, as it implies that the principles of economic organization cannot be detached from the general principles of social organization. Of course, the reason why they thought so could be attributed to their ignorance of the extent and complexity of economic systems. However, given that the period in history when economics was perceived as an independent subject of inquiry was very short indeed, ignorance is probably not the main reason for the way in which both Plato and Aristotle treated economics.

Both Plato and Aristotle were broadly concerned with the organization of a just society. In as much as there was a well-defined economic problem in their writings it would probably have been defined in the same terms, which is, how to organize economic activity in a way that would be consistent with the principles of a just society and would promote virtuous behaviour.

But while both of them probably conceived of the economic problem in the same manner, they came up with extremely different recommendations with regard to economic organization. Plato, on the one hand, in his *Republic*, promoted a social division of labour (society was equated to the human body). The division into social classes was based on productivity principles. People who are wise should rule, those who are strong and shrewd should guard and the others should use their skills to supply the rest.[1] What leads Plato to this particular institutional solution is his epistemology, that is, his theory of knowledge. Plato believes that we cannot always trust our senses (read his simile of the cave in *Republic*, part 7, section 7) and that there is a difference between the appearance of things and their substance. Thus, while we can all identify a just action, only the educated (the philosophers) know what justice is. Hence, his social division of labour is geared up to let those, who know what justice is, rule. Aristotle, on the other hand, examines the question of what constitutes justice from a more down to earth perspective. He examines it from the point of view of what ordinary people would consider to be a virtuous character.

He thus reaches the conclusion that virtue lies in 'lying in the mean', namely, moderation. Consequently, he feels that the organization of society should be geared to support moderate behaviour. While a division of labour within the household would be beneficent as it will help each household satisfy their need, a division of labour across households is not recommended as it would promote greed. In books 7–8 of his *Politics* Aristotle debates the relationship between happiness and prosperity. In his view, of course, happiness is a virtue which may, sometimes, dictate imprudent actions. Thus we observe that (a) the Greeks had an economic problem, very different from ours, in mind and (b) that although both Plato and Aristotle tried to solve the same economic problem, their solutions differed considerably.

In more modern times, throughout the industrial revolution, a new perception of the economic problem took hold. The economic problem of classical economics was, broadly speaking, one of output maximization and growth. Adam Smith wrote in his *Wealth of Nations*[2] that the objective of political economy is, 'to provide a plentiful revenue or subsistence for the people' (*Wealth of Nations* (WN), p. 428). However, for him, one of the most important elements was the ability of society to supply all individuals with their needs.[3] But even here, a schism emerged. Marx too, was interested in how to best organize society so that all needs are met. However, posing the question led Smith (and others) to suggest a system of decentralized decisionmaking where competition is dominant as a means to resolve the problem, Marx argued that such a system would not be effective. Instead, he argued, only when society becomes successful in organizing its social division of labour consciously (and a priori, via some sort of planning) will it move out of its naturalist state into real autonomy.

Thus again, we see that classical economics which, by and large, tried to resolve the problem of satisfying the needs of a people who had increasingly become dependent on each other, managed to come up with completely the opposite form of social organization. This is yet another example that the economic problem has not always been perceived in the same manner as we see it today and that, even when perceived in a particular manner, the institutional recommendation which follows the attempts to resolve it are not necessarily of the same nature.

Evidently, the answers to questions like 'how much to produce', 'what determines prices' and 'how can I make money' are going to be fundamentally different in the different types of system mentioned above. In the end, the advice and the recommendations of the economist are all derivatives of the perceived principles which guide and direct the social organization of economic activities.

1.1.2 What is a theory?

The philosophy of science is a broad and complex area. I do not attempt to summarize it here but merely to demonstrate some of the difficulties.

The world around us seems complex and irregular. Human beings, however, have always been drawn to the idea that there is some order in this apparent chaos. The way to go about it is to try and create an order in our mind about the world around us. Whether, or not, and how such an order relates to the real world are complex questions. At this stage I would like to demonstrate the issue with a little, and specific, example.

Suppose that the political party in government of a certain country wishes to devise a strategy for reelection. They turn to some analysts to ask for recommendations on how to develop a suitable strategy. In order to advise the party in power, the analysts must find what it is that makes people vote for the government. They distribute questionnaires in which they ask people about their general dispositions and economic circumstances. They have discovered two rules:

1. Rich people are Happy people.
2. Happy people vote for the government.

Note that these assertions do not have to be a result of the use of questionnaires. The analysts could have made these statements as assumptions: statements which most people will be willing to accept as being generally true.

Moreover, to make these assertions the analysts would need to explain what exactly they mean by 'Happy' and 'Rich'. Does 'Happy' describe someone who is jumping up and down from joy at least three times a day or someone who is just not looking for a new job? Does 'Rich' mean having a lot of money with huge debt to the Mafia or simply having no debt at all? In other words, there is a need to agree on what exactly it is that we are talking about. This primary stage of any theory is where the subject matters of the investigation are defined.

The first phase, therefore, in building a theory which—our analysts hope—will explain why and how governments win elections is to define the relevant components which we believe are likely to influence the outcome.

Let us suppose that one way or another our analysts propose clear definitions of what they believe will affect the reelection of the party in power: Riches, Happiness, Government, and Money. Adding to this our two observations from above, we have the foundation of a theory:

Definition 'Rich people' (denoted by R), 'Happiness' (denoted by H), 'Government' (denoted by G), 'Money' (denoted by M).

Axioms[4] 1. 'Rich people are Happy', or 'R are H';
            2. 'Happy people vote for the Government', or 'H vote G'.

What we need now is a rule of inference: a method by which we can enrich our understanding beyond the two axioms that we, presumably, know. Aristotelian syllogism, for instance, is an example of such a rule of inference. It works in the following way:

Premise 1   all humans are mortal;
Premise 2   Aristotle is human;

Conclusion   *Aristotle is Mortal.*

In our case this will become the following:

Axiom 1   R is H

Axiom 2   H votes G

Conclusion   R (Rich people) vote for G (the government)

We call such a conclusion a **Theorem**:

Theorem   Rich people vote for the government; (or, R vote for G).

What we have created here is a **system of logic**. Axioms plus a rule of inference define a logical system. The conclusions of logical systems are always *logically true* provided that there has been no mistake in the application of the rule of inference. However, this does not mean that these conclusions are also *empirically*[5] *true*. Namely, some statements may be logically true but they might not be confirmable in reality.

The system of logic that we have described yields a set of theorems (or propositions) which are the main body of the theory. As I said before, the theory will be logically true provided that we have applied the rules of inference correctly. This, however, will not tell us whether or not reality supports the theory.

On the whole, the theory produces two types of statements: *explanations* and *predictions*. A prediction is something which we may be able to confirm by some sort of testing. In such a case we may say that the theory is *verifiable*, or *confirmable*. However, the fact that a theory produces good prediction does not automatically confirm its explanation. In our case, the following propositions will be derived from the above theorem:

Prediction   If you give people M they will vote G;

Explanation   People vote G *because* they have M.

In our theory, the prediction is that if we gave people money the government would win the election. This may also be confirmed by observations. We may find that throughout history people were given more money before the election and the party in government consistently returned to power. Does it mean that people vote for the government *because* they had been given more money? Not necessarily.

Suppose now that all elections throughout history took place during spring. Suppose also that there is a flower called Eternum subjugatum which blooms for a short period in the spring and that its bloom produces a certain scent in the air which acts like a drug. Every spring, people act as if they were collectively intoxicated and they all become subjugated and timid. They accept authority without question and do all that the people in power tell them to do. Can we still say that the empirical truth of our prediction also confirms our explanation? Not really.

Naturally, in this case it would be easy to design an experiment by setting the elections on a different date and sometimes give people money and sometimes not. But in more complex situations, where experimentation may not be possible, a situation like the above means that we cannot really trust the evidence to lend empirical truth to our prediction.

The problem here is that *causality*, basically, is not observable. What we normally see are two events occurring in a given sequence. Always B comes after A. Can we say that

A causes B? Well, this is a big question. I am not the man, and this is not the place, to answer it. Nevertheless, it is important to bear this in mind and always be cautious not to confuse correlation (the systematic relation in the occurrence of events) with causality. Therefore, the explanatory content of a theory is many times more difficult to handle.

Naturally, if we believed that the premises of the theory were empirically true, then we would been more inclined to believe the explanation which is offered by the theory (by expecting the logical structure of the theory to carry the empirical truth value of the premises to the propositions). For this, of course, we must also believe that nature is, indeed, governed by logic and this is not necessarily obvious.

Whenever the premises are not believed to be necessarily empirically true, the explanatory side of the theory remains questionable. In the end, it will be these properties of the theory which will determine its limitations.

To a great extent, the problem of **normative** and **positive** economics developed around these questions. What exactly is meant by 'positive' is highly debatable, like the questions surrounding our perceptions and our ability to observe. Generally speaking, people tend to associate the 'is' statement with what is 'positive'. Once we understand what is meant by positive we shall be able to see immediately what is normative.

Here is an 'is' statement: 'John is tall'. This appears to be an innocent enough statement of fact which would, generally speaking, appear 'positive'. Still, the meaning of this statement cannot be considered as universally true. Among short people John may be tall but in a different environment he may not really be 'tall'. Therefore, perhaps a truly positive statement would be 'John is 6' 10'''.

Now, suppose that the price level in an economy is comprised of the prices of five goods. Let each good have a different weight in our price level according to the relative amount of spending on that good. If only one good is purchased and everybody spends their entire income on it, its weight in the price level should be 1. A good that nobody consumes will have a weight of zero. Let α_i represent the weight of good i (i will be a number between 1 and 5):

$$P = \alpha_1 p_1 + \alpha_2 p_2 + \alpha_3 p_3 + \alpha_4 p_4 + \alpha_5 p_5 = \sum_{i=1}^{5} \alpha_i p_i$$

where

$$\alpha_1 + \alpha_2 + \alpha_3 + \alpha_4 + \alpha_5 = 1.$$

A change in the general price level will reflect the weighted sum of the changes in individual prices in the price index. We denoted a change in the price level by: dP. Hence, the general price level will change according to the following equation:

$$dP = \alpha_1 dp_1 + \alpha_2 dp_2 + \alpha_3 dp_3 + \alpha_4 dp_4 + \alpha_5 dp_5 = \sum_{i=1}^{5} \alpha_i dp_i$$

Example   Let the goods and weights be given as in Table 1.1

Now, suppose that the prices of the various goods have changed in the following way: Bread + 20% (hence, $dp_1 = 0.2$); Fuel + 20% ($dp_2 = 0.2$); Transport + 10%; Holidays (ski) −40% (hence, $dp_4 = -0.4$); Health + 10%.

The general price level will then rise by 11%. (Can you explain why?)

Table 1.1 Various goods and weights

	Good	Weight (α_i)
1	Bread	0.4
2	Fuel	0.2
3	Transport	0.1
4	Holiday	0.1
5	Health	0.2

How much of an 'is' statement would it be if I said, The 'prices have gone up by 11%'? For families who never go on a skiing holiday, this will be far from the reality of their lives. For them, the price of their typical consumption bundle will rise by more than 11%. Moreover, if I now chose to change the weights of the various goods in the price index then the statement, 'The prices have gone up by 11%', would simply be incorrect. But the reason it would be incorrect is not because it failed to describe reality. Rather, it would be wrong, because to begin with it was describing a socially constructed reality. As the convention about that which goes into the price index changes, so will the 'positive' nature of any socially constructed 'is' statement about changes in the price level. In short, the crucial point here is that a choice was involved in the formulation of this 'positive' statement. Each particular weighing system reflected what a particular person felt to be a better conception of 'price'. 'Price' here is more an 'idea' than a fact.

It is true that a statement like 'the price of bread has gone up by 20%' may appear as a more convincing positive statement. We all know exactly what is meant by the price of bread and we can observe that it has gone up by 20%. Nevertheless, this is a bit of an empty exercise. What it is that we observe is that the money price of bread has gone up but the meaning of this money price may vary according to the interpretation one gives to the concepts of 'money' and 'price'. So it is true that we can agree that the money price of bread has risen by 20%, but we will not necessarily agree on what it means. In the end, it is the meaning that counts and this, after all, is a matter of choice.

Some people tend to think of normative statements as those statements which reflect value judgement; for example, 'It is good that the price of bread has gone up by 20%'. This, evidently, is a blatantly normative statement. But 'good' and 'bad' seem to have a distinct status simply because we think of these concepts as being subjective. That is to say, it is a matter of individual choice which generates their value system. However, it is also a matter of individual choice which generates the conceptual framework which pours meaningful content into the statement 'the price of bread has gone up by 20%'.

What I am trying to say is that while the standard interpretation of the normative–positive divide is based on the difference between description and judgement, the world of economic theory is full of 'judgemental descriptions'. I would, therefore, recommend caution with apparent positive statements as well as respect to blatant normative judgements. After all, we are all human.

All the above arguments may appear to be dismissive of economics, but if this is your impression you cannot be further from the truth. It is the strength and beauty of the social sciences that they combine our natural social dispositions with the way we form and understand the institutions of society.

1.2 The fundamental economic problem

The first step in understanding economics is to form an idea of its domain. In other words, what makes something a subject of economic investigation? Or, which is almost the same thing, what is an economic good?

There may be different answers to this question which, in turn, will suggest different economic theories. Although it is important to consider different definitions of economic goods, I will concentrate on what I will term the **neoclassical** interpretation.

Definition   Everything which is both **scarce** and **desirable** is an **economic good**.

What is meant by scarcity is not difficult to imagine. Still, it must be noted that scarcity is defined in space and time. When in a certain place and at a certain point of time something is scarce, then it is an economic good. It will remain one even if plenty of the stuff is available either elsewhere or in due course.

What is meant by desirability is a bit more complex. In general it is everything which we desire. However, we do not distinguish between what we desire because we *need* it and what we desire because we *want* it. Some would argue that this is a deficiency of the definition but we shall overlook this problem throughout this course.

Moreover, there is the question of what exactly we mean by desirability. Is it merely wanting a thing or is it the quantity of a thing that we want? The mere want of a thing suggests that the quantity of it we desire is finite (and sometimes very small indeed). In reality, this may indeed be what we mean by this. However, the desirability we refer to here is the want of more things. Our experience seems to suggest that people have some sort of unlimited want, which does not mean that they want an endless amount of one particular good, but rather, endless amounts of all goods. This means that we may want only one pair of shoes (for walking) but we also want a pair of rollerblades, a pair of shoes with flashing lights (for the night), a pair of amphibian shoes, a pair of flying shoes etc. Namely, we want new goods rather than more of the same goods.

Whether or not this want is an innate feature of human character or the cultural consequence of commercial society where the self-interested pursuit of material wealth has been exonerated and even transformed into a force for social good, is an open question. In most of the modelling that we shall be doing in this book, we will usually discuss a world where the number of goods is finite. This means that the pursuit of material wealth, i.e. desirability, will have to be translated into a want of greater quantities of the same set of goods.

The last point about this definition is the emphasis on the simultaneity of scarcity and desirability in our definition of the economic problem. We need both scarcity and desirability for something to become an economic good. There are things which we desire that are not scarce. Air, for instance, is a need (and thus desirable) but, *at the moment*, is not scarce. Therefore, air is not an economic good. But when it becomes scarce, we would be willing to act in order to get it. When pollution levels in Paris rose significantly during a heat wave one summer, people were willing to refrain from using their cars. This willingness came from the realization that fresh air had become scarce. Equally, love is desirable but when we have plenty of it (it is not scarce) it is not an economic good. However, in each big city in the world there are areas where love is becoming an economic good.

On the other hand, the mere scarcity of something does not make it the subject matter of economic investigation. Leprosy, for instance, is scarce yet people are not willing to do anything to acquire its germs. Unless, of course, there are people who wish to inflict pain on others. In such a case, leprosy would become an economic good.

1.2.1 Modelling the problem

Having defined economic goods we have also defined an economic problem: it is the problem of reconciling unlimited wants (defined in quantities of goods in a world of finite goods) with scarce means.

The next step is to ask ourselves what are the implications of this definition. What can we learn from it which cannot be seen simply by staring at it? To do so, we must use our common sense up to a point where things get too complex. From that point onwards, we want to use tools which will preserve the logical truth of our initial intuition. We may not intuitively understand the mechanism of our system but we can rest assured that it carries on the logic of our initial observation. In the end, by looking at what the system yields we may find an explanation which may then appear obvious to us. Nevertheless, this will not make our system redundant as this apparent 'intuition' would only be reached after the event (a posteriori). Constructing such a system is what we call **modelling**, and the logical language most commonly used is that of mathematics.

To see what exactly is meant by all this let us begin by modelling the first component of the definition of economic goods: scarcity. This model is called the **production possibility frontier (PPF)** or the **transformation curve**. We shall see that by adding to it the second element of the definition of the economic problem (i.e. desirability) we can generate two of the most important concepts in economic analysis: the concepts of *price* and *efficiency*.

1.2.2 Production possibility frontier: opportunity cost and efficiency

We begin by setting the premises. Consider an economy where only two commodities are produced (x and y). Let there be only one means of production (labour) which is measured in terms of labour hours. The *technology* of production is given as follows:

Each labour unit can produce *Either* 2 units of y *or* 1 unit of x^6.

Suppose also that there are 100 *homogeneous* units of labour in the economy. Table 1.2 depicts some of the allocations allowed by this technology.

In Figure 1.1 we draw the line which depicts all these points. This line, which we also call the **production possibilities frontier**, describes the highest quantity of y which can produce in conjunction with various quantities of x (or the other way around). It was constructed in the following manner. If all units of labour were engaged in the production of y they would have produced 200 units of it (each unit of labour can produce 2 units of y and there are 100 labour units). As they can *either* produce 2 ys *or* 1 x, this means that with 200 units of y there will be no x produced at all. If, on the other hand, they were all engaged in the production of x alone they would have produced 100 units of it (each unit of labour can produce 1 unit of X and there are 100 units of labour). As labour units are homogeneous—this means of equal ability—they will also be able to produce

Table 1.2 Technology of production

Labour units in the production of x	Labour units in the production of y	Quantity of x	Quantity of y
0	100	0	200
1	99	1	198
2	98	2	196
3	97	3	194
.			
.			
.			
.			
.			
99	1	99	2
100	0	100	0

combinations of x and y along the line that connects the two extremes. For instance, if one unit of labour is transferred from the production of y to the production of x, the economy will lose the 2 units of y it had been producing while working on y but gain a unit of x. If we assume that the unit of labour is divisible (i.e. we can transfer any fraction of labour time from one engagement to another) the Production Possibility Frontier of the economy will be the one depicted in Figure 1.1.

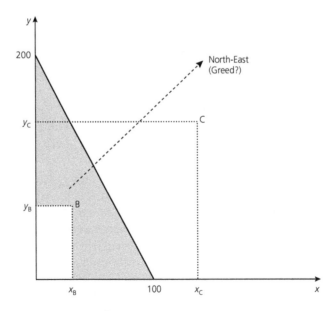

Figure 1.1 The production possibility frontiers.

The subspace of positive quantities of both x and y (depicted in Figure 1.1) constitutes the space of all possible combinations of economic goods. A point in this space, like B, depicts a bundle containing x_B units of commodity x and y_B units of commodity y. Point C, on the other hand, describes a bundle containing only x_C units of x and y_C units of y. From the position of x_B and x_C you can see that there are more units of x in C than there are in B. Similarly, there are more units of y in C than there are in B.

As our initial task was merely to model scarcity, what we can learn from this is that scarcity divides the world economic goods (the positive quadrant) into those combinations (bundles) which are feasible, like B, and those which are not, like C. We have enough labour hours to produce the bundle B (this is reflected by the fact that B is below the line depicting the production possibilities frontier). But we do not have enough hours to produce C which lies above the frontier. As far as we can tell from modelling scarcity alone, this is all we can learn (and you may well say, 'hey, this is obvious'; it is always good to start an analysis with things that are obvious).

However, as we insisted that economic goods must simultaneously be scarce and desirable we must add the desirability assumption into our story. As I explained earlier, in this world of finite goods, we interpret desirability as a measure of the wish to have greater *quantities* of everything (representing the general wish for material wealth). This means, in our model, the wish to always go north-east (the arrow in Figure 1.1).

With this additional element, our story becomes slightly more interesting. Scarcity forces a distinction between feasible bundles (like B) and unfeasible bundles (like C) by imposing a limit on what society can have (the heavy black line in Figure 1.1). Desirability (the journey north-east), on the other hand, requires that we go as far north-east as possible. In terms of resolving the economic problem we cannot rest until we have gone as far north-east as possible. This, of course, forces upon us a further distinction between two types of feasible bundles. Those bundles from which we can go north-east, and those from which we cannot. Recall that by 'going north-east' we mean being able to have more of both economic goods, x and y, simultaneously. The word we use to make this distinction is **efficiency**. This is not such an excellent choice of a word, as it is already used in daily language to describe something more akin to the mechanical notion of efficiency. Yet economic efficiency is not the same as mechanical efficiency.

Let us recap our story in full. The production possibility frontier (PPF), representing scarcity, demarcates that which is feasible from that which is not. As we desire to have more of everything (desirability), the PPF represents a **constraint**. We can only have those things below or on the PPF (the shaded area in Figure 1.1). The PPF constraint, the line connecting point $(x = 0, y = 200)$ with point $(x = 100, y = 0)$ can also be described algebraically as:

$$y = 200 - 2x. \tag{1}$$

This can be reached simply by looking at the constraints on production in this economy. We know that each labour unit can produce either 2 ys or 1 x. Namely, a unit of y requires 1/2 a unit of labour and a unit of x requires 1 unit of labour. The total number of labour units available is 100. Thus, the economy can produce any combination of x and y that requires up to 100 units of labour. Beyond that, the economy will not be able to produce.

Such a constraint is generally expressed in the following way:

$$(1/2)y + (1)x \leq 100. \tag{2}$$

Any combination of x and y which satisfies (2) is a feasible combination. Thus (2) defines the production possibilities set (the shaded area in Figure 1.2). Hence, for instance, a combination of 50 units of y and 50 units of x will satisfy (2) and will fit the feasible set. To produce 50 units of y, when each unit of y requires 1/2 a unit of labour, means that we will need 25 units of labour. For 50 units of x we will need 50 units of labour, as each x requires a full unit of labour. Together, therefore, we will need 75 units of labour, which is much less than the 100 units of it which we have at our disposal. We cannot, however, produce 100 units of both x and y. (Why?)

The PPF itself (i.e. points of the frontier), on the other hand, depicts those combinations of x and y which exhaust our resources (the equality sign in equation (2) means that the total number of labour units required is exactly the same as our constraint: 100). From a point *on* the PPF we cannot increase the production of any one of the commodities without giving up some of the other commodity (Fig. 1.2). In other words, we cannot go north-east. It is there, we say, that the constraint is binding.

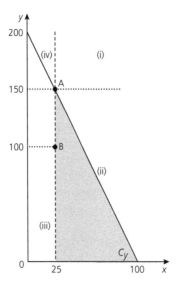

Figure 1.2 Efficiency and the PPF.

At point B we produce 100 units of y and 25 units of x. Checking with (2) we can see that this combination is feasible though it does not exhaust all labour units that are available.[7] At point A, on the other hand, we produce 150 units of y and 25 units of x. This combination is feasible too but it is different from point B in that it exhausts all labour units that were available to the economy.

If we look at the four quadrants around A we can see that we can always produce less of at least one commodity (quadrant (iii)). Hence quadrant (iii) is always feasible if the economy is at A. In particular, we can always move from A to B only by rearranging production. Quadrant (i), on the other hand, is not feasible at all. Had any point in (i) been feasible it would mean that from A we can produce more of one commodity without having to give up any other commodity. This would imply that at A not all our resources have been utilized, which, obviously, is not the case. Moving into quadrant (i), however, will be consistent with desirability (the journey north-east).

Points in quadrants (ii) and (iv) are such that to get there from A we must give up some amount of one commodity in order to get more of the other. Hence, if at A we have 150 units of y and 25 units of x, a point, like C, where we have one more unit of x will require a 'sacrifice' of some units of y. To have 1 more x (i.e. 26 x altogether) we will need 26 units of labour engaged in the production of x. This will leave $100 - 26 = 74$ units of labour with which we can produce only 148 units of y (recall that each unit of labour can produce up to 2 units of y). This means that from A, an extra unit of x means 2 units less of y.

While both A and B are feasible, from the point of view of resolving the economic problem of reconciling unlimited wants with scarcity, the distinction between A and B is significant. At B we can have more of all goods (in our case, x and y), while at point A we cannot go north-east. This means, at A, that we cannot have more of one good without giving up another. We distinguish a feasible point such as A from other feasible points by calling it an **efficiency allocation**.

Definition 1   An allocation of means of production which yields a combination of outputs where it is not possible to increase the output of one *economic good* without reducing the output of at least one other economic good is called **efficient**.

Suppose now that labour is not the only means of production and that one needs machines as well as labour in order to produce both x and y. Suppose, also, that there is only one kind of machine and that machine hours are homogeneous. Let one machine unit (say, one **machine hour**) produce *either* 1 unit of y *or* 2 units of x and let there be 100 units of machine hours altogether. We assume the labour requirements to be the same as before (i.e. one unit of labour can do either 2 units of y or 1 unit of x). We cannot produce either x or y by simply using one means of production. This means that if we want 1 unit of x we would need 1 unit of labour *and* 1/2 a machine hour. If we do not have one of those inputs, we shall not be able to produce the unit of x.

We now have two constraints which affect our feasible set. The first is the labour constraint which we have explored above. It meant that for each unit of x we would need 1 unit of labour and for each unit of y we would need 1/2 a unit of labour:

$$(1/2)y + x \le 100 \tag{3}$$

Now we have an additional constraint—the machine constraint:

$$y + (1/2)x \le 100 \tag{4}$$

As both labour and machines are needed for the production process of both x and y, the two constraints must be considered *simultaneously*. This means that every pair of x and y will be feasible only if equations (2) and (3) are satisfied simultaneously. Figure 1.3 depicts the space of economic goods with the two constraints.

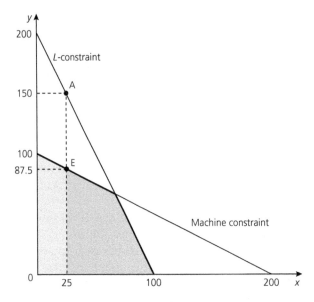

Figure 1.3 Economic goods *x* and *y* under two constraints.

Let us now look at point A again (it is the same A as in Figure 1.2 where we had only one constraint). The combination of 150 *y*s and 25 *x*s satisfies equation (2) (i.e. there is enough labour to produce it). But it does not satisfy equation (3).

$$150 \times 1 + 25 \times (1/2) > 100$$

It means that although there is enough labour to produce the combination of *x* and *y* at A, there is not enough machine hours for that purpose. Hence, A is no more feasible.

If we insist on producing 25 units of *x*, it is the machine constraint which becomes binding (the labour constraints allow us to produce 150 *y*s with it). Hence, according to (3), 25 units of *x* are consistent with up to 87.5 units of *y* (point E).

■ **QUESTION**

Is E an efficient allocation, given that some labour hours are not used (i.e. there is unemployment)?

Answer

This is obviously a tricky business. I am sure that you intuitively feel that E cannot be efficient. How can it be efficient, you can ask, if there is unemployment? You may feel this way out of sympathy with the unemployed, or, if you are differently inclined, out of concern for wasted labour hours. Either way, there is something that makes you feel uncomfortable with an assertion that E is efficient.

However, the difference between working on intuition alone and subjecting it to the laws of reason is that once a definition has been given—and I am sure that you did not object when we defined efficiency—we must work with it. According to the definition of efficiency, an allocation where we cannot have more of one economic good without giving up another is an efficient allocation. At point E we cannot have more of one good without giving up another (i.e. the journey north-east is not possible) simply because there are not enough machine hours. Therefore, by definition, E is an efficient allocation. Namely, it is an allocation which resolves the economic problem.

But while we have to work with definitions, it does not mean that we should remain unmoved by their implications and not be ready to reexamine them. Clearly there is something which does not feel right about an allocation which is deemed efficient (i.e. a solution to the economic problem) even though some people are unemployed. It is as if we are saying that the interest or the feelings of those who are unemployed are outside the domain of society's objectives.

However, the way we feel about the unemployed is mainly driven by our own experience, which has been formed within a given institutional set up. To us, an unemployed person is someone who is unable to access national income, or the more broadly defined social wealth. This is so because, in many economies, distribution is the mechanism of allocation (we'll come back to this later). But if, for instance, society acted like a sort of collective where everyone is entitled to, say, basic income and some people really would rather not work (I can equally think of people whom society would rather that they not work.) and others work because they want to work. Would we have felt so bad about E being an efficient allocation in such circumstances?

What is clear from this is that we must be more careful in the way we employ the concept of efficiency. We leave the definition as it is, but we make the following modification. In the definition it says that an allocation is efficient if we cannot have more of one economic good without giving up another. If by *economic goods* we mean tangible goods and services (like bread or telephone service), the definition is that of what we may call **productive efficiency**. If, however, by economic goods we refer to the well-being of all individuals (which is by definition an economic good as it is both scarce and desirable), the concept of efficiency we examine is that of **allocative efficiency**.

Thus, point E in Figure 1.3 is indeed productive efficient but not necessarily allocative efficient. Resolving the economic problem, therefore, cannot be summarized by examining the productive efficiency of the system. We must also examine its allocative efficiency.

We will discuss the concept of individual well-being in Chapter 2, but here I would like to make one preliminary comment. If we assume that there is a direct relation between material wealth and well-being, productive efficiency is a necessary condition for allocative efficiency. Namely, as by desirability we mean that we want to have more of everything, it means that we would feel better with more of everything. We have thus already set up a connection between material wealth and well-being. In such a case we cannot have an allocation which is allocatively inefficient but productively efficient. (Please try to prove this by yourself.)

Hence, to resolve the economic problems means to find the institutions that will produce allocations which are allocatively efficient. Given our assumption about well-being, it implies that such allocations are also productive efficient.

We are thus ready for our next definition:

Definition 2 The set of all productively efficient allocations is called the **Production Possibility Frontier**

Thus we know that the socially desirable allocation will have to be located on the PPF. In the case of Figure 1.1 and 1.2 we only had one constraint. The PPF then was the straight line connecting point (0,200) and (100,0). When we have the two constraints, the set of feasible allocations becomes the shaded area in Figure 1.3. In accordance, the PPF will now be the heavy line moving from point (0,100) to (100,0).

Opportunity costs

We go back to the original set-up where there is only one constraint (Figure 1.1). Suppose now that the economy is producing at point A. Is there any *cost* that the economy is paying for this choice? Given that we want more of everything, any choice suggests that we had given up something that we wanted. Choosing to produce 25 units of *x* means that we had to forgo 50 units of *y* which we could have had, had we not produced any *x* at all. Conversely, the production of 150 units of *y cost* us 75 units of *x* which we could have produced, had we not produced any *y* at all. As we want more of everything this is a *price* that society pays for its choices. It is called the opportunity cost.

Definition 3 What is lost by not using resources in their best alternatives is called **opportunity cost.**

Note that, so far, we talked about opportunity cost as a general notion of price. To make it slightly more concrete, let us examine the opportunity cost of a unit of *x*. At point A we gave up 50 units of *y* in order to be able to produce 25 units of *x*. On average, therefore, the opportunity cost of a unit of *x* is:

(what we had given up)/(what we got in return) = 50/25 = 2 units of *y* per unit of *x*
(The converse will be true to *y*.)

This opportunity cost, or the real price of *x*, will be the same wherever we choose to be on the PPF. This is so because of the specific technology we employed and the homogeneity of our labour force. So it does not matter whether we produce 25 units of *x* or 50 units of it. In both cases, an extra unit of *x* would require the transfer of 1 unit of labour from *y* to *x*. This is so because according to our technology we need 1 unit of labour to produce 1 unit of *x*. As, on the PPF, we have exhausted our resources, the extra unit of labour would have to come from those who are working in the production of *y*. As each worker can either do 2 *y*s or 1 *x*, the opportunity cost of *x* will always be 2 units of *y*. Note that this is exactly the slope α of the PPF in Figure 1.2.

Let us review what we have seen so far by way of theorizing. We started with a set of definitions. These included the definitions of scarcity, desirability, economic goods, efficiency, Production Possibility Frontier, and opportunity cost. The very basic modelling of scarcity has thus produced the following theory:

Premise 1 All the efficient allocations are on the Production Possibility Frontier;
Premise 2 Only goods produced on the Production Possibilities Frontier have an opportunity cost which is greater than zero;

Theorem Only goods which are produced efficiently have an opportunity cost which is greater than zero.

In the presence of scarcity there are two possible allocations of resources. One where the constraint is not binding (i.e. not on the possibilities frontier), the other, well inside the feasible set. Only allocations where the constraint is binding are efficient and the production of each unit of any good will have an opportunity cost. Inefficient allocations mean that we can go north-east and produce more of both goods. Thus, we do not have to forgo any good to produce more of the other. This means that when we are producing inefficiently there is no opportunity cost to the production of an extra unit of any good.

Naturally, as observers we all know that even when there are clear productive ineffi-ciencies, all economic goods seem to have a *price*. This means that when we pay money for one good, we are basically giving up something else that we could have purchased with the same amount of money. This seems to suggest that there is an opportunity cost to all economic goods regardless of whether or not they are produced efficiently. How then, you may wonder, does this correspond to the above theorem?

To understand this in full we must examine very carefully the definition of opportunity cost. We define these costs to be the cost from not using resources in their *best* altern-ative. Recall point B in Figure 1.2. There we produced 100 units of y and 25 units of x. According to equation (2) we know that this means a total of 75 units of labour. Suppose now that we want an extra unit of x. According to our production technology we would need 1 unit of labour for 1 unit of x. If we transferred one unit of labour which is currently engaged in the production of y to work on x we will lose 2 units of y. It will appear as if the opportunity cost of one unit of x at B is 2 units of y. This is in clear contradic-tion to the above theorem, according to which only efficient allocations are associated with opportunity cost. B, as it is well inside the feasible set, is clearly an inefficient allocation.

But is the opportunity cost of x really 2 units of y? Note that the definition of opportun-ity cost refers to those costs that arise from not using resources in their best alternative. When there are 25 units of labour which produce nothing, will the cost of 2 units of y per unit of x really be associated with not using resources in their best alternatives? If we could choose a unit of labour which is currently unemployed for the production of an extra unit of x and leave those units working for y unaffected, what will be the opportun-ity cost of an extra unit of x? The answer is clearly zero. To choose to employ a worker who is currently producing y when there are workers who do not produce anything does not satisfy the requirement of cost incurred from not using resources in their best alternative. The worker we have just moved from y to x would be best allocated to the production of y, while the labour unit which produces nothing will be best allocated to work in x. Hence, the opportunity cost of a unit of x is zero.

All this does not alter the fact that when we are being asked to pay for a good in a shop we do so regardless of the efficiency status of the economy. While this is obviously true, we must notice that there is a difference between paying for x with any quantity of y (determined by the market or in any other form of negotiation) and paying for x with its *opportunity cost*. Whenever we pay for x with more or less units of y than its opportunity cost, we are paying for x with more, or less, than *it really costs to produce it*. In such a case we may say that the economy is inefficient. If the *price* of x is greater than its opportunity cost, it means that to get a certain quantity of x we must produce a sufficient amount of y that will allow us to purchase x. But this sufficient amount will be many more units of y which are really needed to pay for x. Those resources which are now employed in producing the extra quantity of y required for paying for x could have been used to produce more of both x and y. As both goods are desirable (and we want more of them) any allocation where prices do not reflect the opportunity cost is inefficient. Indeed, one of the most important questions confronting economists is: which form of organization will yield prices (or exchanges) which reflect the real cost: i.e. the opportunity cost?

1.2.3 The shape of the PPF and the importance of marginalistic considerations

Let us now consider the effect having more than one constraint on opportunity cost. We refer back to the case where one needed both labour and machine time to produce both X and Y. Figure 1.4 below depicts such a case where the feasible set is the shaded area. Consider now two allocations: $A = (40, 80)$ and $B = (80, 40)$. Both A and B are productively efficient allocations. What is the opportunity cost (or the 'real price') of an extra unit of x in the cases of A and B?

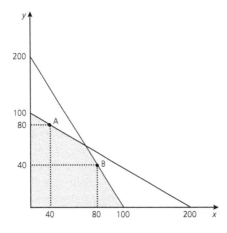

Figure 1.4 The importance of considering the margins.

At A, the overall opportunity cost for the production of 40 xs is 20 ys (note that if the economy did not produce any X at all, the quantity of y it could produce would have been 100, according to the *binding* constraint). The opportunity cost of producing one more x can be calculated as the average cost: $20/40 = 1/2$ a unit of y per unit of x. If we now add one unit of x we shall lose 1/2 a unit of y. Here, as in the previous case, the **average opportunity cost** was a good measure of the *marginal* opportunity cost. The **marginal opportunity cost** is the cost associated with the production of the next, or the last, unit of a good. So far we paid little attention to this as the average and the marginal were very much the same. At point A in Figure 1.4 this is still the case. But the significance of the special attention to considerations at the margin can be learnt through the examination of point B.

At B, if we follow the same principle (of the averages) to derive the opportunity cost per unit we shall get the result that the average cost of one unit of x at B is $60/80 = 3/4$ of a unit of y per unit of x. This can lead us to believe that the cost of an additional unit of x will be 3/4 a unit of y. However, if we do produce the extra unit of x we shall find that it, as a matter of fact, costs us 2 units of y rather than 3/4 a unit of y. At point A the binding constraint is that of machines. Therefore, transferring one machine from y to x will reduce the production of y by 1 and increase that production of x by 2 (hence, 1/2 of y per x). In case B the binding constraint was that of labour. A transfer of one worker from producing y to x will cause a loss of 2 ys and a gain of 1 x. Namely, the cost of an extra unit depends on how much we are already producing. Instead of the average, we shall have to be more careful and look at what is going on at the margins. The reason for that is the convex shape (towards the origin) of the PPF in Figure 1.4. In Figure 1.2, for instance, we would not have encountered such problems.

So why is the PPF convex towards the origin? The reason that we have discussed above is the existence of multiple constraints. However, even if there were only one factor of production to consider, the PPF would have been convex had we not assumed the homogeneity of that factor of production. A third reason, not entirely unrelated to the previous ones is the existence of diminishing marginal productivity. We shall discuss the role of the latter reason in more details as we go along (Chapter 3).

1.3 Specialization and trade

So far we examined a direct conclusion from modelling scarcity (and applying the notion of desirability) according to which the solution to the economic problem of reconciling unlimited wants with scarcity is to find the institutions that will allocate resources efficiently. We noted that efficient allocations are also associated with a particular notion of price, namely, opportunity costs. This, which is one way to examine whether an allocation is efficient, is to ask whether the price of goods reflect their true social costs. But there is another implication which arises from our modelling of scarcity (and the notion of desirability). This is the principle of specialization and trade.

If we accept the definition of economic goods, as those goods that are both scarce and desirable, and that we have unsatiated wants[8], then it can be easily established that it is always best for everybody to specialize and trade. Best, here, means that everyone will be able to have more of everything once they specialize and trade. I will demonstrate this point with an example:

Consider two individuals who head households I and II. Each household produces all its life necessities by itself[9]. Assume too, that these necessities include only two types of goods: food (F) and clothes (C). Household I can produce, and consume, either 6 units of clothes (C) or 2 units of food (F) or any convex combination of these two extremes. The circumstances of the second household (II) allow it to produce, and consume, either 6 units of clothes (C) or 6 units of food (F), or any convex combination of these two extremes.

This means that the production possibilities curve of each household is as given in Figure 1.5.

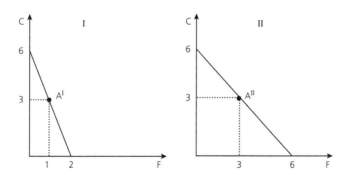

Figure 1.5 Autarky: each household consumes exactly what they produce.

Suppose now that the two individuals (representing the households) choose to be at points $A^I = (1, 3)$ (producing and consuming 1 unit of food and 3 units of clothes) and $A^{II} = (3, 3)$, respectively. The two individuals, therefore, have organized their households in a productively efficient manner.

Not that the opportunity cost (or, the price) of food in household I is 3 units of C per unit of F (the slope of the PPF in the left-hand side of Figure 1.5). In household II, however, the opportunity cost (or, the price) of food is only 1 unit of C per unit of F (the slope of the PPF in the right hand side diagram). Conversely, the opportunity cost of clothes in household I is 1/3 of a unit of F per unit of C while in household II it is 1 unit of F per unit of C.

To summarize, this is where the two households stand when each is self-sufficient (see Table 1.3).

Table 1.3 Opportunity cost when the two household are self-sufficient

	Clothes (C)		Food (F)		Totals	
	I	II	I	II	C	F
Production	3	3	1	3	4	6
Consumption	3	3	1	3	4	6
Opportunity cost	1/3 F per C	1 F per C	3 C per F	1 C per F		

Clearly one can see that it is cheaper to produce C in household I where the opportunity cost is 1/3 F per unit of C against 1 F per unit of C in household II. We say in such a case, that household I has a *comparative advantage* in the production of C. When an individual (or a household) has a comparative advantage in the production of any good, we mean to say that it costs less, in terms of other goods, to produce that good in that household.

For exactly the same reasons, household II has a comparative advantage in the production of food (F). The opportunity cost of a unit of F in II is 1 C per F while it is 3 Cs per F in household I.

This seems to suggest that if every unit of C produced at I had instead been produced at II, and every unit of F produced at II had instead been produced at I, the total amount of F and C available for both households would have been much greater. This, of course, can only happen if each individual **specializes** in production and if the two households then **trade** for consumption. In other words, that the two households move away from their states of self-sufficiency and become dependent on one another. You can clearly see that this makes sense only if we wish (individually and collectively) to have more of everything (desirability). If you recall Aristotle, from the first section of this chapter, while he did promote efficiency within the household (i.e. each one of our households should produce at A), if all needs could thus be satisfied, he saw no reason to specialize and trade. But Aristotle was trying to solve a very different economic problem.

Coming back to our case, it stands to reason that each household should specialize in producing that good in which it has a comparative advantage. Household I, therefore, will specialize in C and household II will specialize in F. So household I will produce 6 units of C while II will produce 6 units of F. Suppose now that each household should want to carry on consuming 3 units of C (due to the harsh winter conditions). This means that household II will have to buy 3 units of C from household I. How many units of F will household I be willing to pay for a unit of C?

We cannot here establish the exact price that will emerge. However, we know the limits of this price. Household I will not be willing to buy F for more than 3 units of C. The reason is that this is how much it would have cost household I to produce a unit of F, had it not specialized. So we know that the price of F in terms of C must be less than its opportunity cost to the buyer. Similarly, household I will not be willing to sell F for less than 1 unit of C because this is what it would have cost it, had the individual decided to produce C by himself. Hence, what we get here is that the price of F must lie between 1 unit of C (the opportunity cost to the seller) and 3 units of C (the opportunity cost to the buyer). Hence,

Buyer's opportunity cost ≤ price ≤ Seller's opportunity cost

$$1\,C\,per\,F \leq p_F \leq 3\,C\,per\,F$$

Whether the agreed price falls closer to the buyer's opportunity cost or to the seller's opportunity cost depends on the institution of exchange and the relative bargaining power of the two households. We shall deal with these issues later in the course. At this stage, suppose that the agreed price is 2 units of C per F. This exchange rate between C and F is depicted by the broken line in the two graphs below in Figure 1.6.

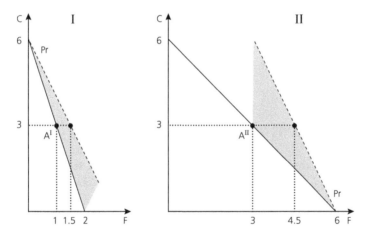

Figure 1.6 Feasible sets after specialization and trade with an agreed price of 2 Cs per F.

It is easy to see that both households have now consumption opportunities which they did not have before (the shaded areas in Figure 1.6). We therefore conclude that trade will benefit *both* households. It is also easy to see that if the two households insist on consuming 3 Cs each, they will now be able to consume more food with it (1.5 units of F in comparison with 1 unit of F for I and 4.5 units of F in comparison with 3 units of F for II).

Table 1.4 Allocation after trade

	Clothes (C)		Food (F)		Totals	
	I	II	I	II	C	F
Production	6	0	0	6	6	6
Consumption	3	3	1.5	4.5	6	6
Price	1/2 F per C	1/2 F per C	2 C per F	2 C per F		

Table 1.4 is a summary of the situation after trade. Evidently, the two households are better off (assuming that having more of all goods is indeed equivalent to being better off) after specializing and trade. The logic that by specializing and trading everyone is a winner is one of the more important messages derived from the initial modelling of the economic problem. It implies that the best form of economic organization should be based on interdependency between all agents in society. The same argument is also forwarded in the discussion about international trade. Naturally, the keen observer will see that there is a hidden condition for specialization and trade to become a win–win situation. This condition is the right (and ability) to say no. What made the outcome beneficent to everyone was the fact that the price fell between the opportunity costs (or reservation price) of the two individuals. But if for some reason, one agent managed to persuade the other one to specialize, and somehow managed to force a price which was below that agents opportunity cost (as a seller), the 'oppressed' agent could say no. However, if it were far too costly for that agent to revert back to his state of self-sufficiency, he may be obliged to trade at a price by which he becomes worse off. This notion of individual sovereignty and the ability to say no should become an important part of the institutional arrangements which we propose to put into place in order to resolve the economic problem.

1.4 Self-assessment and applications

In this section you are given first a set of questions. If you really wish to improve your knowledge you should try and answer each of the following questions by yourself, without looking at the answers. After you have answered all the questions, compare your answers with someone else who is studying with you. If there is no one in your area with whom you may consult, choose a patient member of your family or a friend and try to explain to that person the issues in each of these questions. The fact that they may not know anything about economics will force you to explain the subject in a way that will make you understand things that you would not have understood otherwise. Only after all these trials may you compare your answers with the answers in the book.

QUESTION 1

An economy produces two goods, X and Y, with two means of production: labour and capital. A unit of labour can produce either 1 unit of X or 4 units of Y (or any linear combination of the two). A unit of capital can produce either 4 units of X or 1 unit of Y (or any linear combination of the two). There are 100 units of each means of production.

(a) Draw the production possibility curve of the economy when the two goods can only be produced by a mixture of both factors;

(b) What will be the opportunity cost of X if the economy produces 50 units of it?

(c) Given that the production technology is linear, will the opportunity cost of X remain unchanged when we produce 90 units of it?

Answer

This is a straightforward question which tests your understanding of the principles behind the modelling of scarcity.

(a) The graph shown in Figure 1.7 should have emerged:

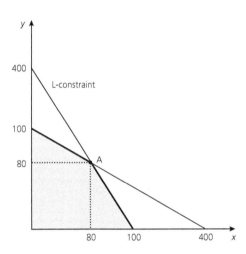

Figure 1.7 Modelling scarcity when both means of production are needed simultaneously.

This could have been established either by simply drawing each constraint according to the available information (i.e. 100 L can do either 400 Y or 100 X etc.), or by setting the two equations of the constraint:

$$\text{Labour} \quad x + \frac{1}{4}y = 100$$

$$\text{Capital} \quad \frac{1}{4}x + y = 100$$

From the symmetry of the model it is easy to see that the two lines intersect at (80,80). The PPF is clearly the heavy line in the diagram as both capital and labour (at fixed proportions) are required for the production of each unit of X and Y.

(b) When the economy produces 50 units of X we are to the left of point A. The binding constraint is that of labour and hence, the opportunity cost (the slope of the PPF) is 1/4 units of Y per X.

(c) When we produce 90 units of X we are to the right of point A and hence, the opportunity cost of X is 4 units of Y per X.

■ QUESTION 2

In the above economy where a unit of labour can produce either 1 unit of X or 4 units of Y (or any linear combination of the two) and a unit of capital can produce either 4 units of X or 1 unit of Y (or any linear combination of the two). There are 100 units of each means of production. Suppose now that the discovery of new production technologies allowed the production of both X and Y by using only one of the two means of production (without a change in their respective productivity).

(a) What will now be the production possibility curve?

(b) What will now be the opportunity cost of producing 50 units of X? Will it change if we produced 90 units of X?

Answer

The conditions of this question are similar to those of question 1. There is, however, a technological change:

(a) We assume now that a change in technology allows us to produce X or Y by using only one of the means of production (capital *or* labour) at their initial productivity (i.e. 1 L can do *either* 1 X *or* 4 Y, etc).

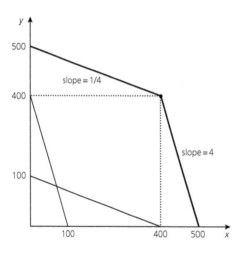

Figure 1.8 Modelling scarcity when only one means of production can produce either goods.

If we produce only Y we can produce 400 units of Y by using 100 L and an extra 100 Ys by using 100 K (which can produce 1 Y each). Altogether, if all resources are directed to the production of Y we will be able to produce 500 units of Y (see Figure 1.8). If we now wish to have X as well we shall first transfer to its production the input which has comparative advantage in producing X (i.e. capital).

(b) The opportunity cost of X at 50 or 90 will be the same. It will be 1/4 units of Y per X. If, however, we produced 401 units of X, the opportunity cost of X becomes 4 units of Y per X.

▦ QUESTION 3

Robinson Crusoe can bake 10 loaves of bread in one hour or peel 20 potatoes. Friday can bake 5 loaves of bread in an hour or peel 30 potatoes. If they believe in equality of consumption, would they specialize and trade? If so, at what price will they exchange bread for potatoes?

Answer

Figure 1.9 the PPF should be drawn for Robinson Crusoe (on the left) and for Friday (on the right)

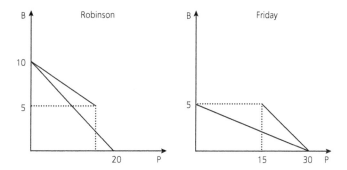

Figure 1.9 Crusoe and Friday before and after trade.

Clearly, Robinson has a comparative advantage in baking bread (his opportunity cost for it is 2 potatoes per loaf). Friday has a comparative advantage in potatoes (his opportunity cost for potatoes is 1/6 loaf of bread). It is worthwhile for both of them to specialize and trade.

If they wish to be better off from a material point of view, but still pursue other values like equality, the distribution which they must aim for is that of 5 loaves of bread and 15 potatoes each. To achieve this they must exchange 5 loaves for 15 potatoes. Hence, the price of a loaf of bread is 3 potatoes and the price of a single potato is 1/3 of a loaf of bread. Here we can see an attempt to bring together principles of ethics with the resolution of the economic problem. In the case which we had set here, there is no tension between resolving the economic problem and complying with a basic ethical principle. Whether this is universally true is a far more complex question.

▦ QUESTION 4

'Developed countries get very little from trade with less developed countries. The reason for this is that all means of production in the developed world are capable of producing much more than any of their counterparts in less developed countries'. Discuss this statement.

Answer

The question is written in simple daily language. Economists would want to make sense of it by translating it into the language of economic modelling. The point of the question is made by many people who are not well-versed in the meaning and significant of economic concepts. We must discipline our thoughts and try to put it all in a framework that would make sense.

It is not very difficult to realize that the appropriate framework of analysis is that of the PPF. It is in this context that we analysed specialization and trade as a derivative of modelling scarcity and desirability.

The quote in the question states that the factors of production of one country are better than some others in the production of all goods. This means that the developed country has what we call *absolute advantage*. But we have come to learn to be very careful of things with 'absolute' attached to them. The point of this question is to show that while this may be true the developing country will still have comparative advantage. From the point of view of economic analysis, only comparative advantage matters; not absolute advantage. It is yet another demonstration of the difference between the daily use of the word efficiency (in its mechanical sense) and the economic concept of efficiency.

To make the exposition easier we should focus on a world of two goods. If, say, the developed country can produce 100 units of *x* or 100 units of *y*, its opportunity cost in producing *x* is 1 unit of *y* per *x* and in producing *y*, it is 1 unit of *x* per *y*.

The less developed country can produce either 40 units of *y* or 20 units of *x* (it is small too). Its opportunity cost in producing *x* is 2 units of *y* per *x* (which is more than the opportunity cost of the developed country) but only 1/2 unit of *x* per *y* (which is evidently less than that of the developed country). The PPF of both economies are drawn in the diagram below. The PPF of the developed country is the straight line from (0,100) to (100,0). The PPF of the developing country is drawn between (0,40) and (20,0). Let us assume that *y* is a luxury good that is of no use to the less developed country at this stage (say, *y* is fine whisky). *x* on the other hand is an essential good like, say, food (see Figure 1.10).

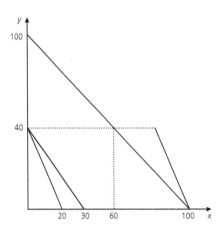

Figure 1.10 The two economies before and after trade.

Suppose now that the larger economy consumes (and produces) before trade 40 units of *y* and 60 units of *x*. The less developed country produces (and consumes) 0 *y* and 20 *x*.

If the larger economy carries on consuming 40 Y, it would be better off buying them from the smaller economy. If they do, they can transfer all their means of production to x. In such a case, they will produce 100 units of x. They will have to pay the smaller country part of this in return for their 40 units of y. As long as they pay the smaller country more than 1/2 x per y (which is what it costs the smaller country to produce y), the smaller country will be better off. The larger economy, on the other hand, will not be willing to pay more than 1 x per y as this is what it would have cost them had they produced y themselves. Hence, the price of y in terms of x (P_y):

$$1/2 \text{ units of } x \text{ per } y < P_y < 1 \text{ unit of } x \text{ per } y.$$

If the price happens to be, say, 3/4 x per y (or 4/3 y per x) then the larger economy will buy 40 y at the price of 30 x. It will now be able to consume 40 y with 70 x which was not possible before trade. The smaller economy too will benefit as they will be able, through specializing in what they do not need, to increase their consumption of what they are dependent on, namely, x. They will now be able to consume 30 units of x instead of 20.

NOTES

1. While Plato does not explicitly write about an economic division of labour, he does insist that Justice, among other things, means that people should do that which they are good at (see part five of the *Republic*). Given that the rulers and the soldiers have no property of their own and that the rulers do not allow great inequality among the supplying class, it is not unlikely that economic division of labour was closely associated with the social one.

2. Smith, A, (1976) [1776] *An inqury into the nature and causes of Wealth of Nations*, Liberty Press.

3. His famous 'invisible hand' is usually quoted to suggest that social good may come out of people seeking their own interest. However, it appeared before *Wealth of Nations* in his *Theory of Moral Sentiments* where he uses the idea of the invisible hand to suggest that life's necessities will always be supplied irrespective of ownership structures.

4. *Axioms (or premises)* are the fundamentals of our theory. In this example, we learn the axioms from our questionnaires (i.e. observations) but, as I indicated earlier, we could have simply suggested this as a piece of 'common wisdom'. In any case, we accept axioms to be *true* without looking for further confirmation. We have to ask ourselves what exactly we mean by 'true' but as we have enough on our plate as it is we shall not deal with this question here.

5. Empirical means something that can learn through our senses, and more generally, from experience. The word empirical comes from the Greek word *empeirikos*, which comes from *empeiria* (experience). Interestingly enough, in the third century, Sextus Empiricus, claimed that deductive reasoning *a la* Aristotle does not add anything to our knowledge. In the given example, for instance, it was only through knowing that Aristotle is mortal that we constructed the first premise. Hence, the conclusion is embedded in the assumption (this is the problem of 'petitio principii'—assuming the required). Arguments on whether or not Sextus Empiricus was right have invoked a great deal of writing. An example of the difficulty with his statement will soon be given in connection with the theory which we develop here.

6. Given that the labour unit (measured in time) is divisible, any linear combination of the two is also possible.

7. The constraint in (2) is: $(1/2)y + x \leq 100$. Set $y = 100$ and $x = 25$ and the economy is using only 75 units of labour (25 units short of what is available). Equation (2) then holds and B is feasible.

8. There is another reason why the notion of unsatiated wants is an integral part of our theory. It prevents the situation where goods cease to be economic goods when they cease to be desirable. It is important to note that once we change our perception of the economic problem (or even modify the notion of desirability) efficiency and opportunity cost will cease to be the criteria by which we examine economic performance.

9. A state of **autarky** or **self-sufficiency**.

PART ONE

Preface to microeconomics

Once we understood, more or less, what constitutes an economic problem we come to the question of choosing the institutional arrangements that will resolve it. Namely, we are looking for institutional arrangements that will produce allocations which are *allocatively efficient* (and thus are also *productively efficient*). The answer should be relevant to any organization seeking to resolve an economic problem, be it the economy in its entirety, a corporation, or even a household.

To answer this question we need to understand, first of all, how the world around us would look if things were left to themselves. Naturally, to enable us to understand such a concept we have to identify the unit which is the prime mover of the social world. In other words, we have to identify the *agent* whose behaviour is detrimental to the understanding of social outcomes.

There are various possible answers to this question. The unit may be the 'individual' or it may be a collective of individuals (for instance, 'society', the 'nation', a 'class'). But if it is a collective of individuals, could its behaviour be deduced from the sum of the behaviours of its components? Or could its behaviour be governed by other things than the sum of its components? If the answer to the first question is yes (and no to the second one), then we need not worry about the group as it too is explained by the behaviour of the individual agent. If the answer to the second question is yes (and no to the first one), then we must base our analysis on the behaviour of the collective. For instance, consider a notorious gang of youths in the streets of a city. The gang has been around for many years and has a reputation for tough behaviour and 'bravery'. At a point in time, the people who make up the group may individually not be so brave or tough. However, when the group faces a decision whether to engage in street battles with a rising new gang or withdraw, the group will go to battle even though most of its members would rather it did not. In other words, someone could have predicted that the battle would take place, without knowing anything about the individual members of the group, merely by examining its history. In fact, examining each individual in separation without any reference to those elements in his, or her, character which subjugated him, or her, to the will of the collective could yield the wrong prediction.

All these are very difficult questions and issues, for which many different answers have been given over the years. Modern economics, however, is fundamentally an individualistic theory. That is to say, it is a theory that is based almost entirely on the analysis of the behaviour of a single individual and his, or her, interaction with others. Any group analysis including things like our street gang, or the firm, or the corporation, are all viewed as a consequence of complex individuals' interactions. The group as such (and its own history) has no significance in our analysis.

I am not saying all this to persuade you that this is indeed how things should be. I simply feel that it is important for you to understand the economist's world. Many important methodological decisions are embedded in economic analysis, and while we cannot study them in any reasonable way here, being conscious of them is a step in the right direction. Hence, when some politicians defend themselves against criticism levelled against them for supporting individuals and not society (through, say, tax cutting policies) by saying, 'there is no such thing as society', they do not mean to say that society does not exist. What they mean is that society is indistinguishable from its individual agents.

The question of whether the group, or the collective, is always a simple reflection of the sum of its components had been critically raised in the debate about the philosophy of physics. In the second part of the nineteenth century the belief in the atom as the basic component of the physical world was widely accepted. Yet, there was a school of thought (positivism), which included physicists such as Ernst Mach (1838–1916), which argued that science should be based only on those things that we know beyond any doubt and that are based on experience. Clearly, many positivists refused to accept that atoms were real, since nobody had ever seen them. They admitted that atoms are quite useful in generating good predictions but argued that they were not real and therefore, were not sufficient to generate explanations. The crux of the debate was the famous dilemma about the consistency of thermo-dynamics with Newtonian classical mechanics. In mechanics, all actions were revers-ible. In thermodynamics, the direction of time is unique. For instance, when you put a hot object next to a cold one, the heat will move from the hot object to the cold one until both bodies have the same temperature. For the arrow of time to move in the other direction, we must be able to see two bodies with the same temperature where one of them is getting hotter while the other is getting colder. The query that was raised was this: how can atoms, which are subject to the Newtonian principle of reversibility, constitute the foundation of matter which is subject to the laws of thermodynamics? (Here, the 'group' is matter and the 'individuals' are the atoms.) The Austrian physicist Ludwig Boltzmann (1844–1906) devised an experiment in which he examined the behaviour of a gas in an empty container. Thermodynamics suggests that the gas should spread in the empty container while the Newtonian expectation is that it does not. He showed that while each atom followed the Newtonian principle, as a collective, the gas did spread. To reconcile the two contrast-ing images it was suggested that the collective too could behave according to the Newtonian principle and be reversible in time, but that the probability of it following the thermodynamic rules was simply greater. Thus it was shown that it is quite con-ceivable that the atoms of gas will act according to Newtonian mechanics but the *statistical* behaviour of the collective will be subject to the laws of thermodynamics.

This insight developed in physics has not been seriously taken on board by economists. But if we would take a lesson from Boltzmann's experiment, it would be to highlight the possibility that even in society, the collective may be working (at least statistically) according to rules different from those controlling its individual components. At the same time, it also leaves the door open to try to find a mechanism which connects the individual with the group.

Whichever way physics has gone in trying to conceptualize the world around us, economics is far behind. The theory unfolded below is, as I said, individualistic through and through. Economic analysis begins and ends with the individual, and sadly, there is barely any role to anything which is a reflection of the collective, such as institutions. I hasten to say that this has not always been the case. Classical economics, for example, which dominated economic thinking in the eighteenth and nineteenth centuries, is extremely conscious of the role of society and its institutions in the behaviour of individuals.

I am not sure whether economic analysis became poorer for abandoning social institutions. In certain respects, this was necessary in order to allow the language of economics to develop fully. Indeed, most recent research in economics (notably, new institutional economics) reflects a return of economics into the fold of the social sciences.

In our exposition below we shall follow the individualistic nature of neoclassical economics. We depart from this principle only in our analysis of the firm. I shall comment on this when we get there, but in current economic analysis there is a clear recognition that the firm is also a nexus of individual interactions.

A subject map: synopsis

As was indicated above, at this level of your studies we introduce an artificial distinction between two types of agents. The first is the consumer, who also supplies the means of production (such as the labour or other assets which he, or she, may possess). The second is the firm. However, despite the apparent difference between the two types of agents, the method by which we analyse their behaviour is basically identical.

A general 'map' regarding the various components and their relationship in microeconomics makes clearer the purpose of each component of your study (Figure 1.1). You can treat it as a synopsis of what lies ahead. On the left and right side of Figure 1.1 you can see the individual and the firm, respectively, at the heart of the system. Each agent has the appearance of a machine: something which swallows economic goods of one type and turns them into economic goods of another type. Thus the individual on the left takes in an economic good and turns it into another, though intangible, economic good called **utility**: we call this process **consumption** (explored in Chapter 2). The individual on the right (the firm) takes in economic goods (such as labour and capital) and turns them into other tangible economic goods. We call this process **production** (explored in Chapter 3).

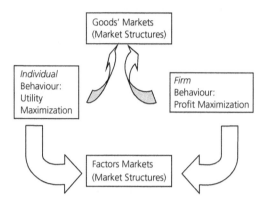

Figure 1.1 General maps regarding components and their relationship in microeconomics.

We assume all agents to be **rational** in the sense that they will want to maximize their output for any given level of inputs (for the individual on the left this means **utility maximization**, for the individual on the right, this means **profit maximization**). The technologies with which all agents convert one type of economic good into another is captured by the **utility function** for the agent on the left and by the **production function** for the agent on the right. Analytically, the analyses of the behaviour of the two agents are almost identical.

The internal arrows leading from each agent into the other boxes suggest inference. Namely, what is it that we derive from the study of the behaviour of both agents? The arrow leading up from the individual's box suggests that from the process of utility maximization we derive the **demand** for goods, and the arrow leading up from the firm's box that we derive the **supply** of goods. The box on top is the place where the two meet, which we call the analysis of market structures (explored in Chapter 4).

Note that there are arrows leading down from the boxes of each agent. This means that by exactly the same analytical mechanism we also derive the *supply of factors* (i.e. of labour and other assets) by the individuals. These are bought by the firms as means of production. We also derive from the firm's behaviour its *demand for factors*. The box at the bottom describes the meeting place between the two, or the factor markets (explored in Chapter 5). Analytically, again, there is no great difference between analysing market structures at the top and at the bottom of the diagram. Thus, while economics may look intimidating, it is, actually, very simple and well defined. There is a complete symmetry between the analytical instruments used to analyse the left-hand side and those which we use to analyse the right-hand side. Equally, there is complete symmetry between the analytical tools we use to analyse the top and the bottom of the diagram.

What comes out of this diagram is that everything seems to be connected. The decisions made by each agent will affect all other agents. This, it must be noted, is not an obvious conclusion about the world. There is no obvious reason to believe that the domains of individual decision-making are identical for all individuals, namely, that we all make decisions about all commodities at the same time. Nevertheless, in an important sense, the idea that everything is connected does capture the essence, or indeed the limit, of an organization where people specialize and thus become dependent on each other.

So if all are dependent on each other, the question which immediately arises is that of coordination. Can a system where all agents are dependent on each other work without interference or help? The answer given by economics is in the affirmative. The question of coordination is the subject of general equilibrium: Chapter 6 below explores this issue.

Once we have established that the system can work without interference and that the way it works resolves the economic problem (i.e. coordination without interference leads to an efficient allocation of resources), we are ready to consider other elements which may be important to society: notably, the question of distribution. We ask, then, whether what coordination without intervention produced is also consistent with other ethical dimensions of social organizations. This is the subject matter of what is generally called **welfare economics** (also explored in Chapter 6). In Chapter 7 we begin to reflect on whether or not all of this is useful given some problems which are endemic to the world and which cannot be entirely resolved by the simple story above.

2 The individual's behaviour

■ **MAJOR POINTS IN SUMMARY**

- We will explore the significance of **preferences-based utility** as a means to investigate the relationship between individuals and the world of economic goods
- We will examine the notion of rational behaviour and the idea of **utility maximization**
- We will show how demand is derived from such behaviour and what we can learn from it about the nature of goods, the relationship between them, and our ability to evaluate the outcome of market interactions.

We begin our analysis of the individual by examining how he or she makes a decision about how much he, or she, wants of any economic good and why. You may say, 'But we know already that individuals want to buy more of a good when its price is low and less of it when its price is high; why do we need to complicate the story?' I would like to begin by tapping into what is apparently known to you and see why we need to develop a more comprehensive theory of individual behaviour.

2.1 The role of demand

One of the most famous illustrations associated with the study of economics is shown in Figure 2.1.

The vertical axis gives real number values to the price of this good (say, x). The horizontal axis gives real number values denoting the quantities of the good. The demand schedule (D) depicts the quantity demanded at each possible price while the supply schedule (S) relates the quantity that will be supplied at any possible price. There is one point (A) where, at a given price, the quantity demanded equals the quantity supplied.

Embedded in this picture is a vision of economics which is very similar to the Newtonian vision of mechanics. The world of economic interaction is conceptualized as a world of opposing forces (demand and supply) which are constantly drawn to a balancing point (equilibrium).[1] It is therefore obvious that we would like to examine how each of these forces operates. In modern economics it is utility, which provides an explanation of how demand operates.

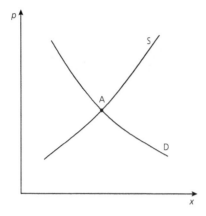

Figure 2.1 Supply and demand curves.

However, the notion of a downward sloping demand schedule is very old indeed. It is possible to find some evidence of it in the ideas of Aristotle, St. Thomas Aquinas, and certainly among classical economists like Smith, J.S. Mill, and Marx. However, none of the above economists connected the notion of demand and utility in the same way as we do in neoclassical economics. For many, the downward sloping demand schedule was more of a certainty—like a law of nature—than a derivative of a more complex structure. Why then, you still wonder, do we need such a complex structure to derive something with which many people seem to be willing to agree anyway?

There are two aspects to the answer. First, although many people may feel that demand schedules are downward sloping, such a schedule cannot be constructed as an empirical fact. At any point in time we can only establish what people actually do at a given price. If price changes over time, people may act differently for numerous reasons including reasons which are not at all connected to the demand for a particular good. Put differently, to be completely certain that demand schedules are downward sloping, we must be able to observe an individual, or individuals, acting at two points in time where the only thing different is the price. This is obviously impossible. We can try and estimate[2] demand schedules empirically but as a schedule, they do not really exist. Therefore, we cannot be certain that demand schedules are always downward sloping and we must be in a position where we can provide an explanation even if we come across an estimated upward sloping demand.

Second, there is the question of the usefulness of our theory. As I argued earlier, economics is a language with which we discuss social issues. This means that we cannot only be interested in the predictive power of our theory. We must also be able to interpret situations in a way that will allow us to judge them. For instance, consider the following story. The government considers whether to build a bridge over a certain river. It orders a market research where a demand schedule is being constructed (assume, for the sake of simplicity that the demand was constructed through a questionnaire where people were asked how many times they would use the bridge at different crossing prices). At the same time, it commissions an investigation into the engineering side where it is discovered that given the size of the river, the smallest bridge that could be built is of a capacity for T crossings per day. The graph in figure 2.2 captures these findings.

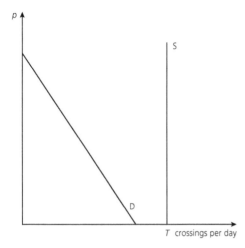

Figure 2.2 Demand and supply for bridge crossings per day.

The cost of the smallest bridge is £C billion but demand and supply do not intersect with a meaningful positive price. Ignoring now the implications of the failure of demand and supply to meet, how can the government—pursuing the interest of the public—form an opinion on whether it is worthwhile building the bridge? If the only use of demand and supply is to predict the price in a market then we will not be able to say anything about whether, or not, the government should build the bridge. However, if we understood the meaning of the area underneath the demand schedule, we could be wiser. But to make sense of this area we must derive the demand schedule from a certain construct rather than assume it. We shall come back to this point at the end of the chapter.

Alternatively, consider the following two scenarios shown in Figure 2.3.

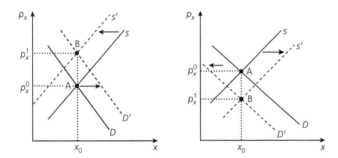

Figure 2.3

If we merely accept the downward sloping nature of demand and the upward sloping nature of supply as premises (or 'laws') then we would be able to make predictions in exactly the same way as we would, had we had a theory to explain them. Hence, it may be conceivable that for prediction purposes we do not need to develop our understanding of these concepts further. In the above diagrams we see two cases. In the left-hand side diagram, owing to an increase in demand and a fall in supply, the new equilibrium would be at a higher price but without any change to the equilibrium quantity of the good which will be traded in the market. In the right-hand side diagram we can see that a fall in demand and an increase in supply would cause a fall in the equilibrium price without changing the quantity of the good traded in the market. The prediction about the equilibrium quantity and price depended entirely on the analysis of the shift of both the demand and supply schedules. However, can we as economists (and thus, social commentators) say which of the changes is better?

By merely assuming the demand and supply there is very little we can say in trying to compare the two situations. In both cases the quantity of the good *x* which is now traded in the market had not changed. The only difference between the two cases is that in one of them, the price had gone up and in the other, it had gone down. You may say, clearly a lower price must be better than a higher price, therefore the change described in the right-hand side diagram is better than the one described in the left-hand side diagram.

But is it? Let us try to examine the changes more carefully. In the right-hand side diagram demand fell. Namely, people want to buy less of the good at any given price. What could this mean? Could it mean that people's income fell dramatically so that they can no longer afford to buy as much of the good as they wanted originally? Could it be that demand fell because half of those who usually bought the good *x* have run into money and are no longer interested in this type of good? Alternatively, did demand for good *x* fall because the price of another good fell?

And what can we say about supply? Has it increased because wages have gone down, or has it increased because technology has improved? It is not at all clear that the fall in the price of the good is such a blessing. Of course, if the change is a result of the fact that the prices of other goods fell and technology improved, the fall in the price may be a good thing. But how do we know how other prices affect demand and whether the ultimate effects constitute an improvement for consumers? We have no obvious way of telling.

Equally, in the left-hand side diagram the price has gone up. Intuition tells us that higher prices are no good. However, could it be that the price has gone up because the increase in demand reflects an increase in consumers' income? Could the fall in supply be a result of an increase in the wages of workers? Would the subsequent increase in price necessarily mean that the position of consumers in this market had deteriorated?

Here is yet another case, shown in Figure 2.4. Again, if we merely accepted the downward sloping demand schedule as a premise (or axiom), thus completely disassociating it from utility or any other explanation, we would still be able to predict exactly as we would, had we derived demand from a more complex structure. In the left-hand side diagram we can predict that if the demand for a commodity increased (a shift to the right of the demand schedule, which means that the quantity demanded at each price will be greater) without any other changes (as, for instance, in supply) the new equilibrium price will be higher. But as demonstrated in the right-hand side diagram, we would also predict an increase in price if the supply fell (the supply schedule moves to the left which means that at any price, the quantity of good supplied will be smaller). Considering only these two changes, how can we, as economists, distinguish between these two changes which have similar predictions with regard to the price but different predictions with regard to quantities? Can we judge one to be in anyway a 'better' outcome than the other?

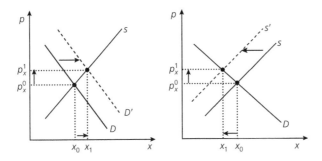

Figure 2.4 Shifting the demand and supply schedules.

Can we advise the public—and the government—on the social implications of these two changes?

On the face of it, the answer is clear. In the case of an increase in demand, price increased but so did the equilibrium quantity. In the case of a fall in supply the increase in price was accompanied by a fall in the equilibrium quantity. Hence, you may say, the change on the left is 'better' than the change in the right-hand side diagram.

But this is not so obvious. Let us suppose that the fall in supply resulted from an increase in wages. These would increase the cost of production which means that a seller will sell less at any given price (we shall explore this further in Chapter 3). If you then examine carefully the case of the fall in supply you will find that while there is a fall in equilibrium quantity, there is also an increase in wages. Surely the interest of workers as members of the community cannot be ignored. In addition, it is clear that in the left-hand side diagram people buy more of the good but they also spend more on it. What would they do with the amount of money left for them to spend on other goods? In the right-hand side diagram, the consumers buy less of the good but pay more for every unit. This, in turn, could mean either that they spend more or less on the good. Would it make a difference if it were more rather than less? If you go to a shop and find that the price of brown rice has gone up and you buy the cheaper white rice instead, should this be interpreted as a deterioration in circumstances? In particular if, at the same time, workers earn more money?

As for the increase in quantity in the case of increased demand, can we say for sure that it is a better sign than a fall in quantity? Suppose that the good in question is a certain fruit: *Nonesensatioualis*, which is found growing only in one place in the world, namely, the island of *Neverland*. It is considered common food among the indigenous population and there is an equilibrium at point A. One day, it was discovered that the fruit has immense powers of sexual regeneration. All of Hollywood moved to the island and the demand for *Nonesensatioualis* rose. As there are too many rich-and-famous (rafs), the new equilibrium will be at a higher level of both price and quantity. Does this mean that the indigenous population is necessarily better off?

In all these cases we only examined the effects of the changes on the equilibrium level of price and quantity, which is ultimately traded in the market. However, from an analytical point of view there are many more components of the diagrams which may help us judge the effects of the changes. For instance, we can clearly see that there are definite effects on the areas underneath the various functions; could this have any significance? Could this be the reason why we may be able to give a more definitive answer to the question of whether the changes represent an improvement or not?

Had we only assumed the shape of the demand schedule (as well as that of the supply schedule) we could not attempt any serious *interpretation* of the areas underneath both the demand and the supply schedules. We do have an explanation of the outcome (In one case the price increased because of an increase in the demand while in the other, the price increased because of a fall in the supply) but as we have no explanation of what demand (or supply) is we cannot make sense of the outcome.

The use of utility to explain the demand schedule (as opposed to assuming it) will provide an immediate and coherent interpretation of what the area underneath the demand schedule represents. It will also allow us to investigate the relationship between what is happening in one market and the rest of the economic arena. **Production functions** (or technology) would be equally useful in explaining the supply schedule (as opposed to assuming it) and, subsequently, allow us to interpret the area underneath it in a meaningful manner. In such a way, a prediction of an increase in price will have completely different significance when we are able to pour more content into those tools that we feel are nearest to what can be empirically observed or estimated.

There are many more important implications which can be derived from the way in which we explain those simple tools fundamental to the economics psyche. We shall see later on that the support for market institutions is very much embedded in the utility interpretation of demand. This means that the study of utility is very important indeed. It will provide a useful means of making sense of economic outcomes as well as a justification for a certain kind of organization of economic activities. At the same time, we must all be conscious of its role as a means of interpretation rather than a confirmed empirical truth.

2.2 Rationality

2.2.1 Definition

As we emphasized earlier, the first thing that we must bear in mind is that modern economics is an individualistic theory. This means that everything is a consequence of motivation and human interaction. Hence, the most important foundation of modern economic analysis is the analysis of that which motivates individuals.

However, what exactly it is that motivates individuals is a very difficult subject about which there have been numerous alternative observations. Economists chose to circumvent this problem by asking a slightly different question: how would people execute that which they want to achieve? Their answer was basically simple: they would behave rationally.

Some economists think that by saying this they are not committed to any particular objective (i.e. motivation). The only thing economics is focused on, they argue, is how best to achieve this objective. This led some of them to even conclude that economics is so universal that it can accommodate any sort of motivation one could imagine.

However, without getting deeper into this extremely complex, yet significantly important, issue I would like to say that this could not be further from the truth. There are two elements in this conception of rationality in economics which need examination. One is the implicit assumption (to which we will refer again later) that individuals would always prefer more material wealth to less (whether in terms of new products or, in the case of finite goods, greater quantities). The other, far more significant in nature, is the presumption that there is no connection between the means to an end and the end itself. Max Weber (1864–1920), for instance, who is considered to be one of the most significant sociologists (or social theorists) argues (quite convincingly, I hasten to add) that there are two forms of rational actions. One is the type of action that is captured by the 'best means to end' approach and which he calls instrumental rationality (*Zweckrationalitat*). The other, is a form of action where the agent is sort of overwhelmed by the objective and does not pay attention to the details of the means (expressive rationality or, *Wertrationalitat*).[3] In the second case we may find people who act out of commitment to an idea in a manner which is not necessarily optimal. I suppose that there must be some sort of connection between the natures of those objectives that allow you to cold-heartedly seek the best means to an end and those that overwhelm you.

Though this is an important question, this is not the place to develop the discussion. I just want to make sure that as we progress in modelling individual behaviour you are constantly aware of the limitations and the difficulties (as well as benefits, of course) of our enterprise.

Thus there are two elements to the concept of rationality which is used by economists. First, the assumption that whatever one wishes to achieve, he, or she, would like to achieve the most of it that is feasible. In normal language, this means that rational people will always choose the means which are most likely to successfully achieve their aim. Second, they will behave in a consistent manner.

Consider the following example shown in Figure 2.5: suppose that an individual lives in isolation and can either produce (by his labour) 3 units of X (tomatoes) or 6 units

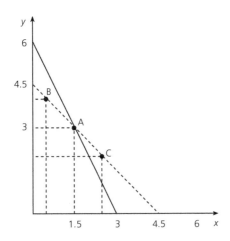

Figure 2.5 An example of individual rationality.

of Y (cucumbers) in a season's work. Assume further that as these goods are economic goods they are desirable and the individual would, therefore, like to have a lot of them. Obviously he cannot have a lot of both so what exactly it is that he wants a lot of? In such a sterile world, where there is clearly nothing else to think about—there are only tomatoes and cucumbers in the world—what our individual wants is... *a salad*! The first element of rationality would be for him to choose the combination of tomatoes and cucumbers which will produce the most quantity of his favourite salad. Suppose his tastes in salads are such that given all which is available to him (i.e. all possible combinations of tomatoes and cucumbers which he can grow in a season), he best prefers the salad which is made of 1.5 tomatoes (X) and 3 cucumbers (Y) (point A in Figure 2.4). He could, of course, have a similar type of salad (in terms of combination) if he only produced 1 tomato and 2 cucumbers. However, this will violate the presumption of the desirability of all economic goods. Thus, embedded in the wish to choose the best means to an end is the presumption that the end must be an efficient choice.

One day, our farmer's wife got cross with him and hit him on the head. As a result, our farmer discovered that his *abilities* (but not taste!) have changed completely. He is now much better at producing tomatoes than cucumbers. With his labour he can now produce either 4.5 X or 4.5 Y (the broken line in Figure 2.5). Assuming, as we said, that the hit on the head did not affect his taste, which combination of X and Y should he produce now?

It is clear that he can carry on producing exactly the same salad as before. However, he cannot ignore the new opportunities which have now been created (those combinations of X and Y which were not available before). The question is, what kinds of salad mix will prove to be rational? Here, of course, we are considering the second element of rationality: the consistency issue.

Had he chosen to move to a point like B we would say that our individual is not rational. The reason for this is that he had already made a choice between A and B. When he chose to produce A, B was a feasible option. By choosing A the individual is implicitly telling us that he prefers A to B. If now he chooses to move to B when A is feasible he would be telling us that he prefers B to A. This means that he is behaving inconsistently. Consequently, the only rational option would be either to stay at A or to move to a point like C where he has fewer cucumbers but where he has more than compensated by producing more tomatoes.

A move to C would be consistent because it would mean that he is now choosing a salad which is either as good as the one at A or even more to his liking, but which was not available to him before when he chose A. Suppose for a moment that our farmer considers the salad at C to be as tasty as the salad at A. Suppose also that on another occasion his neighbour hit him on the head and his abilities (but not taste) have changed again (Figure 2.6): now he can produce either 2.5 tomatoes (x) or 7.5 cucumber (y). Again, point A is still feasible but along a similar line of reasoning it would be irrational to move to a point like D but perfectly consistent to move to a point like E, where though he consumes fewer tomatoes he can more than compensate by adding cucumbers.

As before, suppose he considers the salad at E to be as tasty as the salad at A (and by implication, as tasty as the salad at C). Looking at all the developments in one diagram (Figure 2.7), we can clearly see that the implication of rationality (and, in

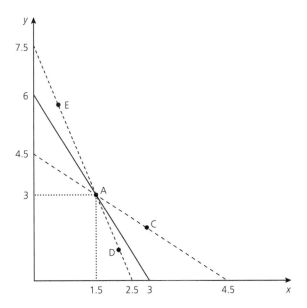

Figure 2.6 Individual rationality in changed conditions.

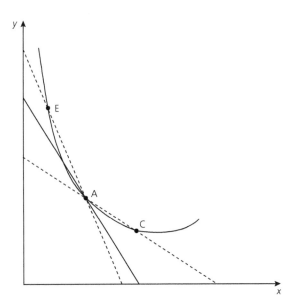

Figure 2.7 Rationality and revealed preferences.

particular, consistency) is that individuals will find points of equal taste arranged along a line like the heavy curve in Figure 2.7. Bearing this very simple implication of rationality we will now try to give more body to this idea through preferences and utility functions.

2.2.2 Preferences and the properties of utility functions

(i) The relationship individuals have with the world of economic goods
Satisfaction and All That...
To analyse the way in which individuals behave when dealing with economic goods (those scarce and desirable things) we must find out how they relate to them. Imagine an old lady with a basket standing in front of the butter and margarine counter. In her basket she already has a loaf of sliced wholesome bread. She is looking at the butter and the margarine, trying to decide whether to take butter, or margarine, or a bit of both. How will she choose?

In the late eighteenth and the nineteenth century the school of Utilitarianism was quite prominent in moral philosophy. What is relevant to our purpose is that according to this theory people derived a real and measurable degree of *satisfaction* from their being, and, in particular, from their consumption of goods.

According to this belief, our old lady will choose butter and margarine according to how much 'joy' or satisfaction they will give her. Therefore, to choose what to do we must simply measure her, say, pulse to find out what she will take. If eating the entire loaf of wholesome bread with thick layers of butter spread over it would raise her pulse to 80 beats a minute while having the same loaf of bread with margarine would induce only a pulse rate of 70 per minute, she would probably choose the butter.

The meaning of this is that our choices are based on some measure of gratification. It also means that if next to the old lady stands an old man whose pulse would rise to 100 beats if he had the butter while it would stay at 60 if he had the margarine, and there is only one pack of butter and one pack of margarine left, we should give the butter to the old man and the margarine to the old lady. Put differently, if each bundle of economic goods produces measurable degrees of satisfaction, we can easily compare any two individuals and choose a distribution which gives the highest degree of overall satisfaction.

But the idea of having a measurable degree of satisfaction is far from obvious and certainly lacks in appeal. People are different and there is no clear means by which they can quantify their feelings. So economists needed a different story to explain how the old lady makes her choice. The solution was the notion of **preferences**. In simple words, this means that if the lady takes the pack of butter she is merely indicating that she would rather have wholesome bread with butter than wholesome bread with margarine. So the issue is not one of quantifying her pleasure but rather a question of ranking. While measurable pleasures could be a means by which bundles are ranked, ranking bundles does not necessarily mean the pursuit of pleasure. Therefore, interpreting the relationship between individuals and the world of economic goods as that of ranking (i.e. whenever an individual confronts two bundles of goods he, or she, will always say either 'I prefer this to that', 'I prefer that to this', or 'I like them both') allows a much broader set of motivations to be considered. This, in principle, lends the theory an important degree of generality which is much more appealing than the narrow and intellectually unacceptable notion of measurable satisfaction.

Representation of preferences

For the purpose of analysing the relationship which individuals have with the world of economic goods we wish to begin with a straightforward and descriptive instrument. For instance, we may want to describe what people will say (literally speaking) when confronted with at least two bundles of economic goods.

Let A and B be such bundles. An individual is bound to say either 'I prefer A to B' or 'I prefer B to A' or 'I like A and B equally'. But while this depiction of the attitudes that people have towards the world of economic goods is intuitively appealing, it generates a great deal of analytical problems.

It is true that most of the time people will be confronted with binary choices (like the one between A and B). But what concerns us is not only the choice of a single individual but simultaneous choices made by many. To that end, we must be aware of what our individual would do had he, or she, confronted a different choice. If, say, a child is offered a choice between a Train Set (TS) and a game of Snakes and Ladders (SL) he may choose TS (which means that he prefers TS to SL). However, when offered a choice between TS and a Pottery Wheel (PW) he may choose PW (which means that he prefers PW to TS). If now he is being offered a choice between PW and SL he may choose SL, which means that he prefers SL to PW. So what have we got in the end? TS is preferred to SL; PW is preferred to TS; and SL is preferred to PW. This means that if the child goes into a toy shop where he is confronted with *all* the goods at once he will have a problem: PW > TS > SL > PW, so what will he choose?

In other words, it is not sufficient to ask the individual to rank only two bundles, we need to know his or her preferences with regard to the other bundles. That is, we want a *complete* ordering (ranking) over the whole space of economic goods. People, however, are highly unlikely to have such comprehensive a priori knowledge about their preferences. We therefore depart from the basic description of people's attitudes towards economic goods into a more abstract depiction of these attitudes.

However, departing from the more intuitive description of people's preferences poses some more problems which need to be addressed. For instance, what will the child do were he to face choosing between TS, PW, and SL when offered all three at the same time? Resolving those issues will inevitably require imposing greater structure on the preferences that rational people may have. Among other things, since we have rejected the utilitarian pleasure quantification, it would be very useful if we can find a mechanism to translate these preferences into numbers. After all, we all know that $7 > 5$ so if an individual assigns the number 7 to bundle A and the number 5 to bundle B it means that he prefers A over B as $7 > 5$.

The most important assumptions about the nature of preferences that we make in order to facilitate the improvement in our conception of them are the ones on completeness and transitivity. **Completeness** is both a technical and substantive assumption. On the one hand it is an important assumption which facilitates the use of a continuous real number function to represent our preferences. On the other, it is a necessary extension of the idea of choice which confronts individuals. We can always easily rank two or more things but most of the time we are confronted with much more delicate and comprehensive choices.

The other assumption, in spite of having important technical implications, is first and foremost a substantive one. **Transitivity** is one way of introducing rationality (in the sense of consistency) into our analysis. By assuming that preferences are transitive we exclude the possibility of the child's predicament illustrated above. Our child's preferences are: PW ≻ TS ≻ SL ≻ PW, which are inconsistent, and, hence, the dilemma. Had his preferences been consistent they would have satisfied transitivity: PW ≻ TS ≻ SL would imply PW ≻ SL if offered this binary choice. Preferences, one can say, must reflect consistency which, one may argue, is the most fundamental principle of rationality as captured by economics.

In addition to ensuring that preferences satisfy the rules of rationality (in the sense of consistency), completeness and transitivity along with a few more technical assumptions also allow us to convert the preference sign into an analytical more familiar one: that of greater than (>); that is, to be able to represent certain preferences by using a real number function which assigns numbers to bundles. Thus, as we said before, A would be preferred over B according to certain preferences if the number assigned to A is greater than the one assigned to B.

The transition works like this: consider a world of two economic goods, x and y. The space of all possible bundles of economic goods is the positive quadrant of the plane shown in Figure 2.8. A point like A depicts a bundle which is comprised of x_0 units of x and y_0 units of y. We write A as A $= (x_0, y_0)$. Similarly B is a point where we have x_1 units of x and y_1 units of y (B $= (x_1, y_1)$).

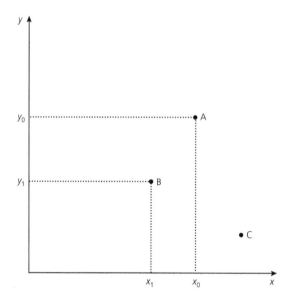

Figure 2.8 The consumption space.

Stage 1: Write down what people can say when faced with having to choose between the two bundles A and B:

'I prefer A to B'.

Stage 2: In order to transfer it into a logically coherent system, write it in symbols:
$A \succ B$ (read: A is preferred by individual i over B).

Stage 3: To allow easy transformation, transform the ranking that individuals have over the space of economic goods into something which will allow statements like: 'I am indifferent to a choice between A and C' (or 'A is at least as good as C'), Denote this as $A \succsim C$.

Stage 4: Extend the ordering 'over the entire set of economic goods (i.e. each individual can at all times rank all possible bundles).

Stage 5: Assume that the above ranking satisfies transitivity; ($A \succsim B$, $B \succsim C$ then $A \succsim C$).

Stage 6: It can be shown that the above ranking can be represented by a real number function: $u(x, y)$. This means that we can always say that $A \succsim B$ if the value of the function (the number that will be associated with A) is greater than the number associated with B. In other words, $A \succsim B$ if $u(A) \succsim u(B)$. We call the function that uses numbers to represent preferences, the **ordinal utility function**. By the word *ordinal* we mean that the function only tells us about the order, or ranking, of all bundles by a certain individual. The numbers themselves, therefore, have no significance of their own.

Hence, if we examine two bundles, say $A = (5, 6)$ (i.e. at A $x = 5$ and $y = 6$) and $B = (6, 4)$ and if our utility function is $u(x, y) = xy$; then we clearly prefer A over B. Why? Because the number we assign to A is $u(A) = u(5, 6) = 5 \times 6 = 30$ whereas the number we assign to B is $u(B) = u(6, 4) = 6 \times 4 = 24$. If instead of this form of representation I chose another utility function v such that $v(x, y) = [u(x, y)]^\alpha + c = (xy)^\alpha + c$. Let $\alpha = 2$ and $c = 1000$; so $v(A) = v(5, 6) = (5 \times 6)^2 + 1000 = (30)^2 + 1000 = 900 + 1000 = 1900$, while $v(B) = v(6, 4) = (6 \times 4)^2 + 1000 = (24)^2 + 1000 = 576 + 1000 = 1576$. Hence, using v instead of u will not alter the ranking. A is preferred over B if we use either u or v although the numbers generated by u are different from the numbers generated by v. In fact, it is easy to see that for any pair of bundles, the one that generates a higher number with u will also generate a higher number with v. Therefore, both u and v represent the same preferences.

To understand the significance of this, consider two individuals 1 and 2, with u_1 and u_2 as their respective utility functions. Society has two bundles only, A and B, and it must decide on who gets A and who gets B. If $u_1(A) = 1000$ and $u_1(B) = 20$ we know that individual 1 prefers A to B ($u_1(A) = 1000 > u_1(B) = 20$); if $u_2(A) = 100$ and $u_2(B) = 20$ we know that individual 2 prefers A over B, also. However the actual numbers have no extra significance. If, for instance, individual 1 is allocated B and individual 2 is allocated A, can we say that it is desirable to ask individual 1 and 2 to swap their bundles?

The answer is that we cannot say such a thing. One reason why we might have wanted such a swap is that we believe that society should maximize the total amount of utility. In such a case, the present allocation of A to 2 and B to 1 gives us a total utility of $u_1(B) + u_2(A) = 20 + 100 = 120$. Giving B to 2 and A to 1 would change that sum to $u_1(A) + u_2(B) = 1000 + 20 = 1020$. As 1020 is so much greater, you are tempted to shout that society should choose the option of giving A to 1 and B to 2. However, these numbers have no meaning whatsoever. The fact that individual 1's preferences are represented by 1000 against 20 and individual 2's preferences are represented by 100 to 20 is insignificant. The only thing we do know is that both individuals prefer A to B and one way or another, injustice will be done.

When we choose to allow numbers to represent the intensity of our preferences we see in the utility function more than just ranking. We call such a function **cardinal utility**. Naturally, in such a case, the comparison of utilities between the two individuals would have been meaningful. Whether we want to treat the utility function in such a way or whether we think society should maximize the total sum of utilities is an entirely different matter that will be dealt with in your future studies.

Properties of Utility Functions
The utility function, therefore, simply represents individual's preferences over the space of economic goods. Given the various properties of those preferences which we have discussed before, let us now examine the properties of the utility function which represents them.

Let us begin by looking at point A in Figure 2.9. From what we have said so far about preferences, A immediately defines 4 quadrants.

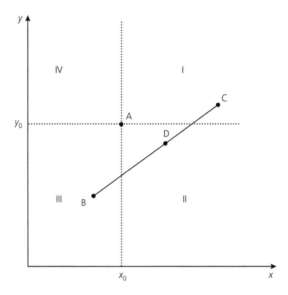

Figure 2.9 Preferences.

This means:

- A is preferred over all points in III (A $\succ$ B);
- All points in I are preferred over A (C $\succ$ A).
- The line connecting B and C goes through quadrant II. Therefore, as we move from an inferior point to a superior one, we must go through a point where we are said to

be indifferent between the two bundles (point D). All such points must be either in quadrant II or IV.

A function u is said to represent these preferences if $A \succsim B$ implies that $U(A) \geq U(B)$. Therefore:

(a) The function u must be increasing in both x and y thus representing the **desirability** feature of economic goods. It means that we always prefer to have more of at least one good[4] (See Figure 2.9). Thus, as we move from quadrant III to I, in Figure 2.9, the value of u increases. We always prefer bundles in quadrant I over bundles in quadrant III.

Now that we have borrowed an analytical instrument from the tool-kit of mathematics, we must make sure that all the elements of that tool have an economic significance. In our case, we borrowed the real number function. Such functions could be continuous and differentiable. Unless we wish to preclude the family of such functions, we must give an economic interpretation to these properties (i.e. derivatives).

(b) There is such a thing called **marginal utility** (MU_x) and it is diminishing for given levels of the other good; $MU_x(y_0) \equiv du/dx$ at x_0

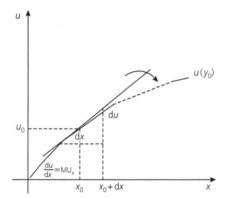

Figure 2.10 Marginal utility.

The meaning of a derivative in the context of a utility function is the analysis of how utility will change if we increased consumption of one good without changing the quantity consumed of any other good. Intuition tells us that at a given situation we cannot equally prefer increases in the consumption of the same good. Consider for instance that the two goods in question are (y) the size of a home (measured in number of bedrooms) and (x) the number of TV sets in the home. Surely we would not feel the same when the number of TV sets increased from 0 to 1 as we would have had the number increased from 14 to 15 sets. Can you imagine the excitement of moving from a situation where you cannot watch TV at all to a situation where all 2bn channels are available? How could such excitement compare with the addition of the fifteenth TV set? You may not even notice it at all. Moreover, the way one treats the increase from 14 to 15 (as well as from 0 to 1) also depend on the size of one's home. With a three bedroom house, 14 sets might become somewhat of a burden. If, however, the increase in the number of sets from 14 to 15 were accompanied by a move into a 32 bedroom mansion, I dare say that the fifteenth set might come in handy (for instance, to lift the spirit of the staff). In other words, **marginal utility** is defined as the increase in utility with a small change in the consumption of one good only. As the consumption of the other goods is unchanged we assume that utility will rise in diminishing increments.

Formally, the concept of marginal utility corresponds to the derivative of the utility function or, which is the same thing, the slope of the function as is depicted in the Figure 2.10. In that diagram we start at the consumption of x_0 units of x and y_0 units of y. In the figure we only depict the changes in utility when consumption of x increases. Hence, at x_0 we will have a utility of u_0 which is really the value which the utility function will yield if we plugged into it the present specific levels of consumption: $u_0 = u(x_0, y_0)$.

There is, however, a 'slight' problem with marginal utility if we consider utility as a mere representation of preferences. Above, we discussed at some length the possibility of representing the same preference-ranking using a whole host of functions which produce different numbers yet preserve the order of preferences over the bundle of goods.[5] This meant that the actual number were insignificant. How then, you may query, can we talk in a meaningful way about diminishing marginal utility? Well, the simple answer is that we cannot do this. Yet, there is something which seems to us intrinsically correct about the assertion of diminishing marginal utility.

For one, recall that we are dealing with the specific case where the number of economic goods in the system is fixed. As I explained when we discussed desirability, the idea of unsatiated wants may appear more reasonable if we talked about the desire for new commodities. Many of us are in constant search for new goods. In this context, the idea of diminishing marginal utility may not be the right one. If, say, x represented 'home entertainment' then increasing x by adding 'home-cinema' to the already existing TV may not yield a diminishing marginal utility as would a simple increase in the number of TV sets.

However, in a world of fixed number of goods where we translate unsatiated wants into a desire of greater quantities of the same thing, we would be intuitively right to expect the utility of an extra unit to diminish.

Still, this does not resolve the problem we have with the meaningful numerical representation of marginal utility in the context of meaningless numerical values of utility. Luckily, the problem has a great and useful solution in the form of marginal utility which is measured in terms of the other good. I will explain this in (d) below.

(c) Indifference points are arranged along a downward sloping curve in quadrants II and IV (see Figure 2.11). As was noted before, the line connecting B and C goes through quadrant II. Therefore, as we move from an inferior point (A ≻ B) to a superior one (C ≻ A) we go through a point where we are said to be indifferent between the two bundles (point D). All such points, therefore, must be either in quadrants II or IV.

The reason why we can make such an assertion is the assumption about the *continuity* of preferences. That is, if we take the line connecting points B with C we can see that there are many bundles strewn along it. We know that at B $u(B) < u(A)$ and at C $u(C) > u(A)$ (see Figure 2.12).

On the vertical axis we write the value of $u(A) - u(\alpha)$ (where α denotes combinations of x and y along the line between B and C). On the left-hand side of the graph, $\alpha = B$ and $u(A) - u(B)$ is greater than zero. At the other end of the diagram, $\alpha = C$. Here, $u(A) - u(C)$ is negative. As we move gradually from B to C, we move from a less preferred to a more preferred bundle. On our way, we must cross the point where $u(A) - u(\alpha) = 0$. This is the

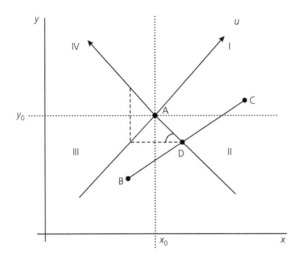

Figure 2.11 Utility increasing in both x and y.

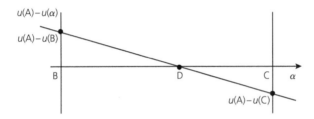

Figure 2.12 Differences in utility for different bundles.

point where $\alpha = $ D and it means that $u(A) = u(\alpha)$ or, that the individual is indifferent between A and D.

(d) The slope of the indifference curve is defined geometrically as $-(dy/dx)$ when the level of u is unchanged (Figure 2.13).

If we give up one unit of $x(dx = 1)$ we shall lose the utility of that unit (MU_x) which is the marginal utility of x at that point. Hence, the total change in utilities will be:

$$(dxMU_x).$$

If at the same time we change the consumption of y also (dy), the overall change in utility will be:

$$(dyMU_y)$$

Therefore, if we give up x and add y there will be a point where the loss of utility will be fully compensated by the increased utility from the extra consumption of y. At that point:

$$-dxMU_x = dyMU_y$$

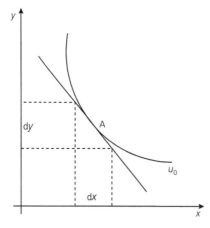

Figure 2.13 The slope of the indifference curve.

Geometry tells us that the slope of the indifference curve is $-(dy/dx)$. We can extract this from the above equation:

$$-dxMU_x = dyMU_y$$

$$-\frac{dy}{dx} = \frac{MU_x}{MU_y}$$

What does it really mean? After all, MU_x/MU_y is a number, say 5, what is the meaning of this number? The answer is very simple and should be borne in mind at all times. Let MU_x be 10 (the number which is generated by the specific utility function which we are using) and MU_y be 2. In such a case, $10/2 = 5$ means that the individual will be willing to substitute 5 units of y with 1 unit of x as he, or she, will have the same utility before and after the change, or, which is almost the same thing, they will be indifferent to the change.

Consider a situation where an elder brother is taking one of his sister's dolls. The girl will immediately cry. The intensity of her displeasure is captured by the marginal utility of dolls (say dolls are commodity x). As the brother hears the key turning in the door (which means that their parents are back) he will try to pacify his sister either by returning the doll (which is not good as he needs the doll to experiment with friends) or by giving her chocolate (commodity y) instead. The slope of the indifference curve tells us how many chocolate bars he will have to give to his sister for her to stop crying. Evidently, if she has a collection of a 1000 dolls, she would barely notice the missing doll and if she does, she would whimper rather than cry. If, at the same time, chocolate is banned from the house, sneaking her a small chocolate bar may be sufficient to appease her. On the other hand, had this been her only doll and the house was full of chocolate, the brother would probably need to give her 2 tonnes of chocolate for the same doll.

In other words, the slope of the indifference curve MU_x/MU_y, which is measured in units of y per x (if the numerator is 10 and the denominator 2, the slope means 5 units of y per 1 unit of x), is really the **marginal utility of x measured in units of y**. It represents the individual's willingness to pay for x in units of y. All individuals are quite willing to pay less; the willingness to pay as represented by the indifference curves measures the upper limit of this willingness. We may say that 5 units of y per x is a real measure of our utility from x. It is our subjective evaluation of x in terms of y. It is therefore referred to as the MRS: **marginal rate of subjective substitution**. The way you should really think about it is as the 'willingness to pay' or the 'subjective exchange rate' between y and x.

But, you may ask, what about the problem of meaningful marginal utility numbers in the context of meaningless overall utility numbers? The answer is quite simple. Once we have established the concept of **real marginal utility** we no longer depend on the numerical value of marginal utility which is produced by the utility function.

The rest of this subsection may appear a little complex to you. It assumes that you know how to differentiate a simple function. If you are uncomfortable with this, you may skip to section (e) below without fear of being in any way left behind.

Consider Figure 2.14:

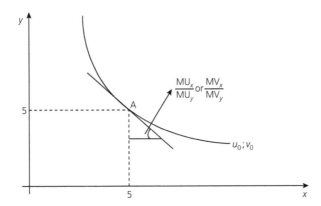

Figure 2.14

At point A we have a combination of 5 units of x and 5 units of y($A = (5, 5)$). Suppose now that our preferences are represented by the utility function: $u(x, y) = xy$. What would be the marginal utility of x if we just looked at the derivative of the function? The answer is: $MU_x = (\partial u/\partial x) = y$ which at point A means 5. What would be the marginal utility of x had we used the function v to represent the same preferences? Recall that $v(x, y) = [u(x, y)]^\alpha + c = (xy)^\alpha + c$, hence the marginal utility of x will be: $MV_x = (\partial v/\partial x) = \alpha(xy)^{\alpha-1}y$. At point A where $x = y = 5$ and assuming $\alpha = 2$: $MV_x = 2 \times (5 \times 5)^{2-1}5 = 2 \times 25 \times 5 = 250$. Clearly 250 is greater than 5 and in fact, if you checked it you will find that in terms of pure marginal utility numbers, the marginal utility of x in neither u nor v is falling. But what about the real marginal utility, namely, the marginal utility of x as measured in units of y (or the marginal rate of subjective substitution)? The answer here is a bit surprising. The real marginal utility of x at point A when we use u to represent our preferences is given by:

$$\frac{MU_x}{MU_y} = \frac{\partial u/\partial x}{\partial u/\partial y} = \frac{y}{x} \text{ units of } y \text{ per } x,$$

which at point A yields the number $5/5 = 1$ unit of y per x. What, then, would be the real marginal utility of x at point A when we use v to represent our preferences?

$$\frac{MV_x}{MV_y} = \frac{\partial v/\partial x}{\partial v/\partial y} = \frac{\alpha(x \cdot y)^{\alpha-1}y}{\alpha(x \cdot y)^{\alpha-1}x} = \frac{y}{x} \text{ units of } y \text{ per } x,$$

which is exactly the same answer as we got by using u. Namely, the real marginal utility of x at A is $5/5 = 1$ unit of y per x. This means that while the numerical representation of utility produces meaningless numbers, the real marginal utility is not subjected to the same difficulties. There will be only one number representing the marginal utility of x measured in units of y (and, of course, vice versa) for all possible numerical representation of the same preferences!

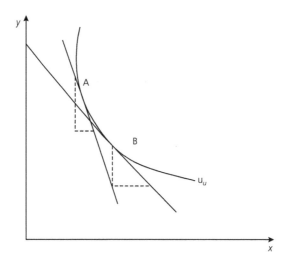

Figure 2.15

(e) The shape of the indifference curve: indifference curves are convex due to the diminishing nature of the real marginal utility. Let us compare the situation at points A and B in Figure 2.15. The slope of the indifference curve, as was established in the previous subsection is: MU_x/MU_y units of y per x (see Figure 2.13). It is the real measure of the marginal utility of x (and the inverse, for y) which is independent of the numerical representation of our preferences but apparently unique to each specific set of preferences. What would we expect the marginal utility of x, measured in units of y, to be at point A? At A, we have a lot of y and very few units of x. In terms of the brother and sister story from before, it is a situation where the sister has only one doll (x) but enjoys plenty of chocolates (y). In such an event, it stands to reason that the brother will have to give her a lot of chocolate to compensate for one doll. Namely, he will have to give her a lot of y to compensate for the loss of one unit of x. In terms of the slope it means that MU_x/MU_y is a large number at A (many units of y per x). A large number, geometrically, means a steep slope. At point B, on the other hand, the sister has a number of dolls but rarely eats any chocolate. If the brother takes her doll she may barely notice it. A tiny bit of chocolate can easily stop her crying. This means that when x is plentiful relative to y, we are likely to need a small quantity of y to compensate per unit of x. Hence at B, MU_x/MU_y is small. One needs very few units of y (which is rare) to replace x (which is in plenty). A small number for the real marginal utility means a flat slope. From this we can deduce that the shape of the indifference curve will be convex towards the origin.

Individual behaviour

Describing the relationship which individuals have with the world of economic goods as represented by the utility function is describing the '**desirability**' element of what constitute economic goods. We still have to add the sense of **scarcity** to complete the picture. Clearly, at the level of the individual, the budget we have represents the scarcity we face.

In a world of two goods, the **budget constraint** presents itself in the following way:

$$p_x x + p_y y \leq I,$$

where p_x and p_y are the respective money price of x and y and I is the individual's income (in money).[6] When the individual chooses a combination of x and y such that the total amount of money needed is less than their income (I), the constraint will not be binding: $p_x x + p_y y < I$. If, however, the individual chooses a bundle that exhausts his or her income then there will be no money left and $p_x x + p_y y = I$.

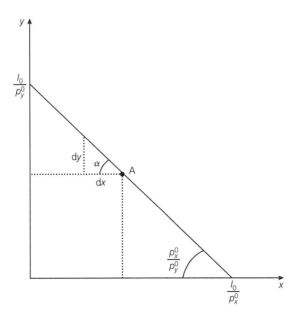

Figure 2.16 The budget line.

The budget line (see Figure 2.16), a bit like the production possibility frontier, divides the world of economic goods facing the individual to that which is possible and that which is not. The intercepts are the points where the individual uses his or her entire income for the consumption of one good only. In such a case, the individual will be able to buy I/p_i units of good i (where $i = x,y$).

The slope of the budget line reveals yet another concept of exchange. Recall that so far we have talked about two such concepts. First there is the slope of the production possibility curve which represents the *opportunity cost* or, the **technological rate of substitution**. As the technology is assumed to be given, this exchange rate between x and y represents the social cost; how many units of y (or x) we really need to give up in order to obtain one more unit of x (or y).

The second concept of *price*, or exchange rate, is the **subjective rate of substitution** or, what one is willing to pay for one unit of x (and y) in terms of the other good. This exchange rate was entirely dependent on individuals' preferences.

Now we have the slope of the budget line which will give us the **market rate of exchange** between x and y or, which is the same thing, the price of x in terms of y (and naturally, the price of y in terms of x). If we are consuming x and y such that our income is exhausted, we are said to be on the budget line. The total spending on x ($p_x x$) plus the total spending on y ($p_y y$) equals our income (I).

If we now choose to consume 1 unit less of x, how many more units of y will we be able to buy? If $p_x = 10$ and $p_y = 5$ then giving up one unit of x will leave £10 which we can now spend on y. Given that the price of y is £5 we will be able to buy two units of y if we gave up one unit of x ($p_x/p_y = 10/5 = 2$ units of y per x). Therefore, the slope of the budget line reveals the exchange rate between x and y that will be facilitated by the market.

Utility maximization

Given that the individual always wants more of all economic goods he, or she, would want to choose the most preferred bundle from the set of feasible bundles. We know that utility is increasing in both x and y (see property (a) above). We also know that each level of utility corresponds to a convex indifference curve. Hence, to translate the above into the language of the model we say that the individual wants to maximize utility (i.e. choose the most preferred bundle) subject to the budget constraint (i.e. from the set of feasible bundles). Graphically it means to choose the highest indifference curve possible (see Figure 2.17).

Given the shape of the indifference curve, the highest level of utility will be achieved whenever the indifference curve is only tangent to the budget line.

What does this mean? Note that tangency means that the slope of the indifference curve is the same as the slope of the budget line at the point of tangency. Therefore, a consumer chooses the optimal consumption bundle whenever his subjective rate of substitution (MU_x/MU_y) equals the market rate of exchange (p_x/p_y). Namely, the real marginal utility of x equals the price of x, in units of y, in the market place. In other words, the individual pays for a unit of x in the market place exactly that much which he or she is willing to pay!

The utility maximizing individual will therefore want to consume x_0 units of x and y_0 units of y (point A in Figure 2.17) in the world of two economic goods. A point like A

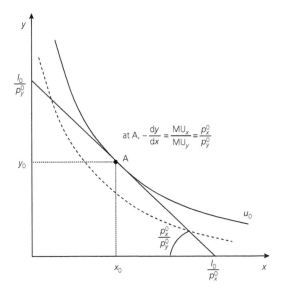

Figure 2.17 Utility maximization.

represents an optimal choice because there is nothing the individual can do—within this framework—that will bring about a higher level of utility (or a more preferred bundle). At A, the subjective rate of substitution (MU_x/MU_y) is the same as the market rate of exchange between x and y (i.e. p_x/p_y).

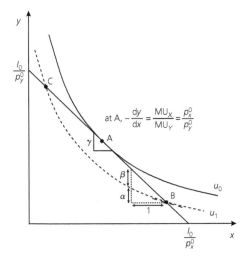

Figure 2.18 Suboptimal bundles.

Had the individual been at a point like B the subjective rate of substitution is lower than the market rate of exchange. The slope of the indifference curve (MU_x/MU_y) is smaller than the slope of the budget constraint (p_x/p_y). This means, in words, that at B if the individual gave up one unit of x, he or she would need α units of y to regain the same level of utility as in B. However, if they do give up one unit of x they will get in the market place $\alpha + \beta$ units of y per unit of x. This means that they will be better off exchanging x for y. This will be true as long as the subjective rate of substitution differs from the market rate of exchange.[7] A similar situation can be seen at C. At A, however, the subjective rate of exchange equals the market rate of exchange. Hence, if the individual gives up one unit of x at A, he or she will need more than γ units of y per unit of x to be able to increase their utility. However, in the market place they will get precisely γ units of y per unit of x. Therefore, if their aim is to increase their utility they will do no such thing once they get to a point like A. Therefore, A is the point where they maximize their utility given the budget constraint.

2.3 Deriving demand for economic goods

2.3.1 Substitution and income effects

Having explained how individuals are making their choices we could also try to establish how universal is the downward sloping demand curve in the plane of quantity and price. Figure 2.19 depicts this analysis:

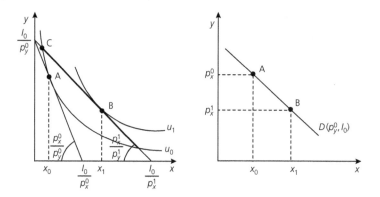

Figure 2.19 Utility maximization and the demand function.

At A, the price of x is given as p_x^0 and (for a given price of y (p_y^0) and a given income I_0) the quantity of x that would be demanded is x_0. To analyse the impact of a change in the price of x alone on the quantity demanded we have to keep the price of y, as well as income, unchanged.[8] We simply set $p_x^1 (< p_x^0)$ as the new price and repeat the analysis from before to reach point B as the new optimal choice. To reach point B we had to follow the following steps. First, the fall in the price of x would have affected the budget constraint facing the individual. As the price of x falls, the agent would be able to buy many more units of x had he or she used their entire income to buy only x. The intercept of the budget constraint with the y-axis would not change as the change in the price of x would have no impact on the quantity of y the person can purchase with his or her entire income. Equally, the price of x is also an element defining the slope of the budget constraint. Hence, as the money price of x falls, the price of x in terms of y falls too (a flatter slope).

The first thing to notice is that an action would be rational if the agent chooses a new allocation where he is better off than he was before, and from where he can have no more of one economic good without giving up another. Thus, all the points on the heavy line suggest allocations which satisfy this. Notice, however, that this includes allocations (like C) where the individual buys less of x as a result of the fall in the price of x. The meaning of it is quite significant. Not only it is untrue that anyone had seen a downward sloping demand schedule, rationality itself does not necessarily dictate such a relationship between quantity demanded and the price. The origin of the widespread belief that demand schedules are downward sloping is thus a greater puzzle than we thought.

Evidently, this means that there are some conditions that make an individual choose point B rather than C and that these are derived from his or her preferences.

At B, clearly, the quantity demanded of x is greater than before and the downward sloping demand curve is now a conclusion rather than an assumption.

But now we have to establish what it is that leads us to a point such as B instead of a point such as C. We can see that the fall in the price of x will shift the budget constraint as shown in Figure 2.20 (the fall in the price of x means that we can buy more of x if we spend our income on x alone but there will be no change in the quantity of y we could purchase with the same money income and the same money price of y).

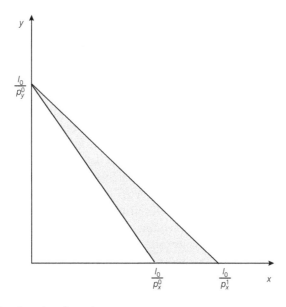

Figure 2.20 Changing the price of good x.

This means that the shaded area reflects a whole new range of opportunities which were not feasible to the individual before. Thus, without a change in the individual's nominal income there seems to be a rise in his or her real income. Namely, the individual can now buy more of all goods and not only good x. Given that individuals find the two goods desirable, a change in the price of x (which brings about a change in real income) will therefore generate a change in the demand for y too. We are therefore confronted with the question of how the effects of the rise in the price of x would be distributed between the two goods.

Moreover, if the change in the price of x has an income effect it means that many of the government policies which affect prices (like taxation or subsidies) will make all people either richer or poorer, and not only those people whom the government would like to help or penalize. Assuming that such policies are also concerned with redistribution of income, this is an important new insight that we could not have derived by treating the downward sloping demand curve as a 'law'.

There are now clearly two reasons why we may buy more of x when its price falls. First there is the obvious reason: it is cheaper (in terms of y). Namely, if we forgo one extra unit of y we will be able to get more x for it than we need to compensate for the loss of utility. Second, in real terms we are now richer. We can buy more of both goods! To distinguish the substitution effect from the income effect, we must first establish what **real income** is. By simply looking at Figure 2.20 it is evident that in terms of x alone there was a significant rise in real income but in terms of y alone there was really no rise at all. So has real income gone up or not?

Two suggestions are now being considered. One, following Hicks, suggests that the measure for real income is **utility**. The other, following Slutsky, points at the **initial bundle** as the reference point for real income. Let us examine them in turn.

According to Hicks, the real income is measured in terms of utility. Hence, the substitution effect can be established by looking at the individual's optimal choice had he or she confronted the new relative price (the new exchange rate between x and y) while keeping utility at the initial level. This can be achieved by finding the point of tangency of the new relative price with the initial indifference curve. This is point C in Figure 2.21. The move from A to C is what we may call as a pure (or, sometimes, net) **substitution effect**. It is simply how a utility maximizing individual would have responded had he or she been confronted with a new market exchange rate between x and y while their real income remained unchanged. Given the Hicksian definition of real income at both A and C the individual enjoys the same level of real income (which is u_0).

Note that what dominates the move from A to C is the shape of the indifference curve. Namely, the reason why an individual will consume more of x as the price of it (in terms of y) falls is that now at A he is being required in the market to pay for x less than what he is willing to pay for it. Evidently, he cannot be considered as behaving optimally if in such circumstances he does not buy more of x.

As the individual buys more of x (and for the same reasons consumes less of y), the composition of x and y in his bundle changes. He moves from a situation where there were fewer units of x relative to y to a situation where there are relatively more x to y. Hence, the real marginal utility or the **marginal rate of subjective substitution** will now decrease. In other words, MU_x/MU_y is now a smaller number; as we have plenty of x and only a small amount of y the willingness to pay for x will be reduced until the

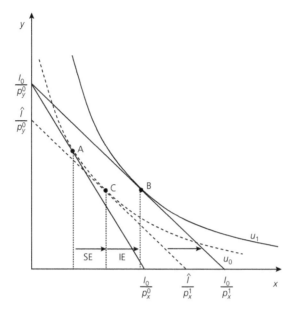

Figure 2.21 The Hicks substitution and income effects.

individual gets to the point where his willingness to pay is the same as what he is being required to pay in the market place.

So due to the convexity of the indifference curve we always confront an inverse net-substitution relationship. Namely, because of diminishing nature of the real marginal utilities we will buy more of the good, the price of which will fall.

Let us now consider the move from C to B. Naturally, since both A and C are on the same indifference curve (i.e. the same utility level) and at B we are on a higher level of utility, the move from C to B must be the *income effect*.

Moreover, the move from C to B in the Figure 2.21 can be brought about by a parallel shift of the budget line. Such a shift can be constructed by an increase in nominal income between points C and B. Recall that there is no change in nominal income and that the budget lines at B and at A are for the same level of nominal income. Evidently, at C the income which can be associated with the budget line must be lower than the one at A (as the price of x falls, we need less money to maintain the original level of real income). The difference between the income we need at C and the one at A (our actual income) could be considered as a nominal equivalent to the real income effect.

For instance, let $I_0 = 100$, $p_x^0 = 10$ and $p_y^0 = 10$. Point A in Figure 2.22 captures the initial position where the consumer chooses the bundle (5,5).

Now the price of x has changed to $p_x^1 = 5$. The individual will move to the new choice, which is point B, where he consumes (8,6). Following Hicks we want to isolate the substitution effect by looking at the individual's choice had he confronted the new relative price at the original level of utility. Point C in Figure 2.22 is such a point where the individual choice is, say, (7,3). We can now calculate the level of nominal income that would

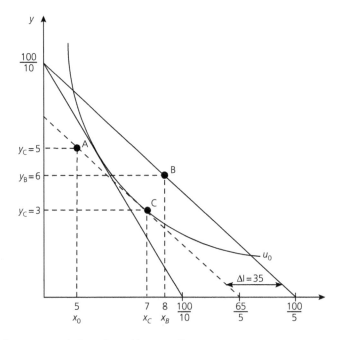

Figure 2.22 The money equivalent of a real income effect.

have been needed to be at point C.

$$\text{At } A:$$

$$p_x^0 x_0 + p_y^0 y_0 = I_0$$

$$10.5 + 10.5 = 100$$

$$\text{At } C:$$

$$p_x^1 x^c + p_y^0 y^c = I_c$$

$$5.7 + 10.3 = 65.$$

This means that once the price of x falls from 10 to 5, the individual will need less money to maintain the original level of real income. Before the change he needed £100 (point A) and now he only needs £65 (point C). This means that as he is still earning £100, the fall in the price of x has made him richer by the equivalent of £35. The shift from C to B, therefore, measures the money equivalent to the increase in real income (which is measured in utilities). Notice, however, that there was no actual change in nominal income during the move from A to B.

What invoked the need to use alternative definitions for real income are two major issues. The first one is that utilities are not an observed phenomenon so we may need something more tangible in order to be able to make sensible policy recommendations. Actual levels of consumption (i.e. points like A) are observed and may serve better as benchmarks for one's real income. Second, there is a certain anomaly in the Hicksian definition of real income. As you can see from Figure 2.22, an individual would only need £65 to be at his, or her, original level of real income once the price of x fell to £5.

If the fall in the price of x were, for instance, due to a subsidy for bread (x being bread) the government may wish to tax away the income benefits that the rich are experiencing. Suppose that it taxed away the £35 difference. Would those individuals be able to consume their initial bundle (A) if they wanted? Well, to buy A at the new prices we will need: $5 \times 5 + 10 \times 5 = £75$. But the income needed under Hicks to maintain the original level of real income was only £65. This means that if the government taxed away the difference, people will no longer be able to consume that which they used to consume before the change.[9] This is why we also examine an alternative definition: that of Slutsky.

In the case of the Slutsky definition we would have simply asked ourselves what would have been the individual's choice had he confronted the new relative prices while being able to maintain his present consumption. This would reveal the net-substitution effect, as the real income (measured in terms of the ability to buy the initial bundle) remain unchanged. In Figure 2.23 this idea is captured by the use of an imaginary budget line that goes through A but that reflects the new price ratio:

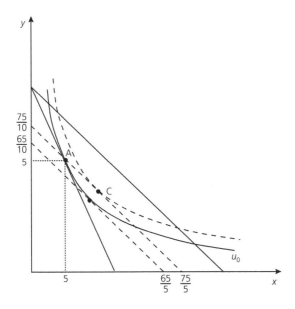

Figure 2.23 The Slutsky analysis.

As the new budget line goes through point A it cannot be tangent to the same indifference curve to which the original line was tangent to. Thus the bundle A can no longer be considered as the optimal choice (i.e. the subjective rate of substitution at A is greater than the new market exchange rate between x and y). Hence, the individual would adjust his choice to that which is optimal and where he pays for x, in terms of y, its real marginal utility. He would thus choose to be at point C which is on a higher utility level.[10]

To calculate the nominal equivalent to the real income effect we can now simply ask how much money would have been needed to consume the bundle at A at the new prices. As we saw earlier the answer to this is £75. Therefore, according to Slutsky's definition of real income, the nominal equivalent to the income effect is only $£100 - £75 = £25$ while under Hicksian's definition of real income, the money equivalent was $£100 - £65 = £35$.

Can one therefore argue that under Slutsky's definition of real income the substitution effect is *always greater* than under the Hicksian definition of it? Well, we cannot answer this question before we examine the next section. But can we say that the real income effect of a change in price under Slutsky's definition of it is always smaller than the one that would emerge under the Hicksian definition of real income?

2.3.2 Normal and inferior goods

We have seen thus far that had substitution effect been the only cause of a change in choice once the price of x changes, the rationality of preferences (as manifested in the convex shape of the indifference curve) would have dictated an inverse relationship between price and quantity demanded. The downward sloping demand would have then been the only conclusion we could then derive from rational behaviour. However, we saw at the beginning of the previous subsection that in fact, it is possible to make a rational choice where we buy less of x when its price falls (point C in Figure 2.19). As this could not be established as a result of the pure substitution effect, it must be the result of the income effect.

In Figure 2.24, the price of x fell from p_x^0 to p_x^1. Net-substitution suggests that the individual will move from point A to point C. This is always true regardless of the nature of the good.

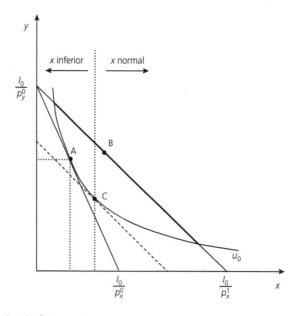

Figure 2.24 Normal and inferior goods.

Now, the move from the broken line at C to the new budget line is a parallel shift which we had seen is an equivalent to an increase in nominal income. This, therefore, is the pure income effect. The increase in real income means that the individual would have needed less money to maintain his original level of real income (under any definition of real income) and subsequently, as his nominal income remains unchanged, he can now buy more of all goods. It would be perfectly rational on the part of the individual if he now chooses to move to a point B, anywhere on the heavy line, where utility is higher.

There are now two main possibilities. The first possibility is that the individual would move to the right of point C which means that as real income increases the individual would want to consume more of x. The second possibility is that the individual would choose to be on the left of C which means that as real income increases the individual would want to consume less of x. In the former case we say that x is a **normal good**; namely, a good, the consumption of which increases with income. In the latter case we say that x is an **inferior good**; in the sense that the consumption of x decreases as income increases.

The actual position of B on the new budget line, in the end, depends on the specific positions of indifference curves. This means that whether the individual chooses to be to the left or to the right of point C is entirely a matter of preferences. Therefore, whether a good is an inferior or normal good is not an intrinsic characteristic of the good itself. It is the way individuals see economic goods which make them either normal or inferior. What may be a normal good to one person may be considered an inferior good in the eyes of the other. In some cultures fish may be considered as basic food, while meat may be rare. It is possible that in such cultures fish may be considered as an inferior good. The manifestation of this will be that the rich would consume meat while the poor would eat fish. Thus, some people, when their income increases they would see themselves as rich and would reduce the consumption of fish. The opposite can be the case in a different culture. Moreover, even within the same culture, it is possible that some people will be more inclined to emulate the rich than others. Hence, when the real income of two agents increases, the response of the one could be to consume less fish so that other sees him or her as belonging to the rich layer of society, the other, on the other hand, a rebellious and proud working-class agent may prefer to stick to his own diet (which in this case is also healthier) rather than become something he is not. Thus, fish would be an inferior good for the first agent and a normal good for the second one.

There are now three possible effects to a change in the price of a good on the quantity of it which will be demanded. Figure 2.25 offers a summary of these cases:

In the case of a normal good, the net-substitution and the income effects seem to be working in the same direction (A to B^N). In the case of an inferior good the income effect appears to work in the opposite direction of the net-substitution effect. There are now two possibilities: (i) the net-substitution effect is greater (in absolute values) than the income effect (A to B^I) or (ii) the net-substitution effect is smaller (in absolute values) than the income effect (A to B^G). We distinguish the latter from the general group of inferior goods by naming it a **Giffen good**.

The demand for the normal good will therefore tend to be flatter than the demand for an inferior good. The demand for an inferior good, where the net-substitution effect is more dominant, is still downward sloping while that of an inferior good, where the income effect is more dominant (a Giffen good), is upward sloping.

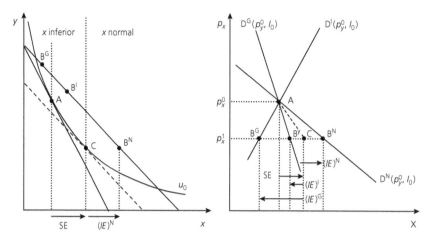

Figure 2.25 Normal, inferior, and Giffen goods and their demand schedules.

2.3.3 Complements and gross substitutes

So far, the **rational utility maximizer** taught us that the intuitive presumption about the downward sloping nature of demand is by no means universal. It allowed us to decompose the changes affecting the demand and to distinguish between two different types of goods. You can imagine that such developments are very useful indeed. If you were a seller of a commodity would you not have wanted to know whether the demand you face is that for a normal or inferior good? You can imagine that the kind of advertising you may wish to pursue if the good you sell is perceived by most customers as an inferior good would be very different indeed from the one you would wish to pursue had the good been perceived as a normal good.

But there is another function which the rational utility maximizer is playing in our system. Recall that in the first chapter, I discussed the idea that specialization and trade are the best way to proceed in order to resolve the economic problem. A consequence of this is that everyone becomes immediately dependent on each other. This is one of the reasons we end up with a system where everything is so tightly connected.

Independent of this problem, we also noticed that in order to be able to represent preferences by a real number function, preferences must be complete. Namely, we must have preferences which are well-defined over the entire set of possible bundles. This means that when I choose how many units of x I want, I had already made a choice about all other goods. While we are all painfully aware that by so doing, we depart from the level of description to the level of the abstract, it turned out to be a useful means to capture the notion of interdependence. As the agent who drives the entire system is the 'individual' he or she must hold the buttons for all the elements in the system. Hence, the effect of a change in the price of any good would reverberate in the system because it will affect the choice of all individuals with regard to all economic goods: those which they consume and those which they sell.

In the case of two goods, all of this means simply that choosing the quantity of x also implies choosing the quantity of y. Therefore, the demands for the two goods are interrelated.

Consider again the fall in the price of *x* as discussed above but now, let us concentrate on what happens to the quantity demanded of *y* (see Figure 2.26).

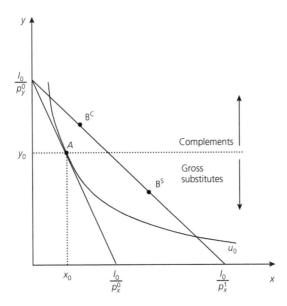

Figure 2.26 Complements and gross substitutes.

There are, in principle, two possibilities with regard to the effects of the change on the quantity demanded of *y*. Either B—the new optimal point—falls above A, where we increase the consumption of *y* when the price of *x* falls. Or, B falls below A, where we reduce the consumption of *y* as the price of *x* falls.

In the case where the consumption of *y* increases when the price of *x* falls, we say that *x* and *y* are **complements**. It is so because a fall in the price of *x* suggests (in general) that people will buy more of *x*. If at the same time they also buy more of *y* it must mean that individuals feel that consumption of *x* 'goes well' with *y*. An example for complements are biscuits and coffee. In some cultures common practice dictates that when guests come to your house you should offer them coffee and biscuits. Therefore, when the price of coffee goes down, you are likely to entertain more and as a result, increase your demand for biscuits too. However, notice again that this is not so because of the intrinsic nature of the goods themselves. For one, it is a cultural thing which connects coffee and biscuits while entertaining. Moreover, it is possible that even within this culture some people may not consider coffee and biscuits as complements. For instance, if someone, who is very conscious about justice, thinks that the fall in the price of coffee reflects the exploitation of coffee growers in a poor country by some multinationals, he or she may choose either to entertain less (and thus, offer less biscuits) or to offer only coffee when guests arrive (thinking that in so doing he would help the coffee growers in spite of their exploitation). Either way, the relationship between the changes in the price of *x* and the change in demand of the other good will no longer correspond to that which had been culturally generated.

In the case where the consumption of y falls with the fall in the price of x we say that x and y are **gross substitutes**.[11] A fall in the price of x suggests that we will consume more of x (x being cheaper). If consuming more of x means consuming less of y, it must be that we feel that we can substitute x for y. A typical example is the use of private cars and public transport. When the price of public transport drops, people will tend to reduce the use of their private car and go more on public transport. Here again, some may say that the fall in the price of public transport would turn them unbearably crowded and thus, choose to use their car more rather than less (hence treating cars and public transport as complements).

A generalized demand function

Let us now summarize, and generalize, the derivation of demand which we have pursued so far:

(a) The desirability of economic goods presents itself in the form of preferring more to less; a rational individual has consistent preferences over the world of economic goods which could be represented by a real number function called the **Utility Function**;

(b) This means that individuals' demand for all goods is determined simultaneously;

(c) The individual confronts scarcity in the form of a **Budget Constraint**;

(d) A utility maximizing individual will choose that bundle where one's **willingness to pay** equals the market **price**, or the market exchange rate between the goods;

(e) The choice of both x_0 and y_0 in Figure 2.27 reflects the individual's demand for x and y;

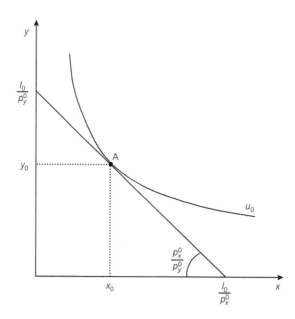

Figure 2.27 Deriving demand.

(f) The demand for x, therefore, depends on those parameters which determine the position of point A;

(g) Point A is determined simultaneously by the utility function (which determined the shape and position of the indifference curve), and by the position of the budget line;

(h) The position of the budget line is determined by Income (I) and the prices p_x and p_y;

(i) Hence we can write:

$$x^d = D(p_x, p_y, I, U)$$

As throughout our analysis we will always assume that tastes, or utility, are unchanged, we may ignore it and only consider those things which are likely to change in our analysis:

$$x^d = D(p_x, p_y, I)$$

A small matter of semantics: D is the **demand function** and x^d is the **quantity demanded**.

(j) The first and immediate property of this demand function is that it is homogeneous of degree zero. This means that if we, say, doubled all variables (p_x, p_y and I), the choice of x will remain unchanged as the position of the budget line[12] is unaffected by such a change; the meaning of this is that we assume rational agents to make decisions in real terms only. They are not impressed if their income doubled at the same time that all prices have doubled too. For them, the nominal values of prices and income are not the parameters for decisionmaking. Instead, it is the real values of these concepts which guide the decisionmaking of the rational agent.

(k) A **normal good** is a good the consumption of which increases when income increases; an **inferior good** is a good the consumption of which decreases when income increases.

(l) The quantity demanded of x is directly related to the price of y if x and y are **gross substitutes** and inversely related if x and y are complements;

(m) The analysis can be generalized in the following way: if there are n goods in the economy denoted by ($x_1, \ldots, x_n$), the demand for good 1 will be of the following form:

$$x_1^d = D(p_1, p_2, \ldots, p_n, I)$$

This D too is homogenous of degree 0; everything we said about p_x holds here to p_1; everything we said about p_y, is true here to any of the other prices;

2.4 Market demand and its properties

From the analysis of the rational utility maximizer we have derived the demand schedule: the most common one is the inverse relationship between quantity demanded and price.

The market demand is nothing else but the total of that quantity demanded. It is the sum of quantity demanded by each individual when their willingness to pay equals the market price.

Technically, what has just been described is called **horizontal summation**. Here is a geometrical presentation of this idea: there are three individuals (or groups of individuals) and a total market demand (on the right), where x_0^1, x_0^2, and x_0^3 are the quantities demanded by each individual at the price of p_x^0 and $x_0^T = x_0^1 + x_0^2 + x_0^3$ (see Figure 2.28).

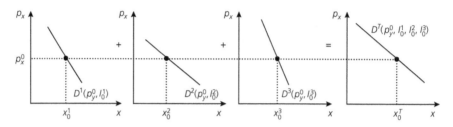

Figure 2.28 Market demand.

Note that there is a great deal of difference between treating the demand in the market place as representing the preferences of a **representative agent** (as we have done up to this section) and treating it as a sum of demands representing the preferences of *all agents*. In an idea world we should focus on the demand as the horizontal sum of individuals' demand schedules. However, this is an almost impossible empirical task. We would need to know each agent's exact preferences and how they translate into a demand function. This, in turn, amounts to almost saying that we know for sure that people actually have consistent preferences over the world of economic goods.

While it is rather clear that it is virtually impossible to collect information about the preferences of each individual, it must also be noted that it is quite conceivable that most people do not have such well-defined consistent preferences over the entire world of economic goods. You may ask, then, why exactly are we doing this? This is of course, an important and complex question. I will not attempt to answer it here but I will give you something to think about. At the beginning of this book I emphasized that economics is a sophisticated analytical language. The question we face, therefore, is not whether or not people are actually rational in the way we modelled them. Instead, the question is whether people will understand arguments about rationality. If, for instance, we tax away from the rich the income effect generated by a subsidy for food they will want to know why. We would answer by saying 'had you been rational, the fall in the price of x (food) would have made you richer by the equivalent of £T (calculated using, say, the Slutsky method). By taxing you at £T we will bring you back to your original level of real income'. It does not really matter whether each person in the economy behaves according to our depiction of rationality. The secret of rationality is that it is based on reason and people understand arguments which are based on reason. Thus, the logic of the government action will become apparent to the public whether or not people actually have consistent preferences over the space of economic goods which can be represented by a real number function!

You may say, but how can we calculate the income effect if people are not really rational? The answer is that this is why we prefer not to treat the market demand as the horizontal sum of the demand functions of all the people in society. Instead, we prefer to think of a representative agent whose preferences generated the market demand. As I suggested earlier, while the market demand is not an observed phenomenon, there are means at our disposal to estimate it empirically. If this empirically estimated demand is the manifestation of the preferences of a representative agent, we can reverse the operation we used to derive demand and pour some empirical content into the preferences parameters of this representative agent. In this way we can assess, based on empirical evidence, the impact of changes on this representative agent. We can then go to the public and say again, 'had you been rational, the effect of this policy on your well-being would be such and such'.

But there is one aspect of using the idea of the representative agent which may be too 'costly' from an analytical point of view. While we may not be able to capture the demand of each agent, we must recognize that there are distributional implications to changes in the market. When the price of a good goes above a certain level, some people would simply have to leave the market. Their departure may be more costly in terms of well-being than a simple analysis of moving from one indifference curve to another. The compromise we make is to identify the demand of certain groups of people if we feel that there are clear distributional elements to the problem under investigation. We will see how this is being done in the application and self-assessment section below.

Demand price elasticity
Consider the following demand schedule (Figure 2.29) which represents the relationship between the quantity demanded of x and its own price. Naturally, we assume all other prices and income to be fixed.

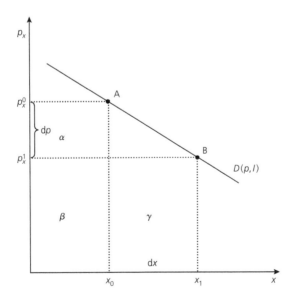

Figure 2.29 Deriving demand price elasticity (p is the vector of all other prices and I is a vector of income).

The total spending on commodity x is obviously: $p_x^0 x_0$. This represents the equivalent concepts of **consumers' expenditure** and **firms' revenue**.

If the price of x came down to p_x^1 and the quantity demanded increased to x_1, total consumers' spending will now become: $p_x^1 x_1$. As the price has gone down but the quantity gone up, the overall spending by consumer (or revenue raised by firms) may either increase or decrease. As you can imagine, this is a question of great significance both to private agents (like firms) and for government policy. When an action brings down the price, everyone would like to know whether or not this means more or less spending (revenues). We shall later see, in the application and self-assessment, what kind of relationship may exist between the properties of commodities which were derived from the optimal choice of the rational utility maximizer, and the properties of the demand schedule.

Geometrically we can say that the total spending at point A is $\alpha + \beta$ and at point B the total spending is $\beta + \gamma$.

The question which we wish to investigate is what would happen to consumers' spending (or firms' revenue) if the price of x fell. We want to know under which conditions would spending (revenue) change in direct or inverse relation to the change in price. In other words, we would like to know whether a fall in price will lead to an increase or decrease in consumers' spending (firms' revenue).

Let us begin by investigating the direct relation; that is, revenues (and spending) fall when the price comes down. Namely, we are asking the question when the revenue at A, in the above diagram, would be greater than the revenue at B. Given our previous notation we are really asking when will $\alpha + \beta > \beta + \gamma$?

Naturally, as β is an area common to revenues at A and B, whether $\alpha + \beta > \beta + \gamma$ really depends on whether $\alpha > \gamma$. But what exactly are these areas? In our case, there was a fall in the price and an increase in quantity. Notice that demand depicts quantity purchased repeatedly. So when we compare A to B we see that in B consumers would buy as much x as in A + more! Therefore, α: is the area which depicts the loss of revenue on previous sales (or, from the point of view of the consumer, the savings on previous purchases). Namely, before the price of x fell, the same quantity was sold at a higher price. After the fall in price of x consumers still buy that quantity but at a lower price. Therefore, we can write $\alpha = dp\, x$.

Similarly, γ represents the gains on the new sales (or the extra spending on the added consumption). In other words: $\gamma = dx\, p$.

To answer whether $\alpha > \gamma$ we must ask ourselves whether $dp\, x > dx\, p$.[13]

$$\alpha = |dp\, x| > |dx\, p| = \gamma \quad / : |dp\, x|$$

$$1 > |\frac{dx\, p}{dp\, x}| = |\frac{dx/x}{dp/p}| \equiv |\eta|$$

By dividing both sides of the initial equation by $(dp\, x)$ we generated a strange relation $(dx\, p)/(dp\, x)$. However, this relationship can be written in a meaningful way:

$$\frac{dx/x}{dp/p}$$

This is a ratio between the proportional change in quantity and the proportional change in price. We call this ratio **price elasticity** and we denote it by the Greek letter: η.

We can thus see that $\alpha > \gamma$ whenever η is less than 1. As price elasticity is really the relationship between the proportional changes in quantity over the proportional change in price. Being less than unity means that when the proportional change in price (in absolute values) is greater than the proportional change in quantity, revenues (or consumer spending) will change in direct relation to the change in price. In other words, when price elasticity is less than unity a fall in the price of x will bring about a decrease in revenue or consumers' spending. (Equally, an increase in the price of x will bring about an increase in revenues (or consumers' spending). Figure 2.30 depicts this property of demand. Clearly $\alpha > \gamma$ and the revenue at A is greater than at B. However, notice that the elasticity is a property of a point on the demand function (dx/dp is the inverse of the slope of the demand schedule) and a single demand schedule may have different regimes of price elasticity. I develop this point further in Chapter 4 (in connection with the monopolist) but at this stage, I would just like to draw your attention to the fact that price elasticity is normally attributed to a point or a segment of the demand. So in Figure 2.30, the shape of the demand gives us a sense of what it means to have price elasticity which is less than unity.

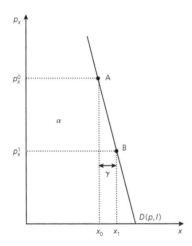

Figure 2.30 Inelastic demand.

It is equally easy to establish when a fall in price will bring about an increase in the overall consumers' spending (or firms' revenue). We are now looking for the case where the savings on the quantity we used to purchase before (recall that at point B we buy again that quantity and more) is less than the extra spending on the new part of purchase. Namely, $\alpha < \gamma$ (or $|\eta| > 1$).

$$\alpha = |dp\, x| < |dx\, p| = \gamma \ / : |dp\, x|$$

$$1 < |\frac{dx\, p}{dp\, x}| = |\frac{dx/x}{dp/p}| \equiv |\eta|$$

Hence, when price elasticity (in absolute values) is greater than unity, a fall in the price of a commodity will be associated with an increase in revenues (or consumers' spending). This property of demand is described in Figure 2.31: $((\alpha < \gamma | \eta | > 1))$.

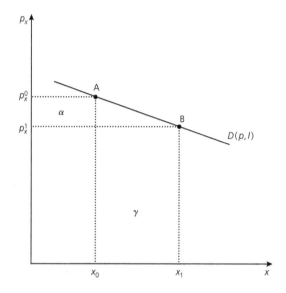

Figure 2.31 Elastic demand.

Here we get a sense of what it means for the demand to demonstrate price elasticity which is greater than unity.

In general, the concept of elasticity is a very important element in economic analysis. It does not, as such, have a theoretical value but it does allow us to be able both predict as well as explain some of the results of various changes. In simple terms one can say that elasticity is a measure of sensitivity. It measures the responsiveness of a variable to changes in another variable. In the above case, we looked at how sensitive is the quantity demanded to changes in price (notice that in our model, prices are given and individuals make their choices in terms of quantity; put differently, the general demand function tells us what would be the quantity of x demanded and not the other way around). We noticed that when price elasticity is low, or 'inelastic' (i.e. $|\eta| < 1$), it means that quantity demanded is not very responsive to changes in price. If price goes down, the quantity demanded will hardly change. It is not surprising, therefore, that revenues (or consumers' spending) fall too.

We can equally apply the concept of elasticity to anything else in our model. Recall that our generalized demand function was

$$x_1^{\text{d}} = D(p_1, p_2, \ldots, p_n, I).$$

This means that we can examine the sensitivity of quantity demanded to any of its determinants. Hence we may have **cross price elasticity**: $\eta_{x_1, p_1} = (dx_1/dp_2)(p_2/x_1)$ which measures the sensitivity of the quantity demanded for good 1 to the change in the price of good 2. Can you tell what will be the sign of the cross price elasticity had goods 1 and 2 been gross substitutes? Would it be the same had they been complements?

Similarly, we can find the **income elasticity**: $\eta_{x_1,I} = (dx_1/dI)\, I/x_1$ which measures the sensitivity of the quantity demanded to changes in nominal income.

The bridge again

Let us return now to the problem posed at the beginning of this chapter. To remind you, what we had there was a government having to decide on whether or not to build a bridge where demand and supply do not intersect. Market research has produced a demand schedule as depicted in Figure 2.32 and the engineering investigation produced a bridge of minimum capacity of T crossings per day at a cost of £C million. We saw that merely by assuming that all demand schedules are downward sloping we would not be able to say something meaningful to advise the government on whether or not to build the bridge. It is clear that in this case the 'market' (or private agents) would not build the bridge, should we treat the market as the ultimate arbitrator? Is it possible that there could be something beneficial to society which is not produced by the market? This, of course, is a much broader question to which we will return in Chapter 7. At this stage, we simply ask ourselves, how a government should decide on whether or not to build the bridge. How should the government decide whether the absence of the bridge is or is not, a market failure? To answer this we must assume that the government only seeks to maximize the well-being of its citizens and that it is not corrupt.

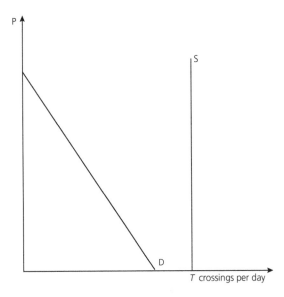

Figure 2.32 A bridge revisited.

Luckily, the answer is easily at hand. Now that we have derived demand from the rational behaviour of a utility maximizer, we know that when a rational individual chooses a quantity at any given price he, or she, has maximized his, or her, utility. Namely, the individual chose that which is most preferred by him, or her. We also know that the significance of such a choice is that it is at the quantity where his, or her, **subjective rate of substitution** is the same as the **market rate of exchange**:

$$(MU_x/MU_y) = p_x/p_y \text{ units of } y \text{ per } x.$$

Suppose that crossing the bridge is x and that y represents an aggregate of all other goods. So when an individual answers the questionnaire by saying that he, or she, would cross 5 times a day had the price per crossing been £10, it means that for a given price of y—representing all other goods—(say, £5):

$$(MU_x/MU_y) = p_x/p_y = £10/£5 = 2 \text{ units of } y \text{ per } x.$$

Put differently, at 5 crossings a day, the real marginal utility of crossing (measured in terms of the units of y which the individual is willing to give up for the last crossing) equals to 2 units of y per crossing. As the price of y is £5, in money terms this means that the individual is willing to pay (2 units of $y \times$ £5 per unit =) £10. These £10 are effectively the money value of the real marginal utility[14] from crossings at the point where you cross 5 times. Namely, if $MU_x/MU_y = p_x/p_y$ units of y per x then clearly: $p_y \cdot MU_x/MU_y = p_x$. This means that the individual always chooses to buy the quantity where the money value of the real marginal utility of the good equals the money price of the good.

This means that the money price which individuals are willing to pay for the first crossing represents the money value of the real marginal utility derived from one crossing. The money price which they are willing to pay for two crossings represents the money value of the real marginal utility of the second crossing and so on and so forth. This means that if you look at the diagram below the line from $x = 1$ to the demand schedule represents the money price which people are willing to pay for the first crossing (and hence, the money value of the real marginal utility of that crossing). The line rising from $x = 2$ up to the demand represents the willingness to pay for two crossings and thus, the money value of the real marginal utility from the second crossing. Hence, if you add all this lines (continuously instead of discretely) you get that the area under the demand schedule is a sum of such lines. In other words, it is the money value of the real marginal utility from the first crossing + the money value of the real marginal utility from the second crossing and so on. When we add the money values of the real marginal utilities, we are actually adding up the utility which we derive from each unit of the good. It is, therefore, the total utility. In other words, the area underneath the demand gives us a money value of the utility which is generated by the consumption of any quantity of the good. Obviously, this is not an accurate measure of utility as the quantity we consume of the other good is also changing when the price of x goes down. Nevertheless, at this stage of your study we will not worry about the complete accuracy of this measure. I will only say that it is, at least, a very good proxy to that which we are trying to capture. In our case of the bridge, the government is deliberating whether to raise taxes to pay for the construction of the bridge even if the crossing is free (which means that the government will be unable to collect the money from people who are crossing the bridge (see Figure 2.33).

If the government builds the bridge and offers free crossing, a proxy for the money value of utility (or benefits (B)) that would be accrued to the public is captured by the area underneath the demand schedule (shaded in the diagram below). Clearly, if B > C

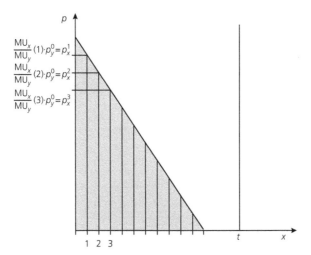

Figure 2.33

it means that the total amount of benefit (or utility) will be greater than the cost. Hence, even if the government has to raise the money via taxation and offer free crossing, it knows that altogether the public would be better off. The money value of the utility generated by the bridge would be, in such a case, greater than the loss of money to the public due to taxation. If, however, B < C the government should not build the bridge as it would mean that the money it would have to raise by tax is more than people are willing to pay in order to have a bridge.

Naturally, the problem is a bit more complex than that as the issues of benefits and financing are far more complex. For one, there is the distributional question about the relationship between those who pay the tax and those who use the bridge. In our world of representative agent this problem is intractable. But in reality, it may constitute a far more serious obstacle.

Still, what I hope that you were able to see is how the use of utility functions and the rational utility maximizer helped us in better understanding what is so commonly attributed to economics: the demand schedule. In addition, note that it does not require for all agents to be rational. What we have done here is to create a framework with which we may be able to convince other people along the following line of argument: had people been rational, building the bridge would have increased overall benefits in society.

Self-assessment and applications

▓ QUESTION 1

When the price of x is 3 and the price of y is 3, an individual consumes a bundle of $x = 4$, $y = 4$. When the price of x has become 1 and the price of y 5, the individual chooses a bundle of $x = 3$, $y = 5$. Therefore, the consumer prefers (3,5) over (4,4). True or False, explain.

Answer

This is a simple question about the rationality of actions. The framework within which this question should be analysed is that of individuals' choice (see Figure 2.34).

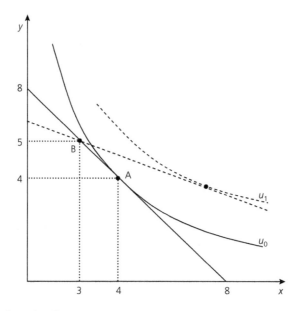

Figure 2.34 Analysing rationality.

We have the following situation: At point $A = (4,4)$, if the consumer is rational his choice would exhaust the following budget constraint:

$$p_x^0 x_0 + p_y^0 y_0 = 3 \times 4 + 3 \times 4 = 24$$

From the information given about the new allocation we know that at B his income would obviously be greater:

$$p_x^1 x_1 + p_y^1 y_1 = 1 \times 3 + 5 \times 5 = 28$$

We must now ask ourselves whether or not the individual could have bought the new bundle when he made his original choice to buy A. In other words, had he purchased the new bundle (B) at the original prices we would have:

$$p_x^0 x_1 + p_y^0 y_1 = 3 \times 3 + 3 \times 5 = 24,$$

which means that point B lies on the original budget line (£24 was the income of the agent when he chose point A). This means that the individual chose A when B was available. Given that he chose A it must mean that the individual prefers A over B. This is also easy to see by using indifference curves. If the highest indifference curve feasible under the original budget constraint is tangent to the budget line at point A, there must be a lower indifference curve which goes through B.

QUESTION 2

In a world of two goods, when the demand elasticity of good x is greater than unity, x and y must be gross substitutes and x is more likely to be a normal good. True or False, explain.

Answer

In order to analyse the nature of x and its relationship with y we must investigate how an agent would respond to a change in the price of x. Suppose that the price of x fell. As the appropriate framework of analysis is that of individuals' choice, you begin by setting the scene (Figure 2.35).

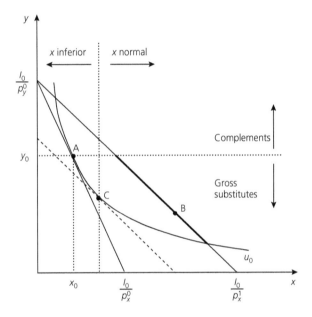

Figure 2.35

We start at A. When the price of x falls, the realm of feasible economic goods is extended. The intercept of the budget line with the x-axis shifts to the right as we can now buy many more units of x if we choose to spend our entire income on it ($I_0/p_x^0 < I_0/p_x^1$). However, if we chose to spend our entire income on y we would not be able to buy more of it as the price of y has not changed.

In order to establish the character of the good (in the eyes of the consumer) and its relationship with the other good we must do two things. First, we must draw the line that will delineate the response when x and y are perceived to be complements from when x and y are perceived to be gross substitutes. This is the heavy horizontal line going through A. A choice on the new budget line which lies above it suggests that the response to a fall in the price of x was to increase the consumption of y (Complements). A choice which lies below it suggests that the response to the fall in the price of x was a fall in the consumption of y (gross substitutes).

To delineate the nature of the good, we examine the pure substitution effect (point C) and we draw the vertical line through C that will distinguish between choices suggesting that the increase in real income brought about an increase in the consumption of x (normal good) and choice suggesting the opposite (inferior good).

We now refer back to the information given in the question in order to conduct our analysis. Accordingly, we are told that the price elasticity of demand for x is greater than unity. We know that price elasticity, which measures the responsiveness of changes in quantity demanded to changes in price, also indicates the effect of a change in the price on consumers' spending. This, in turn is concerned with the management of our budget.

At A (the initial stage), the budget we faced was as follows:

$$p_x^0 x_0 + p_y^0 y_0 = I_0$$

Whatever the final choice of point B would be, the following constraint will have to be satisfied:

$$p_x^1 x_1 + p_y^0 y_1 = I_0$$

where p_x^1 is the new price of x and (x_1, y_1) is the optimal choice at B (on the new budget constraint.

Given that $|\eta_{p,x}| > 1$ we know that quantities demanded are very sensitive to changes in price and therefore, a fall in the price of x will cause an increase in the total amount of spending on it. Hence: $p_x^1 x_1 > p_x^0 x_0$. But as nominal income remains unchanged, an increase in the spending of x must mean a decrease in the spending on y. Hence: $p_y^0 y_1 < p_y^0 y_0$. But as the price of y too, is unchanged, it must mean that $y_1 < y_0$ and the two goods are necessarily gross substitutes. We can also see that in this context, it means that x is more likely (though not necessarily) to be a normal good.

▪ QUESTION 3

Consider an economy with two types of consumers (P and R) and two types of good (bread (B) and wine (W)). Type P are those individuals who derive their income mainly from being someone's employee. Their income is therefore determined in money terms (a salary). Type R are those individuals who earn their income mainly from ownership of vineyards and bakeries. The income of R is therefore dependent in some ways on the price of bread and the price of wine, as these affect profits. To make it simpler, suppose that type R get their income in kind. Namely, the ownership of a vineyard gives the person an entitlement to so many bottle of wines while the ownership of a bakery gives an entitlement to so many loaves of bread. What I mean by this is that their income is calculated as the value of a certain amount of bread and wine. Initially, the money value of income of both types of agents is the same.

(a) Draw the budget constraint of both type of individuals and show how they choose the combination of good they would like to consume;

(b) What would happen to the real income of both types of individuals if the prices of bread and wine rose by the same proportion? Would the composition of the type R income in kind make a difference to the outcome?

(c) What would happen to the real income of both types of individuals if the price of bread rose by 20% and that of wine by 5%? Will your answer depend on whether we follow the Hicks or the Slustky definition of real income?

(d) Would the composition of type R's income in kind affect your answer?

(e) Would it be right to say that those who treat bread as a normal good will end up worse off in (b) and (c) while those who treat it as an inferior good end up being better off in both cases?

Answer

In this question we are trying to enrich our perception of the circumstances in which individuals make choices. I would like you to learn from this not only how to adjust the model to different circumstances but also how sensitive are many of our answers to the circumstances which we describe.

We have two types of agents here. One gets his income in money (type P) and the other gets his income in kind (type R). The two goods are bread and wine. Initially, we are told, the money income of both individuals was the same. That is to say:

$$p_B^0\overline{B} + p_W^0\overline{W} = I_R^0 = I_P^0$$

where $\omega_R = (\overline{B}, \overline{W})$ is the in-kind bundle from which we derive type R's money income (Figure 2.36).

(a) The initial situation is straightforward:

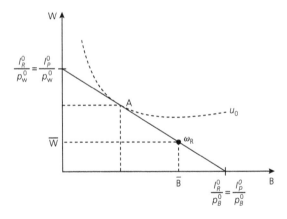

Figure 2.36

$\acute{\omega}_R$ is the in-kind bundle for individual R and as both of them have the same money income, they will face the same budget constraint. If we assume also that they have the same preferences, they will also choose the same bundle (point A).

(b) When the price of both bread and wine rise by the same proportion, this will mean no real change for individual of the type R and a fall in real income for individual of the type P (see Figure 2.37).

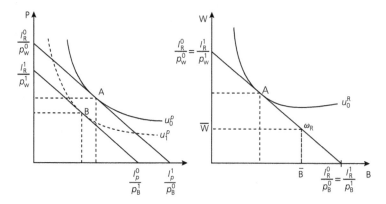

Figure 2.37

The left-hand side of the above figure shows how the change will affect an individual of the type P. As his nominal income remains the same, the increase in the price of both B and W will shift his budget constraint inward. As prices have changed by the same proportion, there will be no change in the slope of the new budget line.

The right-hand side diagram shows what will happen to an individual of the type R. For him,

$$p_B^1 = \lambda p_B^0 \quad p_W^1 = \lambda p_W^0$$

$$I_R^1 = p_B^1 B + p_W^1 W =$$

$$\lambda p_B^0 B + \lambda p_W^0 W = \lambda [p_B^0 B + p_W^0 W] = \lambda I_R^0.$$

This means that although his nominal income increased, there will be no real change:

$$\frac{I_R^1}{p_i^1} = \frac{\lambda I_R^0}{\lambda p_i^1} = \frac{I_R^0}{p_i^0} \qquad i = \overline{B, W}.$$

Naturally, the absence of any real change will not be affected by the position of $\dot{\omega}_R$.

(c) Now we examine the effects of a non-symmetrical increase in the prices of bread and wine (see Figure 2.38). The price of bread rose by 20%; that of wine by 5%. Hence, $p_B^1 = 1.2\, p_B^0$ and $p_W^1 = 1.05\, p_W^0$.

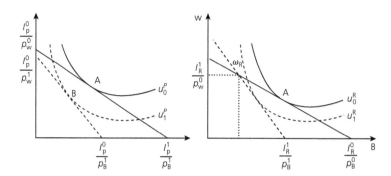

Figure 2.38

Again, the left-hand side diagram in the above figure depicts the effects of the change on an individual of the type P. As the price of bread increased by more than the price of wine the relative price of bread will increase (steeper budget constraints). The individual will end up on a lower indifference curve (at point B).

What will happen to an individual of the type R depends on the position of $\hat{\omega}_R$. In the above diagram we show the effect of the change when the in-kind bundle is mainly comprised of wine. Assuming that his initial choice was to the right of $\hat{\omega}_R$, he will be made worse off too.

Before we show the other possibilities, let us look at the second element in question (c). Here you were asked whether the change in the real income depends on whether we use the Hicksian or the Slutsky definition of it. From the Hicksian point of view, it is clear that the fall in real income is captured by the move to a lower indifference curve. The amount of money which we need to compensate for the loss of utility is dl_H in the diagrams below. The Slutsky measure of change in real income is captured by the amount of money needed to compensate the individual so that he can carry on purchasing his initial bundle (dl_S in the Figure 2.39).

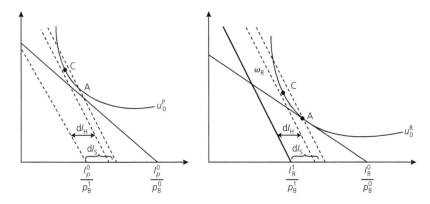

Figure 2.39

In the case of type R individuals, you might have confused the fact that income is calculated on the base of an initial bundle with the Slutsky idea of real income. You might have recognized that the fall in utility clearly signifies a fall in real income according to the Hicksian definition but you might have failed to do so using the Slutsky definition. You might argue that the reference bundle for real income is $\hat{\omega}_R$, thus, there will be no change in real income as long as $\hat{\omega}_R$ remain unchanged. This, of course, is false as the individual's initial choice was not to be at point $\hat{\omega}_R$.

(d) Does the answer to (c) depend on the position of $\hat{\omega}_R$?

In this case, when there is a real change, the position of $\hat{\omega}_R$ matters. The left-hand diagram in Figure 2.40 shows the case where the wine component is greater while the right-hand diagram represents the case where the bread component is greater. As the increase in the price of bread was greater than the increase in the price of wine, the right-hand diagram shows that the individual will become better off relative to his, or her, initial position. In such a case, the effect of the increase in the relative price of bread on individuals of type R will be different for its effect on individuals of type P. The latter will become worse off, the former will become better (see Figure 2.40).

(e) Does the question of whether bread is a normal or inferior good matter?

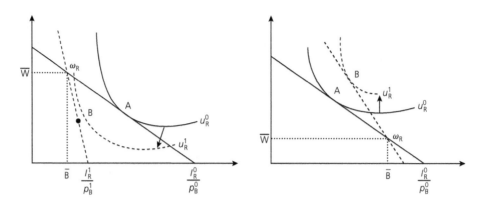

Figure 2.40

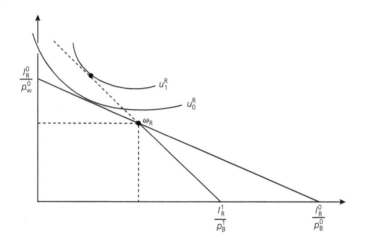

Figure 2.41

In the case of a synchronized change in the prices of bread and wine (section (b)) it makes no difference whatsoever. Individuals of type R will experience no change in their real income and welfare while individuals of type P are clearly worse off (see Figure 2.41).

In the case of section (c), the only difference that may exist is the one described above. If bread being an inferior good means that the initial choice of an individual of type R will be at a point to the left of $\hat{\omega}_R$ while bread being normal implies a choice to the right of $\hat{\omega}_R$ then the conclusion does depend on the type of good. If bread is inferior, the individual of type R will become better off even if his initial bundle has a greater wine composition.

■ QUESTION 4

There are two types of goods in the economy: books (x: measured in number of books read per period) and club dancing (y: measured in number of visits to a club per period). There are also two types of individuals: a reader (R) and a dancer (D). Both individuals receive their income in terms of books and club visits allowance. Let (x, y), where $x = y$, be the initial allowance each of the individuals receives.

(a) Draw the initial choice of these two individuals which reflects their different characters (and preferences) assuming that both goods are consumed;

(b) Derive the demand for books for each type of individual;

(c) The introduction of the internet has made book purchasing much easier (and cheaper). How will this affect both individuals? Will the quantity demanded of books (generated by these two types of individuals) be greater or smaller had the Dancer considered books to be an inferior good?

Answer

This is a question about income in kind and diverse preferences. In section **(a)** you were expected to draw the initial set-up, where (x_E, y_E) is the initial endowment, R represents the reader, and D represents the dancer (see Figure 2.42).

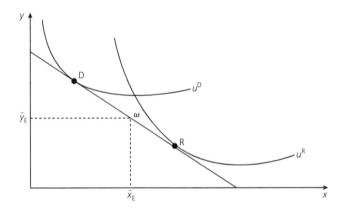

Figure 2.42

(b) Here we have two difference cases of deriving demand. In order to do so, you must examine the effects of a change in one of the prices. Suppose that the price of x fell. First we examine the trivial case:

The reader

As the price of x falls, substitution effect takes us from A to C and as long as books (x) are normal goods, the demand for books by the reader will increase (see Figure 2.43).

The dancer

In this case the story is slightly more complex (see Figure 2.44). As the price of x falls substitution effect will bring us to point C. However, as real income falls, assuming that x is normal will lead us

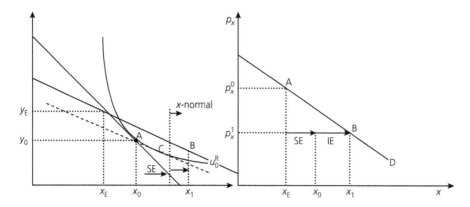

Figure 2.43

either to point B or N. If we end up at N we have an **upward sloping demand schedule for a normal good** while at B it will still be downward sloping.

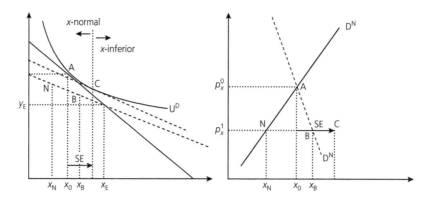

Figure 2.44

(c) In this question we ask what will happen to both individuals when the price of x falls. The analysis of the change was conducted in (b) and what remains to be said is that:

(i) The dancer will be worse off while the reader will be better off;

(ii) If the dancer treats books as an inferior good the quantity demanded of books will definitely increase.

▨ QUESTION 5

A good is a normal good whenever the substitution and income effects work in the same direction. True or false, explain.

Answer

False. A simple counterexample like the case where income is given in kind (as shown in Figure 2.45) should be sufficient:

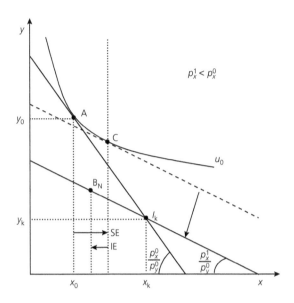

Figure 2.45

The individual gets his income as the money value of a given bundle: $I_K = (x_K, y_K)$. Let A be the initial choice of this individual. When the price of x falls, the new budget line will have to go through his point of income (because he can never have more of both goods relative to his income in kind because this would have meant that his income is actually higher). Substitution considerations will lead him to C while the fall in real income will mean that the good is normal only if the income and substitution effects work in the opposite directions.

▓ QUESTION 6

The Slutsky substitution effect is always greater than the Hicksian substitution effect. True or false, explain.

Answer

False. There are three components to this question

(a) the difference between Hicks's and Slutsky's definition of 'real income';

(b) analysing the fall in the price of x and showing that the Slutsky substitution effect is greater when utility functions are homothetic and the good is normal (the left-hand side of Figure 2.46);

(c) analysing the fall in the price of x and showing that in the case of an inferior good, the Hicksian substitution effect is greater.

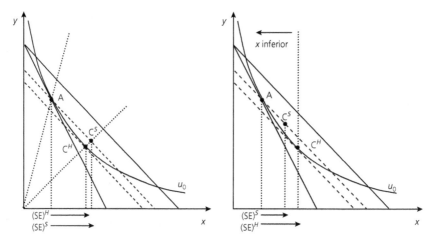

Figure 2.46

We have thus rejected the statement by providing a counterexample.

▥ QUESTION 7

A consumer spends 30% of his income on good x and the rest on good y. The income elasticity of the demand for both x and y will be unity. True or false, explain.

Answer

This is a somewhat technical question which requires the understanding of the budget constraint and elasticities.

(i) The information gives is:

$$p_x x = 0.3I \qquad p_y y = 0.7I$$

hence,

$$x = \frac{0.3I}{p_x} \qquad y = \frac{0.7I}{p_y}$$

(ii) Let us examine the income elasticity of the demand for x. Namely, we are looking at the sensitivity of the quantity demanded to changes in nominal income:

$$\eta_{x,I} = \frac{dx}{dI}\frac{I}{x} = \frac{0.3\, p_x x}{p_x}\frac{1}{0.3\, x} = 1$$

And the same should be done for y.

QUESTION 8

A company considers a package to help employees in the running cost of their cars. It considers two options:

(1) to offer a fixed amount of money towards the use of the car in addition to a cost-free usage for the first x_0 miles;

(2) to participate in the actual cost of running the car (i.e. pay a certain amount, a_0, per mile used);

    (a) Let x represent the mileage of car usage and y all other goods. Draw each of the options while analysing the individual's response to the proposed change (i.e. discuss the income and substitution effects);

    (b) which of the two options will the employee prefer had the company decided to spend the same amount of money under the two options;

    (c) will your answer to (b) change had option (1) included **only** free mileage?

    (d) which of the two options would the company prefer if it aims at achieving the same real income improvement at a lower cost?

Answer

This question examines your command of the budget line and your knowledge of consumer's choice. In the latter part, the main point of knowledge to be demonstrated is the analysis of income and substitution effects.

(a) An employee is offered by a company a package to help in the running cost of his company car. There are two options:

    (1) A lump-sum payment (L) towards the use of the car as well as a certain free mileage. This option is captured in the left-hand diagram below;

    (2) a 'subsidy' per mile used. This option is captured in the right-hand diagram of Figure 2.47.

    In both cases the individual will increase the use of his car. In the case of the lump-sum payment, there will be no substitution effect while in the case of the subsidy there will be both income and substitution effects.

(b) To spend the same on the two schemes means that the amount of money paid out to the individual according to the use of his car should be the same as the money paid to him when the payment is independent of that use. This means: $a_0 x_0 = L$.

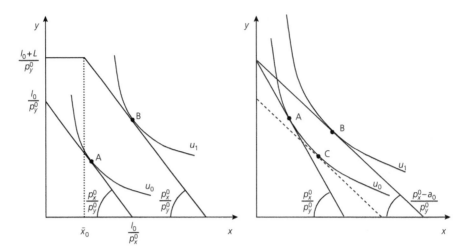

Figure 2.47

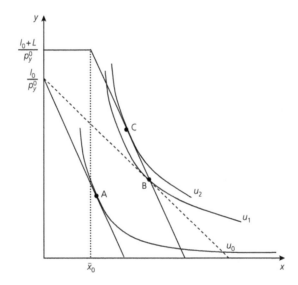

Figure 2.48

In other words, the budget line under offer (1) must cross the budget line under offer (2) at the point where the individual would choose to be had he received offer (2) . We can show this formally:

At B(option 2) : $(p_x^0 - a_0)x_0 + p_y^0 y = l_0$
hence: $p_x^0 x_0 + p_y^0 y = l_0 + a_0 x_0$
Option (1) $p_x^0 x_0 + p_y^0 y = l_0 + L$ where $a_0 x_0 = L$.

Point B, therefore, must be on both budget lines for the two offers to be of equal money value. It is evident that the individual will prefer option 1.

(c) The answer will not change but there will be a need for more free miles to be offered;

(d) If the company wants to achieve a certain real income improvement, say u_1, then it is easy to see that the cheapest option for the firm will be option 1 (Figure 2.49):

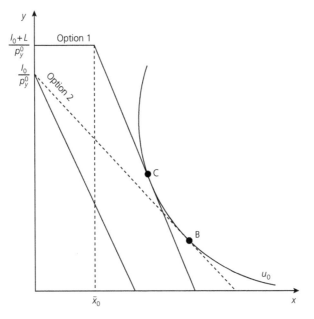

Figure 2.49

As the budget line of option 1 is tangent to the indifference curve upon which the choice of option 2 has been made, the choice under option 2 will not be feasible had option 1 been finally offered. Therefore, the money which the company will spend under option 1 to achieve the same utility as under option 2 will be much reduced.

▨ QUESTION 9

To reduce congestion on the roads, the government decides to introduce congestion charges. This means the price of using the road increases. To ensure that the public is not worse off as a result of the change (elections looming), the government proposes to subsidize the use of public transport.

(a) Analyse the effects of introducing congestion charges;

(b) How would the introduction of public transport subsidy affect the outcome?

(c) Will the level of congestion increase or decrease relative to the effects at (a)? On what does the outcome depend?

(d) Will the combined scheme raise revenue or incur costs for the government?

Answer

The focus of this question, which can be derived from the main issue, is the effects of government's intervention on the welfare of agents. Many students confused the issues and thought the question to be dealing with the relationship between the markets for public transport and the use of roads. However, as the main concern is 'to ensure that the public is not worse off', the appropriate framework of analysis can only be that of individual choice. It is there where we study agents' response to prices and its affects on their welfare.

(a) The introduction of congestion charges can be considered as a tax on the use of roads. It is not a lump sum tax as it depends on whether or not people choose to travel. In many places, such charges depend on the distance travelled but even if not, they can be seen, for simplicity sake, as an average increase in the cost of the use of road.

Let x be the use of road (measured in distance travelled) and p_x the price per unit of use. Let y and p_y be the use and price of public transport. The introduction of the charge will have the following effect (Figure 2.50):

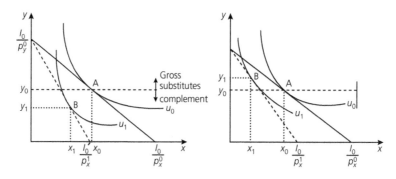

Figure 2.50

The price of road use increased from p_x^0 to $p_x^1 = p_x^0 + c$. A typical individual will move from A to B in the right-hand diagram if he or she treats x and y as gross substitutes and from A to B in the left-hand diagram if they treat x and y as complements. The total amount of money raised by the government per agent will be $[c x_1]$.

(b) + (c) The introduction of a subsidy for the use of public transport will reduce the price of y from p_y^0 to $p_y^1 = p_y^0 - s$. The changes must be such that the individual is not worse off (i.e. the new choice must be at the original level of utility).

We now move from A through B to C. In the left-hand diagram of Figure, x and y are treated as complements. Hence, when the price of y falls, the quantity demanded of x will increase. Congestion, therefore, at C will be greater than at B (which the case in subsection (a)). However, in the right hand diagram, x and y are treated as gross substitutes. The fall in the price of y suggests a fall in the quantity demanded of x. Hence, congestions at C will be even lower than at B.

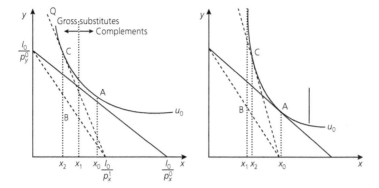

Figure 2.51

(d) At points A and C, the following equation holds:

At A $p_x^0 x_0 + p_y^0 y_0 = I_0$
At C $p_x^1 x_2 + p_y^1 y_2 = I_0$
Hence: $(p_x^0 + C)x_2 + (p_y^0 - s)y_2 = I_0$
$p_x^0 x_2 + p_y^0 y_2 = I_0 + s y_2 - C x_2$

The left-hand side of the last equation represents the amount of money (I) we need to be at C at the original prices. As C is outside the original budget constraint, this means that this amount of money is greater than I_0. Hence, $s y_2 - C x_2 > 0$ which means that the cost (i.e. subsidy per agent) is greater than the revenue. The scheme will therefore be costly to the government.

QUESTION 10

A telephone company charges its customers a fixed sum of T for the first x calls they make in a given period. Every extra call is then charged at the price of p_x a call. The company would like to replace the existing arrangement with a new one. It considers two alternatives:

(a) abolish the fixed payment and charge a lower price for each call;

(b) increase the number of calls allowed under the same fixed payment and increase the price of every extra call.

Assume that customers always use more calls than what is covered by the fixed payment.

(i) Draw the budget constraint confronting customers under the initial scheme;

(ii) Draw option (a) and consider whether customers are likely to be better or worse off. Can the company choose a price where customers are equally well off as under the original scheme? What will happen to the number of calls in such a case?

(iii) Draw option (b) and consider whether customers are likely to be better or worse off. Had the option been designed in such a way as to allow individuals to consume the number of calls they would under (a), will it be a better or worse option for the consumer?

(iv) If you knew that most customers use the phone only slightly above what is covered by the fixed payment, which of the schemes would you recommend? How would you advise the company if this was not the case?

Answer

This question has two major components. One is the budget constraint and its possible shapes; the other, a comparative analysis of individual's choice. It aims at showing how economists may use abstract frameworks to provide practical recommendations. The pretext is the pricing policy of a telephone company. As no information is provided regarding differences in costs or the market structure, it implies that the criterion for choosing a scheme is a different one. From reading the question in its entirety, the student can deduce that this is a firm which is more concerned with its public image than with its position in the market.

In terms of choosing the right framework of analysis students could have seen at once that this is an indifference curves analysis. It is so, simply because the main question here is whether or not the customer (a representative individual) will be better or worse off. The next step, therefore, is to translate the question into the language of the model. Here, the real 'jump' for you is the transformation of the three pricing policies (the existing one + (a) and (b)) into forms of budget constraints. This is what should have emerged:

(i) Drawing the initial budget constraint, (see Figure 2.52).

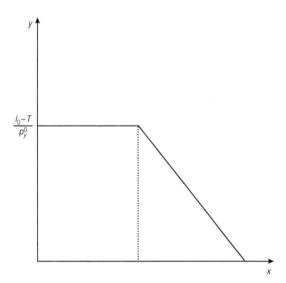

Figure 2.52

(ii) The Figure 2.53 should emerge.

Scheme (a) is drawn in the left diagram. You should note that if consumers were initially at P they *might* be worse off. Had they been initially at T they *will* definitely be better off. In the

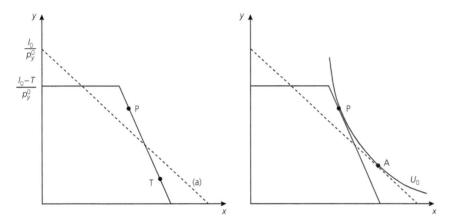

Figure 2.53

right-hand diagram, it is shown how a price can be set such that their utility remained unchanged (this is an example how at point like P individuals will *not* be made worse off).

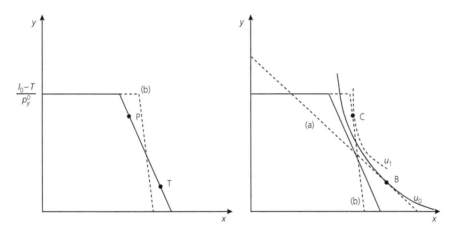

Figure 2.54

(iii) The general principle is depicted in the left diagram of Figure 2.54. At point P they will definitely be better off. Had they been initially at point T they *might* be worse off. This is exactly the opposite of the previous scheme. In the diagram on the right we can see the circumstances where scheme (b) is designed in such a way as to ensure the feasibility of the choice under scheme (a). It is clear from this that in such a case, individuals would rather have scheme (b).

(iv) Here you were expected to give a general answer: had the consumers been initially at point P, scheme (b) is likely to appeal to them more. Had they been initially at point T scheme (a) would be more appealing. One must bear in mind that we have no information about the

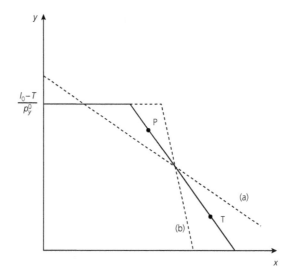

Figure 2.55

costs of the two schemes (see Figure 2.55). Assuming that they cost the same, the company would want to appear as having consumers' benefit in mind.

■ QUESTION 11

'It is better to give the poor a subsidy for food rather than an income supplement which they are likely to spend on other goods and alcohol.'

Suppose individuals consume only two goods, x:food and y:other goods (including alcohol), and they have an income of I.

(a) Show the effects on consumption of paying a subsidy of s per unit of x consumed;

(b) Show the effects on consumption of paying income supplement of S;

(c) Compare the effects of the two schemes assuming that government spending on each individual is the same in both cases (this means that if under the subsidy scheme the individual chooses x_s then $sx_s = S$);

(d) Comment on the statement.

Answer

As in question 10, this question has the same major components: the budget constraint and the comparative analysis of individual's choice. The pretext here is the famous problem of subsidizing goods or individuals. Here, the analysis is conducted from the point of view of the affected individuals. Other social issues and the difference in administration costs are neglected. Students should have been able to establish this by the lack of any information regarding the cost side of the two schemes.

In terms of choosing the right framework of analysis you can easily see that this is an indifference curves analysis. It is so, simply because the main question here is whether or not a representative individual will be better or worse off. The next step, therefore, is to translate the question into the language of the model. This is what should have emerged.

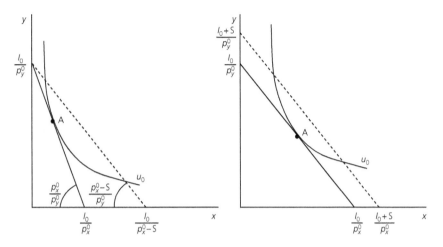

Figure 2.56

(a) and (b) The diagram in Figure 2.56 on the left depicts the effects of a subsidy (s) on the budget line and the possible consumption of x. The diagram on the right depicts the effects of an income supplement S on the budget line.

(c) Here, the main test lies in interpreting the equal spending (i.e. $sx_s = S$) and the relative positions of the two budget lines as seen in Figure 2.57.

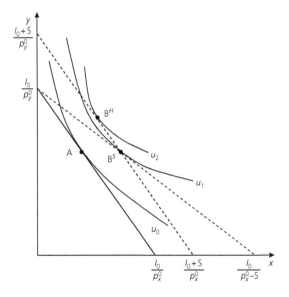

Figure 2.57

Notice that $sx_s = S$ means that the income-supplement budget line will always go through whichever choice the individual would have made under the subsidy scheme.

(d) With reference to the above diagram, students were expected to use indifference curves analysis to show that income supplement will be preferred by individuals. Many students failed to see this and expected the same indifference curve to be tangent to both budget line. This means that they have entirely missed the point raised in (c).

▓ QUESTION 12

Consider a world of two goods, x and y:

(a) When individuals receive a given money income and the two goods are complements, can we conclude that the price elasticity of the demand for x is smaller than unity?

(b) Suppose now that instead of money income, the individual receives income in kind (a bundle of x_k, y_k, units of the two goods):

    (i) If the two goods are complements, can x be an inferior good?

    (ii) If the two goods are complements, will the price elasticity of demand for x be smaller than unity?

    (iii) Would your answer to (ii) depend on whether the individual is selling or buying x?

Answer

(a) The question is about how the nature of relationship between goods may influence the demand facing one of them. The question asks whether the price elasticity of the demand for x will necessarily be less than unity if the two goods are complements. You are expected to realize that an answer to such a question can only be derived through the analysis of the change in the price of one good (say, x):

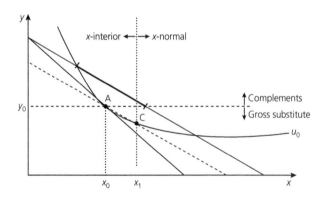

Figure 2.58

At first, you must explain what is the meaning of price elasticity being less than unity. Then you should conduct the following analysis: this is the normal case with exogenous income where it is clear that if the two goods are complements, spending on y will have to increase. Consequently, spending on x will have to fall (as money income is exogenous). This means that the price elasticity of the demand for x will indeed by less than unity (see Figure 2.58).

(b) Here the story is a bit more complex as individuals get their income in kind. There are two possible situations: either the component of x in their income bundle (endowment) is dominant or that of y. (Had they actually received their income in goods rather than the money equivalent of the bundle, the former case would have been the case where the individual is selling x and buying y which the latter case is exactly the reverse). The question covers both cases so we may begin with the former (see Figure 2.59).

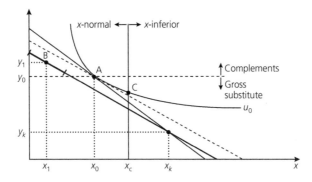

Figure 2.59

(i) In this case, it is clear that if it is at all possible for the goods to be complements, x will necessarily be a normal good;

(ii) It is also evident that if the two goods are complements, the demand for x will be upwards sloping. There is not particular significance, in such a case, to whether price elasticity is greater or smaller than unity. The only thing we would learn is whether the demand schedule is flatter or steeper than the slope of the ray from the origin (see Figure 2.60).

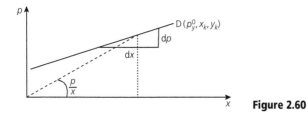

Figure 2.60

$$\frac{dx}{dp}\frac{p}{x} \geq 1 \Rightarrow \frac{p}{x} \geq \frac{dp}{dx}$$

(iii) In the latter case where y is the dominant element in the income bundle, the answers are very different indeed (Figure 2.61).

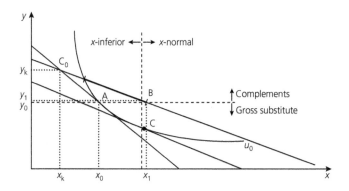

Figure 2.61

Here, the effects of the fall in the price of x are such that x may either be normal or inferior when x and y are complements. As long as x is not a Giffen good, the fact that x and y are complements suggests that price elasticity of demand will be greater than unity:

At first (at A) we have the following:

$$p_x^0 x_0 + p_y^0 y_0 = p_x^0 x_k + p_y^0 y_k$$

or:

$$p_x^0 (x_0 - x_k) = p_y^0 (y_k - y_0)$$

Now, at B we have the following:

$$p_x^1 (x_1 - x_k) = p_y^0 (y_k - y_1)$$

As $p_y^0 (y_k - y_0) > p_y^0 (y_k - y_1)$ then $p_x^0 (x_0 - x_k) > p_x^1 (x_1 - x_k)$

Hence,

$$p_x^0 x_0 - p_x^1 x_1 > p_x^0 x_k - p_x^1 x_k = x_k (p_x^0 - p_x^1) > 0$$

and

$$p_x^0 x_0 > p_x^1 x_1$$

Thus, the spending on x must decrease and price elasticity of demand will be less than unity.

■ NOTES

1. Notice that while conceiving of society as a nexus of opposing forces is essential for modern economics, the Newtonian view is not the only form that such an interaction can take. As an example you may wish to consider the Hegelian–Marxian view of the dynamics of opposing forces or, consider the possibility of viewing society as a cooperative rather than a framework for conflicting forces.

2. In the most intuitive way, you can think of a survey where people are asked how much of a good they will consume at different prices. Naturally, there are more sophisticated econometric methods of estimating demand that are based on observations. In either case, we must always bear in mind that this is an estimation which is not the same as observation.

3. A discussion of the social action appears in the first chapter of Weber's *Economy and Society*, which came out after his death in 1922.

4. Economists proudly argue that their conception of rationality is sufficiently general as they say nothing about the objective function (the purpose of actions). However, this is not entirely true. Economists will always acknowledge that individuals will want more goods (either of the same type, in a world where the number of goods is given exogenously, or of different types if economic goods are defined endogenously).

5. The operation of moving from $u(x, y)$ and $v(x, y)$ is what we call a *monotonic transformation*. We mean by this that every function that takes $u(x, y)$ as an argument and blows up its parameters will yield the same ranking. Recall that in our specific case: $v(x, y) = [u(x, y)]^\alpha + c$.

6. Notice that as there is no time dimension to the model, x and y are the only goods around and, therefore, savings does not come into the picture. In your future studies you will see that when we wish to consider intertemporal choice we will define one of the goods as current consumption and the other as future consumption. This will introduce savings into the system. At this stage, however, I think that we have enough on our plate to contend with.

7. Or, in technical terms, they will exchange x for y as long as the slope of the indifference curve differs from the slope of the budget constraint.

8. This method of analysis is very important in a complex world like that of society. We know that normally, a lot of things change simultaneously and this is why it is difficult to establish which one, of all the things that had changed, causes any particular effect. To analyse an isolated change we try to conduct an analysis assuming that all other factors which may influence the outcome remain unchanged. The Latin word for leaving all other things unchanged is *Ceteris Paribus*.

9. Needless to say, moving back to A will not constitute a rational move but the idea that you will not be able to consume that which you used to, seems powerful enough to make one wonder whether one's income has not really fallen.

10. Clearly this means that the pure substitution effect under Slutsky's definition, contains an element of a Hicksian income effect (a higher level of utility than at A).

11. We use 'gross' to distinguish it from the substitution which we discussed before.

12. Determined by the intercepts: $I/p_x, I/p_y$ and the slope: p_x/p_y.

13. Note here that, as we relate to the graph, both α and γ are positive numbers. The truth is, however, that when $dp > 0$, $dx < 0$ (why?). Therefore, what we are really looking at are the absolute values of dp and dx.

14. Recall that the real marginal utility does not suffer from the problem of different numerical representation. Whichever utility function we use to represent a certain preferences profile, the slope of the indifference curve will not be affected by these monotonic transformation.

3 | Production and the behaviour of the firm

Although I emphasized at the beginning that the basic unit underlying economic analysis is the individual, we are slightly departing from this by assuming that firms too, are units which can be analysed in separation from the individual we have discussed in Chapter 2. Technically, this departure is not of great substance as we are simply going to use the same analytical tool to describe the behaviour of a 'thing' called the firm. So instead of having an individual who wishes to maximize the quantity of an economic good (utility) through the use of other economic goods, we now have a 'firm' trying to maximize the quantity of one economic good (say, x) through the use of other economic goods (say, labour and capital). This last bit, as you will soon see, is an equivalent statement to the pursuit of profit maximization.

Why do we do this and why does it matter? I think that it would not be far fetched to say that the most obvious and known economic institution is that of the market. Markets have been around for as many centuries as humanity can recall. In the market there are buyers and sellers. With the rise of enlightenment and the search for social systems of natural balances which emulate the world of matter, the notion of equilibrium as the holding mechanism of the system became dominant. As far as economics is concerned, what would be more natural than to think of the buyers and sellers as representing opposing forces? However, for them to be opposing forces we must analyse them in separation.

So, you may ask, what is wrong with this? Well, if in the end, as we said earlier, all boils down to the behaviour of the individual, the idea of opposing forces becomes somewhat more complex. If the agent who buys the good is also the worker in the firm which produces it as well as being a shareholder how can we describe the working of opposing forces? Naturally, the answer to this question is fundamentally institutional as the position of agents within such a system is not necessarily symmetrical. Moreover, in such a world, the opposing forces seem to be between the agents themselves. If we are all buyers, workers, and owners at the same time, we are competing against everyone else in order to secure a greater share of social produce for ourselves. This is by no means a happy picture. It is interesting to note that Adam Smith, who is usually associated with the promotion of competition, had commented on this point exactly. He said in the *Theory of Moral Sentiments* (which was first published in 1759, before the *Wealth of Nations*) that people are in constant need of each other's assistance. If the assistance is given out of love and benevolence, society will flourish. However, when people are self-interested, society may still subsist due to the utility of the system where the assistance we so naturally need is provided through 'mercenary exchange'. Such a society, he argued, would be a much less happy place.

Therefore, if competition is between individuals, what is the point of distinguishing one particular institution (the firm) from the many others which exist in society? Put differently, if the competition is between all individuals and on all fronts, is there no competition within the firm? Are the workers not competing against each other to climb the ladder of pay? Are the managers not competing with the shareholders for their share in what the firm produces? In short, there are too many potential internal conflicts within the firm for an assumption about its unity to be of great value.

Nevertheless, there is something to be said in favour of trying to conceive of the firm as a single agent. For one, given the current structure of ownership, the description of the firm as a 'profit maximizer' agent may not be so far fetched. It is true that the interests of the managers and those of the shareholders may not be the same but there are external pressures on managers too. For instance, suppose that you are a manager of a company which is traded in the stock markets. The value of your shares reflects, among other things, the profitability of your company. If you choose to produce in a way that profits are lower, this will be reflected in your share having lower than potential value. There will be someone out there who is familiar with the production technology of what you produce who would know that he can do this with greater profits. Such a person will have an interest in buying your low value shares so that he can oust you as a manager and then, raise the profits and the value of his own shares. Thus, while it is true that the internal organization of the firm is crucial to its performance, there could still be powerful pressures from outside to maximize profits. While this will not alter the fact that if the corporation is poorly organized, the ability to maximize profit would be seriously diminished, we can still learn something about the more abstract implications of such pressures. Consequently, while the importance of understanding the institutional structure of the firm cannot be denied, the reductionist approach which we use here is not such an enormous crime. It is certainly a valuable exercise in terms of understanding the underlying principles of such an important motivation.

3.1 Production functions

Technology and organization

The activity of production is one of the most important elements in the attempt to resolve the economic problem. If we wish to reconcile unsatiated wants with scarcity, we must endeavour to get as much as possible from existing resources. In Chapter 1, we talked about technology as given (i.e. one unit of labour can produce so many units of y or so many units of x). Namely, we did not ask ourselves whether or not the way we organize production may influence our ability to extract output from our inputs. It should, of course, be evident that both the internal organization of production and the organization of exchange (i.e. markets)—which govern the remunerations to our efforts—have a great influence in this matter. What I mean by this is that for any given technology, the way the firm is organized is bound to have an effect on the productivity of the various agents who participate in the process of production. Hence, different answers to questions like 'Who makes the decision?' or 'Who gets what?' or, which is really the essence of it all, 'Who hires who?' are very likely to affect the willingness of agents to fully participate in the process of production. By saying 'fully participate' I am trying to draw your attention to the human dimension of production, namely, that there is a difference between 'being at work' and 'working'. In other words, if, for instance, you drive a cab, does it matter whether or not you drive your own car? Does the way in which your remuneration is calculated affect your dexterity?

If indeed the organization of production has an impact on our productivity, what then do we mean by 'given technology'? Referring back to Chapter 1, we called 'technology' that which described the way in which a commodity, or a service, can be produced. Thus we had statements like 'We need half a unit of labour and one unit of machine to produce one unit of good x'. This is clearly independent of any organization of production and the productivity of either input is assumed to be given. If, however, we say that under some circumstances (such as, for instance, when workers own the assets with which they work), the productivity of labour is greater, then, to say that one simply needs half a unit of labour is not a proper description of the technology.

Put differently, given that the behaviour of some elements in the production process (notably, people) may be influenced by social questions, 'technology' may not be something which we can assume as given. One could say, of course, that technology describes the upper bounds of productivity. This means that when we say that we need half a unit of labour for the production of x we are saying that if labour were at its best, this is how much of it we would have needed. The internal organization of production will then simply tell us whether or not we were successful in extracting this ultimate productivity. Thus, when we say 'given technology' we are referring to the boundaries of human knowledge. At any point in time, human knowledge tells us about our potential: the best we can extract from our resources. We may indeed treat it as given, as at any point in time we would be unable to perform miracles. If our knowledge, say, of the physical world is such that we need 1 ha of land, 2 labour days, 300 g of wheat seeds and 6 machine hours (tractors, plough and combine) to produce 500 kg of wheat, we could not produce more than that whichever way we organize production. This is exactly what the production possibility frontier is showing us. It is showing us that given what we know about the world in terms of how to produce say, x and y, these are the combinations of the two which can be extracted from our resources had people contributed what they can to the production process.

But technology itself does not tell us whether or not we are going to be successful in getting the best out of our resources. This, as I suggested above, depends on how we organize the process of production. Thus, the combination of 1 ha of land, 2 labour days, 300 g wheat seeds and 6 machine hours may be what we need if labour was at its best but when would it be at its best? Had the land belonged to someone else and the reward for labour were low, it is unlikely that workers will give their best to the process. They are more likely to sit by the sideway and discuss a recent TV show than work very hard. Had they owned the land, would they work harder? The answer to this, of course, depends on the risk they face and the comparison between their return and what they would receive from a landlord. Had circumstances been so volatile (weather wise) as to make the harvest so uncertain, the spirit of the worker (who owns the land) may be dampened. At the same time, if the owner of the land rewards labour handsomely, would you necessarily withhold your best effort from your place of work?

Moreover, the current level of our knowledge too, may be influenced by the way society is organized and in particular, by the way it was organized in the previous period. Simple issues like the spread and depth of education, and the reward for innovation are bound to influence our ability as well as our drive to extract more out of our limited resources.

Means of production

From a technological point of view, production may appear as a cold calculation according to which we determine how much of different goods are needed to produce one unit of yet another economic good. Thus, if we want to produce a certain quantity of, say, wheat, technology tells us that we need so much acres of land; so many seeds of wheat; so many hours-use of different types of machines (like a plough, a tractor, and a combine) and, we need workers who would direct the machines and do other things. From the point of view of the production technology, all means of production are treated equally in the sense that they are all needed (in different proportions) to produce wheat. But if wheat is all that is being produced, you can imagine that a fierce argument may develop between the providers of each means of production with regard to the distribution of the produce of their collective work among them. In the past, there seemed to be some form of identity between individuals and their position in the production process. This meant that people were either workers (labour), or owners of land (landlords), or owners of capital (capitalists) but they were not more of one of these things at any point in time. Thus, whatever was distributed to workers of the final produce constituted the only source of income for these people. Whatever was given to the capitalist was his or her only source of income and the same for the landlord. The competition for a share in output was therefore quite bloody.

You may ask, but what has this got to do with production? Inasmuch as the actual process of creating a new economic good is concerned, this, of course, is of no particular interest. However, as we noted in the previous section, our ability to produce at full potential depends on the willingness of the human element in the production process (i.e. labour or management) to fully participate. This, in turn, is very likely to be influenced by what they get out of their participation. In other words, the distribution of the outcome of their collective effort may influence their productivity. Naturally, the question is not that of the absolute level of income they derive from their participation but more a question of social justice.[1] Namely, the role individuals play in bringing about the collective output (determined by technology) is of great significance to the question of what should anyone get out of the production process. Indeed much of the debate surrounding the question of distribution was associated with an examination of the relative contribution of each means of production to the production process. But while this contribution depends on technology there were also other characteristics of each means of production which influenced the debate. For instance, if we look at all factors mentioned above there are some intrinsic differences between them.

Consider first the less obvious means of production: seeds (representing here raw materials). What typifies seeds in our production process is being a produced good which is entirely consumed in the production process. Namely, there is no intrinsic difference if I buy the seeds in the market place in order to bake bread or in order to sow in the field. At the end of either process, the seeds themselves—in their form as seeds—would be no more. In such a case, the owners of the seeds cannot make any claim for the produce of seeds beyond the claim they could make of someone who buys seeds to feed the birds. What makes land unique are the following three properties. It is immoveable, it is, basically, fully renewable, and it is not itself a produced good. By the end of the season, with the appropriate treatment, the land will be there ready for us to start all over again. It may need to rest a year or so occasionally but in the end, it will be available to us for generations.[2] So land is quite a unique means of production. If it is scarce at any point in time (and recall that we are talking here about fertile land and not the vast expanses of the Sahara desert), then there is clearly an **opportunity cost** for using it for any particular purpose. However, there are no obvious **intrinsic costs** in the sense that we would have less land in the next period if we use it in this period.

Then we have the three produced means of production which would last our production period but will remain diminished at the end of it. I refer here to the tractor, the plough and the combine. All three are produced goods and are, predominantly, moveable. They will also outlast the production process but unlike land, their 'lives' would be shortened. If we think of goods such as machines, we know that they have a long yet finite life. This means that the more we use them, the quicker they get to the end of their lives. Hence, using the tractor will shorten the remains of its life and the same is true for the plough and the combine. So while they are not entirely consumed in the production process, they are consumed in part. We call such factors, **capital**.

Last, but not least, we have labour: the hours of work invested in bringing all the previous means of production together. The hours of labour are, of course, renewable but they would not be renewed by themselves. The land needs only be left by itself for it to be ready for the next period. The worker must be fed and rested so that he can live through the period in which he is giving his work to the field.

Thus we have identified four categories of means of production based on their intrinsic differences: Land, Capital, Raw Material, and Labour. The question with which many scholars struggled for many years is whether these intrinsic differences are a reason to influence the distribution of what has been produced. Marx, for instance, argued that there is basically only one means of production and that is labour. In the end, he claimed, everything is a product of labour (raw material as much as capital). The implications of such a view are far reaching and we shall not deal with this here but I draw your attention to the fact that the innocent appearance of production as a socially neutral application of human knowledge may be somewhat misleading.

Naturally, this is not how things are viewed in modern economics where the concept of price, or cost—derived from our current conception of the economic problem—is basically that of the opportunity costs. Thus, from this point of view, there is no real difference between the various factors of production. The only criterion which is of any interest with regard to the employment of any of these factors in the production process is that of their opportunity cost. In other words, for modern economics, the organization of production is solely about productive efficiency. We leave the question of distribution to be dealt with separately. However, given that the ability to extract full participation (i.e. highest productivity) may be influenced by the debate on distribution which, in turn, may be influenced by some intrinsic properties of some means of production, this may be a misguided view. In part, the purely productive efficiency approach is due to development in economic theory itself where (as you have seen at the beginning of the section on microeconomics) we no longer associate individuals with a specific element in the production process. In modern economics, all agents are all things. They are workers, owners of capital and land as well as consumers. To talk, then, about the claims to the output which are derived from the intrinsic differences between the inputs seems a bit misplaced. Whether or not this is indeed the case, remains an open question.

The process of production

In very simple terms, a production process is a blueprint which tells us how many units of various inputs (economic goods) are needed in order to produce one unit of another economic good. To simplify, let us concentrate on the two types of economic goods whose relationship with the production process are, perhaps, the most significant. I refer here to labour (L) and capital (K). Naturally to facilitate a reasonable presentation, we shall assume that both are acceptable **aggregates**. That is, although there may be many different types of workers, we assume that we can abstract the notion of labour into one type of labour. Thus there is one means of production called labour and it is measured in terms of hours given to the production process. Equally, while there are different machines, we treat them all as one means of production. Aggregation, I hasten to say, is not such a trivial exercise and there are serious ramifications to it. Therefore, to make our life easier, we have simply assumed that there are only two inputs consisting of one type of labour and one type of capital.

The process of production relates a set of quantities of inputs to a quantity of output. This is precisely what is meant by the formal notation of functions. When we say that $x = f(K, L)$ we mean to say that for any combined level of capital and labour, there is a level of output x which is the outcome of the process. From an analytical point of view, the production function is very much the same as the utility function. In both cases we use economic goods to produce another economic good. In the case of the production function we produce tangible economics goods (hence related to productive efficiency) while in the case of utility we produced a non-tangible economic good of that name. Assuming that utility is scarce and desirable, it is an economic good to which the concept of efficiency can be applied. Distinct from productive efficiency, utility is the subject of allocative efficiency.

We begin our investigation by examining the circumstances of production. Suppose that a commodity x is being produced by labour and capital. Let us first examine the meaning of this.

In the Figure 3.1 we set the horizontal axis to denote quantity of labour (L) used (which can be measured in work-hours) while on the horizontal axis we denote quantities of capital (K) used (again, measured in machine hours).

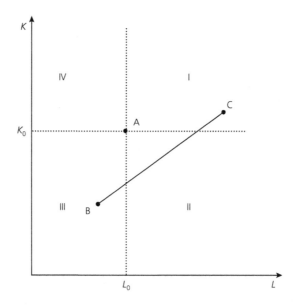

Figure 3.1 The product space.

At A, the combination of L_0 units of labour (measured in hours) and K_0 units of capital (measured in hours) can produce x_0 units of x.[3] At any point in quadrant III any combination of labour and capital will yield less units of x than x_0. All points in quadrant I suggest combinations of inputs which yield $x \geq x_0$. There are points in quadrants IV and II where the loss of output as a result of a fall in the level of one input may be compensated by an increase in the use of the other input. Put differently, output would be rising when we increase both inputs or one of them. However, by saying this we are making the following implicit assumptions: first, that the technology is **continuous** and second, that the two inputs can be **divided** and **substituted** at all levels. Namely, that moving from a point like B in quadrant III to a point like C in quadrant I will yield a continuous increase in output as we continuously increase both inputs. Hence, as at B $x < x_0$ and at C $x > x_0$, there is a point like D where $x = x_0$. This means that points of equal output (iso-quants) are located in quadrants IV and II. Like indifference curves, they will be located on a downward sloping line. Like the indifference curves in the case of utility, the iso-quants describe all possible combinations of input with which we can produce a particular level of output.

The assumptions of **divisibility** and **substitutability** which are implied by the existence of such iso-quants, are not as straightforward as in the case of utility analysis. Divisibility simply means that we can measure inputs in terms of their time contribution. If so, we can talk of any fraction of a unit that can affect output. While some may have difficulties with this, we shall not consider it as a serious problem. Substitutability is a much more serious problem.

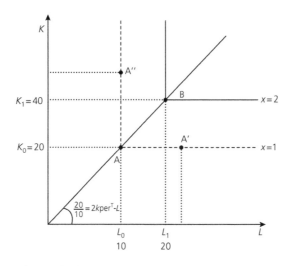

Figure 3.2 Fixed proportion production process

To make sense of it all let us begin by describing a simple production process as shown in Figure 3.2. As before, the horizontal axis describes quantities of labour (measured in hours) while the vertical axis describes quantities of capital (also measured in hours). The line from the origin describes the technology of production. This process is what we call a **fixed proportion process** and is, perhaps, the most realistic description of any particular production technology. We can see that at point A we would need, 10 units of labour and 20 units of capital to produce one unit of x. The L-shaped broken line is what we call the iso-quant. Recall that the iso-quant describes the different combinations of input needed for the production of a particular level of output. The L-shape of the iso-quant suggests that there is no substitutability between labour and capital. If we start at A and we increase only the amount of labour we employ at A'), we would not be able to produce a single extra unit of x (we thus remain on the iso-quant which describes all combinations of input with which we can produce one unit of x). Equally, if we increase only capital (point A'') we would not be able to produce more than one unit of x. How can we increase the output? We can do so only by increasing both inputs by the same proportion. Hence, if we double both labour and machines to (20,40) we could produce two units of x (the higher broken line (B)). As the proportion of labour and capital in the production process are constant, we can identify this technology by the capital–labour ratio it requires. In our case, this ratio of K/L is $20/10 = 2$ units of K per unit of labour (L).

However, at any point in time there is more than just one technology available. What I would like to show now is how the notion of substitutability can become meaningful if we think of it as a switch between technologies.

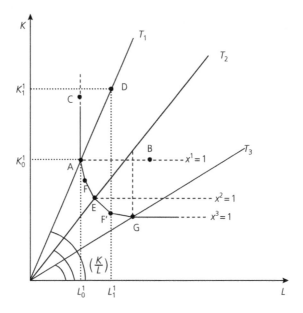

Figure 3.3 Mixing fixed proportion technologies.

If we think about production as being made up of linear processes (fixed proportions), and we have three different technologies (T_1, T_2, and T_3, (Figure 3.3)), it would mean that we could produce x by using one of these technologies at any particular point in time. Each technology requires a different combination of inputs in the production process, and as we saw earlier, you cannot increase output by merely changing one input. You must use both inputs and maintain the same proportion between them if you wish to affect the level of output. Hence, if you look at A in process 1, it means that you need L_0^1 units of labour and K_0^1 units of capital to produce one unit of x. The iso-quant is L-shaped, because increasing only labour or capital (points B and C) will not increase the output. In such a case, there is clearly no substitutability between the means of production. If you want to produce 2 units of x using process 1, you will need to move to a point like D where both labour and capital have been increased to L_1^1 units of labour and K_1^1 units of capital.

The fixed proportion between the two means of production is captured by the ratio of capital to labour (K/L) which is depicted by the slope of the ray from the origin. At both A and D

$$\left(\frac{K_0^1}{L_0^1}\right)^A = \left(\frac{K_1^1}{L_1^1}\right)^D.$$

However, if substitutability is taken to mean that we can choose combinations of technology then we may be able to move closer to the notion of substitutability. If points A and E represent the combination of capital and labour required for the production of one unit of x under technologies 1 and 2, respectively, point F represents the inputs required to produce one unit of x by a combination of technologies. The greater the share of technology 1 in the production, the nearer will F be to A. The greater the share of technology 2 in the production, the nearer will F get to E. If, in addition, we have technology 3 to consider, F' depicts the level of inputs required for the production of one unit of x with the combination of technologies 2 and 3. As before, the more of technology 2 we use, the nearer will F' be to E. The more of technology 3 we use, the nearer will F' be to G. If, indeed, we can mix technologies, we can see that the levels of inputs required for the production of one unit of output are arranged along the heavy line in the above diagram which reminds us of the indifference curve. This means that if we have a very large number of technologies available, the move from one technology to another can constitute a meaningful notion of input substitutability.

Therefore, we claim that while smooth functions may not directly capture the nature of the production process, they, nevertheless, constitute a good abstraction of it. We will obviously be looking for a function that will be able to generate similar properties as the mixture of processes (i.e. smooth iso-quants which are convex). $x = f(K, L)$, where f is a real number, continuous, and twice differentiable function, is a description of exactly such a production function.

3.1.1 Properties of the production function

(a) It is increasing in L and K ($\rightarrow$) If we increase all inputs, the output also will have to increase (see Figure 3.4).

(b) As in the case of utility, by using a real number function that is differentiable as an abstraction of the production process, we must make sense of all that comes with it. Notably, we must provide an economic interpretation for the concept of the derivative. In the case of the utility function we identified this to be the marginal utility, but we faced serious difficulties given the ordinal nature of preference representation. Here we do not have a similar problem, as the production function is cardinal. Namely, the quantity of output produced is the actual quantity and not merely a representation of it. Hence, the concept of marginal product too is quite self-evident. We define marginal product (MP_L) as dx/dL (at L_0) which should be read as, 'a change of dL units in input L will increase output by dx units' (see Figure 3.5). In other words, it is the effects on output of a change in the units of inputs.

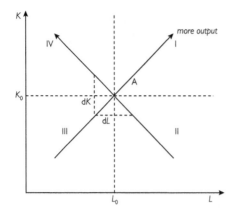

Figure 3.4 Delineating product functions.

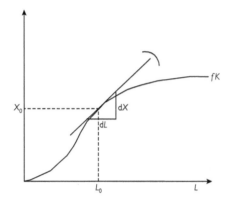

Figure 3.5 Marginal product.

A broader way to think about marginal product is by referring to it as the contribution of the last unit of input. Hence, if we remove, or add, one unit of an input (leaving the others unchanged), the marginal product will measure the subsequent increase in the output. There is, however, something quite misleading in calling the marginal product the contribution of an input, as this is not determined only by the ability and dexterity of that input (labour in particular). The level of marginal product depends on how many people are already at work and what is the level of other inputs employment. If, for instance, you are producing computer games, you would need a room, a computer (with the right software), and a teenager. Suppose that hiring the first teenager generated an output of one new game per week. The teenager was spending a lot of time checking his e-mail and chatting on the net as he was bored being alone in the building. Then, you hire another teenager but you do not hire an extra room or computer. So the two of them will have to work together using the same computer. Given what we said earlier, the two teenagers will now find company in each other and they will fire each other's imagination. As a result, they will work a lot and their total output will be four new games per week. Thus, the marginal product of the first teenager was 1 and that of the second teenager was 3.

When we introduce the third teenager into the same room (with the single computer)—namely, we are varying only one of our inputs—this will become a bit crowded. Although they will still excite each other's imagination, some arguments may develop with regard to which is the better idea. On the other hand, whenever there is a problem a solution would be found more easily. Hence, the three of them together can produce 7 new games a week. Thus the marginal product of the third teenager is 3 (which is less than the marginal product of the second teenager). Note, however, that the fact that the third teenager contributed less has nothing to do with his identity. Implicitly, we assumed that all teenagers are alike and of equal talent and ability. If the third teenager were to be, instead, the first one to be employed, his marginal product would have been 1 new game rather than 3.

You can imagine what might happen to the output of games if we kept crowding the room with its single computer with hormone-driven teenagers. The contribution (the marginal product) of every consecutive teenager is bound to be lower than the one before as they spend more time arguing and fighting than writing new games.

Note, however, that if we had ten teenagers in one room with one computer and the marginal product of the 10th teenager was 1/2 a game, this is primarily due to the fact that other factors are fixed. If we now hire 9 more rooms and 9 more computers so that each teenager has a room and a computer yet, they do not lose their proximity, the output of the 10th teenager is likely to be considerably higher. Thus we emphasize that the marginal product of a factor represents its contribution to the output for a given level of other factors. The notion of diminishing marginal product, in such a case, makes perfect sense.

(c) There are combinations of K and L which yield the same level of output and they are arranged along a line that goes through IV and II. Thus, the iso-quants are downward sloping (see Figure 3.4).

(d) The slope of the iso-quant is defined as dK/dL when x is unchanged (see Figure 3.6). If we change geometrically L by dL, the output will change according to $dL \cdot MP_L$ (i.e. the number of new units of labour times the contribution of such a unit to output). If we change K by dK, the output will change by $dK \cdot MP_K$. Along the iso-quant the change in output as a result of a change in $K =$ the change in output as a result of a change in L. Hence $-dL \cdot MP_L = dK \cdot MP_K \implies -dK/dL = MP_L/MP_K$ units of K per units of L (see Figure 3.6). In other words, if the marginal product of labour is 10 units of x and the marginal product of capital is 5 units of x, the slope of the iso-quant would be ($MP_L/MP_K = 2$.) It means that if we choose to substitute one unit of L (which contributes $10x$) with capital (which only contributes $5x$ each) we would need to replace it by 2 units of K so that output remains unchanged.

(e) The iso-quants, like the indifference curves, are convex. The reason for this could be explained (inaccurately, from a purely mathematical point of view, but nevertheless quite usefully) through the marginal product. Compare the slopes of the iso-quant at points A and B. At A we have a lot of capital (K) and very few workers (L). Thus, the slope at A is given by: MP_L^A/MP_K^A where both marginal products are determined by the quantities of K and L at point A. As we move to B we move to a point where there is less capital and far more labour employed. Both these factors suggest that the marginal product of

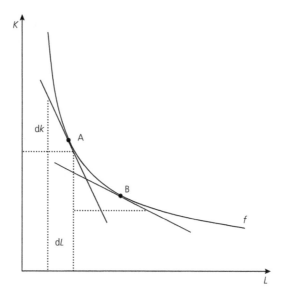

Figure 3.6 Difference in slopes of iso-quant.

labour would be much smaller (many more teenagers and fewer computers and rooms). Thus, it is likely that $\text{MP}_L^A > \text{MP}_L^B$. Equally, as we have far more labour at B and fewer units of capital, the productivity of K must be higher at B. Hence, as we move from A to B we move to a technology, which uses more labour (L) and less capital (K). Therefore, the productivity of labour will be lower than before while the productivity of capital greater ($\downarrow \text{MP}_L / \uparrow \text{MP}_K$)| and the slope of the iso-quant becomes flatter.

3.1.2 Returns to scale

So we have a production function $x = f(K, L)$. We have examined so far how the output would increase along a fixed proportion of technologies and what would happen to the returns to a single factor when we allow switching from one technology to another. To complete the picture we must return to the question of what will happen to the output as we increase all inputs. The concept which deals with this issue is called the 'return to scale'.

The return to scale is a measure of how effective is an increase in the scale of operation. When we say that there are **increasing returns to scale** we mean to say that the output will rise by a greater proportion than that by which we have increased our operation. Thus, if we double the quantity of capital and labour which we employ, the output will rise by more than twice. In our computer game factory it would mean that if one room, one computer, and one teenager produce 1 game a week then two rooms, two computers, and two teenagers produce more than 2, say 3, new games a week. **Constant returns to scale** mean that the output will rise by exactly the same proportion as that by which we have increased the scale of operation. Thus, two rooms, two computers, and two teenagers will produce 2 new games a week. **Decreasing returns to scale** mean that the proportionate increase in output is less than the proportionate expansion of operation.

Thus, two rooms, two computers, and two teenagers would only produce, say, 1.5 new games a week.

In the context of production functions, the **scale of operation** is captured by the amounts of inputs which we use. When we talk about changes in scale we normally mean a change across the board. You will see later on that the composition of inputs depends on their relative prices; the scale of operation would normally relate to the price of the output.

Therefore, a change in scale does not alter the composition of inputs, it only affects the level of their employment. An increase in the scale of production means that we have increased all inputs by a certain proportion. The **returns** to this change are measured by the proportionate increase in the output.

Let us examine again what we know about the production function. We know that the output rises as we employ more of both inputs. We also know that there is a certain substitutability which is captured by the iso-quant. For each level of output there is a unique iso-quant. Therefore, there are an infinite number of iso-quants. Figure 3.7 below represents two of them.

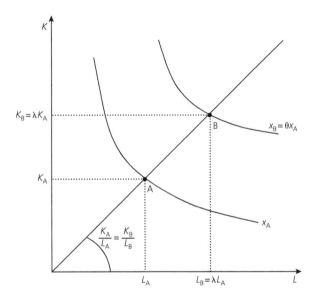

Figure 3.7 Increasing production and returns to scale.

Increases in scale are depicted by a movement along a ray from the origin. The slope of such rays, in this figure, represents a given capital to labour ratio (K/L) (the composition of inputs). As we move along such a ray, the levels of inputs are increased[4] and output (represented by the relevant iso-quants) will rise too.

We began at point A in the above diagram. We may now wish to increase the scale of our operation by a certain proportion, say $\lambda(\lambda > 1)$. We therefore increase both Labour and Capital by λ such that $K_B = \lambda K_A$ and $L_B = \lambda L_A$. Clearly,

$$\left(\frac{K}{L}\right)_A = \left(\frac{\lambda K}{\lambda L}\right)_B.$$

At point B the output also has increased. Let us suppose that $x_B = \theta x_A$, which means that the output has increased by θ. Whether there are increasing, constant, or decreasing returns to scale now depends on whether θ is greater, equal, or less than λ.

A simple way to look at this issue is by examining functions which have a special property: homogeneity.[5]

A homogenous production function means that if we increase all inputs by a certain proportion, the increase in output can be described as a function of the increase in inputs. That is to say, θ can be written as $\theta(\lambda)$. For instance, if we multiply all inputs by λ, the output will rise by $(\theta =)\lambda^t$. We can write this as follows: $f(\lambda L, \lambda K) = \lambda^t f(L, K) = \lambda^t x$.

If $t = 1$, it means that an increase in all inputs by a certain proportion will increase the output by the same proportion ($\theta = \lambda^1 = \lambda$). This is the property of **constant returns to scale**; it means that as we increase the scale of our operation by increasing all inputs, the output will rise by exactly the same proportion as the increase in inputs.

If $t > 1$, it means that an increase in all inputs by a certain proportion will increase the output by a greater proportion($\theta = \lambda^t > \lambda$). This is the property of **increasing returns to scale**.

If $t < 1$, then output will increase by a lesser proportion than the increase in inputs ($\theta = \lambda^t < \lambda$). This is the property of **decreasing returns to scale**.

Generally, we assume that all types of returns to scale are present in the process of production. We believe that increasing returns to scale are likely to be present at the first stages of production, and decreasing returns to scale will have to appear as output grows.[6]

The following graph depicts the production function where there are increasing returns to scale at the beginning and decreasing returns to scale towards the end. To make it simple, suppose that v is a composite input comprised of both labour and capital. Thus increases in v correspond to movements along the ray in Figure 3.6. In other words, $v_0 = (L_0, K_0)$, $v_1 = (L_1, K_1)$. We thus get the following relations as shown in Figure 3.8.

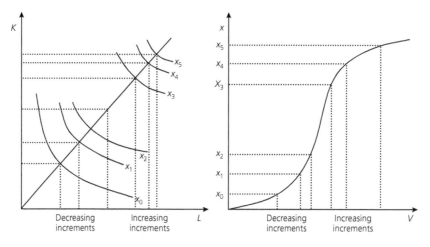

Figure 3.8 A typical production function, derived from iso-quants.

Note (on the right-hand side diagram) that, at first, fixed increments in output require ever decreasing increases in inputs (i.e. increasing returns to scale). Later, one can see that fixed increases in output require ever increasing increases in inputs (i.e. decreasing returns to scale).

The corresponding points in the left-hand side diagram depict the firm's growth of output when inputs are increased by the same proportion. When production functions have the property of homogeneity, it will also become the firm's **expansion path**. This path depicts all the optimal combinations of input with which one can produce a chosen level of output for given factor prices.

3.1.3 Returns to factor (marginal product): the short run

We have so far examined the properties of the production function when we increase all means of production, simultaneously. If we think about it in terms of the degree of freedom which the producer has in terms of varying his inputs, being able to vary all inputs is the ultimate degree of freedom. Thus, if we go back to our computer games producer, it would mean that he can vary at whim the number of hours the teenagers work for him, the duration of renting a room and the number of rooms rented at any point in time and, of course, the number of computer hours used. You can imagine that, in reality, there is nothing like it. When you rent property you usually have a relatively long-term contract (which means that you have to pay for the room so you might as well use it). So when we are in a position to change and adjust the level of any input, we say that we are employing **long run** considerations. When we are unable to alter the quantity of the input available to us because we have already committed ourselves to using it, we say that we are employing **short run** considerations.

Interestingly enough, it is always labour which is considered to be the most dispensable means of production; the means of production we can vary in the long, as well as in the short, run. This means that labour will be first to be hired (because there is an embedded short term commitment to it) as well as first to be fired. Put differently, of all the contracts signed by the producer with various forms of inputs (land, capital, and labour), the fact that one can vary only labour in the short run means that the contracts with workers are the least significant from the producer's point of view. Whether or not this is a result of historical development or simply a realistic observation, it is not obvious that this is how things should be.

When we examine the long run circumstances of production we know that all inputs are variables and therefore, the key property of the production function is that of **returns to scale**. We assumed that the long run development of production suggests increasing returns to scale at first and when the operation becomes too big, due to difficulty of monitoring and control, the returns will diminish.

In the short run, we only vary one factor (labour). The effects of varying one factor on the level of output is measured through the concept of **marginal return to factor** (marginal product) which we have begun to study earlier.

Recall that we said that marginal product is the contribution of a single factor (dx/dL) and that we thought that while it may be increasing at first, it too will be diminishing as we increase the quantity of input employed (the case of increasing number of teenagers working in one room and on the same computer).

◼ QUESTION FOR REFLECTION

Can a function exhibit increasing returns to scale and diminishing marginal product at the same time?

We know that the particulars of any production process are very difficult to establish. This is why economists are always looking at the relationship between things which we could easily see and things which are more difficult to measure. For instance, to measure marginal product may be very difficult indeed. One would need to know the specifics of the production function. However, it is very easy to compute the **average product per factor**. The average product per factor is simply, $AP_L = x/L$; namely, total output divided by the number of workers (or hours worked). Let us now examine the properties of the average product and its relationship with the less obvious concept of marginal product.

As we are examining the returns to a factor, we are working in the short run. This means that while we vary labour (L), we do not change the quantity of capital employed (K_0). Figure 3.9 depicts the production function when capital is fixed.

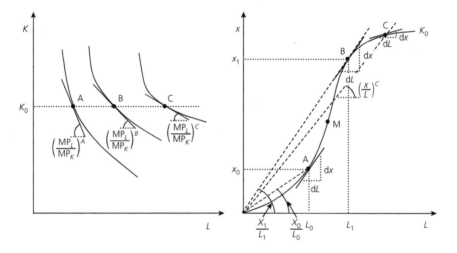

Figure 3.9 Short-run Production functions.

At first, it is reasonable to suppose that any increase in the variable input will add to output in increasing increments (i.e. increasing marginal product). At a certain point the amount of the variable input, relative to the fixed input, will increase so much that its contribution to the output will have to fall.

Thus, at first, the function exhibits increasing MP_L, and then, diminishing MP_L. We can now clearly see that the $MP_L (= dX/dL)$ is the slope of the function. Up to A it increases, then, it diminishes.

On the left-hand diagram of the figure we can see the corresponding points of production. These form what one may consider as the **Short run expansion path**. Along this expansion path the level of capital is fixed and the only way to increase the output is through increases in labour inputs.

In the right-hand diagram, the slope of the rays from the origin is always x/L, therefore, it is by definition, the average product (AP). For instance, if we look at the ray from the origin to point A we can see that the slope of the angle created by this line is given by the opposite side over the adjacent side: $x_0/L_0 = AP_L(x_0)$. We can thus see how the slope of the ray from the origin increases from A to B and diminishes further onwards. At point B, at which the slope is at its highest, it equals the gradient of f, which by definition is the MP_L of (L_1, X_1). There are, therefore, two slopes to be examined. The first one is the slope of the production function itself, which, as we saw earlier, gives us the change in output resulting from a slight change in input. We called this, the marginal product. The other slope is that of the ray from the origin to any particular point on the production function, like point A. We can clearly see that the ray from the origin is rising up to B and then diminishes. But we can also see that the same thing happens to the slope of the function. At first, the slope is rising (becoming steeper) indicating increasing marginal productivity. Then, at M, it begins to fall (see what happens to the slope as we move from B to C). The remaining question is about their relationship. By looking at A, B, and C we can see that as long as the ray from the origin is rising, the slope of the function (i.e. the marginal product) is steeper than the slope of the ray from the origin. Namely, at a point like A, where average product is rising, marginal product will be greater than average product. At B, when the average product is at its highest, it has the same slope as the function itself and is thus the same as the marginal product. After that, when the average product is falling (B to C), the marginal product is smaller than average product (the slope of the ray from the origin at C is greater than the slope of the function itself at that point. Figure 3.10 depicts these relationships.

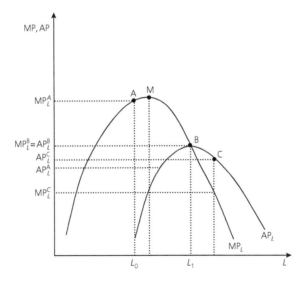

Figure 3.10 Average and marginal product.

Thus, if we were to investigate a particular firm and we do not know the exact production function, we may be able to infer that if the average product is rising, the marginal product will be lower and rising too. At this stage this may not mean much, but as you will see later, this is a significant piece of information.

3.2 The behaviour of the firm

Firms have to make two choices: how much to produce and by which technology to produce (inputs composition). The choice of technology is, in principle, very similar to the way individuals choose their consumption basket. The production function is to the firm like the utility function is to the consumer.

We generally assume that firms wish to maximize profit. Whether or not this is really the case and what might be the consequences if it is not is an interesting subject which, at this stage, will be left out.

Consider for a moment the profit function:

$$\Pi = p_x x - c(x),$$

where $p_x x$ is revenue while $c(x)$ represent the cost.[7] We shall assume at this stage that prices (of the product as well as the inputs) are all given exogenously.

It is easy to see that one way of presenting profit maximization is to think of choosing the highest output level for any given level of costs (a bit like utility maximization; for any budget constraint (cost level) we want to get the most preferred bundle). The graph in Figure 3.11 depicts this choice.

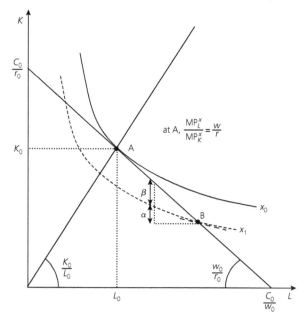

Figure 3.11 Profit maximization: maximizing output for given cost.

For a given level of cost c_0, the firm can choose all combinations of labour (L) and capital (K) which are within its 'budget constraint' (the cost allowance, if you wish). The rate at which the firm can substitute capital for labour is given by the market exchange rate. Exactly as consumers could exchange goods according to their relative price p_x/p_y, the firm can exchange inputs according to their market rates. Given that w denotes the wage level and r the return on capital,[8] the market rate of exchange between the labour and capital for given prices will be: w_0/r_0 units of capital per labour. If the cost of labour (w) is 10 and the cost of capital (r) is 5, you can replace a unit of labour with 2 units of capital.

The highest level of output which is now feasible is given by the highest iso-quant. The choice of inputs' combination is therefore determined at the point where the iso-quant is tangent to the iso-cost (the firm's budget constraint). At that point, the slope of the iso-cost, which is the **market** rate of exchange between capital and labour, is the same as the slope of the iso-quant. The latter, as we explained earlier, is really the **technological rate of substitution** between capital and labour. It means that at its optimal point, the firm will gain no extra output by exchanging labour and capital at the margin. It means that if the firm gives up some labour, it will be able to buy only that much capital which will add to its output exactly that much which has been lost by giving up labour. At point B above, we can see a point which is not optimal. If the firm gave up one unit of labour it would need α units of capital to remain at the same level of output (the technological rate of substitution). But in the market place, it can get $\alpha + \beta$ units of capital per labour. It means that the firm can improve its performance through market operations.

For any given relative factors prices we can get the set of all points where the firm is producing optimally. These points, captured in Figure 3.12, are what we call the firm's **expansion path**. It is a long run expansion path, as all means of production vary in the process of expansion.

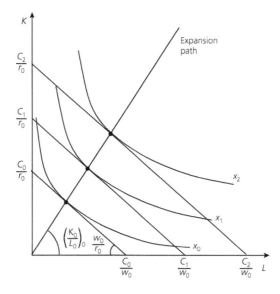

Figure 3.12 Long run expansion paths.

In the case where the production function is homogeneous, the expansion path will be a straight line.

So far, however, we only talked about the choice of technology (inputs' composition) which constitutes optimal choice. We have not yet dealt with the question of how much x to produce. The answer to this depends on the relationship between output (x) and the iso-cost lines. This relationship is explored in the next section.

3.2.1 The cost functions

To establish the relationship between the level of costs (c) and the level of output x, we are asking a general question about the relationship between the properties of the production function and the properties of the cost functions. As we know the former, if we knew how they relate to each other we would have known the latter too.

To see this, consider a very primitive case where there is only one input. Namely, $x = f(L)$. In such a case (this is a bit similar to the short run story but here we say nothing about any other factor), the production function will have increasing marginal product at first and diminishing marginal productivity as the output increases. This is depicted in the left-hand diagram (Figure 3.13).

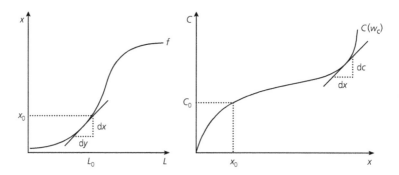

Figure 3.13 Production-cost relationships.

Clearly, the slope of the production function is: $dx/dL = MP_L$. Now, what would be the cost of producing x? Clearly, this is the cost of labour. Hence, $c(x) = wL(x) = wf^{-1}(L)$ which means that we are looking at the inverse of the production function. Recall that, by definition, a production function was telling us how many units of x we would have if we employed, say, L_0 units of labour. In our case, it would be $x_0 = f(L_0)$. But sometimes we can reverse the question and ask how much labour would we need to produce so many units of x. So our costs are defined as $c(x) = wL(x)$. To examine the cost function diagrammatically, we need to look at the intercept and the slope. As L is the only means of production $f(0) = 0$ and equally $L(0) = 0$.

We now examine the slope. The geometrical definition of the slope in the space of (x, c) (in the above right-hand diagram) is always dc/dx. This represents a change in the cost level resulting from a small change in the level of output. We call such a concept the **marginal cost**. We return now to our cost function and ask how can we change the level of cost? The answer is very simple. Here, as we have only one input, the change in the level of cost could only result from a change in the number of units of L employed (as we assume the wages to be fixed): thus, $dc = wdL$. However, we are looking for an expression like dc/dx. We therefore divide both sides of the equation with dx:

$$\frac{dc}{dx} = w\frac{dL}{dx}$$

$$MC(x) \equiv \frac{dc}{dx} = w\frac{1}{dx/dL} = w\frac{1}{MP_L}.$$

This means that the marginal cost is inversely related to the marginal product. This makes perfect sense, if you think about it. If the productivity of labour is low one would need a lot of labour time to produce one extra unit of x. As the cost of each unit of labour is the same (w), it will be very high. If, in contrast, we have very high productivity, we would only need a short time to produce the extra unit of x. The cost of that unit will therefore be low.

As the marginal product is the slope of the production function, it means that the shape of the cost function (determined by the marginal costs) will be the mirror image of the production function. The level of wages will determine the position of the cost function in the (x, c) space but its shape is determined by the properties of the production function.

The general form
The cost function in the general form of our two inputs model is:

$$C(K, L) = wL + rK$$

where w, r are the market prices of labour and capital respectively. We shall assume that these prices are fixed.

Long run cost function
In the long run, it is assumed that all inputs are variable. We assumed, when discussing production functions, that at first it is most likely that the process of production will be characterized by increasing returns to scale, hence, an increase of a unit of output will require a decreasing increase in inputs, thus, a decreasing increase in cost. This is depicted in Figure 3.14 between the origin and point A.

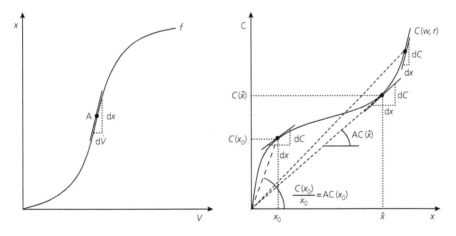

Figure 3.14 Production functions and the total cost curve.

This is very similar to the case of single input, with the difference that the slope of the production function gives the marginal returns to scale while the input is the mixed bundle v. As the output increases, we assumed that the process will exhibit decreasing returns to scale. That is, every further increase by a unit of output will require ever increasing increases in inputs. As prices are fixed it also means that the cost of each unit (the Marginal Cost) will be rising.

Marginal costs (long-run)
The change in total cost that results from a change in output. MC is therefore dC/dX. We can clearly see that this is the gradient of the cost function in the lower part of the above diagram. Notice that marginal cost and returns to scale are inversely related. When there are increasing returns to scale there will be a diminishing marginal cost. The production of every extra unit of output will require decreasing increases in inputs and, thus, decreasing cost per extra unit.

Average costs: the cost per unit of output
Again, as average costs are expressed as: C/X, we can see that they can be represented by the slope of the ray from the origin in Figure 3.14.

As was the case in the relationship between the average and marginal product, we can clearly see that when the average cost is at its lowest it corresponds to the point where the ray from the origin is tangent to the cost function. Hence, the slope of the cost function (i.e. the marginal cost) will be the same as the average cost at the point where average cost is at its minimum level.

As the marginal and average cost represent the slopes of the function and the ray from the origin, respectively, it is easy to examine their relationship (Figure 3.15).

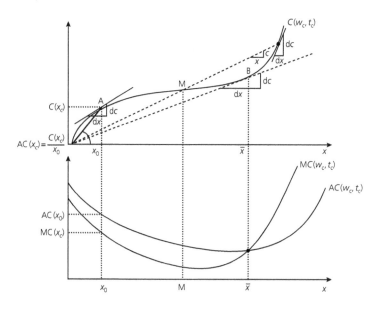

Figure 3.15

First, we can see that the average cost (the ray from the origin) is falling all the way up to point B from whence, the ray from the origin to the function will have increasing slope. This U-shape of the average cost is captured in the diagram below with B being its minimum point. Equally, when we look at the slope of the function itself (marginal cost) we can see that this will fall all the way to M and start rising again later. This represents the increasing returns property at the beginning (which means, diminishing marginal cost) and the diminishing returns to scale at the end (increasing marginal cost).

The relationship between the two curves can be easily established. When the average cost is falling (as for instance, at point A), the slope of the ray from the origin (average cost) is greater than that of the function (dc/dx). This is true all the way up to point B. Hence, the average cost is higher the marginal cost as long as the average cost is falling. At the minimum average cost the slope of the ray from the origin is the same as the slope of the cost function. Therefore, the average and marginal costs are the same at point B. Beyond B, when the average cost is rising, the marginal cost is clearly greater (steeper slope of the function) than the average cost.

The intuition here is also quite evident. If we have increasing returns to scale at the beginning it means that for every additional unit of output we would need decreasing increases in inputs (as every increase in input produces an increasing increase in output). Thus, the cost of the extra unit is falling (marginal cost). If the cost of every extra unit is falling, so will the average cost. However, the average cost will be higher, as it still takes into account the previous higher levels of marginal cost. For the same reason, when the marginal cost begins to rise as a result of diminishing returns to scale setting in, the average cost will take time to catch up as it is still taking into account the previous lower marginal costs. Further down I shall provide you with a numerical example that will clarify the issue completely.

Short run cost function
In the short run, one of the means of production is fixed, hence, its costs are independent of the quantity produced. The cost function, therefore, is divided into two: **fixed costs**[9] (FC) and **variable cost** (VC(x))

$$SRC = FC + VC(x).$$

To see how the SRC function behaves one needs only to recall the short run production function. The short run production function has the same shape as the long run production function but for different reasons. Translating it into a cost function means repeating the argument we presented for the long run cost function, with one important difference. The long run marginal and average costs began, more or less, at the same point. When we produce our first unit, the concepts of the marginal and the average are the same. In the short run this is not the case, as already when we produce the first unit we have the cost of the fixed stock of capital to consider.

Whenever the marginal product is rising the cost of an extra unit (the marginal cost) will be decreasing. This is so because increased productivity means that one would need less labour than one needed before for an extra unit of output. Therefore, the VC(x) part of the SRC behaves exactly in the same way as the long run cost. The difference, therefore, will lie in the position of the SRC. Figure 3.16 depicts the relationship between the long and the short run cost functions.

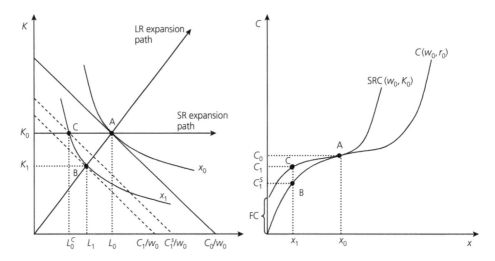

Figure 3.16 Long and short run production and cost functions.

In the long run, given the input prices ratio, we would have produced x with a ratio K_0/L_0 according to our LR-expansion path, which connects all points where the slopes of the iso-cost lines are tangent to the slope of the iso-quant curves (which is determined by factor prices). When K is fixed, in the short run, it means that only at point A will the output be produced by the same combination of K and L in the long run and in the short run. (A is both on the long run and on the short run expansion paths). Any output below x is produced, in the short run, by a combination that is more expensive than the one that would have been used in the long run. For instance, to produce x_1 in the long run, we could have used the combination of K_1, L_1 at point B. In the short run, however, we are stuck with K_0 so we might as well use it. This means that we can only produce x_1 if we choose the corresponding level of labour with which it can be produced. This is described by point C. But at C, under the current inputs prices, the cost of producing x_1 is much higher (the broken iso-cost line) than the cost needed to produce x_1 at point B. The same would be true for any output above X (try to show it yourself).

LRAC and SRAC Relationship

In Figure 3.17 we have reconstructed the long run and short run total costs function. The average costs are shown by the rays from the origin. The slope of such a ray is, as we saw earlier, the value of C/x which is exactly the average cost (AC). It is easy to see that for any level of output, except one, the level of cost in the short run is greater than it is in the long run. Subsequently, it should come as no surprise when the average cost of the long run is always below the short run average cost (except at one point). We can also see that at any level of output, the slope of the ray that reaches the SRC at a given level of output is greater than the one that reaches the LRC. Therefore, short run average costs

(SRAC) are generally greater or equal to the long run average costs (LRAC). The only point where the long run and short run levels of costs are the same is at point A which is also the point where the LR-expansion path intersects with the SR-expansion path. It is easy to see that such an intersection occurs at only one level of output x_0.

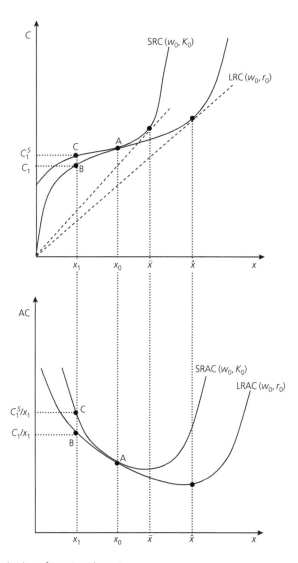

Figure 3.17 The derivation of SRAC and LRAC.

At point A (above and in the previous set of diagrams) the long run and the short run produce the same optimal choice of technology. This means that short run average costs and long run average costs are at the same level. To the left of x_0 we see that the long run considerations are different from the short run considerations. This means that as the short run is the period where the number of constraints is greater, any short run choice would be inferior to the one made in the long run. The level of cost with which we could produce x_1 in the long run is identified by point B. In the short run, the level of cost would be higher (identified by point C). Thus the average cost in the short run will lie above the long run average costs.

As the shape of the short run cost function is not different from the shape of the long run cost function (but for different reasons), the corresponding shapes of the cost functions is similar too. This means that while the long run average cost function is U-shaped due to increasing returns to scale at the beginning and diminishing returns to scale at the end, the short run average cost function is U-shaped due to increasing marginal productivity at early stages of production and diminishing marginal productivity at a higher level of output.

If we now add the marginal costs into the diagram we can see the entire picture. We have already explored the shape of the long run marginal costs (LRMC). It starts more or less at the same level of the average cost and then falls, up to a certain point where diminishing returns to scale kick in.

The short run marginal cost (SRMC) is the slope of the SRC. We can see that even at very low levels of output where the average costs are very high (due to the fixed costs), the slope of the function is very flat. Namely, the short run marginal costs are very low at first. The intuition is evident. Will one teenager in a building full of computers not have a feast in designing computer games?

At the level of output of x_1 the slope of the LRC (at B) is steeper than that of the SRC (at C). This means that everywhere before point A the slope of the SRC is flatter than that of the LRC. From a geometrical perspective this makes perfect sense, as SRC began higher than LRC and they have to converge to the same value at A.

Thus, SRMC < LRMC at all points before A. At A, as the SRC is tangent to the LRC the two functions will have the same slope. This means that the SRMC (at A) = LRMC (at A). Everywhere to the right of A it is easy to see that the slope of the SRC is bound to be steeper than that of the LRC. Hence, SRMC (to the right of A) > LRMC (to the right of A). As usual, both short run and long run marginal costs intersect with their respective average costs at the minimum of the latter.

The analysis conducted thus far assumed that capital was fixed at a particular level (K_0). This, of course, is only one possibility. We could have had the level of capital fixed at any initial quantity. For instance, this would be the difference between starting our computer games operation with one room and one computer or starting it with 10 rooms and 10 computers.

While the analysis of the shape of the short run costs and their relationship with the long run costs is sufficiently general, it is worth our while to examine the differences between different levels of initial capital.

In Figure 3.18 we compare the short run–long run relationships at two different levels of initial capital. The derivation of the various costs functions and their relationship for each level of initial capital is the same as before. The shape of the corresponding short run cost functions is the same but the one with higher initial capital will also have higher fixed costs. Therefore, $SRC(0, K_1) > SRC(0, K_0)$. So one difference is that the greater is the initial capital (the level of fixed costs) the higher will be the starting point of the short run cost function.

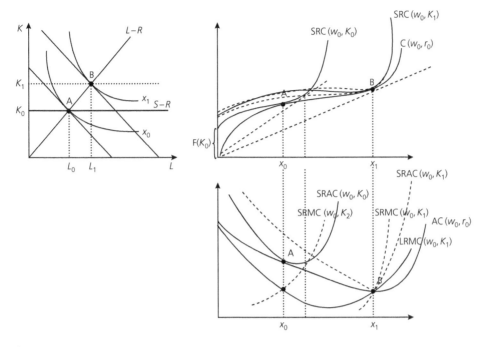

Figure 3.18

The second difference is the point where long run and short run considerations meet. Point A denotes the level of output at which the long run expansion path intersects with the short run expansion path when the fixed level of capital is K_0. Point B represents the corresponding point in the case where the initial stock of capital is K_1. Clearly if the quantity of initial capital is so great, the level of output for which this would have been our optimal choice even if we could vary it would necessarily be very large indeed.

If we now engage in the same type of operation we conducted earlier to derive the corresponding marginal and average cost function, we should get the picture in the bottom diagram. All ACs will have their typical U-shape but what will be different is that for at least one level of initial stock the point where the short run and long run meet is the point where the LRAC is at its minimum. This would also mean that the corresponding SRAC would be at its minimum at the same level of output.

The question is, of course, whether there is any significance to this particular level of capital which yields an average cost function which is tangent to the long run average costs at its minimum. Moreover, is there any significance to the minimum of the average cost function?

Suppose that the manager of the computer games company invites you to evaluate the efficiency of his operations. He asks you only to look at the question of whether *that which he is doing, he is doing efficiently*. Naturally, on your first day in the office, he provides you with all the information you need (i.e. production function and factor prices). Note that he does not want you to tell him whether or not he should produce more or less of computer games. You know that he is producing a certain quantity (say, x_0) and he wants to know whether he is doing it efficiently. Naturally, from his point of view he is only interested in whether he can produce the same quantity at a lower cost (i.e. he is interested in profit maximization). In that sense, he is really asking you whether his operation is optimally organized. Suppose that you discover the following situation as shown in Figure 3.19:

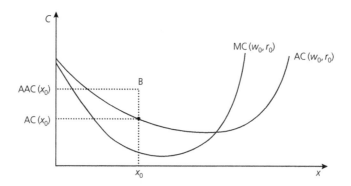

Figure 3.19

You discover that he is producing x_0 at an average cost of $AC(x_0)$. What would you say? Is he producing optimally? Is this efficient?

When students look at this diagram their attention is being attracted by the minimum average costs. There is something alluring about this point; after all, if this is a point where average costs are at their minimum, should we not want to be there? The answer, of course, is no, we do not necessarily want to be there.

Given the production function of the company and the factor prices, producing x_0 at $AC(x_0)$ simply means that *you cannot produce x_0 at a lower level of costs.* Recall that each point on the average costs was derived from a point on the cost function. This level of cost was derived from the profit maximization operation. Namely, it represents the minimal level of cost with which each level of output can be produced. By definition, therefore, all points on the average costs are **equally optimal** in the sense that we cannot produce any level of output at lower costs. If the company is producing at a level of cost which corresponds to their production function, the company is producing x_0 optimally. Had the company produced x_0 at a level of **actual average costs** (AAC) which is higher (point B in the above diagram), we would have said that the organization of production is not optimal.

Is producing on the average costs efficient? Well, recall that efficiency was defined in terms of other goods, namely, an *efficient allocation is an allocation where we cannot have more of one good without giving up another.* We know that all points on the PPF represent efficient allocations.

To know whether x_0 is produced efficiently, we should ask ourselves whether it is possible to carry on producing x_0 while releasing some inputs to go and work in the production of y. Being on the average cost means that our organization is optimal in the sense that we cannot produce x_0 at lower costs (Figure 3.11). We cannot release any input without reducing the quantity of x we produce. Thus, we cannot have more y when we produce x in this manner (point A in Figure 3.20). However, if we were producing at point B where AAC are greater than AC, it would mean that we could produce x_0 at lower costs. These resources which we would have released could have helped in producing more y. Thus, being on the average cost function means that the organization of production is efficient.

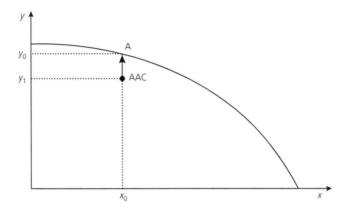

Figure 3.20 A fall in the wage rate.

So what about the minimum average cost? From the point of view of choosing the right initial capital, to produce at the minimum average cost means a full utilization of our capital. However, as we saw in the first chapter, the full employment of all means of production is not, in itself, a criterion of efficiency.

3.3 Producers' behaviour with respect to output

So far we have mainly looked at the question of how a producer will choose the combination of labour and capital which will bring about maximum profit regardless of how much of x he intends to produce. These are, therefore, more general conditions for optimal production. Naturally, there is also the question of how much to produce? To analyse this we simply have to rewrite the profit function and take a closer look at the role of x (the level of output) in determining the maximum profit.

The producer's problem will now be written as

$$\text{Max } \Pi(x) = R(x) - C(x)$$

By now we know all that we need to know about the cost function $C(x)$. However, we do not know much about the **revenue function**: $R(x)$.

The revenue each firm earns is simply the price multiplied by the quantity sold. Its general form is

$$R(x) = p_x(x)x$$

where $p_x(x)$ is the inverse demand function which the producer confronts. Namely, the demand schedules tell us what people are willing to pay for any quantity of x.

How can we change our revenue? Well, in principle we can change our revenue by selling more or less x. The question that will arise is whether selling more x would reduce the price so that we lose the difference on quantities we used to sell before. For instance, if we sell 20 units of x at a price of £2 each our revenue will be $R(20) = 2 \times 20 = 40$. If we now sell 5 more units of x (i.e. $dx = 5$ and we sell 25 altogether) but as a result of this the price of x has gone down by 20 p (i.e. $dp = 0.20$) to £1.80, we would gain £1.80 $\times$ 5 on the new sale (i.e. $dx\,p$) but we will lose 20 p on the 20 units which, until now, we used to sell at £2. Thus we would lose 0.20×20 (i.e. $dp\,x$). Hence, in general, a change in R means:

$$dR = dp\,x + dx\,p$$

where $dp\,x$ is the loss of revenue on previous sales (if the price of x came down) and $dx\,p$ is the gain on new sales. By now, this should sound very familiar. If not, read again the section on the price elasticity of demand in Chapter 2.

We now want to know how revenue changes when we choose to produce one more unit of x. We call this change in revenue the **marginal revenue** and we denote it by dR/dx. In the case of competition, where the firm's behaviour does not directly influence the price, the sale of one more unit will not affect the price, hence, it will increase the revenue by the price we get for that extra unit. In other words, the competitive firm's revenue will change according to the change in sales. Hence, as $dp.\,x = 0$,

$$dR = p_x dx$$

Divide both sides by dx to get the marginal revenue, MR $= dR/dx$; we get

$$MR = dR/dx = p_x$$

which simply means that if you sell one more unit your revenue will increase by the price. In the more general revenue function we can find the marginal revenue in a similar way. Divide $dR = dp \cdot x + dx \cdot p$ by dx and we get

$$MR(x) = dR/dx = (dp/dx)x + p_x(x)$$

where dp/dx is the derivative of the demand function, that is, it shows how the price will change if output is changed. As dp/dx is usually < 0 (inverse relation) it is clear that $MR(x) < p_x(x)$; namely, the MR(x) curve will normally lie below the demand schedule.

Now, if we multiply and divide $(dp/dx\,x)$ by p/p, we can write:

$$MR(x) = \frac{dR}{dx} = \frac{dp}{dx}\frac{x}{p}p + p_x(x)$$

$$= p_x(x)\left[1 + \frac{1}{\eta}\right] = p_x(x)\left[1 - \frac{1}{|\eta|}\right] = p_x(x)\left[1 + \frac{1}{(dx/dp)\cdot(p/x)}\right]$$

where η is the price elasticity of demand.

Now, in a perfectly competitive market we assume that the firm will not influence the price, hence the price elasticity of demand which the individual producer confronts goes to infinity, the reason why price elasticity will be infinite is that a small increase in price will lose the seller *all* his customers. We shall explore this point again in Chapter 4. Therefore,

$$\left. \begin{array}{l} \text{when} \quad |\eta| \to \infty \; \frac{1}{|\eta|} \to 0 \\ \quad \text{MR}(x) \to p_x(x) \end{array} \right\} :$$

Now that we have studied the revenue function we can add it to the cost function which we had studied before. Recall that $\Pi(x) = R(x) - C(x)$, see Figure 3.21.

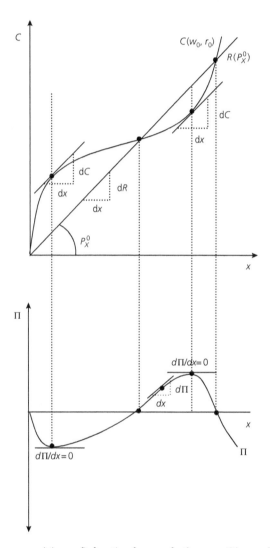

Figure 3.21 Cost, revenue, and the profit function for a perfectly competitive market.

The R function of a competitive industry has a constant slope, p_x, which is the MR = (dR/dx). The greatest distance between it and the cost function is always where the gradient of $C(x)$ (i.e. MC(x)) equals to the gradient of R (i.e. MR). However, there are two points where the distance is the furthest. In the one case we will be minimizing profit; in the other, we will be maximizing it. A necessary condition, therefore, for profit maximization is that $MR(x) = MC(x)$ but it is not a sufficient one.

Instead of exploring the mathematical second-order conditions let us take another look at the profit function. Clearly what distinguishes the profit maximization point from the other optimal solution (albeit to a different problem) is that profits are positive.

We can rewrite the profit function in the following way:

$$\Pi(x) = p_x x - C(x) = x\left(p_x - \frac{C(x)}{x}\right)$$

$$= x(p_x - AC(x)).$$

Clearly, for $\Pi > 0, p_x > AC(x)$.

We therefore have two principles which guide the behaviour of the firm:

(i) How much to produce?

The answer is to produce so much x such that

$$MC(x) = MR^c = p_x.$$

(ii) Whether to produce?

The answer is this is to produce as long as

$$p_x \geq AC(x).$$

Hence, the supply of the firm will be guided by the $MC(x)$ function which is above the average cost (Figure 3.22). It is also the segment of output where the marginal cost is rising. Indeed, the real second-order condition to ensure that profit is maximized is that the point where $MR(x) = MC(x)$ lies where MC is rising. But as we saw now, while this may be sufficient mathematically it is not terribly meaningful from an economic point of view, (as −£1 m is certainly greater than -£2 m but who would rejoice at a maximum profit which is negative?). As firms seek positive profits, the point where $MC(x) = MR(x) = p$ must also satisfy that $p \geq AC(x)$.

In the short run, this condition is somewhat modified (Figure 3.23). The costs in the short run are comprised of two elements: variable and fixed costs. $SRC(x) = FC + VC(x)$. The short run average costs are then simply derived by dividing the cost function by output. Hence:

$$SRAC(x) = \frac{SRC(x)}{x} = \frac{FC}{x} + \frac{VC(x)}{x} = AFC + AVC.$$

It is easy to see that the AFC will be declining as x increased but $VC(x)$ will be rising due to the diminishing marginal product. The difference between $AVC(x)$ and the $SRAC(x)$ is really the AFC. As output increases this expression becomes insignificant and the $AVC(x)$ asymptotically approaches $SRAC(x)$ (Figure 3.23).

Suppose now that the price is such that profit maximization dictates that one choose point A where

$$MR(x_0) = p_x = MC(x_0).$$

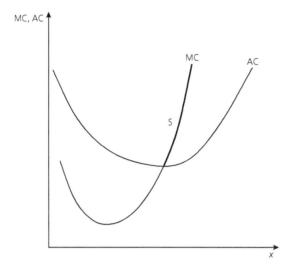

Figure 3.22 The firm's supply curve.

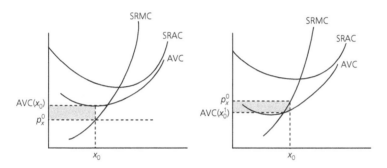

Figure 3.23

But here, $SRAC(x_0) > MC(x_0) = p_x$, which means that the profits are negative. Notice that the profit/loss is always the geometrical area between total revenue (captured by the rectangular created by $p_x^0 \cdot x_0$) and the total cost (the rectangular created $AC(x_0) \cdot x_0 = \frac{C(x_0)}{x_0} \cdot x_0 = C(x_0)$). According to the long run principle established above the firm should not produce at all. However, in the short run, the firm is bound by contracts and while it may not have paid the rent for the building in full, it would have to do so until the end of the year. Should the firm shut its operation?

The answer here depends on the position of point A relative to the AVC. The average variable costs tell us what are the operational costs involved in producing x_0 units over the year. If $AVC(x_0) > MC(x_0) = p_x$ it means that in addition to the fixed cost which you have to pay by the end of the year, you will have additional losses derived from producing x_0 units of x. These additional losses are captured by the shaded area in the left-hand diagram. If, on the other hand, $AVC(x_0) < MC(x_0) = p_x$ then the shaded area in the right-hand diagram depicts profits that you would make from producing over the year. These profits could be used to pay for the fixed costs but they will not be sufficient to offset your losses. Hence, in the short run, there is a further type of consideration but the principle remains the same. As long as the price is below average costs (or average variable costs in the short run) the firm should leave the market.

3.4 A simple numerical example

Consider the production circumstances of a good x which requires only one input (labour) for production. The technology available is the following one:

L	$TP = x$	$AP = x/L$	$MP = dx/dL$
0	0	0	0
1	9	9	9
2	24	12	15
3	42	14	18
4	60	15	18
5	75	15	15
6	87	14.5	12
7	96	13.7	9
8	101	12.6	5
9	101	11.2	0
10	95	9.5	−6

Figure 3.24 depicts how total product (TP), average and marginal product (AP and MP) change with the change in input (L). You will also see how they relate to each other.

Note that as long as the marginal product is greater than the average product, the latter is rising. This is so because the marginal product describes the contribution of the last unit of input. As long as this contribution is greater than the average product, the average will have to rise. In brief, what you see is that the AP is at its highest when it is the same as the marginal product. Given diminishing marginal product, every extra unit of output will require more and more inputs. Thus, the product per input will have to fall. The reason why it does not fall immediately when the marginal product begins to fall is that the increases in output at the beginning were so great that it takes a much sharper decline in productivity to change the direction of the average product.

Cost functions

Suppose now that the production of x requires a license which costs £1130. A labour unit costs £900 (for the duration of the production process). We therefore distinguish between fixed costs (FC) which are unaffected by the level of output produced and variable costs (VC) which reflect the level of production. The average cost (AC) is simply TC/TP or TC/x. Naturally, the average cost is the sum of the AFC(= FC/x) and AVC(= VC/x). The marginal cost is the change in cost per extra unit of output. Evidently, this change will depend on the productivity of labour. The more productive labour is, the less labour units will be required for the production of one unit of output. For instance, one unit of labour produces 9 units of x. Hence, one x requires 1/9 unit of labour. Note from the previous table that 9 is the marginal product of the first labour unit. Hence, the amount of labour

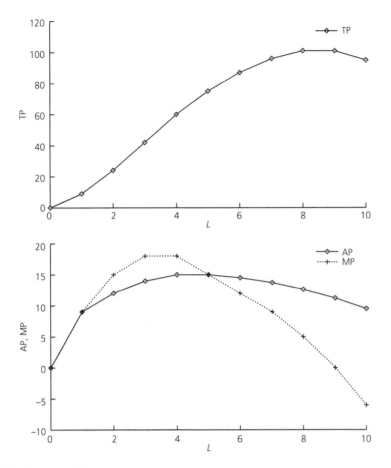

Figure 3.24 TP, AP, and MP: a numerical example.

required for the production of one unit is always $1/MP$. As we pay $W = 900$ per labour unit, the cost of one unit of output will be $[900 \times 1/9] = 100$. In general, therefore, we can write $MC = W \times (1/MP)$.

The various cost functions are described below:

L	TP (X)	FC	VC	TC	AFC	AVC	AC	MC
0	0	0	0	0	0	0	0	0
1	9	1130	900	2030	125.5	100	225.5	100
2	24	1130	1800	2930	47	75	122	60
3	42	1130	2700	3830	26.9	64.3	91.2	50
4	60	1130	3600	4730	18.8	60	78.8	50
5	75	1130	4500	5630	15	60	75	60
6	87	1130	5400	6530	12.9	62.1	75	75
7	96	1130	6300	7430	11.8	65.6	77.4	100
8	101	1130	7200	8330	11.2	71.3	82.5	180

The graph which depicts the relationship between the various cost functions is depicted in Figure 3.25.

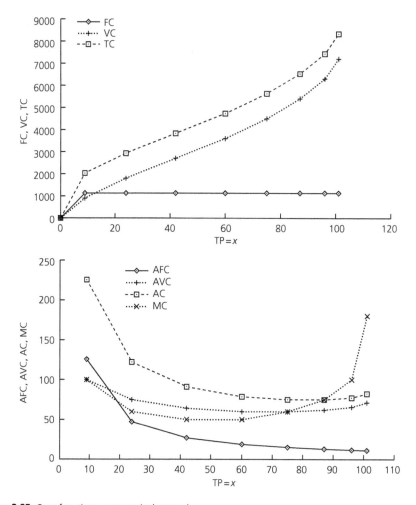

Figure 3.25 Cost functions: a numerical example.

The general generation of the U-shaped AC function is depicted above. Clearly, AC = AFC + AVC. One can see that as FC is unchanged when output is increased. Hence, FC/x will be declining the greater becomes x. Due to diminishing marginal product, every extra unit of output will require ever increasing cost. Hence, VC/x is rising with output. For very low levels of x, FC/x is a large number while VC/x is small. The shape of the AC will thus be dominated by AFC. For large x, FC/x is almost zero. The shape of AC is thus dominated by AVC.

Profit maximization

Suppose now that the firm can sell a unit of x for £100. We shall also assume that whatever the firm does, it will not affect the market price as the firm is too small. Hence, the revenue of the firm is $p_x x$ and the marginal revenue (the revenue of the last unit sold) will be the price *Px*. The following table describes the situation of the firm under various level of production.

TP	P	R	TVC	TC	П	MR	MC	MП	AVC	AC
0	100	0	0	1130	−1130	0	0	0	—	—
9	100	900	900	2030	−1130	100	100	0	100	225.5
24	100	2400	1800	2930	−530	100	60	40	75	122
42	100	4200	2700	3830	370	100	50	50	64.3	91.2
60	100	6000	3600	4730	1270	100	50	50	60	78.8
75	100	7500	4500	5630	1870	100	60	40	60	75
87	100	8700	5400	6530	2170	100	75	25	62.1	75
96	100	9600	6300	7430	2170	100	100	0	65.6	77.4
01	100	10 100	7200	8330	1770	100	180	−80	71.3	82.5

Notice that profit is maximized when the MR = MC and when the *p* > AC.

3.5 The firm as an organization: A note

We began this chapter with a thought about the purpose and significance of treating the firm as an agent in a world where theory begins and ends with the analysis of individual behaviour. For the principles of individual behaviour we had already devoted Chapter 2. Nevertheless, I gave a few reasons why the study of the firm as an abstract profit maximizing agent may serve some purpose. Notably, this allows us to understand the presumably opposing forces at work in a market place. I said presumably as it is not clear that in a theory where the atoms are individuals, the opposing forces are necessarily operating through the markets. As all agents are consumers, workers as well as owners, the market place does not clearly identify the opposing forces. If I own shares in a supermarket chain which regularly distributes profits, would I necessarily seek cheaper alternatives if the price of food in my chain rises? Instead, the opposing forces—individuals against all other individuals in their effort to secure themselves a share of the community's product—could be played out everywhere, including within the firm itself. Indeed, many firms are large scale organizations involving a great number of people with different skills, wants, and backgrounds. The conflicting interests of the various groups may be of some significance to the ability of the firm to achieve the objectives of its owners, or managers.

The implication of this is not necessarily that firms are not profit maximizers. As I said before, at the end of the day, when there is competition for ownership via the stock markets, every manager has to ensure that he has at least been seen to perform well, lest someone else steps in. However, the fact that firms are large organizations means that the ability of the manager to extract that profit maximizing output very much depends on the structure of the organization.

Recall that the entire analysis which we conducted in this chapter was based on the properties of the production function. Namely, we assumed—as was explained at the beginning of the chapter—that the productivity of all means of production is at its best. Thus, the only 'decision', as it were, the manager had to take is how much *x* to produce and how many units of labour and capital to hire. However, if we perceive the firm as an organization, we would realise that whether or not the productivity of labour is such that we can produce on the production function (and subsequently, on the cost and appropriate average and marginal costs) depends on whether the workers are putting all their effort into their work. This, however, depends on two things: **motivation** and **incentives**.

From the way we have formulated the behaviour of agents in Chapter 2, it is evident that modern economics does not seem to say much about motives apart from that we are all seeking the best way to get that which we most preferred. However, that which we most prefer seems to be open to a variety of options. The question which we face here is whether or not seeking the best means to an end regardless of what that end is, constitutes a unique type of motivation. Many tend to equate the rational utility maximizer with the motive of self-interest but they do so not because it means that we search for the best means to an end but because the end we seek is *our* most preferred situation. But this is not entirely accurate. It is because people tend to conflate utility with pleasure that the notion of maximizing our utility translates itself so easily to self-interested, nay, selfish, behaviour. But if we understood utility for what it really, is—a representation of preference ranking—this would not follow immediately. That which we prefer most, in principle, could be the well being of others. I do not think that it is possible to say that the motivation of the person who seeks his own material well being is the same as that of a person who seeks the material well being of others. Both may, in principle, try to achieve their aim using the best means available.

However, while it is true that, in principle, to seek the best means to an end does not confine the model to a particular motivation, it is not at all evident that all sorts of preferences could be represented by a real number utility function. The conditions for such representation were quite stringent and when we argued for the validity of such representation, the analysis was based on representing the preferences of a person who seeks his own material well being. This, by all means, must be read as the pursuit of self-interest. As such, we tend to attribute the same type of motivation to all economic agents even though the instrument we use to capture it may not necessarily be confined to such a motivation.

The reason why the 'self-interest' interpretation of motivation matters is because it means that people have no opinion about processes, institutions, and the like. All they care about is the end result and not the mechanism which produced it. Therefore, a worker in a firm does not care about the relative share of his wages from the total output to which he had contributed. He only thinks about it in terms of his utility which is defined in terms of what he consumes himself. Naturally, for such a worker, the organization of production does not matter at all.

So, if all are similarly motivated how can we influence their actions? The answer is, of course, through their constraints. Namely, if we cannot influence the objectives of an individual, we can interfere in their incentives. In a world where everything is substitutable we can always push people away from one thing towards another. Hence, if we want people to put more effort we can give them an incentive by rewarding effort well. Thus, whatever they pursue they will find the detour into greater effort worth their while.

There is nowadays considerable amount of evidence that may cast a doubt on whether all individuals are really uniformly motivated. Naturally, if they are not uniformly

THE FIRM AS AN ORGANIZATION: A NOTE

motivated their response to changes in their constraints (incentives) may be very different indeed. Some research in social psychology suggests that motivation could be affected by one's self-attribution. This means that the way in which we judge others through their actions could also be applied to our self-assessment. That is to say, if, for instance, we do not shoulder the burden with others, we may view ourselves as exploiters of others. Consequently, even in the absence of *external* causes (i.e. incentives) we may choose not to shirk. Deci and Ryan (1985),[10] for instance, provide evidence that external motivation (i.e. incentives) may be less effective than an internal one. Offering a large bonus for a job to be finished on time may not result in the employee being more motivated than if he had simply liked his job. Frey and Goette (1999)[11] found that even a simple change from internal to external motivation might have performance implications. Offering a reward for something which, until then, had not been rewarded may lead to a decline in performance. Frey and Jegen (1999)[12] provide a survey of empirical evidence which supports this motivation crowding theory.

However, one does not need to alter the assumption about human motivation in order for the organization of production to be of any significance for the output produced. Classical economists who were much less formal (though not necessarily less rigorous) than modern economists have always acknowledged the role of institutions. John Stuart Mill, for instance, offers a lengthy discussion of how ownership and control may influence the productivity of labour.[13] He claims that when workers own the land they toil their efforts would be much greater than if they only received a fixed share of the product (namely, that which they get depends on their action) and greater still than if they merely received a fixed wage.

This association of effort (and thus, production functions) with ownership of the various assets involved in the process of production is now the foundation of the modern (?!) 'property right' approach to the theory of the firm. The fact that the modern is not so new is something to ponder but I shall refrain from doing it here.

According to this approach, the distribution of property rights is the single most important factor to explain both the structure of firms and their competitiveness (i.e. their ability to work on the production function). The reason for this is that property rights are the source of power and that they allow the people who own the assets to cream off a great deal even in a world where clear contracts exist. For instance, if you are driving a cab which is owned by another and you are promised in the contract to receive, say, 80% of the intake, the owner of the car may come to you at the end of the period and say that he had unexpected expenses which are not covered by the contract and which he has to subtract from the earning before allocating you your 80%. Clearly, if you owned the cab yourself, you would have been able to recoup all of what you have earned. This, according to standard theory should, in principle, give you a greater incentive to work.

The fact that ownership structures govern the flow of returns and the fact that the returns are the incentives for people's behaviour means that we can no longer simply assume an agent called a firm. There are two separate issues emanating from this. First, there is the question of how can incentives be regulated for a given ownership structure. In other words, how shareholders who are not the managers, make the managers take the interest of the shareholders close to their heart. How, for instance, can you make the person who drives your cab put his greatest effort in running the business efficiently? Should you offer him a fixed sum (so that he faces no uncertainty)? Should you offer him a percentage of the intake? Or, perhaps, should you offer him part of the ownership of the car? Second, there is the broader social question of how did the current typical ownership structure emerge and whether it is something which is socially (and economically) desirable. Is the pursuit of the shareholders' interest socially desirable in terms of the competitiveness and distribution which it generates?

There is little doubt that the shareholders would want the manager to maximize profit. As most of them are not involved in the firm, they have no other consideration apart from profit maximization. The manager, on the other hand, is working in the corporation and must consider the interests of other groups with whom he is in daily contact. Being salaried would also mean that his earnings may be slightly less sensitive to changes in the performance of the corporation.

Consequently, the shareholders who have the power to appoint or sack the manager will face what is called the 'principal-agent' problem. The shareholders are the principal who want their agent (the manager) to maximize profit. The manager has a great advantage over the shareholders as they are less familiar with the issues associated with running the corporation and are therefore susceptible to all kind of excuses and stories which the manager can put forward to justify his action (and the subsequent reduced profit). The question for the shareholders, therefore, is how to write a contract that would give the manager the incentive to maximize profits. One of the most common of such incentives is the 'performance related pay' but whether or not this is working is a different story altogether.

The second and far more important issue is the ownership structure itself. Namely, who has the a priori right to the fruits of the collective action or, which is very much the same thing, who hires whom. On this question one can either take a historical perspective or a more analytical one. Put differently, one can ask how did the dominant form of ownership structure evolve and why? Or one can set out and alternative question about the optimal ownership structure. Naturally, the two questions could be combined but I would rather leave this out at this stage.

The historical development of the modern corporation is a complex issue which cannot be easily summarized. In many respects, these developments are closely linked to the development of actual private possession and the legitimacy of private property. The legal historian Henry Maine has argued that the development of private property is the story of disentangling collective ownership which was common, in his view, in primitive societies. In part, this disentanglement was a result of the faltering sense of kinship which served as the cement of society, as communities grew bigger. Nevertheless, when he compares the effect that this process had on different communities, it was not universal. Maine observes that while there was a crumbling sense of kinship among the Indian village community which was located in a relatively populated area, the Russian village community kept a sense of kinship which could be explained by the vastness of the country which allowed hordes of people to move from a village community to form a new community. The consequences of this difference to the evolution of the institution of private property were immense. In India the outcome was the emergence of private ownership of land while in Russia, the arable land had been periodically redistributed and, as he puts it, 'the village artificer, even should he carry his tool to a distance, works for the profit of his co-villager'.[14]

The significance of this type of investigation is that it sheds some light on the social function of private property in human development and human interaction. It allows us to better understand the attitudes which people may have towards the institutional structure which is based on it. These attitudes are bound to have some significance for the ability of the firm to extract the best effort from all its participants. Naturally, this is only relevant if we assume that attitudes towards institutions may affect the motivation of agents. As things stand, we are not particularly concerned about the legitimacy, or otherwise, of various institutional set-ups as all our agents are equally motivated by self-interested motivations.

The second approach is basically trying to explain the corporation from an analytical point of view. Recall that in Chapter 1, we discussed specialization and trade. We saw there that once people specialize there will be a gap between how much it cost them to produce and how much the others are willing to pay for it. Suppose that you specialize in potato production and you come to the market once a week with your sack of potatoes. Suppose also that you would like to find in the market, in return for your potatoes, a nourishing breakfast. There is a very large gap between what you are willing to pay for that breakfast and what it really cost to produce it. However, you would need to visit all other producers in the community and ask them about the properties of the goods which they produce. You will need to study nutrition to create the bundle of goods which will constitute your breakfast. Throughout that time in which you research into the question you are either not selling potatoes and if you have to go to the library in the village you will even be producing less potatoes. So matching your desires with what is brought to the market will cost you a great deal.

If instead someone assumed the role of the entrepreneur he would do the work for you. He will find out that which you want (while you carry on producing potatoes) and roam the village to discover whether the combination of goods can be produced. If not he may convince someone to produce these goods so that the next time you get to the market he will be able to offer you that which you wanted. Given the difference between what you were willing to pay and what it costs other to produce, the entrepreneur can make a profit. This is a case where the 'middle man' is most important, without him, it would cost you much more to exchange potatoes for breakfast. The entrepreneur could operate because he was cutting your **transaction cost**. As long as he can do it, there will be room for an organization like the firm which will do, as it were, the work for you.

Viewed as such, the organization has an additional problem. If what the entrepreneur does is to sign contracts with different agents who provide a good at a lower rate than it would cost the customers if they did it by themselves, the source of efficiency of the organization becomes the contracts. Here again we have a whole problem of designing contracts which will create the incentive for the people connected with the corporation to do their best. However, as contracts do not cover all eventualities it became apparent that when contracts are incomplete, in the sense that, in some instances, the contract does not specify who gets what, the question of ownership emerges.

To summarize, under the assumption of uniform motivation, we are not particularly concerned with the way in which particular institutions are perceived by those who participate in them. As we assume these preferences to be self-interested we exclude any institutional element from them. In such a case, the history and the legitimacy of property rights do not matter to the efficiency of the operation. The only thing which matters is the organization of these rights (i.e. who owns what) and/or the set of contracts which are designed to extract as much as effort from each participant for any given ownership structure.

If, however, we assume that people's attitude towards institutions matters, the history and legitimacy of property rights may matter a great deal. In such a case, different distribution of attitudes would suggest that different arrangements of property rights may facilitate efficiency. The ability of contracts to deliver, in such a case, is likely to be influenced by the acceptability of the ownership structure.

All of this is far more complex than the story we have told throughout this chapter. However, as we explained at the beginning, the purpose of this chapter is to explore the implications for production and costs of the general principle of profit maximization. We have done so assuming that none of the participating agents owns the assets and that all of them are nevertheless participating in full. This, as it were, is the benchmark against which we could then examine different forms of organization.

Self-assessment and applications

■ QUESTION 1

'Short run average cost always lies above long run average cost except at one point. However, while it is clear that with a fixed amount of one input the firm cannot expand along its long run expansion path, it can always use less of it and follow its long run expansion path. Therefore, short run average cost should be exactly the same as long run average cost up to a certain point.'

(a) Derive the long run average cost schedule;

(b) What is the difference between the short and the long runs?

(c) Derive the short run average cost schedule;

(d) Comment on the above statement.

Answer

This question had been structured in such a way as to allow you to show that you are familiar with the cost functions. However, this does not mean that the question of choice of framework disappears.

(a) Deriving long-run average cost. The key issues here are: associating the shape of the long run cost function with the relevant properties of the production function; recognizing that the average costs can be depicted by the ray from the origin; deriving the average cost from the change in the slope of that ray from the origin. All of these are in the domain of testing one's familiarity with various models.

Sections **(b)** and **(c)**—like (a)— required simple exposition of material which is covered in great details in the above. First, you should demonstrate that you recognize the role of fixed costs in the distinction between the long and the short runs. An explanation of the short run cost curve and its position relative to the long run curve is essential. And so is the derivation process where we compare the ray from the origin (the average cost) which is associated with the long run cost curve with that ray which is associated with the short run curve.

In section **(d)** the more analytical part of the question begins. The statement suggests that as we can always produce less with those means of production which we have, there is no reason why producing less than the level of output for which both short and long run cost coincide, should cost more than it would if we could vary all means of production.

The choice of framework here is crucial and, as you see below, it is the firm's optimal choices in the production factors plane (see Figure 3.26):

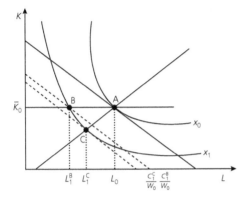

Figure 3.26

Translating the question into the language of the model. It is proposed in the statement that there is no reason why the firm should not produce at point C (with the long run optimal mix of inputs) as it can always reduce the amount of capital it uses. Obviously, while it is true that the firm can use less capital it will still have to pay for the idle means of production. If at B the short run total costs are:

$$c_1^B = r_0\overline{K}_0 + w_0 L_1^B$$

at C they will be:

$$c_1^C = r_0\overline{K}_0 + w_0 L_1^C$$

as $L_1^C > L_1^B$, the actual costs at C are higher than at B and the configuration around point C is not really feasible. It is not necessary to construct the argument in this formal way but as you can see it is clearer and shorter.

QUESTION 2

(a) Under which conditions will the long run average cost and marginal cost be the same?

(b) Will the short run average cost be the same as the long run average cost?

(c) Will the short run marginal cost be the same as the short run average cost?

Answer

This is a question about (i) a constant return to scale production function; (ii) about the relationship between the properties of production functions and those of the cost functions; and (iii) about the difference between the short and the long runs.

(a) The main points here were as follows: (i) an understanding of the properties of the CRS production function and its significance to the derivation of the corresponding long run cost function with its constant slope and 0-origin; (ii) the derivation of the long run average and marginal cost functions as depicted in Figure 3.27.

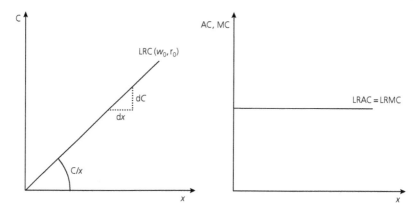

Figure 3.27

You are expected to demonstrate that you understand the geometrical representation of both the average and marginal cost in the left-hand side diagram.

(b) and **(c)** An understanding is required here that returns to scale is a long run property of production and that it does not affect the short run principle of diminishing returns to factor:
The answers to (b) and (c) are self-evident in Figure 3.28.

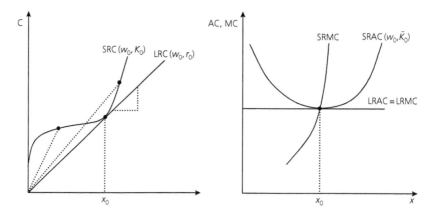

Figure 3.28

QUESTION 3

(a) Explain, using diagrams, why the short run cost function is tangent to the long run cost function at one point only.

(b) Assuming upward sloping expansion paths, what will happen to the level of output at which such tangency occurs, the higher is the level of fixed capital? Does it mean that the level of capital which generates the coincidence of the short run and the long run minimum average costs is an optimal level of fixed capital?

(c) Will the long and the short run average cost of a production process which exhibits only increasing returns to scale (at the relevant section of output) have similar U-shapes? Explain.

Answer

(a) The issue here is a recurring one: why should the short run cost lie everywhere above the long run cost except one point only? I am sure that you will produce here the following familiar picture (see Figure 3.29).

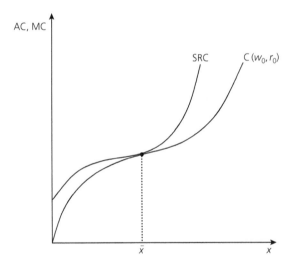

Figure 3.29

But this merely constitutes a restatement of what needs to be explained. A verbal explanation is needed here along the line that there is only one combination of inputs which is optimal in the long run for each level of output. The short run means that one of the means of production is fixed. Hence, there will be only one level of output the production of which will be conducted in the same manner in both the long and the short runs. At any other level of output, as the short run *adds* a constraint, the cost of production will have to be higher.

Figure 3.29 is fully acceptable if accompanied by a graphic explanation in the L, K space where you are expected to produce the long run and the short run expansion paths:

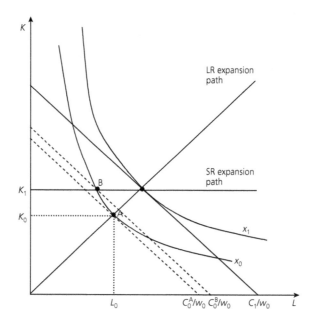

Figure 3.30

We normally assume the long run expansion path to be upward sloping. The short run expansion path is horizontal (see Figure 3.30). It is easy to see that there is only one level of output for which the choice of inputs will be on both the long run and the short run expansion path (point C above). In addition, we expect you to show why at any other point, the short run costs are higher than the long run costs. Comparing the long run cost of producing, say, x_0 (A) with that of the short run cost for producing the same level of output (B) will yield:

$$c_0^A = r_0 K_0 + w_0 L_0^A < c_0^B = r_0 \overline{K}_0 + w_0 L_0^B$$

hence, the short run cost lies everywhere above long run cost with the exception of point C which is common to both expansion paths.

(b) There are two elements to this section: (i) To show that the tangency between the long run and the short run occurs at higher levels of output the higher is the level of fixed capital. This should be fairly obvious (a move from A to B) (see Figure 3.31). (ii) The second element is a much more important component in this sub-question. It is the question whether the level of K which produces a tangency between the long run and the short run average costs curves at their minimum can be considered as an optimal level of fixed capital.

Here you are expected to demonstrate that you understand the relationship between section (a) and the average costs curve. Ideally, you are expected to produce the diagrams as seen in Figure 3.32 where you explain how the short run average cost relates to the long run average cost. In addition, we would like you to demonstrate that you understand that at the minimum of the long run average costs, the short run average costs is at the minimum too.

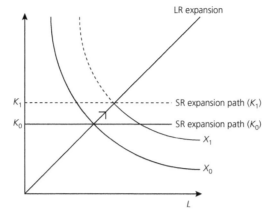

Figure 3.31

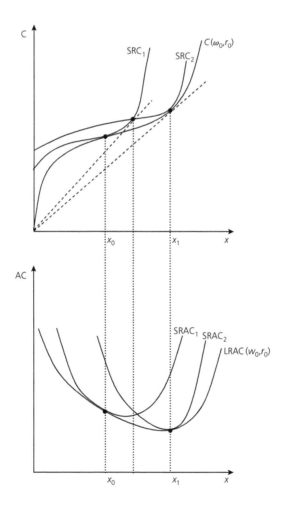

Figure 3.32

The main part of the answer is the explanation of the significance of producing at the minimum average cost. We expect you to say that only if the objective of the firm is to fully utilize its resources will the minimum average cost be an optimal solution. As such, it can be said that the level of capital which facilitates production at this level of cost in the short run can be considered as optimal. *However* as this is not really the objective function of the firm, the statement according to which the level of capital for which the short run average cost is tangent to the long run average cost at the minimum of both functions, can be considered as 'optimal' is misleading!

(c) This section is the more demanding in the question. In this section, we expect you to produce the cost functions for the long run as well as the short run in the case of increasing returns to scale. Figure 3.33 should emerge.

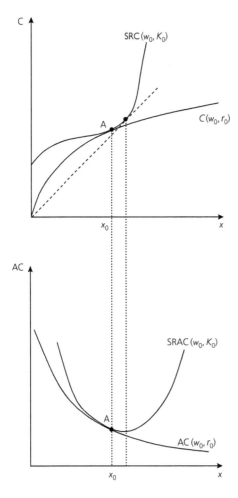

Figure 3.33

Clearly, while the long run average cost will be falling, the short run average cost should have its normal U-shape as increasing returns to scale is a long run property of the cost function.

■ QUESTION 4

Short run marginal costs will always intersect the long run marginal costs at the same level of output at which short run average costs equal the long run average costs. True or false? Explain.

Answer

This is quite straightforward if you understand how to derive all these functions. There is no point in trying to memorize it or to guess the answer, simply derive it yourself. You should have produced the following Figure 3.34.

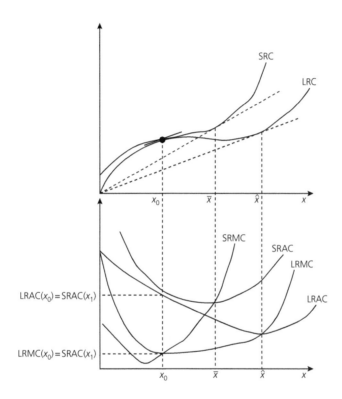

Figure 3.34

It is easy to see that, indeed, whenever the long run average costs are the same as the short run average costs it is so because the SRC is tangent to the LRC. This means that they have the same slope at that point which also means that the LRMC will be the same as the SRMC.

■ NOTES

1. There is mounting evidence to suggest that job satisfaction (as a proxy for utility) depends on relative earnings. Namely, the level of one's earning is not the key parameter in the reports on job

satisfaction as is the view people may have on the distribution of earnings. See, for instance, Clark, A.E and Oswald, A.J. (1996), Satisfaction and comparison income, *Journal of Public Economics*, vol. 61 pp. 359–381; Easterlin, R. (1995), Will raising the incomes of all increase the happiness of all? *Journal of Economic Behaviour and Organisation*, vol. 27 pp. 35–47.

2. Not forgetting of course, that it is possible for us to ruin land as a means of production through certain abuses of the environment.

3. We cannot see x, as this is a two-dimensional drawing.

4. The levels of inputs are increased by the same proportion; otherwise inputs' composition will change and we will be doing more than merely expanding our operation.

5. *Definition:* $f(x_1, \ldots, x_n)$ will be called homogenous of degree t if for all $x_1, \ldots, x_n$ in its domain and for all λ,

$$f(\lambda x_1, \ldots, \lambda x_n) = \lambda^t f(x_1, \ldots, x_n).$$

Examples

(i)

$$f(x, y) = xy$$
$$f(\lambda x, \lambda y) = (\lambda x)(\lambda y) = \lambda^2 xy = \lambda^2 f(x, y).$$

(ii)

$$f(x, y) = x^{1/2} y^{1/2}$$
$$f(\lambda x, \lambda y) = (\lambda x)^{1/2} (\lambda y)^{1/2} = \lambda^{1/2} x^{1/2} \lambda^{1/2} y^{1/2} = \lambda^{1/2+1/2} f(x, y) = \lambda^1 f(x, y).$$

6. You can think of organization problems (i.e. hierarchy) as well as issues of control as some of the reasons why any operation is bound to encounter deceasing returns at some stage.

7. We have not yet explored costs but, even without knowing the details, generally speaking costs are a function of how much we produce (and they rise with the output).

8. While it is clear that wages are the recompense for labour, it is less evident why r (the interest rate) is the return to capital. At this stage think of the following: remember that capital is a machine. Why would anyone use their money to buy a machine? Only if they can rent it out at an annual fee which is greater or equal to what they would have received for the money in the bank (i.e. the opportunity cost). Clearly, had the return on capital been less than the market return on money, people would not have bought machines and allowed others to rent them.

9. In general, we refer to all those expenses which are independent of how much we produce (in the short run) as fixed costs. They may include things like license fees and other regulatory costs. We also draw a distinction between **sunk cost** and other fixed costs. The former are conceived to be costs which have already been paid and cannot be recovered. So if you buy a plant at the place where you wish to produce, the difference between what you have paid for it and its re-sell value constitutes the sunk cost in this case. Sunk costs are a very important element in the analysis of industrial structure (as they represent an entry cost into an industry) but we shall not pay much attention to them at this level.

10. Deci, E.L. and Ryan, R.M. (1985), *Intrinsic Motivation and Self-determination in Human Behaviour*, Plenum, NY.

11. Frey, B.S. and Goette, L. (1999), Does Pay Motivate Volunteers? *for Empirical Research in Economics*, Working Paper No 27.

12. Frey, B.S. and Jegen, R. (1999), Motivation Crowding Theory: A Survey of Empirical Evidence *Institute for Empirical Research in Economics* Working Paper.

13. Mill, J.S. (1909 [1848]), *Principles of Political Economy*, Ed. W. Ashley, Augustus M. Kelley Publishers, (reprint, 1987). See in particular book 2 chapters 6–9 where he discusses three forms of land ownership: Peasant proprietor, Metayers, and Cottiers.

14. Maine, H. (1897), *The Early History of Institution*, John Murray, London, p. 81.

4 | **Market structures**

This is a point where we must take stock of what it is that we have learnt so far. First, we have established that the economic problem in modern economics is how to reconcile the tension between scarcity and unsatiated wants. The immediate consequence of modelling scarcity was the realization of the significance of efficiency (that allocation where we cannot have more of one thing without giving up another) and opportunity cost (price) to economic analysis.

We have also emphasized that, unlike other traditions in the analysis of social phenomena, modern economics takes an individualistic approach to the analysis of social organization. Hence, we began by concentrating on the behaviour of the 'atom' of economic analysis: the individual. We have assumed that individuals are rational in the sense that they will behave in a consistent manner and that they will be trying to obtain their most preferred outcome. In terms of economic goods, they would wish to choose the bundle of goods which they prefer most.

Notwithstanding the qualifications of section 3.5 above, we chose to treat the firms as another form of an 'atom'. This is clearly not right, as firms also are the culmination of human interaction. Still, at this level of your studies, we are trying to explore basic concepts rather than get a comprehensive picture of the many dimensions to which economic analysis can be applied. As the other fundamental feature of economics is that it pursued the notion of a naturally balanced social system, it adopted the notion of equilibrium from the natural sciences and sought to explore the working of opposing forces (equilibrium). Thus the need arose to set up a clear counterforce to the aims

THE BASIC PRINCIPLE OF EQUILIBRIUM IN ECONOMICS

of the individuals. The firm, as a profit maximizing agent, presented us with such an opportunity.

From the utility maximizing behaviour of individuals we derived the demand; from the profit maximizing behaviour of firms we derived the supply. The opposition of forces here is quite clear and well depicted by the traditional demand and supply analysis to which we referred at the beginning of Chapter 2. It is now time, therefore, to investigate what happens when these two opposing forces meet.

4.1 The basic principle of equilibrium in economics

The notion of equilibrium is a complex and intriguing concept. It was borrowed from physics (classical mechanics to be precise) but what exactly it means in economics remains somewhat obscure and contentious. To be sure, it means some kind of a resting point but what exactly are the forces at work is not so easy to ascertain.

Fascinating as this may be, we have no time (nor the background) to dwell on this problem beyond that which had already been said in the previous chapters. Instead we shall think of it in most simple terms as the point where *all rational plans coincide*. Namely, a situation where an individual examines the values of the exogenous variables[1] (which, in his case, are all the prices) and decides on the quantities of x and y he would like to purchase so as to maximize his utility. If, indeed, the agent can go to the market place and get exactly those quantities at these prices, their rational plans have materialized. Given that there are many agents in the market, equilibrium means that the rational plans of all of them can be materialized equally.

So far we have explored two types of agents: consumers and producers. The former choose quantities they want to buy and the latter choose quantities they want to sell. Equilibrium here will simply mean that the total quantity desired by consumers equals the total quantity producers want to sell. These decisions, as we saw in the previous chapters, are made according to given prices. Hence, that which may facilitate equilibrium is the appropriate system of prices.

In Figure 4.1 you will find again, the most famous picture which in the eyes of many epitomizes economics.

The demand function represents the quantities which individuals will want to consume at various market prices (or more precisely, their willingness to pay for—or the marginal utility of—each quantity of the good). Recall that such decisions are based on equating the price one is being asked to pay with the price one is willing to pay (indifference curves tangent to the budget constraint).

The supply function represents the quantities which producers are willing to sell at various market prices. Recall that such decisions are based on equating the price one gets (marginal revenue) with what it costs one to produce (marginal costs).

There is, as you can see, no dynamics behind this graph. Therefore, the only thing we can say is this:

(a) at p_x^1 the quantity demanded is greater than the quantity supplied; we call such a situation: **excess demand.**

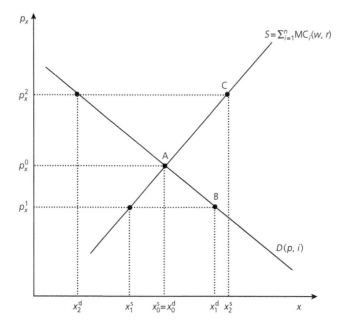

Figure 4.1 Demand, supply, and the concept of equilibrium.

(b) at p_x^2 the quantity demanded is less than the quantity supplied; we call such a situation: **excess supply**.

(c) at p_x^0 the quantity demanded equals the quantity supplied; we call such a situation: **equilibrium**.

For this to be a meaningful depiction of anything, we have to distinguish between points A, B, and C in the above diagram. Clearly, the difference between point A and points B and C is that at A there is *equilibrium*. This means that A is a resting point. All rational plans are fulfilled. The quantity of x which individuals wanted to buy at the price p_x^0 (given the prices of other goods is held fixed) is exactly the same quantity which producers wanted to sell at that price. Consumers wanted this quantity because the marginal utility of x at x_0, measured in units of, say, y, multiplied by the price of y equals the money value of x (p_x^0).[2] Put differently, because at these prices x_0 is the quantity of x which maximizes individual's utility.

Producers want to sell this quantity because at this price of x, x_0 is the quantity of x which maximizes their profit. No agent (individual or firm) will have an incentive to do anything other than go into the marketplace and buy or sell the amount which they intended to buy or sell.

At B and C, on the other hand, these rational plans do not coincide. Rational consumers will fail (at B) to obtain in the market that which they intended to purchase. At the price of p_x^1 the quantity which they want to buy—which will maximize their utility—is x_1^d. The quantity which will maximize producers' profits is x_1^s. As $x_1^d - x_1^s > 0$, some agents will not be able to find what they want in the market. As a result, some of them might choose to act and, say, offer to pay a higher price for the good. They thus prefer having somewhat less of the good to not having any of it at all.

At C, the opposite is true. At the price of p_x^2 producers want to sell x_2^s, because this is the quantity of x which will maximize their profit at the given price of x (and the given prices of the means of production). Consumers, on the other hand, will only want to buy x_2^d, which is the quantity of x that will maximize their utility (evidently, for their willingness to pay to be as high as the price of x, their marginal utility of x must be high also. This, given the diminishing nature of marginal utility, will only happen at lower levels of consumption). As $x_2^s - x_2^d > 0$, some sellers will not be able to sell the goods which they have brought to the market. This is when the signs of **sale** come up in shop windows.

The mere fact that individuals have incentives to act in order to alter one of the exogenous elements instead of just doing what they initially intended is what we call **disequilibrium**. But the question that immediately follows is whether what they do will bring about equilibrium or merely make things worse.

The model itself does not give us any information with regard to the kind of activity individuals will pursue when unable to fulfil their rational plans. We therefore 'wave our hands', as it were, and tell stories. One such story is the one I have mentioned above. Namely, when an individual comes to the market place and is unable to purchase the quantity he wants to buy at the given price, he might offer to pay a higher price knowing that the seller will sell to the highest bidder.

As a particular individual offers a higher price, the seller will wish to sell at that higher price. At the higher price, all individuals—the bidder included—will revise their rational plan and will want to buy a smaller quantity of the good as they are expected to pay more in terms of other goods.

Sellers too will revise their plans. At a higher price they are willing to produce more (and sell more) as long as the price is greater than or equal to the cost of the last unit (marginal cost).

Hence, the quantity demanded declines as well as the quantity supplied increases. This is working in the right direction bearing in mind that the initial quantity demanded exceeded the initial quantity supplied.

Similarly, had we started at point C where the quantity demanded is less than the quantity supplied the sellers would now be in a position where their rational plan cannot materialize. At the given price they will be left with a quantity of the good which they intended to sell but failed to do so.

One seller may wish to attract the buyers, and will, therefore, offer to sell the goods for a lower price (i.e. a sale). Naturally, other sellers will want to offer even better sales. As a result, the price will begin to come down. This will bring about a revision of rational plans. Consumers will want to buy more and sellers will want to sell less. Again, the dynamic of the story appears to be working in the right direction: reduction of the difference between the quantity demanded and the quantity supplied.

What we have assumed here about the dynamics of disequilibrium is that prices will change (over time) in direct relation with the excess demand.[3] At B excess demand was positive and therefore price increased. At C, on the other hand, excess demand is negative (i.e. excess supply) and the price changed in the same direction as the sign of the excess demand (i.e. it fell). We can write it in general as:

$$\frac{\partial p}{\partial t} = \dot{p} = F[x^d(p) - x^s(p)]$$

which means that the change in price over time is a function F of the difference between the quantity demanded and the quantity supplied at the prevailing price. Clearly, when $\dot{p} = F(0) = 0$ we have equilibrium.

All this, however, may not always work. Consider, for a moment, a demand for a Giffen good or a demand for normal good when the income is in kind. There are now two possible relations between such an upward sloping demand and the upward sloping nature of supply (see Figure 4.2).

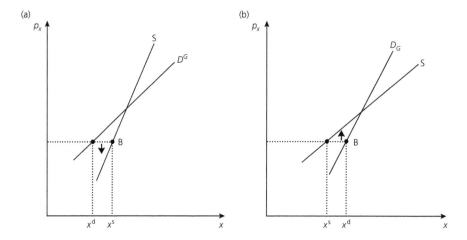

Figure 4.2 Demand and supply for a Giffen good.

We can clearly see in Figure 4.2(a) that when the price is below equilibrium level (point B) we have an excess supply of the good (negative excess demand). Hence, according to the rule which we had laid before, this means that the price of x would fall. However, if the price of x fell, it would get further away from the equilibrium price rather than converge to it. In the right-hand diagram we can see that a similar level of price would generate positive excess demand. Hence, according to the rules, the price of x would rise. It is therefore moving in the direction of the equilibrium price.

In general, what we are saying here is that, sometimes, it may be the case that there is an equilibrium in both Figure 4.2(a) and (b). However, the fact that there exists an equilibrium does not mean that it is a meaningful economic concept. Economists know that systems fluctuate a great deal. The concept of equilibrium, in a sense, is a reference point. But this reference point is of use only if we can derive from it the dynamics of the system. In Figure 4.2(a) we have no idea what will happen to prices, and the equilibrium point is, therefore, not greatly significant. Figure 4.2(b) suggests that there are forces which are pushing the price of x towards its equilibrium values. Therefore, knowing the equilibrium price will be of some value even if the system is not in equilibrium at the moment.

4.2 The determinants of market structures

Market is where the conflicting forces meet. The most basic question we need to ask is what might influence the outcome of an encounter between a consumer and a seller? We list the following as those things which are likely to affect the outcome:

- Number of agents
- Information and mobility
- Nature of product
- Entry and exit.

Number of agents. The number of agents refers to both buyers and sellers. Imagine yourself walking into an empty shopping mall. You are the only customer around and it has been days without any shopper before you arrived. Can you imagine what will happen? Will you walk into a shop finding indifferent sellers waiting for you to choose a good at the marked price?

Most probably your appearance in the mall will create a commotion, as all sellers are trying to convince you to buy their goods. Your ability to influence the price will be immense.

Alternatively, imagine a kiosk selling water in the middle of a desert when a convoy of silk traders who have not come across an oasis for 6 days arrives. What will happen now? Assuming that the 6 days travel had not affected the civility of the silk traders, would the water seller be able to buy a silk shirt for his daughter? Put differently, the power over price will now rest with the seller.

There are many other possible combinations but what should become clear is that the number of agents and the relative size of each 'force' in the market, is bound to affect the distribution of power over the determination of equilibrium price.

Information and mobility. Information is one of the most important sources of influence on the outcome of any interaction. If you walk into a shop and examine the new CD you wish to buy, whether or not you pay the cashier the amount printed on the CD depends on whether you know how much it costs elsewhere. If you knew that exactly the same CD can be bought in the next shop for 2p less, you would immediately walk into the other shop.

Notice that two things have influenced your action: first, knowing about the price of the good elsewhere (information) and, second, your ability to act on it (mobility). If, while you are visiting the shop and about to purchase a CD at a price of £11–75, someone calls you on the mobile phone to tell you that, next door, the CD can be bought at £11–73, whether or not this will influence the outcome of trade depends on whether there is someone preventing you from going to the other shop. Put differently, sometimes you may have the information but due to various reasons, you may not be able to act on it. Similarly, being able to act but not having the information will also produce a different outcome from the original situation where you have the information and you can act on it.

Nature of product. When you walk into a car dealer's show room you will probably meet an elegantly dressed person who would wish to convey to you—through the way he, or she, is dressed—that they are serious people who not only understand their business, but who are also truly ready to divulge any information to you. You examine a car and you are impressed. Not only is this a make about which you have recently read that it can withstand all sorts of accidents, it also has air-conditioner, CD player, CDROM, a small toilet, and a breakfast bar.

When you come round—after hearing the price—you will say that only yesterday you saw a similar car elsewhere at half the price. The dealer will smile and quietly tell you to go ahead and purchase the other car. The source of his confidence will be, simply, the knowledge that the other car is so different from what he is offering that, if you even consider the other car as an option, you could not be a serious customer in the first place. Put differently, when you wish to buy a Rolls-Royce you will not compare its price with that of, say, a mini. Hence, it is important that we recognize that, sometimes, there is more than one dimension to a product. In such a case, the fact that one may have the information (as well as the ability to act) with regard to only one dimension of the product, may not influence the trade as it would in the case of having information about all dimensions. A seller of a Rolls-Royce knows that you have not come to his shop to buy a means of transportation. The fact that you can purchase cheaper means of transportation will have no bearings on your dealing with the dealer. However, if you told him that you saw a cheaper Bentley, you will find the smile of his face being wiped out and it is then that he will order some tea for you.

Entry and exit. This determinant of market structure is closely linked to the number of agents. When there is free entry and exit we are likely to have many buyers as well as sellers. When, on the other hand, there are some barriers to entry the number of sellers may not be as large.

Behind this notion of entry and exit lies a very important component in the analysis of market's structures. This is the concept of **barriers to entry**. Barriers to entry could be exogenous, like license fees or very high set-up costs which may deter many from even contemplating to join the market. The other, more interesting types of barriers to entry are endogenous. These barriers can be created through various forms of strategic behaviour on the part of the incumbents. These can include price wars, R&D investment (to facilitate a reduction in cost) etc. Naturally, entry conditions are bound to influence both the long-term and the short-term kind of interaction between buyers and sellers.

4.3 The model of perfect competition

Perfect competition is a model which aims at exploring the most fundamental properties of competition. What we mean by competition here is the collective interaction of agents who are only seeking that which they prefer without any reference to what this may do to the others. Naturally, as resources are scarce, this means that they are implicitly competing against each other.

The model of perfect competition is an attempt to analyse two main issues. First, could a world where self-interested individuals are left to themselves to compete for limited resources work? Second, if it does, what is the nature of the outcome? Naturally, the answer to the first question is simply the answer to the question of whether or not there is equilibrium in a perfectly competitive market. The answer to the second question would be measured in terms of the efficiency of the outcome.

To be able to explore the essence of competition we must try and rid ourselves from all possible influences, as described in the previous section. It is not as if economists think that this is how the world really looks. Instead, it is an effort to understand what lies at the heart of the idea of competition. We begin, therefore, by specifying the determinants of an abstract notion of competition. We call it, **perfect competition**.

(a) Number of agents: a very large number of agents (both buyers and sellers) so that the particulars of no single agent can be the cause of the outcome.

(b) Information and mobility: perfect information and perfect mobility so that the outcome cannot be attributed to any of these.

(c) Nature of product: homogenous product so that we cannot explain the outcome by the difference in the goods themselves.

(d) Free entry and exit.

There are two conclusions which are immediate:

C1: All agents are **price takers**;

C2: There will be a **single price** in the market.

C1 is quite straightforward. As there is a large number of agents $(a + d)$, each agent will feel that (i) he can buy (or sell) whatever quantity he wishes. Whatever fits a single agent's rational plan cannot be significant when there are so many other participants. If you wish to buy 20 loaves of bread instead of 2 are you likely to be able to execute your wish without affecting the price? (ii) none of the agents can, on his own, change the market price.

C2 follows mainly from (b). The fact that everyone knows, at all times, the price of a good everywhere in the market, plus that everyone can actually go and get the good at the place where it is cheapest, suggests that there must be a single price.

To analyse the case of the perfectly competitive industry we must always look separately at each individual firm and at the cumulative outcome of all firms' actions: the market. For simplicity of exposition, let us assume that all firms are identical. In such a case, the analysis of a perfectly competitive industry should be based on Figure 4.3 where the figure on the left depicts a representative firm; the one on the right depicts the market.

The demand schedule in the right-hand diagram can either be seen as the sum of all individuals' demand schedules or, for simplicity's sake as the demand schedule which would have been derived from the utility maximization of a single, representative agent. The idea of price taking manifests itself in consumers' behaviour through the shape of the budget constraint. Recall that, in Chapter 2, we derived the demand schedule from the behaviour of rational agents. The budget line, which captures the notion of scarcity, was a straight line. This means that the slope of the budget line (p_x/p_y units of y per x) was the same regardless of how many units of x or y the individual chose to consume. When a consumer makes choices thinking that these choices will not affect the price, the consumer is a price taker. Otherwise, the slope of the budget line (i.e. the price of x in terms of y) should change according to how many units of x the individual

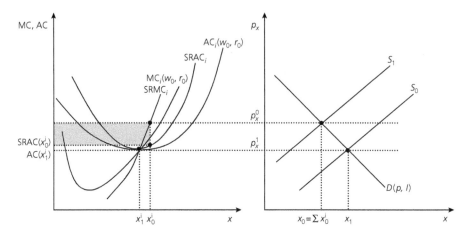

Figure 4.3 Suppliers in a perfectly competitive market.

intends to consume. Consequently, we may say that this downward sloping demand is representative of the behaviour of a rational agent who is a price taker.

On the side of the producers we made a similar assumption regarding the prices of inputs. Recall from Chapter 3 how we derived the cost functions by relating optimal choice of inputs with different levels of output. Whether in the short run or the long run, the expansion path of the firm was dominated by the iso-cost function where the price of labour in terms of capital remained unaffected by the actual choices made by the firm.

In the left-hand side we can see both the long run and the short run cost functions for given factor prices and, for the short run, for a given level of fixed capital. In this case we are examining a situation where the fixed level of capital is such that the minimum of the short run average cost and the long run average cost occur at the same level of output. This is not at all necessary but it will make the exposition simpler.

We begin with a short run situation. The supply curve in the market (right-hand diagram) is the sum of all the short run marginal costs which are above the minimum average variable cost. Although all agents are price takers, it is through the dynamics of the group that prices are formed in the market. In our case, there will be an initial equilibrium at p_x^0 and each firm will sell x_0^i units of x where its $\mathrm{SRMC}(x_0^i) = p_x^0$, which is what a profit maximizing policy requires. Altogether, the market will be supplied by $(nx_0^i) = x_0$, where n is the number of the firms in the market.

At this stage, as $\mathrm{SRMC}(x_0^i) = p_x^0 > \mathrm{SRAC}(x_0^i)$, each firm is making profits above the market rate of return to capital (r). This is the shaded area in the left-hand diagram. The reason why the return on capital is higher than the market rate of returns is simply due to the legal separation between the firm and its owners. The owners of the firm (those who have shares) are being paid for the capital which they offered. To pay them as much as all capital is being paid (the opportunity cost of putting £1 in the company instead of in the bank) is part of the costs to the firm. However, when, after deducting the cost ($wL + rK$) from the revenue, the firm has still a surplus, it can choose either to invest it (keep it) or distribute it among its shareholders (dividend). Namely, it can pay its shareholders. If it does, then the shareholders are getting more than the market rate of return on their capital. However, in the long run the opportunity to earn profits which are above the market rate of return will draw more capital into the industry and new firms will appear. As firms enter the market, there will now be greater supply at any given price. This means a shift in the supply schedule to the right.

The entry of new firms will create excess supply at the initial price. In such a case, the dynamics of the market will push the price down as some sellers fail to achieve what they intended. As long as firms enter the market—and they will do so as long as there are profits above the normal to be given to their owners—the supply will carry on shifting to the right and the price will carry on falling. The process will reach its conclusion at the point where firms are maximizing their profits but the profits which they get are not sufficient to pay their owners more than the market rate of return on their capital. This is the point where the price equals both the marginal and the average costs (and where long run and short run considerations will coincide):

$$\text{Min } AC(x_1^i) = MC(x_1^i) = p_x^1.$$

At this point, the total cost $[AC(x_1^i)x_1^i = c(x_1^i)]^4$ equals the total revenue $[p_x^1 x_1^i]$ and, therefore, profits above the normal are zero. This means that the firm, as a legal entity, does not retain any profits at all. Its owners, on the other hand, get the market rate of return on their capital. There is, therefore, no particular benefit from share ownership in this industry. This is where the flow of entry will stop.

At the new equilibrium $x_1 = x_1^i (n + k)$, where k is the number of firms which entered the industry. Note that it would make very little difference if we described the movement towards the minimum long run average cost along the short run or the long run marginal cost functions.

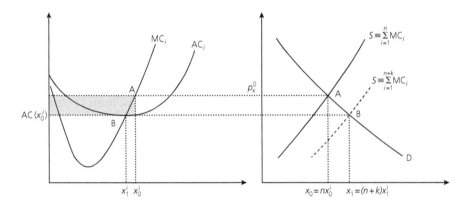

Figure 4.4

At A the firm makes profits above the normal (Figure 4.4). When firms enter, we end up at point B. In both cases (Figures 4.3 and 4.4), existing firms will produce less as new entrants bring about a further reduction in price. Here as there is no qualitative difference between an analysis using S-R cost functions and the one that doesn't, you will find that many times, for the brevity of the exposition, the analysis of the movement towards the long run equilibrium is conducted only on the set of the long run cost function. Whether this is entirely appropriate or not depends on what exactly it is which you are trying to analyse.

Consider the effects of an increase in demand for a good sold in a perfectly competitive market.

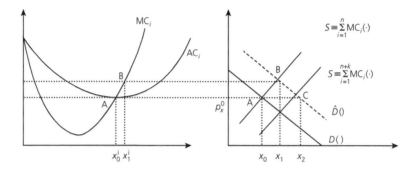

Figure 4.5

We begin at a long run equilibrium at point A. Note that we shall conduct all the analysis in terms of the long run cost functions, as in the end we would want to compare long run equilibria. The increase in demand (shift outwards of the demand in the right-hand diagram of Figure 4.5) will cause excess demand for the good at the given price. This, in turn, will cause an increase in the price as those whose rational plans failed would try to out bid the others. As price increases, firms will adjust their output to the profit maximizing condition (i.e. $MC(x) = p$). This will bring an increase in sales which will bridge the gap created at first by both reducing the quantity demanded (higher price) and increasing the quantity supplied. We thus move to point B. At B, firms are making profits above the normal (the shaded area) and pay their shareholders more than the market rate of return on their capital. This attracts further capital and new firms. The new firms will want to sell the profit maximizing level of output (x_1^i) and thus push supply further out creating excess supply. This, in turn, will push prices down, cause firms to change their output plans, and reduce profits. The process will carry on until we get to point C where each firm produces at the same level of output as at the beginning but there are more firms in the market.

In general, one must be careful here as there is an element of the story which is hidden. Both when existing firms wish to produce more and when new firms enter the industry, the demand for the specific means of production increases. If the industry is just a small element of the total (global?) demand for a particular input, then the expansion of the industry will have no impact on factor prices and we will indeed end up at C. If, however, the expansion of the industry generates an increase in factor prices, it would push the AC and MC functions up. This means that the final equilibrium will be at a higher price than at the beginning, and the new equilibrium will be somewhere between B and C.

If there are increasing returns to scale in the factors market, the expansion of the industry will bring down factor prices. This will reduce the levels of AC and MC and yield an equilibrium at a point to the right and below point C.

4.3.1 **The significance of the perfectly competitive model**

The existence of a meaningful equilibrium seems to suggest that the unrelated pursuits of self-interest can work, in the sense that all rational plans coincide. However, we must bear in mind that this is only a partial equilibrium because we examine the actions of agent in one market only while we know that they simultaneously act in others. In terms of our description of individual behaviour we saw that choosing a quantity for x happens at the same time that we choose the quantity for y and whatever else we wish to buy or sell. We shall come back to this general equilibrium question in Chapter 6. Here, we are trying to derive some basic lessons from the partial equilibrium set-up.

The main feature of competitive equilibrium (both in the short and in the long run) is the principle of **marginal cost pricing**. What does it imply? As we are still in the business of resolving the economic problem, the criterion for economic performance is that of efficiency. We saw, however, that there are two different concepts of efficiency. Productive efficiency, which is derived by applying the definition of efficiency to tangible goods and services, and, allocative efficiency, which is derived by applying the definition to non-tangible goods such as utility. We saw that the production possibility frontier provides us with a collection of productive efficient allocations and that the selection of the allocatively efficient allocation must be made out of the set of productive efficient allocations. In other words, the allocatively efficient allocation is on the PPF. We shall begin by asking the question whether, in perfect competition, the outcome is efficient in the productive sense of the word.

Productive efficiency

As this is a partial equilibrium model we only see the effects of competition on one good only. However, we have noticed in Chapter 3 that to be able to produce on the relevant cost functions means that we are producing efficiently. Namely, as in competition price always equals marginal costs, it means that we pay for the last unit no more than it really costs to produce. The corresponding average cost tells us that this is the lowest level of costs with which we can produce that quantity which we sell in the market place. Hence, as these costs functions are derived from the optimal conditions of profit maximization (or cost minimization), it means that we cannot release resources for the production of any other good without reducing the quantity of x we produce. Thus, by definition, we are on the PPF. The outcome of competitive interaction is definitely **productively efficient**.

Allocative efficiency

The next question is whether or not the outcome is also allocatively efficient. As the choices which are made by individuals reflect their preferences (utility), to have an **efficient allocation** means not being able to change the allocation in such a way that someone will be better off without making someone else worse off. We have thus applied the concept of efficiency to look across members of society in terms of their desires.

In the context of a single industry (partial equilibrium analysis) the utility, the two 'types' of agents we have are consumers and producers. We propose to capture their respective benefits, or well-being, by the terms of **consumers'** and **producers' surpluses**.

Let us begin with consumers. In the diagram below we have equilibrium at point A where: $p_x^0(x_0) = \mathrm{MC}(x_0)$. For the sake of exposition we assume that the demand schedule we see represents the optimal choices of a representative agent. This means that when the individual wants to buy x_0 units of x, the marginal utility of the last unit of x (measured in units of y and for a given price of y, in money[5]) is equal to the price $p_x^0(x_0)$. So a vertical line from the x-axis to point A measures the money equivalent of the utility of the last unit of x. Equally, the vertical line to $p_x^1(x_1)$ on the demand schedule is the money equivalent of the marginal utility (the utility of the last unit) at x_1. This means that each vertical line from the x-axis to the demand schedule depicts the marginal utility at that point measured in money terms. Hence, if we add up the marginal utilities—the marginal utility of the first unit + the marginal utility of the second etc.—we get the total utility. However, as I explained in Chapter 2, the problem is that as the price of x falls we change the quantity of y we consume. Therefore, the marginal utility of x is not well-defined (as it requires all other components of utility to be constant). However, I argued that in spite of this analytical difficulty we can still treat the area underneath the demand schedule as a **proxy** to the total utility.

Thus, if equilibrium is at point A the entire area underneath the demand schedule captures a proxy to the total amount of utility generated in the market. As there is a single price $(p_x^0(x_0))$, it means that consumers are paying a lower price than they are willing to pay for all x below x_0. For instance, they were willing to pay $p_x^1(x_1)$ for x_1 but they only pay $p_x^0(x_0)$. This means that they pay for the last unit of the quantity x_1 less than the value of its marginal utility. This difference is pure gain for the consumer. In other words, the difference between what consumers are willing to pay and what they actually pay (due to the fact that there is a single price in the market) constitutes the consumer surplus. In terms of the complete picture, the whole area under the demand is the total utility generated from consuming x_0 units of x. But consumers pay $p_x^0(x_0) \cdot x_0$ which is the rectangular region ACOE in the diagram below. Namely, of all the utility they derive from the equilibrium consumption of x they are only left with the triangle ABC.

In this set-up we created an artificial agent called the Producer. Producers also, in principle, are members of society and their benefits matter too. We represent their benefits in terms of what we call the **producers' surplus**. The simplest way of thinking about producers' surplus is simply to apply to producers the same idea we applied to consumers. Namely, to consider as their benefit, the difference between what they actually get and what they were willing to sell their goods for. Thus, as we know that marginal costs represent the cost of each additional unit, we can say that while the marginal costs of all units before x_0 is less than the price $p_x^0(x_0)$, the producers benefited from selling these units at a higher price than it costs to produce them (Figure 4.6). Thus the areas between the marginal cost curve and the AC line represent producers' surplus. It is important to note that producers' surplus is not synonymous with profits and I do not wish to spend too much time on this as it is, as I said before, an artificial construction. We use the notion of producers' surplus to show you something in partial equilibrium which should, in fact, be shown only in general equilibrium. So while the concept of consumers' surplus is a meaningful construction, this is not entirely the case with producers' surplus. This is particularly so as the whole notion of producers is not an obvious construction.

Thus, if producers' surplus represents the benefits of producers and consumers' surplus represents the benefits to consumers, we can clearly see that an efficient allocation would be one where these two benefits are efficiently distributed. Namely, consumer and producer surpluses are efficiently distributed if we cannot increase the one without

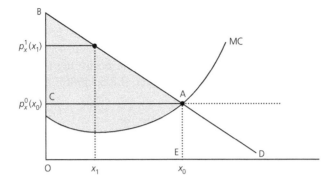

Figure 4.6 Consumer and producer surpluses.

reducing the other. It is clear that at point A, where $p_x^0(x_0) = \mathrm{MC}(x_0)$, this is indeed the case. If we moved up along the MC curve we could increase producers' surplus but at the expense of consumers' surplus. Equally, if we moved down along the demand schedule, we could increase consumers' surplus but at the expense of producers' surplus. Thus point A represents an allocation which is both productive and allocative efficient. Naturally, the great message that seems to come out of it is that if you let people who are self-interested compete against each other without any impediment and without any of them having an advantage over the other an allocation will emerge which is both allocative and productive efficient.

4.4 The monopolist

Although in the mind of many the monopolist is the exact opposite of perfect competition we must be cautious with such an assertion. Recall that we have counted **four determinants** of market structures. To say that one structure is the exact opposite of the other, we must be able to show that in all four categories this is indeed the case. If we examine what exactly is entailed in the monopolist market structure we will find that it is only in one dimension that the monopolist is the opposite of perfect competition. This is the number of agents dimension. For the monopolist we change assumptions (a) and (d) to allow for a market where there is a *single seller* and a large number of buyers. The change in (d) (entry and exit) is required to facilitate this state of affairs. We therefore assume that there are *exogenous* barriers to entry. Note, however, that all other assumptions about the nature of the product and about information and mobility remain unchanged.

The analysis of the monopolist, in principle, is similar to the analysis of the single firm in competition. The monopolist too maximizes profits, and profits are still the difference between revenues and cost:

$$\Pi = R(x) - C(x).$$

As long as we do not specify any special conditions about the position of the monopolist in the inputs' markets, the cost function which the monopolist confronts is exactly the same as the one which the competitive firm confronts (Figure 4.7). That is, a function which reflects the increasing returns to scale at the beginning of production which then turns into diminishing returns to scale when the operation becomes increasingly complex:

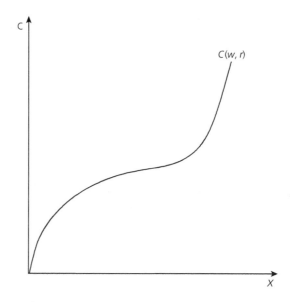

Figure 4.7 Cost function for a monopolist.

Naturally, the difference between the monopolist and the competitive firm is in the revenue function. Let us write the revenue function in its most general form:

$$R^m(x) = p_x(x)x.$$

Note that $p_x(x)$ is simply the inverse demand function; it tells us how much people are willing to pay for each quantity of x.

How will revenue change, say, from point A to B in Figure 4.8?

At A the revenue is $p_x^0 x_0$, at B it is $p_x^1 x_1$. Clearly, as price came down the seller lost the area α, which is the difference between the higher and the lower price (dp) multiplied by previous sales. α, therefore, is really $dp\, x$. On the other hand, the lower price attracted more sales so the above loss might be offset by new sales which are captured by the area β. β, therefore, is really the new price (p) multiplied by the additional quantity which is now sold (dx): $\beta = dx\, p$.

We can now say that the change in revenue will be the following:

$$dR = \alpha + \beta$$

$$dR = dp\, x + dx\, p$$

where dp will have the opposite sign of dx (the inverse nature of demand).

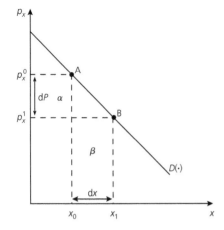

Figure 4.8 Demand function and marginal revenue.

Marginal revenue (MR) is defined as dR/dx. Divide the above equation by dx:

$$dR = dpx + dxp/: dx$$

$$\frac{dR}{dx} \equiv MR(x) = \frac{dp}{dx}x + p(x).$$

As $p(x)$ represents that willingness to pay for any quantity of x (i.e. the demand schedule), as long as the demand is downward sloping ($dp/dx < 0$), the marginal revenue will lie below the demand schedule. Namely, what we get for an extra unit sold is the price which people are willing to pay for it (denoted by the demand schedule) minus that which we lose on those quantities we used to sell at a higher price. When demand is linear dp/dx is constant, so as x increases the distance between the MR and demand increases too (Figure 4.9).

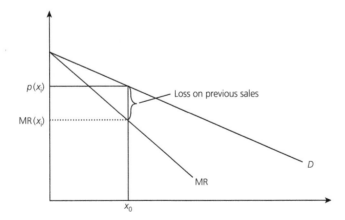

Figure 4.9

If we investigate the marginal revenue further we shall find that

$$dR = dp\,x + dx\,p/dx$$

$$\frac{dR}{dx} \equiv \text{MR}(x) = \frac{dp}{dx}x + p$$

$$= p\left[1 + \frac{dp}{dx}\frac{x}{p}\right]$$

$$= p\left[1 + \frac{1}{dx/dp(p/x)}\right]$$

$$= p\left[1 + \frac{1}{\eta}\right] = p\left[1 - \frac{1}{|\eta|}\right]^{*}.$$

Geometrically, elasticity is simply the product of the inverse of the slope of the demand schedule and the slope of the ray from the origin (Figure 4.10).

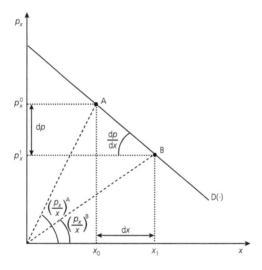

Figure 4.10 Linear demand and demand elasticity.

Consider for a moment the linear demand function. The slope of the function at A and at B is exactly the same. Yet, demand elasticity will be different because of the ray from the origin. While $(dp/dx)^A = (dp/dx)^B$ (hence $(dx/dp)^A = (dx/dp)^B$), $(p/x)^A > (p/x)^B$. Therefore:

$$\left|\left(\frac{dx}{dp}\right)^A \left(\frac{p}{x}\right)^A\right| > \left|\left(\frac{dx}{dp}\right)^B \left(\frac{p}{x}\right)^B\right|$$

hence, $|\eta|^A > |\eta|^B$

This suggests that demand elasticity, in absolute values, is diminishing as output increases. Consequently, given its position in the MR function, the MR will be diminishing too. In the end, MR is basically the slope of the revenue function. We can now add this

---

* I use p and $p(x)$ interchangeably.

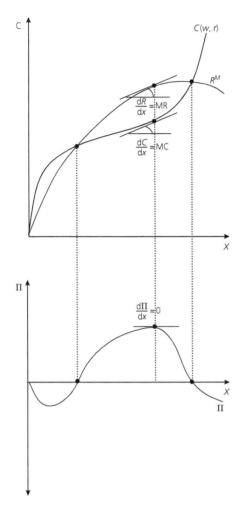

Figure 4.11 Profit maximization for the monopolist.

function to the cost function to find the point where the monopolist will be maximizing profits (see Figure 4.11).

Again, as in the case of the competitive firm the point where profit is maximized is where the slopes of the two functions are the same. Therefore, the monopolist too confronts the same two questions as the competitive firm: (i) How much to produce?

Produce so much x such that

$$MR(x) = MC(x).$$

Specifically,

$$MR(x) = p\left[1 - \frac{1}{|\eta|}\right] = MC(x).$$

(ii) Whether to produce? The monopolist wants positive profits. Therefore, a similar condition will apply here; namely, produce as long as:

$$p > AC(x).$$

The final market configuration of the monopolist will, therefore, be the following one as shown in Figure 4.12.

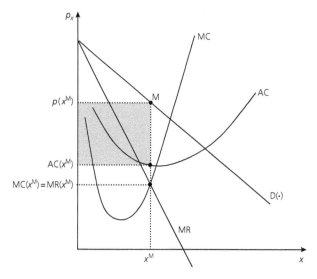

Figure 4.12 Equilibrium for the monopolist.

The shaded area represents the profit above the normal as total revenues are given by $p(x^M)x^M$ and total costs by $AC(x^M)x^M$. The difference between the two (the shaded area) therefore represents the profits above the normal.

The inefficiency of the monopolist

To evaluate the efficiency of the monopolist we must again distinguish between productive and allocative efficiency.

Productive efficiency

Note that throughout the above analysis we assumed that the monopolist operates on the appropriate cost functions. Namely, when the monopolist chooses how much to produce by equating marginal revenue to marginal costs, these marginal costs represent the minimal costs with which the last unit could be produced. Had these not been the genuine marginal costs as derived from the production function and the proper optimization problem this would not be the point where profits are maximized.

In competition, we know why firms will produce at the real cost functions. This is so because they will incur losses if they do not. In the long run when firms are producing at the minimum average cost, no firm can afford to produce at higher costs. So, would a monopolist do so if he does not face similar competition? The answer is that the monopolist faces competition in the ownership market. Namely, if a manager is running a monopolist at a profit level which is short of the potential, the value of the monopolist's shares would be lower than they could be. There is bound to be someone in the market to know enough about the specifics of producing the commodity the monopolist is producing, to see the gains for himself. Namely, he will buy the cheap shares, introduce the proper production process, and increase profits. The value of the shares will increase and, of course, he would sack the manager. Therefore, we do not suppose that there is an inherent reason for the monopolist not to be productive efficient.

Allocative efficiency

In the left-hand diagram of (Figure 4.13) we have the perfect competition equilibrium. In the right-hand diagram we have the monopoly market structure. Recall that the demand schedule represents individuals' willingness to pay (or the marginal utility from the consumption of different quantities of the good x) and that the area underneath the demand schedule provides a proxy for the pecuniary value of the overall utility of our representative agent. Hence, the triangle ABC in both diagrams depicts what we called the **consumer surplus**, in the sense that this is part of what he, or she, was willing to pay and ended up not paying. Put differently, this is the portion of their utility from consuming x which they have not passed on to the producers.

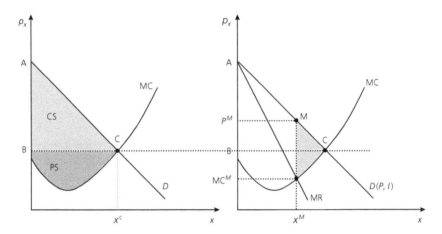

Figure 4.13 Consumer surplus, producer surplus, and the inefficiency of the monopolist.

Similarly, the marginal cost schedule represents, as it were, the seller's willingness to sell. We called the difference between the price he gets for each unit and the price for which he, was willing to sell it the **producer surplus**. We interpret both surpluses to be the benefits generated by the market. If we now compare the two equilibria we can clearly see in what way the monopolist is inefficient.

We saw earlier that the competitive allocation is both productive and allocative efficient because the solution was on the production possibilities frontier and benefits have been efficiently allocated in the sense that we cannot increase consumer surplus without reducing producer surplus and we cannot increase producer surplus without reducing consumer surplus.

In the case of the monopolist, it can be clearly shown that by moving from point M (which is the monopolist allocation) to point C both consumer and producer surpluses can be increased. Hence, the monopolist solution is inefficient in the sense that we can have more of one thing (benefits of either consumers or producers) without giving up another.

4.5 A note on price discrimination

Given that the monopolist is a sole seller, there are situations where the monopolist can take advantage of the difference in willingness to pay of different groups of its customers. Consider, for instance, the following simple case. A monopolist operates in a market where, for some reason, import is not allowed but the monopolist can, nevertheless, export. This is clearly not a realistic state of affairs but it will help us explain the nature of price discrimination. Figure 4.14 will emerge:

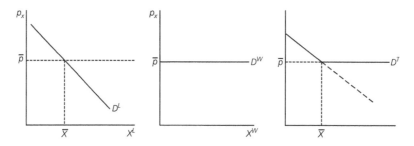

Figure 4.14

The first group of consumers (local consumers) have the demand in the left-hand diagram. The price elasticity of their demand is greater than unity. The middle diagram depicts the international demand for the good, which, assuming that the monopolist is only one of many sellers in the international arena, is perfectly horizontal. Namely, in the international scene, the monopolist is part of a competitive market and the price elasticity it faces approaches infinity. The right-hand diagram shows how the two add up. For any price above $\bar{p}$, the monopolist can only sell to the local population. At $\bar{p}$ the monopolist can sell both locally up to $\bar{x}$ and to the rest of the world beyond this point. The lower part of the local demand is basically irrelevant as the monopolist would always prefer to sell abroad at a higher price than locally at a lower price. We now add the relevant marginal revenue curves to the picture.

It is clear that up to $\bar{x}$ sales are only local. Therefore, the relevant demand for the monopolist is the local one. Therefore, up to this point, marginal revenue is derived from the properties of the local demand schedule. As price elasticity is greater than unity, the marginal revenue is positive, yet falling. Beyond point $\bar{x}$, the monopolist is only selling abroad. This means that the relevant marginal revenue must be derived from the perfectly horizontal international demand. However, when price elasticity approaches infinity, the marginal revenue becomes the same as the demand. In other words, if the monopolist sells an extra unit abroad, it will get the international price for it but as the price itself stays the same, there will be no loss on the sale of the previous quantity.

We now add the monopolist cost functions (Figure 4.15).

Suppose, first, that the monopolist cannot discriminate between local and foreign customers. In such a case, will the monopolist sell only locally or would it sell abroad as well? Let us begin with the left-hand diagram at point A where the monopolist is only selling locally. Is it worth the monopolist's while to sell extra units? Well, the first few

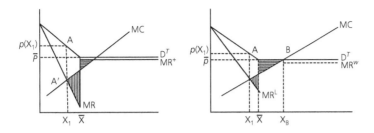

Figure 4.15

units up to point $\bar{x}$ mean that the monopolist will see the price fall to $\bar{p}$. Thus, he will make a loss on these extra units. The easy way to see this is to look at the relationship between the marginal revenue and the marginal costs. Start at A' (where MR = MC). This means that the additional revenue on the last unit was exactly the same as the additional cost for it. If we now move further to the right, this means that for the next unit MR<MC. Namely, the addition to the revenue from producing the extra unit will be lower than the addition to the costs. Hence, these are losses which would need to be subtracted from the profits originally made at point A. This will be true all the way up to point $\bar{x}$. However, from this point onwards, the monopolist can sell additional units at a constant marginal revenue (abroad). Therefore, from $\bar{x}$ to point B, MR > MC. The revenue increases by more than the cost. This is pure addition to the profits at A. Therefore, whether or not the monopolist will sell abroad depends on whether the triangle created to the left of $\bar{x}$ is greater or smaller than the triangle created to the right of it. If the triangle to the left is greater than the triangle to the right (the left-hand diagram), the monopolist will not sell abroad as the additional losses on local sales will exceed the additional gains from selling abroad. If he cannot discriminate, the monopolist will only sell locally. On the right-hand diagram we can see the case where the loss on local sales is smaller than the gain on foreign sales. Here the monopolist will move to point B and will export the difference between the quantity at B and $\bar{x}$.

Suppose now that the monopolist can discriminate:

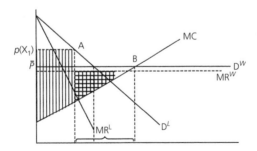

Figure 4.16

It is easy to see that, in such a case, the monopolist will equate its marginal cost to the marginal revenue of each group separately. The monopolist will then sell at point A locally and will sell abroad the whole quantity between A and B at the international price

$\bar{p}$ (Figure 4.16). This means that up to point A the marginal revenue was greater than the marginal cost for all units sold locally. Quantities beyond that are all sold abroad and this means that the marginal revenue on all the additional sales is greater than the marginal costs. It is easy to see that in such a case, the total profits of the monopolist would be greater as the only difference between this situation and the one in which the monopolist sold abroad without discrimination is the destination of the sales between A and $\bar{x}$. Without discrimination, it would have been sold locally at a loss (the left-hand triangle in the diagram before). Now it is sold abroad at a gain. Total profits, therefore, will be greater when the monopolist can discriminate.

4.6 Monopolistic competition

We have so far examined two main forms of market structures: perfect competition and monopoly. They differed in only one of the basic fundamentals which influence market structures: the number of agents. In perfect competition we had many buyers and sellers (facilitated by the free entry assumption), while in monopoly there are as many buyers as there are in competition but only one seller. To facilitate such a configuration in the long run, we also assumed that there are barriers to entry. This meant that although the monopolist enjoys profits above the normal, other firms cannot enter the industry.

We now move to a point in between these two extremes with regard to the number of agents. We would like to investigate the case of a situation where there are many buyers but the number of sellers is greater than in the case of monopoly but considerably smaller than in case of a perfect competition. Put differently, we would like to investigate the situation where a monopoly, in the short run, does not become a perfectly competitive market structure once the barriers to entry have been removed (in the long run).

To understand this point, let us begin by analysing the case where the removal of barriers to entry does produce a perfectly competitive outcome. Consider the following situation. In the previous section we discussed the market configuration of a monopolist without inquiring into the origin of its powers. One way in which a firm can gain such a monopolistic power is through innovations which could constitute barriers to entry. By 'innovation' we normally mean a technological development that leads to a reduction in the cost of production (notably, the marginal cost). This means that the firm with the innovation can sell the good at a lower price than the minimum average cost of the existing technology. Consequently, other firms, if they cannot access the new technology, will be making losses and will have to leave the market. Indeed, whether, or not, such innovations erect barriers to entry and drive out existing firms depends on how available is the new technology to other firms. In the world of perfect competition we also assume perfect information, which implies that information is widely available. Hence, technological developments cannot remain the exclusive right of those who generated them, which, in turn, raises a serious problem of incentives.

Why would a perfectly competitive firm invest in R&D and innovate if it cannot make sufficient gains from it? Had we had an explicit dynamic depiction of the model, one could have argued, even if everyone has access to the new technology the gains made by the inventor depends on how quick the other firms are in learning the new information. If knowledge is instantly disseminated then no firm in perfect competition will have an incentive to innovate. As you can appreciate this could be a serious source of difficulty for the competitive paradigm. Recall the production possibilities frontier from Chapter 1.

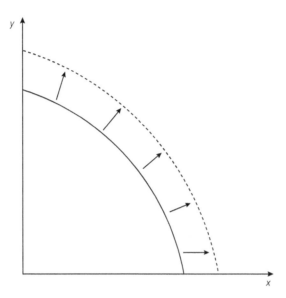

Figure 4.17 Innovation and the production possibility frontier.

The position of the frontier depends on the stock of means of production (i.e. how much labour and capital there is in the economy at a certain point in time) and technology. Consequently, there are two ways in which this frontier can be pushed outwards and the availability of goods for the economy increased (this is what we call growth; see Figure 4.17). First it can be done through an increase in the stock of means of production (notably, capital). Second, the shift can be achieved through technological development. The former suggests that with the same technology we can produce more of both goods while the latter is based on the ability to produce more with the same stock of means of production. If we find that the competitive paradigm—as depicted by the model of perfect competition—implies a disincentive to innovate, we may have a problem in discussing its intertemporal efficiency. We saw in the previous section that perfect competition yields a productive as well as allocative efficient allocation. But if it means that this will yield less growth, then in terms of future possibilities, the competitive paradigm may not really be efficient.

One way of dealing with this incentive problem is to allow the innovator to enjoy the fruits of his invention through legislation. This is what patenting laws are trying to achieve. For further discussion of innovation in a competitive environment see question 6 in the self-assessment section below.

So we have a market with a single producer whose monopolistic position is protected through the command over a new technology which is protected by law (it is registered as a patent) and which no other firm can use. This means that we have effective barriers to entry as new entrants will only be able to use the old technology (with higher marginal cost of production). The incumbent will be able to lower the price below their minimum average cost price and thus drive them out of the market.

Naturally, if patenting is there to allow innovators to enjoy the fruits of their invention in such a way that the incentive to innovate will not be affected by the competitive environment, this can only be a temporary measure. After due returns, society may wish to have the benefits of the new technology spread around. Hence, fees are sometimes attached to a prolonged registration of patents.

Suppose now, that for this reason, the monopolist is required to pay a fee to keep the invention as a registered patent. In a way, this resembles the idea of using a lump sum tax to try and rectify the inefficiencies of the monopolist. When the monopolist must pay to keep the exclusive right for its innovation, there might be a problem if it renders the new technology as more expensive than the prevailing one. This, of course, may not be a good policy as it will stifle innovation but if the charges are such that only profits are squeezed, the possibility arises for the monopolist to make more profits by allowing other firms to use the new technology.

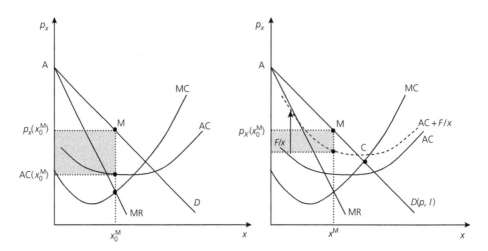

Figure 4.18 Patent registration fees in a monopoly.

In the left-hand of Figure 4.18 we have the monopolist set-up before the application of patenting fees. In the right-hand diagram we see the effect of charging patenting fees. Note that the introduction of registration fees constitutes a fixed cost element as the fees are independent of the level of production. Hence, the average cost curve will shift upward but the marginal cost will not change at all. This is so because the cost of producing an extra unit of x had not changed as a result of the fees. Had the fees been dependent on output, the marginal cost would have changed too.

As the fees are part of the fixed cost, the increase in the average cost falls the greater the quantity of output produced. If we produce only a few units of x, the fees per unit will be high, and thus, the average cost will shift by F/x (where F represents the fees). As F

remains constant and x is increasing F/x (the difference between the old and new average costs) will be decreasing.

The fact that marginal cost remained unchanged means that there will be no change in the profit maximizing allocation. This suggests that there will be no direct improvement in terms of the inefficiency of the monopolist as price is still different from marginal costs. The only direct effect of the introduction of these fees will be a fall in the profit as can be seen in the smaller shaded area in the left-hand diagram. Note, however, that we cannot see in this context the overall effect of the fees as there is a transfer of profits from producers to the government. Whether, or not, the loss of benefits in this market can be compensated by a government transfer remains, at this stage, an open question.

With the introduction of registration fees, the monopolist may decide to allow other firms access to its technology provided they paid the firm a user license fee. What will now happen to the market's structure and what will be its long run equilibrium? Could it be worthwhile for the firm to lose its monopolistic power?

When the monopolist allows other firms to use the new technology for a fee, this will reduce its own cost and increase the cost of possible entrants. Put differently, it facilitates a long run situation where one firm (the ex-monopolist) can make profits above the normal while others cannot. The market will emerge as shown in Figure 4.19.

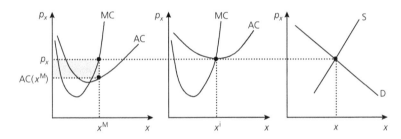

Figure 4.19 The emerging competition.

The left-hand diagram depicts the ex-monopolist. While everyone is now using the same (new) technology, everyone is paying a fee towards this use. The monopolist also pays the government but other producers pay the monopolist. With every entrant, the monopolist's AC is falling as part of its fixed cost is being paid by another. The minimal rate that the monopolist will set is that rate at which its own AC curve will end up lying below the entrants' AC. The above diagram depicts such a long run configuration. Firms will enter as long as there are profits to be made. How many firms enter depends on the fees which the monopolist will charge the entrants. The optimal fee level for the ex-monopolist will be the one that will generate a profit in the left-hand diagram which is greater than or equal to the profits before other firms entered and the burden of the fees laid entirely with the monopolist. Naturally, when the patent registration can no longer be re-renewed, more firms will enter and all firms will have the same technology and the same fixed costs (if any). We then end up with the normal competitive market allocation as the one described in Section 4.3.

Note that, as other firms entered and are free to do so, the demand confronting each one of them becomes completely elastic (a horizontal demand). The reason for this is that if any one firm charged a higher price than the market rate, it will lose all its customers who will move to buy the good with the other firm. Implicit in this story is the assumption that a single firm can, in principle, supply the entire market. Had this not been the case, the demand confronting each firm would not be completely elastic. If it raised its price it may lose many customers, but as the other firm would not be able to supply the entire market equilibrium price will increase. Put differently, the firm will be able to influence the market price.

However, this situation cannot be sustained. In the long run, the other firm will be able to adjust its production in such a way as to supply the market. Consequently, the demand each firm confronts (in the long run) will inevitably become completely elastic.

Indeed, it is in the type of demand elasticity which each firm confronts where the difference lies between monopolistic competition and other market structures. If the implications of the process of entry are that each firm confronts a completely elastic demand, it will mean that no firm can exercise any monopolistic power. It cannot raise its own price without losing its entire share in the market. But the reason why, in perfect competition, firms lose their entire market share in response to any slightest increase in their price is that the good they sell is exactly the same as the one that can be purchased by another. Namely, it is the **homogenous product** assumption about the nature of the good which facilitates this kind of development. As the move from perfect competition to monopoly represented changes in the 'number of agents' element of the determinant of markets structure, monopolistic competition represents a change in yet another element of those determinants: the nature of goods.

To fully understand this let us go back to the monopolist and ask what exactly will happen to it when firms enter the market.

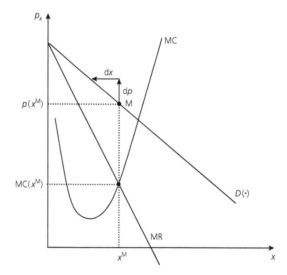

Figure 4.20 Monopolist demand schedule and new entry.

Initially, the monopolist is the sole producer and it confronts the above demand schedule (see Figure 4.20). If it raised the price by dp, it will lose dx because people are willing to pay so much only for a smaller quantity of x (when marginal utility is higher). Suppose also that the commodity which the monopolist produces is a simple type of white bread.

If you were considering entering the market for carbohydrate (in the form of bread) consumption given that there is a monopolist producing white bread, would you choose to produce white bread too? The answer to this question is actually fairly complex and we shall deal with some of the principles behind it in the next section. At this stage, we shall assume that since you know that there is a demand for all sorts of carbohydrates, you may choose to produce something which is slightly different, say, wholemeal bread. What will happen to the producer of white bread as you enter the market?

Among the people who want to consume carbohydrates there are those who are more health conscious than others. In addition, they may have different tastes in carbohydrates which may have nothing to do with health (some like white bread some like brown bread). When there was only one producer in the market, there was not much choice. If you wanted carbohydrate (in the form of bread) it had to be white bread. With the new entrants, some would immediately shift from white bread consumption to wholemeal bread consumption even if the latter is not cheaper. In fact, some may shift to wholemeal bread even if it were dearer simply because this is nearer to what they really want to consume when buying bread.

At the same time, there are people who would never abandon white bread even if there was a cheaper option of wholemeal bread. For them, life is not worth living if you cannot dip a piece of white bread in your soup! Therefore, both kinds of bread have a following which would remain loyal to it even in the face of a price differential. For them, the commodity is not 'carbohydrates' or 'bread', it is rather 'white bread' or 'wholemeal bread'. This means that each of the firms can raise the price without losing all its customers, as is the case in perfect competition. The demand elasticity which they confront even when there is entry will not be perfectly elastic. In other words, each of these firms has a certain degree of monopolistic power over some section of the market.

Consider for a moment that the taste in 'bread' products can vary from the extremely healthy ('Wheat on the Stick' type) to the much less healthy ('Bleached Bagels'). Let these tastes be arranged along the [0, 1] segment where 0 represents 'Bleached Bagels' while 1 represents 'Wheat on the Stick' (see Figure 4.21).

The horizontal axis gives the taste variation. The vertical lines from White Bread and Wholemeal represent the price of each of the commodity. Let us suppose that the distribution of individuals with different taste variants is uniform. This means that each variation of taste as the same number of people who like it most. Thus, when only White Bread is in the market—and we shall assume that everyone must eat bread—every one will buy White Bread. However, for those for whom White Bread is the dream bread, the price they pay (in terms of utilities) is exactly their willingness to pay (*Pwb*). However, for all the others who buy the bread but this is not exactly what they wanted, they are paying a higher price. They are paying the price *Pwb* + the disutility from having to buy something which is not exactly what they wanted. The further one is, in terms of taste, from the position of White Bread, the costlier will White Bread be for them (in terms of utilities, as everyone will be paying exactly the same money price). Thus, a health freak

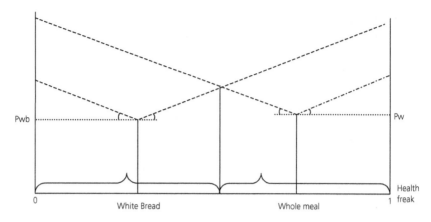

Pwb

Pw

0

White Bread

Whole meal

1

Health freak

Figure 4.21

will buy a loaf of White Bread and eat it as if it were a medicine. This utility price, which people pay, is captured by the rays from the top of the price line. The further one is from the top of the price line the higher will be one's cost of consuming White Bread.

Before we examine the implication of the introduction of Wholemeal for White Bread we must note that everything we had said about White Bread also applies to Wholemeal. For some people, this is their dream bread and paying Pw is exactly what they wanted to pay. People, whose tastes variants are further from Wholemeal will be paying much more as they, also, do not get what they wanted. The rays from the top of the Wholemeal price line capture the cost of buying Wholemeal (in utility terms). Thus, the introduction of Wholemeal will have the following effects on White Bread. When the producer of Wholemeal bread enters the market, the demand confronting the producer of White Bread, who until this point was the sole producer of carbohydrates, will shift to the left (see Figure 4.22). At any given price, some customers will shift to the other good, even if

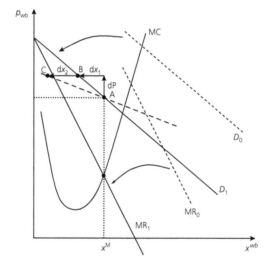

Figure 4.22 Monopolistic competition and new entry.

the price of the other good is higher. In the taste diagram we can see this in the following way. The moment Wholemeal enters the market, all those with taste variations which are to the right of the intersection of the two rays (more or less, at the middle) will prefer to buy Wholemeal. Until now they bought White Bread but at great cost (utility wise). Now they can buy a bread which is closer to their taste. Thus, White Bread at once will lose a whole section of the market regardless of its initial price. This is, of course, equivalent to a shift to the left of the demand schedule.

In addition, if the producer of White Bread were to raise the price of the good by the same dp as before, he will lose a much greater dx now than he would had he been the sole producer in the market. If you look at the taste diagram you can see that raising the price line for White Bread will shift both rays stemming from it upwards. This means that the intersection between the rays from White Bread and the rays from Whole-meal is now further to the left. It means that more people who until now were more or less indifferent between the two goods (neither was what they wanted) will now switch to Wholemeal. What this means is that with the entry of new firms, not only will the incumbents lose a market share, they will also confront a more elastic demand schedule.

If you think carefully about the meaning of elasticity you will realize that among other things, elasticity represents choice. The more choice you have, the more elastic will be the demand confronting a single producer. If the producer of our White Bread increases the price he will first lose dx_1 according to the willingness to pay of all his loyal customers (the move from A to B in Figure 4.22). However, some of his customers stayed with him simply because for them neither White Bread nor Wholemeal bread were what they really liked. Given the price of both goods, they chose to buy White Bread because they would be paying for it in money terms as well as in terms of not getting exactly what they want which is less than what they would get if they bought Wholemeal bread. When the producer of White Bread raises the price, some of these people will shift to the Wholemeal bread because this would now be cheaper in terms of the money cost as well as the cost of not getting that which you really want (the move from B to C).

Consequently, we may conclude that as new firms enter the market, the demand sched-ule confronting existing firms will move inside and become more elastic. As long as there is profit to be made, firms will enter the market until that point where the demand sched-ule is tangent to the average cost. When the demand schedule is tangent to the average cost, the price will be equal to the average cost. The level of output for which demand is tangent to the average costs is also the profit maximizing choice, where marginal revenue equals marginal cost. The intuition here is fairly straightforward. At any other price the average cost is greater than the price. This means that at any other price the firm will be making losses. Hence, the profit maximizing price must be the one where the price equals average cost. At the same time we know that profit maximization also requires equating marginal cost with marginal revenue. Hence, the long run equilibrium in the monopol-istic competition case will be at the point where marginal revenue equals marginal cost but the price is greater than the marginal cost and equals the average cost.[6] Had there been no product differentiation (Figure 4.23), the demand schedule would have become completely elastic and the long run solution would have been the same as in perfect competition (the tangency of the average cost with the demand would have occurred

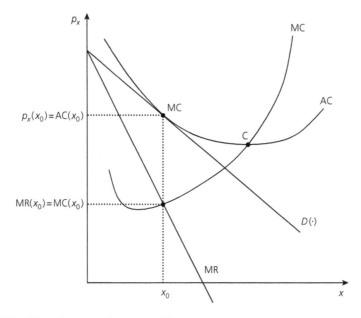

Figure 4.23 Equilibrium in monopolistic competition.

at the minimum of the average cost). This means that the difference between perfect competition and monopolistic competition is in the demand elasticity which firms confront in the long run. In the case of monopolistic competition, firms have, even in the long run, some monopolistic power over some people to allow them to be able, in principle, to vary their price without either losing their entire market share if they raise the price or gaining the entire market if they reduce the price. The extent of their monopolistic power can then be measured in terms of the deviation of the market price from the marginal cost.

We may use this framework of product differentiation to gain some further insight into the significance of the competitive outcome. What distinguishes the monopolistic competition in the long run from the long run perfectly competitive equilibrium is, in our case, the distribution of tastes. If you consider the taste segment we examined earlier, you may ask the question what it would mean, in this set-up, if the demand facing the individual firm were to be perfectly elastic? The answer, quite clearly, is the presence of very near taste variants. Namely, if next to White Bread a new company began to sell Spotted White Bread (i.e. white bread with one grain of health) this would mean that the people who were very close in their taste to White Bread would find it as a good alternative. If White Bread then raised its price, it might indeed lose all its customers. Put differently, the monopolistic competition long run equilibrium will approach the competitive one as the diversity in provision increases. You can guess how keen various companies are to admit that their products are similar to those of others. In many respects, among other things, the purpose of advertising is to prevent the perfectly competitive solution to emerge.

4.7 A note on strategic behaviour

Up to this point, our analysis was dominated by a sort of passive behaviour. All agents were rational utility (or profit) maximizers but in all the cases which we have discussed, they made their choices assuming that their own choice will not influence the choice of the other agents. However, if we consider the case of monopolistic competition to be a more realistic depiction of market structures, we must acknowledge that when there are a few firms in the market they are unlikely to ignore each other when they make their own choices. We call such a behaviour **strategic**.

Consider a simple case where there is a market with the following inverse demand function for the good x:

$$p(x) = \alpha - \beta x$$

Suppose, for simplicity's sake, that the marginal cost of producing x is constant and equals to zero. The revenue function will be

$$R(x) = p(x)x = (\alpha - \beta x)x = \alpha x - \beta^2 x$$

and the marginal revenue,

$$\delta R / \delta x = \mathrm{MR}(x) = \alpha - 2\beta x.$$

The demand for good x is shown in Figure 4.24. The competitive solution is at the point where $p(x) = \mathrm{MC}\,(x)$. As we assumed MC to be zero, the competitive equilibrium is at the point where $p(x) = \mathrm{MC}(x) = 0$:

$$p(x) = \alpha - \beta x = 0 \text{ means that } x^c = \alpha/\beta$$

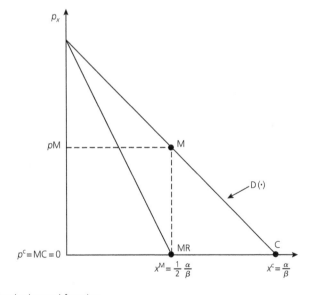

Figure 4.24 A simple demand function.

This point is denoted by the letter C in the above diagram.

Had there been a single producer (a monopolist) the equilibrium would be at the point where $MR(x) = MC(x)$. Again, as $MC = 0$, the condition becomes:

$$\delta R/\delta x = MR(x) = \alpha - 2\beta x = 0 \text{ which means: } x^M = \alpha/2\beta$$

This point is denoted by the letter M in the above figure.

Suppose now that there are two producers in the market. Had they ignored each other and acted as monopolists (in a similar vein as in monopolistic competition), each of them would have produced the monopolist output which is $\alpha/2\beta$. As there are two such agents, the total quantity of x brought to the market will be $2(\alpha/2\beta) = \alpha/\beta$. But $\alpha/\beta = x^c$ which means that they will end up at point C where both will make no profits above the normal.

It is clear from Figure 4.24 that if each firm produced a bit less, they will both enjoy greater profits (the price will be above zero and revenues, which in our case are equal to profits above the normal, will be positive too). But how much will each of them produce? Everyone would want the other one to produce less and himself more so that he gets the greater share of the profit. Is there a possible solution to this situation?

To understand this let us deviate from our story and discuss a similar situation which is captured by the famous prisoner's dilemma. Two suspects of a cheating in an examination were caught by the police and are held in different cells. They cannot communicate with each other. Their interrogators tell each one of them that if he blows the whistle on the other, he will get only 20 days in jail while the other will get 10 years. Each suspect also knows that if both of them confessed each one will get only 1 year in jail, while if they keep silent, for the lack of evidence, they will be tried on a minor offence which carries a sentence of 3 months each. What should they do?

The following matrix captures all possibilities. The rows represent the choices of individual 1 while the columns represent the choices of individual 2. Each box represents the outcome where the left-hand number is the outcome for individual 1 and the right-hand number is the outcome for individual 2.

	Confess	Do not confess
Confess	(1 year, 1 year)	(20 days, 10 years)
Do not confess	(10 years, 20 days)	(3 months, 3 months)

The question which individual 1 will ask himself is the following one: what will be my best response for each choice of action by individual 2? If individual 2 chooses to confess we must examine column 1. If individual 1 responds to the confession by 2 by confessing as well, the outcome will be that both will sit in jail for 1 year. If, instead, individual 1 responded to 2's confession by not confessing, he will get 10 years in jail. Clearly, 1 year is preferred over 10 years, and individual 1 knows that his best response to individual 2's confession would be to confess as well.

But what if individual 2 chose not to confess? Here we must examine column 2 of the above matrix. If individual 1 responded to 2's refusal to cooperate with the police by confessing, he will get only 20 days in jail. If, instead, he chose not to confess, he would end up with 3 months in jail. Clearly, 20 days is preferred over 3 months and individual's 1 best response to individual 2's cooperation with the police would be to confess.

In other words, whatever individual 2 chooses to do, individual 1's best response is to confess. We say in such a case that confession is a dominating strategy. For symmetry reasons you can appreciate that individual 2 will reach exactly the same conclusion. Consequently, both will choose to confess and will end up spending 1 year in jail each. This equilibrium is called a **Nash equilibrium** and it represents each agent's best response to whatever the other agent might do.

However, one can clearly see from the above that there is a better solution, from the individual's point of view, than the Nash equilibrium. This would be the outcome in the case where both choose not to confess. The reason why this is not an equilibrium is the incentive which each agent will have to renege on the choice of strategy. Were you able to agree with your partner not to confess, you will have an incentive to confess as this will reduce the number of days in jail from 3 months to 20 days. As your partner is likely to do the same, you will end up confessing anyway. The above description of Nash equilibrium presupposes a form of competitive behaviour and it does not provide a full account to what might happen if cooperation were possible.[7] In this sense, the notion of Nash equilibrium is a perfectly good method to resolve the problem of the two producers with which we started.

We know that as a monopolist, profits will be maximized whenever output equals to $(\alpha/2\beta)$ which is where $MR = MC = 0$. The geometry of our tale suggests that as the monopolist's optimal choice will be at the point where the MR equals to zero, this will happen at half the size of the market. Indeed, under competition, the output would have been (α/β) which is exactly $2\,(\alpha/2\beta)$.

Consider now the situation where, like in the prisoner's dilemma, each firm is conscious of the other. What would then be its best policy?

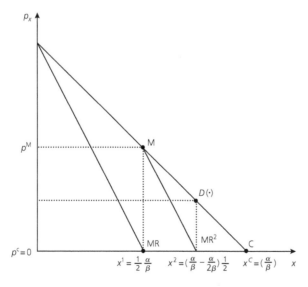

Figure 4.25 Best responses.

The simple answer to this will be that the best response to the choice of output by the other firm will be to exploit as much as possible the monopolistic power over the remaining of the market (see Figure 4.25). Hence, if one firm was first in the market and, as a monopolist, chose to produce $x^1 = (\alpha/2\beta)$, the second firm's best response will be to behave as a monopolist on the residual of the market at the point: $x^2 = ((\alpha/\beta) - (\alpha/2\beta))/2$; where $(\alpha/\beta) - (\alpha/2\beta)$ is the residual of the market demand at the competitive price.

But if this is what firm 2 chooses to do, will firm 1 not change its choice? Well, like firm 2, firm 1 wishes to maintain its monopolistic power over the remainder of the market. This would mean that it too would want to choose the quantity which is half the residual (where MR = MC = 0). Hence, we can write the rule of best response for each firm. That rule is to produce half the size of what is left of the market given the choice of output by the other firm. This would mean the following.

$$x^1 = \left(\frac{\alpha}{\beta} - x^2\right)\frac{1}{2}$$

$$x^2 = \left(\frac{\alpha}{\beta} - x^1\right)\frac{1}{2}.$$

Figure 4.26, depicts these equations.

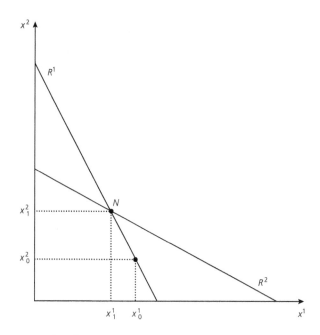

Figure 4.26 Best response functions.

The horizontal axis denotes the quantity produced by 2 while the vertical axis denotes the quantity produced by 1. Had 2 produced nothing, $x^1 = (\alpha/2\beta)$, which is exactly the monopolist solution. Had firm 2 increased its output, the best response of firm 1 will be a lower level of output. In particular, if firm 2 chose x_0^2 then the line denoted by R^1

(response function for 1) tells us what level of output will maximize 1's profit (1's best response to x_0^2). This will be x_0^1. In the same way, we can construct the response function of firm 2 (denoted by R^2). Clearly there is a pair of strategies (output) which constitute each agent's best response to the other agent's choice. This is the pair (x_1^1, x_1^2). From the above equations we are able to calculate these values:

$$x^1 = \left(\frac{\alpha}{\beta} - x^2\right)\frac{1}{2}$$

$$x^2 = \left(\frac{\alpha}{\beta} - x^1\right)\frac{1}{2},$$

hence,

$$x^2 = \left(\frac{\alpha}{\beta} - x^1\right)\frac{1}{2} = \frac{\alpha}{2\beta} - \frac{1}{2}\left[\frac{\alpha}{2\beta} - \frac{1}{2}x^2\right]$$

$$x^2 = \frac{\alpha}{2\beta} - \frac{\alpha}{4\beta} + \frac{1}{4}x^2$$

$$x^2 = \frac{1}{3}\frac{\alpha}{\beta}$$

for symmetry reasons this will also be the value of x^1.

From what we know about the Nash equilibrium in the prisoner's dilemma, we may conclude that while the pair (x_1^1, x_1^2) may be an equilibrium, the two firms could have increased their profits had they cooperated. One famous case of such cooperation is the Oil Producing and Exporting Countries (OPEC) cartel. Representatives of these countries used to meet in order to decide on the quantity of output which will keep the price sufficiently high, so that they can share a greater profit. However, on many occasions, some of the countries which were more in need of funds chose to slightly increase their output so that they will gain more from the higher price. The more the countries behaved in this way, the less effective became the cartel.

As I said earlier, cooperation is a very broad and complicated field of investigation and it may not be insightful to analyse it using the existing framework. However, I would like to draw your attention to a certain gap that has arisen due to our analysis of strategic behaviour. While the Nash solution may not produce the highest profits for the agents, it is, from a social point of view, preferred to the cooperative solution. This, of course, does not mean that cooperation is an inferior form of social organization. What it does mean is that in a world of self-interested individuals, competition may be a means by which such desires are tamed. In the non-strategic analysis we could see this in the fact that the long run solution meant that firms will make no profits above the normal, and in the strategic case we see this through the fact that a conspiracy (which is a form of cooperation) by agents to increase their gain at the expense of the others will be socially undesirable as well as unsustainable.

There is, however, a much more alarming conclusion which follows the analysis in strategic behaviour. This is the conclusion that agents fail to achieve that which they want. In the case of the prisoner's dilemma this is quite clear. The interests of the agents is to get to the box of (3 months, 3 months) which would have been obtained had both of them cooperated with each other and refused to confess. The fact that a competitive behaviour brought them to a less desirable outcome suggests a serious failure in the working of competition.

In the non-strategic framework, firms want to maximize profits and they achieve this outcome even in the long run, when the normal profit is that maximum. But in the case of strategic behaviour, it is clear to us that the firms did not achieve the highest profits which were feasible. If the meaning of competition is that it allows through decentralized decisionmaking, the coincidence of wants, then Nash equilibrium has demonstrated that this may not always be the case. The question which one would need to follow is whether this is a result of failure in the working of markets, or a failure which is due to the absence of some markets. The answer to this question will be given in further studies.

Self-assessment and applications

▓ QUESTION 1

(a) Analyse the short run and long run effects of a unit tax on a competitive industry;

(b) Compare the effects of such a tax (in the short run and in the long run) on a competitive industry confronting an elastic demand schedule ($|\eta| > 1$) with an industry confronting an inelastic demand schedule($|\eta| < 1$). Examine the effects from the point of view of:

  (i) consumers;

  (ii) producers;

  (iii) governments.

(c) 'The inefficiency of the unit tax can only be justified in a partial equilibrium analysis. If we consider the economy as a whole, the deadweight loss will be offset by the increase in demand for other goods.' Comment on this statement.

Answer

(a) Before we get into this section let us examine how would a unit tax of, say, t per unit of output affect the cost functions:

$$c^U(x) = c(x) + tx$$

$$AC^U(x) = \frac{c^U(x)}{x} = \frac{c(x)}{x} + \frac{tx}{x} = AC(x) + t$$

$$MC^U(x) = \frac{dc^U}{dx} = \frac{dc}{dx} + \frac{dT}{dx} = MC(x) + t.$$

Hence, with a unit tax, both average cost and marginal cost are higher by the tax (t). This means that as there is a parallel shift of both average and marginal costs, the minimum average cost would be exactly at the same level of output as before the tax.

(i)   The first point is the direct effect of the unit tax on a representative firm. In our case, this should be an upward shift of both the average and marginal cost curves. Also, as it is a unit tax, the new minimum average cost will intersect the new marginal cost at exactly the same level of output as before the change;

(ii) A short run analysis as shown in Figure 4.27. Note that as we analyse a move from one long run equilibrium to another, we only examine the effects on the long run cost function. From a qualitative point of view, our analysis would not be much different had we moved continuously between short run and long run cost functions.

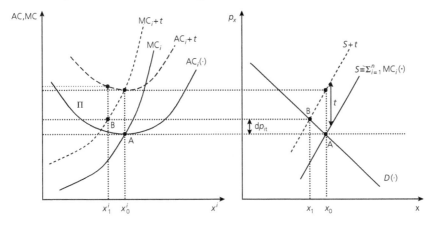

Figure 4.27

Notice that the supply curve shifts upwards and, as a result, equilibrium price rises by less than the value of the unit tax, total output falls, and each firm produces less while making losses (A → B).

(iii) The long run analysis (see Figure 4.28). Some firms will now leave the market (an explanation of why only some firms, and not all of them at once, had been awarded extra points). The price will rise by the full value of the tax and each firm will produce exactly as it did before the change;

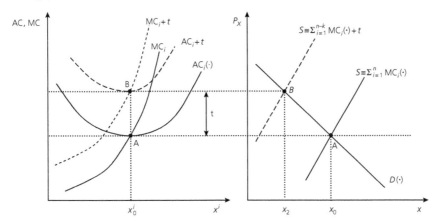

Figure 4.28

(b) It is sufficient here to examine the situation by looking at the market alone. The left-hand diagram Figure 4.29 depicts the elastic demand schedule while the right-hand diagram deals with the inelastic one. A to B is the short run. C is the long run.

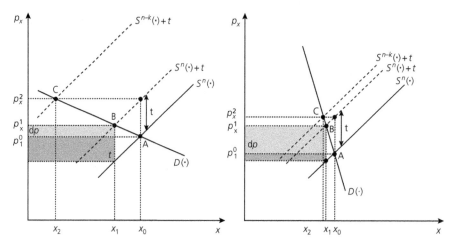

Figure 4.29

Short run

(i) Consumers: when demand elasticity is greater than unity, the price increases by a small fraction of the magnitude of the tax ($dp < t$)(Figure 4.29). When it is less than unity, while the price still increases by less than the full tax, the increase in price will be much greater (right-hand diagram). At point B (the new equilibrium) we also see the total amount of tax revenue ($T(x) = t \cdot x_1$), which is the shaded area. Who, you may ask, pays the tax? The answer is very simple. That part of consumer surplus which falls into the shaded area (the lighter shade), is a transfer of utility (in its money equivalent form) from consumers to the government. Equally, the darker shaded area which used to be part of the producer surplus is now transferred to the government. Thus, the distribution of the burden of taxation (i.e. who pays it) depends on the relative size of these two shaded areas. To determine the relative size of these two areas, one would need to know both changes in price as well as the overall quantity exchanged. A simpler, more immediate way of assessing this is simply by looking at the change in price. As a result of the tax the market moves (in the short run) from point A to point B. Thus, the increase in the price for consumers is $p_x^1 - p_x^0 = dp^c$. Before the tax, the price which consumers paid was the same as the price received by the producer. Once there is a tax, it means that a part of the price goes to the government. Therefore, at B, the price received by the producers is different from that which is paid by the consumers. It is $p_x^1 - t = p^p$. Hence, relative to the original position, the change in the price which the producer receives becomes $p_x^0 - (t - dp^c) = dp^p$. As $t = |dp^p| + dp^c$ the distribution of the burden can be assessed through the composition of the tax. The greater is the change in consumer price, the greater will be the share of the consumers. Looking at these two cases it is clear that the burden of tax, in the short run, is greater on consumers when price elasticity of demand is less than unity than it is when price elasticity of demand is greater than unity.

(ii) Producers: exactly the reverse is true.

(iii) The tax raised with a greater price elasticity of demand will be smaller, as quantity is very responsive to slight changes in price.

Long Run

(i) Consumers: in both cases the long run increase in consumers' price will be at the full value of the unit tax. This means that the entire tax revenues are coming now from what used to be consumers' surplus.

(ii) Producers: for those staying in the market it will make no difference. As a group, however, there will be more producers leaving the market under the elastic demand schedule than under the less elastic one. The reason, as before, is that the long run equilibrium output under the elastic demand schedule will be much smaller than under the less elastic demand schedule.

(iii) As in the short run.

(c) This is the part of the question where you are expected to comment on the efficiency of taxes:

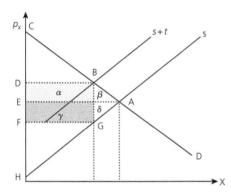

Figure 4.30

Before the tax was imposed, the equilibrium was at point A. The benefits were roughly distributed as follows: the consumer's surplus was the triangle ACE, the producer's surplus was the triangle AEH. After the tax was imposed, the market reached its short run equilibrium at point B (see Figure 4.30). We now have four new areas denoted by the Greek letters. The area α used to be the consumer surplus and is now transferred to the government. The area β used to be part of the consumer surplus but is now lost. The area γ used to be part of producer surplus and is now transferred to the government, and the area δ used to be part of the producer surplus and is now lost, namely, not transferred to anyone. The two areas which have been lost represent benefits to both consumers and producers which were available before the tax and are no longer available after the tax. We, therefore, call the triangle ABG **deadweight loss**. Clearly, this is the cost of the tax in terms of its efficiency. Naturally, what we assume here is that the transfers from the consumers and producers of commodity *x* to the government is a neutral act. Namely, that the utility transferred from the consumers to the government would be, in the end, passed on by the government to other members of society. As we are all equally important from the social point of view, this transfer is neither a loss nor a gain from society's general point of view. Therefore, the deadweight loss is indeed a pure loss.

However, it is not difficult to imagine that this may not be so trivial. If commodity *x*, for instance, were fast cars and the demand for such cars came mainly from the rich and famous, the transfer of utility from them to poorer members of society (through the government) could be seen as an increase in the society's welfare. We know that we have difficulties comparing individuals but it is not so complicated to imagine that from a collective social point of view the gain in welfare of the poor is more important than the loss in utility for the rich. Even the rich may be willing to accept this social criterion. If so, the transfer of benefits from consumers and producers of fast cars to the more needy elements may be sufficiently desirable as to offset the deadweight loss.

Nevertheless, there is one important element which generates inefficiency of this type of tax. It is the fact that the price no longer equals marginal cost of production (it equals MC + *t*). As we saw earlier, marginal cost pricing is the benchmark of efficiency. What we have not seen yet are the general equilibrium implications of departing from marginal cost function for the economy in general. We shall visit this issue in Chapter 6.

QUESTION 2

The competitive market for new homes is in long run equilibrium. Its demand is comprised of two groups: first time buyers and second home buyers.

(a) Describe the long run equilibrium paying attention to the distribution of surplus between first time buyers and second home buyers.

(b) Analyse the effects on the total output, each firm's output, the number of firms, and prices in the short run and the long run when the cost of labour increases.

(c) What will happen (in the case of (b)) to the capital to labour ratio, to all consumers' expenditures, and to the expenditures of each group of consumers?

(d) Analyse the effects on the total output, each firm's output, the number of firms, and prices in the short run and the long run when the government offers a subsidy to first time buyers.

(e) What will happen (in the case of (d)) to the capital to labour ratio, to all consumers' expenditures, and to the expenditures of each group of consumers?

Answer

In this question you can test your ability to analyse markets when the composition of agents is more complex. Here we have a market for new homes (flow!) but a clear distinction between first and second time buyers. We may assume that the demand elasticity of first time buyers is less than unity and that of second time buyers, greater than unity. This is not a necessary assumption but you should have an opinion about this. The analysis should then be consistent with what you chose.

(a) Figure 4.31 depicts the market, the demand of first time buyers, demand of second time buyers, and the market as a whole, from left to right. Clearly the market demand schedule should have an elasticity which represents the relative size of each group of consumers.

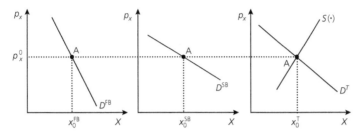

Figure 4.31

The long run equilibrium is at points A:

(b) and **(c)** Let there be an increase in the cost of labour: the increase in labour costs will push up both average and marginal cost. As each firm adjusts its output to the profit maximizing level

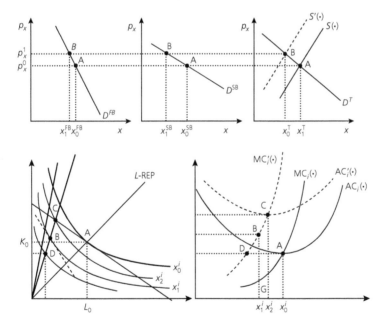

Figure 4.32

(where MC = the existing price, at point D), the output of each firm (and so, the total in the short run) will fall. This will show up in the market through the inward shift of the supply schedule. This, in turn, will bring about a short run increase in equilibrium price. Under the assumptions which we have made second time buyers' spending will decrease while first time buyers' spending will increase. The overall spending depends on the total demand elasticity (Figure 4.32).

It is perfectly reasonable for you to explain the changes under different demand elasticity considerations without committing yourself to a particular situation.

The capital to labour ratio will rise when labour becomes more expensive and this will generate a new long run expansion path. We now have a bit of a difficulty in representing the exact process, as we chose to analyse everything based on the long run cost functions and adding the short run costs would clog the view. In the short run, the stock of capital remains fixed. We, therefore, move at first to a point such as D which is already on the new technology but we shall assume that it corresponds to a short phase when some of the existing capital remains idle. This is a slight inaccuracy but it does not have any qualitative influence on our analysis. One can think about it in the following way. The immediate response to the increase in cost would be to lay off workers and as there is a need to readjust production, there is an adjustment period where some of the capital is not fully used. We thus move from A to D. Then, as price increases and as we manage the appropriate adjustment we end up at point B.

In the long run, firms will leave the market. This will push the supply further to the left bringing about an increase in long run equilibrium price. The consumers' spending will change further in the same direction as it did in the short run.

(d) and **(e)** Let the government offer a subsidy to first time buyers: a subsidy to first time buyers will shift their demand upwards. The reason for this is that with a subsidy, it is as if individuals are

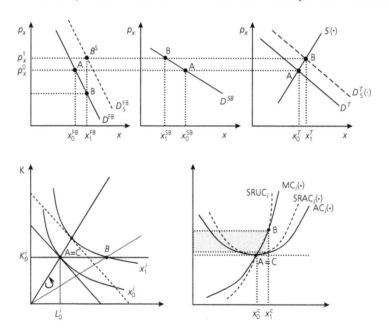

Figure 4.33

willing to pay more for any quantity of the good. For any quantity of the good, the demand schedule depicts our willingness to pay, captured through the concept of the money equivalent of our marginal utility. When we receive a subsidy, it is as if the government tops this willingness to pay by an extra amount s. Naturally, we could also depict subsidy through a change in the supply schedule (the opposite of what we did in question 1 where we had a tax). However, when the policy is aimed at a segment of the market, using the supply schedule to depict the policy will be misleading. It is therefore important to be able to examine the effects of policies by shifting both supply and demand (Figure 4.33).

This means that the overall demand will shift upwards also, but at a lesser proportion, given that only some people receive the subsidy. The short run equilibrium prices will rise and overall consumers' spending will rise too. Spending by second time buyers depend on their demand elasticity. Assuming, as we did, that it is greater than unity, their spending will fall.

First time buyers need more attention. Their direct spending, that is, that which they spend from their own pocket, is given by point B. Recall that the market price is B^S but consumers only pay the price at B which is the price at B^S minus the subsidy ($B^S - S$). Hence, as far as the first time buyers are concerned, they move from point A to point B on their demand schedule (without the government supplementary willingness to pay). As their price elasticity is less than unity, their spending will fall. The increase in overall spending will come from the government. The total spending on subsidy would be $S(x) = (B^S - B)x_1^{FB} = s \cdot x_1^{FB}$.

In the short run, the output will increase and firms will be making profits. The capital to labour ratio will fall in the short run, (point B), but will remain unchanged in the long run (point C). Also, in the long run, firms will enter the market and push the supply schedule to the right. Assuming a horizontal long run industry supply, the price will fall back to its original level and so will the spending by second time buyers. First time buyers will spend (directly) even less (assuming demand elasticity less than unity) and overall spending will rise or fall according to the overall demand elasticity. Each firm's output remains unchanged relative to the initial position. The capital to labour ratio, also, remains unchanged.

QUESTION 3

(a) Analyse the short run and the long run effects of a lump sum tax on a competitive industry;

(b) Compare the effects in (a) to those of a unit tax which raises the same amount of revenue for the government. What will happen to the number of firms remaining in the market?

(c) 'While in the short run, the lump sum tax is clearly efficient and the unit tax is not, in the long run, both taxes are equally inefficient as the burden of tax is shifted onto consumers.' Comment on this statement making a clear distinction between productive and allocative efficiency and bearing in mind some general equilibrium considerations.

Answer

(a) First we must examine how would a lump sum tax affect our original cost functions. Suppose that originally we had the cost function $c(x)$. This means that the corresponding average and marginal costs are

$$AC(x) = \frac{c(x)}{x}$$

$$MC(x) = \frac{dc}{dx}.$$

A lump sum tax is a tax which must be paid irrespective of how much of the good is being produced. Hence, a lump sum tax has the form of a fixed costs:

$$c^L(x) = c(x) + T$$

$$AC^L(x) = \frac{c^L(x)}{x} = \frac{c(x)}{x} + \frac{T}{x} = AC(x) + \frac{T}{x}$$

$$MC^L(x) = \frac{dc^L}{dx} = \frac{dc}{dx} + \frac{dT}{dx} = MC(x) + 0 = MC(x).$$

This means that the new average costs are really just the old one + an expression (T/x) which is very large for small xs and almost zero for large xs. The new average costs, therefore, lies above the old one and the difference between them (T/x) is shrinking the more output is being produced. Clearly, as the tax is independent of output, the production of an extra unit of x would not increase the tax liability. This means that $dT/dx = 0$. Hence, the marginal cost remains as before. Consequently, the new average cost will reach its minimum when it equals to the old marginal cost function.

(i) The first point is the direct effect of the lump tax on a representative firm. In our case, this should be a shift upwards of the average cost curve alone. Also, as the marginal cost remains unchanged the minimum average cost will be at a higher level of output. The distance between the new and old average cost is given by T/x;

(ii) A short run analysis is shown in Figure 4.34.

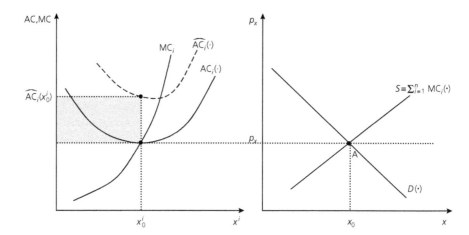

Figure 4.34

Note that the Supply curve does not move and, as a result, equilibrium price will remain unchanged. Each firm will carry on producing as before but they will now be making losses.

(iii) In the long run (Figure 4.35), some firms will now leave the market (an explanation is expected as to why only some firms and not all at once leave the market). Supply will fall and equilibrium price will rise by more than the average tax. Each of the remaining firms will now produce more than they did before the tax.

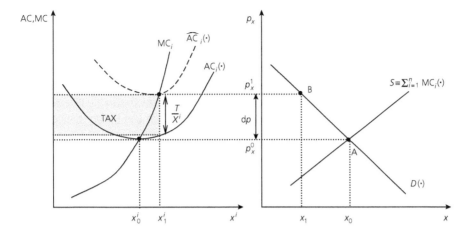

Figure 4.35

(b) This part of the question is considerably more difficult. The question here is about comparing the lump sum and unit tax (see question 1 for details). To see the relationship between the two tax systems in terms of the revenues which they raise, let us begin by assuming a unit tax of the size t and a lump-sum tax (T) such that the revenue raised through each firm is the same. This will be a convenient benchmark which implies that the number of firms remaining in the market will be the same under the two schemes (for the overall tax revenues to be the same):

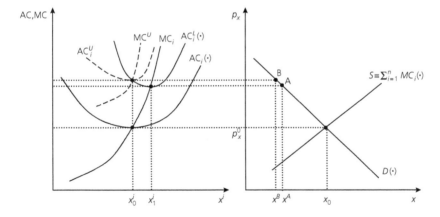

Figure 4.36

If each firm were to pay the same amount of tax under the lump sum scheme (T) as under the unit tax, then

$$T = tx_0^i \quad t = \frac{T}{x_0^i},$$

where x_0^i is the representative firm's pre-tax level of output (as well as long run level with a unit tax). This means that the average lump sum tax at that point of initial output must be the same as the unit tax. Naturally, under a lump sum tax each firm will produce more (x_1^i) so the average lump sum tax which such a firm will pay will be smaller (Figure 4.36).

The long run effects of a unit tax t are denoted by points B. Those of the corresponding lump sum are denoted by points A. In both cases there will be fewer firms in the market than before the tax. Under the unit tax each firm will produce as before and overall output will fall. Under the lump sum tax each firm will produce more than before the tax but overall output will fall. Equilibrium price under a unit tax will rise by the full value of the tax (t) where each firm will pay the government the amount (tx_0^i) in tax. Under the lump sum tax which generates the same overall revenue with the same number of firms after the imposition of the tax as in the case of unit tax, price will rise by more than the average tax but by less than the equivalent unit tax. Output under unit tax will fall by more than under the lump sum tax.

Generally speaking, we know that for the two systems to produce the same tax revenues we must have

$$Tn^L = tx_0^i n^U,$$

where T is the lump sum tax per firm; n^L, the number of firms remaining in the long run with a lump sum tax; n^U, the number of firms remaining in the long run with a unit tax. Hence, the relative number of firms depend on the level of tax per firm:

$$\frac{T}{tx_0^i} = \frac{n^U}{n^L}$$

If the tax per firm under lump sum is greater than under a unit tax, the $n^U > n^L$ and the opposite if the tax per firm under the lump sum scheme is smaller than under the unit tax.

(c) This is the part of the question where you are expected to comment on the efficiency of taxes. It is clear that in the partial equilibrium setting, in the long run, there will be a dead weight loss to the unit tax as well as the lump sum tax. Nevertheless, the reason we know that the unit tax will remain inefficient is that even in the long run, the price in the market for x no longer equals the marginal cost. Hence, had a full compensation of the deadweight loss been feasible (through increases in demand elsewhere), equating price to marginal cost could not have been the benchmark of efficiency. In the case of the lump sum tax, because the benchmark of efficiency (price equals marginal cost) has not been violated even in the long run, there is room to believe that the increase in price will cause increases in demand elsewhere that might compensate for the apparent deadweight loss.

QUESTION 4

The overall demand schedule for cigarettes has an elasticity which is greater than unity. The demand elasticity of 'heavy smokers' is less than unity.

(a) What will be the demand elasticity of the 'light smoker' if the demand for cigarettes is comprised of these two groups alone?

(b) Analyse the effects on the total output, each firm's output, the number of firms and prices in the short and long run when the government has a way of taxing only 'heavy smokers'.

(c) What will happen (in the case of (b)) to the capital to labour ratio, to all consumers' expenditures, and the expenditures of each group of consumers?

Answer

Here we have a market for cigarettes but a clear distinction between 'heavy' and 'light' smokers. The demand elasticity of 'heavy smokers' is less than unity and that of second time buyers, greater than unity. But the overall demand elasticity for cigarettes is greater than unity.

(a) The demand elasticity of the 'light' smokers must be greater than unity (Figure 4.37),

(b) and (c) Taxing 'heavy smokers'. A tax on 'heavy smokers' will shift their demand downward. This is the exact opposite to what we did when we introduced a subsidy for first time buyers in

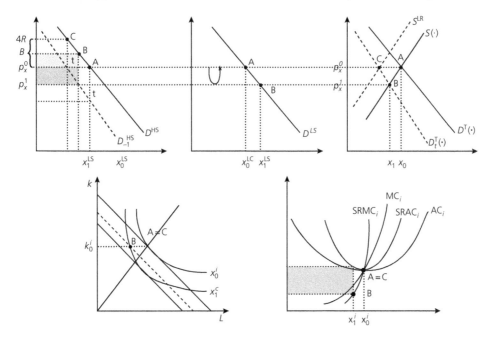

Figure 4.37

question (2). It is as if the willingness to pay is reduced by a tax that will have to be directed to the government. This means that overall demand will shift downwards also, but at a lesser proportion. Short run equilibrium prices will fall and overall consumers' spending will fall also. Spending by 'light smokers' will increase. Overall spending by 'heavy smokers' (including taxes) will rise.

In the short run, output will fall and firms will be making losses. Capital to labour ratio will rise in the short run (from A to B) but will remain unchanged in the long run (point C). Also, in the long run, firms will leave the market and push the supply schedule to the left. Assuming a horizontal long run industry supply, the price will rise back to its original level and so will the spending by 'light smokers'. 'Heavy smokers', however, will be spending more on cigarettes. Each firm's output remains unchanged relative to the initial position. The capital to labour ratio, also, remains unchanged.

■ QUESTION 5

Two groups of producers supply one competitive industry with a commodity (say, x) which requires skilled labour. One group is located in an underdeveloped area A with a high level of unemployment amongst unskilled labour. The other is located in a relatively well off area B where there is not much unskilled labour.

The government would like to pursue a 'welfare to work' policy and to induce firms to hire and train the unskilled workers. To that end, the government proposes to pay part of the wages for all workers in area A. To prevent firms from moving their plants from area B to area A, only existing firms in area A will qualify.

(a) Analyse the effects of the proposal on market price, output, and consumers' spending. How will it affect output, profits, and the number of firms in each area?

(b) What will be the effects of the proposal on the choice of technology of firms in area A? Will the proposal achieve its aim?

(c) 'Instead of forcing people to work for welfare, the government could have achieved the same result by taxing wages in area B.' Discuss this statement while reviewing your answers to (a) and (b).

Answer

The first feature of the case is that there are two groups of suppliers for the same commodity (x). Group A produces the good in an underdeveloped area with high unemployment among unskilled labour. Group B produces in a developed part of the community where there is no unskilled labour unemployment. By implication, good x is produced by skilled labour (hence there will be no difference in wages due to the difference in level of unemployment among unskilled labour). We begin, therefore, with a long run equilibrium in the industry (Figure 4.38).

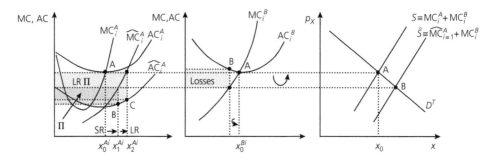

Figure 4.38

The government wishes to deal with the problem of unemployment in area A by pursuing a welfare to work approach. It proposes to subsidize wages in area A to allow firms to take on unskilled workers and to train them. For simplicity's sake, we may assume that the subsidy applies to the entire wage bill of the firm rather than to specific individuals.

In addition, to prevent the movement of firms across regions, only existing firms qualify.

(a) The effects of the proposal on the industry are as depicted in the above diagrams. Both AC and MC of firms in A will shift downward.

Short run: In the first instance, the fall in the MC in area A will bring about a shift outwards of the aggregate supply depending on the market share of area A. This will cause a fall in market price of x and we end up at points B in the above diagrams where firms in A make profits and produce more of x each; firms in B make losses and produce less each. Consumers' spending will change according to demand elasticity. Had the price elasticity of demand been greater than unity, spending will increase; if it were less than unity, spending will fall.

Long run: In the long run, firms in B will leave the market. This will shift the supply backward and cause an increase in the market price. The process will continue as long as there are losses in area B. When the price returns to its original level, we will reach the new long run equilibrium. Now, there will be less firms in area B and they will all make normal profits. Each firm in area B will produce as much as it did before the implementation of the policy.

In area A each firm will produce more (point C) than it did before the change and they will all be making profits above the normal (which are used for the purpose of retraining).

(b) The effect of the change on the choice of technology (Figure 4.39).

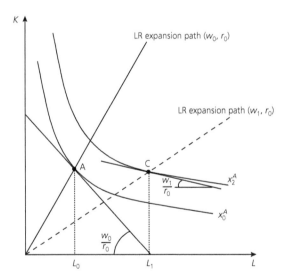

Figure 4.39

The change in relative factor prices will introduce a new, flatter long run expansion path. As a firm in area A is now producing more, the move is from A to C in the above diagram where more workers are employed. The policy will achieve its aim.

(c) Taxing wages in area B (Figure 4.40).

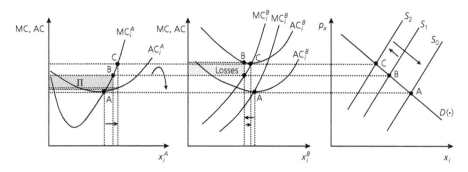

Figure 4.40

Short run: Taxes on wages in area B will lead to a shift upwards of both AC and MC. This will cause the aggregate supply to shift upwards depending on the relative share of area B in the market. Equilibrium price will increase and consumers' spending will change according to price elasticity of demand.

Each firm in area B will produce less and make losses. Each firm in area B will produce more and make profits above the normal.

Long run: Phase 1: In the long run, firms in B will leave the market and price will rise until it equals the minimum of the new AC curve in area B. At this stage, each firm in area B will produce more or less of x depending on how the minimum of new AC relates to the pre-tax function; and each firm will make normal profits. There will be less firms in area B; *Phase 2:* In area A there will be profits to be made. Firms from area B, therefore, will move their plants to area B. Hence, in the end, all firms from area B will move to area A, supply will increase and we will return to the original price and quantity only this time, supply will come from area A only. There will be no tax revenues for the government and there will be more job opportunities in area A. This time, however, the opportunities may arise as demand for labour in area A will rise and push up the wages (as it will be more costly to hire the unskilled labour). Consequently, MC will increase which will lead to an increase in price and a subsequent adjustment of consumers' surplus. In spite of the increase in the wage bill, firms will not return to area B as long as the tax liability is in place.

To some extent the critics were right (achieving more employment opportunity without spending government funds). However, the cost of such a change are perhaps greater than using tax payers money to subsidize area A. The costs are in the devastating effects which such a policy will have on area B.

■ QUESTION 6

A technological discovery had been made in one of the firms in a competitive industry. By registering the discovery as a patent, the inventing firm will have to pay registration fees but it could allow other firms the use of the new technology provided that they paid the inventing firm a license fee.

(a) Beginning with a long run equilibrium, describe the short run effects of the discovery prior to any patenting arrangements, and before other firms could use the new technology, on the industry's price and output and on each firm's output and profits.

(b) What will be the short run and the long run effects of introducing a patent registration fee on the inventing firm and a licence fee on all other users of the new technology?

(c) Could the license fee be set in such a way that none of the other firms will be willing to pay them? What will then happen to output and price in the industry in the long run?

(d) 'Allowing firms to patent their innovations works against allocative efficiency. Even in a case like (b), the existence of license fees could even bring about an increase in price. This means that the benefits of the innovation are not shared.' Discuss this statement.

Answer

In this question we examine some possible relationship between market structures. We have a competitive industry where one producer had made a technological innovation which must now be registered and paid for.

(a) Beginning with the long run equilibrium we now investigate the short run effects of the discovery before it is registered as a patent and before anyone else can access it (Figure 4.41).

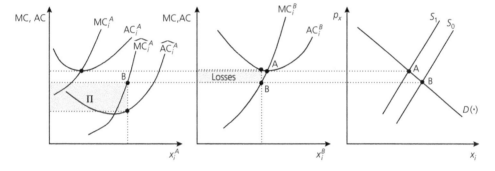

Figure 4.41

The discovering firm (left-hand diagram) will be able to reduce both its AC and MC of production. If the number of firms is very large indeed, this should have an infinitesimal effect on the aggregate supply unless, of course, the discovery is such that allows the inventor to leave its mark on the market.

We shall simply assume that this is a competitive environment where the discovery is significant enough to influence the aggregate supply. Hence, price will fall, and while the inventor is making profits, other firms may suffer losses (points B above). (Had we assumed that the inventor is too small, it would simply mean that the inventor will now make profits above the normal while others will not: both stories are accepted at this stage.)

(b) When the inventor allows other firms to use the new technology for a fee, this will reduce its own cost and increase the cost of others. Put differently, it facilitates a long run situation where one firm (the inventor) can make profits above the normal while others cannot. The following market will emerge (Figure 4.42).

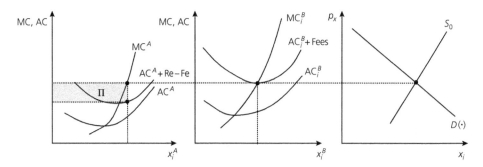

Figure 4.42

The left-hand diagram depicts the inventor. While everyone is now using the same technology, everyone is paying a fee towards this use. The inventor pays the government, the other producers pay the inventor. With every new user, the inventor's AC is falling. The minimal rate that the inventor will set is that rate at which its own AC curve will end up lying below the others' AC. The above diagram depicts such a long run configuration. Firms will swap technologies or new firms will enter as long as there are profits to be made. How many firms enter, depends on the fees which the inventor will charge the users.

(c) If the inventor sets a very high license fee and his technology is such that it can flood the market, it will create a monopolist situation. Whether, or not, it's worth the inventor's while depends on the profits it will make as a monopolist who has to pay the full patenting fees (there will be no license fees to offset these costs) against the profit it can make in the case like (b). You are expected here to show how the inventor will set the price and quantity if it remains the sole producer, but they must draw attention to the fact that the monopolist price might be higher than the price charged by a competitive block using the old technology. Nevertheless, you should then point out that given that the inventor can engage in a price war, its new technology can become an effective barrier to entry.

(d) This is a question about the incentives which competitive firms have to invest in R&D. Had there been no patenting right, the long run equilibrium suggests that firms will only have normal profits. In a regime of perfect information, this would mean that the firm will have neither the funds nor the incentive to engage in R&D. In a case like (b) above we can see how the benefits of the invention are shared. After all, even if other firms make normal profits, with the new technology market price will be lower than before. Hence, at least some of the benefits from the invention are passed on to consumers directly. Naturally, the problem hidden in this question is about how to reconcile the commonly used static concept of efficiency, with its dynamic consequences.

▓ QUESTION 7

Consider a monopolist who faces a demand with constant price elasticity.

(a) Draw the initial equilibrium in the market.

(b) Suppose now that there is an increase in the marginal cost. What will now be the new equilibrium in the market? What will happen to consumers' expenditure and to the operational profits (i.e. assume no fixed costs) per unit of output?

(c) Suppose that the cost function can be written as: $C(x) = MC(x)/2x$, 10. By how much will the profit per unit of output change, had marginal costs risen by 20%?

Answer

This is a slightly more demanding question than usual. It deals with a monopolist who faces a non-linear demand. For simplicity's sake, we chose a demand with constant price elasticity.

(a) The initial set-up:

Constructing demand

To understand the implications of constant price elasticity for the demand schedule we must look at the concept of elasticity:

$$|\eta| = |\frac{dx}{dp} \frac{p}{x}|,$$

as

$$\eta = \text{constant} \quad \frac{p}{x} = \eta \frac{dp}{dx}.$$

This means that there is a constant relationship between the slope of the demand schedule (dp/dx) and the ray from the origin (p/x) see Figure 4.43.

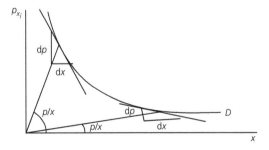

Figure 4.43

As p/x falls, so must (in absolute terms) the slope of the demand schedule.

Constructing the MR

The position of the MR relative to the demand schedule requires close examination. Assuming, of course that price elasticity is greater than unity, we have

$$MR = p_x \left[1 - \frac{1}{|\eta|} \right]$$

as

$$\frac{1}{|\eta|} = \alpha (< 1)$$

$$\left[1 - \frac{1}{|\eta|} \right] = \beta (< 1),$$

hence,

$$MR = \beta p_x,$$

where α and β are constants.

This means that the MR is a fixed proportion of the price. This means that we have Figure 4.44. The complete initial set-up is therefore:

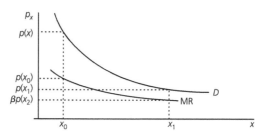

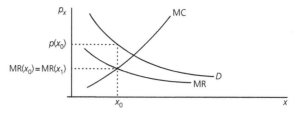

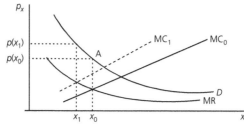

Figure 4.44

(b) An increase in the marginal cost.

We move from A to B. Price will increase and the quantity supplied will decrease. As the constant price elasticity is greater than unity, consumers' expenditures will fall. To see what will happen to profits per unit, we must examine the following expression:

$$\pi(x_0) = \frac{p_x^0 x_0 - c_0}{x_0} <> \pi(x_1) = \frac{p_x^1 x_0 - c_1}{x_1},$$

which is

$$p_x^0 - AC(x_0) <> p_x^1 - \hat{A}C(x_1).$$

We know that the price has gone up and that the quantity of x is now smaller. However, as there has been an increase in costs, we cannot be sure what will happen to the profit per unit.

(c) We now have a specific cost function to consider.

We begin by writing the conditions of optimal production:

$$\pi(x^*) = p_x(x^*)x^* - c(x^*)$$

$$= p_x(x^*)x^* - mc(x^*)\frac{x^*}{2}$$

as

$$mc(x^*) = \beta p_x(x^*) \quad \text{thus} \quad \frac{mc(x^*)}{\beta} = p_x$$

$$\pi(x^*) = \frac{mc(x^*)}{\beta}x^* - mc(x^*)\frac{x^*}{2}$$

$$= mc(x^*)x^*\left[\frac{1}{\beta} - \frac{1}{2}\right] = mc(x^*)x^*\gamma.$$

Thus the profit per unit becomes:

$$\frac{\pi(x^*)}{x^*} = mc(x^*)\gamma,$$

where γ is a constant. Hence, if marginal costs increase by 20% (which will lead to a fall in output and an increase in price as described in (b)), profits per unit will increase by 20%.

QUESTION 8

A unique art gallery for postdeconstructionalist neo-postmodernist art, Pomposity, faces a particular demand. One group of people may visit the gallery provided that the price of a visit is never below p. The other, will not visit the gallery if the price is above p. Thus, the demand facing the art gallery is kinked at price p.

(a) Under which conditions is the marginal cost likely to intersect the marginal revenue twice? What will be the equilibrium outcome in such a case?

(b) Under which conditions is the marginal cost likely not to intersect with the marginal revenue at all? What will be the equilibrium outcome in such a case?

Answer

This is a question about a monopolist which faces a kinked demand schedule. There are, therefore, two possibilities:

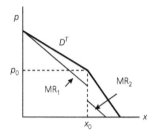 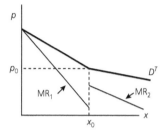

Figure 4.45

At $p = p_0$ the price elasticities of the two sections of demand are different (see Figure 4.45). The question is when will the MR of group 1 lie above MR of group 2 and when will it lie below it.

Recall that:

$$MR_1(x_0) = p_0 \left(1 - \frac{1}{|\eta_1|}\right) > MR_2(x_0) = p_0 \left(1 - \frac{1}{|\eta_2|}\right),$$

when

$$|\eta_1| > |\eta_2|.$$

This case is depicted in the left-hand diagram. The opposite case is depicted in the right-hand diagram.

(a) The answer to this question depends on whether $MR_1 < MR_2$. This is clearly the case in the above right-hand diagram shown in Figure 4.46.

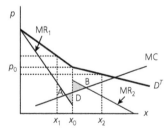

Figure 4.46

There are now two possible situations. One, where the equilibrium is at A, and another, when equilibrium is at B. In both cases, MR=MC. To determine the correct equilibrium we start from A, to the left of which it is evidently in the interest of the producer to produce more (when MR is above MC it means that every extra unit produced will raise profits). Should the producer move from A to B? As we begin moving from A to B we see that between A and D, MC > MR. It means that every unit produced between A and D will reduce profits. This loss is captured by the shaded triangle between A and D. However, as we move from D to B, the MR > MC and profits accumulate. Thus, the answer to whether the producer will produce at A or B depends on whether the shaded loss triangle is greater or smaller than the clear gain triangle between D and B.

(b) In this case, the price elasticity of demand for group 1 is greater than that of group 2.

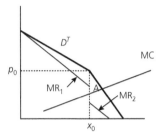

Figure 4.47

We can see again that up to point A in Figure 4.47, the producer accumulates profits (MR > MC). Any extra unit will have to be sold to group 2 and for them, the MC > MR. Hence, the equilibrium will be at A when the monopolist only sells to group 1.

▓ QUESTION 9

Consider a monopolist who faces a linear demand ($p(x) = \alpha - \beta x$) and a cost function $C(x) = cx$.

(a) Describe the initial equilibrium.

(b) How can one measure the inefficiency generated by the monopolist if $\alpha = 1000$ $\beta = 2$ and $c = 100$?

(c) In general, what will happen to price elasticity of demand, equilibrium price and quantity if there was an increase in β?

(d) What, in such a case, will happen to the inefficiency created by the monopolist?

Answer

A simple monopolist question.

(a) Given the shape of the cost function ($C(x) = cx$) the marginal cost is a constant c as shown in Figure 4.48.

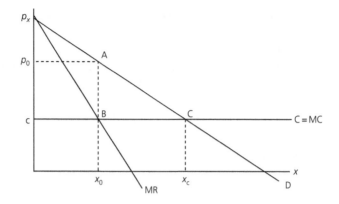

Figure 4.48

The initial equilibrium is given by

$$R(x) = p(x)x \quad \text{hence} \quad R(x) = (\alpha - \beta x)x = \alpha x - \beta x^2$$

$$MR(x) = \frac{dR}{dx} = \alpha - 2\beta x.$$

At equilibrium:

$$MR(x) = MC(x)$$

$$\alpha - 2\beta x = c,$$

hence

$$x_0 = \frac{\alpha - c}{2\beta}$$

$$p_0 = \alpha - \beta x_0 = \alpha - \beta \frac{\alpha - c}{2\beta} = \frac{\alpha + c}{2}.$$

(b) To calculate the deadweight loss we must calculate the area of the triangle ABC. To do this, we must calculate the distance between C and B and the distance between A and B:

The distance CB:

$$x_c = \frac{\alpha - c}{\beta} \quad \text{hence} \quad x_c - x_0 = \frac{\alpha - c}{2\beta}.$$

The distance AB:

$$p_0 - c = \frac{\alpha + c}{2} - c = \frac{\alpha - c}{2}$$

$$\text{Area} \quad \Delta = \frac{1}{2}\left[\frac{(\alpha - c)}{2}\frac{(\alpha - c)}{2\beta}\right] = \frac{(\alpha - c)^2}{8\beta}$$

(c) Price elasticity:

$$\eta_{x,p} = \frac{dx}{dp}\frac{p}{x}$$

$$\frac{dp}{dx} = -\beta \quad \frac{dx}{dp} = \frac{1}{dp/dx} = -\frac{1}{\beta}3,$$

hence

$$\eta_{x,p} = -\frac{1}{\beta}\left[\frac{\alpha - \beta x}{x}\right] = -\frac{1}{\beta x} + 1.$$

Clearly, an increase in β (which will make the slope of the demand schedule steeper) will increase the number associated with price elasticity (which means, in absolute values, that demand becomes less elastic). The equilibrium quantity will fall, but the price will remain unchanged!

(d) It is easy to see that an increase in β will reduce the inefficiency created by the monopolist in the sense that the deadweight loss will be smaller.

▤ QUESTION 10

The demand for pop music CDs is comprised of the 'young' who are addicted to music and the 'young at heart' who have a more discerning taste. The industry is competitive, but for the 'young' the purchase of new CDs is also a cause for disruptive and unsocial behaviour. A pressure group, 'the sound of silence' which is combating noise pollution proposes to levy a unit tax on the 'young', in order to reduce the amount of new CDs purchased.

(a) Describe the initial set-up of the industry.

(b) Analyse the effects of the proposal on CD price, consumers' spending, number of firms, and the quantity of CDs purchased by each group. Will the objective of the pressure group be achieved?

(c) A young support group argued that the objectives of the pressure group could be better fulfilled if instead of taxing the young, a subsidy per CD were to be offered to the older group (young at heart). In this way, claim the support group, the industry will not suffer and the composition of the market will serve as an inducement for more 'moderate' music.

    (i) Analyse the effect of such a proposal and compare it with your answer to (b).

    (ii) Evaluate the claim of the support group.

Answer

In this question students were expected to conduct an analysis of a competitive industry where there are two different groups of consumers. It is important to note that although the two groups of consumers differ in their taste for pop music, they are all consumers of the same type of music. The difference in their taste will therefore manifest itself through difference in price elasticity. The 'young at heart' are more likely to have a demand with price elasticity greater than unity while the brutally 'young' will have an inelastic demand schedule.

(a) The initial set-up (Figure 4.49).

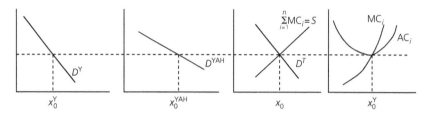

Figure 4.49

(b) The imposition of a unit tax on the young will cause a shift to the left of their demand (Figure 4.50).

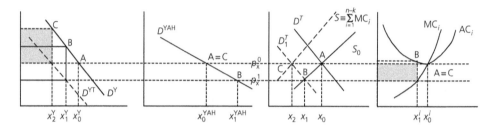

Figure 4.50

In the short run, this will cause a fall in aggregate demand for pop music which will reduce the equilibrium price. We move from A to B in Figure 4.50.

The total amount of pop CD in the market will fall and firms will be making losses. The 'young at heart', however, who have an elastic demand will purchase more of the music and will spend more on it. The 'young' will buy less, but their spending on music (including taxes) will be greater than it was originally (at A).

In the long run, if taxes are not used to fund the firms' losses, some firms will leave the market and supply will shift to the left. This will cause an increase in the equilibrium price until we end at point C. The total amount of pop CDs will be smaller, though the price returns to its original level. Firms will be in long run equilibrium, producing as much as before but with fewer firms in the industry. The 'young at heart' will be in the same position as before the tax while the 'young' will buy even fewer CDs and their spending on them will increase further.

(c) A subsidy to the 'young at heart' will increase their demand at any given price (Figure 4.51).

In the short run, aggregate demand will increase leading to an increase in equilibrium price. Firms will increase their output (to match MC with the new price) and total amount of CDs in equilibrium will rise (A to B). The 'young' will now buy fewer CDs and spend more on pop music. The 'young at heart' will buy more and spend more too (their private spending is denoted by the move from A to B', the subsidy is paid by the government).

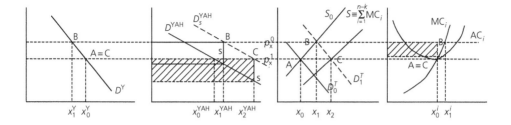

Figure 4.51

In the long run, firms will enter the industry and supply will increase. Equilibrium price will fall back to its original level but at a higher level of output (each firm produces as before but there are more firms). The 'young' will return to their original position while the 'young at heart' will spend more (at C') and buy more CDs.

(ii) Evaluating the claim of the young support group: taxing the 'young' will yield an outcome where the market will be smaller with the same quantity demanded from the 'young at heart'. The 'young' will buy less and therefore, the market share of the 'young at heart' will have to be greater. A similar result will emerge from the second proposal. However, if the total number of CDs purchased by the 'young' has an impact on the noise (as one would expect), then only the first option will have an absolute effect on the number of CDs bought by the 'young'.

■ QUESTION 11

The R&D department of a monopolist discovered a new technology with which commodity x can be produced. The good news about the new technology is that it considerably reduces the marginal cost. The bad news is that due to the delicacy of the new technique, the maintenance costs of the new technology are very high indeed.

(a) Describe the initial monopolist equilibrium.

(b) How would the introduction of the new technology affect the equilibrium outcome?

(c) Is it possible that the monopolist will refuse to employ the new technology in spite of the low level of marginal costs which are associated with it?

Answer

(a) The initial monopolist equilibrium is merely a reproduction of a standard textbook diagram. We shall not repeat it here.

(b) and **(c)** The monopolist must decide whether to employ a new technology. The main characteristics of this new technology are that they reduce the marginal costs but due to its technological delicacy, the cost of maintenance is very high. The first things we expected students to observe is that the new technology has higher fixed costs (at the beginning) and lower marginal costs. This means that the monopolist must choose between points A and B in Figure 4.52.

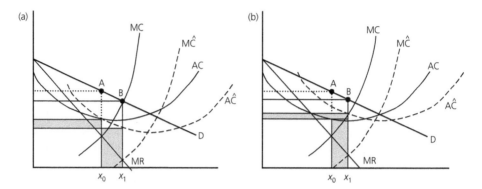

Figure 4.52

There are now two possible situations. In Figure 4.52(a) we have the case where it will not be in the interest of the monopolist to employ the new technology. I am afraid that the diagrams are not very clear but I will try and explain it clearly. In this case, Figure 4.52(a), the level of new average costs at the higher level of output is clearly higher than the level of AC at the initial optimal output. As we move from A to B, the increase in revenue will be captured by the area under the MR. However, comparing to the original situation, total costs will have risen by the area around the edges of the old cost box (AC multiplied by x). In this case, the entire increase in revenue is contained (and thus offset) in the increase in costs. Therefore, comparing the profits at A and B it is clear that as the move will cause greater increases in costs than in revenue, profits at B will be lower than at A.

In Figure 4.52(b), the level of average costs at the new optimal output is lower than that at A. Again, the area under the marginal revenue denotes the increase in revenue. The change in costs, however, contains a decrease (which the area above the original cost box) as well as an increase (the area to the right of the original box). The former depicts fall in costs and the latter increase. It is easy to see that while the answer is not definite, only in such a case can the profits at B be greater than the profits at A.

■ **QUESTION 12**

A competitive market for commodity x is supplied by two types of firms: private profit making corporations and charities. Because charities employ people with special needs, the government pays part of their wages. Price elasticity of demand for x is greater than unity.

(a) Describe the initial long run equilibrium in the market for x.

(b) Compare the input mix used by a typical corporation and the mix used by charities.

(c) To help charities further, the government considers whether to increase its wage subsidy to charities or to tax wages in private corporations:

   (i) analyse the effects of each option on the market price, consumers' spending and the output of each group of suppliers;

   (ii) if the aim of the government is to increase the employment of special needs individuals, which of the two options would be a better policy and why?

Answer

A competitive industry is supplied by profit maximizing firms as well as charities. We do not spell out the objective function of the charities except for noting that they employ people with special needs. We assume that the government supports the charities by offering a wage subsidy for the special needs employees.

   (a) *The long run set-up* (Figure 4.53).

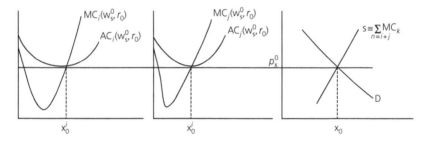

Figure 4.53

The type of labour employed by the charities suggests that they produce x with an inferior technology. Namely, the cost of producing any quantity of x is greater for the charities than it is for the profit maximizing agent. Without the government subsidy they will not be able to stay in the market. We therefore assume that the subsidy is sufficiently large to allow all charities to operate at the same equilibrium level of cost as the profit maximizing firms. The left-hand diagram depicts a typical charity while the diagram in the middle represents the profit maximizing agent. The right-hand diagram captures the entire market. We start at initial equilibrium where price equals marginal and minimum average cost for all agents. Note, however, that the wage bill facing the charities is different from the one which is paid out by profit maximizing agents.

   (b) The choice of input mix (technology) (Figure 4.54).

   The profit maximizing agent will choose the input mix as described in the left-hand diagram. The right-hand diagram depicts the choice made by the charity. As the cost of labour for the charity is lower than the cost of labour for the competitive industry, they will choose a more labour intensive technology.

   (c) We now consider the effects of an increase in wage subsidy for charities (Figure 4.55).

An increase in subsidy for the charities will shift their AC and MC downwards (see Figure 4.55).

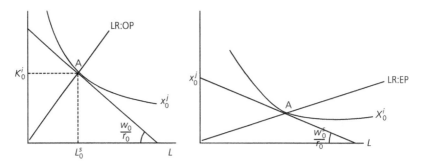

Figure 4.54

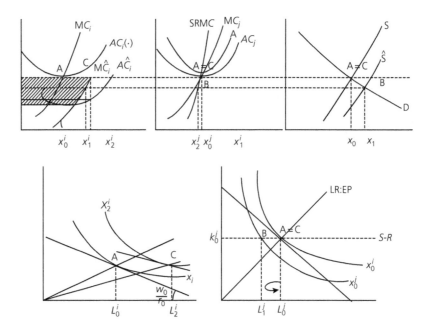

Figure 4.55

The short run analysis: At the given market price, charities may be willing to sell more of the good (we implicitly suggest that they wish to maximise their profits although these are not distributed to any shareholder). This will cause excess supply in the market which will reduce equilibrium price to p_x^1. At the new price, the charities will now produce x_1^i each while the other agents will produce at x_1^j. Charities now have a small surplus while the other agents make losses.

In the choice of inputs diagram it is clear that charities will now move to point B where they employ more workers per unit of output as well as produce more x. Profit maximizing agents will face the same factor prices but will produce less. As the total output in the industry increases from

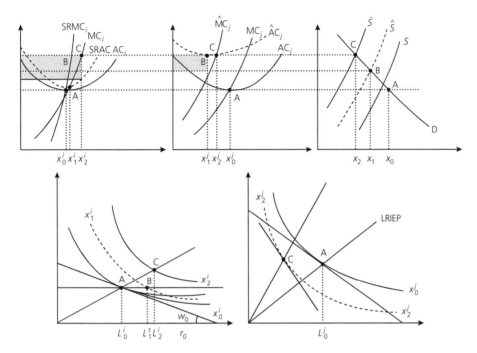

Figure 4.56

x_0 to x_1 the share of charities increased and therefore, the number of people employed in the industry will increase too.

The long run analysis: Some of the profit maximizing agents will leave the markets. As they do so, the supply will shift to the left and prices will begin to rise. This, in turn, will reduce the losses of the remaining firms and increase the surplus of charities. As charities are not guided by surplus maximization when they choose their field of work (although they may, in our story, try and maximize this surplus wherever they work) there will be no entry of new charities. Thus, long run equilibrium will be established at point C where the price will return to its original level. Profit maximizing agents will make zero profits above the normal, while charities will have a considerable surplus. As price increases, so will the output produced by each charity. Hence, the effect of the policy will be to increase the market share of charities, and, subsequently, increase the level of employment of special need individuals in the industry.

Taxes on the wages bill of private-corporations

A tax on wages paid by the private corporations will cause a shift upward of both AC and MC (Figure 4.57).

The short run analysis: Private firms will now wish to reduce their production to equate their new MC with the existing price. A fall in output will cause excess demand for the good and price will rise to p_x^1. At this price, private firms will produce x_1^i and will make losses while charities will produce x_1^i and make a surplus.

The long run analysis: Private firms will now leave the market until the price reaches p_x^2. Here, the remaining private firms will make zero profits above the normal and produce less than they did before the policy was implements. Charities will have a surplus and produce much more (point C).

Altogether, the subsidy to wages case produced a greater share for charities, more employment of people with special needs and an increase in consumers' spending in the market for x (price elasticity of demand greater than unity). In the case of tax on wages, the share of charities increased, employment of people with special needs increased, and consumers' spending on x fell.

It seems as if the employment of people with special needs under the wage subsidy will be greater than under the tax scheme, as a similar increase in the charities market share will be supported not only by an increase in number of people with special needs employed which is due to the increase in output, but also because the entire production by charities will be more labour intensive.

On the other hand, this is a costly option. In the tax case the government managed to improve the position of charities and people with special needs, and, at the same time, raise taxes.

NOTES

1. Exogenous variables are those elements of the problem the values of which are known. Endogenous variables are those elements of the problem the values of which are determined by the model. Hence, in our analysis of consumers, individuals chose the quantities of x and y (which are the endogenous variables) for any given level of prices and income (which are the exogenous variables). In a system of simultaneous equations: $ax + by = c$ and $dx + ey = f$, x and y are the endogenous variables while (a, b, c, d, e, f) are the exogenous variables.

2. $\frac{MU_x}{MU_y} = \frac{p_x}{p_y} \Rightarrow p_x = \frac{MU_x}{MU_y} p_y$.

3. Excess supply is simply a negative excess demand.

4. $AC(x) \cdot x = \frac{c}{x} \cdot x = C$.

5. $\frac{MU_x}{MU_y} = \frac{p_x^0}{p_y^0} \Rightarrow p_x^0 = \frac{MU_x}{MU_y} p_y^0$, where $\frac{MU_x}{MU_y}$ is measuring units of y per x.

6. We can also show this point formally. At the tangency point, the slope of the average costs curve (dAC/dx) equals to the slope of the demand schedule (dp/dc). Hence:

$$\frac{dp}{dx} = \frac{dAC}{dx} = \frac{d(c(x)/x)}{dx} = \frac{(dc/dx)x - c(x)}{x^2} = \frac{MC}{x} - \frac{c(x)}{x^2}.$$

We must now multiply both sides by x:

$$\frac{dp}{dx}x = MC - \frac{c(x)}{x} = MC - AC$$

$$\Rightarrow \quad AC + \frac{dp}{dx}x = MC.$$

We can now see that if $AC = p$, MR must be equal to MC. Recall that $MR(x) = p + (dp/dx)x$.

$$\frac{dp}{dx}x = MC - \frac{c(x)}{x} = MC - AC$$

Hence:

$$\Rightarrow \quad AC + \frac{dp}{dx}x = p + \frac{dp}{dx}x = MR(x) = MC(x)$$

7. Naturally, our answers regarding the effectiveness of the Nash equilibrium may change if we considered the fact that most games are not played once. Had the game been a repeated game than other issues of commitment and reputation may come into play. If our two criminals faced the same ordeal every year and a half, they will learn from each other actions. This is a very rich a full theory which we shall not develop at this stage of your learning.

5 | The market for factors

MAJOR POINTS IN SUMMARY

- Demand and supply of labour derived from the behavioural models of consumers and firms (utility maximization and the supply of labour, profit maximization and the demand for labour)
- Factors affecting labour market equilibrium (unions).

5.1 Capital, labour, and distribution

Up to this stage we have investigated how individuals and firms make their decisions with regard to demand and supply of goods but we have not discussed what it is that determines the prices of factors of production (like labour and capital). To some extent, there is no obvious reason why we should devote a special chapter to factor markets. In a world where the economic problem is that of reconciling unsatiated wants with scarcity, the concept of price which is derived from this definition is that of opportunity cost. It means that only those things which are both scarce and desirable will have a price tag attached to them in terms of other goods. Subsequently, means of production with a price tag attached to them must simply be economic goods. All of Chapter 4 was devoted to how economic goods are being priced under different forms of market structure. Why, then, must we discuss the market for means of production separately?

There are three main reasons for this need:

(a) The reversal in the position of agents: in the factor market it is the behaviour of the firm from which demand is derived while the behaviour of individuals is the origin of supply.

(b) The differences in the type of goods used in the production process (for instance, the difference between labour and capital).

(c) The effects of market equilibrium on the distribution of income are much more evident than in other markets.

The reversal in the position of agents (a) is not a matter of substance in itself. In a sense, we devote a special chapter to factor markets simply in order to consolidate your command over market analysis. However, at the same time there are some basic differences between the derivation of demand in the markets for final goods and the derivation of demand in markets of intermediate goods. While both consumption and production can be characterized as processes where agents use economic goods to produce other economic goods, in the case of consumption, the produced economic good is a non-tangible good (utility) without a clear market.

In production, however, we use economic goods (factors) to produce other economic goods which are clearly traded in the market. Hence, when we derive the optimal behaviour of an agent we must be conscious of the optimal conditions being maintained both in the market for factors as well as in the market for the produced good. This is not a serious departure from the type of market analysis conducted in Chapters 2 and 4, but it is a slightly more complex angle which will contribute to a better understanding of market analysis.

From the point of view of the difference in the type of means of production (b) this is obviously a much more serious issue. It is inevitably closely linked to point (c) about distribution. We have briefly discussed some of the intrinsic differences between the types of means of production in Chapter 3. We saw there that while there are clear intrinsic differences between them, from neoclassical perspectives this is irrelevant. Still, there are some difficulties which may become significant.

We can easily imagine what it means to use so much petrol in the process of production. This, being a **raw material** is simply paid the market price per unit of consumption. There is no conceptual difference between buying petrol for production and filling your car at the pump.

However, there is obviously a problem when we come to discuss capital. In principle, capital is a **stock**. At any point of time there are so many machines. But the production process is a **flow**. It describes the use of things over a given period of time determined by the time required for the production of each unit of output. In other words, at any point of time there could be a certain number of machines but the demand is not really for machines but rather for machine hours. How the need for machine hours relates to the demand for machines as such is a matter which we will not discuss here. In fact, the problem with some means of production being 'durable' (i.e. goods with a life span which covers more than one period) is not necessarily unique to the factor markets. There are durables in the consumption market as well. So while the markets for such goods require special attention, it is not specific to factor markets. It is also beyond the scope of this course.

Therefore, as far as capital is concerned we confine ourselves to the discussion of the use of capital in production rather than with machines themselves. We would want to know how many machine hours a firm would want to use during a period of time rather than how many machines it would buy. The best way of thinking about it is in terms of whether one would want to buy a good or to rent one. The considerations regarding the purchase of a good which lives over a long period of time are different but not unrelated to the considerations to rent it. When you visit a foreign country you would normally rent a car. But there are conditions under which you may prefer to buy a car at the beginning of the holiday and sell it at the end. Similarly, a firm operating in certain premises would not necessarily want either to buy or to rent the place. But from the point of view of the pure production process, we only consider the use of machine hours consumed in the production process. What, then, should determine the price (reward?) of such use?

As we said before, the only criterion in the use of means of production is that of efficiency (i.e. opportunity cost). But how easy is it to establish these criteria in the face of such different forms of means of production, and will factor markets deliver a satisfactory solution to this problem? Some of these issues are extremely difficult and this is not the right place to fully explore them. I would like you, however, to bear in mind that the appropriateness of the returns to factor may be of great significance. The ability of an organization to produce on its production function, or to reach the frontier of its technology (i.e. for means of production to generate the highest productivity), depends on the general acceptability of the principle which directs the distribution of the outcome of the collective action. In simple words, the question who gets what once output has been produced is very likely to influence whether one wants to put a lot or little effort at work.

To be sure, *Capital* is a complex notion which caused great feuds and drew a lot of blood. But the reason for this is not directly related to our current analysis. Recall that when we wrote the cost function we wrote w-wages as the return to labour and we wrote r-interest rate as the return to capital. With zero profits above the normal in a competitive environment this means that the national income is divided between a reward to work and a reward to capital. Naturally, this would not be a problem if all agents were both workers and owners of capital at the same time.[1] However, if there is a clear division between those who derive their income from wages and those who derive it from capital then dividing income between returns to labour and returns to capital immediately creates an obvious tension between labour and capital.

There are basically two layers to this problem. First there is the question of what is it that justifies rewarding capital at all. Second, there is a question of whether the parameter which governs the returns to capital is the right one. Namely, has the interest rate anything to do with capital's contribution to output?

Consider, for a moment, a plot of land with two individuals. Both of them had an initial stock of wheat seeds. One of them consumed the whole lot and the other chose not to turn all his stock into bread. In order to grow wheat, there is a need for both seeds and labour. The person who had no seeds left could not grow wheat. The person who had seeds left could now offer some seeds to maintain the worker (and himself) during the production period as well as seeds to be sown. Who, then, should get the yield of the field (note that no one owns the land)? Should it be the worker, who did all the work, or should it be the person who advanced the seeds (the capital)? The answer is far from obvious and scholars have argued about this endlessly. Whatever one thinks, it is important to bear in mind that even without ownership of land there could be reasons to justify returns to both workers and capitalists. The returns to work is obvious but the returns on the capital can be justified on the grounds of abstinence as well as risk. For one, the capitalist abstained from consuming that part of his stock which was then used for the production of the new crop. Second, while the worker entered a contract whereby his return was agreed and guaranteed, the capitalist could not have known whether the field will yield any crops at all. Hence, while the worker has a secured return, the return to capital depends on nature.

For those who believe that goods have intrinsic value and that value is the labour embodied in them, the idea that someone else (other than the workers) should be rewarded for it is unacceptable. But even if one believes that the essence of economic goods is the fact that they are all products of human efforts (not, of course, the neoclassical view which we are exploring here), this does not necessitate the conclusion that people who contribute indirectly to the production process should not be rewarded. There were quite a few liberal classical economists who felt that the value of things must reflect their labour values but they still thought that there is a good reason to reward the 'capitalist'.

There are further issues associated with the significance of the remuneration which the factors receive. We are not currently trying to understand this in full, but as the concept of price in our story is that of opportunity cost we can see why the price of capital is based on the interest rate. This is so because when someone buys a machine and rents it out, he expects to get for it at least as much as he would have received had he saved the money for the machine in a bank instead. In such a case, he would have received the interest rate for this money (we shall discuss this further in the section of money and banks). The interest rate for using the machine over the year is, therefore, the owner's opportunity cost. Strangely enough, while the return for capital can quite easily be explained through the concept of opportunity cost, this is far more complex as far as labour is concerned. As we shall see further below, wages are the opportunity cost of leisure and not of work. So, unlike capital, the wages are not what workers would get if they worked; it is what they will lose if they had more leisure. This means that whether on the grounds of intrinsic differences or for the way in which we examine their remuneration, there are some asymmetries in the system of production which may need further examination.

These are all very important issues and although there is a great deal more to be said about them, they are not part of the domain of this course. Nevertheless, as economics is a language, the intellectual context from where its concepts have been derived is very important for a proper understanding of many contemporary debates. Nowadays, as the perception of the firm becomes more institutionally oriented, many elements representing the real competition between members of society for the greater share in the collective output may resurface. However, instead of basing this on the intrinsic properties of the agents or the position in the production process, it all becomes a question of power which is derived from ownership. The questions, however, of who should get what and why remain unchanged.

5.2 The demand for factors

The demand for factors of production comes from the firm: the producing agent. It is, in our case, the other side of the coin in the analysis of profit maximization. Recall that the profit function is

$$\pi = R(x) - C(x) = p_x x - wL - rK$$

where L stands for labour and K for capital.

Table 5.1 Technology of wheat production

Units of labour	Output in wheat (kg)
0	0
1	1100
2	2000
3	2750
4	3200
5	3600
6	3900
7	4100
8	4000
9	4000

As was suggested in the previous section, the price of labour is wages (w) and the price of capital is the interest rate (r). The aim of the firm is to maximize profit. We must now inquire what that would mean in terms of choosing a certain input.

Consider a field of a given size where only wheat is grown. Suppose, also, that only labour, in addition to land, is required for the production of wheat. Table 5.1 is the technology of wheat production.

How many workers will an owner of a field wish to employ if his objective is to maximize the output (as we have only one commodity here, maximizing profit and maximizing output will be the same thing)? If he could, he would want to employ eight and pay each one of them nothing. But as people will only work for him if he agreed in advance to pay them something, his considerations are slightly more complex.

To begin with we must assume something about the market for labour. The assumption with which we will start is that it is a competitive market. From what we have established earlier, this would mean that there is a *single* price in the market. In other words, all workers get the same wages. Given the property of diminishing returns to factor it is clear which principle should guide the land owner in his hiring policy.

Diminishing marginal product means that the contribution of each worker is different. As all of them get the same wages, some would contribute more than they get, some might contribute less than what they get. Those who contribute more will increase the land owner's profit and those who contribute less will reduce his profits. Let us, therefore, examine the contribution of the workers. Figure 5.1 depicts the marginal product of workers measured in terms of wheat. As you must be aware by now, the area underneath the marginal product curve denotes the total output. Hence, if you look at four workers, the marginal product of the fourth worker is 450 kg of wheat. If we employed four workers the total product will be the sum of all the workers' contributions. The contribution of the first worker (which is $1100 \times 1 = 1100$) is given by the first column in the above diagram. The contribution of the second worker ($900 \times 1 = 900$) is the second column. Altogether, the total output will be the sum of these four columns, which is nothing else but the sum of the workers' marginal products. It is, therefore, $1100 + 900 + 750 + 450 = 3200$ which is indeed the output of four workers as given by the technology Table 5.1.

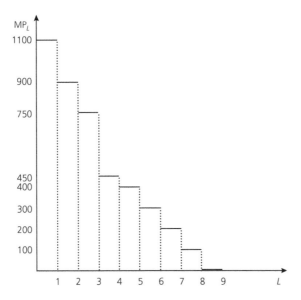

Figure 5.1 Returns to labour as a factor.

Suppose now that the wage level is 700 kg per worker. If we employed one worker only, his contribution will be 1100 and what we must pay him will only be 700. This means that we shall have a profit of $1100 - 700 = 400$. Hence, it is worth our while to employ at least one worker. If we chose to employ two workers we would still have to pay them 700 kg each. We know that the first worker will contribute (i.e. his marginal product) more than he will be taking away (his wages). The second worker contributes 900 which is still more than he takes home. Hence, by employing two workers we will have 400 kg profit on the first worker and $900 - 700 = 200$ kg profit on the second worker (600 altogether). The third worker contributes 750 kg so his contribution to profit is $750 - 700 = 50$ kg. The left-hand side of Figure 5.2, depicts the distribution of wages and profits when wages are at 700 kg and we employ three workers. The figure on the right depicts the case of employing four workers. As you can see, the contribution of the fourth worker is only 450 kg. As we must pay him the going rate he will take away 700 kg in wages. Our profits, which we have accumulated on the previous three workers will now have to fall in order to pay the fourth worker the difference between his contribution and his wages. As his contribution is only 450 kg and we must pay him 700 kg, our profits will have to fall by 250 kg.

Note that the area between the marginal product line and the wage line depicts our profit, it will therefore be maximized with three workers as the difference between the fourth worker's contribution and wages will have to be deducted from the accumulated profit. In other words, employing three workers will give us the profits of $(1100 - 700) + (900 - 700) + (750 - 700) = 650$ kg. The profit when employing four workers will be $(1100 - 700) + (900 - 700) + (750 - 700) + (450 - 700) = 650 - 250 = 400$ kg.

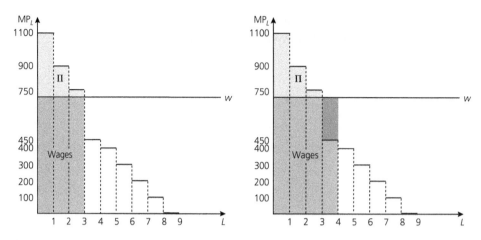

Figure 5.2 Wage bills and profits.

With a more general and smooth production function the above situation will look as shown in Figure 5.3.

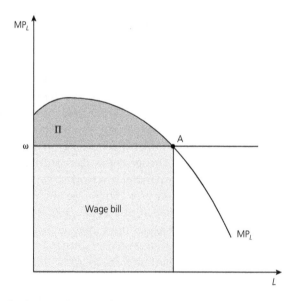

Figure 5.3 A generalized marginal product function.

If we employ L_0 workers at the wages of ω (which is the wages in terms of the good produced, like wheat in our story), the total output will be the area underneath the curve up to point A (this is simply the summing up of all contributions). Of this area, ωL_0 is the total size of the wage bill and the difference is the profit. As is quite clear from the above, profits will be maximized whenever we choose to employ so many workers as to equate the marginal product of the last worker with his, or her, wages. This is so because of the diminishing nature of the returns to factor. The unit labour before L_0 has a marginal product which is above the wage level while the unit labour above L_0 has a marginal product which is below the wage level. In the former case profits are augmented, in the latter, they diminish.

What if there are more than one means of production? The answer remains unchanged. Assuming interdependence in the production process (i.e. that we cannot produce the good with only one means of production), whether or not there is another factor of production does not alter the fact that the area underneath the marginal product of any means of production depicts the total output. The difference in our analysis will be that the area between the wage line and the marginal product will no longer depict profits alone. Instead, it will be that part of our output which will be used to pay the other means of production as well as profit. Hence, if in our previous story employing three workers generates a profit of 650 kg, but we needed to hire tractor hours (capital) as well, then the profit will be 650 (the cost of capital). Nevertheless, the principle according to which labour should be employed optimally remains unchanged: we should employ so many workers up to the point where wages (measured in terms of output) = marginal product (which too, is measured in units of output). The same can be extended to all means of production.

We have already discussed the principles which will guide the firm in choosing the optimal mix of means of production. These were that the market rate of exchange between labour and capital would be the same as their technological rate of exchange. Namely, $w/r = MP_L(K)/MP_K(L)$ units of capital per labour.[2] This is depicted Figure 5.4.

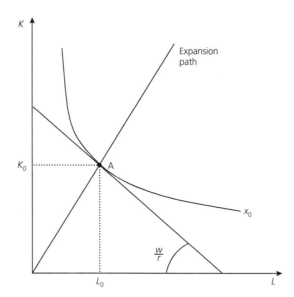

Figure 5.4 Optimal input mix.

But the **demand for factors** is derived by answering the following question: how many units of a particular input would you want to use assuming all other factors to the fixed?

The answer which we produced was very simple and straightforward. If you only vary one means of production and the market for it is competitive, employ so many units of that means of production as to equate its marginal product with its wages.

If we produce good x with K and L then this would mean the following:

(i) that the wages (in terms of the good we produce) is $\omega = w/p_x$ which is the nominal wages (w) divided by the price of the good; and it must be the same as marginal product of labour for any given level of capital (K):

$$\omega = w/p_x = \mathrm{MP}_L(K).$$

Or, in slight different terms, that:

$$p_x\mathrm{MP}_L(K) = w$$

which means that the *money value* of the marginal product (or the **Marginal Revenue Product of Labour**) equals the nominal wages.

(ii) that the return to capital (in terms of the good we produce) is $\rho = r/p_x$ which is the return to capital measured in terms of the specific good produced; and it must be the same as the marginal product of capital for any given level of labour (L):

$$\rho = r/p_x = \mathrm{MP}_K(L).$$

Or, in slight different terms, that:

$$p_x\mathrm{MP}_K(L) = r$$

which means that the *money value* of the marginal product (or the **Marginal Revenue Product of Capital**) equals the nominal return to factors. Note that the two conditions which we have just set are perfectly consistent with the profit maximizing principle which guided our choice of input mix. We can rewrite the above two conditions that $p_x\mathrm{MP}_K(L) = r$ and $p_x\mathrm{MP}_L(K) = w$ as

$$p_x = \frac{w}{\mathrm{MP}_L(K)} = \frac{r}{\mathrm{MP}_K(L)}$$

$$\frac{w}{r} = \frac{\mathrm{MP}_L(K)}{\mathrm{MP}_K(L)}$$

which means choosing a combination of labour and capital such that the units of capital one would need to pay per unit of labour will be exactly the same as the quantity of capital which is needed to substitute the productivity of one unit of labour.

In the short run, the quantity of capital is fixed. Hence, every increase in labour input will cause a greater fall in productivity than the case where an increase in labour is accompanied by an increase in capital. The left-hand side of Figure 5.5 depicts the firm's profit maximization considerations in terms of both goods. The right-hand diagram depicts the demand for labour in the short and in the long run assuming the price of output as fixed (this allows us to look at the real wage and the physical marginal product rather than the nominal wage and the Marginal Revenue Product. We begin at A. When the quantity of

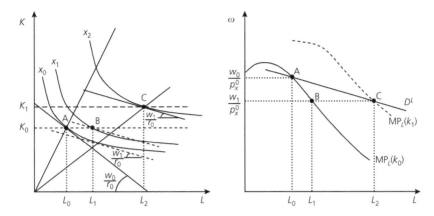

Figure 5.5 When short-term capital is fixed.

capital is fixed, increase in labour will produce a fall in productivity (as many more people are using a fixed number of machines) as depicted by $MP_L(K_0)$.

When there is a fall in the nominal wage (w), for a given output price, real wages ($\omega = w/p_x$) will fall too. In the left-hand diagram this means that we should now follow a new expansion path, but as we cannot change the capital in the short run we will now move to produce at point B where the *short run marginal cost equals the price*. At that point we use more labour with the initial level of capital. Hence, we move along the marginal product curve which corresponds to the initial level of capital from A to B.

However, had we been able to change the quantity of capital then for the same price of output we will move to point C which is the new long run optimal mix along the new expansion path. However, at C we use more capital too. This means that the productivity of any labour input would now be different as they have more capital at their disposal. As we did before, we can now draw the physical marginal product of labour when there is more capital at hand. Clearly, this marginal product will lie above the original marginal product curve. We therefore move from point B to point C. The long-run demand for labour by an individual firm will thus be crossing through different short run demands representing different levels of fixed capital. Obviously, the long run demand for labour will be more elastic than the short run demand for it.

The industry's demand

Unlike the market for final goods, in the factors' markets, market demand cannot be reached by the mere summation of the individual demand schedules which we have described above. The reason for this is that when, say, nominal wage falls, the cost of production of any quantity of output will fall. Subsequently, both marginal and average cost will fall and as a result there will be a change in the market price. A change in the market price will change the **marginal revenue product of labour**, or, in the alternative approach, will raise the real wages. Figure 5.6 captures this feature. In the left-hand side we conduct the analysis in terms of 'real wages'. In the right-hand side the analysis follows the more traditional marginal revenue product. Both figures depict the optimal conditions as given by

$$\omega = w/p_x = MP_L(K) \text{ ('real wage' approach)}$$

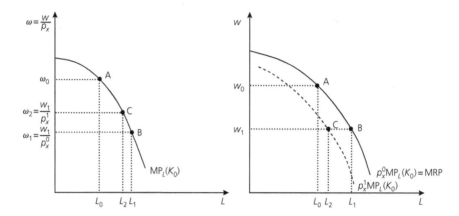

Figure 5.6 A change in nominal wages and the marginal product.

and

$$p_x MP_L(K) = w \text{ (marginal revenue product approach).}$$

This means that the left-hand side is measured in terms of the produced good (i.e. real terms) while the right-hand side is measured nominally (in money terms). The benefit of the marginal revenue product approach is that it allows the demand for factors to be comprised of agents from different industries. The 'real wage' approach is easier from the point of view of exposition but if there is more than one industry demanding the factor, we may run into serious problems of defining the price index.

We begin at an initial equilibrium at point A and we shall now examine how the comparative statics of a change in the wage level affects the individual demand for factors differently from the way it affects the industry's demand. When nominal wage (w) falls, for a given price of x, we will, in the short run, move to B in both figures. This means that every firm will want to produce more x (as we have more labour at B than we have at A but we have the same amount of capital).

Another way of seeing this is in recalling what the marginal cost of producing x will be when labour is the only variable factor.

$$MC(x) = w/MPL$$

as nominal wage (w) falls, the marginal costs of x fall too. This means that at any given price, each firm will want to produce more x so as to satisfy the profit maximization principle of producing so much x such that the marginal cost equals the price. Figure 5.7 depicts this situation.

As each firm produces more there is now excess supply in the market and the price of x will fall in the short run. As the price of x falls, we know from the analysis of the industry

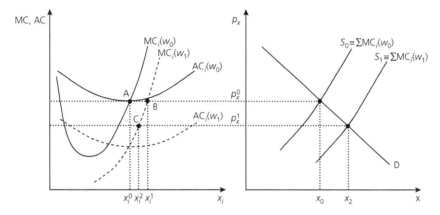

Figure 5.7 A change in the wage rate and optimal production.

that each firm will produce less than it did at B but more than it had done in A. Looking at the first set of figures we can see that this would mean a rise in the real wage such that instead of B, the firm will move in the short run to point C. In the right-hand side, the same story will be captured through the effect of the fall in the price of x on the marginal revenue product. As the price of x falls, the money value of the marginal product falls with it. The marginal revenue product will move to the left and the short run choice of the firm will be at point C.

Both diagrams yield the same conclusion. The demand for factor by each firm when the short run circumstances of industry are taken into consideration will be the move from A to C rather than from A to B. In the case of the MRP approach this means that the MRP cannot be simply summarized over all firms but in the case of the real wage approach this is very much the case: the move from A to C is still a move along the marginal product curve.

To some extent this is a bit of a 'red herring'. After all, when we derived the demand for goods by each individual, the demand schedule depended on the price of other goods. Naturally, when the price of a good falls, individuals will want to buy more of it but at the same time they will also change their demand for the other good. Hence, the price of the other good will change, also, and there will be a need to readjust the individual's demand schedule. These are important considerations but they are all part of our general equilibrium analysis. There is, as a matter of principle, no reason why we should not be able to conduct the analysis of a factor market while assuming the price of the output as unchanged.

5.3 Supply of labour

The supply of produced goods like capital or raw material is basically subject to the same principles of supply which we had set up in Chapters 3–4. There are, of course, the additional alterations needed to deal with durable as well as exhaustible resources but the fundamental principles will not be any different. We shall therefore skip the discussion of the supply of produced good and concentrate on the most specific and difficult means of production: labour.

5.3.1 Preferences

For labour to be an economic good it must be both desirable and scarce. While this is very much the case from the point of view of producers, as far as individuals are concerned its scarcity is evident but the desirability of labour is slightly more complex. Do we like to work? Would we prefer a combination of economic goods with a greater labour input on our part over the same combination when we need to work less? Alternatively, if we do like to work, and labour facilitates greater consumption opportunity, why do we not all exhaust ourselves? Or, do we?

To address these issues economists chose to look at labour as a *residual* of the decision-making process rather than the actual subject of it. To circumvent the problem whereby labour may not be a desirable good for individuals, we ask ourselves why people work and why they differ in the amount of work they do and, sometimes, in their response to changes in their wages? The answer we provide is that we work to earn and be able to buy economic goods but this does not make work itself an economic good. Work, for us, is nothing more than a bundle of goods which we can purchase with its returns. In addition, work comes at the expense of our leisure which, in the eyes of many, is an obvious economic good. We desire leisure and it is scarce. Hence, leisure is an economic good. Labour, then, becomes not a thing in itself but a transformation mechanism. That is, when we choose to have an extra hour in bed we forgo an hour of work with the return of which we could have purchased other economic goods. This implies that work in itself is meaningless to us. We only consider it as a means of getting other economic goods and as such it constitutes the opportunity cost of the only activity which can be construed as economic good: leisure.

I will not hide my view that this is unsatisfactory; that not only we have debased the notion of work below that which many people will be willing to accept, we have also raised a serious question mark on the ability of the rational utility maximizer to deal with the behaviour of economic agents. Still, at this stage we are merely setting the framework and in future studies one will be able to see that some attempts have been made to address these difficulties.

Setting, thus, a framework where labour is a residual and the subject of preferences is leisure, we must now turn to examine how this affects our analysis. To begin with, recall that when we described preferences and their representation by a utility function we said that in order for preferences to be representable they have to be *complete*. That is to say, at any point in time we can rank all possible bundles (consumption combinations) of all economic goods. We have now added one economic good called *leisure* which we will denote by L_e. Assuming that all other economic goods can be represented by an aggregate good called x, we can now write the utility function that will represent the preferences individuals have over the entire set of economic goods as follows:

$$u(x, L_e)$$

This function will have exactly the same properties as the utility function defined in Chapter 2. There, preferences were defined over the world of economic goods comprising of two types of clearly tangible goods (x and y). We have not really changed anything concerning that function. In a sense, what we have now is simply a function with one additional economic goods (i.e. $u(x, y, L_e)$) but as we wish to draw diagrams in two dimensions we have substituted x and y by one composite good—representing all such goods—called x. Figure 5.8 depicts these preferences in the new plane of leisure and consumption.

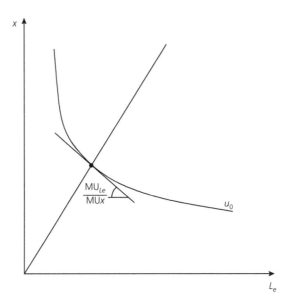

Figure 5.8 Preferences in consumption-leisure space.

Hence utility is rising when we have more of both goods (consumption (x) and leisure) and there is such a thing called marginal utility of leisure which we assume to be diminishing. As in Chapter 2, there are indifference points where we are equally satisfied with less consumption and more leisure or more consumption and less leisure. Indifference curves are convex and their slope is denoted by the subjective rate of substitution MU_{Le}/MU_x units of x per hour of leisure.

5.3.2 Scarcity (constraint)

What makes leisure different from produced goods is that its availability is fixed. It is, so to speak, restricted by nature. As we measure leisure by the hour, there are only 24 h of fun to be had. If we allow for the necessary 6 h beauty sleep, we are left with a maximum of 18 h of leisure. This, as can be easily understood, has nothing to do with the price of leisure. From what we said earlier, the opportunity cost (hence, the price) of leisure is the consumption of other goods which have been forgone by not using the same time to work and earn hourly wages. If w is the money wage per hour then it follows quite simply that the budget constraint which an individual confronts is the following:

$$p_x x = w(\bar{L} - L_e)$$

where $\bar{L}$ is the maximum level of leisure possible (our 18 h out of bed). This means that the amount of money we spend on consumption cannot exceed the amount of income we earn. The income we earn (in this world where there are no assets apart from our natural gifts) is simply the product of the hour wage rate and the number of hours worked. The latter is the difference between the natural length of the day and that part of it which we wish to use for leisure. Consequently, labour gets into the picture as being the residual of the decision to have leisure: $\bar{L} - L_e = L$ (labour). This means that individuals' supply of labour depends on their choice of leisure.

Rewriting our budget constraint will yield the following:

$$p_x x + w L_e = w\bar{L}$$

which suggests clearly that as p_x is the price of x, w (wages) is the price (the **opportunity cost**) of leisure.

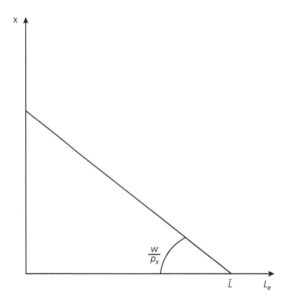

Figure 5.9 The budget constraint in consumption-leisure space.

Notice that the intercept of the budget line with the leisure axis is fixed by $\bar{L}$ and unlike the case in Chapter 2, nothing can move it. In Chapter 2 the intercept would be $I/p_i (i = x, y)$ which meant that a change in the price of one of the goods would affect the quantity of that good which an individual could purchase had he, or she, chosen to use their entire income to buy that good. In Figure 5.9 you can see that the amount of leisure to be had cannot exceed $\bar{L}$ regardless of either the price of the other good or the price of leisure itself.

The slope of the budget line can be easily understood if we start at $\bar{L}$. If we choose to stay in bed all day, we will be able to earn nothing and, subsequently, we will not be able to buy any quantity of the other good (x). Leaving home for one hour (moving to the left on the leisure axis) will produce a wage of an hour (w) with which we will be able to buy w/p_x units of x. Hence, the slope of the budget line, which represents the quantity of the other good which an hour of labour can command, is what we call the 'real wage'; it is the hourly wages measured in terms of consumption.[3]

5.3.3 Behaviour

Apart from the difference in the nature of the budget constraint, there is no difference between the way we analyse individual behaviour in the context of tangible goods and in the context of leisure. Hence, our individual will want to choose the most preferred combination of consumption and leisure. Given the shape of indifference curves and the fact that utility is rising with an increase in both leisure and consumption, such an optimal point is captured in the Figure 5.10. The highest indifference curves (hence, utility) which are feasible (within the budget set) is the one that is tangent to the budget constraint. At this point (A) the slopes of the indifference curve will be the same as the slope of the budget line. This means that the subjective rate of substitution between leisure and consumption will be the same as the market rate of substitution. In other words, at A, we are willing to pay MU_{Le}/MU_x units of consumption good x per hour of leisure. This, at A, is the same as the slope of the budget line which is the quantity of x we will pay, as a matter of fact, per hour of leisure we take. If we forgo one hour of work we will lose w/p_x units of x. If you are playing golf and all of a sudden your mobile phone

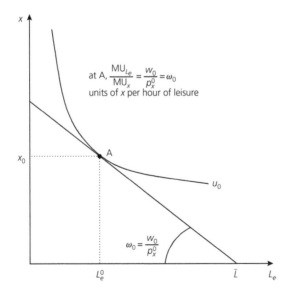

Figure 5.10 Optimality in consumption-leisure space.

rings and someone tells you that if you came to work for him for one hour he will pay you £2000. If the price of a holiday is £1000 not going to work for that hour and carrying on playing golf would have cost you two holidays. As you already take four holidays you may feel that you are willing to pay two holidays for the pleasure of one extra hour on the golf course. If you had had no holiday by the time the phone rings, you may feel that paying two holidays for one hour of golf is a price which you are not willing to pay. This would mean that the slope of your indifference curve is less than the market price (point B in the above diagram).

Formally, this problem takes the shape of

$$\max \quad u(x, L_e)$$
$$\text{s.t.} \quad p_x x = w(\bar{L} - L_e)$$

and its solution is exactly point A in the figure.

5.3.4 Deriving the supply of labour

Having established how rational agents choose their allocation of time, we must examine now how the time devoted to work varies when the cost of leisure (wages) changes (see Figure 5.11).

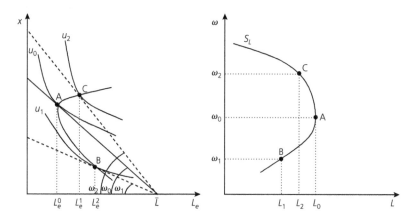

Figure 5.11 Deriving the supply of labour.

On the left we have the choices individuals make in the space of consumption and leisure. On the right we have the subsequent supply of labour.

We begin at point A. When the real wage is ω_0 (which means that the nominal wage is w_0) the choice of leisure is L_e^0 and, subsequently, the choice of labour is $L_0 = \bar{L} - L_e^0$.

When the wage level falls to ω_1 the nature of the indifference curves and the budget constraints suggests that we will choose a point like B where we have more leisure (L_e^1 and less work (L^1). Intuitively this will not cause any difficulty. When the opportunity cost of leisure is falling, we would like to have more leisure and work less.

We now go back to A. When the wage level increases to ω_2 we can see again that due to the specific nature of the budget constraint (we cannot have more than $\bar{L}$ hours of fun per day regardless of prices), we are likely to choose a point like C. Here, again, we have more leisure than at A and we work less. If we now vary wage level continuously we will get a set of all the optimal choices along the heavy curve in the left-hand diagram. The mirror of this curve in the labour–wage plane depicts exactly how much work the individual will want to supply at any level of wages.

How is it, you may wonder, that both fall and increase in wage levels produced the same response in relation to the initial point A?

The intuition for this is quite simple. Unlike previous cases where the price of a good represented only its opportunity costs (in terms of other goods), the wage we earn is both the price of leisure and a source of income. Hence, when ever the wage level rises leisure becomes more expensive but at the same time we earn more money. As a price, an increase in the wage level should make us reduce our leisure as it is more expensive. As an income, an increase in the wage level should make us want more leisure (if it is a normal good). So we have conflicting forces at work and it is therefore not at all surprising that the supply of labour is backward bending. At the lower end of wage levels it is clear that income is very low, so the more influential force will be wage as a price of leisure. When you have little to eat and someone tells you 'I will give you a raise' you are unlikely to drop it all and run to the golf course. You are more likely to see the opportunity in work to alleviate your poverty and respond to the increase in the wage level by working more.

At the other end, when your hourly wage is enormous you are unlikely to be impressed by a proposed increase in your hourly wage. You are more likely to think to yourself, 'If I am paid more, I'd better spend more time at the golf course so that other people can see that I am a high flyer.'

5.4 Market equilibrium

Given the shape of the supply of labour which we have derived in the previous section, there is a potential problem in the analysis of competitive outcomes. Consider the aggregate demand for labour based on the marginal product of labour and the supply of labour which is based on the simple horizontal summation of individuals' supply curves.

Figure 5.12 depicts a situation where the demand for labour cuts the backward bending supply of labour twice. On the face of it this may cause a problem. As was explained earlier, it is important not to have too many equilibria as we may risk the predicament of being able to explain everything while we explain nothing. If we have a few, the first question which we must ask ourselves is whether the two are equally meaningful.

As was explained at some length in Chapter 4, it is important not only to identify the existence of equilibrium but also to establish an idea of *stability*. Namely, as the real world is not really in any equilibrium situation, we need the equilibrium point to tell us

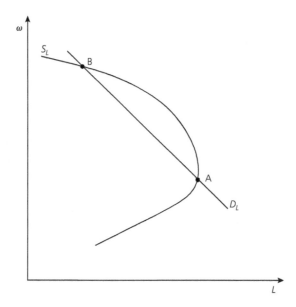

Figure 5.12 Equilibrium in the labour market with a backward-bending supply curve.

something about the direction which the developments in the market will take. These directions, it is assumed, are dominated by the position of the equilibrium point. For such a point to be a meaningful reference point we would need to be able to point at forces that will drive the market towards the equilibrium point.

At this stage we have only recognized one such force: excess demand. When the quantity demanded exceeds the quantity supplied, we assume that prices will tend to rise. When the quantity supplied exceeds the quantity demanded, we expect prices to fall. If you examine both our equilibrium candidates you will find that around point B excess demand will drive us away from that point. This means that if we were at B, this will be an equilibrium provided that nothing rocks the boat. A certain shock that pushes wages down will create a situation of excess supply which will push prices further down towards A. Any wage level above B and we are in an excess demand regime that will push prices up. Put differently, there are no market forces that can lead us back to an equilibrium at B and we, therefore, deem this point as an irrelevance. Around A there is a different story. Here it is clear that from any other wage level market forces will push wages to its level at A. A, therefore, will be the equilibrium point even if it so happens that the demand cuts twice through the supply.

But even when we have only one equilibrium there are two possibilities to be considered (Figure 5.13). In the left-hand side, the unique equilibrium lies at the upward sloping part of the labour supply. In the right-hand side it lies at the backward bending part of the labour supply. Consider next the effect of a wage tax on the competitive equilibrium in the labour market. From what we said about the labour supply, we know that it mirrors *all* possible choices of leisure and consumption. This means that, as such, an introduction of a tax will have no direct impact on this curve. However, the introduction of a wage tax creates a difference between **gross** and **net** wages. The individual

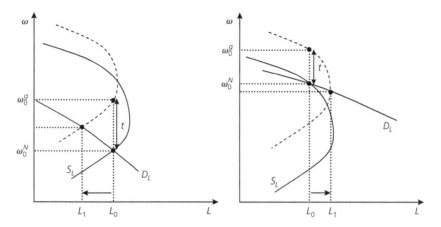

Figure 5.13 Equilibrium considerations in the labour market.

makes his choices based on his net income. However, to get, say, ω_0, the gross wage must be much higher. Namely, if our individual received ω_0^g then $\omega_0^n = \omega_0^g(1 - t)$ where t is the tax rate. Which means that for the individual to take home ω_0 and to choose to work L^0 he will have to get ω_0^g as wages. When we apply the rule everywhere we shall see that the effect of a tax on wages will be to shift the supply schedule upward. The results of such an event on the equilibrium level of labour supplied will depend on whether the equilibrium is at the upward or backward sloping part of the labour supply. As can be seen from the above, if the equilibrium is at the upward sloping part of the labour supply, equilibrium level of labour will fall. However, if the equilibrium were at the backward bending part of the labour supply the effect of the tax will be to increase labour supply.

The assumption is that, normally, labour supply is more likely to be rising with wages at the point of equilibrium. Consequently, we can see that a wage tax can create productive inefficiency in addition to the allocative inefficiencies which we have already discussed in Chapter 4. However, you can also see from the above analyses the delicacy of this framework. This is why labour market analyses require greater attention and this is why there are so many different opinions with regard to the effectiveness of various tax policies.

Self-assessment and applications

▦ QUESTION 1

'The fact that the supply of labour increases with wages (income) suggests that labour is a normal good while leisure is an inferior good. Whenever labour supply falls with increase in wages, the reverse is true.' Comment on this statement.

Answer

This is a question where students are expected to provide a more detailed derivation of the supply of labour:

Let us first examine the case when we are on the upward sloping part of the labour supply (Figure 5.14).

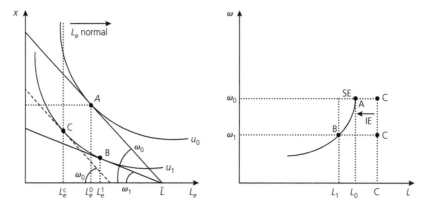

Figure 5.14 Upward sloping supply of labour.

As we move from B to A the wage level has risen. The substitution effect is the move from B to C and it suggests that as leisure becomes more expensive we will want to have less of it. From C to A this is a pure income effect (emphasized by the parallel shift of the budget line from C to A). As real income increased, having more leisure than what we have at C will imply that leisure is a normal good. A choice of less leisure as a response to an increase in real income implies that leisure is an inferior good. In the end, point A suggests that we will have less leisure than we had at B. This will be consistent with leisure being either normal (point B^N) or inferior (point B^I).

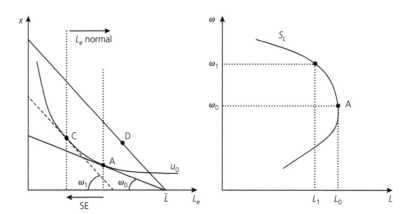

Figure 5.15 Backward sloping supply of labour.

Let us examine now the backward bending part of the labour supply, see Figure 5.15. We now describe the move from A to D. The substitution effect is the move from A to C and it suggests that as leisure becomes more expensive we will want to have less of it. From C to D this is a pure income effect (again, emphasized by the parallel shift of the budget line from C to D). As real income increased, having more leisure than what we have at C will imply that leisure is a normal good. A choice of less leisure as a response to an increase in real income implies that leisure is an inferior good. In the end, point D suggests that we will have more leisure than we had at A. This can only be consistent with leisure being a normal good.

QUESTION 2

Will the fact that workers are unionized have an implication for the structure of the labour market?

Answer

Unions are a complex case for analysis. We do not yet possess all the necessary tools of analysis by which the behaviour of unions and their impact on the market can be properly analysed. The intention of this question, therefore, is to test some basic analytical skills. For instance, from what we have studied so far it is clear that if workers form a union they turn the labour market structure into a monopolist. Assuming that the union has enough power to ensure that all its members obey the rules, what might the union try and achieve?

So far we have analysed monopolist in the context of profit maximization. This, however, will not be applicable to the labour market. As an organization which seeks the benefits of its members (and I exclude all discussions regarding power structures, control, and the like) a possible aim could be to maximize overall wage bill (revenues) (which are then distributed to members of the union). Ignoring here the question of insiders and outsiders (i.e. those who earn wages and those who are out of work), Figure 5.16 will emerge.

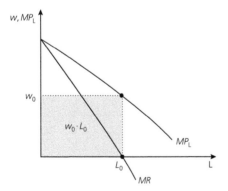

Figure 5.16 Unions as monopolists in labour market.

As long as there is a positive marginal revenue, sending an extra worker into the market will cause excess supply and reduce the level of wages but the loss of earnings by those who are already in the market will be smaller than the gain in earning by the new people at work. At the point where marginal revenue is zero, this is the point where an increase in the supply of labour will bring down the wage level as to leave the level of total wages unchanged. Hence, the wage bill will be maximized at the point where the marginal revenue equals zero.

The outcome of such behaviour will be to raise the level of wages (relative to the competitive outcome) and reduce the amount of employment. Whether this will be a successful policy depends on whether everyone is a member of the union and whether or not the union can prevent agents from trying to make gains for themselves at the expense of the group.

▨ QUESTION 3

What will be the equilibrium wage level and employment in a labour market where employers act as one?

Answer

This is a case which we have not discussed in any form and which requires greater attention that we can give at this level of our studies. Nevertheless, I would like to use this application opportunity to show to you how we gain some insight into a model which we have not discussed but for which we already have some basic tools to understand. This is the case of a **monopsony**.

A monopsony is a market structure which is very similar to that of the monopoly. The only difference is that instead of one seller and many buyers, we have one buyer and many sellers. Recall that the logic of the monopolist was to take into account the effect on price that any decision on output will have. Therefore, the marginal revenue of the monopolist differed from that of competition. Consider first the competitive solution in the labour market (Figure 5.17). As we saw in this chapter, equilibrium will be achieved when, for each firm,

$$w = p_x MP_L \quad \text{or} \quad \omega \equiv \frac{w}{p_x} = MP_L.$$

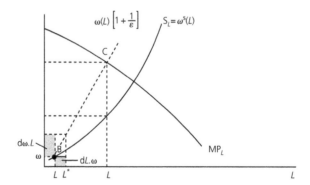

Figure 5.17 Monopsonist solution in the labour market.

Namely, the market is in equilibrium when we pay workers the value of their marginal product. In other words, we equate the return from labour (marginal revenue product of labour) to its cost (wages). Now, as we have a single buyer (the collective of employers) they know that if, say, from B, they want to hire an extra worker this will cause excess demand and raise the wage level which has to be paid now to all the workers. Namely, the cost of hiring the extra worker is both the wages we have to pay that worker + the increase in wages we have to pay to all the other workers who have been working for us: $\omega(L)dL + d\omega L$ (where dL is the extra worker). To examine the costs per worker we must divide it all by dL:

$$\omega(L) + \frac{d\omega}{dL}L = \omega(L) + \frac{d\omega}{dL}L\frac{\omega}{\omega} = \omega(L)\left[1 + \frac{d\omega}{dL}\frac{L}{\omega}\right] = \omega(L)\left[1 + \frac{1}{\varepsilon}\right].$$

(where ε represents the elasticity of labour supply and it is positive in value).

Hence, instead of equating the marginal revenue product of labour to the wage level (which in competition is not affected directly by our action) which is just the cost of the last worker, we equate it to the full extra costs:

$$p_x MP_L = w(L)\left[1 + \frac{1}{\varepsilon}\right] \quad \text{or} \quad MP_L = \omega(L)\left[1 + \frac{1}{\varepsilon}\right].$$

This is point C in the figure.

This is a mirror image of our analysis of the monopolist. The monopolist, to maximize his profit, took into account the lost of revenues as he sells extra units. The monopsonist, to maximize profits, takes into account the extra cost.

QUESTION 4

(a) An individual has to use public transport to get to his workplace. Employers do not pay for either the time or the money which the individual spends on his way to work. Suppose that initially a worker spends T_0 hours a day commuting at a cost of C_0. Show the initial choice of labour in the plane of leisure and other goods.

(b) What will happen to labour supply as the government allows public transport to deteriorate (i.e. longer travel times at higher cost)?

Answer

(a) This is a question about the position of the budget line which is given in Figure 5.18. When the time it takes to go to work is not paid for and the cost of transport are not covered by the employer, the budget line begins at a deficit if we assume that transport to work is not part of the individuals' consumption. That is, before one can use his earning to purchase goods one would have to use it to cover the cost of getting to work.

Clearly, the time it takes to get to work will reduce the availability of paid hours (shift leftwards). The cost of commuting will put the individual in the red if he does not earn enough (the shift downward).

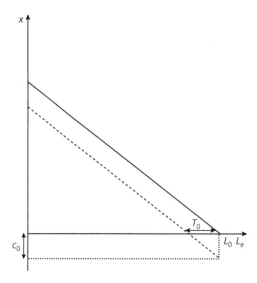

Figure 5.18

(b) Longer travel time and higher cost of commuting will shift the budget line further to the left and down. While at each level of wages individuals will choose to have less leisure, this will not necessarily translate into more work as the extra time is used for commuting.

QUESTION 5

In a proposed cost cutting exercise, a firm offers its workforce the following deal: a cut in regular wages but a considerable increase for all overtime work. Suppose that a labourer initially worked L_0 hours at the going real wage of $\acute{\omega}_0 (\acute{\omega} = w/p)$ and that overtime is paid for all hours above L_0.

(a)   What will happen to the labour supplied by this individual?

(b)   Does your answer depend on whether the worker was initially at the upward sloping part of his labour supply or at the backward bending part of it?

(c)   Will the firm end up paying an individual more or less than it did originally? Will workers be better or worse off?

Answer

This is a rather simple question regarding the labour supplied by an individual. It is not a question about the shape of the labour supply and it must, therefore, be entirely analysed in the context of an individual's choice of leisure.

(a) and **(c)** There are basically four possible situations as seen in Figure 5.19.

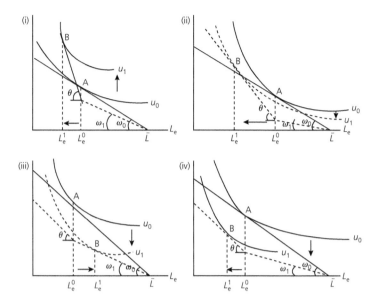

Figure 5.19

(i) the individual will supply more working hours and will be better off. The cost of this worker to the firm (in real terms) before the change will be

$$\omega_0(\bar{L} - L_e^0)$$

which is the vertical line from the horizontal axis to point A.

Now we have a lower wage rate $\hat{\omega}_1$ to be paid for the normal working hours and θ is the overtime pay. In such a case, the spending by the firm on the individual in case I will be

$$\omega_1(\bar{L} - L_e^0) + \theta(L_e^0 - L_e^1)$$

which is the vertical line to point B. This is clearly an increase in the cost of the worker.

(ii) Here point B indicates a greater supply of working hours but the individual will be worse off. As in the previous case, the vertical line to point B is greater than the line to A.

(iii) Point B indicates a reduction in hours of work supplied together with a fall in the worker's welfare. Evidently, in such a case, the spending on this worker will fall.

(iv) Here the supply of working hours will increase together with a fall in the worker's welfare but the cost to the firm will fall too!

(b) It is fairly clear that the fact that we are at the upward sloping segment of the labour supply or the backward bending segment of it has only limited influence on the result. Most of it really depends on the extent of the fall in regular wages and the size of the overtime pay. One possible way of making sense of this is to look at the average wage per hour (the ray to point B from the origin).

In cases I and II, the average wage per hour has increased. In case I the person is better off, which means that his real income increased. Therefore, the substitution effect should have induced him to work more while the income effect should have encouraged more leisure. As he ends up working more, his substitution effect seems more dominant and it is likely that the individual is on the upward sloping segment of his labour supply.

In case II, the average wage per hour increased but the individual is worse off. The substitution effect suggests an increase in labour supplied and so does the income effect. It is possible that leisure is an inferior good and we must therefore be at the upward sloping section of the labour supply.

In case III, average wage per hour fell. The substitution effect directs the individual to work less but a fall in real income will increase his supply of labour if leisure is a normal good. As the substitution effect dominates the income effect, we must be at the upward sloping section of the labour supply.

In case IV, the average pay per hour fell but the individual offers more labour. The substitution effect directs the individual to reduce his labour supply while the income effect proposes an increase if leisure is a normal good. Here, the income effect dominates the substitution effect, so we may say that the individual is at the backward bending section of his labour supply.

▨ QUESTION 6

Suppose that a labourer has chosen to work L_0 hours at the going real wage of $\acute{\omega}_0$ ($\omega = w/p$). He is now offered the following:

(i) An increase in his real wages to ω_1 per hour,

(ii) An increase of £B per hour (which is greater than the increase in the first option: $B > (\acute{\omega}_1 - \acute{\omega}_0)$) but only for overtime (the hours above L_0);

(a) What will happen to the labour supplied by this individual under each of these proposals assuming that his choice is in the upward sloping region of his labour supply?

(b) Will your answer be different if he was at the backward bending region of their labour supply?

(c) Is it possible that the labourer might be indifferent between the two schemes?

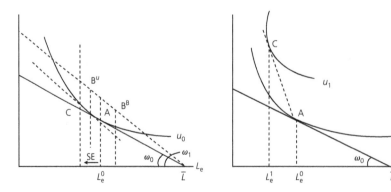

Figure 5.20

Answer

The context of this question is clearly the choices individual makes in the leisure consumption space (Figure 5.20). The left-hand diagram depicts option (i) while the right hand diagram represents option (ii) where B^B and B^u represents the effects depicted or whether they are at the upward sloping or backward bending part of the labour supply. The information with regard to $B > (\acute{\omega}_1 - \acute{\omega}_0)$ simply suggests that the increase in hourly wages beyond L_0 is greater than the increase in the hourly wage under option (i).

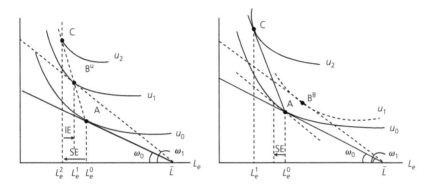

Figure 5.21

(a) and **(b)** The left-hand diagram in Figure 5.21 represents the case when labour supply is upward sloping. The substitution effect is greater than the income effect. Hence, the workers response to option (i) will be point B where the individual chooses to have less leisure and supply more labour time. The worker is more likely to be better off with option (ii) but his supply of labour will not be that much different under the two options.

In the right-hand diagram we have the case where wages are at the backward bending segment of the labour supply. Here, income effect exceeds (in absolute values) the substitution effect. Hence, we end up at point B. Again, the individual is likely to prefer option (ii) but here, his supply of labour under this option is clearly greater (point C).

(c) Can the individual be indifferent between the two options? (Figure 5.22). This is clearly possible (see Figure 5.21). In such a case, his supply of labour hours will be much greater if offered option (ii) than if he were to be offered option (i).

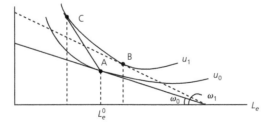

Figure 5.22

QUESTION 7

'Competitive labour markets are really a ploy' argue some commentators. 'Any level of real income (measured in utility terms) achieved through equilibrium wages in the market, could have been obtained if agents were given instead, a bonus which would be independent of the number of hours they work, + a much lower level of wage per hour.'

(a) Explain how individuals choose how many hours to work;

(b) How will the proposed change affect the supply of labour?

(c) Evaluate the commentator's claim.

Answer

Although the language of this question is referring to a very complex problem of the difference between motives and incentives, at this level, it boils down to a simple analytical query. The question is whether transferring a greater part of the remuneration to a non-performance related pay will produce similar outcomes as when remuneration is entirely performance related (we think of hours at work as a measure of effort).

(a) To begin with, you must ensure that you know how the choice of hours worked (as a residual to the decision on leisure) is being taken.

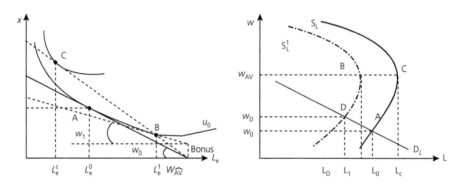

Figure 5.23

(b) and **(c)** Here you must translate the question into the language of the model. We are initially at point A (see Figure 5.23). According to the question, the same amount of utility (as a measure of real income) can be achieved by an alternative method of payment which is comprised of a general bonus B and a lower wage ($w_1 < w_0$). This can clearly be demonstrated by the move from A to B. It is important to note, however, that the bonus B will not be paid to the individual if he did not work at all. The way the diagram is drawn one might think that an individual can earn B without any work at all. This is, of course, not the case but saying that the individual must work some hours before being entitled to the bonus would not have changed the answer in any significant manner.

While the move from A to B suggests that the claim in question is correct; i.e. that we can obtain the same utility with this kind of remuneration structure, the full answer depends on the effects on the labour supply and the market. What is determined there is the wage per hour. The move to the new scheme does not tell us, from the point of view of the employer, what is the cost per hour worked (we exclude other types of costs). We can clearly see that the cost per hour under B will be the slope of the line drawn up to B ($w_{AV} > w_0$). To see what will be the effect of the change on the supply of labour we must compare the supply of labour under the initial scheme at w_{AV} (which is, at C, L_C) and the new scheme (at point B). Clearly, under the new scheme the supply of labour hours will be smaller. The intuition here is clear too. As the bonus is independent of how many hours an individual works, it is, virtually, a pure income effect. At each level of wages, it would mean that the quantity of hours worked will fall, as leisure is a normal good.

Consequently, the supply of labour will shift to the left and there will be a new equilibrium (ignoring all the subsequent effects on other markets) at point D where effective hourly wages are higher but the total amount of labour supplied lower.

QUESTION 8

'Competitive labour markets are really a folly', argue some commentators. 'For any given level of real wages, one can both substantially increase real income from labour as well as increase the labour supply if, instead of the single wage level, one offered workers a lower wage for their first hours of work and a higher wage for their subsequent hours' contribution. Workers will be as well off as before while their material income will increase.'

(a) Explain how individuals choose how many hours to work;

(b) How will the proposed change affect the supply of labour?

(c) Evaluate the commentator's claim.

Answer

This is a question about the notion of real income and the cost of labour.

(a) As before, you must first establish that you know well how decisions are made.

(b) and **(c)** Here is the point where you translate the question into the language of the model (Figure 5.24). We begin at point A. The new proposal shows that agents will receive less $w_1 < w_0$ (we assume prices of goods to be constant) for the first hours and $w_2 > w_0$ for any additional hour.

Evidently, as the level of real income (i.e. utility) remains the same (we move from A to B), we can see that the agent will want to work more and, consequently, will also be able to consume more. The total consumption before was x_0 and it is x_2 now (again, ignoring the effects on prices). In terms of labour as a cost, we know that the initial wage per hour was w_0. At this level of remuneration, agents would want to offer L_0 hours of work. The new scheme requires a new calculation of the wage per hour (which is the cost for the employers if we ignore all other possible components). The total wage bill per worker is now:

$$w_1 L_1 + w_2 (L_2 - L_1) = p x_2.$$

Thus, the actual cost of labour, real wage per hour, is the slope of the line reaching B which is clearly greater than the initial cost ($w_A > w_0$).

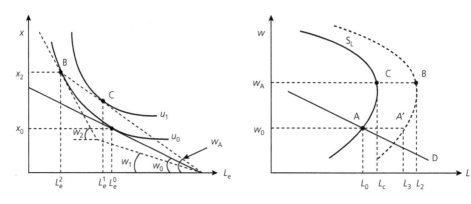

Figure 5.24

The effect that this will have on the labour market depends on what it is precisely that is traded in that market. Standard analysis tell us that it is hours of work at the price of a single hour. To analyse the effect that the offer will have on the labour market we must ask the question: what would be the choice of working hours, if w_A were to be offered as a simple hourly wage. The answer is given at point C in the above diagram. However, the new offer would produce the same hourly pay but will generate more hours of work (point B). This will be true for each level of wage. If we replace w_0 by a similar scheme we will end up at point A' (Figure 5.25).

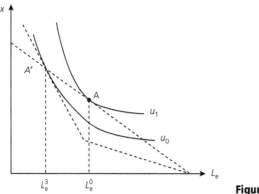

Figure 5.25

For each level of hourly pay, there will now be a corresponding scheme which generates a greater supply of working hours. Consequently, there will be excess supply of labour and the average hourly wage will decline. Workers will inevitably be on a much lower level of real income (they would have experienced the same thing had wages remained at w_0, the move from A to A'). Naturally, to examine the full impact of such a change we would need to take into consideration all other markets. In general, however, we can see that there will be more resources available and thus, greater output. The fall in workers' real income may be offset by such a growth (and through the fall in prices) but whether or not this happens is a big distributional question.

■ NOTES

1. An assumption clearly made by neoclassical economics. According to the US Census Bureau, in 2000, 65% of households held some interest earning assets in financial institutions. This, of course, includes various forms of savings and pensions but the median value of such holding was $4000. At the same time, only 30.4% of households held stocks or shares and other interest earning assets. This does not seem to suggest that the majority of households in the United States are equally concerned about returns from capital as they are about returns from wages. The UK Family Expenditure Survey from 2001 shows that 76% of income comes from people's direct efforts (i.e. wages and self-employment). Only 4% come from investment and 7% from annuities and pensions. Given the distribution of wealth in the United Kingdom it is more likely that there is a clear division between those who earn their income from work and those who earn it from capital.

2. Note that the marginal product of labour—its productivity—is determined for a given level of capital ($MP_L(K_0)$). Equally, the marginal productivity of capital depends on the number of people employed.

3. Note, however, that while we mentioned 'real wage' in the case of the demand for labour, this is not the same concept as the 'real wage' in the supply of labour. In the case of demand, the producer wants to equate the marginal product of whatever it is that he is producing with the wage he pays workers in terms of the same product. If the producer is in the business of nuclear waste management, the 'real wage' which he is looking at is the quantity of nuclear waste shifted by the last worker; surely the 'real wage' for the worker cannot be the same thing. For the worker, his real wage is the amount of consumption goods which he can purchase. It is highly unlikely that he will consider nuclear waste as part of his consumption bundle.

   Nevertheless, for ease of exposition we shall assume that x is a composite consumption good and p_x is the consumption goods price index. In the last chapter (in the 'macro' section) we shall spend more time discussing the possible implications of the difference between real wages as cost (for the producers) and real wages as income (for the workers) but we shall not discuss these issues any further here. To circumvent the problem we shall assume that all prices, except wages are fixed.

<table>
<tr><td>**6**</td><td># General equilibrium and welfare economics</td></tr>
</table>

General equilibrium is one of the most important aspects of neoclassical microeconomic analysis. However, it is not so much because of its added value to the understanding of the principles which guide economic analysis as it is for its service as the ultimate test of those ideas.

Microeconomic analysis has been based on the principle of rational behaviour but the most important aspect of it is the concept of equilibrium. It means that rational plans of individuals can coincide in such a way that no rational being will have the incentive to act so as to change the outcome.

However, while the considerations (i.e. choices) of the rational individual are made with reference to all economic goods,[1] the concept of equilibrium which we have encountered so far had been constructed with reference to a single good. It reflected the coincidence of rational plans—made by consumers and producers—regarding a single good while assuming that all other prices are fixed. Yet, we did see that the demand for each good by each individual is dependent on the prices of the other goods. Similarly, the quantity of labour supplied (which affects the equilibrium level of wages and, subsequently, income and the supply schedule of all goods) is dependent on the prices of other goods. The test, therefore, of the idea of harmonious rational interaction lies in showing that even when we allow all prices to change there will exist a set of prices for which all rational plans—across all goods and factors—will coincide. Showing this is the task of general equilibrium theory.

It is the existence of such an equilibrium which is the prime driving force behind the modern advocacy of the free markets system. General equilibrium, if it exists, suggests that a decentralized system with rational agents can work if agents are given freedom to pursuit their own interests. Naturally, this is far from being the final word as it is not clear whether the rationality assumption was descriptive (i.e. describing how people behave) or functional (a means of getting testable propositions). Second, even if equilibrium exists, are there any processes of exchange which lead us to this point? Third, what are the social implications of being at a point of general equilibrium?

We shall neglect entirely the first and second questions but we will say something with regard to the third one. Before that, however, we shall elaborate on the meaning of general equilibrium.

6.1 'Vertical' and 'horizontal' dimensions of general equilibrium

The distinction between what I call 'vertical' and 'horizontal' dimensions is not a distinction of substance. By the latter I refer to the relationship between equilibria across final goods markets which are connected directly through demand (and which one may call 'inter-markets' equilibrium). By 'vertical' I refer to the relationship between markets which are connected through production (and which one may call intra-market equilibrium). The reason I draw this distinction is to allow a simpler analysis of the circumstances and meaning of general equilibrium.

6.1.1 Horizontal or inter-markets equilibrium

We begin the analysis by examining how markets become connected through consumers' behaviour. To do so we shall start with something more familiar: the partial equilibrium analysis as described in Chapter 4. We shall assume that there are only two goods in the economy (x and y):

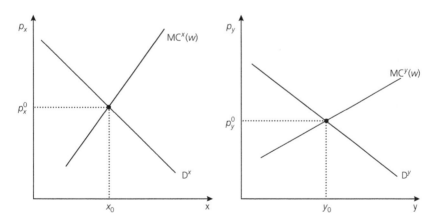

Figure 6.1 Equilibria in two-goods markets.

In Figure 6.1 the left-hand diagram describes the equilibrium conditions in the market for x while the right-hand diagram describes the equilibrium condition in the market for y. At the price p_x^0 the quantity demanded of x (which is x_0 units of x) is the same as the quantity of x which producers will want to supply (because it is the marginal cost of x_0 which equals the price of p_x^0 and we assume this price to be above the average cost). Similarly, in the market for y it is at the price of p_y^0 that the quantity demand (y_0) is exactly the same as the quantity supplied. The question which will concern us here is whether or not the two equilibria are dependent on each other and if so, how?

To make our life easy we shall only concentrate on the more obvious and direct relationship between the two markets. In this case, as the two goods are final goods in the sense that none of them is used in the production of the other, the direct relationship between them can only come from consumption. To understand why the two goods are related we need to remind ourselves of how we derived the demand for each good. Recall from Chapter 2 that the choice regarding how much x or how much y the individual will want to consume is determined simultaneously by the process of utility maximization (or the choice of the most preferred bundle), see Figure 6.2.

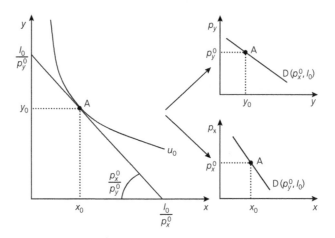

Figure 6.2 Utility maximization and demand for two goods.

This means that the quantity of x (x_0) which the individual wants to consume at the price of p_x^0 is chosen together with the quantity y_0 of y at the price p_y^0. In addition, the decision regarding both x and y had been made at a given level of income (I_0). Hence, the demand schedule in each market depends on the price of the good itself, the price of the other good, and income. When, in Chapter 2, we derived demand for good x we changed only the price of good x assuming that the price of y remained unchanged. But the actual price of each good is a result of the equilibrium conditions in that good's market. This equilibrium, which we call 'partial equilibrium', is only telling us how the price of one good is being determined for any given price of the other good. It does not explain how a change in the equilibrium condition in one market may influence the equilibrium condition in the other market. The fact that markets are related in such a close way may not be easy to establish. Still, one of the most obvious examples is that of markets for bonds and the markets for shares. I am sure that you have heard people argue, many times, that an increase in interest rates (which means a fall in the price of bonds) will have a 'devastating' effect on the price of shares. Surely the reason one can make such statements is the belief in the existence of a clear connection between the equilibrium condition in one market and those of another. However, while in some cases these connections may appear intuitively clear, in many cases such connections are not obvious. Nevertheless, bearing in mind the nature of modern economics, where individuals are sovereign, things have no intrinsic value and whether or not goods are related to one another is a matter of consumer's choice.

To capture the idea of such interdependence let us elaborate the equilibrium condition within each of the above markets bearing in mind that the demand for each good depends on the price of the other good. As income remains unchanged throughout our analysis we shall drop it from our exposition.

We begin by examining the equilibrium in the market for x. The following equation describes the demand for x which could be derived from a consumer's rational choices for any given price of y:

$$x^d = D^x(p_x, p_y) = a - bp_x + ep_y$$

where the sign of e depends on whether the two goods are gross substitutes or complements. If the individual views the two goods as gross substitutes then an increase in the price of the other good (y) will produce an increase in the demand for good x. Therefore:

$$e > 0 \quad \text{if } x \text{ and } y \text{ are gross substitutes};$$
$$e < 0 \quad \text{if } x \text{ and } y \text{ are complements}.$$

To make it easier to follow I shall conduct the discussion in general as well as specific terms. Let us, therefore, suppose that $a = 100$, $b = 3$, and $e = 1$. Hence,

$$x^d = D^x(p_x, p_y) = a - bp_x + ep_y = 100 - 3p_x + 1p_y.$$

(I recommend that you draw this function on a separate sheet of paper assuming a certain price for y, say $p_y^0 = 5$. To test your understanding, see what will happen to demand if the price of y increased to 6.)

The supply of x which is the marginal cost of x, is given by the following:

$$x^s = S^x(p_x, w) = cp_x - dw = 2p_x - 4w$$

where an increase in the price of x will induce producers to sell more as the cost of the current last unit (the marginal cost) will become smaller than the price. Given diminishing marginal product (and rising marginal cost), profit maximizing behaviour implies an increase in the output. As wages increase, the marginal cost of the current last unit will be greater. This, in turn, will induce producers to sell less at any given price.

Equilibrium in the market for x can now be easily calculated:

$$x^d = D^x(p_x, p_y) = a - bp_x + ep_y = x^s = S^x(p_x, w) = cp_x - dw$$

or:

$$100 - 3p_x + 1p_y = 2p_x - 4w$$

Had $p_y = 5$ and $w = 5$, then we get

$$100 + 5 + (4 \times 5) = p_x(2 + 3)$$
$$125 = 5p_x$$
$$25 = p_x^0$$

which is the equilibrium price in the market for x for a given price of y (5) and a given level of wage (5).

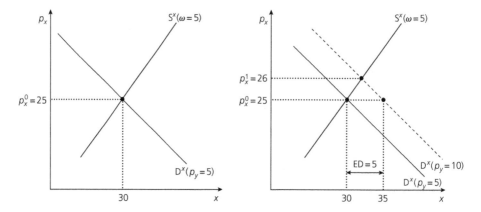

Figure 6.3 Partial equilibrium in a two-goods market.

The left-hand diagram in Figure 6.3 depicts the equilibrium in the market for x which we have calculated above. The right-hand diagram depicts the equilibrium price of x had the price of y been 10. What would have been the equilibrium price of x had the price of y been 15?

We can clearly see how the equilibrium price of x depends on the price of y but the market of y, also, is subject to similar influences by the price of x. We must therefore develop a tool that will clearly relate the two prices. We know that in equilibrium the quantity demanded equals the quantity supplied. Hence, there is no excess demand or excess supply in the market. Recall from Chapter 4 that the notion of equilibrium was strongly related to the notion of excess demand. When there is excess demand or excess supply (which is just a negative excess demand) there will be someone in the economy who will be willing to pay more (or sell for less) depending on their personal circumstances. In such a case, we do not have an equilibrium as prices will carry on changing. Only when there is no excess demand (positive or negative) will there be no incentive to anyone to alter the situation. All rational plans will be fulfilled.

Let us examine the notion of excess demand more carefully. In Figure 6.3 we had clear demand and supply functions. In the left-hand diagram we know that when the price of x equals 25, the quantity demanded is exactly the same as the quantity supplied:

$$x^d = D^x(p_x, p_y) = a - bp_x + ep_y = 100 - 3p_x + 1p_y$$
$$= 100 - 3 \times 25 + 1 \times 5 = 30 \text{ units of } x$$
$$x^s = S^x(p_x, w) = cp_x - dw = 2p_x - 4w = 2 \times 25 - 4 \times 5 = 30 \text{ units of } x.$$

On the right-hand diagram we can see that when the price of y had risen to 10, $p_x^0 = 25$ is no longer a point where excess demand is zero:

$$x^d = D^x(p_x, p_y) = a - bp_x + ep_y = 100 - 3p_x + 1p_y$$
$$= 100 - 3 \times 25 + 1 \times 10 = 35 \text{ units of } x$$
$$x^s = S^x(p_x, w) = cp_x - dw = 2p_x - 4w = 2 \times 25 - 4 \times 5 = 30 \text{ units of } x.$$

As excess demand is the difference between the quantity demanded and the quantity supplied we can write it as

$$ED = x^d - x^s = 35 - 30 = 5.$$

We know from the above calculations that had the price of y been 10, the price of x for which there will be no excess demand (i.e there will be equilibrium in the market for x) is 26.

We can write the excess demand for x as a more general function. It will have the following form:

$$ED^x(p_x, p_y, I, w) = x^d - x^s = D^x(p_x, p_y, I) - S^x(p_x, w).$$

In our case (ignoring income completely) it becomes:

$$ED^x(p_x, p_y, w) = x^d - x^s = D^x(p_x, p_y) - S^x(p_x, w) = a - bp_x + ep_y - [cp_x - dw]$$
$$ED^x(p_x, p_y, w) = a + ep_y + dw - p_x(b + c) = 100 + 1p_y + 4w - 5p_x$$

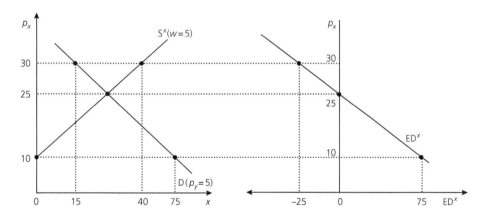

Figure 6.4 Deriving the excess demand function.

The left-hand diagram in Figure 6.4 depicts the equilibrium condition in the market for x when the price of y is 5 and $w = 5$. The right-hand diagram depicts the excess demand for x at different prices of x for a given price of y. On the vertical axis we have the price of x while the horizontal axis denotes the level of excess demand. Therefore, when $p_x = 25$, $ED^x = 0$. When $p_x = 30$ the quantity demanded will be $x^d = 100 - 3 \times 30 + 1 \times 5 = 15$, the quantity supplied will be $x^s = 2 \times 30 - 4 \times 5 = 40$ and thus, $ED^x = 15 - 40 = -25$ (which means excess supply). When the price of x is 10, however, $x^d = 100 - 3 \times 10 + 1 \times 5 = 75$, $x^s = 2 \times 10 - 4 \times 5 = 0$ so that $ED^x = 75 - 0 = 75$.

As the focus of our interest is the relationship between the equilibrium price of x and the price of y, we can see in the diagram below what will be the effect on the excess demand curve if the price of y changed.

We start with the original situation where the price of y is 5 and $w = 5$. The equilibrium in the market for x will then be at the point where the price of $x = 25$ and this is where excess demand for x will be equal to zero. We now increase the price of y to 10. The intuition is very clear. When the price of y increases and the two goods are gross substitutes, this means that the demand for x will increase. At the initial price there will now be excess demand the result of which will be an increase in the equilibrium price of x (See Figure 6.5).

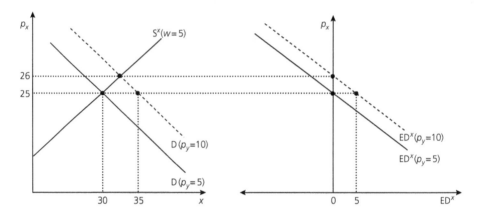

Figure 6.5 The effect of a change in p_y.

When the price of y was 5, equilibrium occurred at $p_x = 25$. This means that excess demand was zero at these prices. Now, when the price of y increased to 10, excess demand for the same price of x (25) will be 5:

$$x^d = D^x(p_x, p_y) = a - bp_x + ep_y = 100 - 3p_x + 1p_y$$
$$= 100 - 3 \times 25 + 1 \times 10 = 35 \text{ units of } x$$
$$x^s = S^x(p_x, w) = cp_x - dw = 2p_x - 4w = 2 \times 25 - 4 \times 5 = 30 \text{ units of } x$$

Hence,

$$ED^x(p_x, p_y) = ED^x(25, 10) = 35 - 30 = 5.$$

When $p_x = 26$ excess demand will be

$$x^d = D^x(p_x, p_y) = a - bp_x + ep_y = 100 - 3p_x + 1p_y$$

$$= 100 - 3 \times 26 + 1 \times 10 = 32 \text{ units of } x$$

$$x^s = S^x(p_x, w) = cp_x - dw = 2p_x - 4w = 2 \times 26 - 4 \times 5 = 32 \text{ units of } x.$$

Hence,

$$ED^x(p_x, p_y) = ED^x(26, 10) = 32 - 32 = 0.$$

Thus, we can see that an increase in the price of y will shift the ED curve to the right. When the price of y was 5, $ED^x(25, 5) = 0$; when p_y became 10, $ED^x(25, 10) = 5$. Note, however, that this is so simply because the other good's price coefficient e was greater than zero. This meant that x and y are gross substitutes. Had the goods been complements, we would have used a negative number for e. By way of an exercise, I recommend that you repeat the analysis from above assuming that $e = -1$. How will then the excess demand function change when the price of y increases?

We are now ready for a clear representation of the relationship between the price of y and the equilibrium price of x. We know that for any given price of y, the equilibrium price of x will be the price at which the excess demand for x will be zero. From what we saw above it is clear to us that an increase in the price of y will cause an increase in the equilibrium price of x. Figure 6.6 depicts the relationship between the price of y and the equilibrium price of x.

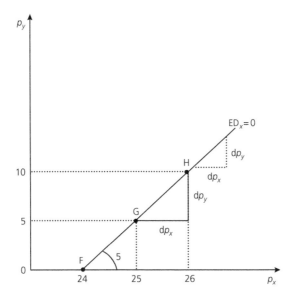

Figure 6.6 The relationship between p_y and the equilibrium p_x.

We start with $p_y = 0$. Even if the price of the other good had been zero, there will still be a downward sloping demand for x and an equilibrium price for x which is greater than zero. Using our previous calculations, this would mean

$$x^d = D^x(p_x, p_y) = a - bp_x + ep_y = x^s = S^x(p_x, w) = cp_x - dw$$

and when $p_y = 0$:

$$100 - 3p_x = 2p_x - 4w$$

as $w = 5$ we get:

$$100 + (4 \times 5) = p_x(2 + 3)$$

$$120 = 5p_x$$

$$24 = p_x.$$

In general terms the equilibrium conditions mean that:

$$(x^d =)a - bp_x + ep_y = cp_x - dw(= x^s)$$

hence

$$p_x^e = \frac{a + ep_y + dw}{c + b}$$

where p_x^e is the equilibrium price in the market for x. It is easy to see that even when $p_y = 0$, there will be a positive number for p_x^e. Hence, we start at point F in the above figure which depicts the price of x for which there will be an equilibrium in the market for x when the price of y equals zero. We now want to see what will happen to the **equilibrium price of x** when we increase the price of y. In other words, we are looking for the price of x which will yield a zero excess demand for x for any given price of y.

From our previous analysis we can see that when the price of y was 5, equilibrium price of x was 25 (point G in Figure 6.6). For $p_y = 10$, equilibrium price of x was 26 (point H in the above figure). It is easy to see that the slope of the $ED^x = 0$ line is really (dp_y/dp_x). From our numerical example this is clearly 5. For a 5 point increase in the price of y, there is only 1 point of an increase in the price of x ($5/1 = 5$).

In more general terms, from the equilibrium price equation in the market for x (which implies zero excess demand for x) we can see that an increase in the price of y will cause an increase in the price of x as long as $e > 0$. Hence, we will have an upward sloping line to depict the combinations of p_x and p_y for which there is zero excess demand in the market for x. It is easy to see that an increase by dp_y units in the price of y will increase the equilibrium price of x by $[e/(b+c)]$:

$$dp_x^e = p_{x_1}^e - p_{x_2}^e = \frac{a + e(p_{y_0} + dp_y) + dw}{c + b} - \frac{a + ep_{y_0} + dw}{c + b}$$

$$= \left[\frac{a + dw}{c + b} + \frac{e}{c + b}(p_{y_0} + dp_y)\right] - \left[\frac{a + dw}{c + b} + \frac{e}{c + b}(p_{y_0})\right] = dp_y\frac{e}{c + b}$$

hence

$$dp_x^e = dp_y\frac{e}{c + b}$$

$$\frac{dp_x^e}{dp_y} = \frac{e}{c + b}.$$

In our case, this will be a 1/5. As I pointed out above, the slope of the $ED^x = 0$ line is given by (dp_y/dp_x). The expression $[e/(b+c)]$ which represents the change in the equilibrium values of p_x resulting from a change in the values of p_y is really dp_x/dp_y. Hence, the slope of the line is $1/[e/(b+c)]$ which is $(b+c)/e$. The reason for the positively sloped line is equally clear. When the price of y increases and the two goods are gross substitutes, there will be an increase in the demand for x which, in turn, suggests that equilibrium will be obtained at higher price for x.

Whatever we said about the market for x given the price of y can be said about the market for y for any given price of x. That is to say, there is a demand function for y which is a function of the price of x:

$$y^d = D^y(p_x, p_y) = f - gp_y + mp_x = 90 - 2p_y + 1p_x$$

a supply function:

$$y^s = S^y(p_y, w) = hp_y - jw = 3p_y - 3w$$

and an excess demand function:

$$ED^y(p_x, p_y, w) = y^d - y^s = D^y(p_x, p_y) - S^y(p_y, w) = f - gp_y + mp_x - [hp_y - jw]$$
$$ED^y(p_x, p_y, w) = f + mp_x + jw - p_y(g + h) = 90 + 1p_x + 3w - 5p_x.$$

The equilibrium price for y (that price for which excess demand for y is zero for any given price of x will be:

$$(y^d =)f - gp_y + mp_x = hp_y - jw(= y^s)$$

hence

$$p_y^e = \frac{f + mp_x + jw}{g + h}.$$

From where we get that even when the price of x is zero, there will still be a positive price of y for which the market for y will clear.

As the price of x increases, demand for y will increase, also (see Figure 6.7). This means that at the existing price of y there will be excess demand for y and the price will increase until it reaches its new equilibrium level.

Combining the two graphs together will give us the solution to the problem to this 'vertical' dimension of general equilibrium (Figure 6.8).

Existence
As you can clearly see from Figure 6.8, provided that the slopes of the two ED functions are such that they intersect, there exist a pair of prices (p_x^*, p_y^*) such that there is no excess demand in either markets. Put differently, both the market for x and the market for y are in equilibrium.

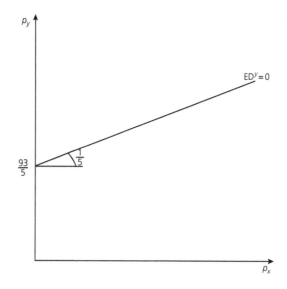

Figure 6.7 The $ED^y = 0$ line.

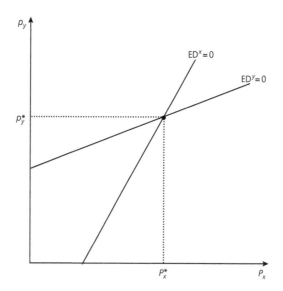

Figure 6.8 General equilibrium in markets for x and y.

Algebraically, the solution is also fairly straightforward. We wish the two excess demand functions to be equal to zero at the same time. That is, we are looking for the prices of x and y such that

$$x^d - x^s = a - bp_x + ep_y - [cp_x - dw] = 0$$
$$y^d - y^s = f - gp_y + mp_x = hp_y - jw = 0.$$

Rearranging,

$$(b + c)p_x - ep_y = a + dw$$

$$-mp_x + (g + h)\, p_y = f + jw.$$

This is a simple set of simultaneous equations where there two endogenous variables (p_x and p_y) and a set of exogenous coefficients ($a, b, c, d, e, f, g, h, j$). Endogenous variables are the variables the values of which are determined in the model. Exogenous variables are those components of the system the values of which are known before we solve the model. In our example, the only endogenous variables are the prices of x and y. All other values are known in advance. This, of course, suggests that it is not really the price of x which determines the price of y or the price of y which determines the price of x. Instead, both prices are determined by the other coefficients like taste (which will affect a, and e in the case of x and f and m in the case of y), technology (c and d in the case of x and h and j in the case of y) and wages. In a complete system, wages represent a price and they also will be determined endogenously. Therefore, what determines the equilibrium values of all prices are tastes and technology.

I leave it to you to solve the system but there is an easy way of doing it (using the Cramer method) from which we get that

$$p_x = \frac{(a + dw)(h + g) + (f + jw)e}{(c + d)(h + g) - (me)}$$

$$p_y = \frac{(c + d)(f + jw) + (a + dw)m}{(c + d)(h + g) - (me)}$$

which means that the value of the endogenous variables is determined only by the values of the exogenous variables. As long as the two expressions on the right-hand side of the above equations are greater than zero, there exists an equilibrium.

Exercise
Use different methods to calculate the equilibrium values of the prices of x and y in our specific example.

Stability
If you recall from the discussion in Chapter 4, we said there that the existence of equilibrium is by no means sufficient from our point of view. If there are no forces which will direct the economy back to an equilibrium price once the system is thrown out of equilibrium, the equilibrium itself is meaningless. Let us briefly examine whether or not there is a potential for stability in our system (see Figure 6.9).

Suppose that, initially, both markets are not in equilibrium and we start at point A with the pair of prices p_x^A and p_y^A. From the point of view of the market for x, at the price of p_y^A, the equilibrium price of x would be higher (p_x^{AE}). Therefore, as the actual price of x is lower ($p_x^A < p_x^{AE}$) it means that there is excess demand for x. Whenever there is excess demand, we expect someone to bid up the price and thus push the price of x towards its equilibrium level, which lies to the right of point A. The position of A relative to the $ED^X = 0$ line corresponds to its position relative to $ED^Y = 0$ line. Hence, as the actual price of y is less than its equilibrium value (p_y^{AE}), there is excess demand for y as well.

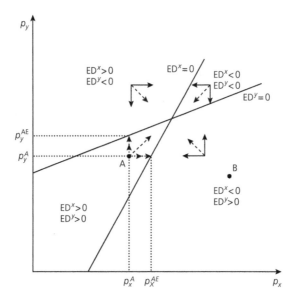

Figure 6.9 Stability of equilibrium.

Hence, the price of y will be pushed to its equilibrium value (the upward arrow from A) while the price of x will be pushed to the right towards its equilibrium value. As the time path of these changes is not clear, we can imagine that both prices will change at a similar speed. This means that both prices will change in the direction to which the third arrow is pointing. This direction is clearly the one that will lead the markets to the general equilibrium solution.

Once you understand that the ED = 0 lines represent equilibrium values, you can see that a similar principle will apply from whichever point we choose to start from. If we start at B it is clear that for any given price of y the price of x will be moving in the direction of its equilibrium value (i.e., to the left). The price of y will tend to its equilibrium value of any given price of x (which is upwards). Again, the arrow in between represents this change in both prices over time and it also points towards the general equilibrium values of both the price of x and the price of y.

6.1.2 The 'vertical' dimension of general equilibrium

Until now we have looked at the question of the existence (and stability) of the inter-dependence across markets of final goods. The immediate cause for their interdependence is clearly the fact that consumers have preferences over the complete world of economic goods. Consequently, the price of every good is bound to influence their behaviour in other markets. At the same time when individuals make decisions regarding consumption they also make decisions regarding the supply of factors and, in particular, the supply of labour. It is this supply—coupled with technology—which eventually determines the equilibrium level of wages (which is one source of income) which, in turn, affects the marginal cost and the supply of final goods.

As I said earlier, there is no real substance to the distinction between 'vertical' and 'horizontal' dimension. As individuals make simultaneous decisions with regard to consumption and the supply of factors, the equilibrium values of all prices (including those goods which are used in the production of others) are determined simultaneously. Still, the aim of the distinction between the vertical and the horizontal was mainly to reduce slightly the complexity of the analysis.

To be precise, what I mean by the vertical dimension of equilibrium is the relationship between the consumption decision and the supply of factor decision (which, in turn, determines the availability of goods for consumption). To some extent, we are describing here the world of Robinson Crusoe.

Suppose that an individual lives on an island where he can rely on his work alone to generate consumption. There is only one good which can be produced on the island. The technology of its production is based on labour alone and has the form of a normal production function where $x = f(L)$. There are, therefore, two economic goods on the island. One is the good x and the other, leisure. The production possibilities frontier confronting this individual is shown in Figure 6.10.

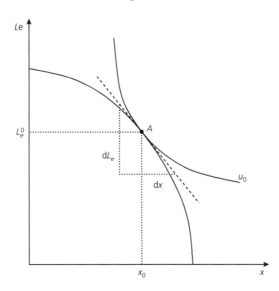

Figure 6.10 Robinson Crusoe's PPF and indifference curves.

If the individual chooses to lie on a beach all day, he will have the maximum level of leisure with zero consumption from the other good. When, eventually, he decides that lying on the beach is not what he wants and that he would like to have some x, he will face the following situation. If he gives up one unit of leisure ($dL_e = 1$ h), he will be able to produce x according to the productivity of his first hour of work ($dx = MP_L$ units of x). Hence, the slope of the PPF which is given geometrically as dL_e/dx, equals to $1/MP_L$ units of leisure hours per unit of x. As the marginal product of labour is diminishing, the slope of the PPF becomes steeper the more he works. In other words, when he only starts working his productivity is high. An hour of leisure, therefore, forgoes a lot of x (a very high opportunity cost for leisure). Equivalently, the opportunity cost of a unit of x is very low (as his productivity is high, he can produce a unit of x in a fraction of an hour).

Therefore, as the price of leisure is very high, the price of one unit of x (in terms of leisure) is very small indeed. Hence, the slope of the PPF is almost flat when we start producing x (reflecting the price of x) and becomes steeper the more x we produce. At the beginning, each unit of x requires a small fraction of our leisure time (as we are very productive when we work). But when we have slaved in the field all day, we are tired and our productivity is reduced. Every extra unit of x will require an increasing fraction of our time which could have otherwise been spent on the beach.

In addition, the individual has utility which is defined over x and leisure. As both are economic goods, in the sense that they are scarce and desirable, utility is rising with more of both goods and there are downward sloping indifference curves. For our individual, the PPF constitutes the 'budget' constraint, and if he is rational he will choose the allocation of time between labour and leisure in such a way as to maximize his utility from both x and leisure. This is point A in the figure. At this point, the slope of the indifference curve (which is his willingness to pay for x in terms of leisure or his marginal utility of x measured in terms of leisure) will be the same as the slope of the PPF:

$$-\frac{dL_e}{dx} = \frac{1}{MP_L^x} = \frac{MU_x}{MU_{Lei}}$$

units of leisure per unit of x.

In Chapter 5 we established that the individual's choice with regard to consumption and leisure means that a rational agent will choose a combination of leisure and consumption such that the subjective rate of substitution (or, his willingness to pay for the good in terms of leisure) will be equal to the market rate of exchange between the two. Had there been markets for labour and x (as this is an island), the price of leisure would have been the wage level per unit of labour and there would have been a price for x: p_x. Hence, we know that optimal consumption means that

$$-\frac{dL_e}{dx} = \frac{1}{MP_L^x} = \frac{MU_x}{MU_{Lei}} = \frac{p_x}{w}$$

Hence,

$$w = p_x MP_L.$$

This means that the nominal wage will be equal to the value of marginal product. Again, recall from Chapter 5 that these are the equilibrium conditions in the labour market. We have thus established the general equilibrium conditions for competitive markets along the process of production. The consumer chooses his supply of labour and demand for consumption according to the principle which equates the subjective rate of substitution with the market rate of exchange. Producers will produce according to the profit maximization principle where they equate the marginal rate of technological substitution with the market rate of exchange for factors.

6.1.3 The complete picture

Suppose that we have a two goods economy (x and y) which are produced by a single means of production. What can we say now about the conditions for equilibrium across all markets and within the production relations of each commodity? We begin by summing up the conditions across the two figures.

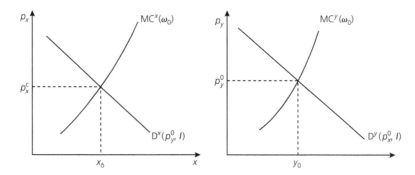

Figure 6.11

In each of the markets for final goods we have an excess demand function of the following general character (see Figure 6.11).

$$ED^x = x^d(p_x, p_y, I) - x^S(p_x, w, r) \equiv ED^x(p_x, p_y, I, w, r)$$

$$ED^y = y^d(p_y, p_x, I) - y^S(p_y, w, r) \equiv ED^y(p_y, p_x, I, w, r)$$

clearly

$$\dot{p}_x = F(ED^x) \qquad \dot{p}_y = G(ED^y).$$

Where the dynamics is assumed to be such that whenever there is **excess demand** in a market, prices will rise and whenever there is excess supply (**negative excess demand**), prices will fall. In Figure 6.12 we recap the existence of the general conditions in both markets. Together with the vertical considerations (when labour is the only means of production) we will get the following complete picture (see Figure 6.13).

   Competitive equilibrium means that in each separate market:

(a) Prices are equal to marginal costs.

(b) The distribution of surpluses is efficient.

I will show now that the meaning of (a) is that the competitive prices, that is, the market rate of exchange between x and y reflects the true technological (social[2]) circumstances. In geometrical terms, I will show that it equals the slope of the PPF.

   What exactly is the slope of the PPF? In the plane of (x, y), the slope of the PPF is geometrically defined as: $-dy/dx$. The negative sign represents the negative slope. This means that if we increase $y(dy > 0)$ we will have to decrease $x(dx < 0)$. Any point on the PPF represents that quantities of x and y which can be produced simultaneously

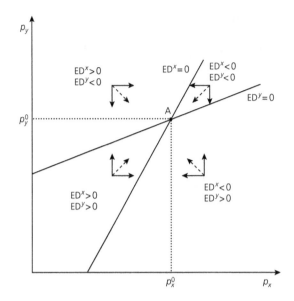

Figure 6.12 General equilibrium in the final goods market.

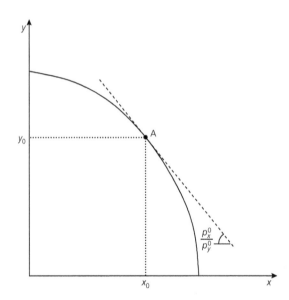

Figure 6.13 Equilibrium in production.

and where we cannot have more of one good (either x or y) without giving up another (i.e. productive efficient). Thus, the meaning of the slope is the amount of y we have to forgo in order to produce one more unit of x. As we chose to define technology (in Chapter 3) as the boundaries of human knowledge which assume the full participation of all agents (i.e. productivity is at its highest level), the position of the PPF is independent of the way production (or society) is organized. In this sense, the quantity of y we have to forgo to produce one extra unit of x which is derived from the PPF is really a neutral measure. It tells us what is the technological cost of x measured in units of y. This cost is independent of the way we organize our economic activities.

So how do we measure this 'technological cost' or what is known in the literature as the **marginal rate of technological substitution**? Well, suppose that you take one labourer away from y and you reallocate him to produce x. The loss of y (dy) will be exactly the marginal product of that labourer in the production of y; the gains in x (dx) will be exactly the marginal product of that labourer in x. Hence,

$$dy = dL \, MP_L^y$$

$$dx = dL \, MP_L^x$$

In our case, as we move one worker, $dL = 1$. Recall that geometry tells us that, by definition, the slope of the PPF in the plane of (x, y) is given by $-dy/dx$. Given what we had said about dy and dx, this slope becomes:

$$-\frac{dy}{dx} = \frac{dL \cdot MP_L^y}{dL \cdot MP_L^x} = \frac{MP_L^y}{MP_L^x}.$$

Measured in units of y per x. We saw the PPF in the case of Robinson Crusoe. Figure 6.14 is our case.

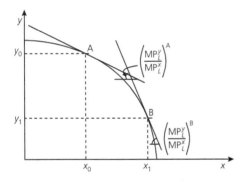

Figure 6.14

At A, we produce a lot of y and very little of x. This means that the productivity of factors in the production of x is greater than their productivity in the production of y. Either from the point of view of an individual input (which is what we assume here) or from the point of view of returns to scale, the production of x takes place when we still have increasing returns while that of y where returns are diminishing. This is why the slope is so flat and, indeed, transferring a worker from y to x will cause such a small loss in y in return for such a high gain in x that the opportunity cost of one unit of x is bound to be very small indeed (flat slope). When we move to B, the whole picture is reversed.

Bearing all this in mind, let us examine now what it means to say that that all markets are perfectly competitive.

$$p_x = \text{MC}(x) = \frac{\overline{w}}{\text{MP}_L^x}$$

$$p_y = \text{MC}(y) = \frac{\overline{w}}{\text{MP}_L^y}$$

Hence

$$\frac{p_x}{p_y} = \frac{\text{MC}(x)}{\text{MC}(y)} = \frac{\overline{w}/\text{MP}_L^x}{\overline{w}/\text{MP}_L^y} = \frac{\text{MP}_L^y}{\text{MP}_L^x} = \frac{\mathrm{d}y}{\mathrm{d}x}.$$

This means that when all markets are perfectly competitive market prices will reflect the true technological/social costs.[3] This means that by allowing markets to operate competitively, we were able to produce an exchange rate between the goods which represents exactly how much they cost society to produce. This has been achieved without having to resort to any central collection of information or guidance.

When, in Chapter 4, we discussed the significance of competitive markets we concluded that they are productive efficient as all firms produce on their cost functions which represent optimal choices such that the output they produced could not have been produced at lower costs. This was, inherently, a general equilibrium claim.

When we come to discuss allocative efficiency, things get much more complex. We have established that we can use the area underneath the demand schedule to represent the welfare of consumers in what we called the consumers' surplus. We chose to look at the area above the MC (and below the price) as representing the benefits of producers in what we called producers' surplus. We argued that in terms of these surpluses, competitive equilibrium represents an efficient distribution of them. Can we rely on this to claim that the general equilibrium nature of competition is also allocatively efficient? The problem of using surpluses is that these are partial equilibrium considerations. It is very difficult to move from this type of consideration to the general equilibrium type of consideration. In particular, this is problematic as it is based on the presumption that there exists such an agent called a firm which is distinct from the consumers and the participants in the process of production. In order to understand whether the competition is allocative efficient, we would need to investigate, head on, the competition between individuals. We shall do so in the next section but before this, we would like to highlight another insight into the benefits of competition. However, we shall have to base this insight on a serious inaccuracy. Namely, we would like to associate the competitive outcome with that which society desires but to establish that which society desires is a very complicated problem. So instead of struggling with the question of how to capture social preference we shall assume that we are able to capture the preferences of all members of society through the preferences of a representative agent. We can thus learn something about what society's choices between x and y would be.

As the representative agent would also make choices in a rational way, he would choose the combination of x and y which maximizes their utility. They do so by equating the slope of the budget constraint (market prices) with the highest indifference curve (subjective valuation). Thus, we know that a competitive equilibrium is characterized by the following trinity:

$$\frac{MP_L^y}{MP_L^x} = \frac{p_x}{p_y} = \frac{MU_x^{RA}}{MU_y^{RA}}.$$

The technological rate of exchange between x and y (MP_L^y/MP_L^x units of y per x), which is entirely due to technology, is equal to the market rate of exchange between x and y (p_x/p_y units of y per x) as well as to the representative agent's marginal utility of x measured in units of y. This is exactly what happens at point A in Figure 6.15.

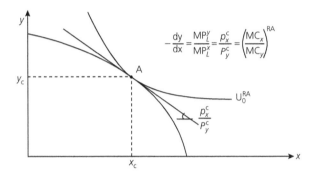

Figure 6.15

This picture suggests that by allowing individuals to pursue their own interests, assuming that they are all rational, the outcome of this decentralized system in which the government is only needed to uphold law and order is both productive and allocative efficient. Here, we represent the allocative efficiency nature of the solution by showing that the competitive solution would also constitute the most preferred bundle of the agent who represents all social preferences. Namely, that which society desires seems to be consistent with the outcome of the free reign of rational self-interest. Naturally, if the competitive solution is the one society desires, it must also be allocative efficient—why would society prefer an allocation where someone can be made better off without anyone else becoming worse off?

Notwithstanding the difficulty of thinking of a representative agent as a means of aggregating social preferences, we can use this presentation of the efficiency of competitive equilibrium to better understand inefficiencies created by, say, monopolists or through taxation. The figure below demonstrates the inefficiency of the monopolist market structure. As this is a general equilibrium model we must also assume something about the other markets. We shall assume that the market for y is perfectly competitive and so is the labour market.

As we said in Chapter 4, there is no a priori reason to believe that the monopolist is productively inefficient. As long as there is competition via ownership (stock markets), managers would be under pressure to keep the cost of producing whatever they produce at the lowest level. As the market for y is perfectly competitive and so is the labour market, we can clearly assume that the economy would be productive efficient (see Figure 6.16).

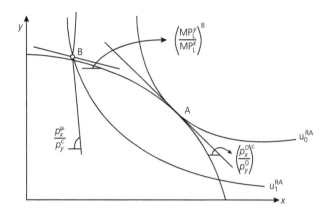

Figure 6.16

Suppose that at first all markets are perfectly competitive. We are, therefore, at point A where as all prices equal marginal costs, market prices reflect their true social cost. It is also the point where our representative agent would have maximized his utility. Now, the market for x became a monopolist. This means that there will be less x produced and the price of x will rise. Relative to the competitive solution we know that there will now be a loss of utility (deadweight loss). However, we must be more careful here. As the price of x increases, so will demand for y (if they were gross substitutes). This means that consumer surplus in y may increase to offset some of the losses. So how can we argue that the deadweight loss is indeed a loss? Well, in terms of general equilibrium we have less x but more y. So the economy moves from point A to point B in the above PPF. But will the new prices carry on reflecting the true social costs?

As in the monopolist case: $p_x^M > \text{MR}(x) = \text{MC}(x)$, it means that

$$p_x > \text{MC}(x) = \frac{\overline{w}}{\text{MP}_L^x} \text{ monopolist}$$

$$p_y = \text{MC}(y) = \frac{\overline{w}}{\text{MP}_L^y} \text{ competitive}$$

hence

$$\frac{p_x}{p_y} > \frac{\text{MC}(x)}{\text{MC}(y)} = \frac{\overline{w}/\text{MP}_L^x}{\overline{w}/\text{MP}_L^y} = \frac{\text{MP}_L^y}{\text{MP}_L^x} = \frac{dy}{dx}.$$

Hence, the slope representing the market rate of exchange at B is greater than the slope of the PPF at that point. It means that we pay for x, in terms of y, more than it really costs to produce. Moreover, not only do we pay more for x (and less for y), the representative agent would want to maximize his utility by looking for the bundle which equates his marginal rate of substitution with the market rate of exchange. Thus the indifference curve of the representative agent would be tangent to the price ratio at point B. But this, as you can clearly see, is a lower level of utility. Thus, the monopolist allocation is productively efficient but allocatively inefficient. The total amount of utility available for society would be lower than in the case of competition. The deadweight loss, therefore, is indeed a loss.

But while this highlights the greatness of the competitive solution we must take note of an important corollary. In our discussion, we focused on the monopolized market. However, in the economy we described there are three markets. There is the market for x, for labour (leisure), and for y. Out of the three markets, two were competitive (the market for y and for labour). So, does this mean that if we examined competitive industry y, in spite of our conviction that it is efficient (in a partial equilibrium set up) it is not? The answer, I am afraid, is affirmative. While testing the working of decentralized decision-making systems at the limit of competition suggests that they can work, it also suggests that the conditions for this are very stringent indeed. All markets must be competitive at the same time for the benefits of competition to be accrued. You can imagine that point B could have been a result of a situation where all markets are monopolized. How can we argue that the benefits of y are genuine when only one other market is monopolized if a situation where all markets are monopolized produces the same general equilibrium outcome? We shall come back to this point in Chapter 7. Now, let us take our investigation of allocative efficiency to a more appropriate level. As I said earlier, one of the problems we have in studying allocative efficiency in markets is because of the presumption that the opposing forces are those of consumers and producers. In our individualistic theory, both the identification of agents as being either consumers or producers and the presumption that there is such an 'agent' called the firms are misguided. Thus, to better understand the significance of competition to allocative efficiency, we move now to examine economies where individuals are not identified with any aspect of the market. In addition, such a framework facilitates an answer to the question of allocative efficiency without resorting to the abstract notion of a representative agent.

6.2 An exchange economy and Pareto efficiency

Suppose that we have two individuals (1 and 2) and two commodities (x and y). Suppose too, that each individual has his income in kind (i.e. in goods). Thus, the bundles $(\bar{x}_1, \bar{y}_1)$ and $(\bar{x}_2, \bar{y}_2)$ represent the income of individuals 1 and 2, respectively. This means that before any trade takes place, individuals have at their disposal a certain quantity of each good. They could, therefore, choose not to trade if as rational agents they would feel that they only wish to consume that which they have earned. The two diagrams of Figure 6.17 depict (at point A) the initial endowment (income) of each individual. To make things easy, let us add numbers to our story. Let the initial bundles be: $(\bar{x}_1, \bar{y}_1) = (10, 20)$ (which means that individual 1 gets his income as a bundle of 10 units of x and 20 units of y). Let $(\bar{x}_2, \bar{y}_2) = (40, 10)$ which means that individual 2 gets 40 units of x and only 10 units of y. Altogether, there are $\bar{x}_1 + \bar{x}_2 = 10 + 40 = 50$ units of x in the economy and $\bar{y}_1 + \bar{y}_2 = 20 + 10 = 30$ units of y.

Suppose that both individuals have the same utility function $u(x_i, y_i) = x_i y_i$ (which means that if $i = 1$ we are looking at individual 1 and if $i = 2$, this is the utility function of individual 2). From a general analysis of such a utility function we can establish whether

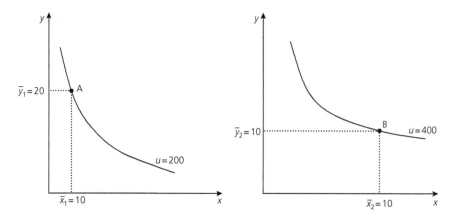

Figure 6.17 Indifference curve of two individuals in an exchange economy.

an individual would want to keep his income in kind or trade it for a more preferred mix of the two goods. Recall that an optimal choice is a choice where the subjective rate of substitution equals the market rate of exchange:

$$\frac{MU_x}{MU_y} = \frac{p_x}{p_y} \text{ units of } y \text{ per } x.$$

What is the marginal utility of x in our case? Suppose that we have x_0 units of x and y_0 units of y. Our utility will be: $u(x_0, y_0) = x_0 y_0$. The marginal utility of x will be the increase in utility which will result from increasing the consumption of x by 1 unit. Let $x_1 = x_0 + 1$. Therefore, $u(x_1, y_0) = x_1 y_0 = (x_0 + 1)y_0$. The marginal utility of the extra unit of x will be the difference between the utility with it and the utility without it:

$$MU_x = u(x_1, y_0) - u(x_0, y_0)$$
$$= x_1 y_0 - x_0 y_0 = (x_0 + 1)y_0 - x_0 y_0$$
$$= x_0 y_0 + y_0 - x_0 y_0 = y_0.$$

In general, therefore, the marginal utility of x is y and for a similar type of argument, the marginal utility of y is x. Hence, the conditions for optimal consumption become

$$\frac{MU_x}{MU_y} = \frac{y}{x} = \frac{p_x}{p_y} \text{ units of } y \text{ per } x.$$

At point A in the above diagrams, the utility from the initial bundle is as follows: for individual 1 $u(10, 20) = 200$ and for individual 2 $u(40, 10) = 400$.[4] Had the prices been: $p_x = 4$ and $p_y = 2$, would individual 1 wish to trade?

Now, $p_x/p_y = 4/2 = 2$ units of y per x. At point A individual 1 has 20 units of y and 10 units of x. The individual's rate of subjective substitution y/x equals $20/10 = 2$ units of y per x. Hence, as the marginal rate of subjective substitution equals the market rate of exchange, the individual will be consuming at an optimal point and will not wish to trade.

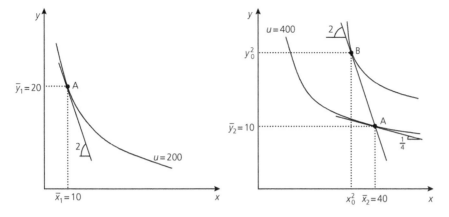

Figure 6.18 Prices and marginal rate of substitution.

In the left-hand diagram of Figure 6.18, the budget constraint at A is tangent to the slope of the indifference curve. Hence, A would constitute a rational choice.

For individual 2 the story will be slightly different. At A in the right-hand diagram, $y/x = 10/40 = 1/4$ units of y per x. This is clearly less than the market rate of exchange which means that individual 2 is willing to pay for y more than it costs in the market place. As the price is 2 units of y per x or $1/2$ unit of x per y, this is clearly less than his willingness to pay for y as measured by the subjective rate of substitution. For an x, he is willing to pay y/x units of y (or $1/4$ y per x). Hence, he is willing to pay 4 units of x per y. As he is willing to pay so much more for y, it is unlikely that the price of y will remain $1/4$. Individual 2 would like to move to a different point (like B) where he sells x and buys y.

How much would individual 1 want to sell or buy of x and y as the prices change? To see this we must establish how much x (or y) will he want to consume given his utility function. We know that the rule of optimal choice suggests that

$$\frac{MU_x}{MU_y} = \frac{y}{x} = \frac{p_x}{p_y}$$

hence,

$$x = \frac{p_y}{p_x}y.$$

The money income of this individual will be

$$I_0 = p_x\bar{x}_1 + p_y\bar{y}_1$$

and his budget constraint

$$I_0 = p_x\bar{x}_1 + p_y\bar{y}_1 = p_xx + p_yy$$

where x_1 and y_1 on the right-hand side of the equation denote the quantities of x and y which he wishes to consume. Given that his income is in kind, this means that the individual can always choose not to trade. Put differently, he can always choose to consume his income. Thus, all budget lines will have to go through point A.

From the budget line we can now extract y:

$$y = \frac{p_x \bar{x}_1 + p_y \bar{y}_1}{p_y} = \frac{p_x}{p_y}\bar{x}_1 + \bar{y}_1$$

and add this to the optimal condition where the marginal rate of subjective substitution equals the market rate of exchange:

$$x_1 = \frac{p_y}{p_x}\left(\frac{p_x \bar{x}_1 + p_y \bar{y}_1}{p_y} - \frac{p_x}{p_y}x_1\right)$$

$$= \bar{x}_1 + \frac{p_y}{p_x}\bar{y}_1 - x_1$$

$$2x_1 = \bar{x}_1 + \frac{p_y}{p_x}\bar{y}_1$$

$$x_1 = \frac{\bar{x}_1}{2} + \frac{1}{2}\frac{p_y}{p_x}\bar{y}_1$$

which means that the quantity of x which the individual will want to consume is a function of his income and the relative prices. This is consistent with everything we said in Chapter 2 about the parameters of demand. Similarly, we can get an equivalent equation to describe how much y the individual will want to consume:

$$y_1 = \frac{\bar{y}_1}{2} + \frac{1}{2}\frac{p_x}{p_y}\bar{x}_1.$$

Again, due to the fact that both individuals have the same utility function and that the function is symmetrical, everything we said here about individual 1 is also true of individual 2. Namely, we will have the same corresponding equations to describe x_2 and y_2.

Let us describe now how the decision is made with regard to how much of each good we want to buy or sell. Consider the good x_1. Initially, we have x_1 units of the good. We know from above that we will want to consume $x_1 = (x_1/2) + (1/2)(p_y/p_x)y_1$. So whether we want to buy or sell x depends on whether our initial bundle contains more or less units of x. Let E_x describe the difference between the quantity of x we have and the quantity of x we want:

$$E_x = \bar{x}_1 - x_1 = \bar{x}_1 - \frac{1}{2}\bar{x}_1 - \frac{1}{2}\frac{p_y}{p_x}\bar{y}_1$$

$$E_x = \frac{1}{2}\bar{x}_1 - \frac{1}{2}\frac{p_y}{p_x}\bar{y}_1$$

similarly,

$$E_y = \frac{1}{2}\bar{y}_1 - \frac{1}{2}\frac{p_x}{p_y}\bar{x}_1.$$

Hence, if $E > 0$ it means that we want to sell the good as the quantity of it which we have is greater than the quantity of it which we want. If $E < 0$, we will want to sell the good as the quantity of it which we already have is smaller than the quantity of the good which we wish to consume. Let us go back to our example (see Figure 6.19).

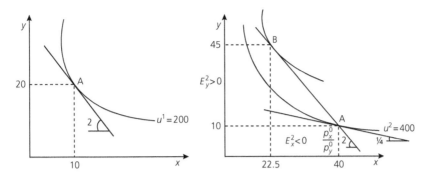

Figure 6.19 Edgeworth box with relative price equal to 2.

We saw that when $p_x/p_y = 4/2 = 2$ units of y per x, individual 1 would not want to move from point A which constitutes an optimal choice. Individual 2, however, would have liked to buy some y and sell some x. Let us verify these conclusions.
At the relative price of 2, what will E_x^1 be? Given the above equation we know that

$$E_x^1 = \frac{1}{2}\bar{x}_1 - \frac{1}{2}\frac{p_y}{p_x}\bar{y}_1 = \frac{10}{2} - \frac{1}{2}\frac{2}{4}20 = 5 - 5 = 0$$

$$E_y^1 = \frac{1}{2}\bar{y}_1 - \frac{1}{2}\frac{p_x}{p_y}\bar{x}_1 = \frac{1}{2}20 - \frac{1}{2}\frac{4}{2}10 = 10 - 10 = 0$$

which means that individual 1 will not choose to trade. Individual 2, on the other hand would have wanted to move to a point like B in the right-hand diagram of the figure as this is where his utility is maximized. Indeed, using these equations would give us the answer to the question of how much of the good he would have wanted to trade:

$$E_x^2 = \frac{1}{2}\bar{x}_2 - \frac{1}{2}\frac{p_y}{p_x}\bar{y}_2 = \frac{1}{2}40 - \frac{1}{2}\frac{2}{4}10 = 20 - 2.5 = 17.5$$

$$E_y^2 = \frac{1}{2}\bar{y}_2 - \frac{1}{2}\frac{p_x}{p_y}\bar{x}_2 = \frac{1}{2}10 - \frac{1}{2}\frac{4}{2}40 = 5 - 40 = -35$$

which means that he wants to sell 17.5 units of x and buy 35 units of y. In the figure above, you can clearly see that the individual wishes to exchange y for x at the market rate of exchange.

Naturally, the fact that one of the individuals wants to bring about a change is sufficient for us to suppose that the given relative prices will not be sustained. Individual 2 is very likely to make an offer to individual 1 that will make both of them better off.

In simple terminology, individual 2 wants to buy y while individual 1 does not wish to sell (thus, we have excess demand which means that the price of y will have to rise). In the market for x individual 2 wants to sell but individual 1 does not wish to buy. We have excess supply of x and its price must fall. Suppose that the prices have changed such that $p_x = p_y = 3$. This means that we now have a market rate of exchange of $p_x/p_y = 3/3 = 1$ unit y per x. What will now happen to the choices of both our individuals?

Clearly, at A there is no longer correspondence between the slope of the indifference curve and the relative market price (Figure 6.20). The slope of the indifference curve (for

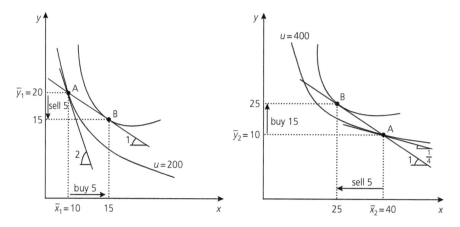

Figure 6.20 Consumption and endowments for $p_x/p_y = 1$.

individual 1) will be $y/x = 20/10 = 2$ units of y per x while the market price of x in terms of y is only 1 unit of y. As we have to pay less than what we are willing to pay, we would choose to have more of x. Similarly, individual 2's subjective rate of substitution is still 10/40=1/4 units of y per x (at A) or 4 units of x per y. As the market price of y is now only 1 unit of y per x, individual 2 will want to buy more units of y.

Following our equations we can see that both individuals will want to move to a point like B in Figure 6.16. At B the situation will be as follows:

At the relative price of 2, what will E_x^1 be? Given the above equation we know that:

$$E_x^1 = \frac{1}{2}\bar{x}_1 - \frac{1}{2}\frac{p_y}{p_x}\bar{y}_1 = \frac{10}{2} - \frac{1}{2}\frac{3}{3}20 = 5 - 10 = -5,$$

$$E_y^1 = \frac{1}{2}\bar{y}_1 - \frac{1}{2}\frac{p_x}{p_y}\bar{x}_1 = \frac{1}{2}20 - \frac{1}{2}\frac{3}{3}10 = 10 - 5 = 5,$$

which means that individual 1 will want to buy 5 units of x and sell 5 units of y. Individual 2, on the other hand would want the following:

$$E_x^2 = \frac{1}{2}\bar{x}_2 - \frac{1}{2}\frac{p_y}{p_x}\bar{y}_2 = \frac{1}{2}40 - \frac{1}{2}\frac{3}{3}10 = 20 - 5 = 15,$$

$$E_y^2 = \frac{1}{2}\bar{y}_2 - \frac{1}{2}\frac{p_x}{p_y}\bar{x}_2 = \frac{1}{2}10 - \frac{1}{2}\frac{3}{3}40 = 5 - 20 = -15,$$

which means that he wants to sell 15 units of x and buy 15 units of y. While this is clearly not an equilibrium situation as the quantity demanded of, say x, is not the same as the quantity offered, it is important to note that had this been the price, points B in the above diagram depict the trade in which each of these individuals will be interested. For any price, therefore, there is a corresponding point like B in the above diagram which depicts the trade position of each individual. As the price rotates, the trade offered will change (Figure 6.21).

The line connecting all such points is called the **offer curve**. Each individual will have an offer curve which starts at the initial endowment (where they do not wish to trade)

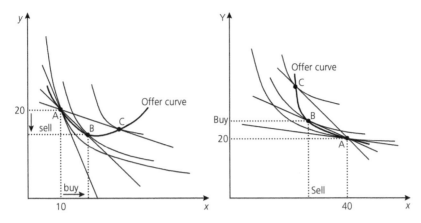

Figure 6.21 The offer curve.

and changes according to the change in the relative market price. A point on the offer curve will have the features of point B, above, where it tells us how much of each good individuals will want to buy or sell. Note that at each point on the offer curve (like B above) each individual is maximizing his utility. The idea of **general equilibrium** in this context is the existence of a price for which the good which individual 1 wishes to sell is the same as that which individual 2 wishes to buy and vice versa.

To study the existence of such an equilibrium we must examine the offer curves of both individuals within the same diagram. To achieve this we propose to superimpose one graph (say the left-hand diagram) onto the right-hand diagram. We take the right-hand diagram from above, rotate it, and impose it on the left-hand diagram:

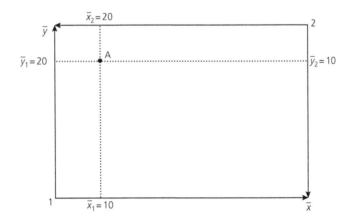

Figure 6.22 The Edgeworth box.

What we have here is what is called the **Edgeworth Box** (Figure 6.22). The bottom left end of the box represents individual 1's point of view while the point at the top right-hand side of the box represents individual 2's point of view. Point A, now, is the common initial point which we had in our previous diagrams. It depicts the initial bundle of both individuals when read from their respective 'corners'. From the point of view of individual 1 we can see that he has 10 units of x and 20 units of y. Individual 2 (from the top right) has 40 units of x and 10 units of y. Altogether, the box defines the domain of trade: that which there is in the economy. In our case, there are altogether 50 units of x and 30 units of y. Point A, therefore, describes a certain initial distribution between the two agents. Figure 6.23 depicts the two agents positions when the relative price is 2.

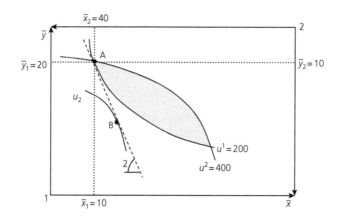

Figure 6.23 Edgeworth box with relative price level equal to 2.

It is easy to see that individual 1 will not want to trade while individual 2 will want to exchange x for y. At the same time, it is also clear that all the allocations trapped between the two initial indifference curves (the shaded area) represent greater utility to both individuals (unlike point B where only individual 2 will be made better off). This suggests that both individuals will have an incentive to find a way to trade.

Note that the indifference curves of each individual is convex in the opposite direction. Utility, also, is rising in the opposite direction. Individual 1's highest utility is the top right-hand end of the box while individual 2's highest utility is at the bottom left-hand end of the diagram. Figure 6.24 has the case when the relative price is 1.

It is clear that if the individuals traded to their respective point B each one of them will be made better off. At A, individual 1's utility is $u(10, 20) = 10 \times 20 = 200$. If he had his way he would want to buy 5 extra units of x and sell 5 units of y. This means that he will have 15 units of x and only 15 units of y. Clearly, $u(10, 20) < u(15, 15) = 225$. You can do the same calculation for 2.

Indeed, you can easily verify that all the points within the shaded area represent allocations where both individuals are on a higher indifference curve. This is a reiteration of the point we made in Chapter 1 regarding the notion of benefits from trade. For each initial position like A, there are allocations where both sides can make gains. Let us now examine the existence of the general equilibrium price where all rational plans coincide (Figure 6.25).

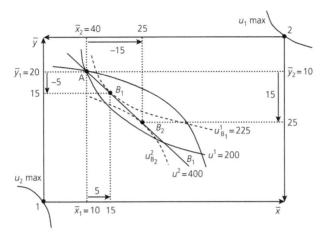

Figure 6.24 The Edgeworth box with relative price equal to 1.

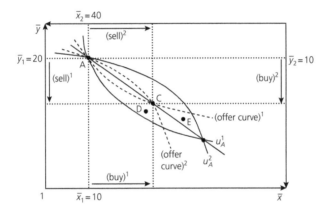

Figure 6.25 The Edgeworth box and general equilibrium.

We start from A and we draw the offer curve for each individual. These offer curves contain the points B from above. However, as is clear from the figure, there is a point C where the offer curves intersect. This is clearly an equilibrium point as its significance is that the quantity of y which individual 1 will want to sell equals exactly the quantity of that good which individuals 2 wants to buy. Conversely, the quantity of x which individual 2 wants to sell exactly equals to the quantity of the good which individual 1 wants to buy. Hence, if they go ahead and exchange at this price, all rational plans will coincide. The price is also easy to observe. It will be the line connecting the initial position to the point of intersection. It is the price because the slope of this line has exactly the meaning of the price: how many units of y were exchanged with how many units of x. It is also the equilibrium price because it is on both individuals' offer curves. This means that at this price each one of them had made an optimal choice.[5]

As each individual at C is at an optimal position, it means that the indifference curve is tangent to the price. Hence, the indifference curves of both individuals are also tangent to each other (as they both face the same price). It is therefore clear that it is no longer possible for both individuals to agree on a different allocation. At any other point (say D or E), either individual 1 will be worse off as he will end on a lower indifference curve (D) than at C, or individual 2 will be made worse off at a point like E. As there will always be at least one of the two agents who will refuse to trade, there will be no trade and C is the final point of negotiation. We therefore say that C lies on the *contract curve* (see Figure 6.26).

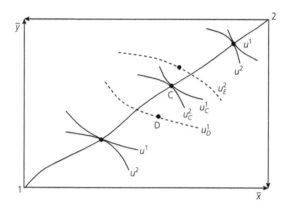

Figure 6.26 The Edgeworth box and the contract curve.

Within the Edgeworth box there are maps of indifference curves for both individuals. This means that every indifference curve of individual 1 will have a corresponding indifference curve of individual 2, which will be tangent to each other at a certain allocation. The line connecting all such points of tangency is called a contract curve for the reason we gave above to why the trade will stop at C. At any point on the contract curve, we can no longer move to a point where both agents are made better off. Put differently, if we move away from a point on the contract curve, at least someone will be made worse off. Given our initial definition of efficiency, we can now say that when we are on the contract curve: we cannot make anyone better off without making someone else worse off. Thus, all points on the contract curve are allocative efficient. We call this efficiency **Pareto efficiency**[6] and note that everything is measured in terms of one's own utility. There is no need to compare utilities here and in this sense we can avoid all the problems associated with the cardinal nature of utility. Whether or not the contract curve is a straight line depends on the nature of individuals' utility functions and their relationship. We shall not explore this point at this stage of our study.

What we see from all this elaborate exercise is that it does not matter whether we conceive competition (or the opposing forces) to be between consumers and producers or, between all agents. The outcome remains the same: there exists an equilibrium—a balancing of all opposing forces—which is, in terms of the economic problem which we are trying to solve, efficient.

6.3 A note on welfare economics

When we began our investigation into the notion of general equilibrium, I suggested that perhaps the best way of looking at it is as a logical exercise rather than as a description of the world. Its static nature, more than anything else, suggests something which is quite unreasonable. Do we really expect all markets to be in equilibrium at the same time? Nevertheless, if we do ask ourselves whether it is possible for a system of *laissez faire* to work in a world where agents are self-interested yet thoroughly dependent on each other, the question of coordination becomes central. What we mean by coordination is a mechanism which directs resources in such a way as to ensure that all individuals can execute their own plans; a general coincidence of wants. Obviously, when we talk about wants we mean **rational** wants and this, in a way, could become a point of contention. If agents are rational in a different way (say, the notion, *a la* Weber, of expressive rationality (*Zweckrationalitat*); see Chapter 2), could competition coordinates these wants? What if there was more than one form of rationality, would markets be the mechanism to coordinate the successful execution of these, very diverse, wants?

In essence, the model of general equilibrium which we examined above suggests that when people are rational (in the instrumental fashion) and pursue their own interest, the competition between all individuals could be resolved through the markets, in the sense that there exists a vector of prices for which all their rational plans would coincide. In simple words, competition between rational individuals (and not just between consumers and producers) can work. Does this mean that we should recommend competition as a form of economic organization?

In terms of the economic problem which we had set out to resolve, the answer should be yes. What we have discovered is not only that through competition there can be some sort of coordination among individuals. We discovered that the outcome is both productive and allocative efficient. As such, competition resolves the economic problem.

This sounds very cheerful indeed but here is also where the significance of a **logical test** kicks in. Had the world really been comprised of individuals whose rationality can be captured by real number utility functions, the existence of general equilibrium and its efficiency would have been sufficient to persuade us to recommend this form of economic organization. However, as a logical exercise it also reveals the flaws in the argument.

Let us begin with, perhaps, the most obvious one as it rests entirely within the assumptions of the models, see Figure 6.27.

Our theory tells us that for any initial position like A, there exists a price where all rational plans coincide. Such a price will lead us to an allocation which will always be Pareto efficient. First of all we can see that it reiterates our conclusion from Chapter 1 that there are always benefits to be had from trade and that all parties are winners. Whatever reason could there be for anyone to oppose the introduction of free trade institutions?

The first question we may wish to ask is what do we mean by 'free'? When we say that all agents benefit from trade (i.e. from the move from A to C) we assume (a) that the

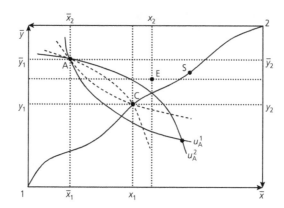

Figure 6.27 General equilibrium and welfare.

process of trade makes no difference to individuals; and (b) that if prices emerge which are not beneficial to one of the agents, he, or she can say no. Indeed, if our preferences are only defined on the end-state and if, as is always assumed in competition, the number of agents is very large indeed, these assumptions are quite plausible. But there are serious question marks hanging over the consequentialist nature of our preferences. I do not wish to develop these here but it is not difficult to imagine that someone would refuse a good material consequence if the method by which it arrives is considered by him or her to be, say, immoral.

In terms of the sovereignty of agents to say no, there is a certain paradox in this model. We saw that what characterizes competition is the large number of agents. This means that while we have a system of decentralized decisionmaking, individuals have little power. This means that to say no implies withdrawing from the game altogether. In a world of interdependence this does not seem to be such a feasible option.

We are satisfied that competition resolves the economic problem because we end up at a point like C which is allocatively (Pareto) efficient. But what does allocative efficiency mean? As you know, all the points on the contract curve are allocatively efficient. This also includes the extreme ends. Namely, if agent 1 has everything and agent 2 has nothing, this is a Pareto efficient allocation. We cannot improve the lot of the poor without making the rich worse off. Is this an appropriate resolution of the economic problem?

We mentioned in Chapter 1 and in one of the previous sections that in the end, society must choose the allocation which is consistent with the opinion of all its members. That this is a difficult process is quite evident but instead of establishing what exactly it is that society wishes to achieve we may ask ourselves whether it would make sense for such a choice to be always allocatively efficient. Intuitively, this seems plausible. If there is an allocation which is socially desirable but Pareto inefficient, should society object to making someone better off, if this comes at no one's expense? The answer depends on whether our preferences are only end-state preferences. It is not impossible to envisage objections to making someone, who, say, is already very rich, better off even if it does not come at anyone's expense.

Consider, for a moment point E in the above figure. E represents an allocation where both agents get the same quantities of both goods (equality in consumption). Naturally, when people talk about equality they refer to far more complex structures but let us suppose that as none of the goods are produced goods and as the two agents are different only in the preferences, society equates equality with equality in consumption. In such a case, the socially desirable allocation would be E which is not on the contract curve. Clearly if society believes that there is no justification for any other distribution, one would object to give more to any agent even if it comes at no one's expense. The problem is that there would be some inconsistency here between the agents' private preferences and their social choice. It is difficult to envisage that both of them may prefer another distribution to E yet both think that this is where society should be.

So if we accept that what is socially desirable must be allocatively efficient also, then there is the question of how can we get there. Suppose that society wants to be at point S in the above diagram but the initial distribution would lead us to C if we do not interfere. Luckily, we can demonstrate that if lump sum were feasible, we can direct the economy to point S without having to change the competitive structure. To understand this best think of the lump sum tax as a means by which we can rearrange the initial endowment in such a way as to make point S our competitive outcome. In other words, everything that society may choose can be obtained by competitive means if we could use lump sum transfers.

This means that not only is competition efficient, it is consistent with whatever may constitute a social choice. This is almost the same as saying that allowing the free reign of competition is value free as it is not associated with a particular social choice. This means that on paper, the competitive paradigm is doing extremely well. Not only does it resolve the economic problem, it is consistent with almost all sensible forms of social preferences. However, how much of this is due to the fact that it is logical exercise and not a description of the world?

Well, we can name a few issues which may cast doubt on whether or not the consequences of competition are as wonderful as this.

(a) There is the problem of the consequentialist nature of preferences which I mentioned earlier.

(b) There is the problem of whether social choice should necessarily be Pareto efficient and what it would mean to individuals' private preferences.

(c) There is the problem of 'price formation'. Namely, what general equilibrium tells us is that there exists a vector of prices for which all rational wants would coincide but we have no idea whether there exists any mechanism of trade or exchange which yields these prices. The fact that there are prices for which there is general equilibrium is not a proof that such prices will ever be formed. If there is not such clear mechanism, general equilibrium becomes a bit of an impossibility theorem. It shows that the conditions for rational wants to coincide under competition are so stringent that they are virtually impossible.

(d) There is the problem that we observed in one of the previous sections about the need for *all* markets to be equally competitive for the efficiency of general equilibrium to emerge. Is it really possible for all markets to be equally efficient? If not, what is the justification for the pursuit of greater competition?

(e) There is a question of complete markets but I shall leave this to Chapter 7.

(f) There is the question of the dynamic consequences of competition. As we noted in Chapter 1, one way of resolving the economic problem is to push the frontier (PPF) out. There are two ways in which the frontier can be pushed out. The first is through more resources and the other, through greater innovative activity (technological improvements which means that you can extract more from existing resources). Will competitive structures be more or less conducive to encouraging investment in R&D?

(g) It is, in some sense, a strange social system. As general equilibrium is usually conceived in contemporaneous simultaneity, it means that what explains the outcomes are the exogenous variables (endowments and tastes) rather than the actions of agents. This, in turn, creates a serious difficulty in trying to construct an ethical view of how the system operates. Such a view would surely have some bearing on what we consider to be society's preferred outcome.

Self-assessment and applications

▓ QUESTION 1

Assume an economy with two goods (x and y) and one means of production (say, labour). All markets are perfectly competitive:

(a) Describe the short run and the long run market equilibrium of a typical competitive industry (say, the market and industry for commodity x).

(b) What is the relationship between the efficiency conditions of competition in the markets for x and y and social efficiency as captured by the production possibility curve? (**hint**: do not analyse the labour market but simply assume a unique, and fixed, wage level.) Does this mean that competitive markets are efficient only in the long run?

There is now a technological improvement in the production of x:

(c) What will happen to the real price of x in terms of y if the two goods were gross substitutes?

(d) Will your answer be the same had the two goods been complements?

(e) Are both answers in (c) and (d)) consistent with the analysis of the change in the framework of the production possibility curve?

Answer

This is a question which combines understanding of competitive equilibrium as well as the general equilibrium dimension of cross industry analysis. We assume here an economy with two goods and one means of production (labour):

(a) An initial description of a typical competitive industry in both the short and the long runs (see Chapter 4);

(b) Here you are expected to explain the relationship between marginal cost pricing and allocative efficiency in the sense that if all markets priced at marginal cost (with labour as the only means of production), relative market prices will reveal the true social cost (the slope of the production possibility frontier):

$$p_x = MC(x) = \frac{\overline{w}}{MP_L^x}$$

$$p_y = MC(y) = \frac{\overline{w}}{MP_L^y}.$$

hence,

$$\frac{p_x}{p_y} = \frac{MC(x)}{MC(y)} = \frac{\overline{w}/MP_L^x}{\overline{w}/MP_L^y} = \frac{MP_L^y}{MP_L^x} = -\frac{dy}{dx}.$$

Obviously, you must be aware of the independence of efficiency from the concept of the long run.

Now the question becomes slightly more complex: there is a technological improvement in the production of x and students were expected to analyse the general equilibrium implications to the relative price of x in terms of y.

(c) and (d) (i) The choice of framework: as the question deals with relative prices in a world of two goods, the student must recognize that this is a general equilibrium question; the question is about cross markets equilibrium (a 'horizontal' notion of general equilibrium). The tool of analysis which is required here is that of **excess demand (ED) functions**. Ideally, students should have explained how they construct the ED functions (see above) for both cases of gross substitute and complements. This, however, was less significant than getting the models right.

(ii) Presenting the tool of analysis.

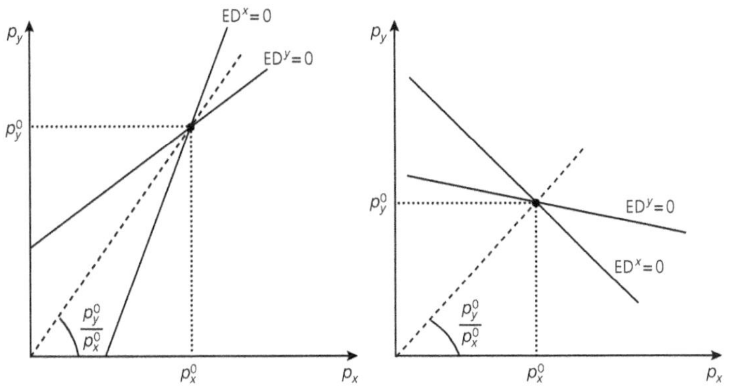

Figure 6.28

The left-hand diagram in Figure 6.28 depicts the case of gross substitutes while the right-hand diagram depicts the case of the complements;

(iii) Analysing the effect of the technological change (Figure 6.29):

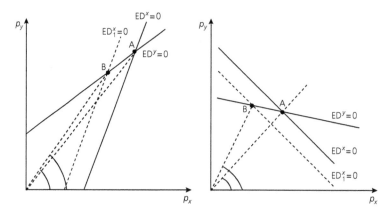

Figure 6.29

The two diagrams describe the effects of the technological improvement in x on the relative price of x in terms of y when they are gross substitutes (left) and when they are complements (right). As the case of question 5(c) in the home paper, the implications on the direction of change in relative price of x in terms of y is independent on whether the goods are gross substitute or complements;

(e) Here you should note that the result of the technological improvement is a 'pivotal' shift outward of the PPF and hence, the changes in (c) and (d) are consistent with the earlier efficiency considerations (Figure 6.30).

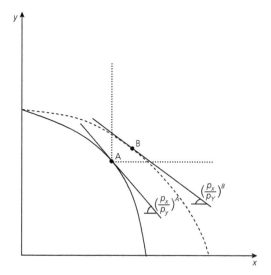

Figure 6.30

QUESTION 2

What will be the effect on general equilibrium prices of x and y (when x and y are gross substitutes) of an increase in the demand for x?

Answer

This is a question where you must use the excess demand functions:

$$ED^x = x^d(p_x, p_y, I) - x^S(p_x, w, r) \equiv ED^x(p_x, p_y, I, w, r)$$
$$ED^y = y^d(p_y, p_x, I) - y^S(p_y, w, r) \equiv ED^y(p_y, p_x, I, w, r)$$

clearly

$$\dot{p}_x = F(ED^x) \qquad \dot{p}_y = G(ED^y)$$

and as we assume that x and y are gross substitutes, we end up with the diagram on the left below depicting equilibrium conditions in each market as a function of the other good's price (Figure 6.31).

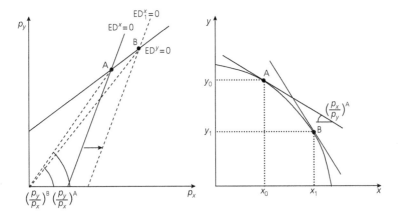

Figure 6.31

The relative prices are captured by the ray from the origin to point A. When there is a change in tastes which brings about an exogenous increase in demand for x, it means that for any given price of y, equilibrium in the market for x will only be obtained at a higher price of x (a shift to the right of the x excess demand schedule). These changes and their subsequent effect on equilibrium prices are captured by point B in the right-hand diagram of Figure 6.27.

QUESTION 3

What will be the effect on general equilibrium prices of x and y (when x and y are complements) of a decrease in the demand for x?

Answer

As in the previous question a proper exposition of the excess demand functions is required:

$$ED^x = x^d(p_x, p_y, l) - x^S(p_x, w, r) \equiv ED^x(p_x, p_y, l, w, r)$$

$$ED^y = y^d(p_y, p_x, l) - y^S(p_y, w, r) \equiv ED^y(p_y, p_x, l, w, r)$$

clearly

$$\dot{p}_x = F(ED^x) \qquad \dot{p}_y = G(ED^y).$$

As we assume that x and y are complements, we end up with the diagram on the left (Figure 6.32) depicting equilibrium conditions in each market as a function of the other good's price:

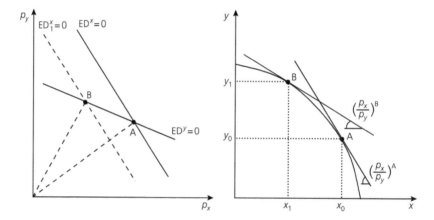

Figure 6.32

The relative prices are captured by the ray from the origin to point A. When there is a change in tastes which brings about an exogenous decrease in demand for x, it means that for any given price of y, equilibrium in the market for x will only be obtained at a lower price of x (a shift to the left of the x excess demand schedule). These changes and their subsequent effect on equilibrium prices are captured by point B in the right-hand diagram in Figure 6.32.

▩ NOTES

1. See the conditions for utility representation of preferences in Chapter 2.
2. Recall that in the PPF curve we assume technology to be exogenous. It means that technology is *not* a social issue.
3. The relationship with leisure is captured by the competitive nature of the labour market. Here, this would mean that there is a single price for leisure and it is the going wage level w. Had the labour market not been competitive, we would not have been able to argue that the wage rate confronting industry x is the same as the wage rate confronting industry y. Hence, the ratio of marginal costs would not have been converted into the slope of the PPF.

4. Does this mean that individual 2 is better off than individual 1? If you are not sure about your answer, please read Chapter 2 again.

5. I urge you to try and calculate this equilibrium using the equations we have used to construct the offer curves.

6. Named after the Italian sociologist/economist Vilifredo Pareto who insisted on conducting welfare analysis without interpersonal comparisons.

7 Market failures: natural monopoly, externalities, and public goods

In the previous chapter, we have discussed at some length the apparent merits of the competitive paradigm. We have demonstrated through the existence of **general equilibrium,** that a system of decentralized decisionmaking can work, in the sense that all rational plans will coincide. The meaning of this is that there exists a set of prices for which no individual, if rational, will have an incentive to act so as to change the outcome. In addition, we noted that competitive outcomes produce a price system which reflects the real social cost and, thus, the more apparent aspect of the working of competitive markets is the equality which emerges between that which consumers wish to pay (the subjective side), that which they have to pay (i.e. the market price, or the institutional side) and that which it really costs to produce (the technology, or social side).[1]

Given all this, one may wonder what role, if any, do governments have in the economic sphere of our lives? This is obviously a very important question to which we are unable to devote the appropriate attention. Still, the purpose of this section is to demonstrate how, in spite of the self-regulating impression which can be derived from the competitive paradigm, there are many obvious incidents which suggest otherwise.

For one, even if there were no obvious impediments to the working of decentralized decisionmaking, governments would still be essential in upholding the legal framework within which competition operates. It is important to bear in mind that the model of perfect competition is not describing a 'natural' state of affairs. It is far from obvious that people will not act in such a way as to change the outcome or even the rules of the game, if they feel that the consequences of the system are not favourable to them. In that sense, the role of the government is not only to maintain the order of the systems against a tide of disaffection, but also to interfere in the distribution of income which could be the source of such disaffections.

But there are less heroic reasons why a government may have a greater role than expected within a competitive world. Three of them will be discussed in this section. One is the problem of **natural monopoly**, another is the problem of **public good**, and the last is the problem of **externalities**. Broadly speaking, all these problems fall into the category of what is called **market failure**. What we mean by market failure, as distinct from mere market imperfection, is a situation where the competitive solution (with all its attached benefits) cannot emerge if things were left to themselves. Recall that one of the great attractions of the competitive paradigm is that, at least theoretically, efficiency can be obtained (i.e. the economic problem can be resolved) by simply letting people pursue their own interest without interference (*laissez faire*). Market failures are those cases where the competitive solution will not emerge without intervention. Given the overall interdependence of all markets, it is enough for a failure to exist in one market for the overall benefits of competition to be almost entirely held back. In the previous section we saw that if one market out of three were monopolized, the fact that the other two are perfectly competitive will not yield an allocation on the PPF which either market prices reflect the social cost or that the utility of a representative agent would be maximized.

In principle, we distinguish between two major types of market failures. There are those failures which are derived from the circumstances of production (like the case of the natural monopoly), and those which are due to the incompleteness of the market system. When we said, in Chapter 6, that the general equilibrium condition for efficiency to emerge is that all markets, without exception, should be competitive, we meant to say all markets that **should** exist as distinct from those which actually do. We will come to this point later.

7.1 Natural monopoly

What exactly is meant by natural monopoly is an interesting question in itself. We would consider as a natural monopoly any situation where market demand is such that it intersects with the marginal cost (thus facilitating $p = mc$, the condition for allocative efficiency) at a level of marginal cost which is below the average costs.

In the left-hand diagram of Figure 7.1 we have a case where the presumption behind the model is that the technology is such that there are increasing returns to scale everywhere. In other words, a technology where there are large set-up costs but the cost of an extra unit is small and constant and will always remain below the average costs, will exhibit increasing returns to scale. In the right-hand diagram we have the normal cost structure which we assumed in Chapters 3 and 4 but that which introduces the problem is the size of the market. The demand is not sufficiently large to offset the large set-up costs and to facilitate production at a level where marginal costs are above average costs. In both cases, it is clear that the efficient competitive equilibrium (the point where $p = \mathrm{MC}(x)$) is at a level of price which is below the average costs. This means that firms will be making losses. Recall that $\pi = p \cdot x - c(x) = p \cdot x - ((c(x)/x)x) = p \cdot x - \mathrm{AC}(x)x$. In the diagram below

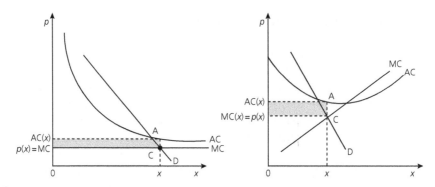

Figure 7.1

the price equals to the marginal costs. The revenue, therefore, is the rectangular region $p, C, x, 0$. The total costs are captured by multiplying average costs by output which is the rectangular region AC, A, x, 0. It is easy to see that the cost rectangular is greater and the difference between them, the shaded area, represent the losses. In the long run, competitive firms will not supply such a market.

Which of these two explanations (i.e. technology as such or the size of the market) is at the root of the problem is an important question. You can imagine that if technologies which exhibit increasing returns everywhere exist, the success of competition as a means of resolving the problem of reconciling unsatiated wants with scarcity may not be so self-evident. As marginal cost pricing makes competition efficient, the presence of an increasing number of industries with increasing returns to scale may no longer mean that interdependence and the free pursuit of one's own interests yield an efficient outcome.

Typically, when people talk about natural monopolies they refer to large public utilities such as, water supplies or railways. You can imagine that to open a railway line you would need first to have tracks, stations, and rolling stock before the first passenger can come on board. You can imagine that the cost of an extra passenger is likely to be very low but the average costs (including all the set up costs) are enormous if the number of passengers does not rise sufficiently.

Why is such a case called **natural monopoly**? The reason for this is, very simply, that the competitive solution is at a price which is below average costs, hence, competitive outcomes imply that firms would be making losses. Would a monopolist be willing to sell the good? Of course, as long as its own price is above the average costs.

In the left-hand diagram (Figure 7.2) we can see a case where there is a monopolist solution with profits above the normal due to the fact that the monopolist price would be above the average costs. In the right-hand diagram we can see a case where even a monopolist may not produce the good. As the latter is an extreme case, a bit like our bridge story from Chapter 2, where the question is whether the government should provide the service if it is not provided by a private firm, I would rather leave this out from our discussion here. The more interesting question is whether a good or a service which would have been provided by private firms (albeit a monopolist), should be controlled by the government in one form or another.

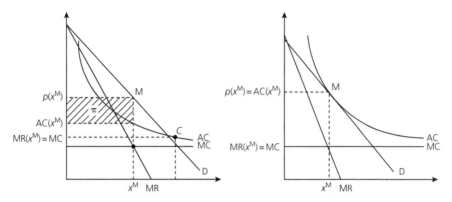

Figure 7.2

Evidently, allowing a private monopolist to provide the service would generate all the typical inefficiencies which are associated with monopolists. You may say, 'But without the monopolist the good, or service, would not have been provided, surely this should be an overriding consideration.' Well, there are two issues here. First, the good or service could always be provided by the government which could offer more of it at a lower price (at, for instance, a break even point where average costs intersect demand). Second, by allowing one industry to remain monopolized, the overall benefits of competition (as manifested in the idea that market prices reflect the true social costs) would not be accrued.

To have an appropriate bench mark, let us suppose that the government—who, we assume, is interested in promoting the well-being of the public—produces the good itself. What would be the optimal pricing policy it would pursue?

The answer to this question is a bit complex and beyond the tools of analysis introduced in this book. I shall, therefore, only say that we can show that if the government can choose the price and charge a special tax to cover losses if the price is below average costs, it would choose the marginal cost pricing. Not surprisingly, this conclusion is also consistent with the overall benefits of competition. If commodity x is a natural monopolist but it is offered at marginal cost pricing, the conditions of efficiency across all markets are not violated. Namely, the fact that one good is offered by a single producer (the government) would not violate the efficiency condition which would have emerged if all markets were competitive. Note, however, that this can only be achieved if a public enterprise is producing the good. A private natural monopoly would never be willing to produce at a marginal cost where the most efficient organization will only yield losses.

So, you may ask, why is it not the policy pursued by governments around the world? There are two main reasons for this. First of all, governments are usually not in a position to levy designated taxes. Namely, decisions about taxation are not usually taken in conjunction with the pricing decision concerning a particular enterprise. Hence, the actual decisionmaking process of a government does not correspond to the ideal from which we drew our conclusion. We considered a government deciding a tax for the sole purpose of covering the losses of the enterprise when prices are below average costs, but this is not how it works. A more typical way of dealing with the problem is to consider an enterprise (in public hands) deciding a price without the power of raising extra taxes to cover its possible losses.

Consider the following story: in Plutonia there are only two cities, Northside and Southside. A very large desert separates the two cities and the government was pressed into considering the renewal of a railway link between the two cities. There is an old track connecting the two cities; suppose that it is costless to renew but it will cost £100,000 a year to maintain. The track is such that it facilitates 2000 trips a year between the two cities. For the sake of simplicity, let us suppose that the marginal costs are zero. The demand for travel is given by: $p = 1000 - x$, where p is the price of travel and x is the number of trips per year.

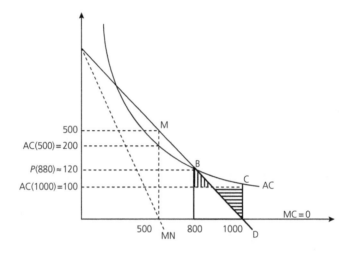

Figure 7.3

We begin at the break even point B (see Figure 7.3). At this point, as price equals average costs, profits (or surplus, if we do not wish to use the word profit in connection with government) will be zero ($\pi = px - c(x) = x(p - (c(x)/x)) = x(p - AC(x)) = 0$). The revenue area equals the costs area.

What will now happen if the government decides to reduce the price to zero (the level of marginal costs). Let us first identify all the points. At B, the price equals average costs. Our demand schedule is: $p = 1000 - x$. Our cost function is: $C = 100,000$ hence, $AC(x) = 100,000/x$. At B:

$$p = 1000 - x = \frac{100,000}{x} = AC(x)$$

$$\Rightarrow 1000x - x^2 = 100,000 \Rightarrow x^2 - 1000x + 100,000 = 0$$

$$\Rightarrow x = \frac{1000 \pm \sqrt{1,000,000 - 400,000}}{2} = \frac{1000 \pm \sqrt{600,000}}{2} = 887,259 \approx 880$$

$$\Rightarrow p(880) = 1000 - 880 = 120.$$

For the sake of comparison we can see that had there been a private monopolist, it would have offered the profit maximizing output which is where marginal revenue equals marginal costs (= zero). This will be at point $x = 500$ and the price of $p = 1000 - 500 = 500$. This is point M in the above diagram. So merely by replacing the monopolist by a break even public enterprise seems a better way of organizing the market. But this, of course, is not the whole story.

As the public enterprise reduces the price to the level of marginal cost (point C) we know that the conditions for efficient general equilibrium would be upheld. Is this something which is in the interest of the public? What we mean by 'interest of the public' is whether the public would be willing to use tax money to cover the losses of a cheaply provided service?

As in the story of the bridge in Chapter 2, we examine the cost benefit of such a policy. Naturally, we ignore here the implication that such a policy would have for the general use of taxation but we will nevertheless be able to get a feel of the issue at stake.

Moving from the B to C will increase consumer surplus by the following areas (the rectangular below $B = 120 \times 880$ + the triangle to the right of $B = (120 \times 120)/2$. Hence we have $105,600 + 7200 = 112,800$. Hence, the consumer surplus increased by the value of £112,800.

At point C, the average cost of producing a 1000 is $100,000/1000 = 100$. The total losses now would be $[AC - p(= MC)] \times 1000 = £100,000$. This means that the gains in consumer surplus are greater than the losses for offering the service at marginal cost pricing. Does this mean that we should go ahead and produce at point C exactly in the same way that we made the decision in the bridge story in Chapter 2?

The answer, of course, is no. In the bridge story, building the bridge would have generated new utility. Here, this is not the case. All the area captured by the rectangular shape below and to the left of B is merely a transfer within the economy. Some of it used to be money paid as salaries to people working in providing the service. This is now given as consumer surplus to the consumers of the service. It is by no means a gain to the economy unless we believe that the consumers of the service matter more than the workers in it. So, in order to answer the question whether or not cutting the price to marginal costs is beneficial to society we must only examine the **extra utility** and **extra costs**. These are captured by the triangle to the right and below point B and the rectangle (within the triangle) from C. Clearly the extra consumer surplus is the area of the triangle to the right of B. When the price was at B, this area was not in anyone's hands. The area is clearly $(120 \times 120)/2 = 7200$. The extra costs for producing 120 more units by moving from 880 to 1000 is: $100 \times 120 = 12,000$. This means that the extra cost exceeds the additional benefits. In such a case, pursuing a marginal cost pricing policy would not be to the benefit of the public. If you look carefully at Figure 7.4 you will see that whether or not the extra benefits are greater or smaller than the extra costs depends on the relative size of the two shaded little triangles. The top triangle represents net utility gains and the triangle on the right, the net costs gain. It is easy to see that whether the one is greater than the other is merely a question of price elasticity of demand.

You can easily see that when price elasticity of demand is greater, the cost triangle will be relatively smaller in comparison with the pure gain triangle. In such a case, the extra benefit of producing at marginal cost pricing would be greater than the extra cost. When

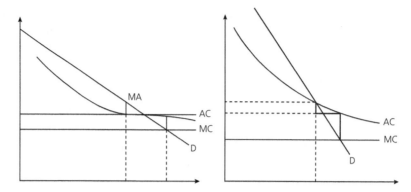

Figure 7.4

this happens then the optimal pricing policy would be the marginal cost pricing even though the enterprise could not affect the level of tax paid by the consumers. In our case, you can see that the price elasticity of demand at point C is so low that we face the case of the right-hand diagram when it would not be in the public interest to deviate from the break even point.

However, while the government may, indeed, be pursuing the interest of the public, if the price is not the same as the marginal cost, the conditions for the overall benefits of competition to be accrued are still violated; in terms of the PPF we would end up at an allocation where market prices do not reflect the social costs and the economy would remain inefficient even if all other markets were to be perfectly competitive.

Nevertheless, you may say, as a public enterprise would either produce at B or at C or anywhere in between, it is clearly a better state of affairs than that of a private monopolist. Does it not mean that privatization is inefficient? Would it not be better to allow the state to run natural monopolies, preferably, at marginal cost pricing and thus, ensure that the overall benefits of competition do not elude society? But even if the public enterprise would not sell at marginal cost pricing, the outcome of its optimal pricing policy is surely better than that of a private monopolist.

The main drive for privatization and for the arguments in favour of the private mono-polist and against public ownership is based on the presumption that the main problem of state run enterprises is that they are inherently productive inefficient. Namely, as the managers of public enterprise are not driven by profits and are not threatened by the ownership market, they would not have the incentive to operate efficiently (on the cost functions which we derived in Chapter 3 and which corresponded to the minimal cost with which any level of output could be produced). In other words, the argument for privatization is based on the assumption given in Figure 7.5.

The heavy cost lines represent the productive inefficiency of the public enterprise. As managers would not gain from cost minimizing policy, the actual costs of producing the service will always be greater than those which would have been had managers been concerned with minimizing costs.

If, on the base of these actual costs we pursue the policy of marginal cost pricing we would end up at point C. However, had the firm been privatized, even allowing it to

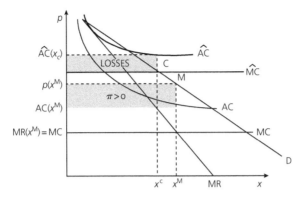

Figure 7.5

simply act as a monopolist could produce an allocation where prices are even lower and output even greater (point M). The reason for this is that once the firm is traded in the stock market, the managers would be forced to operate on the cost functions which correspond to profit maximizing behaviour (cost minimization). Otherwise, as we said earlier, there would be someone in the market who would know that he can produce the good with greater profits and they will buy the shares of the company and sack the manager.

If indeed we are unable to achieve marginal cost pricing because we cannot assign designated tax for each public service, it means that we forgo the opportunity to achieve overall efficiency. In such a case, privately owned monopolists may be the least of two evils. But there are two issues which are not so obvious. First there is the question of how true is the presumption that state owned monopolists are necessarily productive inefficient? Second, there is the broader question of whether specifically designated taxes should not become part of the general taxation policy.

The answer to the second question is complex and requires a long discussion. I shall therefore leave it as a thought with you. The answer to the first question is complex also, but you will learn more about it in your future studies. For one, there is the question of evidence. Is it clear that across the board public enterprises are less productive efficient than private monopolists? But whatever be the evidence there is a far deeper issue here. Can we offer managers a contract that will emulate the working of the market? As you will see in your future studies, there are many occasions where economists believe that some difficulties can be resolved by the appropriate design of a contract or a mechanism. I shall indeed refer to one such issue later in this chapter. But to understand exactly whether, or not, such a design is possible you will need to equip yourself with more tools of economic analysis. At this stage, I will only leave you with these thoughts about the issue.

7.2 Externalities and incomplete markets

An economy lives along the river y. They produce two goods: a fish called y and a mud-car (car which is made of mud) called x. Both goods are produced by labour alone. Suppose that all markets (the markets for x and y as well as the labour market) are perfectly competitive. The general equilibrium condition in this economy (which we have explained in the previous chapter) will be as follows:

The markets for x and y

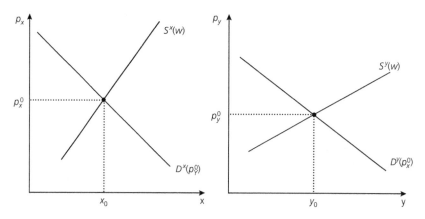

Figure 7.6 Equilibrium in the goods markets.

In each of these markets, price equals marginal cost (see Figure 7.6). Recall from Chapter 3 that the marginal cost when there is only one means of production will be equal to w/MP_L. Hence, the competitive equilibrium in both markets will yield

$$p_x = \mathrm{MC}(x) = \frac{\overline{w}}{\mathrm{MP}_L^x}$$

$$p_y = \mathrm{MC}(y) = \frac{\overline{w}}{\mathrm{MP}_L^y}.$$

The information regarding the competitive nature of the labour market is captured here by the uniqueness of the cost of labour (the equilibrium wage level). The nominal wage for workers in both sectors equals the value of the marginal product.

General equilibrium

Recall that the slope of the PPF measures the effects of a transfer of one labourer from one industry to another. Hence, if you take one labourer away from fishing y and you reallocate him to work in the production of x. The loss of fish y (dy) will be exactly the marginal product of that labourer in the production of y (i.e. the quantity of fish that would have been caught had he gone out fishing with his comrades); the gains in x (dx) will be exactly the marginal product of that labourer in making mud-cars x:

$$dy = dL\,\mathrm{MP}_L^y$$

$$dx = dL\,\mathrm{MP}_L^x$$

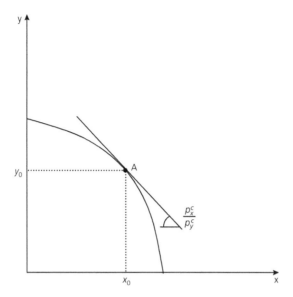

Figure 7.7 General equilibrium with production.

As $dL = 1$ and geometry tells us that the slope of the PPF is $-dy/dx$ or, MP_L^y/MP_L^x units of y per x.

Putting everything together will yield that

$$p_x^c = MC(x) = \frac{\overline{w}}{MP_L^x}$$

$$p_y^c = MC(y) = \frac{\overline{w}}{MP_L^y}$$

hence,

$$\frac{p_x^c}{p_y^c} = \frac{MC(x)}{MC(y)} = \frac{(\overline{w}/MP_L^x)}{(\overline{w}/MP_L^y)} = \frac{MP_L^y}{MP_L^x} = -\frac{dy}{dx}$$

which means that prices in competitive markets reveal the true social costs. As individuals in each market consume that much of each good such that they pay for them the value of their marginal product, the trinity of the subjective (individuals), the institutional (markets), and the technological (society) has been confirmed.

Suppose now that a new technology has been discovered for the production of mud-cars. The new technology is such that it requires spraying the mud-cars with a consolidating material called z which is then washed out into the river. The unfortunate fact is that z is toxic and fish (y or otherwise) do not like z. That is to say, z kills fish. The plant producing mud-cars x is located up the river while the fishing community lives nearer to the sea. What will be the consequences of introducing such a technology? For the sake of simplicity we shall assume that z exists in abundance (relative to the car production requirements) in nature (outside of water) and that, subsequently, it is available for the mud-cars producer at no extra cost.

The first point it that the PPF will shift outward. This, from our point is of less interest, as what concerns us here is the question of efficiency at a given point in time rather than any notion of inter-temporal efficiency. Put differently, the question I wish to ask is whether the economy will be equally efficient with the new technology as it was before given that there had been no institutional change to affect the competitive nature of the markets.

On the face of it, you may think that as there had been no change in the competitive nature of the markets, prices will therefore be equal to the marginal cost and, as this is the benchmark of efficiency, the equilibrium trinity will be preserved. Let us begin by investigating what will now be the situation in each market. I shall only deal with the new technology and forget all about the old technology.

The markets

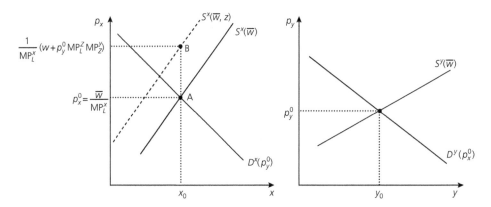

Figure 7.8 Equilibrium in the markets after the introduction of Z.

In the markets for both x and y employers will be hiring workers in the competitive labour market (see Figure 7.8). The conditions for profit maximization from which we derive the demand for labour (see Chapter 5) are the same as before. Namely, one will employ so many workers as to equate the value of their marginal product with the nominal wage level. Hence, as the productivity of a fisherman is measured in the amount of fish he contributes to the catch and the productivity of workers in mud-cars x is measured by the number of cars (or fraction of a car) which their presence at work adds to the total output, we are left with exactly the same markets equilibria in x and y:

$$p_x = MC(x) = \frac{\overline{w}}{MP_L^x}$$

$$p_y = MC(y) = \frac{\overline{w}}{MP_L^y}.$$

However, if you think about this carefully, is it really the case that the marginal product of a worker in x is the quantity of cars (or the fraction of a car) which he contributes to the total output?

When a worker produces a mud-car, what else will he be producing? The answer is obvious. With the new technology, the production of each mud-car requires the use of the consolidating material z. As a worker produces a car, he also increases the quantity of z used according to the amount of z needed for the consolidation of a single vehicle. Hence, when he contributes to the total number of cars produced, he also contributes to the quantity of z which is then washed into the river.

Once in the river, the quantity of z produced by the worker's contribution to the production of mud-cars x will now kill a certain number of fish. Consequently, there are less fish in the river and the quantity of a fish that could be caught by the work of a single fisherman (or by a unit of a fisherman's time) will inevitably be reduced. In other words, the marginal product of a unit of labour when producing mud-cars x is no longer measured only in terms of mud-cars. It should also be measured by the damage which such a unit of labour creates in the fishing industry.

Hence, if we examine the equilibrium point in the market where x_0 units of x are produced and sold at the price of p_x^0, while the marginal cost for the producer is really that much which he has to pay in order to produce a unit of x, the cost for society are different.

To produce one unit of x the employer would need to hire workers according to their marginal product. We have already established that this will be $1/MP_L$ units of labour. The cost of it (i.e. the marginal cost of a unit of x) will thus be w/MP_L. The fact that z is used in the process and that z kills fish, is of no concern to the producer of x. However, it is the concern of the consumers of x who are also the consumers of y. The *real* cost to society of a unit of x when x_0 units of it are produced is not only the marginal product in the production of x. It is the cost of a labour required to produce a unit of x (w/MP_L) + the damage to y. Let MP_L^z be the quantity of z released into the river by the work of a unit of labour employed in the production of a single mud-car x. Let, MP_z^y denote the quantity of fish killed by a unit of z also. Therefore, $MP_L^z MP_z^y$ is the quantity of fish killed by the output of one labour unit employed in the production of x. If, say, a unit of labour employed in the production of x releases 5 kg of z into the river and each kilogram of z kills 2 fish, then the employment of a unit of labour in the production of x kills $5 \times 2 = 10$ fish. When the price of y is p_y^0, the value of that loss equals

$$p_y^0 \, MP_L^z \, MP_z^y.$$

Hence, the **real marginal cost**, or the **social cost**, depends on how much labour we employ in the production of one unit of x. If, at x_0, the quantity of labour required is $1/MP_L^x$, then the **social marginal cost** of x at that point will be

$$(1/MP_L^x)(w + p_y^0 \, MP_L^z MP_z^y).$$

This corresponds to point B Figure 7.3. This would be true everywhere along the marginal cost curve and hence we have a social marginal cost which is above the **private marginal cost** in the market for x.

The fact that the producer of x does not concern himself with the social cost, suggests that the marginal cost which will determine the supply of x is the private one rather than the social one. Hence, the equilibrium conditions in both markets remain exactly as described above (i.e. $MC(x) = w/MP_L^x$).

General equilibrium

Had we not known the details of the above story and simply examined the markets for x and y we would have established that as there are competitive conditions in all markets, and that the benchmark of efficiency (that prices equal marginal cost) will deliver the overall efficiency of the system as captured by the equality of willingness to pay (subjective), actual pay (market prices), and the social cost (the slope of the PPF). Let us, therefore, examine the PPF to see whether indeed this is the case. As before, we do not examine the PPF in relation to its original position before the technological change. Instead, we focus on the new PPF.

The slope of the PPF, as was previously explained, can be examined by the transfer of one unit of labour from the fishing industry to the mud-cars industry. When we take one labour unit from the fishing industry (y) we will lose, immediately, his contribution to the daily catch as measured by his marginal product: MP_L^y. However, this is not the end of the story. When this unit of labour had been reallocated to work in x, they will also produce z and subsequently kill fish. Therefore, the loss of output in the fishing industry as a result of the transfer of one unit of labour from y to x will be the direct loss of output (MP_L^y) + the indirect loss of output that will occur the moment the worker starts producing x (and z):

$$dy = dL[MP_L^y + MP_L^z MP_z^y].$$

The result of this transfer with regard to x will be as before. Output will increase by the marginal product of that worker:

$$dx = dL\, MP_L^x.$$

As $dL = 1$ and geometry tells us that the slope of the PPF is $-dy/dx$ we can clearly see that:

$$-\frac{dy}{dx} = \frac{MP_L^y + MP_L^z MP_z^y}{MP_L^x}$$

units of y per x (see Figure 7.9).

Bringing together the competitive prices of the different market and the PPF will now produce a slightly different picture:

$$p_x = MC(x) = \frac{\overline{w}}{MP_L^x}$$

$$p_y = MC(y) = \frac{\overline{w}}{MP_L^y}$$

hence,

$$\frac{p_x}{p_y} = \frac{MC(x)}{MC(y)} = \frac{(\overline{w}/MP_L^x)}{(\overline{w}/MP_L^y)} = \frac{MP_L^y}{MP_L^x} < \frac{MP_L^y + MP_L^z MP_z^y}{MP_L^x} = -\frac{dy}{dx}$$

which means that prices in competitive markets no longer reveal the true social costs. Although we still pay for each good that much which we are willing to pay, the price we

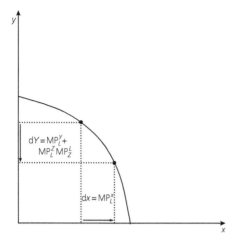

Figure 7.9 The slope of the PPF after the introduction of Z.

pay for x (in terms of y) is much smaller than what it really costs to produce it. Equally, the price of y is much greater than what it really costs (in terms of x) to produce it.

In Chapter 6 we tried to tie the 'trinity condition' (the equality between the marginal rate of subjective substitution, the market rate of exchange and the technological rate of substitution) with the notion of Pareto efficiency in two different ways. First, I have argued that if, at the expense of accuracy, we can imagine social preferences represented by a social utility function (or by the utility of a representative agent), we can see immediately why the above condition means allocative efficiency (Figure 7.10).

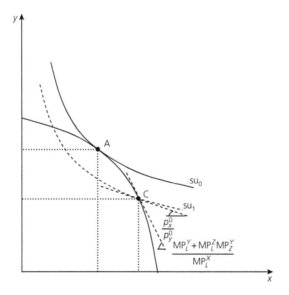

Figure 7.10 Allocative efficiency with negative externalities.

At point A we have the most preferred social allocation. It is associated with the most preferred social choice and as, at that point, the slope of the social indifference curve is the same as the slope of the PPF, it means that what society is willing to pay for a good equals that which it has to pay for it technologically. When, without externalities, market prices too are equal to the same values, we can see that society will not be made better off by any other allocation.

While this is clearly not a proof of Pareto efficiency, it helps in understanding the nature of competitive equilibrium. Recall that Pareto efficiency meant an allocation where no one can be made better off without someone being made worse off. If the social utility function is based on what is good for the individuals in society, the fact that we have achieved the highest social utility could be interpreted as not being able to choose an alternative combination of the goods where at least someone is made better off. Put differently, had there been another allocation (say point D) where someone could have been made better off without anyone being made worse off, why would society not prefer this point over A. If society indeed prefers it to A, the highest 'social indifference curve' would not be tangent to the PPF at A.

In the presence of externalities, with the use of a similar crude tool of social utility, we can easily see how the competitive equilibrium produces a result which is clearly inferior. At point C in Figure 7.10, the condition where people pay for the good that much which they are willing to pay is preserved by the social indifference curve being tangent to the market price. However, as the market price cut through the PPF at that point, we know that this price is not really the price dictated by technological circumstances. We are clearly paying for x less than it really costs to produce it and for y, more than it really costs to produce it. Suppose, for a moment, that the market price of y in terms of x (at C) is 2 units of x per y. The slope of the PPF at that point is, say, 2 y per x or, 1/2 x per y. As individuals are willing to pay 2 x per y, it means that if they paid it they would be equally well off. By simply rearranging production we can ensure that the price of y is only 1/2 a unit of x. This means that they will be able to give up less units of x per y than what they are willing to pay. Hence, they will all become better off by switching some of their x for y. If this happened, they will be moving towards point A and as was just explained, no one will be made worse off. While at C we are producing at a point where the economy is productive efficient, it is not allocative efficient. From the above diagram it is evident that there is an allocation which is socially preferred to the one at C. This clearly suggests that it is possible to find a new allocation (like A) where some will be made better off without anyone becoming worse off. The Pareto efficient allocation, therefore, cannot be obtained by competitive markets.

7.2.1 Externalities, taxation, property rights

It is beyond the scope of this course to deal with the question of how should such a problem be resolved. I will only point out that the main purpose of such a policy will be to make the producers of x take into considerations in their costing, the damage they cause the others. Recall from above that the real marginal cost of producing x is:

$$(1/\mathrm{MP}_L^x)(w + p_y^0 \mathrm{MP}_L^z \mathrm{MP}_z^y).$$

The element which needs to be added is clearly $p_y^0 MP_L^z MP_z^y$. If, for instance, we were able to levy a tax of that nature on the producers of x, the efficiency of competition will reemerge. As in both industries prices equal marginal cost, we will now have the case where

$$p_x = MC(x) = \frac{1}{MP_L^x}[\overline{w} + p_y^0 MP_L^z MP_z^y]$$

$$p_y = MC(y) = \frac{\overline{w}}{MP_L^y}.$$

Hence,

$$\frac{p_x}{p_y} = \frac{MC(x)}{MC(y)} = \frac{(1/MP_L^x)[\overline{w} + p_y^0 MP_L^z MP_z^y]}{\overline{w}/MP_L^y}$$

$$= \frac{MP_L^y}{MP_L^x}\left[1 + \frac{p_y}{\overline{w}}MP_L^z MP_z^y\right] = \frac{MP_L^y}{MP_L^x} + \frac{MP_L^y p_y}{\overline{w}}MP_L^z MP_z^y$$

as $MP_L^y p_y = \overline{w}$

$$= \frac{MP_L^y + MP_L^z MP_z^y}{MP_L^x} = -\frac{dy}{dx}$$

which means that with a tax, the equilibrium condition in each market will produce the expected correspondence between subjective market and technological rates of substitution.

The problem with such a tax (named as **Pigovian**[2] tax) is that the government will need to know quite a lot about the technological circumstances of each industry. As the people who know best are in those industries, the ability of the government to establish what exactly is going on and to devise an accurate tax policy is seriously diminished.

Another method of resolving the problem is associated with the distribution of property rights. This is a rather complex and important issue about which you will learn much more in future years but one which I feel need at least to be stated here. As you can imagine, the main problem we have in our story is that no one owns the river. Suppose, now, that the fishermen owned the river. In such a case, the producers of x would not be able to pollute without permission. As they make profits from selling x they have an interest to go to the fishermen and reach an agreement with them. The producers of x would offer money in return for the right to pollute. There is no obvious reason why the fishermen (who have not yet become environmentalists) should object. Equally, had the property right been given to the producers of x, the fishermen would have an incentive to pay the producers of x to produce less (and so pollute less). Why should the producers of x care if the money comes from the fishermen or from sales of x?

The remarkable thing is that in the absence of **transaction costs** (what you pay to reach an agreement), as agents are equally rational, whichever scheme you follow will produce the Pareto efficient allocation. In other words, the only thing which matters is the allocation of property rights. The distribution of these rights does not matter for efficiency in the absence of transaction costs. This is known in the literature as **Coase theorem**.

What then, is the general significance of the externalities phenomenon. What exactly is the meaning of the problem of externalities?

If you think carefully you will discover that what happens in the presence of externalities is that the institutions of the market fail to deliver. Without externalities, decentralized decisionmaking in the framework of competitive markets produced a result whereby all rational plans coincided in such a way that no one could have achieved more without forcing someone else to achieve less. Put differently, if your aim is to get the most preferred bundle which is feasible, you could have achieved this through the markets. When there are externalities and we get a competitive equilibrium which is, clearly, no longer Pareto efficient, such a description of the system does not hold. If your aim is to achieve the most preferred feasible bundle, the institutions of the market will provide you with an illusion of achieving your goal (in the sense that you will be paying exactly that much which you are willing to pay and that you will be on your budget line) but this will not be true. Through a reorganization of production activities, you could have achieved more at the expense of no one at all.

So, is the efficiency (allocative) of the competitive paradigm merely an illusion? The answer to this question is complex. At this stage I will point out that this is not the case as a matter of principle. Unless there was a mistake in our use of logical instruments, the conclusion according to which a system which is organized on the basis of competitive markets will produce a solution which is both productive and allocative efficient. However, the problem of externalities suggests that for the system to deliver, it must be **complete**.

By complete I mean two different things. First of all, as you have noticed earlier (in Chapter 4) it is sufficient for one industry not to be organized in a competitive fashion for the allocative efficiency of the system to disappear. For instance, had the market for x been a monopoly and the market for y a competitive market, we will end up with a general equilibrium solution which is similar in nature to the externalities outcome. As the price of the monopolist is above the marginal cost price, the efficiency-trinity no longer holds. So the first sense of completeness requires that all markets are fully competitive for the system to deliver that which people are seeking to achieve.

The second notion of completeness—which is what economists normally mean when they talk about it—is that all markets are included. In the above case of externalities, it is clear that the reason for the failure of the competitive system is the lack of any considerations for z. Had the consequences of z for the fishing industry been taken into consideration by the producers of x (as with the tax I proposed earlier), their marginal cost would be the one which correctly corresponds to the social cost. The reason why z does not appear in anyone's considerations is because it has no price tag attached to it. Consequently, there is no market for z in spite of its clear role in resources allocation. The absence of such a market suggest that the system is **incomplete** in the sense that not all things which influence the outcome are considered via a price mechanism.

If, for instance, it had been discovered that while z kills fish, it also solves potency problems ('*zaigra*'). I am sure that you can imagine what will happen to the demand for z. I said at the beginning that z existed in abundance relative to the car production requirements. The discovery of its potency problem will increase the demand for it so much that, we assume, a positive price will emerge. When this happens, the producers of x will no longer be able to use the new technology without buying z. If they do, its price will inevitably enter the costs equation and will subsequently, equate the private cost of producing x with its social cost.

Therefore, to suppose that the institutions of competitive markets deliver that which people seek to achieve will require the assumption that markets are complete. If we think about it, this does not sound like a plausible assumption. The question which we may wish to consider is whether there are alternative means of ensuring that even if markets are incomplete, the allocative efficient solutions can still be obtained. We shall leave this for your further studies and thoughts.

7.3 Public goods and their efficient provision

Our entire discussion of economic interactions and systems has been completely focused on the individual and his behaviour. Implied in this, among other things, is a notion of private consumption. Namely, what one does for himself will remain entirely in his own domain. Subsequently, we assumed that all goods are divisible in the sense that when I consume something, no one else can gain anything from that part which I consumed, and there will be less of the good left for others.

However, it is fairly clear that there are goods which are not divisible. The most obvious example is 'defence'. The quantity of defence available to the public is not divisible in the sense that the amount of security I feel will not reduce the amount of it which is available to you.

The problem which arises with the presence of public goods is that given that everyone can consume the same quantity without affecting that which is available to others, will provide an incentive not to pay for it. Suppose that in one street (*cul de sac*) lives a single man, who is a body-builder and an expert in Judo, kick-boxing, and all other forms of martial art, and a lone mother with a teenaged daughter. The street is in a remote part of town. Will there be street-lighting in this road?

The costs of providing street-lighting are high and above what the lone mother (anxious as she may be, she is not wealthy) is willing to pay. It certainly is above what the body-builder is willing to pay even though he may well be able to afford it. The latter would like to have street-lighting so that people can see his physique but, still, the obsession has not yet reached the level where he will be willing to pay much for it. He probably thinks to himself, the lone mother must be desperate to have it so that her daughter does not walk back home in the dark. Surely, it will be worth his while to wait until the lone mother arranges for street lights which he will then be able to enjoy. After all, there is no way in which the woman can exclude him from using the light.

Suppose that the marginal cost of providing street lights for an hour an evening for one year is equal to £200 (suppose that it is technically impossible to provide less than one hour an evening). The lone mother, given the level of her income, is willing to pay £150 a year. The body-builder is willing to pay £60 a year. Remember that one's willingness to pay reflects one's marginal utility from using street lights. Clearly, providing street lights will increase the utility (or welfare) of the people in the street. Altogether, they are willing to pay £210 while the cost is only £200. This means that the money value of their utility from street lights is greater than its cost.

The question that will now arise is whether or not the market mechanism will provide for what is clearly a socially desirable project. The answer is simply no. The way the market operates is by providing individuals with what they want and charging them its marginal cost. The marginal cost of a year's provision of street light is 200. The profit maximizing firms competing to provide the service will charge each consumer the marginal cost. However, neither the lone mother nor the body-builder are willing to pay that much. Therefore, there will be no market solution to something which will produce a clear Pareto improvement. Having the service will make the two agents better off without making anyone worse off. The fact that the markets fail to provide the service is another example of how the working of competition can fail to deliver what people seek to achieve, in spite of the fact that markets may clear and prices will equal marginal costs everywhere. In a way, this problem is not much different from the previous one (externalities). Here, as there, the problem is really that of a missing market.

If the market does not provide a solution to the problem, how can the government resolve it?

Suppose that the government decides to step in and provide the street lights in that road, how much should it provide? Should it provide the minimum of an hour an evening or should it provide for more hours of street-lighting? In other words, while the markets are a mechanism of allocation, it is more difficult for the government to choose the right allocation which is not only improving the public welfare, but that is at the same time, allocative efficient.

To understand this better let us examine how exactly is the allocation of resources generated by the market in the case of divisible private goods. Consider an economy with a private good x and a public good G. Suppose that both goods are produced by labour only. Figure 7.11 is the PPF of the economy.

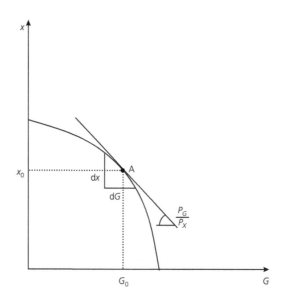

Figure 7.11 The PPF with a public good G.

The slope of the PPF is MP_L^x/MP_L^G units of x per G or, units of private good per unit of public good.

The nature of an allocative efficient point (like A) is that the subjective rate of substitution, the market price and the technological rate of exchange will all be the same. The problem here is that as there is no market for G, what will constitute its price?

We know exactly how individuals make a choice of how much x and y they wish to consume. We derive their demand schedule for, say x, by analysing optimal choices under different prices (Figure 7.12).

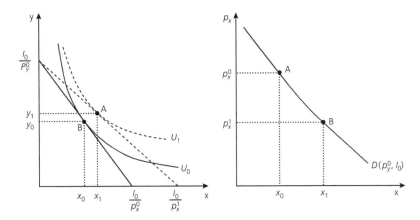

Figure 7.12 Optimal demand for good X.

We then use horizontal summation to find out what will be the quantity demanded by all agents at any given price of x (Figure 7.13).

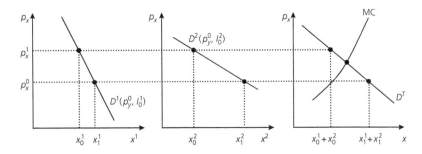

Figure 7.13 Deriving market demand for good x.

Setting the overall demand against the marginal cost of its production (which serves the principle of profit maximization of the producers) we get how much x people want to buy and produce, and we also know what price x will command. As the same thing happens in y we know that the allocative efficient allocation will be that which will equate social and private costs. So the mechanism which brought about the allocation of resources to the production of x (i.e. determined the level of x which should be produced to satisfy the principle of efficiency) is that of the price. But there is no market and no single price for the public good. How can we determine its efficient allocation?

To begin with, we repeat the same process as for the private good. That is to say, as the public good is an economic good, it means that it is both scarce and desirable. Hence, people are willing to pay to have it. How much they are willing to pay will be derived by asking what quantity of G they will want to have had they confronted a certain price for its consumption. We ignore for a moment that the answer could be, 'I do not wish to pay anything as I am waiting for someone else to buy it', and simply refer to the rationality principle of behaviour. If you were asked how much of x and the public good G you will want if their prices were such and such, your answer will give us a demand schedule for the public good G Figure 7.14.

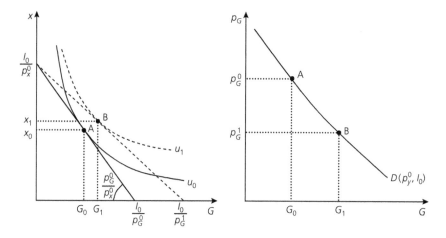

Figure 7.14 Deriving individual demand for the public good.

At A you were willing to pay p_G^0 to have G_0 units of the public good together with x_0 units of the private good at the price of p_x^0. For G_1, however, you are willing to pay fewer units of x as the marginal utility of the public good is diminishing.

Asking now how much of the public good the public would want had the price been p_G^0 is not a meaningful question. If there are n identical agents and all of them would want G_0 of the public good at the given price, we do not need to produce nG_0 units altogether. Having G_1 units of it will be sufficient, as every agent will be able to consume the quantity of the public good he wants without affecting the quantity available for another. Therefore, a horizontal summation will produce an obviously inefficient result. We must, therefore, resort to an alternative technique in order to establish the efficient provision of the public good. As G is indivisible, we know that the only thing different about it is the difference in the willingness to pay for it. Hence, what we want is a vertical summation rather than a horizontal one (see Figure 7.15).

For the level of G_0 of the public good, individual 1 is willing to pay p_1^0 while individual 2 is willing to pay p_2^0. Therefore, the total amount of money the public is willing to pay

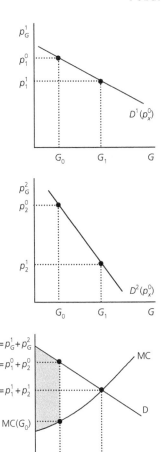

Figure 7.15 Deriving total demand for the public good.

equals $p_1^0 + p_2^0 = p_G^0$. Given the marginal cost of producing G_0 we can see that the marginal cost of the public good is less than the overall willingness to pay.

In the case of the private good, the area underneath the demand schedule represents the utility of a representative agent. It is as if we derived it for a single individual. When, however, we sum the demand schedules vertically, we add up every individual's willingness to pay. Hence, the price p_G^0 denotes the summing up of people's marginal utility. The area underneath the demand for the public good represents a measure of the total amount of social wealth that will be accrued to the public at any given level of public good provision. The area underneath the marginal cost is, as usual, the cost of production (I ignore here questions of short run, long run, and the like).

Looking back at our diagram from above you can clearly see that G_0 is not the efficient level of public good provision. The shaded area represent the social net benefit that will be generated by providing G_0 units of the public good, therefore, it is clear from the diagram that more benefits are there to be had. If we move to produce G_1 units of the public good, the overall willingness to pay will be: $p_1^1 + p_2^1 = p_G^1$. Also we can see that at that point the marginal cost of providing G_1 units of the public good

exactly equals the sum of the willingness to pay. In the case of the street light, we are
in a position similar to G_0. The total willingness to pay was 210 which was greater
than the marginal cost. Therefore, as in G_0, society can clearly be made better off not
only by providing street lights but by also providing more than the minimum of 1h per
evening.

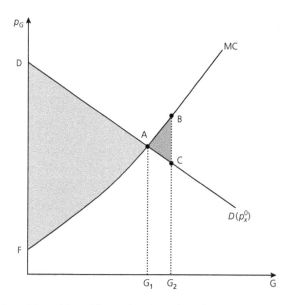

Figure 7.16 Optimal provision of the public good and transfers of benefits.

In Figure 7.16 we can see why equating the sum of willingness to pay with the marginal
cost produces the efficient allocation. Recall that the vertically summarized demand
schedule is the sum of individuals' marginal utility from each unit of public good (given
the price of the private good x). When we add up the marginal utility of each member
of the public, we have the overall utility provided by a single unit of the public good.
Adding these over the different quantities of the public good (i.e. the area underneath
the demand) measures the overall utility of the public (for a given price of x). Part of this
utility (or willingness to pay) is actually paid out to cover the cost (the area underneath the
marginal cost curve) but from a social point of view this is merely a transfer of utility from
consumers to providers of means of production, who, in the end, are also the consumers.
Therefore, we consider the cost section as a transfer from consumers to themselves. The
shaded area to the left of point A represent net benefits. When we move to point B,
the overall utility will be the area $DACG_2$ while the total cost is the area $OFABG_2$. Triangle
ABC represents that part of the cost which is not 'financed' by a transfer from what people
are willing to pay. Naturally, this will have to be paid from some source and this means
that by moving from A to B someone will be made worse off.

Coming back to our PPF, the condition for efficient provision of the public good will
be that quantities of x and G (see Figure 7.17) such that:

$$\mathrm{MP}_L^x/\mathrm{MP}_L^G = \left(p_1^G + p_2^G + \cdots p_n^G\right)/p_x.$$

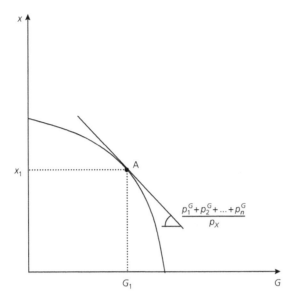

Figure 7.17 Optimal production of public and private goods.

7.4 Information and incentive compatibility: a note

One of the main problems of decentralized decisionmaking systems is that they rely heavily on individuals wishing to participate. As long as all markets are competitive and there are no missing markets of any sort, there is no need for any individual to share what they know with anyone else. The good thing about it is that we have a system which does not depend on the existence of a central office which is responsible to collect and analyse data. One of the major problems confronting central planning was the technological difficulties associated with such operations. It became extremely difficult to analyse product relationships and prices so as to produce an efficient allocation. In the competitive world, however, there is no need for any of this. As everyone pursues their own interests, they are the only ones who need to know about their preferences and technologies.

However, the moment the system ceases to operate smoothly and, despite appearances, fail to deliver what individuals seek to achieve, the decentralized system raises some serious problems regarding the government ability to rectify such situations.

In the case of externalities I have pointed out that if the government wished to levy a tax on a producer who pollutes, it would need to know the technology of this process. In our example, we had the producers of x (mud-cars) and the fishermen who were affected by the polluting effect of z. If the government were to levy a tax that will rectify the situation it would need to know $MP_L^z MP_z^y$. But this information is not readily available and the best people to ask are those people who are least interested in providing an answer (the producers of *x*). When asked, the producers of *x* have no incentive to tell the government the truth about the extent of their polluting activities. They will, therefore, provide the government with information minimizing the effects of their pollution. If the government then approaches the fishermen, it will get a completely different story. While the producers of *x* have the incentive not to tell the truth and minimize the effects of pollution, the fishermen too have no interest in the truth and they would want to exaggerate the effect of the pollution on them. Consequently, if the government fails to retrieve the correct information, the tax it will levy may help in rectifying the situation but will still leave the economy at a point which is still allocative inefficient.

In the case of public good the problem is even more complex. Consider our lone mother with the teenage daughter and the body-builder. If the government wishes to find out individuals' willingness to pay so that it can choose the efficient level of public good provision, both have an interest to exaggerate their willingness to pay (recall that choosing the level of public good provision by equating the sum of individuals' willingness to pay with the marginal cost does not mean that individuals are also asked to pay their respective willingness to pay). If the government cannot get a true measure of individuals' willingness to pay, the level of public good provided is unlikely to be Pareto efficient.

As the issue at hand is that of the incentive, I only wish to draw your attention to the fact that economic theory has means of dealing with such problems. The government may design schemes in such a way as to create the incentive to tell the truth. How are such things done? You will have to be patient and study economic theory further.

▨ NOTES

1. Note that the assumption according to which technology precedes the institutional arrangement of economic activities is far from obvious. At this level, however, we shall nevertheless stick to it.
2. Named after the Cambridge economist Pigou who wrote *Wealth and Welfare* in 1912.

■ PART TWO

PART TWO

8 Aggregation and the macroeconomic problem

8.1 Introduction

Intellectual investigations are most of the time driven by the urge to explain some facts or phenomena. In microeconomics, we saw that the subject matter of our investigation was that of economic goods: those things which are both scarce and desirable. We were asking the question of how to organize economic activities in such a way that would resolve the economic problem. We were concerned with the broad question of resources allocation. The set of economic facts around us was fairly easy to identify. We can all recognize a price (in money)[1] and we can even recognize an exchange rate between, say, tomatoes and cucumbers.

In macroeconomics, while some facts may be easy to identify, it is not at all obvious why they should require a new—and separate—form of investigation. For instance, one of the most prominent facts which had contributed a great deal to the development of an almost separate discipline called macroeconomics is the problem of unemployment. However, one may argue, this should be seen as simply a problem of labour market analysis which is clearly in the domain of microeconomics, why do we need to establish a different form of investigation to analyse it?

A possible answer to this would be that there are imperfections in the labour market which cannot be resolved simply by allowing market forces to operate. But even if this were the case, it is still not clear why there is a need for a special form of investigation. Microeconomic analysis, as we saw in Chapters 4 and 7, is quite capable of dealing with imperfection. Should the study of unemployment not be confined to the study of market imperfection?

To some extent, the development of the separate subject of macroeconomics reflects the exasperation with mere market analysis. The problem of unemployment had been so severe that scholars felt that there must be something more serious than mere market imperfection behind it. What they really meant is that there are institutional reasons behind the problem and neoclassical microeconomics does not really assign an explicit role to institutions. Transferring the weight to a level of discourse where the subject matter of investigation are relationships between the economy as a whole and its biggest institution, the government, felt like a way of circumventing this apparent deficiency of microeconomic analysis.

But there are other reasons to why some economists felt that microeconomic analysis as such is insufficient. Given the model of general equilibrium which we have portrayed in Chapter 6, the role of government is clearly confined to facilitating the achievement of the allocative efficient outcome. However, in the general equilibrium story which we have told, money—an extremely well known phenomenon—played no clear role. Why is there money? Is it, or is it not, an argument in individuals' utility function. Had money been a simple 'commodity' then we could derive a demand for and a supply of it and we can even envisage a competitive market for money. I am sure that all of this sounds very strange to you. 'We do not really want money' you may mutter to yourself, 'We want the things it can buy'. But money is a real fact of life, it is scarce and desirable, yet it is not really a simple commodity. Or is it?

Within the standard general equilibrium theory we cannot find an obvious explanation either of the origin of money or to what affects its provision. This is not to say that microeconomic tools are inherently oblivious of money and indeed, there are attempts to deal with such questions in a microeconomic framework but this is something for future studies. In any case, within the problem of resource allocation, it helped to concentrate minds by assuming that money is a given phenomenon. But as we know from experience we cannot really have a complete economic theory without explaining both the quantity of money and its effects on the system. In addition, from our individualistic framework of analysis it is also not clear how should we account for government's actions. There is no doubt that government actions have an influence on the economy but should we consider the government as a simple rational agent? If so, what kind of an objective function should we attribute to it and why?

Standard textbooks tend to motivate the interest in macroeconomics by pointing at phenomena which are general to the economy as a whole. For instance, business cycles, which depict a known historical phenomenon of fluctuations in total output, have been a major concern in recent years. The standard static model of general equilibrium does not seem to accommodate such a phenomenon and explanations have been sought outside its domain. However, there have been attempts at explaining business cycles from the microeconomic point of view by further investigation of the dynamic aspects of general equilibrium. In some explanations, the focus is on the behaviour of individual firms and their problem of liquidity. When firms face liquidity problems they may not be able to fulfil their contracts and, subsequently, they may face bankruptcy. Naturally, a microeconomics feature of a trough in a business cycle would be the liquidation of firms. If we can find an explanation why this happens in a fashion which generates cycles we will have a micro-theory of the business cycle. Still, as the effects of business cycles are felt throughout, the general belief is that the solution to the problem (as well as its explanation) lies within the analysis of the system as a whole. We must also bear in mind that the prevalence of business cycles as an observed phenomenon does not sit comfortably with the efficiency of competitive market structures. What typifies business cycles is their length. Namely, it is not the fluctuation as such which is the source of concern. When all markets are perfectly competitive there should not be prolonged business cycles as all shocks will be accommodated by the corresponding changes in prices. If, on the other hand, markets are not perfectly competitive, can one explain business cycles merely by looking at the market imperfections?

Recent developments in microeconomic theory suggest that there may not be a need to separate macroeconomics from microeconomic analysis and that we have sufficient tools to incorporate both money and government into our micro-models. Nevertheless, at this stage of our study we will introduce the distinct framework of macro analysis so that, in the future, you may ponder more seriously about the relationship between the two.

8.2 The problem of aggregation

8.2.1 The common denominator and the institution of competition

In the introduction we discussed at some length the problem of identifying variables which constitute the subject matter of our investigation. While in microeconomics this seems less of a problem (to say 'the price of tomatoes is 60 p per lb' is something which we may be able to observe), in macroeconomics the problem is much more pronounced. We do know what a tomato is and we can ascertain its exchange rate in terms of other goods. Do we know what a 'national product' is? And what is the meaning of a 'price level'? In other words, the problem of macroeconomics is exacerbated by the need to **aggregate**: namely, to add up things which have no obvious common denominator. How much is 5 lb of potatoes + 23 loaves of bread?

Evidently there is a need for a common denominator for all goods. But if this common denominator is not neutral we might run into some difficulties. For instance, consider a world of two goods: A and B where a and b are their respective quantities. Suppose that we choose to use good A as the numeraire. Namely, we will measure the economy in terms of one good only. If in year 2 the value of everything produced in the economy in terms of commodity A is twice as much as in year 1, we shall say that the economy grew by a 100%. But is good A really a neutral means by which to measure the economy?

Let $p_t = p_B/p_A$ be the price of good B in terms of A at time t. The total product of the economy in period t will now be:

$$x_t = a + p_t b.$$

Suppose now that due to a technological improvement we can produce more of both A and B. There are now two possibilities:

(i) The technological improvement was equally relevant to both A and B. This means that their relative price will not change: namely, $p_{t+1} = p_t$. The new national product will thus be

$$x_{t+1}^i = (a + \Delta a) + p_t(b + \Delta b)$$

where Δa and Δb represent the change in output.

(ii) The technological improvement was mainly relevant to the production of A. Nevertheless, the fact that such an improvement means that the production possibilities frontier has shifted outwards suggests that we may increase the production of any good. Still, the price of the good, the production of which most benefited from the improvement, will change more than any of the other goods. Hence, p_{t+1} is no more the same as p_t and:

$$x_{t+1}{}^{ii} = (a + \Delta a) + p_{t+1}(b + \Delta b).$$

Clearly, the relationship between $x_{t+1}{}^{ii}$ and $x_{t+1}{}^{i}$ can be anything, so what has really happened to the total level of output?

In this example we have used money prices and good A as a means of aggregation. We were not very successful because the relationship between good A and good B through their money prices, were not unaffected by the changes under consideration. Could we, instead, aggregate by using money values alone? Well, as our interests are focused on the real economy this may not be very helpful. If all prices doubled (as well as individuals' earnings) surely there will be no real change in the economy. However, our index which is based on the money value of all goods, will tell us that output has doubled which, of course, is not true. There are even more complex problems with the use of money as a means of aggregation because we are not quite sure how neutral money really is?

Nevertheless, we must be able to do something and at this stage we shall assume the neutrality of money. This means that we may use the money value of goods as a common denominator for the purpose of adding up things which, otherwise, would have nothing in common.

Consider an economy where two goods are produced: x and y. The PPF, shown in Figure 8.1 depicts the state of the economy at time t.

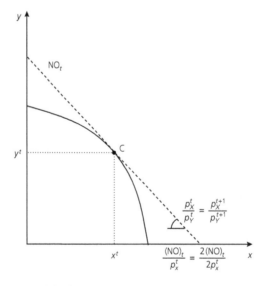

Figure 8.1 The production possibility frontier.

Assuming that the economy is competitive across all industries and factor markets, it is clear that the economy will end up at a point like C where the relative market price reveals the true social cost. If we extend the line tangent to point C we get a sort of 'budget line'. The following equation describes this line:

$$p_x^t x^t + p_y^t y^t = (NO)_t.$$

This means that the value of the output at point C where we produce (x^t units of x and y^t units of y), is the value of all that has been produced in the economy (the national output[2]). This level of output, at the given level of prices cannot be obtained at any other point on the PPF. By implication, you can see another feature of competitive market structures: they maximize the value of national output.

Clearly, if we double the prices of x and y, the relative market price will remain unchanged. If $p_x^{t+1} = 2p_x^t$ and $p_y^{t+1} = 2p_y^t$, then $(p_x^{t+1})/(p_y^{t+1}) = (p_x^t)/(p_y^t)$. Hence, point C will still be the competitive outcome. However,

$$p_x^{t+1} x^t + p_y^{t+1} y^t = 2p_x^t x^t + 2p_y^t y^t = (NO)_{t+1} = 2(NO)_t$$

but you can clearly see that there has been no real growth. The PPF has not moved at all, yet the index of national output suggests that the economy is producing twice as much.

To solve this problem, we say that using money values of goods as their common denominator will only be meaningful if we keep prices unchanged. For instance, let us see what would have happened in the above story had we measured output at the prices at time t? The answer is very simple. If at $t + 1$ we still produce the same level of output for both x and y, then by measuring them in terms of their prices at t, we can see that nothing has happened to the national output.

Consider now the following case in Figure 8.2:

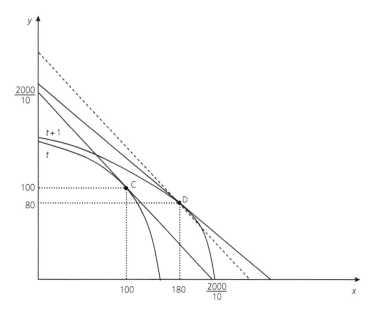

Figure 8.2 Shifting the PPF.

At t if we were at point C where we have 100 units of x and 100 units of y, $p_x^t = p_y^t = 10$; hence, the value of national output will be: $10 \times 100 + 10 \times 100 = 2000$. Now, there has been a technological development which pushed the PPF outward and the economy has moved, at $t + 1$, to point D where they produce 180 units of x and 80 units of y. Has the economy grown or not?

Assuming competitive markets, we know that point D must also be the point where market prices are tangent to the slope of the PPF. Suppose now that the price of x has risen to 11 while the price of y rose to 14. In current prices, the level of national output at $t + 1$ is: $11 \times 180 + 14 \times 80 = 3100$. This means growth of 55%. But this 55% increase also contains an element of the change in relative prices. To rid our analysis from such changes we must ask the following question: how much more money would one have needed to be able to buy today's output at yesterday's income? This should sound familiar enough as this was exactly the subject of establishing a nominal equivalent to the real income effect which resulted when the price of a good changes.

To buy today's output in yesterday's prices we would have needed $10 \times 180 + 10 \times 80 = 2600$, which is only a 30% increase (the broken line going through point D which is parallel to the line going through C). Therefore, if we want to consider money as a common denominator we must avoid problems of relative prices and examine changes in output against a single set of prices. In such a case, all changes in the nominal value of our output could be entirely attributed to changes in the real output.

However, note that there is another problem lurking at the back of this analysis: the assumption about the competitive nature of industry. Consider Figure 8.3. We start at point A, where not all industries are competitive. Therefore, at A, market prices will not necessarily reflect the true social cost. Now, suppose that there is a technological

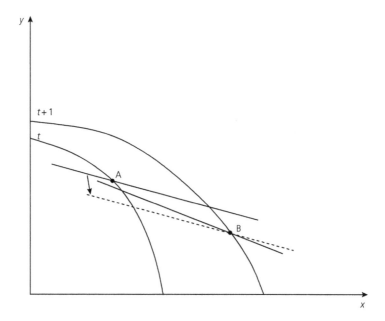

Figure 8.3 Shifting PPF and imperfect competition.

improvement and the economy ends up at point B. Note that as the competitive conditions are no longer binding, we cannot be sure on how exactly the new price will relate to the new PPF. If we measured the money value of today's output at yesterday's prices, we will have the broken line, parallel to the line through A, go through point B. As this broken line lies below the line that goes through A we can be sure that the nominal value of the output at B will be lower than that at A. If we did not know anything about the PPF, the data would read as if the economy has shrunk. Yet as you can clearly see, point B is on a set which was not available when the economy was at A and there had been a clear growth in real term (the shift outwards of the PPF). Equally, institutional changes alone can sometime imply growth although there has been no change in the economy's frontier.

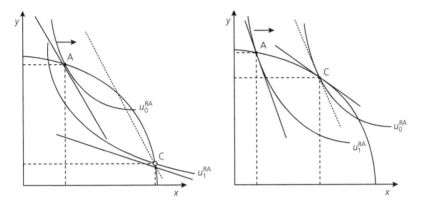

Figure 8.4

Suppose that y is a competitive industry while x is a monopolist (Figure 8.4). The relative price will therefore not reflect the real social cost and the economy will end up at a point like A where we produce less x than we would under a competitive organization of all markets (point C) and we pay for x more than it really costs to produce it. If now a new policy eliminates the circumstances which allowed x to be produced by a monopolist, the economy will move towards point C. However, point C in the left-hand diagram denotes a move to a competitive environment where there are some missing markets (i.e. externalities), while point C in the right-hand diagram assumes a move to the perfectly competitive allocation. If we measure the nominal value of the output at C in terms of A's prices (the broken line through C), looking at the amount of money needed to sustain the new allocation C at the original prices (the broken lines) we can see that in both cases the measure of national output will suggest growth. However, in both cases the PPF has not moved at all. This means that the economy has exactly the same potential as it had the year before.

Some may say, 'But this could mean an improvement in welfare'. If we add to the diagram our crude representative agent we will find that in one case (with externalities) we end up at a lower 'social' utility. In the right-hand diagram, there is, indeed, an improvement in welfare. But this cannot be attributed to the accuracy of our calculation, as we would never be in a position to know whether the economy is in a competitive equilibrium without missing markets. In short, what this shows is that it is not inconceivable that when we try to account for growth based on fixed prices, we may not get a true depiction of what has really happened. Still, as the PPF is not known to us and its estimation is a very difficult thing, we are left with these principles of measurement which are fine provided that we are conscious of the associated difficulties.

I suppose that one could say that a move from A to B or A to C in the above diagrams suggests an enormous institutional change. Such changes are usually unlikely to happen over a short period of time. Hence, the gaps which may create such problems as noted above are not very likely to happen often.

In most cases, economies are more likely to be well inside their frontier. This means that when we talk about growth, we talk about the changes in economic activities rather than the potential of the economy. As the opportunity costs of all goods inside the frontier is zero, we have no benchmark against which to compare the movement of national output. To assess the economic significance of growth inside the frontier would, therefore, be a far more complex task.

8.2.2 The problem with counting

Having established that, in spite of all difficulties, the only way to produce aggregate measures is through their nominal values, we must look more carefully into how we add those values up.

Suppose that a farmer produces the total amount of W tonnes of wheat a year. The baker, who uses wheat to make bread, produces B loaves of bread a year. In money terms, the farmer has produced the value of $p_W W$ and the baker the value of $p_B B$ where p_W and p_B are the respective prices of wheat and bread. So the value of national product is

$$NP = p_W W + p_B B.$$

Bearing in mind that a proportion, say α, of the produce of wheat was used by the baker, the value of the baker's output contains something which has already been accounted for. We call such a problem, the problem of **Double Counting**.

To circumvent this problem we define the national product to be the **value added**. Namely, that much in the value of goods which has been added through the entrepreneurial endeavour of members of our society. In our case, it means that the national product is

$$NP = (p_W W) + (p_B B)[1 - \alpha(p_W W)].$$

The **value added** will appear in each firm's balance sheet as the difference between sales and purchases from other firms. The Balance Sheet of a firm normally looks like this:

$$
\begin{array}{cccccc}
 & \text{purchases} & & & & \\
\text{sales} - & \text{from other} - & \text{depreciation} - & \text{wages} - & \text{interest} = & \text{profit.} \\
\text{(S)} & \text{firms} & \text{(DP)} & \text{(W)} & \text{(IN)} & \text{(P)} \\
 & \text{(PF)} & & & &
\end{array}
$$

Definition The **gross national product** is the total sum of **values added**.

$$GNP = \Sigma VA = \Sigma(S - PF).$$

But $\Sigma(S - PF) = \Sigma(W + IN + P + DP)$. If we now transfer **depreciation** to the other side we get:

$$\Sigma(S - PF - DP) = \Sigma(W + IN + P)$$

or

$$GNP - \Sigma DP = \Sigma(W + IN + P).$$

We call the expression on the left the **net national product** (NNP). On the right-hand side we have all possible ways of earning an income (labour (W), lending capital (IN) and ownership (P)) which is, therefore, the **generated income** by the firms. Summing over all units in the economy and we get the total amount of generated income. This, in other words, is **national income**, which we normally denote by the letter Y.

Hence, what we have here is the following relationship:

$$GNP - \Sigma DP = NNP = Y.$$

The NNP is the total amount of resources available to the economy when there is no trade (i.e. a **closed economy**). But what are the various usages to which these resources can be put to? If, for a moment, we consider a **closed economy without a government**, then the only usages possible are **consumption** and **investment**.

What is the difference between consumption and investment? Are goods inherently one or the other? The answer is no. In a wheat producing economy, there is only one good which can be either used for consumption (making bread) or for investment (stored as seeds to be sown in the next period). So consumption and investment are matters of choice. We shall come back to this later but at present we simply look back at our economy and we ask what have people done rather than what they will do.

We can therefore say that the NNP has been used for consumption (C) and investment (I).

$$NNP = C + I.$$

What do people do with their income? They either use it for consumption or they 'store' it, namely, they save. Hence:

$$Y = C + S.$$

Bearing in mind that $NNP = Y$, we get

$$C + I = C + S$$

or,

$$I = S$$

which means that actual investment always equals actual savings. This last equation is an important one as it tells us about the way capital is formed. After all, those things which we refrain from consuming now may be used as means of producing in the next period; namely, they can increase the means of production and, thus, the potential of the economy. If the investment—the flow of new capital goods—is greater than the rate of depreciation (i.e. the amount of capital (machines) which became unusable during that period), the total means of production for the next period will be greater. This would mean an expansion of the production possibilities frontier or what we call **growth**. If, however, the amount of investment—the flow of new capital goods—is less than what is required to replace the capital which became unusable, the total means of production for the next period will drop. This would mean a contraction of the production possibilities frontier; the economy will be declining. What will happen if the investment equals the rate of depreciation?

■ NOTES

1. Although the meaning of price is more complex. After all, there are still some nagging doubts about what is 'price'? In terms of which good do we measure it? What is the meaning of money? and so on.

2. Note that this 'national output' is not the concept of national income, or GDP which are commonly used to describe the level of economic activity in an economy. We shall define these concepts in the next section. Here, I would only like to draw your attention to some conceptual difficulties associated with measuring changes of aggregates.

9 The determinants of output

In Chapter 8, we have investigated the meaning of one of the most important objects of macroeconomic analysis: **national income**. Given the difficulties in identifying and quantifying the aggregate level of national economic activities, we opted for a pecuniary definition, assuming that money itself is not an economic good of the same nature as all others. Thus we ended up defining national product as the sum of all values added. As a corollary we discovered that the sum of all values added is also the sum of all income generated within the economy. This, of course, has put national product at the heart of our concerns. If income is the means by which we can improve our well-being, then being able to understand what determines its level and what affects its progress (i.e. growth) becomes one of the most crucial questions for economics in general and for macroeconomics in particular.

At the same time, we also know that, in real terms, output is created by means of production such as labour and capital. Without going into the details concerning the possible effects which growth may have on the input mix, it is fairly clear that the level of national product and its progress could also tell us something about employment. In a world where labour is one of the main mechanisms by which people draw from the social wealth, the development of employment is merely the other side of our well-being coin.

It is worth noting, however, that the well-being of an economy is a far more complex subject than the mere aggregate level of national income and employment. I am sure that you can imagine how questions of income or wealth distribution may influence the benefits which can be derived from any given level of national income. For instance, if ownership of corporations was more broadly and evenly spread, the question of employment would lose some of its sting. If all the people had incomes which are derived from both ownership and labour, unemployment would not necessarily deprive people of their ability to extract a reasonable share from the national income. Or, if the government redistributed income via non-work related means (say, universal benefits), it is possible that such an economy, with a lower level of national income, may generate greater well-being than an economy where there is no redistribution at all and most of the national income is concentrated in the hands of the few.

Obviously, considering these alternative institutional arrangements does not reduce our interest in that which determines the level of national income. Whatever institutions we have, we would always prefer to have them with as high a level of income as possible. However, at a more advanced level of study we shall have to ask ourselves whether any particular institutional arrangements have any specific influence on the level of national income which can be obtained. But, before that, we shall concentrate on the more basic question of what is it that determines the level of national income for a given institutional structure. The structure to which I refer here is the one we have emphasized so far: a more or less competitive set-up of the economy.

Indeed, in most textbooks in economics you will find the problem of what determines the level of output posed as a question of demand and supply. This, to be precise, is a question which is a logical extension of the competitive set-up. As what determines the output of individual industries is demand and supply, it seems natural to think that the overall output too, is a matter for demand and supply to determine. However, society is not only a collection of markets. Individuals as members of society may be influenced by the environment within which they operate and this may have an effect on their productivity (and thus, aggregate supply). One can conceive other notions of social organization which may rely on more delicate mechanisms than demand and supply for allocation and distribution. The question of what determines output when markets are not the main mode of either allocation or distribution is bound to be dominated by other analytical tools than demand and supply. However, within the competitive set-up, the world where all agents compete against all others and when all is a matter of exchange, the question of what determines output really boils down to whether the level of output adjusts to fit the level of demand or is output determined by the wishes and considerations of producers.

9.1 Say's law and general equilibrium

In spite of Adam Smith's prominence as the founder of the independent discipline of economics, most people will argue that there is no macroeconomics *per se* in Smith. While they may be right regarding Smith's handling of money and unemployment, this is not at all true with regard to this most crucial question of the determinants of national income.

Adam Smith opens his *Wealth of Nations* with the claim that national income is the produce of the nation's labour or that which has been purchased with it from other nations. However, he goes on to say, the quantity of it depends on (a) the 'skill, dexterity, and judgement with which its labour is generally applied' and (b) on 'the proportion between the number of those who are employed in useful labour, and that of those who are not so employed'.

Put differently, according to Adam Smith the level of national product depends on both demand and supply. By supply, he refers to the way in which labour is organized or, what I would term more generally, the *circumstances of industry*. By demand Smith refers to a distinction between the demand for different employments. For instance, if a landlord, by the end of a year, has a supply of, say, wheat grains, he may either use them to hire labour to work in his fields and produce more wheat, or he may hire people to entertain him or become his servants and so on. If he uses his entire stock of grain to feed his demand for frivolous delights, the total amount of wheat that will be produced in the economy in the next period is bound to be smaller. If he used most of the stock for the purpose of producing more wheat, the amount of output by the end of the period will be much greater. In other words, the same stock of means of production can produce different levels of national income depending on how it is being used.

While we no longer accept Smith's distinction between productive and unproductive labour, this is really about a valid distinction between the demand for consumption and demand for investment. The main difference between Smith and the modern version of demand determined output is that in the latter case, the determination of output was associated with the question of unemployment. In Smith's case, labour is always fully employed and wages are flexible. More specifically, Smith considered the total demand for labour as unaffected by its internal composition. Put differently, contemporary approaches to demand determined output are based on the effects which short falls (or excesses) of demand may have on the level of national income. According to Smith, this is not a direct effect as the level of demand for labour is determined by the output of last period. In this respect, even according to Smith, supply determines demand but as the composition of demand is detrimental to the level of output in the next period, there is the question of which causes what?

In part, some of the confusion about Smith's position is the result of the fact that Smith's analysis is inherently dynamic. He was not really concerned with the question of whether or not there exists a set of prices for which all rational wants coincide. Coordination, which is the essence of the concept of general equilibrium presented in Chapter 6, is not at the heart of Smith's interest. Instead, he was far more interested in the dynamics of competition. Viewed in this way, the role of demand's composition is quite significant. Over time, the composition of demand is detrimental to the level of output.

Unlike Smith, one of his followers did leave his mark on the development of macroeconomic analysis. J.B. Say published in 1803 his *Traite d'economie politique, ou simple exposition de la manniere dont se forment, se distribuent et se consomment les richesses*. Drawing on an implicit notion of general equilibrium where all markets (including the labour market) clear, Say's main claim concerning the level of national income is the famous 'Say's Law' which has been popularized as: *supply creates its own demand*.

The main element in Say's proposition is based on a recognition that the process of production itself generates the income from which demand is derived. In other words, in order to be able to buy goods you must produce goods. Therefore, it is not possible to have a situation of 'over production'. If you produce more, you also generate more income from which a demand will rise for that extra bit of output. This, of course, does not preclude excess demand or supply in individual markets. What is argued in Say's proposition is that the demand for each commodity is generated by the overall production process. Therefore, if there is a market which is oversupplied, there will have to be a market which is undersupplied. In the context of a barter economy this may sound quite simple: whatever people produce and bring to the market, they will exchange for other goods. Hence, it is supply that determines what will be demanded. Say's law is a bit more sophisticated than that and makes the additional connection between production and income generation.

I hope that you are able to observe that some of the discussion on Say corresponds to our own analysis in Chapter 8. There, we defined national income as the sum of values added and discovered that it is thus the same as the generated income. This, to an extent, is what Say argued. However, he made an additional point. That, therefore, what will be demanded (say, for consumption and investment) will always be the same as the value of what has already been produced.

A hidden problem in this discussion is the time dimension and the meaning of causality. In the case of Smith's story it is true that the total demand for productive and unproductive labour will be equal to the amount of wheat produced in the previous year. In this sense, as we said before, supply determines demand. But it is the decision of the landlord about what to do with their wheat which will, in turn, determine the supply of the next period. In that sense, demand (or rather, demand composition) determines output.

In Say's analysis, on the other hand, the emphasis is more on the mechanism which transmits the income generated by production, across all markets to bring about the conclusion that there is no aggregate overproduction. Say's law, therefore, seems to be closely associated with a notion of general equilibrium.[1] The idea which concerned Say (i.e. that overall there cannot be overproduction and thus, output determines demand) became closely linked with the idea of clearing markets. In such a case, it seems almost obvious to say that demand will have no influence on output.

In Chapter 8, we discussed the reasons for the development of new analytical tools for dealing with macroeconomic issues. On the face of it, there is no obvious reason for this as general equilibrium was already a theory which captures the entire economy. However, among other things, money was not part of it while it has been a part of every economy's life. But when we go back to the question of output (or national income), in particular, in the way Say's law proposes, we are back again in the domain of the real economy. Namely, the transmission mechanism across all markets is an essential component of the argument that there cannot be any overproduction and thus, supply creates demand. This is essentially a general equilibrium question and I thought that it would be interesting to examine whether or not there is any correspondence between Say's law and what is embedded in the general equilibrium model.

Let us first examine the relationship between a competitive set-up and the level of national output. Consider an economy where only two commodities are produced (let us call them ... x and y). Assume too, that both are produced by only one means of production called labour according to the following technology: $x = f(L_x); y = g(L_y)$, where L_x, L_y represent the amount of labour employed by industries x and y, respectively. f and g are the respective technologies. Let the total amount of labour available be given by L. Assume too, for simplicity's sake, that labour supply is fixed. Hence, $L_x + L_y = L$. Let us begin at an initial equilibrium set-up shown in Figure 9.1 where all markets (for x, y, and labour) are at equilibrium.

Generally speaking, the potential of the economy (the level of real output) is captured by the production possibilities frontier. The actual level of output (at the competitive equilibrium C) is given by $p_x^0 x_0 + p_y^0 y_0 = N p_0$.

In the labour market we wrote the real wages on the vertical axis (see Chapter 5). However, note that the price level p represents an aggregated price (i.e. $p = \alpha p_x + (1 - \alpha)p_y$). Therefore, the demand for labour too is an aggregated marginal product. It is the horizontal sum of the marginal product of labour in both industries.

In equilibrium, p_0 is the weighted sum of p_x^0 and p_y^0.[2] The area underneath the demand for labour is the sum of the aggregated marginal product of each unit of labour measured

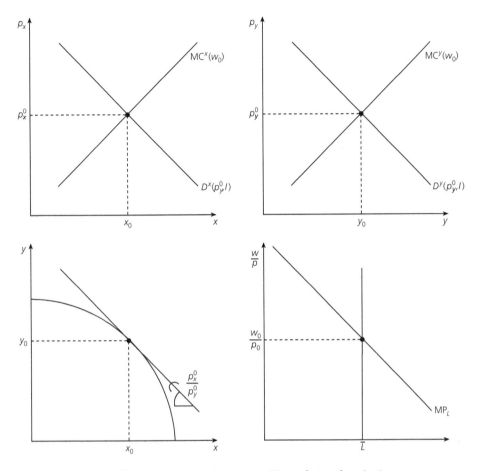

Figure 9.1 General equilibrium in a two-good economy with one factor of production.

in terms of some composite good. It is, therefore, an aggregated notion of total output. With consistent measurements, the area underneath the demand for labour should be the same as $(Np_0)/p_0$.

Note, also, that the rectangular area created by $(w_0/p_0)L_0$ captures the income which has been generated as wages. The rest of the area underneath the demand schedule (i.e. the rest of the national product) is thus the profits (or return to capital had there been capital in our story) which too is a form of income.

Let us examine now what might be the effects on output of an increase in demand for both x and y. As this demand cannot come from nowhere, let us suppose that it was generated by a one-off return on an external asset. However, recall from our microeconomic analysis that all decisions made by agents are connected. Therefore, while the demand for x will increase and cause the price of x to increase too, this will cause a change in demand for y according to whether the goods are gross substitutes or complements. Assuming that the two goods are gross substitutes the following changes shown in Figure 9.2 will occur.

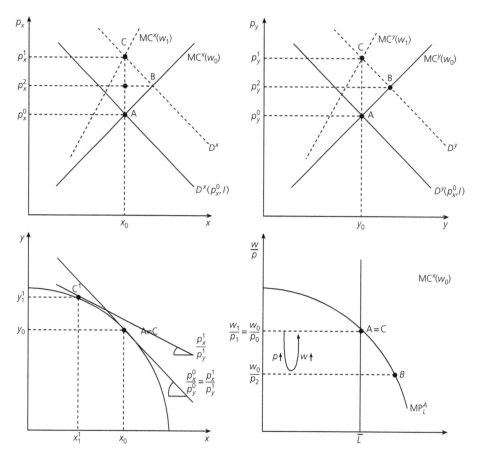

Figure 9.2 A change in tastes.

As the demand for x and y increases, their prices will begin to rise. In turn, real wages (w/p) will fall and labour, as a means of production, has become cheaper. Profit maximization dictates employing so many workers up to the point where their marginal product equals their real wage. This, now, will happen at point B in the labour market. Consequently, there will be excess demand for labour at the initial level of nominal wages w_0. Competition for workers will cause nominal wages to rise until we return to the original point A where nominal wages have risen sufficiently to compensate for the increase in the prices of x and y. In the markets for x and y this will mean that the supply curves will shift to the left (with higher nominal wages, marginal costs will increase). This, in turn, will create excess demand at point B and prices will keep rising further. This will create yet another fall in real wages that will lead to an increase in nominal wages.

To see where all of this is leading us we have to identify the clear process. In the markets for x and y the prices are rising. First, there was an increase due to the demand pull and then, there were further increases due to increase in nominal wages. We can see that the process may end with either the same resource allocation if point C is exactly above A in the markets for x and y. Or at a different allocation (point C' in the PPF diagram) where we produce less x and more y. Whether this is the outcome or a point like D is an outcome very much depends on how the relative prices will change. Using our excess demand analysis (see Chapter 6) we can see that the relative price will either remain the same or change slightly (Figure 9.3).

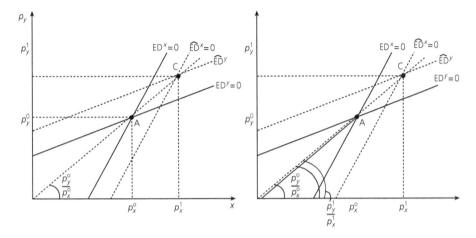

Figure 9.3 Changes in relative prices: the excess demand analysis.

The initial increase in demand for x would mean that for any given price of y equilibrium in the x market will only be possible at a higher price for x. This will cause the $ED^x = 0$ to shift to the right. A similar argument applies to y and thus $ED^y = 0$ will shift upwards. In addition, there will be an increase in wages. This shifts supply in the markets for x and y to the left. Hence, in the market for x equilibrium—for a given price of y—will be obtained at a higher price of x. This will cause the $ED^x = 0$ to shift further to the right. Again, a similar argument for y will shift the $ED^y = 0$ further upwards. Consequently, the new general equilibrium will be reached at point C.

The diagram on the left represents the case where relative prices (the ray from the origin) have not changed. This would mean that the increase in demand will have no real effect on the economy. We will remain at the same point on the PPF ($C = A$). The equilibrium level of real wages also will remain unchanged.

The diagram on the right captures the case where C' is at the point where the ray from the origin has a higher slope. This means $p_x^1/p_y^1 < p_x^0/p_y^0$. Therefore, C' on the PPF will lie to the left of A. In the labour market the real wages will remain unchanged. The fact that a change in the relative price will also change the aggregated price level will only mean a different change in the nominal wages. But whatever is the case, it is clear from the labour market the neither demand for labour (which is a function of labour's productivity) nor the supply of labour will change (we assume that the change in tastes will not affect individuals' preferences with regard to leisure).

Therefore, on the face of it, general equilibrium theory seems to be consistent with the implication of Say's law in the sense that output determines demand, demand does not determine output. We saw how a change in demand for both goods left the level of real income unchanged. This we can learn either from the fact that the PPF itself has not changed. Or, better still, from the fact that in the labour market the total aggregated output (the area underneath the demand for labour) will be the same at A as it is in C or C'. As there was no change in the productivity of labour, the aggregate marginal product curve remains in its position. As the supply of labour also, has not changed, as long as there is equilibrium in the labour market, real national product as well as its distribution will not change.[3]

But this is not the whole story. Note that in the above analysis, the labour supply was vertical. This raises two issues. First, there is the question of whether or not what caused a change in the demand for x and y would also cause a change in the supply of labour. Second, even if the answer to the first question is that there is no connection between the initial change and the supply of labour, would not people's decision about work be affected by prices?

The reason why we may expect the supply of labour to be influenced by what originated the increase in demand for x and y is that, as we saw in Chapter 2, for preferences to be representable in a functional form, they must be complete. Namely, all economic decisions taken by an agent are connected. That which caused the increase in demand for x and y is bound to affect the supply of labour. However, this is only true if we believe that all people are identical. If we allow the fact that some people may derive their income only from ownership (profits) and if we assume that they are those who received the one-off return on the external asset, then it is conceivable that the increase in demand for x and y would not affect the supply of labour.

The second issue, of course, is much more difficult to dismiss. If indeed labour supply is not vertical, the effects of the increase in demand may be very different indeed. I shall come back to this point later.

Whether or not the above finding can be said to be consistent with Say's own formulation of the law named after him is a complex and interesting question which we shall not address here. We will only say that in the broad interpretation of Say's law, the above finding suggests that demand would not affect supply only under very restrictive conditions.

But there is another, more Smithian, reason why one may question this broad interpretation of Say's law. This is the possible effect that the **composition** of demand may have on output. While this clearly goes beyond the immediate question of whether you need to produce something in order to buy something else, it is within the domain of the broader question of whether demand can influence supply. As the change in allocation which resulted from the increase in demand clearly suggested a change in the demand composition (point C' which is the more likely outcome), how may this influence output?

Let us modify our story a bit. Suppose that goods x and y are produced by two types of inputs: machines (K;capital) and labour (L). One way in which we may influence output is by changing the amount of resources available for production.

Suppose that x and y are not just any goods. Let x be machines (M) (or investment goods) and y be consumption goods (C). Within neoclassical economics, goods have no intrinsic value or nature. Goods become investment goods or consumption goods only by the use which individuals choose to put them to. Nevertheless, for the sake of exposition

I will assume that one can distinguish between the two types of good by their more likely use. Implicitly, what we are saying is that all produced machines are used for production purposes rather than as exhibits in a conceptual art gallery.

We can now restructure our model with the following assumptions:

(i) Two goods, C and M

(ii) Technology: $C = f(L,K)$; $M = g(L,K)$ where f and g are production functions the properties of which will be explored later on in our study.

(iii) Scarcity: there is a fixed amount of labour L at all times but the amount of capital may differ across periods. Let K_t be the amount of capital at time t. Every year, there is a certain proportion of those machines which ceases to function. Let $\triangle$ be the rate of depreciation of the stock of capital. This means that at any year t, the quantity of capital available is reduced by $\triangle K_t$ machines.

Figure 9.4 depicts the production possibilities frontier of the economy at time t.

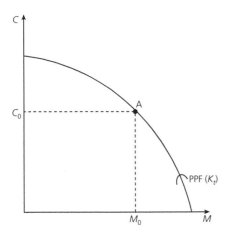

Figure 9.4 The PPF at t, with a capital stock K_t.

Suppose that initial equilibrium is at point A. Here society 'chose' to produce $C_t = C_0$ units of consumption good and $M_t = M_0$ units of capital goods (i.e. investment). At any one point of time, the stock of capital of the economy will be:

$$K_t = K_{t-1} + M_t - \delta K_{t-1},$$

which means the new stock of capital is the old stock of capital—those machines which have gone out of service + new machines. In terms of changes over time we may say that the stock of capital will change according to the balance between new machines and those which have gone out of service:

$$\frac{\partial K}{\partial t} \equiv \dot{K} = M_t - \delta K_{t-1}.$$

The stock of capital (the available resources) will increase whenever the quantity of capital goods produced (investment) is greater than the amount of machines which are taken out of use (depreciation).

When M_t is greater than $\triangle K_{t-1}$ then the stock of capital will increase. The PPF, in such a case, will shift outward and thus increase the feasible set which is available to society (Figure 9.5).

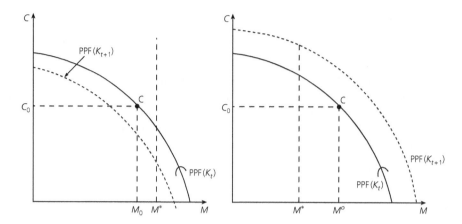

Figure 9.5 Changes in the capital stock and the PPF.

Suppose that the rate of depreciation is such that if the economy produced M^* new machines, it will only be sufficient to replace those machines which had to be taken out of service. In the left-hand side of the figure we see that demand composition had led the economy to choose point C where the amount of investment good M produced is too little ($M_C < M^*$). Hence, the stock of capital for the next period will be smaller. The PPF of the economy will shift inward and point C will no longer be feasible.

The right-hand diagram shows the more happy state when demand composition is such that we produce more M than M^*. Therefore, the stock of capital available to the economy will increase and the PPF will shift outwards.

In other words, while the mere increase in demand may not produce any change at all in the level of national income, it may produce a change in demand's composition. This, in turn, may indeed influence the availability of resources and subsequently, the level of national income.

9.2 Output and markets

As we noticed earlier, at the heart of Say's law and the 'supply determines demand' approach lies a notion of general equilibrium. We have just demonstrated that this claim is far from being universal. Namely, while it may be true that an exogenous demand pull will have no real impact on the economy, there are circumstances when relative prices do change and, thus, demand composition changes too. Consequently, if we may be able to clearly distinguish between the demand for different types of national output usages, demand pull may influence output.

Indeed, some of the criticisms of Say's law was based on exactly the same principle. While it is true that in a barter economy there cannot be excess demand or supply in any market, this is not true in a monetary economy. Even if overproduction is not possible as income is generated by the production process, we may still have excess demand in one market against excess supply in another. In simple terms one can say that in a barter economy if you bring two pints of milk to the market where bread and milk are exchanged, you cannot get more or less bread than what has been brought into the market by the baker. When goods are exchanged for money, agents are less concerned to be left with some of the money which they have brought to the market. Therefore, even though there will be no excess demand or supply in terms of goods which have been brought to the market, there may be pecuniary excess demand or supply.

In terms of consumption and investment, Say's law seems to imply that what people plan to do, they will end up doing. Namely, what they plan to consume and what they plan to invest is a direct derivative of their national income. In a world of barter, he may be right (although we have demonstrated—using Smith's example—that even this is dubious as demand composition in itself could influence output). In a monetary exchange, it is possible that what different people plan to do would not coincide and, subsequently, relative prices will change. When relative prices change, demand composition also will change. Therefore, even if demand composition in itself cannot influence output, a change in it may well do.

There is, however, a much more serious point of contention regarding the reliance of Say's law on the idea of competitive general equilibrium. This is the problem of relationship between market structures and economic performance.

The model we have described in Section 9.1 is basically a competitive general equilibrium. So the claim that demand may not affect output is clearly set against competitive market structures. This raises two main questions: (a) will demand influence output when markets are not perfectly competitive? (b) If so, should government policy focus on promoting competitive structures and refrain from demand management on the assumption that this will become ineffective as we approach perfect competition?

The answer to question (b) is very difficult. It involves a proper examination of both the feasibility of achieving a fully competitive allocation (see some comments in Chapter 7 concerning externalities or missing markets) as well as the desirability of trying to approach it. Here I shall not attempt to deal with any of these. Instead, I would like to comment on another aspect of the relationship between competitive markets and the determinants of output from the supply side point of view.

According to Say's law, in a competitive set-up, demand will be ineffective in determining national output. Now I would like to raise a question concerning the kind of influence which competitive market structures in themselves might have on the level of output. Put differently, if it is the circumstances of industry which determine the level of national income, is perfect competition the best form of organization in the sense that it allows knowledge to be fully utilized? I refer here to our discussion in Chapter 3 about the meaning of technology. Recall that we said there that the production function presupposes that all participating agents will give their best in terms of productivity. Hence, the position of the PPF reflected the most we can get at the current state of human knowledge.

In principle, the fact that the competitive allocation is at the point where relative prices represent the social cost (i.e. the slope of the PPF is the same as relative prices) means that this is the highest level of national income which is obtainable at these prices (see Chapters 7 and 8). The presumption here is that as people are only concerned with their self-interest, they have no opinion about either the process which lands them with their income nor do they have an opinion about the ultimate distribution of the produce of their collective activities.

We know that the position of the equilibrium allocation (which may be interpreted as the demand composition as it tells us how many units of either good we produce and consume) may influence the PPF by changing the stock of capital which is available for the economy. Namely, if the competitive allocation is such where the quantity of new machines produced (investment) is greater than the quantity of machines which cease to operate (depreciation) then the total amount of machines available will increase. The economy would then be able to produce more of all goods.

But there is another element which determines the position of the PPF (and, thus, national output). It is technology itself or, if you wish, the boundaries of human knowledge. When there are technological improvements it means that with the same stock of capital (and labour) we can produce more of everything. Technological improvements, therefore, will push the PPF outwards and thus increase national output and income.

If we look at the aggregate labour market representation of national income (see Figure 9.6), we can see the significance of technology at once.

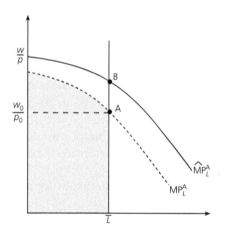

Figure 9.6 The effect of a technological improvement on the labour market.

The demand for labour is an **aggregate marginal product** across industries and the real wages in the nominal wages divided by the aggregate price. Recall that the area underneath the demand for labour (or the marginal product of labour) represents the total output (the shaded area when equilibrium is at A). Technological improvement can be achieved in various ways. The first, and most obvious way, is through what one may call 'learning by doing'. The mere fact that a person is routinely doing a certain job puts him, or her, in a good position to innovate and make the job more productive. This, if you wish, is the more spontaneous way of technological improvement which, since the days of Adam Smith has been attributed to the division of labour.[4] In Figure 9.6 you can see what the meaning of improved productivity will have. The marginal product line will shift upwards and, at point B, real output (the area underneath demand for labour) will increase.

However, the degree to which labour productivity can improve via learning by doing is very limited indeed. At some points, to achieve further technological improvements, which basically means an increase in the marginal product of labour, requires much more knowledge and a greater investment.

This latter method is referred to in current discussions as the problem of R&D. As technology becomes increasingly more sophisticated, it will take a great deal of research to produce an improvement in the marginal product of labour. Therefore, it requires that some people will devote their entire time to that end and subsequently, it requires the appropriate funds.

When a firm invests in R&D there is only a certain probability that their investment will bear fruits and the marginal product of their workers will increase. However, when achieved, this will mean that their marginal cost (as well as average costs) will fall and they will gain a competitive edge. Question 6 in Chapter 4 provides you with an example of the analytical implications of obtaining such a competitive edge.

Earlier in the previous century, a famous economist called Joseph Schumpeter raised an interesting question. Could monopolists employ better technologies than firms in competiton? If R&D is needed in order to increase labour's productivity (and thus increase national output) will the perfectly competitive organization of markets be conducive to such investments?

Recall from Chapter 4 the characteristics of a perfectly competitive industry. Notice that among them is the assumption of perfect information and perfect mobility. On the consumers' side it means that everyone knows all the prices and without any cost can switch from an expensive seller to a cheaper one. On the production side, this means that everyone can access any available technology and adopt it without any cost. Hence, if a certain firm invested in R&D and discovered a technology with a higher labour productivity, it will not have the means to prevent other firms from using it. Consequently, the competitive edge will only be a short run phenomenon.

When a firm invests in R&D and succeeds in reducing its costs, in the short run it will make profits above the normal, but in the long run, other firms will adopt the same technology and profits will return to their normal rates. This raises a question of **incentives**. Is it in the interest of any particular firm to invest in R&D if it knows that any technological breakthrough will be available to everyone else and that the long run profits will remain at their normal rate?

The answer to this depends on three things: first, it depends on the relationship between the size of the required investment and the obtained fall in costs; second, it depends on the magnitude of profits above normal which can be obtained in the short run; and third, it depends on the length of the short run or, in other words, on how long it takes the other firms to obtain and adopt the new technology. This, as you can imagine, creates precarious grounds for any investment in R&D which does not guarantee a significant reduction in costs. As there are very few such investments, there seems to be no incentive to a firm in competitive markets to invest in R&D. It would be a better strategy to sit and wait for someone else to put up the funds for the research which is needed.

But it is not only incentives which suggest a problem with R&D investments by competitive firms. There is also the question of funds. Competitive firms make little profits above the normal which are, in the long run, reduced to the normal rate. This means that for such firms, most profits are used simply to pay their lenders and owners that which they would have received have they transferred their funds elsewhere.

A monopolist, on the other hand, seems to have both the funds and the incentives to invest in R&D. The profits of the monopolist are way above the normal rate which generates funds by which it can reduce its marginal cost. The incentive exists as, by doing so, the monopolist increases his monopolistic power and may prevent other firms from entering the market. R&D, in this way, can even become the barriers to entry for other firms.

The Schumpeterian hypothesis—the essence of which we have just described[5]—has far reaching implications for both the question of efficiency as well as the question of what it is that determines the level of output.

As far as efficiency is concerned, this may raise some doubts about how efficient the competitive solution really is if its inter-temporal effects are worse than those of a more monopolistic market structure. In other words, while a competitive solution produces an allocation where we cannot make anyone better off without making someone worse off, it will also leave the output (as depicted by the PPF) at its original level. If the Schumpeterian hypothesis is right, a more monopolistic market structure will produce an allocation where we can make someone better off without making anyone worse off today but as there will be more output tomorrow, over time, we may be able to compensate for the loss of welfare at any one point of time.

The Schumpeterian hypothesis has important implications for the determinants of output. On the one hand, it seems consistent with the general gist of Say's law, in the sense that the circumstances of production are very significant to the level of output. Namely, they determine the position of the PPF in the next period. On the other hand, it seems to be based on an entirely different mechanism. It is not because production generates the needed income but it is because it generates the appropriate technological development.

Whether the Schumpeterian hypothesis is right or not is a complex, open debate. Naturally, it is easy to see how the difficulties facing competitive firms in investing in R&D may be overcome by appropriate legislation (patenting laws). But the message which is coming out of this is that it is the institutions of production which matter and not, as implied by Say, the mere production.

So far, we have dealt with the problem of the relationship of demand and supply to national income in the context of competitive market structures. This was all included in question (b) above. We now turn to the other question (a), on whether in the case of market imperfections, demand management has an effect on output.

9.3 Market imperfections and unemployment

To begin our investigation we must first modify our set-up a little bit. We argued at first that the real national product is captured by the PPF and that the PPF depends on the supply of labour, stock of capital and technology. To understand that possible implications of market imperfection as well as to enhance our understanding of unemployment, I propose now to resume our normal depiction of the labour supply.[6] If, indeed, this is the case, you should wonder what does it mean that the PPF depends on the supply of labour? (Figure 9.7)

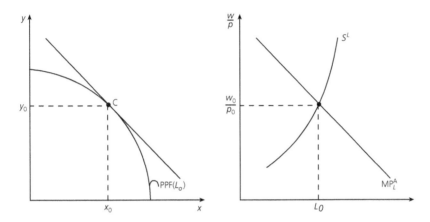

Figure 9.7 An upwards-sloping labour supply curve, the labour market and the PPF.

At any different equilibrium in the labour market, the supply of labour will be different. This means that the amount of resources available to the economy at any point of time is, in itself, a function of market structures. In the above diagram, we see that when markets are competitively organized, the supply of labour will be L_0.

Suppose, now, that in this world of two goods (x and y) y is produced in a competitive market while x is produced by a monopolist. Recall from Chapter 5 that the demand for labour for a competitive firm must satisfy the following principle:

$$w = p_y MP_L^y,$$

namely, you pay workers the value contributed to your revenues by the last unit. A monopolist (in x) who hires labour in a competitive market will also wish to pay workers the value of the last unit's contribution. We know that in real terms the contribution of the last unit is the marginal product of labour. We also know that what we pay workers is a nominal wage w. But while in a competitive firm, each unit of y produced increases revenue by the price, for the monopolist, each unit of x produced by the last unit of labour will only increase its revenue by the marginal revenue. Hence, the monopolist profit maximizing principle of hiring labour will be as shown in Figure 9.8.

$$w = MR \, MP_L^x.$$

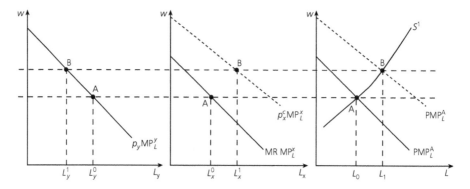

Figure 9.8 Labour demand: competitive firm, monopolist, and the market.

The left-hand diagram in Figure 9.8 depicts the demand for labour by the competitive industry, the diagram in the middle depicts the monopolist's demand while the diagram on the right depicts the labour market in full. Due to the difference in each agents consideration, we now have nominal wages on the vertical line and the demand for labour is really the value of labour's marginal product.

Had the supply of labour been vertical, then from the point of view of labour employed, it will make no difference whether markets are competitive or some of them are monopolists. In such a case, the position of the PPF will be independent of market structures.[7] However, if labour supply was upward sloping the outcome will be different.

When x is a monopolist and y is produced in a competitive industry, the equilibrium in the labour market will be obtained at point A with L_0 labour employed. To this level of L, there will be a corresponding PPF like the one described earlier.

In Figure 9.8 the broken lines depict the demand for labour by industries x and y, had x also been a competitive industry. In such a case, the price of x would have been greater than the monopolists MR[8] (hence, the competitive demand for labour lies above the monopolist demand for labour). This change, in itself, will increase overall demand for labour and subsequently, increase nominal wages. In turn this will cause an increase in the marginal cost of y which will offset the fall in demand for y had x and y been gross substitutes. Therefore, I shall assume that the demand for y will remain unchanged. Altogether, demand for labour will now be the broken line in the right-hand diagram and equilibrium will be at point B where L_1 is the total labour employed (see Figure 9.9).

While we can learn very little about national output from the increase in the area underneath the aggregated demand for labour (as this time, the area denotes the monetary value of marginal product), it is clear that the quantity of labour employed is greater than at A when one industry was not fully competitive. This means that the PPF which corresponds to all industries being competitive lies above the PPF which will emerge if one of the industries was not fully competitive. In this sense, Say's law, interpreted as the **circumstances of industry** as the determinant of output, is confirmed. However, with an upward sloping labour supply, an overall increase in demand too will affect national output even if we achieved what appears to be the limit of the circumstances of industry.

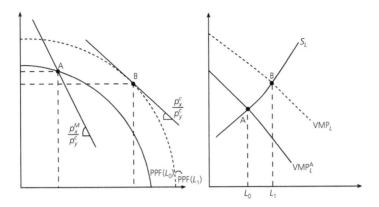

Figure 9.9 Making the x industry competitive: The effect on the labour market and the PPF.

Recall the diagrams in Section 9.1. An increase in demand for both x and y (even without affecting the supply curve of labour) will cause an increase in the equilibrium quantity of labour supplied (Figure 9.10). Consequently, the PPF will shift outwards and the national product will increase.

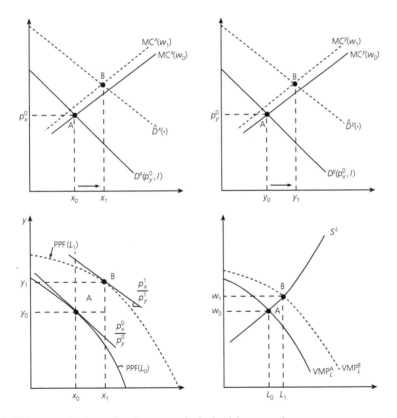

Figure 9.10 Increases in demand and an upwards-sloping labour supply curve.

Much of what we have said so far depends on how exactly one defines the PPF, or, which is almost the same thing, what is the difference between potential output (corresponding to the stock of labour available) and actual output which is an equilibrium notion. This is also one of the major issues in trying to understand the notion of unemployment.

If the PPF is based on the total amount of labour available then the upward sloping supply of labour suggests that most equilibrium points will be at a lower level of employment. Hence, the economy will almost always lie inside its PPF. At the same time, the fact that there is an equilibrium in the labour market suggests that, at the going rate, those who wish to find employment will succeed in so doing. The reason why others are unemployed is simply because they do not wish to work at the going wage level. Some people rightly ask whether we can consider such people as unemployed? In other words, some people question the definition of the potential output. What is the stock of labour which is available to an economy? Is it the total amount of adults between the ages of, say, 16 and 65? If so, do we assume that in every household both partners must work to gain sufficient access to social wealth? Is it, perhaps, the total amount of men between those ages? If so, what about single people or single parent families?

In equilibrium, on the other hand, we do not need any such definition. We simply know that those people who wish to work will find work and they, for all intent and purposes, represent the stock of labour available. According to this approach, in any economy there is always a certain rate of unemployment which captures those people who could have been in the labour market at the equilibrium rate but for some reason choose not to. We may wish to call such a rate the *natural rate of unemployment* but please note that what exactly is meant by it, is still a matter of some disputations.

Naturally, one of the most intriguing questions in economics is associated with this problem. As equilibrium implies the coincidence of rational plans, it means that the decision by those individuals who choose not to seek work at the given wage level, is a rational one. But this looks somewhat strange when it is clear that there are people who are not employed and who should, rationally, seek employment. Put differently, the people who could rationally choose not to seek jobs at the going wage level are either people who have significant alternative sources of income (people who own a lot of assets or, er... criminals) or people who are between jobs, moving cities, training etc. Their 'failure' to seek work is sometimes called **voluntary unemployment**. Yet most unemployed do not seem to fit any of these categories. They are people who do not have alternative sources of income other than what the state provides, and many of them have lived a life of unemployment for some time. Therefore, there must be some imperfection in the labour market itself which prevent it from bringing the economy to its proper competitive equilibrium.

The kind of imperfection to which we allude here is not the same as that produced by a certain imbalance between buyers and sellers (like the case of the monopolist). In such a case, we will simply have people who are seeking jobs at the going rate but cannot find them. We term this, **involuntary unemployment** and we will come back to this soon. The kind of imperfection to which I refer here is really of the type of missing markets, or externalities (as discussed in Chapter 7). Namely, a situation where the labour market does clear but the outcome is inefficient.

It is indeed unclear why people would prefer to stay out of the labour market altogether. Some suggest that the problem is that people who are unemployed become increasingly **unemployable**. In our terminology this would mean that the natural rate of unemployment increases. Others have argued that this is the consequence of the welfare state which offers people a source of income which serves as a disincentive to join the labour market. However, one should bear in mind that the income that people may draw from the labour market may not provide people with a socially acceptable standard of living. Indeed, some of current debates concerning the welfare state have focused on questions like this: how to tie together the joining of the labour market with the provision of minimum social standards? The fact that rational agents would have brought the labour market to an equilibrium with a socially unacceptable level of wages draws our attention again to the role of rationality and institutional arrangements. The supply of labour will always be very large at any given level of wages the more people are solely dependent on their work to access social wealth. Therefore, in a competitive set up, it is in such a situation where the wage level is likely to be the lowest. Put differently, the greater is the number of people dependent on wages, the less likely it becomes for them to be able to draw the necessary provisions from the social wealth.

Rationality tells us that with their meagre wages they should only consume very little but this may either be physically or socially unacceptable. A system of decentralized decisionmaking which is not supported by a welfare state may produce an efficient allocation which for some, may be too hard to bear. One way in which the joining of the labour market can become more attractive is to allow more people to have more than one means to access national income. A redistribution of wealth is a possible method to decrease the labour supply by those who have, thus increasing equilibrium level of wages which, in turn, will make it more attractive to those who have not, to join the labour market and reduce the number of those whose alienation may begin with their resignation from the labour market.

As far as market imperfections in the labour market are concerned, there is a huge amount of literature which tries to explain it. I will not endeavour to summarize the literature but I would simply like to represent some of the problems associated with such imperfection. Suppose that the aggregated labour market is at an initial equilibrium at point A in Figure 9.11.

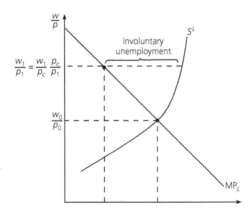

Figure 9.11 A labour market imperfection.

In equilibrium the real wage is w_0/p_0. Suppose that the general price level is comprised of two types of goods: consumer goods (p_c) and investment goods (machinery) (p_p). Hence:

$$p_0 = \alpha_c p_c + \alpha_p p_p,$$

$$\alpha_c + \alpha_p = 1,$$

where α_c and α_p are the weight in the price index of the consumer and investment sectors, respectively.

We know that there is a difference between wages as income (for the workers) and wages as cost (for producers). Workers will care for their real income in terms of consumer goods but producers will have a different notion of cost. Suppose that a unionized labour market agreed on preserving a level of real wages which is measured in terms of consumer goods:

$$\frac{w_0}{p_0} = \left(\frac{\overline{w}_0}{p_c}\right)\frac{p_c}{p_0},$$

W_0/P_c represent the agreed level of fixed real wages.

If now there has been an increase in consumers' price but hardly any increase in capital goods' prices, the labour contract will ensure that w/p_c will not change. This means that the nominal wages will have to rise to compensate for the increase in consumer prices. This means that the expression in parentheses in the above equation will remain constant. As P_c rose by more than P, the right-hand side will therefore increase. Hence:

$$\frac{w_1}{p_1} = \left(\frac{\overline{w}_1}{p_c + \Delta p_c}\right)\frac{p_c + \Delta p_c}{p_1} > \frac{w_0}{p_0},$$

where

$$p_1 = \alpha_c(p_c + \Delta p_c) + \alpha_p(p_p + \Delta p_p).$$

The increase in the price of consumer goods will only affect the overall price level by the fraction α_c. Hence, the general price level will rise by much less than the increase in consumer goods prices. Therefore, the real wages will rise and equilibrium will be at point B in the above diagram.

Clearly, at this level of real wages, there is excess supply of labour. This means that some people who are willing to work at this rate of real wages will not find jobs. This is what we called **involuntary unemployment**. The question that arises is whether market forces are not strong enough to eliminate this gap in the market. Some of those who cannot find jobs are willing to work for these wages or even for less than that. We expect them to offer to do the work at a lower wages and employers will be delighted to hire them if they could.

Whether or not the gap will be closed depends on the nature of the labour contract negotiation as well as on the powers of the union. If wages are negotiated at a national level, it will be difficult for employers to hire people at a lower wage level. If negotiations are localized and the unions have limited power, people may be able to persuade employers to hire them for the lower rate. At the same time, such people (if rational) might be worried about the consequences of their actions to future wage levels. If a reasonable wage level is eroded, they may feel that it serves their interest better (in the long run) to stay out of the market. Having said this, they can only consider such an option if society provides some sort of safety net for people outside the labour market.

But before you jump into conclusion that it is all the fault of the unions, let me balance your view by showing that a similar type of imperfection can be generated by producers in a market where there are no organizations of either workers or producers.

In our analysis of the labour market we had assumed that labour productivity is falling the more labour we employ. However, we are all aware of the fact that workers may respond to incentives and in particular, to wages. If we assume that higher wages mean greater productivity by every worker, a reduction of wages may not always be a good policy for the profit maximizing organization.

Suppose we start at a competitive equilibrium in the labour market at point A in Figure 9.12.

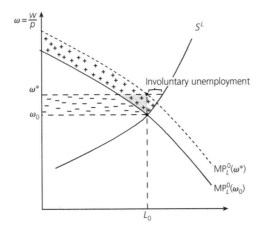

Figure 9.12 Involuntary unemployment through worker incentives.

At A, the marginal product of the last worker is MP_L^0 and, it is a function of the equilibrium level of real wages ω_0 (as we assume the output price to be fixed the only changes in the real wages come from changes in nominal wages). Given that productivity is a function of wages, could it be in the interest of the producer to raise the wages above the equilibrium rate?

When the producer increases wages to ω_1, the marginal product of all the workers will increase. In particular, the productivity of the last worker will rise. As long as the increase in productivity (which contributes towards his profit) is greater than the increase in the wage bill (which reduces his profit) it will be worth his while to raise wages without changing the number of people employed.

Suppose that the level of wages for which the additional contribution in productivity equals to the increase in the real wage bill is ω^*. This means that the areas with $++$ in the above diagram (which describes the gains in productivity) equal in size the area with $---$ (which depicts the increase in cost).

However, at this higher level of wages, more people are willing to work (or people are willing to work longer hours). Hence, there is excess supply of labour in the market. Normally, in a competitive environment, we expect the workers who wish to work at the going rate but cannot find jobs (involuntary unemployed) to bid down the wages by offering themselves for the same jobs at lower rates. However, while in the traditional model reducing wages has only increased profits, now a fall in wages can also reduce profits. If the employer pays everyone less merely to employ a few more people, he may lose the productivity of all those who have been working for him. Such a loss can outweigh the benefits of hiring a few more workers at a lower wage level. Hence, considering all these things together, there could be a level of wages (like ω^*) where the employer will neither seek to increase nor to decrease it even if there were people willing to work for lower wages.

Unlike the case of the unions, involuntary unemployment will be less dependent on the strength of internal associations. We saw earlier that if unions keep the wages above the equilibrium level, involuntary unemployment depends on union power. Here, there is no association among employers and the involuntary unemployment has greater chances to persist.

The fundamental dichotomy

All the above has shown us the difficulties associated with the question of what determines the level of national income. It is evident that institutional arrangements have significant influence both on the circumstances of industry and on the relationship between demand and supply. However, at this stage of your study we shall try to keep things simple. In spite of these obvious complexities, the simple way to identify the main dichotomy in the study of macroeconomics is to distinguish between those who claim, *a la* Say, that supply creates demand and those who claim that demand determines output. The former approach is sometime referred to as 'New Classical' (referring to the widespread beliefs that macroeconomics in classical economics corresponds to Say's interpretation), while the latter is named after J.M. Keynes who was the main advocate of this approach in the first half of the twentieth century.

The significance of this dichotomy is considerable. On the premise side, the 'supply creates demand' approach relies on the presence of competitive markets with prices which are flexible in all directions (i.e. general equilibrium). The 'demand creates supply' approach (Keynesian) assumes that it is possible for the economy to be in equilibrium at the time when labour market is not (not only market imperfection but also non clearing markets).

In terms of policy implications, it is clear that the New Classical approach would propose to refrain from all attempts to influence aggregate demand as this will have no impact on output. Instead, if the government wishes to influence output, it should encourage industry by improving the business environment. According to the Keynesian approach, as demand determines output, the government may influence the level of employment though active demand management activities.

Both approaches face fundamental difficulties. The 'classical' approach faces the difficulty of reconciling flexible clearing markets with persistent business cycles, while the Keynesian approach must reconcile the existence of equilibrium when some markets do not clear.

Evidently, there are deeper differences lurking behind this dichotomy. It is, to some extent, a continuation of the debate about both the validity and the value of *laissez faire*. To some, these differences can be simply reduced into a short run versus long run approach. Accordingly, 'demand determines output' in the short run but 'supply determines demand' in the long run. Put differently, prices may not be as flexible in the short run as they would be in the long run. Therefore, it is possible that in the short run, some of the adjustment will come via changes in output.

This is not the first time when scholars sought to reconcile fundamental differences about the working of the economy by applying one approach to the short run and one to the long run. At the beginning of the twentieth century, some scholars were hoping to reconcile between the classical approach to value (as cost of production, or a reflection of the difficulty of attainment) and the neoclassical one where value is determined subjectively (marginal utility). In spite of the fact that these are fundamental differences, some felt that in the short run, value theory corresponds to the neoclassical perception. In the long run (when prices equal average cost) they reflect the classical view. *Plus ça change?* Perhaps.

▓ NOTES

1. Evidently I do not refer here to the Walrasian notion of general equilibrium which we developed in Chapter 6. Instead, I refer to the general notion of universal interdependence which, at least in my opinion, has been around from at least Adam Smith's days.

2. There is a real difficulty here with the way in which we aggregate. In particular, there is the question of how to determine the weights of different prices. On can expect to find some correspondence between these values and the share of the different goods in national income. However, to keep things simple we shall assume these weights to be determined somewhat arbitrarily.

3. Note that in terms of our discussion in the previous chapter we have again the growth anomaly. While real output has not changed, if we measured growth in terms of A prices then in the case of C' it would mean that the economy has shrunk.

4. In fact, the importance of the division of labour had been recognized many years before Adam Smith. Both Plato and Aristotle acknowledged the significance of the division of labour. However, according to Plato this was a much broader concept of **social** division of labour along the lines that some people are good at different things and they should do that which fits their character. Aristotle, who discussed division of labour within the household, is nearer to Smith in his conception of the division of labour but still has not got far enough as to see a task-based division of labour the way Adam Smith did.

5. There are quite a few formulations of what has become known as Schumpeter hypothesis. To engage in what must have motivated Schumpeter you may wish to read chapter 8 of his book on *Capitalism, Socialism and Democracy*. In this chapter, Schumpeter discusses at some length the argument that monopolist could on many occasions be more efficient than firms in competition.

6. We shall stick, however, to the presumption that those who instigated the changes in demand do not participate in the labour market.

7. In the sense that the PPF depend on the amount of labour supplied. With a vertical labour supply, the amount of resources available will be the same in the case where all industries are competitive as in the case where one of them monopolized.

8. Do not confuse this with the monopolist price being greater than the competitive price.

10 The goods market in the closed economy

In the previous chapter, we have discussed at some length the problem of what it is that determines the level of national output (supply). We now move to a more detailed formulation of what may constitute the aggregate demand for national output. By doing this we are not committing ourselves to any particular theory. Instead, we wish to set a framework where, in the end, we will be able to accommodate alternative explanations to that which affects the aggregate values of important economic variables. From this point onwards we are going to be less concerned with how notions such as aggregate demand relate to the microeconomics analysis of individual markets and their inter-relations. However, I do not wish to suggest by this that the problem has really been solved.

10.1 Closed economy without a government

10.1.1 National accounts

To begin with the simplest possible analysis, let us again ignore the existence of a government. It is always best to start with a view of national accounts where we identify the variables which may be relevant for our analysis. We know that in a world without a government, there are only two conceivable usages for our product and these are consumption (C) and investment (I):

$$NNP = C + I.$$

We now want to look separately at C and I.

From Chapter 8 we recall that NNP and national income (Y) are the two sides of the same coin. Hence, $NNP = Y$. We also know that with our income we can either buy consumption goods (C) or store it for future use (savings: S). Since we have

$$Y = C + S$$

$$NNP = Y$$

then,

$$C + I = C + S$$

hence,

$$I = S$$

which is the capital formation equation. Namely, in such an economy growth through capital accumulation is entirely dependent on the decisions to save which are made by individuals. In other words, if an economy produces only one good, say wheat (W), what can they do with it? They can either use the seeds to make flour and bread (for consumption) or keep the seeds in the basement either in order to make flour and bread in the next period or for the purpose of sowing the fields which, in turn, will yield more wheat. Either way, storing seeds in the basement is the real side manifestation of the idea of savings. Abstaining from consumption is, in principle, savings.

On the usage side, whichever way we use the seeds will constitute investment, in the sense that it facilitates a use in the next period. Those seeds which we had simply stored will be added to the seeds which we will produce throughout the year. However, recall from the previous chapter that investment itself does not imply an increase in the amount of available resources. It also depends on a depletion rate of the existing stock. Therefore, if, in our case, 1/2 of the total amount of seeds is used for consumption, 1/4 for storage, and 1/4 for sowing, whether or not output increases depends on whether the 1/4 used for sowing is capable of producing the initial amount W. If technology is such that it takes 1/4 of W_0 to produce W_0 then in the next period we will have $W_0 (1+1/4)$ which is exactly the output + what we stored for direct consumption in the previous period. However, if we now changed that composition of our investment (say, 3/8 W_0 to be stored for baking bread in the next period and only 1/8 W_0 for sowing) we still save 1/2 W_0 but we will not be able to produce W_0 in the next period. Hence, the same level of investment may be associated with different consequences even for a given technology.

To have a better understanding of how the output is being used in each period, we must investigate what constitutes the demand for different applications. In our limited world there are only two types of usages which we consider: consumption and investment.

10.1.2 **Consumption**

In the model of rational utility maximizers which we analysed in Chapter 2, we have concluded that given the tastes parameters (utility function) that which influences the decision of how much to consume of each good is real income. By real income we mean both nominal income and nominal price levels. This means the position of the budget line was entirely dependent on nominal income and the price of each good. As we are less concerned now with how much of a particular good an individual wants to buy and rather with the more general question of how much would we want to consume, relative prices may not play a role. However, general price levels do matter as they will influence the level of real income (i.e. how far out will the budget constraint lie in the space of economic goods). As we shall assume that prices are given, Y, the national income is defined in real terms. Therefore, the immediate transfer from microeconomic analysis is the assertion that consumption is a function of real income.

We write this as $C(Y)$, where Y is real income. However, even if we do not add any other variable which may influence decisions on consumption, this representation of consumption is problematic. It suggests that consumption is a function of the aggregate level of income and is independent of the *distribution* of income. We shall soon investigate this point.

Let us begin with the simplest representation of the relationship between income and consumption: $C(Y) = c_0 + c_1(Y)$, where c_0 is an autonomous component of consumption. It means that there is a level of consumption which we will want to consume (or *need* to consume) regardless of how much we earn. Then, there is always a fraction of our income which we want to use for consumption ($c_1 < 1$). We call c_1 the **Marginal Propensity to Consume (MPC)**.

The reason why MPC is less than unity dates back to the days of Adam Smith. In the *Wealth of Nations*, when Adam Smith refers to the motives of rational agents he claims that there is always a tension between the wish to enjoy life at present and the need to 'better our conditions' in the future. By insisting that $c_1 < 1$ we suggest that agents will always want to save a certain portion of their earnings for the future.

Figure 10.1 depicts such a function. The intercept with the vertical axis denotes the level of consumption which the economy would need to subsist even when income equals zero. The slope of the consumption curve denotes the change in consumption which will follow an increase in income by one unit. Geometrically, the slope is clearly (dC/dY). From the consumption function it is fairly clear that if Y increases by one unit, consumption will increase by c_1.

One may immediately argue that there is surely a difference between the marginal propensity to consume of the rich and that of the poor. This is clearly true. A poorer

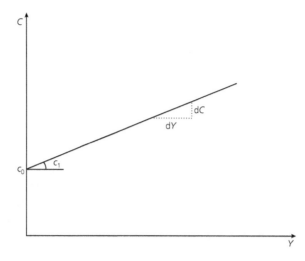

Figure 10.1 The consumption function.

person is more likely to have a greater concern with present consumption than with future consumption. Therefore, a better representation of **consumption** will be when the MPC itself is a function of income. Namely, the richer a person is, the lower will be his, or her, MPC.

There are two issues which require a closer examination. First, from the point of view of a single individual, this will imply the representation as in Figure 10.2. As you can clearly see, there is not much qualitative difference between this function and the linear one from Figure 10.1. In both cases, there is a direct relationship between income and consumption. The more complex representation, does not seem to add any insight which we could not have had from the linear case.

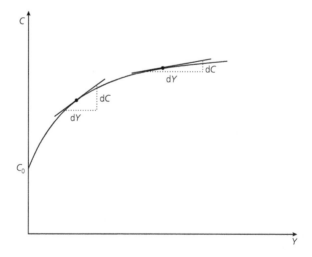

Figure 10.2 The consumption function when MPC is a function of income.

The second issue is that we are really not examining the behaviour of a single individual but rather that of the economy as a whole. It is less obvious why the MPC of an economy should have a strict relationship with income. An economy can get richer but if this also means that there are changes in income distribution, on the average, the MPC may be rising with income rather than falling. In other words, the consumption function which we examine (and its graphic representation) depicts the consumption of the whole economy as a function of the general level of income. Whether or not the MPC of the economy changes depends on whether consumption is a function of income distribution. Suppose that we examine two points of national income Y_0 and Y_1. Suppose also that at each level of income there are two groups of individuals: the poor and the rich. Let $c_1^p > c_1^r$ represent the MPC of the poor and the rich, respectively. Again, we assume that the marginal propensity to consume of the poor is greater than that of the rich not because we think that the poor shop more than the rich. What we mean is that the percentage of income used for consumption by the poor is greater than that of the rich.

The immediate intuition is to say that more of equality will lead to a greater consumption as we transfer income from the rich with a low marginal propensity to consume to the poor with a higher marginal propensity to consume. However, inequality (and equality) evolves in a much more complex manner.

When national income is Y_0 let a proportion α of it belong to the poor and $(1 - \alpha)$ belong to the rich. When α increases it means that a greater share of national income is consumed by people with the higher MPC. This can mean one of two things: either there has been a transfer of income from the rich to the poor but the number of people in each group had not changed, or, that some of the people who were 'rich' have now become poor. Namely, the number of poor people—and, subsequently, their share in the national income—has risen. In the first case we would argue that an increase in α has definitely reduced inequality. In the second case the increase in α represents a probable increase in inequality. When the number of people earning lower levels of income has increased, the share of the poor in total income could rise but intuition tells us that inequality increased.[1] In any case, whenever the share of income earned by the poor increases it is an equivalent state to a transfer of income from the rich to the poor. To avoid confusion we shall therefore simply treat a change in α for what it actually is: an increase in the share of income which is earned by the poor: a change in α is a distributional change.

Each group of individuals has a linear consumption function of the form

$$C(Y^i) = c_0 + c_1^i(Y)$$

where $i = r, p$.

Therefore, the total consumption will be

$$C(Y_0) = \alpha c_0 + c_1^p \alpha Y_0 + (1 - \alpha)c_0 + c_1^r(1 - \alpha)Y_0.$$

$$= c_0 + [\alpha\, c_1^p + (1 - \alpha)c_1^r]Y_0.$$

If the MPC of the poor and the rich are the same (i.e. $c_1^p = c_1^r$), α (our distribution parameter) does not influence the outcome. If, as is reasonable to expect, the MPC of the poor is different from that of the rich, the aggregated MPC $[\alpha c_1^p + (1 - \alpha)c_1^r)$ depends on income distribution. As α increases due, say, to an increase in the number of poor, consumption will increase. Equally, a redistribution policy which reduces inequality by transferring income from the rich to the poor (again, a greater α) will also increase overall consumption although inequality falls.

In the case of an increase in aggregate income $Y(Y_1 > Y_0)$ which is accompanied by a decrease in the share of the poor from α to β, the direct relationship between income and consumption could be broken.

$$C(Y_1) > C(Y_0) \quad \text{if} \quad [\beta c_1^p + (1 - \beta)c_1^r]Y_1 > [\alpha c_1^p + (1 - \alpha)c_1^r]Y_0$$

which means

$$\frac{[\beta c_1^p + (1 - \beta)c_1^r]}{[\alpha c_1^p + (1 - \alpha)c_1^r]} > \frac{Y_0}{Y_1}$$

which means that if initially $\alpha = 0.8$, $c_1^p = 0.8$, and $c_1^r = 0.4$, an increase in income accompanied by a decrease in the proportional share of the poor, say, $\beta = 0.2$, could violate the condition specified in the above equation. We know that $Y_0/Y_1 < 1$ but on the left-hand side we have $[\beta c_1^p + (1 - \beta)c_1^r]/[\alpha c_1^p + (1 - \alpha)c_1^r] = 0.48/0.72 < 1$. It is not inconceivable that the left hand side is smaller than the right hand side. Hence $C(Y_1) < C(Y_0)$ which means that consumption could fall as income increases if the rise in income is associated with a fall in the share of the poor.

What we learn from this is the following: (a) Having a linear consumption function for the economy as a whole does not necessarily imply that the marginal propensities to consume of the rich and the poor are the same. It can simply describe the change in consumption when changes in income have no effect on changes in **income distribution**. Inevitably, a change in income distribution will bring about a change in the level of consumption for any given level of marginal propensities to consume and income.

If we wish to be constantly aware of the distribution of income we may write the consumption function as:

$$C(Y) = c_0 + [\alpha c_1^p + (1 - \alpha)c_1^r]Y$$

A change in income distribution (i.e. α) will constitute a shift in the consumption curve (see Figure 10.3). Whenever the share in the income of the poor increases, for whatever reason, it will have a positive effect on consumption. It all amounts to the same thing. An increase in the share of the poor is like a transfer of income from the rich (with a lower MPC) to a poor (with a higher MPC); (b) If income distribution is changing when the level of income rises, the relationship between income and consumption depend on whether the share of the poor increases or decreases as income increases. In other words, the nature of relationship between consumption and income is not entirely independent of whether higher levels of income also mean higher levels of inequality.

While the significance of income distribution to questions of efficiency and growth has long been recognized, there are, at this stage, too many other things to consider. I would therefore, like you to be aware of the importance of income distribution and of how it may feed into our story. But to make the exposition a bit less cumbersome I will remove this formulation of demand for consumption and stick to the simple form of consumption function which does not capture the effects of income distribution.

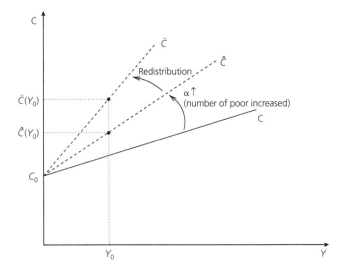

Figure 10.3 Income redistribution, changes in population composition and the consumption function.

In some of the exercises and applications which come at the end of the macro chapters I will return, occasionally, to some of these issues.

So, we go back to the simple form of demand for consumption:

$$C(Y) = c_0 + c_1(Y).$$

But income distribution is not the only thing which may influence consumption and which we chose to omit from the consumption function. Note that, in the above equation everything is measured in **flows**. That is to say, we are talking here about the consumption per *period* of time which is affected by income generated at that period. However, people have **stocks** too. These will include all sorts of assets which have been accumulated over past periods. Put differently, the consumption decision of two individuals with the same income is unlikely to be the same if one of them expects a generous inheritance while the other anticipates debt. Equally, people are likely to take note whether the income they earn is a one-off or a regular earning. In the former case they are unlikely to spend the same as in the latter case.

All these other variables are important for the analysis of macroeconomics. The fact that we omit them at this stage is in no way a reflection of their insignificance. However, as we are only taking our first steps in macro analysis, it is essential to try and focus on the question of income determination. While assets and income distribution are important in this respect, we will have enough on our plate as it is to consider all these additional influences. Nevertheless, I mention all these here so that you do not develop an incorrect picture of the subject which may impede your judgement in the future. In some of the self-study exercises (later in the course) the impacts of some such influences will be considered.

10.1.3 Savings

As our income is used for consumption and saving alone, we can learn something about the saving function from what we have said so far about the consumption function.

Recall that in a closed economy without a government, our income is used for two main purposes current and future consumption:

$$Y = C + S$$

hence,

$$S = Y - C.$$

In terms of behaviour analysis we know already the properties of the consumption function $C(Y)$. Therefore, as savings is the residual of the decision on consumption, savings also are determined by income: $S(Y)$. To be specific:

$$S(Y) = Y - C(Y)$$

$$S(Y) = Y - c_0 - c_1 Y$$

$$S(Y) = -c_0 + (1 - c_1)Y$$

where $(1 - c_1)$ is the **Marginal Propensity to Save (MPS)**. As income is only used for consumption and savings it is fairly evident that each extra unit of income will be used for these two purposes. Therefore,

$$MPC + MPS = 1$$

Or, in terms of our notation, $c_1 + (1 - c_1) = 1$.

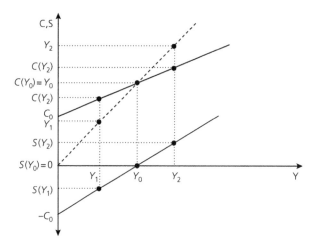

Figure 10.4 Consumption and savings functions.

We can now depict diagrammatically (see Figure 10.4) the relationship between the consumption and savings functions.[2] At Y_1, $C(Y_1) > Y_1$ and this means that consumption is greater than income. In terms of savings this would mean negative savings (or borrowing). At Y_2, $C(Y_2) < Y_2$ which means that income is greater than consumption and thus we are able to save some of our current income for future consumption. Savings, therefore, are positive. At Y_0, $C(Y_0) = Y_0$ which means that consumption (current) equals our income. Hence, we do not save but at the same time we do not borrow. This means that our savings equal zero.

In our discussion of consumption we observed that the level of consumption in an economy may also depend on income distribution. Equally, therefore, the level of savings will also depend on income distribution. We said that for any given level of national income, increase in the share of income which goes to the poor, while assuming that the marginal propensity to consume of the poor is greater than that of the rich, implies an increase in consumption. Subsequently, the level of savings will fall. Figure 10.5 depicts what will happen to the savings of an economy at different level of national income when there is an increase in the share of the poor in national income.

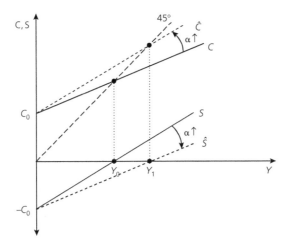

Figure 10.5 Changes in the MPC and the effect on savings.

As α increases (which could either mean an increase in equality or an increase in poverty (and inequality)) at each level of national income there will be a lower share of it in the hands of fewer rich who have a lower marginal propensity to consume than the poor. If you recall from our discussion in Chapter 9 and in the first section of this chapter, at least one form of growth is dependent on savings: capital accumulation. Other things being equal, this would imply that the growth of an economy could be impeded by greater poverty (as the number of poor increases so does their share in income). However, if we consider technological improvement as our major source of growth, this view will have its critics. Some people will argue that if growth comes mainly from technological development and entrepreneurial initiatives, inequality could be a vital force behind it. Inequality, in such a case, would mean that people will be well rewarded for the entrepreneurial activities (which is assumed to be cost reducing; an equivalent to a pure technological improvement). Redistributive policy which aims at equating the reward to all agents will be considered a disincentive for such activities. It would also clearly reduce savings, and thus, affect capital accumulation, as it would transfer income from a low MPC to a higher MPC.

The relationship between growth and inequality is complex and interesting. The evidence—inasmuch as it is observable—is far from conclusive. There are, perhaps, two fundamental questions to think about: (a) Does either of the two basic principles of growth (i.e. capital accumulation or, improved productivity) perform better than the other? and (b) is inequality necessary as an incentive to the pursuit of increased productivity? Naturally, we need more refined tools of analysis to deal with these issues. We can certainly not answer question (a) although we may feel that poorer developing economies will find it more difficult to increase savings given the low level of national income and the relatively higher needs for basic consumption. For such economies, the growth via improved productivity may be the only option which, paradoxically, is not available to them due to lack of education (or human capital). However, you must remember that we say this before considering the influence of international trade. Nevertheless, it is important that at each step of the way you should be able to consider the implications of the model to real life questions.

10.1.4 Investment

From the analysis of national accounts we have established that in a closed economy without a government, savings equal investment. However, we must bear in mind that investment and savings are completely different activities. In the primitive wheat producing economy, suppose that you choose to use only part of your income (in seeds) to make flour and bread. The rest you wish to save. The fact that you chose to save a fraction of your income in seeds does not yet mean either that it will be available for you tomorrow (as proper storage is not a mean thing) or, more importantly, that a farmer will be able to get your seeds so that he can sow them in his fields.

In other words, in a decentralized world, there is a constant need to think about transmission mechanisms. How do savings decisions relate to investment decisions? We will not ponder the question in this course but we must certainly be clear about the difference that exists between the decision to save and the decision to invest.

In very simple terms, we say that **investment** is mainly a function of the rate of interest. There are many ways in which you can think about it. You can think that investment requires taking loans from the bank. Therefore, a higher interest rate will make borrowing expensive and reduce the amount of investment.

Alternatively you can think of it in terms of the **present value** of projects. After all, investment introduces a time dimension into our analysis. We invest today but we reap the fruits of our investment in the future. We must, therefore, compare today's money with money which we will get in the future. When someone asks us to give him, or her, money for a certain project we will have to compare the returns from this project with alternative usages of our money. There is always the option to earn a normal profit on our money by getting the going interest rate (r) which we would receive if we put our money in a deposit account in the bank. How then, do we calculate whether or not we wish to invest our money in a certain project? The key concept here is that of the present value.

The **present value** of T_1 pounds after a year is the amount of money one must allocate today, T_0, such that together with interest it will yield T_1 by the end of the year.

$$T_1 = T_0(1+r) - T_0 = \frac{T_1}{1+r}.$$

Again, T_0 is the amount of money required today to get T_1 by the end of the year. Therefore, we can say that T_0 is the *present value* of T_1; or, T_0 is the *present value* of £T after 1 year.

What, then, will be the *present value* of £T after 2 years (T_2)? It will be the amount of money we need to put in the bank today (T_0) such that if left in the bank for 2 years will yield T_2.

$$T_1 = T_0(1+r)$$

$$T_2 = T_1(1+r) = [T_0(1+r)](1+r) = T_0(1+r)^2.$$

Hence

$$T_0 = \frac{T_2}{(1+r)^2}.$$

Suppose now that a project which yields T pounds every year for five years requires I_0 pounds as investment. How would one decide whether or not to invest in the project?

The answer is very simple. If the amount of money which is required today to yield £T for the next 5 years through the banks, is greater than what is required by the project then one would invest in the project! It is so because in such a case, the project is simply a cheaper method to get £T for the next 5 years. The amount of money required today to earn the yields of the project through the banks is the **present value (PV)**. Hence, the general rule can be written as—invest in the project if

$$I_0 < \text{PV}.$$

But what does PV depend on?

The present value of the stream of income promised by the project is

$$PV\{T\}_{i=1}^5 = \frac{T}{1+r} + \frac{T}{(1+r)^2} + \frac{T}{(1+r)^3} + \frac{T}{(1+r)^4} + \frac{T}{(1+r)^5}$$

$$= \frac{T}{1+r} \sum_{i=0}^4 \left(\frac{1}{1+r}\right)^i.$$

Clearly, the present value depends entirely on the interest rate (r). When the interest rate increases the present value of any project will decline. It will simply mean that at a higher interest rate, the amount of money required today to earn the project's yields is much reduced. Therefore, some projects, the present value of which were only just above I_0 will now be abandoned. In other words, investments in projects will be seriously reduced.[3]

Therefore, we generally assume that the demand for investment is inversely related to interest rates $I(r)$. We may choose to write this function in the following form:

$$I(r) = I_0 - I_1 r$$

where I_0 can be thought of as some basic level of investment which will always be required and I_1 as the sensitivity parameter. I_1 tells us how the level of investment will respond to changes in the interest rate.

10.2 The complete goods market: closed economy without a government

We have now established, in very general terms, what determines the demand for the various usages of national product in a closed economy without a government. The question that will now follow is how does demand relate to what is actually produced.

Recall that, in the end, the following equations must hold:

$$NNP = C + I$$

and

$$I = S.$$

The demand for the various usages of the national product is called the **aggregate demand**. I will denote this demand by the letter E (denoting expenditures) to distinguish it from the aggregate demand function which we will use later on in the price–output plane.

Hence:

$$E(Y,r) = C(Y) + I(r)$$

and in a more explicit form:

$$E(Y,r) = c_0 + c_1 Y + I_0 - I_1 r$$
$$= [c_0 + I_0 - I_1 r] + c_1 Y$$

where the expression in the brackets contains all those elements of the aggregate demand which are not dependent on income (or, which is the same thing here, on the net national product). We can, therefore, write the aggregate demand function as

$$E(y,r) = A(r) + c_1 Y$$

where A is the autonomous component of demand. However, as this autonomous component is not independent of interest rate (r) which determines demand for investment, we write it as a function of interest rate. Clearly A is inversely related to r. (*Why?*)

As we are considering the relationship between demand and output, we must assume that all other things which might affect the outcome remain unchanged. In our case, this 'other thing' is the interest rate (r). We shall assume that it is a given at a certain level which we will denote by r_0.

We can now draw this aggregate demand function but before we do that make sure that you understand the role of the 45° line.

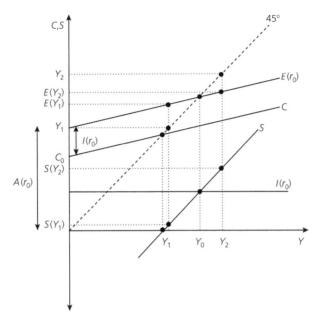

Figure 10.6 Consumption, savings, investment, and aggregate demand.

To have a better insight into the meaning of it all, we draw separately the demand for investment function (which is unchanging with income at a given level of interest rate) and the savings function which is the residual of the demand for consumption function (Figure 10.6). Note that the savings functions does not cross the horizonal axis at the point where the E function crosses the 45° line. In Section 10.1.3 we said that savings will be zero whenever consumption equals income. This happened at the point where the consumption function crossed the 45° line. However, in our case, the E function is not the same as the $C(Y)$ function. It is $C(Y)+I(r)$. Therefore, $S(Y)$ will be zero at a lower level of income than that where $E(Y,r)$ crosses the 45° line. Consider now what will happen at Y_1. At Y_1, the total demand for usages which is a function of both income (Y) and interest rate (r) is greater than what is actually produced. That is, at Y_1,

$$E(Y_1, r_0) > Y_1$$

we call this a state of **excess demand**.

First of all there is the question of how we know about it. What are the symptoms of excess demand? If you were a shop owner who has just received a delivery of canned dolphin-friendly tuna chunks you will make a decision about how much of it to put on the shelf and how much to put in your basement (your stock). That which you put in your basement you intend to use in the next period and it therefore constitutes investment. At 10am, you discover that your dolphin-friendly tuna chunks have all gone and there is an endless queue of people wanting to buy dolphin-friendly tuna chunks outside your store. What would you do? Your most probable action, I believe, would be to go down to the basement and bring up to the shelves some of the tuna which you had put in stock.

If what you did in the morning represents your **planned investment**, the immediate implication of excess demand would be an *unplanned reduction in stocks*.

Excess demand means that we have intended to sell too little. The immediate source from which we may satisfy the hunger for consumption is those things which we have stocked in the basement. Therefore, what we are saying is that whenever there is excess demand, planned investment exceeded planned savings as can be seen in Figure 10.6.

Mechanisms of Adjustment: Perhaps one of the most crucial questions in macroeconomic analysis is the question of how does the system adjust in states of excess demand (or excess supply)? The answer to this question very much depends on one's view on what it is that determines output.

In principle, there are two possible mechanisms of adjustment:

(i) Through increased prices.

(ii) Through increased output.

Naturally, if one believes that output is not influenced by demand, the only mechanism of adjustment would be through prices. As you will soon see, this requires flexibility in both directions. The Keynesian view, on the other hand, is that whenever possible, adjustment will be made through **quantities**. Sellers will increase their orders, and thus, close the gap between demand and supply by means of increased supply.

At Y_2,

$$E(Y_2, r_0) < Y_2$$

which we call a state of **excess supply**.

How would we know that this is the state of affairs? The **symptoms** of this situation are exactly the opposite to the one described before. You now find yourself at the end of the day with shelves overflowing with tuna. Inevitably you will move some of it into your basement. Hence, excess supply corresponds to an *unplanned increase in stocks*. The level of planned investment was lower than the level of planned savings (see Figure 10.6). Again, **adjustment** can either happen through a fall in prices or a reduction in *quantities* (reduced orders). Here, the big question facing the 'price-adjustment' approach is whether prices adjust as easily downwards as they to upwards. The Keynesian view is that in such cases, quantity adjustment is far more likely than price adjustment.

At Y_0:

$$E(Y_0, r_0) = Y_0$$

which we call **equilibrium**.

It means that all rational plans materialized and that much which people wanted to consume they ended up consuming and the same is true with regard to investment. Indeed, you can see from the above graph that at equilibrium, the planned savings also equal the planned investment.

10.2.1 Characterization of the equilibrium and the multiplier

At equilibrium

$$E(Y_0, r_0) = Y_0$$

this means that:

$$E(Y_0, r_0) = A(r_0) + c_1 Y_0 = Y_0$$

hence,

$$Y_0 = A(r_0) \frac{1}{1 - c_1}.$$

As $c_1 < 1$, $1/(1 - c_1) > 1$. This means that a slight change in A will bring about a greater change in Y for which there will be equilibrium in the system. That is why, $1/(1 - c_1)$ is called the *Multiplier*.

For instance, if interest rate fell to $r_1 (< r_0)$ this will mean that now there is a greater demand for investment. The autonomous component of the aggregate demand will now increase:

$$A(r_1) > A(r_0).$$

Let ΔA denote the difference between the two level of investment; that is, $\Delta A = A(r_1) - A(r_0)$. This means that at each level of income (Y) there is now going to be a greater demand for output (Figure 10.7).

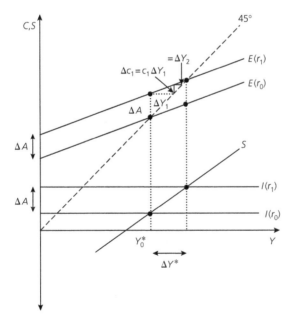

Figure 10.7 An increase in the interest rate and equilibrium.

At the initial level of equilibrium (Y_0^*) there is now excess demand. As output increases to satisfy this increase in demand ($\triangle A = \triangle Y_1$) income too is increased. This, in turn, gives a further push to demand by increasing demand for consumption ($\triangle C_1 = c_1 \triangle Y_1$). Satisfying this increase ($\triangle Y_2 = \triangle C_1$) will further increase demand for consumption and so on and so forth. This is what we call the **multiplier effect**. A single push to demand generates a snow-ball effect. We know that in the end the system converges to an equilibrium because the marginal propensity to consume is less then 1. This means that, each time, consumption increases at a decreasing rate.

Perhaps the most important conclusion which is learnt from this model is that *demand determines output*. This, it must be noted, revolutionized thinking about policy and the role of government. Until those days, macroeconomic analysis was dominated by Say's law where it is supply which determines demand. This, in turn, implies that demand management is completely useless. Till this very day, this is to a great extent the heart of the debate; is demand management useful or not? If yes, then governments have a significant active role in the economy. If demand management is completely ineffective, then government should only worry about creating the proper environment for industry which in turn, will determine the level of output (and thus, employment).

10.3 Closed economy with government

We begin by investigating how the introduction of a government will affect the national accounts:

The usage of the resources is now extended to include public consumption (denoted by G) as well as private consumption (C) and investment (I).

$$NNP = C + I + G.$$

Also, people are now paying taxes (T) before they decide how much to consume and how much to save.

$$Y = C + S + T.$$

Bearing in mind that basic relationship between the value of what has been produced and the generated income (NNP $= Y$) still holds, we get

$$C + I + G = C + S + T$$

or,

$$I = S + (T - G)$$

where ($T - G$) can be thought of as government's savings.

This means that the capital formation equation still identifies the source of capital accumulation (and thus one origin of growth) as savings. However, there are two different sources of savings: private (by individuals) and public (through surpluses in the government budget). Naturally, you can easily see that an economy with a high level of savings may still fail to grow through capital accumulation if at the same time the government is running a large deficit.

In terms of the model, the introduction of government will have the following implications:

First, individuals are now making decisions about consumption with respect to their disposable income (Y_d) rather than the national income Y. Therefore, we must rewrite the aggregate demand for consumption as:

$$C(Y_d) = c_0 + c_1(Y_d).$$

But disposable income is really the difference between income and taxes, or in other words,

$$Y_d = Y - T.$$

So we can rewrite aggregate demand for consumption as:

$$C(Y) = c_0 + c_1(Y - T).$$

The tax function T may be any of the following forms:

Lump-Sum Tax, where $T = T_0$ taxes are raised with no reference to income. As we saw in our microeconomic analysis, lump sum taxes are efficient in the sense that they do not interfere in the decisions of individuals. As your tax liability is independent of what you do, the composition of your choices which you wanted before the tax would stay the same after the tax. When we applied the lump sum tax to industry we saw that such a tax does not interfere in the marginal cost pricing principle and thus, is consistent with the principles of efficiency. In addition, the lump sum tax is very easy to manage. You do not need to know the circumstances of each individual in order to calculate his tax liability. If he breathes, he pays for it! This means that the lump sum tax is both cheap and efficient. Does it have a downside? Of course, as lump sum taxes worsen inequalities. If a poor person and a rich person pay the same amount of money, the proportion of what they pay as tax out of their income is very different indeed. The rich person would pay a very small percentage of his income while the poor person pays a very high percentage of his income. This means that tax is regressive and that the distribution of income becomes more unequal.

Proportional tax: $T(Y) = tY$, where there is a flat rate of tax which is paid by everyone. This is a tax system which does not affect the distribution of income. As everybody pays the same proportion, the proportion of the overall income they earn remains unchanged. However, as the tax liability here depends on what people do the presence of the tax may influence their decision and, thus, generate inefficiency. For instance, if you pay tax according to the amount of income you earn, there may be a point where you would not want to work more if you share the return of your extra hour with the government (or should I say, other members of society). With a lump sum tax you have to pay a certain amount regardless, therefore, there is nothing to deter you from working the extra hour. In addition, the proportional tax is a bit more cumbersome than the lump sum tax as you do have to gather information about how much does each individual earn.

Progressive Tax: $T(Y) = t(Y)Y$ where the rate of tax itself depends on the income earned. It will be progressive if the rate of tax increases with income. This, of course, is the most cumbersome (hence expensive) tax system as you must collect a considerable amount of information and to compute for each individual his tax rate. However, while the system is clearly expensive, it does improve the distribution of income and the rich pay a higher percentage of their income than the poor.

We are not going to comment on, or discuss, the alternative tax systems but it will be useful to have this basic understanding of what distinguishes the one from the other. In terms of modelling the economy, knowing the position of the tax function in the demand for consumption should allow a straightforward incorporation of any form of tax functions. For simplicity, I will normally assume a lump sum tax.

The second addition that follows the introduction of government is that of a government's demand for public consumption (G). The government may adopt any policy it chooses: either to have public consumption increase whenever national income increases (in which case $G(Y) = G_0 + g_1 Y$); or, to reduce spending on public good as the economy becomes richer ($G(Y) = G_0 - g_1 Y$); or, to make public spending independent of output (in which case, $G = G_0$). Again, for simplicity's sake I will assume the latter case.

We now have the complete model in front of us:

$$C(Y) = c_0 + c_1(Y - T)$$

$$I(r) = I_0 - I_1 r$$

$$G = G_0.$$

Hence,

$$E(Y, r) = C(Y, T) + I(r) + G$$

and in a more explicit form

$$E(Y, r) = c_0 - c_1 T_0 + c_1 Y + I_0 - I_1 r + G_0$$

$$= [c_0 - c_1 T_0 + G_0 + I_0 - I_1 r] + c_1 Y.$$

Now, the expression in the brackets (the autonomous component) contains the government spending as well as the effect of lump sum taxes on consumption ($c_1 T_0$). We now write the aggregate demand function as

$$E(y, r) = A(r_0, T_0, G_0) + c_1 Y.$$

We choose to write G and T explicitly as these are the tools of government policy; they constitute what we call **fiscal policy.**

The rest of the analysis is exactly the same as the one we have conducted for the closed economy without a government. We only have to bear in mind that A is now a more extensive argument and that at equilibrium the concept of planned savings which is equated with planned investment contains government savings.

Recall that

$$I = S + (T - G).$$

Therefore, the complete picture is shown in Figure 10.8 and as $A(r_0, T_0, G_0)$ it is easy to see that when economists were mainly concerned with unemployment, the message of the Keynesian model was quite striking. Fiscal policies in the form of either increase spending or decreased taxation can bring about, together with the multiplier effect, considerable increase in output (and employment).

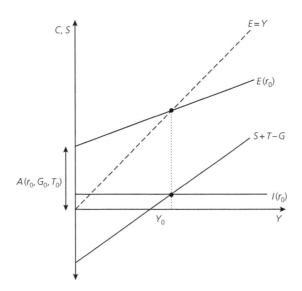

Figure 10.8 Equilibrium with government.

Note that, in our analysis, the multiplier remains as before; I leave it to you to consider what will happen to the multiplier if the tax function was of a proportional nature.

10.4 The IS representation of the goods' market equilibria

The above analysis suggests that the level of national income is determined in the **goods' market** by the aggregate demand. The latter is, among other things, a function of the interest rate. What is particularly interesting about the interest rate is that it is an economic variable which seems to connect the assets (or money) side of the economy with its real side: the actual demand for goods. Think of it in the following way: if you wish to save part of your income you can either hide it in your sock under the mattress or, give it to someone who will promise to give it back to you in the future. However, as you do not know this person you are unlikely to give it to him without being paid for it. But why, you may wonder, would another person want my savings?

There are two kinds of answers which basically mean the same. First of all, some people will want to buy things now but may not have enough money. They do not mind having less in the future as long as they can have more now. To an extent, this is a matter of preferences but also of income distribution. Some people prefer the pleasure of today and are willing to sacrifice future income for that purpose, some people may not have enough now but may have more in the future so they need to even their consumption over time. In addition, there are those people who need money now because they want to buy machinery for a new factory. Those people too, will want to buy your savings. Therefore, at each point in time there will be some people wanting to sell some of their current consumption for future consumption and some people who are willing to sell future consumption for greater current consumption. The balance between these wants, which reflect considerations outside the immediate sphere of our goods' market, affects interest rates. Therefore, by connecting the level of national income with this important variable, we extend the scope of our analysis.

The **IS (Investment–Savings) representation** of the goods' market depicts the relationship between interest rates and levels of national income. When the interest rate is r_0 the equilibrium level of income in the goods' market will be Y_0 (point A in Figure 10.9).

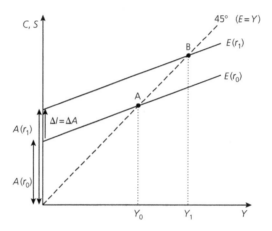

Figure 10.9 The effect of a change in the interest rate r.

Had interest rate fallen to r_1, demand for investment would increase and so will the aggregate demand for goods (the shift upwards of the E schedule). This will create excess demand at point A and with **quantity adjustment** this will mean that increase in orders will bring about an increase in output until equilibrium is restored at point B.

Figure 10.10 depicts the same story in the (Y, r) plane. The initial point A means that when interest rate is r_0, there will be equilibrium in the goods' market at Y_0. Had the interest rate fallen to r_1, there would be an increase in demand for goods and, therefore, excess demand when output remains at Y_0. With quantity adjustment, the output will now increase to Y_1 where the equilibrium in the goods' market had been restored (point B in both diagrams).

Connecting points A and B produces the inverse relationship between interest rates and national income. As interest rates increase, the demand for investment falls (point D). At Y_1 this means that there is an excess supply of goods. With quantity adjustment the output will fall until we reach the level of output on the line connecting A and B.

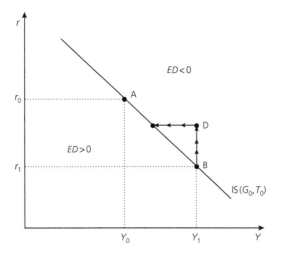

Figure 10.10 The IS schedule: equilibrium (r, Y) combinations in the goods market.

The definition of the IS curve is, therefore, the collection of all pairs of interest rates and national income for which there is equilibrium in the goods' markets. In algebraic terms this would mean that the IS describes the relationship between the values of r and Y when the aggregate demand (E) equals aggregate supply (Y):

$$E(Y,r) = C(Y,T) + I(r) + G = Y$$

and in a more explicit form:

$$E(Y,r) = c_0 - c_1 T_0 + c_1 Y + I_0 - I_1 r + G_0$$
$$= [c_0 - c_1 T_0 + G_0 + I_0 - I_1 r] + c_1 Y$$
$$\text{IS}: A(G_0, T_0) - I_1 r + c_1 Y = Y.$$

In the goods' market we know that Y is a function of r. This would mean that:

$$Y = 1/(1 - c_1)[A(G_0, T_0) - I_1 r].$$

But to get the geometry clear, recall that a slope in the (y,r) plane is defined as dr/dy. To find the expression for the slope let us rewrite the IS equation such that r is a function of Y. This means that we have to write the equation in a different way:

$$A(G, T) + Y(c_1 - 1) = I_1 r$$

or,

$$r = \frac{1}{I_1} A(G, T) + \frac{(c_1 - 1)}{I_1} Y$$

hence,

$$dr = \frac{1}{I_1} A(G, T) + \frac{(c_1 - 1)}{I_1} dy$$

where

$$\frac{dr}{dY} = \frac{c_1 - 1}{I_1}.$$

As $c_1 < 1$ (MPC less than unity) it is clear that $(c_1 - 1)/I_1 < 0$. Therefore, the inverse relationship between Y and r has been confirmed. The expression dr/dY is actually the geometrical definition of the slope of the IS (Figure 10.11). It also tells us by how much interest rate would the fall (and so demand for investment increase) if we increased output by one unit and wished to maintain equilibrium in the goods' market (see Figure 10.11). Recall that the multiplier in the original model was $1/(1 - c_1)$. The greater the marginal propensity to consume, the greater will be the multiplier. However, this means that the denominator $(1 - c_1)$ is smaller which, in turn, means that the slope of the IS is flatter.

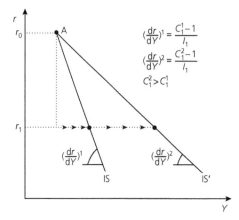

Figure 10.11 The effect of a change in the MPC.

The intuition of it all is very simple too. The greater will be the multiplier, the greater will be the impact on equilibrium level of income (Y) of any slight change in the demand for investment. As the interest falls, the demand for investment will increase and this, with a greater multiplier, will push equilibrium income further to the right; hence leading to a flatter IS.

Self-assessment and applications

QUESTION 1

What will be the effects of an increase in government spending on equilibrium level of output, consumption, savings, and investment?

Answer

Let us begin with simple intuition. What do you think will be the effects of an increase in government spending? In terms of our definitions (and in this sense, this is not really about intuition *per se*), government spending is a measure for government demand for local output. An increase in this demand would mean that, other things being equal, overall demand would increase and at the initial level of output there will now be excess demand.

While it is important to try to have a feel of the general direction of the change, on many occasions it will be more difficult to predict the various consequences. Therefore, it would help you a lot if you develop familiarity with the model which will allow you to set each problem in the full context of the model. In this case, there may not be a need to do so but in order to practise this method, I suggest that you begin by building the model of the goods' market and then investigate the change. We begin by the depiction of the whole model assuming the simplest form of taxes (lump sum):

$$C(y) = c_0 + c_1(Y - T)$$

$$I(r) = I_0 - I_1 r$$

$$G = G_0$$

$$\Rightarrow AE(y, r) = [c_0 + I_0 - I_1 r + G_0 - c_1 T] + c_1 y$$

$$AE(y, r) = A(r_0) + c_1 y$$

$$\Rightarrow \text{In equilibrium} \quad AE(y, r) = y$$

$$y^* = A(r_0) \frac{1}{1 - c_1}.$$

The initial equilibrium is shown in Figure 10.12. At equilibrium, $I(r_0) = S(y^*) + T - G_0$.

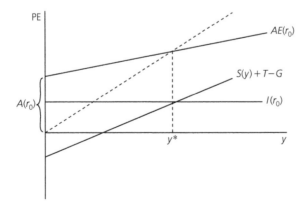

Figure 10.12

Suppose now that G increased to $G_1 > G_0$ but the tax level remained unchanged. How will this affect the model?

$$C(y) = c_0 + c_1(Y - T)$$

$$I(r) = I_0 - I_1 r$$

$$G = G_0 + dG = G_1$$

$$\Rightarrow AE(y, r) = [c_0 + I_0 - I_1 r + G_1 - c_1 T] + c_1 y$$

$$\hat{A}E(y, r) = \hat{A}(r_0) + c_1 y$$

$$\Rightarrow \text{In equilibrium} \quad \widehat{AE}(y, r) = y$$

$$y^{**} = \hat{A}(r_0)\frac{1}{1 - c_1}.$$

Clearly the autonomous component has gone up and this will shift the entire AE line parallelly upwards as in Figure 10.13.

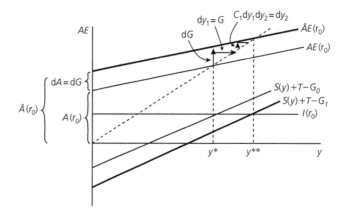

Figure 10.13

We can now follow the dynamics of the change more closely. The initial increase in G (dG) (the first arrow upwards from the initial equilibrium at A) will generate an increase in output of the same magnitude to offset this excess demand (i.e. $dG = dy_1$) (the horizontal arrow which follows). But, as income increases people will want to consume more (i.e. $dAE = c_1 dy_1$) and so on. As the marginal propensity to consume is less than unity, this process converges to the new equilibrium. We could have calculated the new level of equilibrium simply from the following:

$$\text{as} \quad y^* = A(r)\frac{1}{1 - c_1}$$

$$dy = dA\frac{1}{1 - c_1}.$$

In our case, you simply replace dA by dG.

So equilibrium level of output increased by dy (which is greater than dG as the multiplier is greater than 1) say, if the marginal propensity to consume is 0.8, the multiplier will be 5, so the change in output will be five times the initial change in demand.

What will happen to the consumption? Well, as $C(y, T)$ and only y increased, consumption will increase too. What will happen to the level of private savings? As private savings are given by $S(y) = Y - T - C(y, T) = Y(1 - c_1) - c_0 + T(c_1 - 1)$ and as only Y increased, private savings will increase too. But what will happen to the overall savings?

$$S^T = S(y) + T - G = [Y - T - C(y, T)] + T - G = Y(1 - c_1) - c_0 + Tc_1 - G.$$

While y increased, G too increased. As we know that in equilibrium, planned investment equals planned savings, we know that the total level of savings must not change (as the demand for investment had not changed). The overall saving curve, however, shifts down as at any level of output there would be less savings now as G has gone up. The loss of savings at y^* was offset by the increase in private savings as income increased.

What will be the effects of such a change on the IS?

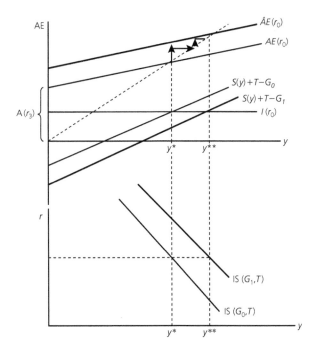

Figure 10.14

For the same level of interest rate, there will now be equilibrium at a higher level of income as see in Figure 10.14. This is a shift to the right of the IS as opposed to shifts along it which are derived from changed in interest rates.

■ QUESTION 2

The multiplier with a proportional tax is smaller than the multiplier with a lump sum tax. Therefore, the slope of the IS schedule with a proportional tax system will be flatter than its slope with a lump sum tax system. True or false? Explain.

Answer

(a) What do you think? If you consider the meaning of the multiplier and the meaning of the tax, it is easy to come to the right conclusion without the full model. As a lump sum tax is independent of income, it means that whenever output increases in response to an initial increase in an autonomous component (say, demand for investment or government spending), the generated income will rise by the full marginal propensity to consume. When the tax is proportional it means that some of the newly generated income would be diverted as tax and the increase in demand for consumption will be smaller. Hence, the multiplier effect is greater with the lump sum than it is with the proportional tax. Let us see this now in full.

Lump sum tax:

$$C(Y) = c_0 + c_1(Y - T)$$

$$I(r) = I(r_0)$$

$$G = G_0$$

$$E(Y_0, r_0) = [c_0 + I(r_0) + G_0 - c_1 T] + c_1 Y = A(r_0) + c_1 Y_0.$$

Equilibrium means

$$E(Y_0, r_0) = A(r_0) + c_1 Y_0 = Y_0$$

hence,

$$Y_0 = A(r_0) \frac{1}{(1 - c_1)}.$$

Proportional tax

$$C(Y) = c_0 + c_1(Y - tY) = c_0 + c_1(1 - t)Y$$

$$I(r) = I(r_0)$$

$$G = G_0$$

$$E(Y_0, r_0) = [c_0 + I(r_0) + G_0] + c_1(1 - t)Y = \hat{A}(r_0) + c_1(1 - t)Y = Y.$$

hence,

$$Y_0 = \hat{A}(r_0) \frac{1}{(1 - c_1(1 - t))}.$$

The multiplier of a closed economy with a lump sum tax (left-hand side) is clearly greater than that of a proportional tax:

$$\frac{1}{1 - c_1} > \frac{1}{1 - c_1(1 - t)}.$$

As the denominator of the right-hand multiplier is greater than that of the left-hand multiplier, the multiplier on the left is greater.

(b) The slope of the IS reflects the sensitivity of the output to changes in demand which are generated by changes in interest rates (see Figure 10.15).

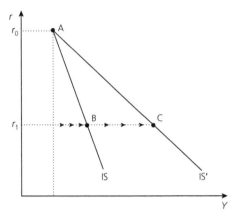

Figure 10.15

We start at A. A fall in the interest rate will increase the demand for investment. A smaller multiplier means that the role on effect of an increase in income (to satisfy the initial increase in demand) is not going to be very large. This will mainly be due to a lower MPC. Hence, the economy will move to point B. With a larger multiplier, the initial increase in income will generate a further increase in demand due to a larger MPC. As income increases to satisfy these extra wants, demand carries on rising. The role on effect, in such a case, will be large and the final increase in output greater. We, therefore, end up at a point like C. That is to say, the flatter will be the IS curve.

▨ QUESTION 3

In a simple Keynesian model of a closed economy, an increased propensity to save will inevitably lead to an increase in national income as there are now more savings which can be invested. True or false? Explain.

Answer

This is a question about the paradox of thrift: what will happen to the economy if people started saving more. The origin of the problem, to remind you, is that savings will affect investment and when focused on capital accumulation as a means of growth, encouraging greater savings at any level of income is a likely government policy.

   However, you can clearly see that there is a problem here. In a model where output is determined by demand, increasing the level of savings at any given level of income means a fall in consumption. This, in turn, reduces aggregate demand and subsequently reduces equilibrium level of output. This fall in income would decrease the overall level of savings and would suggest that by encouraging greater savings, the only thing which the government will achieve is a recession (Figure 10.16).

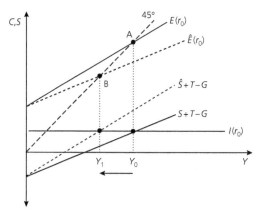

Figure 10.16

Suppose that the government succeeds in convincing the public to save more (an increase in the MPS and a fall in MPC). This will shift the $S + T - G$ function up (for any given set of fiscal policy parameters) and the aggregate demand (E) down to a new equilibrium at point B. This means that people will save more at Y_0 but as income falls to Y_1 they will want to save less because of their reduced income. As, in the end, $I = S + T - G$, the fact that I remains unchanged means that S also will not change (for any given T and G). The 'paradox', so to speak, is that in spite of an increased *demand for savings*, the *level of savings* remained unchanged.

Notice, however, that the assumption as if interest rate is unaffected by the increased demand for savings is unreasonable. Equally, if output falls it is not very likely that interest rates will not be affected. Therefore, this paradox must be viewed as only a part of a story. In later chapters we will return to examine it.

Had, for instance, demand for investment been a rising function of income, the outcome would have been even more pronounced (see Figure 10.17).

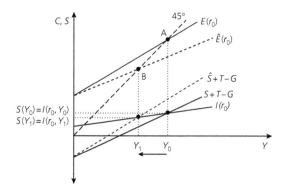

Figure 10.17

In such a case, the increase in the marginal propensity to save will cause—for an unchanged interest rate—a *fall* in the level of savings.

QUESTION 4

Here is a model of a closed economy:

$$C(Y_d) = 80 + 0.8Y_d \text{ (where } Y_d \text{ is disposable income)}$$

$$I(r_0) = 100$$

$$G = 100.$$

Consider two tax systems (and a balanced budget policy); a lump sum tax $(T = G)$ and a proportional tax $(G = T(y) = tY)$. Will the equilibrium level of output be different under the two tax systems? What will be the level of t?

Answer

The equilibrium condition of this system can be written in the following form:

$$E(Y_0, r_0) = Y_0.$$

Lump Sum Tax

$$E(Y_0, r_0) = A(r_0) + c_1 Y_0 = Y_0.$$

Hence,

$$Y_0 = A(r_0)\frac{1}{1 - c_1}$$

where $A(r) = c_0 + I(r_0) + G_0 - c_1 T = 80 + 100 + 100 - 0.8T$.
With a balanced budget $(T = G = 100)$. Therefore:

$$A(r_0) = 80 + 100 + 100 - 0.8 \times 100 = 200.$$

The multiplier is $1/(1 - 0.8) = 1/0.2 = 10/2 = 5$. Therefore,

$$Y_0 = A(r_0)[1/(1 - c_1)] = 200 \times 5 = 1000.$$

Proportional tax

$$C(Y) = c_0 + c_1(Y - tY) = c_0 + c_1(1 - t)Y = 80 + 0.8(1 - t)Y$$

$$I(r) = I(r_0) = 100$$

$$G = G_0 = 100$$

$$E(Y_0, r_0) = [c_0 + I(r_0) + G_0] + c_1(1 - t)Y = \hat{A}(r_0) + c_1(1 - t)Y = Y$$

hence,

$$y_0 = \hat{A}(r_0)\frac{1}{(1 - c_1(1 - t))}.$$

In our case, the new $A(r_0) = 80 + 200 = 280$. The multiplier, however, depends on t. As there is a balanced budget, we know that $G_0 = tY$. This means that the level of t must be decided in the model. So we must simply substitute $t = G_0/y$, wherever there is t. Substituting into the aggregate demand equation will yield the following:

$$E(Y, r) = [c_0 + G_0 + I(r_0)] + c_1(1 - G_0/Y)Y = [c_0 + G_0 + I(r_0)] + c_1 Y - c_1 G_0$$

$$E(Y, r) = [c_0 + G_0 + I(r_0) - c_1 G_0] + c_1 Y.$$

In equilibrium

$$E(Y, r) = [c_0 + G_0 + I(r_0) - c_1 G_0] + c_1 Y = Y$$

$$Y = 1/(1 - c_1)[c_0 + G_0 + I(r_0) - c_1 G_0]$$

which yields a solution similar to the lump sum tax:

$$Y = 1/(1 - 0.8)[80 + 100 + 100 - 0.8 \times 100] = 5 \times 200 = 1000.$$

A distinction must be drawn here between the lump sum multiplier and the proportional tax multiplier. In the case of the lump sum tax, both the level of G as well as the level of T can be decided a priori. With a proportional tax, it is not clear how the balanced budget policy is being decided. The government can set G and then adjust t to accommodate it as we did the above case. Or, alternatively, the government can choose to set the level of expenditure according to its tax revenues. In such a case, the government sets t and adjusts G to be equal to tY. It is easy to establish that there is a rate of the proportional tax ($t = 10\%$) which will yield exactly the same equilibrium (i.e. $y = 1000$). For any $t > 10\%$ equilibrium will be at a lower level of output while for any $t < 10\%$ equilibrium level of output will be greater than 1000 as shown in Figure 10.18.

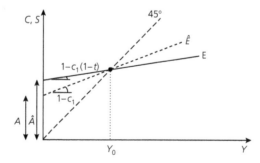

Figure 10.18

QUESTION 5

The balanced budget multiplier suggests that the government's fiscal policy will have no effect on the economy. True or False, explain.

Answer

The intuition here is straightforward. A balanced budget means that the government raises taxes to fund its entire demand. However, when a pound is transferred from an individual who consumed only a fraction of it (the marginal propensity to consume) to someone who spends all of it (the government's marginal propensity to spend is 1), the fall in consumption will be smaller than the increase in government spending. In other words, the amount of resources diverted to government spending is bound to be insufficient.

To see the significance of the balanced budget multiplier let us examine what would happen if the government increased its spending while raising taxes at the same magnitude. Normally, we have the following model:

$$y = [c_0 + I(r_0) + G - c_1 T] \frac{1}{1 - c_1}.$$

Now there is an increase in G and T such that $dG = dT$. What will happen to y? (What will be dy?)

$$dA = dG - c_1 dT$$

$$dY = dA \frac{1}{1 - c_1}$$

as

$$dG = dT$$

$$dY = dA \frac{1}{1 - c_1} = dG(1 - c_1) \frac{1}{1 - c_1} = dG.$$

Therefore, fiscal policy will affect output even though the full extent of government spending was covered by taxes. The reason, as we said earlier, is the difference between the marginal propensity to spend between individuals and government.

QUESTION 6

In a closed economy, the poor earn the fraction α of national income. Their marginal propensity to consume is greater than that of the rich but only the rich pay the proportional tax (t). The government, which is committed to a non-interventionist policy, claims that redistribution occurs naturally through the sympathy of the rich who donate, annually, the fraction β of their income to the poor. In addition, the government has a strict balanced budget policy where government spending depends on the amount of tax raised.

Compare the multipliers of the economy with and without donations.

Answer

This is a question which brings us back to questions of income distribution and the possible effects of various attitudes towards the mechanism of redistribution. It is a bit more difficult than the previous question but I would like to encourage you to try to tackle it. If you feel that this is a bit too much, do not despair. Carry on with your studies and come back to it after you have gained more experience with dealing with the macro models.

We will now compare the multiplier with and without donations:

The poor's disposable income in this model (including potential donations) is, clearly, $\alpha Y + \beta(1 - \alpha)Y$, where the first element is their share in national income while the second element is the proportion β of the income of the rich which is donated to the poor.

The disposable income of the rich is given by $[(1 - \alpha)Y](1 - t) - \beta(1 - \alpha)Y$, where the first element is the net income after tax while the second element is the donation which they transfer *directly* to the poor.

We thus begin by setting all the behavioural functions of the entire economy:

$$C(Y) = c_0 + c_1^p(\alpha + \beta(1 - \alpha))Y + c_1^r((1 - t)(1 - \alpha) - \beta(1 - \alpha))Y$$

$$I(r, Y) = I(r_0)$$

$$G(Y) = t(1 - \alpha)Y$$

$$AE(Y, r) = A + [c_1^p(\alpha + \beta(1 - \alpha)) + c_1^r((1 - t)(1 - \alpha) - \beta(1 - \alpha) + t(1 - \alpha)]Y.$$

Hence, the multiplier

$$Y^* = A(r_0)\frac{1}{1 - [c_1^p(\alpha + \beta(1 - \alpha)) + c_1^r((1 - t)(1 - \alpha) - \beta(1 - \alpha)) + t(1 - \alpha)]}$$

$$= A\frac{1}{1 - M}$$

where, again, αY is the poor's income, $\beta(1 - \alpha)Y$ is the donation made by the rich and t is the tax rate. We call the expression in the squared brackets M.

Without donation ($\beta = 0$) the multiplier will become:

$$\frac{1}{1 - [c_1^p(\alpha) + c_1^r(1 - \alpha)(1 - t) + t(1 - \alpha)]}.$$

It is quite easy to see that:

$$M = [c_1^p(\alpha) + c_1^r(1 - \alpha)(1 - t) + t(1 - \alpha)] + \beta(1 - \alpha)(C_1^p - c_1^r)$$

where the first squared bracket is in the denominator of the multiplier without donation. As the marginal propensity to consume of the poor is greater than the rich, it is clear that M is greater than its equivalent in the no-donation multiplier. Hence, the multiplier with donation is greater than the one without it. The intuitive reason for this is that a transfer from lower MPC to a higher one will increase demand for consumption.

QUESTION 7

To encourage savings, the government proposes to shift from an income tax system to a system of consumption tax. What will be the effects of the change on the multiplier?

Answer

At first you should wonder about the motivation behind the government proposal. Clearly, the problem with income tax is that it takes both consumption and savings. By moving to a tax which is only on consumption, the government hopes that people will be encouraged to save less. But will it be associated with a recession or higher level of income? This is one of those cases where what may appear to us as intuitively self-evident, turns out to be a bit more complex. Naturally, there are a lot of circumstances which affect the result but this should be enough to make you cautious when you apply intuition in these models.

The government proposes a consumption tax. This means that now, instead of a tax function of the following nature,

$$T(Y) = tY$$

we will have a tax system of this nature,

$$T(Y) = tC(Y).$$

Consider the multiplier of a closed economy. We begin by describing the new consumption function:

$$C(Y) = C_0 + c_1(Y - T(Y)) = C_0 + c_1 Y - c_1 t \, C(Y)$$

$$C(Y)(1 + c_1 t) = C_0 + c_1 Y$$

$$C(Y) = \frac{C_0 + c_1 Y}{(1 + c_1 t)}$$

$$C(Y) = \frac{C_0}{(1 + c_1 t)} + \frac{c_1}{(1 + c_1 t)} Y.$$

This means that now, the *AE* function will have the following structure and subsequent multiplier:

$$AE(Y, r) = A(r, t) + \frac{c_1}{(1 + c_1 t)} Y.$$

Equilibrium means

$$AE(Y, r) = Y$$

$$A(r, t) + \frac{c_1}{(1 + c_1 t)} Y = Y$$

$$Y = A(r, t) \frac{1}{1 - (c_1/(1 + c_1 t))}.$$

We must now examine the relationship between this multiplier and the normal proportional tax multiplier:

$$\frac{1}{1-(c_1/(1+c_1t))} > \frac{1}{1-c_1(1-t)} \tag{1}$$

$$1-c_1(1-t) > 1 - \frac{c_1}{(1+c_1t)}$$

$$\frac{c_1}{(1+c_1t)} > c_1(1-t)$$

$$1 > (1-t)(1+c_1t)$$

$$1 > 1-t+c_1t-c_1t^2$$

$$t > t(c_1(1-t))$$

$$1 > c_1(1-t). \tag{2}$$

As (2) is always true, so must be (1).

Namely, the multiplier with consumption tax would be greater than the multiplier with income tax. However, note that the autonomous component becomes smaller! Clearly, a greater multiplier does not seem to bode well for the government but I would suspend judgement until we see the entire picture when we come back to this question in later chapters.

QUESTION 8

'The present value of £10 at the end of every year from now to eternity must be less than 1'. True or false? Explain.

Answer

The answer is straightforward. First, You have to make use of the equation describing the present value of an infinite return. Second, they were expected to show how to calculate the present value of such a deal:

$$PV\{T\}_{i=0}^{\infty} = q\frac{T}{1-q} = \frac{1}{1+r}T\left(\frac{1}{1-(1/1+r)}\right) = \frac{T}{r} = \frac{10}{r} > 1.$$

For all $r < 1$.

QUESTION 9

Derive the multiplier of a closed economy when the government believes that its role in society should increase as national income increases.

Answer

This is simply a case where the government employs a rule of spending which suggests that its spending would increase with income. Inevitably, this will have an effect on the multiplier.

The complete model is,

$$C(Y) = c_0 + c_1(Y - T)$$

$$G(y) = g_0 + g_1 Y$$

$$I(r) = I(r_0),$$

hence in equilibrium:

$$Y = [c_0 + I(r_0) + g_0] \frac{1}{1 - c_1 - g_1}.$$

The multiplier with government spending increasing with income is therefore greater than the multiplier when government spending was independent of income. As $(1 - c_1) > (1 - c_1 - g_1)$ the multiplier with government spending dependent on income would be greater. The logic of this is simple. As the government increases its spending whenever income increases, the push to demand whenever income increases by, say, one, would be much greater. There will now be the demand for consumption as well as the demand for government spending influencing the increase in aggregate demand.

QUESTION 10

Consider a closed economy where the government maintains a policy of a balanced budget by adjusting its spending to tax revenues. There are no transfers in the economy and a proportional tax (t) is levied on household income. Profits constitute 20% of national income and half of it is distributed to shareholders. The rest is used for investment. What will be the economy's multiplier?

Answer

The particular features of this problem are:

(i) Only household income is taxed.

(ii) Profits constitute 20% (we shall denote this by α).

(iii) A share of the profit is being distributed (half in our case; in general, β).

(iv) Non-distributed profits are domestically invested.

(v) The government has a balanced budget policy where spending depend on tax revenues.

(vi) No transfer payments.

What will be the multiplier?

We know that the income which is the public gets (i.e., not kept in corporations) is $(1 - \alpha)Y$. The profits, held initially by the corporations is αY. That part of it which flows to the public is $\alpha \beta Y$. So the total income available for consumption is $(1 - \alpha)Y + \alpha \beta Y$. We begin by setting all the behavioural functions of the economy:

$$C(Y) = c_0 + c_1(1 - t)[1 - \alpha + \alpha \beta]Y$$

$$I(r, Y) = I(r_0) + \alpha(1 - \beta)Y$$

$$G(Y) = t(1 - \alpha + \alpha \beta)Y$$

$$AE(Y, r) = A + [(1 - \alpha + \alpha \beta)(c_1(1 - t) + t) + \alpha(1 - \beta)]Y.$$

Hence the multiplier

$$Y^* = A(r_0)\frac{1}{1 - [(1 - \alpha + \alpha \beta)(c_1(1 - t) + t) + \alpha(1 - \beta)]},$$

where $(1 - \alpha)$ is direct household income; $\alpha \beta$ is the distributed share of profits; $\alpha(1 - \beta)$ the non-distributed share of profits. Indeed, when either $\alpha = 0$ or $\beta = 1$ (namely, all profits have been distributed), we get balanced budget multiplier:

$$\frac{1}{1 - [c_1(1 - t) + t]}$$

Evidently, we assume the expression in brackets to be less than unity.

In our case, $\alpha = 0.2$ and $\beta = 0.5$. Thus, the multiplier becomes:

$$\frac{1}{1 - [0.9(c_1(1 - t) + t) + 0.1]}.$$

NOTES

1. Inequality is a complex concept and there are quite sophisticated ways of measuring it. Here however, we shall not go into depth in the matter. Suppose, for instance, that we have a society with 10 individuals. 5 are poor and earn 10 and 5 are rich and earn 20. Total income is 150. If one of the rich becomes poor we can have 6 poor, earning 10 pounds each (60 altogether). Now the residual 90 is divided over the remaining 4 individuals each of whom will earn 22.5. Intuitively, we would consider the increase in the share of the poor (from 50 to 60) as an increase in inequality. However, an increase in the share of poor can also increase equality. If there are now 6 poor people but their income is 15 pounds per person, their overall share had increased from 50 to 90. The remaining 60 will now be distributed to the 4 rich, who, in turn, will get 15 pounds each. Hence, in this case, an increase in the share of the poor increased equality. However, note that when the increase in share of the earning by the poor leads to greater equality, the MPC or the rich and the poor will tend to be the same.

2. The 45° line helps us transform the values from the x-axis (a general name for the horizontal axis) to the y-axis (a general name for the vertical axis). In Figure 10.5 we examine such a line.

   At point A, we have x_0 on the x-axis and y_0 on the y-axis. The slope of the 45° line is 1. Geometrically, the slope of the above line (tg α) is y_0/x_0. If it is indeed a 45° line then this slope must be equal to 1. For y_0/x_0 to be equal to 1, x_0 must be equal to y_0. Therefore, the 45° line allows us to transform values from the x-axis to the y-axis. We know that at point A, y_0 also represents x_0.

3. Bonds of the **consol type** are such that have an infinite maturity date. When one wishes to consider the purchase of such a bond one would see whether what he says today exceeds, is equal to, or is less

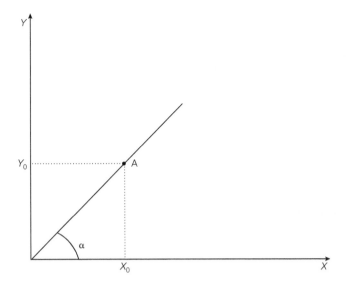

Figure 10.19 The 45° slope.

than the present value of such a bond. The bond yields T pounds by the end of every year from now to infinity. Hence the stream of income one will get in terms of today's money is

$$0 + \frac{T}{1+r} + \frac{T}{(1+r)^2} + \cdots = 0 + qT + q^2T + \cdots = T(0 + q + q^2 + \cdots)$$

where $q = 1/(1+r)$. As $q < 1$ the sum of the infinite series in ( ) is well-defined.

$$T(0 + q + q_2 + \cdots) = T\sum_{i=1}^{\infty} q^i = qT \lim_{n \to \infty} \sum_{i=0}^{n} q^i = qT1(1-q)^{-1}.$$

Therefore, the present value of a consol bond paying T pounds annually is

$$PV\{T\}_{i=0}^{\infty} = q\frac{T}{1-q} = \frac{1}{1+r}T\left(\frac{1}{1-(1/1+r)}\right) = \frac{T}{r}.$$

11 | Money and banking

11.1 Introduction

Money is one of the most difficult concepts in economic analysis. As I explained in Chapter 8, the existence of money and its unclear role in the model of general equilibrium is one of the major reasons for developing an alternative framework of analysis to deal with questions of macroeconomic nature.

In the general equilibrium model we have basically described an **exchange economy** rather than a **monetary economy**. That is to say, in a world of two goods, a general equilibrium price is nothing but an exchange rate between the two goods under discussion. Hence, if the two goods are x and y, the equilibrium price (and indeed any other price) is expressed as: p_x/p_y units of y per x. Recall that, throughout our discussions on microeconomics we have repeatedly emphasized that people have preferences and make choices with respect to real goods rather than any nominal values. Optimal rational behaviour meant that we choose to consume so much of each good such that our willingness to pay for it in terms of the other good equals the market rate of exchange. By willingness to pay we meant that the marginal utility of one good is measured in terms of the other. By market rate of exchange we mean the price, again, measured in terms of the other good.

If instead, we wished to use money value in exactly the same manner we may run into some difficulties. With money, we basically argue that goods are not exchanged against each other but against another commodity called **money**. In terms of our previous discussion this should mean that when the price of good x is 20 pounds, we behave optimally whenever we choose the quantity of x such that our willingness to pay in terms of money for a unit of x equals the market rate of exchange (or price). But for us to measure our marginal utility for x in terms of money would imply that money is an economic good. After all, the whole notion of utility and marginal utility was based on people having preferences regarding all economic goods. Will the move towards a monetary economy mean that money is an economic good? It is certainly scarce, but is it desirable? If it is desirable as such, then should money be an argument in our utility function? Will we be willing to sacrifice other economic goods so that we can have more money? If not, what does it mean, from the point of view of behavioural analysis, to want something merely as a means to get something else? Can we not simply want that something else directly?

The answers to these questions are not at all obvious or simple. At this stage of our study, however, we shall not even attempt to address these issues. I would simply like to make you aware of the complex nature of money and of the difficulties in formulating consistent and coherent theories which deal with it without undermining what we have said before. In any case, what is clear is that money is around and that it has three major functions: as a *numeraire*, a means of exchange, and a store of value.

Money as a *numeraire* means that we use it as a means of counting. When we look at a shoe and a flower we can say that six flowers exchange ($=$) one shoe. When there is another commodity, say toothbrushes, we can count all goods in terms of flowers. If two flowers exchange ($=$) one toothbrush. Hence, three toothbrushes exchange ($=$) one shoe. You can imagine how difficult it all becomes when we have plenty of goods. If the new fashion dictates that you must have as many flowers as possible, people will, all of a sudden, be willing to pay only two flowers per shoe and only one flower per toothbrush. However, given that this is a change in taste, we cannot be sure that the change in the number of flowers the person is willing to pay for one good would be proportional to the number of flowers he, or she, is willing to pay for another. Given that flower is our numeraire, the change in taste also means that now only two toothbrushes will equal one shoe. In other words, the relative price of shoes in terms of toothbrushes will be affected by the fact that people have preferences regarding the unit against which we measured all goods.

Using money as a numeraire proposes a way of circumventing such problems. It means that we measure all goods in terms of money units and, by implication, we assume that money in itself, is not a good like, say, flowers.

Money as a **means of exchange** is fairly obvious. If you want to sell a cow to buy a TV set, you will find it difficult to take your cow into the next shopping mall, squeezing yourself (with the cow) through the gates and land the cow on the counter of the electronics shop. For one, even if you managed not to break the counter, the seller of TVs may not want to have a cow. He, instead, wants to buy diamonds for his wife today (or, if you wish to be politically correct, the seller wishes to buy earrings for her husband...). So the cow is difficult to move around and, the person who owns that which you want may not be particularly interested in having your cow.

But, you may grumble, the electronics seller does not have to keep the cow. If he wants to buy diamonds, he may simply whisk away the cow and take it to the jeweller who has a shop in the other part of town. This is true but as he works late every day except on Fridays, he will have to wait until then before he can take the cow to the jeweller.

While you can clearly see that using money as a means of exchange is far easier than simple barter, the third reason for money follows quite easily from this.

Imagine that our electronics seller has agreed to take the cow in exchange for a wide-screen TV. The day is Monday and we have to wait until Friday to go to the jeweller. Apart from the fact that you must feed your means of exchange, it may also die before Friday or, become ill in some way. Put differently, when paying with simple commodities, the value of what you have received may change without any external change. It is true that the value of money may change too but this will not happen without a change from the outside. The money in your pocket, I am sure, will never become smelly suggesting that it is off and you can no longer use it. But if the cow dies, the value of what the seller had received became zero although there had been no change in the general circumstances. Therefore, money, apart from being a **numeraire** and a **means of exchange**, it is also a **store of value**. It guarantees that, other things being equal, the value of what your received on Monday will stay the same until Friday.

There is, however, one other aspect of money which we need to consider. After all, while it is true that exchanging a cow for a plasma TV may not be such a convenient thing to do we could have promised the TV seller, who is not interested in the cow, that we would pay him at a later date. For him to agree to this, he would have to have a considerable amount of trust in us. Why should he? In other words, giving the seller cash gives him the confidence in the value of what we pay him. He does not need to have trust in us nor have the information about whether, or not, the cow we offer him is ill. In this respect, the role of money is to plug the gap in the market. Put differently, had markets been continuous, in the sense that we run from one deal to another (i.e. the seller does not have to wait till Friday), he might have been willing to accept our cow as soon enough it would have been in someone else's hands. So, altogether, it seems that money is there to resolve a great deal of problems which arise from the reality of exchange and human interaction.

One of the early writers who was, perhaps, one of the first scholars to formulate what may be termed as macroeconomic theory focuses, not surprisingly, on money. In an essay *On Money* published in 1752, David Hume makes the following assertions. First, in line with what we have said above, he writes:

Money is not, properly speaking, one of the subjects of commerce; but only the instrument which men have agreed upon to facilitate the exchange of one commodity for another. It is none of the wheels of trade: It is the oil which renders the motion of the wheels more smooth and easy. (p. 281)[1]

If, then, money is not really part of the real side of the economic system, what is the nature of relationship between this facilitator of trade and actual trade? David Hume himself proposes a formula that suggest a relationship:

It seems a maxim almost self-evident, that the prices of every thing depend on the proportion between commodities and money, and that any alteration on either has the same effect, either of [increasing] or lowering the price. Increase the commodities, they become cheaper; increase the money, they rise in their value. (p. 290)

With some modification we can see that this assertion may lead to the following fixed relationship between the quantity of money and commodities:

$$M = kPY,$$

where M is the total quantity of money, P is the general price level, and Y is the national income (product). The coefficient k represents the specific proportion between the output (commodities in Hume) and prices. Intuitively, this may read as follows: the quantity of money in an economy stands in a given proportion to the value of national product (or the money value of all commodities). Clearly, if Y increases for the equation to hold, P must come down. If M increases, P will rise. Note that this is an early formulation of what is currently known as a monetarist approach. Some economists are of the view that if there is an increase in the quantity of money, this will lead to inflation. In our case, where we do not have a dynamic model, what this means is that when there is an increase in the quantity of money, there will be an increase in prices.

However, for such a view to be correct, it must also be assumed that an increase in the quantity of money (M) will have no effect whatsoever on Y. Returning to Hume, we discover that he himself did not believe this to be the case:

From the whole of this reasoning we may conclude, that it is of no manner of consequence, with regard to the domestic happiness of a state, whether money be in greater or less quantity. The good policy of the magistrate consists only in keeping it, if possible, still increasing; because, by that means, he keeps alive the spirit of industry in the nation, and increases the stock of labour, in which consists all real power and riches. (p. 288)

In a crude fashion we may argue, with reference to Chapter 9, that what exactly the meaning of this equations depends on one's view on what it is that determines output. If Y is independent of demand and if the circumstances of industry are not improved by the supply of money, then the conclusion that an increase in money supply will have no real effect on the economy as it will only cause an increase in prices, can be sustained. If, however, Y is dependent on demand and the latter is related to M, or if the supply of money does affect the circumstances of industry, we may not conclude from the above equation that an increase in M is bound to generate an increase in P. Instead, we will need to contemplate the possibility that an increase in M may cause an increase (or decrease) in Y. In such a case, it is less clear that an increase in money supply will cause increases in price.

Even if we followed Say's 'law', the implication of which is that output is determined by the circumstances of industry (and let us suppose that these have nothing to do with the supply of money), then we end up saying that an increase in the quantity of money will produce an increase in prices. Although this follows immediately from the above equation, we must still inquire into the question how does this happen? Put differently, even if we accept that there is a given relationship between the value of the national product and the quantity of money which is needed to conduct transactions, how is an increase in the quantity of money transformed into an increase in prices?

A primitive form of the answer could be the following one. The reason why people hold money is for the purpose of conducting transactions. If, all of a sudden, they have more money in their hands than they need for their current transactions, they will choose not to keep it in a form of money and use it to buy goods (i.e. increase transactions). When their demand for goods increases, there will be excess demand for goods. In the case of Say's 'law' this would mean that the only possible **mechanism of adjustment** is that of price adjustments. Hence, prices will increase.

The notion of money as a facilitator of trade suggests that money has the role of an asset. **Assets**, normally, are those things which you keep as a stock in order to allow you to consume goods in different circumstances. You buy assets, for instance, to generate consumption when you retire. In a similar sense, money is an asset which facilitates transaction. As such, however, money has a specific nature which we call **liquidity**. As money is the only means of exchange, its availability allows all possible transactions to be performed. If, on the other hand, you think of a house in the country as an asset, it is easy to see in what way it differs from money. When you go to a bar to have a drink, you can always pay in cash. You will find it rather difficult to buy a drink against a time-share scheme which you may offer the bar tender in your house in the country. Alternatively, if you walk in the street and see a beautiful car for sale at an extraordinary low price, you can get it if you have the cash but you may not get it as easily if you have to sell your house first and then come back to buy the car with the cash. The probability that you will find the car with the exceptionally low price waiting for you is almost zero. So when we talk about money, we really talk about a certain kind of an asset: a **liquid asset**.

11.2 The demand for liquid assets

In this course we concentrate on what is called the **liquidity preference approach**. It means that people do not jump from total liquid assets like money, to totally non-liquid assets such as, say, durable goods. Naturally, such an assertion will block the immediate transmission of excess liquidity (resulting, say, from an increase in the quantity of money) into increase in prices as it suggests that people will not move to buy commodities with their 'excess liquidity'. There are degrees of liquidity which various assets represent. Hence, when one finds oneself with more liquid assets than one would have wanted, one can always buy some assets such as bonds, for instance, which are somewhat less liquid but not as non-liquid as, say, a building.

The liquid assets which we have in mind are what we call **real balances** and they are denoted by the real value of our money stock (M/P). We refer to the real value of money because one's wish to hold liquid assets depends on the value of these assets, or, to put it differently, on what they can purchase. If a unit of liquid asset can purchase a mere sandwich you may wish to hold a lot of them. If a unit of liquid asset can purchase a racing car, you are likely to want to hold only a fraction of it.

There are, traditionally, three motives cited to the demand for liquid assets. The first is what we call the **transaction motive**. This simply means that we need liquid assets to conduct transactions. The second motive is what is called the **precautionary motive**. This motive relates to the question of uncertainty surrounding exchange and accordingly we would always like to have some liquid assets available for those transactions for which we have not planned. There is also the **speculative motive** according to which we sometimes like to hold some of our assets in liquid form as we fear the risk of holding our wealth in other assets.

We can, at this stage, reduce it all into our conventional view of that which motivates demand. It should be comprised of two major elements: the price of holding liquid assets and income.[2]

The price, or, as it should be thought of, the opportunity cost, of holding liquid assets is what one could have received had one held his, or her, money in the bank (or lent it to someone else) instead of holding the money in one's pocket. But what is it exactly that one is losing by not putting his, or her, money in the bank. The answer is: the interest rate (r).

Interest rate, like money, is a loaded and complex concept. The most common view of what it is (which we already mentioned in the previous chapter), is that interest rate is the price of present day consumption. If, for instance, one has a certain amount of money, he can choose to use it for immediate consumption or to give it to someone else and, thus, postpone his consumption to a later period.

There are always some people to whom present consumption is more important than it is to others. As they may not have enough means they may want to buy those means (i.e. borrow). Naturally, the person who is being asked to lend will decide on whether to give the money or not according to the compensation which the borrower is willing to offer. This compensation will be the agreed price which inevitably, in our perception of economics, will reflect the balance between the urgency of present consumption to the one, and the willingness to forgo present consumption of the other. Therefore, a decision to hold liquid assets means that one is giving up the interest he, or she, could have earned on that money. Hence, we can say

$$\left(\frac{M}{P}\right)^d = L(r)$$

where the quantity of liquid assets demanded stands in inverse relationship with the price of holding liquid assets. The higher will be the interest rate, the more costly it is to keep one's money in the pocket.

Apart from the price, income, also, plays a role in the determination of the quantity of liquid assets which is demanded. The richer will the economy is, the more will be the opportunities that arise for the use of these liquid assets. One is unlikely to take a lot of cash with him if one is going to spend the next year on a deserted island! Therefore, the general demand function for liquid assets can be written as:

$$\left(\frac{M}{P}\right)^d = L(r, Y).$$

11.3 The supply of liquid assets

Perhaps the most liquid form of assets is 'hard cash'. We call this category of means of payment the **money base** and is denoted by M0. Clearly

$$M0 = PC + R$$

where PC means 'Public Cash' and R is the amount of hard currency which is kept in the Banks as reserve. But people do not use cash only to make payment. They will use the money in their banks' current accounts regardless of its origin. Namely, a cheque is a cheque whether the money in the account is yours or borrowed. We therefore define $M1$ as a more accurate conception of liquid assets:

$$M1 = PC + D$$

where D is the amount of money in deposits which bear no interest (current accounts).

What is D? Suppose now that we bring £K into a bank against which we open an account. Assuming that there was nothing in any of the banks before our arrival and that there are no other assets in the world, the bank balance will appear as follows:

Bank 1

$$\text{Assets:} \quad R_1 = K \quad \text{Liabilities:} \quad D_1 = K$$

Now, suppose that someone comes to the bank and asks for a loan. The manager of the bank will be convinced that we are unlikely to come and ask for all the money we have deposited otherwise why would we have done it in the first place. He therefore calculates the probability of us coming back demanding our money and accordingly will keep that money in reserve. The rest he will be willing to lend.

Normally, the decision of which proportion of one's liabilities should be kept in reserve is made by the central bank. Let α denote that proportion and we call α the **reserve ratio** ($\alpha = R/D$). Suppose that the borrower takes the money and pays it to someone else's account in another bank. Bank 1's balance will now show the following.

Bank 1

$$\text{Assets:} \quad R_1 = \alpha K \quad L_1 = (1 - \alpha)K \quad \text{Liabilities:} \quad D_1 = K$$

We can now repeat the story in Bank 2. First when our borrower brings his loan $(1 - \alpha)K$ to the bank against which he opens an account, and then, when someone else comes to Bank 2 to ask for a loan.

Bank 2 Before further lending

$$\text{Assets:} \quad R_2 = (1 - \alpha)K \quad \text{Liabilities:} \quad D_2 = (1 - \alpha)K$$

Bank 2 After further lending

$$\text{Assets:} \quad R_2 = \alpha(1 - \alpha)K \quad L_2 = (1 - \alpha)^2K \quad \text{Liabilities:} \quad D_2 = (1 - \alpha)K$$

And for the next bank,

Bank 3 Before further lending

$$\text{Assets:} \quad R_3 = 1 - \alpha^2 K \quad \text{Liabilities:} \quad D_3 = 1 - \alpha^2 K$$

Bank 3 After further lending

$$\text{Assets:} \quad R_3 = \alpha(1-\alpha)^2 K \quad L_3 = (1-\alpha)^3 K \quad \text{Liabilities:} \quad D_3 = (1-\alpha)^2 K$$

and so on and so forth. Let us now add it all up. The total amount of deposits (current accounts) is given by the following equation:

$$D = \sum_{i=1}^{\infty} D_i = D_1 + D_2 + D_3 + \cdots$$

$$= K + (1-\alpha)K + (1-\alpha)^2 K + (1-\alpha)^3 K + \cdots$$

$$= K[1 + (1-\alpha) + (1-\alpha)^2 + (1-\alpha)^3 + \cdots].$$

In the brackets we have a progression of the following kind:

$$1 + q + q^2 + q^3 + \cdots.$$

When $q < 1$, the sum of such a progression is always $1/(1-q)$. In the above progression $q = (1-\alpha)$. As α is always less than 1 (reserve ratio) $(1-\alpha)$ too is always less than 1. Hence,

$$\frac{1}{1 - (1-\alpha)} = \frac{1}{\alpha}$$

hence

$$D = K\frac{1}{\alpha}$$

where $(1/\alpha)$ is what we call **deposit multiplier (DM)**. In our case, $R = K$ and therefore, the total amount of deposits in current accounts is: $D = R(\text{DM})$.

In a similar way we can calculate the amount of loans:

$$L = \sum_{i=1}^{\infty} L_i = L_1 + L_2 + L_3 + \cdots$$

$$= (1-\alpha)K + (1-\alpha)^2 K + (1-\alpha)^3 K + \cdots$$

add as well as subtract K

$$L = K + (1-\alpha)K + (1-\alpha)^2 K + \cdots - K$$

$$= K[1 + (1-\alpha) + (1-\alpha)^2 + (1-\alpha)^3 + \cdots] - K$$

$$= K\frac{1}{\alpha} - K = K(\text{DM} - 1)$$

where DM − 1 is the loans multiplier.

From all that we can now go back to our liquid assets $M1$:

$$M1 = \text{PC} + D = \text{PC} + R(\text{DM}).$$

At first this may seem quite remarkable. If part of what constitutes our liquid assets is the total amount of deposits (D), then the government may make us richer by simply reducing the reserve ratio. When the reserve ratio is smaller, banks may lend more against every unit of the hard currency which they keep in their vaults. Subsequently, the deposit multiplier (DM) increases in the quantity of money ($M1$) increases. However, the mere holding of assets does not make one wealthy. If we think, in a very basic way, of the balance sheet of the public in a world where there are only liquid assets, the following picture will emerge:

Assets	Liabilities
PC	L
D	Net Wealth (NW)

The wealth we have is simply the difference between the value of our assets minus our liabilities. In our case:

$$NW = PC + D - L = PC + R(DM) - R(DM - 1) = PC + R(DM - DM + 1) = PC + R = M0$$

where $M0$ is the money base, the coins and notes in circulation. An increase in $M1$ which is not a result of an increase in the money base will leave the public as well of as before (other things being equal).

■ QUESTION FOR REFLECTION

How will the mere introduction of government bonds influence the wealth of the public?

Although $M0$ is the real wealth in the above framework where there are no other assets in the economy, we consider $M1$ as the supply of money. From now on, whenever we write M we mean $M1$.

11.4 Equilibrium in the liquid assets market

We now have the full picture of the market for liquid assets as shown in Figure 11.1.

The demand for liquid assets is falling with its price. This means that the lower the interest rate is, the lower is the opportunity cost of holding liquid assets. Therefore, more people will want to have liquid assets and, implicitly, increase present consumption (as the price of present consumption had fallen).

The supply of liquid assets is not dependent on the interest rates. It is, however, dependent on the policy of the central bank. Equilibrium here means that at interest rate of r_0, the quantity of liquid assets the public wants to hold equals the quantity of it supplied by

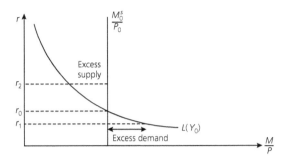

Figure 11.1 Demand and supply for liquid assets.

the banking system.

$$\left(\frac{M}{P}\right)^S = L(r, Y).$$

Implicit in it is an assumption that there is also a balance between demand and supply of present consumption (namely, between borrowers who wish to consume today and lenders who prefer consumption in the future). Demand for present consumption would mean supply of bonds (borrowing money) while supply of present consumption means the demand for bonds by those people who wish to convert their liquid assets into less liquid assets other than goods themselves.

There is a bit of a delicate issue here. When we talk about demand and supply we usually refer to **flows**. That is to say, over a given period there is a demand for so many units of a good and a supply of so many units of a good. When we talk of liquid assets we are talking really about **stocks**. It is not entirely obvious what happens when there is an excess demand or supply for these stocks. To make things simple, let us suppose that behind this market there is some kind of a market for bonds. When there is excess demand for liquid asset (at interest r_1), it means that people want to hold more liquid assets than they have. What they can do is go to the bond market and sell some of their bonds. In that market—which is at least well-defined—there will now be excess supply of bonds. This, in turn, will bring down the price of bonds.

Recall from Chapter 9 that the present value of any bond is inversely related to the interest rates. Normally, the present value would be the reservation price for someone to buy a bond. If you have to pay someone more than is needed to get the same returns through the banks, you would not want to buy the bond. The seller, of course, would not want the price to be any lower. So as a crude measure we may say that in competition the price of the bond would be directly related to its present value. Hence, a fall in the price of the bond means a fall in its present value. The only thing which would be common to all bonds is the interest rate (in the denominator). Thus, a fall in price means an increase in interest rates. So this is the mechanism which will raise the interest rate from its current level r_1 to its new level r_0.

Alternatively, when the interest rate is above r_0 at r_2, there is excess supply of liquid assets. In this case, people would want to convert some of their liquid assets into something less liquid (like bonds). Hence, they will want to buy bonds. As the demand for bonds increases, there will be excess demand for them which, in turn, will raise their price. To increase the present value of all bonds, interest rates will have to fall. This, as it were, is the mechanism behind the adjustment of interest rates in the liquid assets market.

Central banks

In every economy there is now a central bank. The role of the bank is to be the banker for the government as well as for the commercial banks. As such, the central bank may hold the reserves for commercial banks and control their activities through, for instance, the setting of reserve ratios. In addition, the bank serves the government. Among other things, the government may borrow money from the central bank. This is the case when the bank will be printing money. However, whether or not the central bank prints money depends on its independence and commitment to 'backed' money.

In the past, many currencies were based on the gold standard. This meant that a central bank was committed to give gold in return for paper notes. As a result, the bank would not issue too many notes so that at one stage, it may not be able to pay the gold which it is committed to pay to those who may demand it. Nevertheless, the bank issued more notes that it had gold on the presumption that not everyone would come to redeem their claim at once.

During the period between the two world wars, all countries have abandoned the gold standard and money is still used due to its universal acceptability. It is so simply because the government declared such a currency as legal tender (this is referred to, sometimes, as **fiat money**). The role of the central bank is not only important as a regulator of the banking system but also as a source of credibility in the market. The trust which people have in the government may vary according to the their political beliefs and, of course, the degree of their cynicism. When the government promises to act in a particular way, you may have guesses with regard to how this may influence the market. You are likely to act now if you think that this will be harmful for you. Suppose that the public believes that inflation is due to a rise in the quantity of money. Suppose also that this is due to government spending which is funded by borrowing from the central bank. When people expect increases in prices they will go out and buy at once that which they may need much later. This, of course, will help the prophesy come true as the excess demand will increase prices. If the government promised to cut its spending and stop all printing of money, the public should respond by sticking to their original plans and not to raid the shop whenever money becomes available. This, of course, may happen only if they believe the government. If they do not believe the government, they may still go out and buy now and, thus, maintain the rises in prices. If, however, the public knew that the central bank is not the same as the government; namely that it is an independent professional institution they may take the commitment of the bank not to lend money to the government more seriously even if they do not trust the government.

In the aftermath of the First World War, new national states emerged as a result of the Versailles treaty of 1919. Countries like Austria, Hungary, Germany, and Poland experienced dramatic hyperinflations. The interesting things about these hyperinflation is that the winding down process was relatively quick.

A possible reason why hyperinflations started was simple enough. Austria and Hungary became small states after a long history of a very large empire. Poland was new also and Germany (as well as Austria) had a huge reparation bill imposed on it by the Versailles treaty. All of these countries lay in ruins after the long war and the governments found it difficult to raise taxes at a time when there was a need for government actions. As a result, these economies printed money (i.e. borrowed from the central bank) and hyperinflation ensued.

In most cases the hyperinflation seemed to subside within a few months of the setting up of an *independent* central bank which was not allowed to lend money to the government except under very clear rules. This could lead to two interpretations. First, it could suggest that the independence of the central bank could be a crucial factor when monetary policy is concerned. Second, it could be used to argue that people do not follow in their expectation only that which happened before but they can form expectations which are based on logical structures (in this case, that when the printing ends, so would inflation). These are, of course, important issues but we again, this is not the right level to explore them in more details.

Monetary policy

If, for instance, the government pursues an **expansionary monetary policy**, this will cause the supply of liquid assets to increase. In a closed economy this can either happen through a change in the reserve ratio or through the government's borrowing from the central bank (Figure 11.2).

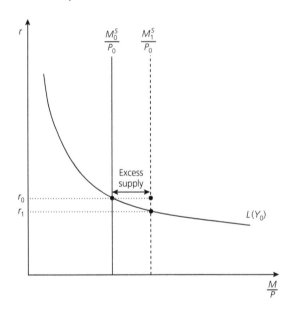

Figure 11.2 Increasing the money supply.

The effect of an increase in M will be a shift to the right of the supply of liquid assets (M/P). When this happens, at the initial level of interest rate (r_0) there is now excess supply of liquid assets. People will wish to convert the excess liquidity they have into less-liquid assets such as, for instance, bonds. Recall from our discussion in Chapter 10 that the price of bonds (their present value) is inversely related to interest rates. When people wish to buy bonds (less liquid assets) it means that there will be excess demand for bonds. Put differently, the demand for future consumption exceeds its supply. Some of those people who want to lend money will not find a borrower. The only way borrowers will be found is a fall in interest rates (which, in turn, increases the price of bonds). Hence, the new equilibrium will be obtained at a lower interest rate (r_1).

11.5 Deriving the liquid assets model

Note that in the liquid assets market (LM), interest rate is determined for any given level of output (Y). In Chapter 10, we discussed the goods market and established that in equilibrium, the level of output is determined for any given level of interest. Evidently, interest rates and output are closely related and influence one another. It is, therefore, useful to try and examine the equilibrium relationship between interest rate and output. We call this presentation of the liquid assets model: the LM curve in Figure 11.3.

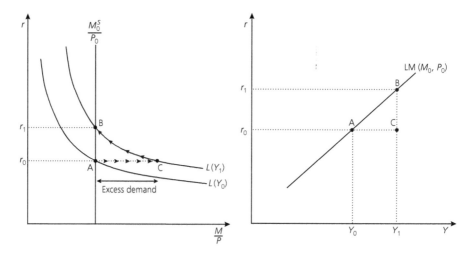

Figure 11.3 Deriving the *LM* curve: liquid asset markets and a change in income.

We begin at point A in the above diagram. We saw that when national income is at Y_0, equilibrium level of interest will be r_0. If we raised the level of output to Y_1, the demand for liquid assets will increase. At point C, in Figure 11.3 we notice that there is excess demand for liquid assets. This means that some people will want to sell their bonds and convert them into cash. Excess supply of bonds will mean that people will need to find lenders. The way to do so is to increase interest rates (the return for the lender) and reduce the price of the bonds. Subsequently, equilibrium interest rate will rise to r_1 (point B in the above diagrams). This means that there is a direct relationship between levels of national income and interest rates for which there is equilibrium in the liquid assets market. Connecting points A and B produce for us the LM curve which depicts these equilibrium relationship. To the right of the LM (points like C) we have excess demand for liquid assets. To the left, by symmetry, we will have excess supply of liquid assets.

Self-assessment and applications

▨ QUESTION 1

Analyse the effects on equilibrium level of interest rate of an increase in the public's tendency to keep a greater share of their liquid assets in the bank.

Answer

What we consider in this framework as liquid assets is, of course, $M1$ which is the total amount of coins and notes in circulation + current accounts. In terms of our notation, $M = PC + D$ where $D = R(1/\alpha)$ where α is the reserve ratio. A shift of £K from PC (public cash) to the bank will have the following effect: $dM = dPC + dD = -dK + dK(1/\alpha) = dK((1/\alpha) - 1) > 0$. In simple terms, a £1 which has been transferred from the pocket to the bank will reduce our liquid asset by a £1 but will allow the bank to lend the difference between it and what is required to remain in the bank (reserve ratio). Given the deposit multiplier effect, the total amount of liquid assets available to the public would have increased. This, in turn, means a shift to the right of the supply of liquid assets, see Figure 11.4.

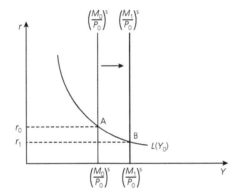

Figure 11.4

As the supply of liquid assets increases, there is now excess supply of liquid assets at the present interest rate. It means that people hold too much of their assets in a liquid form. To move away from the liquid form, people will want to buy, say, bonds. There will therefore be excess demand for bonds and the equilibrium price of bonds will rise. As the price of bonds is inversely related to the interest rate (as the price of bonds corresponds to their present value), it means that interest rate will have to fall to the new level at B.

How will this affect the LM? see Figure 11.5.

For the same level of income there will now be equilibrium at a lower level of interest. The LM would therefore shift downwards.

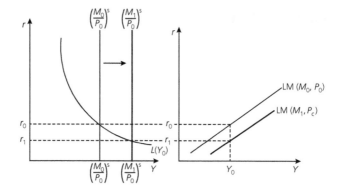

Figure 11.5

▨ QUESTION 2

The total value of loans in an economy is £400 bn and the reserve ratio is 20%. An increase of £50 bn in the money which the public keeps in commercial banks together with an increase of the reserve ratio to 25% will increase the total amount of loans only by £50 bn. True or false? Explain.

Answer

True. We know that $L = K(1 - DM)$. Initially, the deposit multiplier was 5, the loan multiplier is, therefore, 4. As $L = 400$, K must be 100. Now K has been increased to 150. The higher reserve ratio (25%) means a deposit multiplier of 4 and a loan multiplier of 3. Thus, the new $L = 150 \times 3 = 450$. This is an increase of 50 in the total provision of loans.

▨ QUESTION 3

An increase in prices will raise the equilibrium interest rate in the liquid asset market. This, in turn, will shift the LM upwards. True or false? Explain.

Answer

There are two parts to the question which are not, obviously, unrelated. Let us begin with the first part. Here is the equilibrium in the liquid asset market, shown in Figure 11.6.

An increase in prices will reduce the availability of real balances. The supply of (M/P) is decreasing and it shifts to the left in the above diagram. This means that at the existing interest rate there will now be excess demand for liquid assets. In other words, the same quantity of money could buy much less now when prices are higher so individuals may want to hold more (this is the excess demand at the going price-interest rate). Therefore, people will want to sell bonds and get money in return. As we saw earlier, the price of bonds is always inversely related to the interest rate. The present value of a, say, £1 consol bond is $1/r$. Would you be willing to pay more than this to buy such a bond? Would the seller be willing to sell at less than $1/r$? Therefore, in a competitive

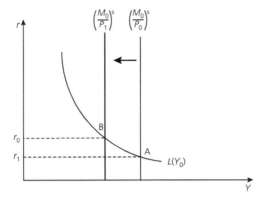

Figure 11.6

world (leaving out all the complexities of the stock market), the price of such a bond would be $1/r$. So when there is excess supply of bonds, the price of bonds would fall and this can only happen through an increase in r. This is the mechanism behind this liquid assets market. We therefore move from A to B.

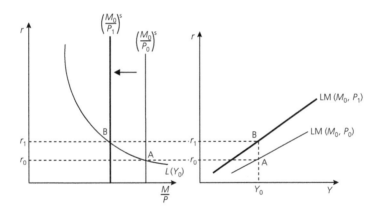

Figure 11.7

In terms of the LM, see Figure 11.7: For any given level of national income there is a demand for liquid assets which is drawn in the previous diagram. This means that as income has not changed, the demand for liquid assets remains in its position in the $(\frac{M}{P}, r)$ plane. Therefore, for any level of Y there will now be an equilibrium at a higher interest rate. This is clearly a shift upwards of the LM schedule.

NOTES

1. The reference here is to a new collection of Hume's essays, entitled, '*Essay: Moral, Political and Literary*', edited by E. Miller, Liberty Press, 1987.
2. We shall ignore here the broader issues of wealth.

12 General equilibrium, employment, and government policy

■ MAJOR POINTS IN SUMMARY

- The complete model: income determination for a given interest rate; interest rate determination for a given income
- The existence of equilibrium and the IS-LM model
- Monetary and fiscal policies in a closed economy.

12.1 The macroeconomic notion of general equilibrium

In Chapters 10 and 11, we have identified two variables which are dependent on each other but are determined in different markets. The first was the level of national income (or output) (Y) which we analysed in the context of the goods market. Notwithstanding the difficulties with the notion of the aggregate goods market which we have discussed in Chapter 9, once we construct such a market we may as well expect output to be determined in that market. However, one of the determinants of equilibrium in the goods market is the demand for investment which, in turn, depends on the willingness of individuals to provide funds for present consumption at the expense of future consumption. This, as we have established, is a function of the interest rate which is really the price of present consumption. In simpler terms, demand for investment is a function of people's willingness to borrow. This, naturally, depends on the interest rate which will determine the cost of such borrowing. We have described in details the equilibrium in such a market in Chapter 10.

The second variable, therefore, is the interest rate. As the interest rate is the price of present consumption it reflects people's wish to hold different sorts of assets at any point in time. With high interest rate, the price of present consumption is great, as on every pound we use to purchase goods today we forgo $(1 + r)$ (with a large r) in the next period. Therefore, the opportunity cost of holding assets in a liquid form to facilitate the purchase of goods, or to 'oil the wheels of commerce', is high. We would rather not hold liquid assets. Hence, it is in the market for liquid assets where interest rate is being determined. But the demand for liquid assets, as we have established, is also a function of the level of national income. The more we produce at any point of time, the more transactions will be required to facilitate it. Hence, the higher is national income, the more liquid assets we would like to hold. The details of the equilibrium in the liquid assets market have been studied in Chapter 11.

So we have two markets: in the goods market Y is determined for any given level of r while in the liquid assets market, r is determined for any level of Y. How, then, do the equilibrium values of Y relate to the equilibrium values of r?

We can now examine the complete model as shown in Figure 12.1.

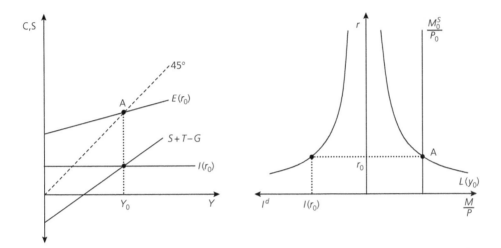

Figure 12.1 Equilibrium in the goods and asset markets.

We can see that at point A in both diagrams there is equilibrium. This means that at interest rate of r_0 there will be equilibrium at Y_0 in the goods market. In the liquid assets market, at Y_0 the demand for liquid assets will be such that given the supply of liquid assets, equilibrium will occur when interest rate is at r_0.

I have added an auxiliary tool of analysis by drawing the demand for investment as a function of interest rates on the left-hand side of the right-hand diagram. The values on the horizontal axis are taken in absolute terms such that at r_0 the demand for investment (which, in turn, constitute part of the autonomous component of the aggregate expenditures function AE) is $I(r_0)$.

The first question we must ask ourselves is whether there exists a simultaneous solution to the equilibrium problem in both markets. It is true that in the above drawing there is such an equilibrium but, if you think about it, it is not intuitively obvious. After all, an increase in output (Y) will cause an increase in r which, in turn, will cause a fall in output (Y) as demand for investment falls. But then, as Y falls, demand for liquid assets will fall too and, subsequently, interest rate will fall and Y will rise ... HELP!

Well, the truth of the matter is that it is very simple to establish that there exists a pair (Y, r) for which both markets will be in equilibrium. The immediate way to see it is by looking at the equations which we have to solve. Equilibrium, in each of these markets is represented by the equation

$$E(Y, r) = Y \quad \text{for the goods market}$$

$$(M/P)^S = L(r, Y). \quad \text{for the liquid assets market.}$$

Hence, we have two equations and two unknown (Y, r). Mathematics tells us that there is a **unique** solution to this problem. At the same time, it also tells us that r and Y, the **endogenous variables** do not determine each other but the two of them are determined by all other variables which are **exogenous** to the model. That is to say, it is not the interest rate which determines the national income in the goods market and it is not national income which determines interest rates in the liquid assets market. Instead, both Y and r are determined by the values we know before we solve the problem. I will demonstrate this point below but if you feel that this is too difficult, you may skip the next section.

When we discussed general equilibrium in microeconomics we said that it is a situation where all rational wants coincide. Can we extend the same notion to the aggregate markets for goods and liquid assets? On the one hand, it is difficult to talk about the rational wants of the government or the rational wants of corporations (in their decision to distribute their profits) without properly studying these institutions. On the other hand, we said that when the goods market is in equilibrium, the demand for consumption is met, the demand for public spending is met, and the demand for investment. However, the fact that demand is met is not necessarily a proof that it is a coincidence of rational wants. There was no clear rational structure behind our demand for consumption other than a general intuition that people would want to consume more the more income they have. So, while we definitely have general equilibrium in the sense that demand and supply are balanced, we cannot really extrapolate from it to assume that like microeconomics, this means that all rational wants coincide. Naturally, if we attach a micro general equilibrium to the macro general equilibrium we may attribute the coincidence of wants to the macro general equilibrium; but, as you have noticed before, in some general equilibria in macroeconomics (the Keynesian ones), not all markets clear.

Recently, there have been attempts to pour more content to the nature of the macro equilibrium through the development of behavioural patterns of a representative agent for whom our aggregate demand functions constitute rational behaviour. However, does it make much sense to apply ideas of rationality to a representative agent who makes decision about aggregates? Have we not abstracted too far?

Whatever is the meaning of the macro general equilibrium, it would be useful to remember this distinction, as to prevent you from searching for the intuition behind some of the outcomes in the wrong place. Yet, if you feel that you have not fully grasped it, there is no need to dwell on it for too long, at this stage of your study.

12.2 The algebra of macroeconomics general equilibrium

Recall that in the basic Keynesian model, equilibrium was depicted by the following equation:

$$E(Y,r) = C(Y,T) + I(r) + G = Y$$

and in a more explicit form, the expenditure function will have the following structure:

$$E(Y,r) = c_0 - c_1 T_0 + c_1 Y + I_0 - I_1 r + G_0$$
$$= [c_0 - c_1 T_0 + G_0 + I_0 - I_1 r] + c_1 Y$$

in equilibrium,

$$A(G_0, T_0) - I_1 r + c_1 Y = Y$$

where A contains the two variables pertaining to *fiscal policy*.

Suppose too, that the liquid assets market has a simple linear demand function for liquid assets of the following nature:

$$L(r, Y) = aY - br$$

where a and b are coefficients representing the strength of influence which a change in both variables will have on the quantity demanded of liquid assets. Note that the equation holds the basic properties of the demand for liquid assets as an increase in Y will increase demand for liquid assets while an increase in interest rate (the price of present consumption) will reduce the demand for liquid assets.

Hence, the equilibrium condition in the assets markets will be

$$(M/P)^s = aY - br.$$

Considering the equilibrium conditions in both market together while isolating Y we get, goods market:

$$Y = \frac{A(G_0, T_0) - I_1 r}{(1 - c_1)}$$

liquid assets market:

$$Y = \frac{M}{P}\frac{1}{a} + \frac{b}{a}r.$$

Equating Y will allow us to isolate r:

$$\frac{A(G_0, T_0) - I_1 r}{(1 - c_1)} = \frac{M}{P}\frac{1}{a} + \frac{b}{a}r$$

$$A(G_0, T_0)\frac{1}{(1 - c_1)} - \frac{M}{P}\frac{1}{a} = \frac{b}{a}r + \frac{I_1}{(1 - c_1)}r$$

$$A(G_0, T_0)\frac{1}{(1 - c_1)} - \frac{M}{p}\frac{1}{a} = r\left[\frac{b}{a} + \frac{I_1}{(1 - c_1)}\right].$$

Let the expression within square brackets on the right-hand side be called γ so we get:

$$\gamma = \left[\frac{b}{a} + \frac{I_1}{1 - c_1} \right].$$

Then,

$$A(G_0, T_0) \frac{1}{(1 - c_1)\gamma} - \frac{M}{P} \frac{1}{a\gamma} = r.$$

Note that the value of r is not determined by Y. It is dependent on the fiscal policy parameters (G and T) as well as the monetary policy parameter M. In addition, it depends on behavioural parameters like the marginal propensity to consume, the sensitivities of the demand for investment to changes in income and interest rates and the price level.

To find the value of Y it is sufficient to place r back into one of the equilibrium equations from above.

liquid assets market:

$$Y = \frac{M}{P} \frac{1}{a} + \frac{b}{a} r = \frac{M}{P} \frac{1}{a} + \frac{b}{a} \left[A(G_0, T_0) \frac{1}{(1 - c_1)\gamma} - \frac{M}{P} \frac{1}{a\gamma} \right]$$

which means that the value of Y, also, is not dependent on r.

Nevertheless, we must not confuse the fact that the general equilibrium values of Y and r are determined by the exogenous factors with the idea that there exists a certain relationship between the equilibrium values of Y and r. If, for instance, there is an increase in A, clearly, the values of both Y and r will increase (if $\gamma > 0$).

12.3 The geometry of general equilibrium: IS–LM

A simpler way of studying the equilibrium relationship between the equilibrium values of the goods market (Y) and the liquid assets market (r) is through the study of the IS–LM framework. Recall from the previous chapters that the IS curve described the relationship between interest rates and the equilibrium values of the goods market (Y) while the LM curve described the relationship between levels of income and the equilibrium values of interest rate (r). Here they are together as in Figure 12.2. Point A, in Figure 12.1 corresponds to the two points A in the figure at the beginning of Section 12.1. Instead of a complex diagram we have a simple representation of the values of Y and r for which there is equilibrium in both markets. As all the points on the IS curve depict values of Y and r for which there is equilibrium in the goods market while the LM curve depicts all the values of Y and r for which there is equilibrium in the liquid assets market; only when the two curves intersect, will there be equilibrium in both markets. The fact that the IS curve is downward sloping while the LM curve is upward sloping suggests, as we said before, that there will be only one pair of Y and r for which there is equilibrium in both markets.

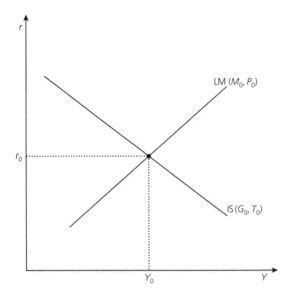

Figure 12.2 General equilibrium using IS–LM analysis.

12.4 Some comparative statics

To see how the system works let us examine a few changes in circumstances using both the basic model and its IS-LM representation. I propose that you should first try and analyse each change yourself. Once you have done it, you may read the corresponding analysis.

12.4.1 Expansionary fiscal policy

When the government decides to increase its spending, it may choose one of the following methods to finance (in real terms) the additional activities:

(a) Raising taxes.

(b) Borrowing from the public.

(c) Borrowing from the central bank.

We shall consider these in turn.

Tax financing

The problem we wish to consider here is an increase in government spending which is financed through an increase in taxation as in (a). Please think about this problem yourself before you read on.

We begin by setting the framework of analysis. The original model is shown in Figure 12.3. An increase in government spending means an increase in G. Recall that

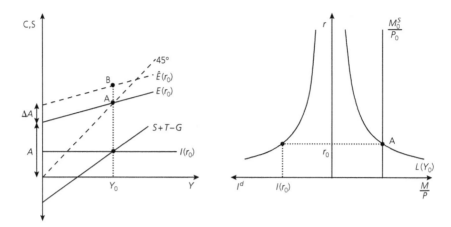

Figure 12.3 An increase in government spending financed through taxes: the initial impact.

the aggregate expenditure function has the following character:

$$E(Y,r) = c_0 - c_1 T_0 + c_1 Y + I(r_0) + G_0$$
$$= [c_0 - c_1 T_0 + G_0 + I_0 - I_1 r] + c_1 Y$$

where the expression in the brackets is the autonomous component:

$$A(G_0, T_0, r_0) = [c_0 - c_1 T_0 + G_0 + I_0 - I_1 r].$$

Therefore, an increase in G from G_0 to G_1 (sometimes we denote the increase in government's spending as $\Delta G > 0$ which, in our case, means $\Delta G = G_1 - G_0 > 0$) will cause an increase in the autonomous component A

$$\Delta A = A(G_1, T_0, r_0) - A(G_0, T_0, r_0)$$
$$= [c_0 - c_1 T_0 + G_1 + I_0 - I_1 r] - [c_0 - c_1 T_0 + G_0 + I_0 - I_1 r]$$
$$= G_1 - G_0 = \Delta G.$$

However, as the government chose to finance the increase in spending via increased taxation, the effect on A will not be as great as ΔG. In the examples which we have set, there is a lump sum tax system. Hence, an increase in taxation means $\Delta T > 0$. Altogether, the impact of the increased spending with the increased taxation will be as follows:

$$\Delta A = A(G_1, T_1, r_0) - A(G_0, T_0, r_0)$$
$$= [c_0 - c_1 T_1 + G_1 + I_0 - I_1 r] - [c_0 - c_1 T_0 + G_0 + I_0 - I_1 r]$$
$$= (G_1 - c_1 T_1) - (G_0 - c_1 T_0)$$
$$= G_1 - G_0 - c_1(T_1 - T_0) = \Delta G - c_1 \Delta T.$$

Whether the increase in government spending which is funded by an increase in taxation will cause an increase or decrease in the aggregate demand for expenditures depends on whether $\Delta G - c_1 \Delta T > 0$. You can clearly see that merely raising the tax to cover the increase in government spending will have an effect on aggregate demand. When $\Delta G = \Delta T$, $\Delta G - c_1 \Delta T = \Delta G(1 - c_1) > 0$. The reason for this, as was discussed in

Chapter 10, is that a transfer of one pound from the public to the government will reduce the demand for consumption by the marginal propensity to consume, while raising the demand for goods and services by the government by a whole pound. Put differently, as the marginal propensity of the government to spend is greater than that of consumers, the transfer of income from the public to the government will raise total demand.

As long as $A(G_1, T_1, r_0) > A(G_0, T_0, r_0)$ we say that the government pursued an **expansionary fiscal policy**. By implication, the mere increase in government spending does not mean an expansionary fiscal policy. Whether such a change amounts to an expansionary or contracting fiscal policy depends on the means by which the government proposes to finance the increase. If the government raised more taxes, it proposes to fund the increase by redirecting resources from consumption to government spending. However, whether the increase will be fully funded by consumption depends on whether the fall in consumption exceeds the increase in government spending.

Suppose that the increase in both G and T was such as to generate an increase in A. This means, in Figure 12.3, a move upwards of the E function. In other words, this means that with an expansionary fiscal policy there will be a greater demand for goods and services (i.e. Y) at any level of interest. In particular, there will be a greater demand for Y at Y_0 and there is now excess demand for goods and services (point B in the figure).

Note that so far there had been no change in the liquid assets market as neither income nor prices nor the supply of money have changed. As a gap develops at point B in the goods market, what exactly will happen depends on the appropriate mechanism of adjustment.

The classical view
According to the classical view, which is derived from Say's law (see Chapter 9), the only mechanism of adjustment will be via prices. This is a manifestation of the view according to which, the level of output is determined by the circumstances of industry and not by demand. This means that the excess demand at point B will cause the price level to increase. When this happens Figure 12.4 will ensue. An increase in prices will reduce the supply of real balances. The same quantity of money (liquid assets)

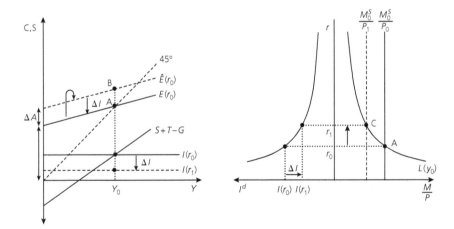

Figure 12.4 Excess demand in the classical view.

commands less goods and services than before. This means that although the quantity of M is unchanged, the supply of liquid assets is much reduced (the $(M/P)^s$ will shift to the left). At A (in the liquid assets market) there is now excess demand for liquid assets. People will sell bonds and there will be excess supply of bonds. To ensure that you succeed in selling your bond, you will be willing to reduce its price. The only way to do so is by raising the interest rate. Raising interest rates makes present consumption more expensive and people will want to buy bonds to facilitate more future consumption.

The increase in interest rate will restore equilibrium in the liquid assets market (point C in the right-hand diagram) but with it, will bring a fall in demand for investment. This, in turn, will reduce the aggregate demand for goods and the E curve will shift back to its original position.

The consequence of the expansionary policy would be that the output remains unchanged while prices, including interest rates, are higher and investment is lower. As the same output must be used to provide for greater demand for public spending, this will now come at the expense of consumption (that part of G which had been covered by the increase in taxation) + a **crowding out** of investment to finance (in real terms) the residual of the increase in government spending which had not been covered by the fall in consumption. We can see from this why the classical economists feel that demand management is not effective in bringing about a real change (i.e. a change in output). Nevertheless, note that a fall in investment may have long term implications as there will be a much smaller increase (depending on depreciation rates) in the stock of capital than would have been had the government refrained from increasing its spending.

The Keynesian view

According to this view, the mechanism of adjustment is more likely to be that of **quantity adjustments** if the economy is in equilibrium with unemployment. This is not to preclude all possible increases in prices but, in general, when there is excess demand orders for goods and services are bound to increase. To make the analysis simple we shall assume no change in prices whatsoever and we shall concentrate on the implications of quantity adjustment.

The initial impact of a simultaneous increase in G and T is very much the same as before. So we are now at point B in the goods market where there is excess demand for goods and services at the level of Y_0 as seen in Figure 12.5. The response to the excess demand for goods will be an increase in orders which, in turn, will cause the output to increase. As the output begins to rise, the demand for liquid assets will increase too. As this happens there is, at the initial interest rate (r_0), excess demand for liquid assets. As in the previous story, interest rates will now rise and, subsequently, demand for investment will fall. This, in turn, reduces the demand for goods and services and pushes AE downward. In the end, equilibrium will be obtained at point C where we have a higher rate of interest together with a higher level of output. The meaning of this is that although there had been an increase in output, it was not sufficient to fully compensate for the residual in the demand for public spending (G) over and above the tax in terms of consumption. Therefore, some investment will have to be reallocated for the purpose of public spending. The outcome of

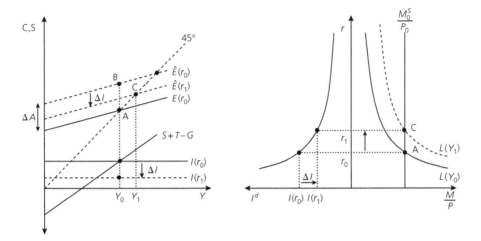

Figure 12.5 Excess demand in the Keynesian view.

this expansionary policy was successful, in the sense that demand management increased output. However, its effect on investment is still negative.

A view from IS–LM

So far, both stories had been told in a slightly complex framework where we had to examine the consequences of each change on two diagrams. By using the IS–LM framework, it all becomes distinctly easier. Recall that initially we have the following situation as shown in Figure 12.6. The IS, which describes equilibrium conditions in the goods market, is

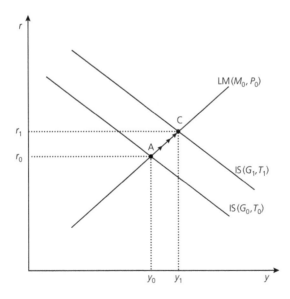

Figure 12.6 Expansionary policy in the IS–LM framework.

downward sloping as every fall in interest rate will increase demand for investment which will require a greater output for equilibrium to be restored. The LM, on the other hand, is upward sloping as every increase in income will cause an increase in demand for liquid assets which will require a higher interest for equilibrium to be restored.

We start at point A. An expansionary fiscal policy means an increase in G or a fall in T (the parameters of the IS curve). In our case, there was an increase in G which was accompanied by an increase in T. Yet, the increase in T was not sufficient to offset (via a fall in consumption) the increase in demand for public spending. Therefore, at each level of output, the demand for goods and services is now greater. In terms of the IS, this means that at any level of interest rate (remember that this is an exogenous variable in the goods market) equilibrium can only be obtained at a higher level of output, namely, a shift to the right of the IS. As the only change was in the parameters of the goods market (the IS), the LM is unaffected.

The Keynesian view. In terms of quantity adjustment, this is the end of the story. The new equilibrium will be at point C which is the new intersection of the new IS and the LM. What is the story about how we get from A to C? Very much the same as the one we told before. In response to the increase in aggregate demand (an increase in government's demand), there will be a quantity adjustment and sellers will increase their orders. This, in turn, will cause an increase in output and, subsequently, in income, which will further feed the increase in aggregate demand through the increase in demand for consumption. At the same time, however, as income increases there is an increase in the demand for liquid assets. This will cause an excess demand for liquid assets which means an excess supply of bonds. The price of bonds will fall through the increase in interest rate. This, in turn, will tame the increases in aggregate demand as the demand for investment will fall. This is, indeed, a complex story but both changes are depicted easily in the above diagram. The properties of our model (i.e. the various marginal propensities and elasticities) ensure that, in the end, this story converges to point C. We can clearly see that the effect of the expansionary fiscal policy will be to raise both output and interest rates. As we know from our earlier discussion that in equilibrium planned investment equals actual investment, we may conclude that if investment is independent of income, investment will fall. The increase in national income has been used both to feed the extra demand for consumption as well as demand for public expenditure.

The classical view. As the adjustment mechanism suggests an increase in price, there will be a change in one of the parameters of the LM function (Figure 12.7). The IS curve shifts to the right for the same reasons as before. However, as prices increase, this means a fall in the supply of liquid assets. Therefore, for any level of output equilibrium will be reached at a higher level of income (check this on the original liquid assets market). Here, this would mean a shift upwards of the LM schedule. This means that we move from point A to point C which is the new intersection between the new IS and the new LM. Again, it is imperative that you learn to rehearse the story behind these diagrams. In this case, we begin at A and the increase in government spending causes excess demand for

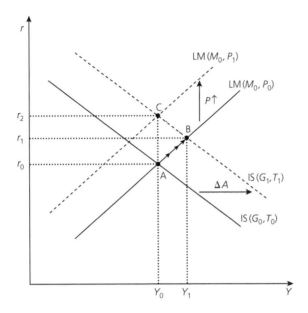

Figure 12.7 IS–LM with an expansionary fiscal policy under the classical view.

goods. Here, we can have some kind of compromise between the different schools; in the sense that even from the classical approach people would accept that it is possible that at first, there will be some quantity adjustment. Namely, the response to the excess demand for goods would come initially from reduced stocks and new orders. Naturally, as output increases so do income and the demand for consumption. However, at the same time the demand for liquid assets will increase. People will sell bonds and cause a fall in bonds' price through an increase in the interest rate. In turn, this will offset some of the increases in demand as demand for investment will fall. We slowly move from A to B. When we get to B, according to the classical school, the economy cannot sustain this overproduction for long. The reason why this was possible at first, they would argue, is simply through the utilization of overtime and part-time workers. But this is only a temporary measure, in the long run, the extra demand would not be satisfied by an increase in output. This will cause the other mechanism of adjustment to kick in. Prices will begin to rise and this will cause the supply of real balances to fall. As it happens, there is excess demand for liquid assets and people will want to sell more bonds. This again will cause interest rates to rise and demand to fall further back due to fall in demand for investment until we reach point C.

Thus, the outcome of the policy had been no change in output but full **crowding out** of investment for the purpose of public consumption. Note that the rise in interest rate in the classical story is much greater than it was in the Keynesian one. According to the Keynesian story the end would have been at point B (with r_1 as the interest rate). According to the classical story, we would end up at point C with $r_2 > r_1$. The fall in investment, in our model, will be greater the higher will be the interest rate.

Internal debt financing

Recall that the initial change which we consider is that where the government wishes to increase its spending (a rise in G). In the previous section we analysed the effects of such a policy when the main source of financing (in real terms, that is, the transfer of resources from one use to another) came from consumption (tax financing). In the case where the government chooses to finance the increase in its expenditure by borrowing from the public, this form of financing will have no real effect on the current demand for goods and services. The aggregate demand for goods and services is comprised of demand for consumption, public spending, and investment. When the government does not levy taxes, it will have no impact on the demand for consumption. From the public's point of view the presence of government bonds (which is how the government borrows from the public) simply means an alternative form of savings but as far as the model goes, there had been no change in any of the parameters which influences the decisions by the public regarding the level of consumption (and subsequently, the level of savings). Therefore, the effect of an increase in government spending on aggregate demand will be:

$$\triangle A = A(G_1, T_0, r_0) - A(G_0, T_0, r_0)$$

$$= [c_0 - c_1 T_0 + G_1 + I_0 - I_1 r] - [c_0 - c_1 T_0 + G_0 + I_0 - I_1 r]$$

$$= G_1 - G_0 = \triangle G.$$

Although the increase in aggregate expenditures will now be greater than in the case where the same increase in government spending was financed by taxes (which reduced consumption), the overall implications are very much the same. The only difference between the two cases will be in the magnitude. With debt financing the expansionary effect of government policy is much greater. Hence, in the classical case this will mean a much greater increase in interest rates and a greater crowding out of investment in favour of public consumption. In the Keynesian story, there will be a greater increase in output and a correspondingly greater increase in interest rate. In the diagram below we compare the effect of the same increase in G when financed by taxation and when financed by borrowing (Figure 12.8).

The move from A to B and B′ represents the Keynesian interpretation when there is tax financing and debt financing, respectively. The move to C and C″ represents the classical story in the corresponding tax and debt financing.

The fact of the matter is that debt financing is a much more complex problem than appears from the above. For one, there is the problem of the long-term effect of debt financing. When the government sells bonds, it will need to service the debt in the future. Equally, some of you may have wondered whether the sale of government bonds should not influence the demand for liquid assets as it may influence the price of bonds (and hence, interest rate). There is, evidently, a lot more to be said about debt financing. However, at this stage we have to confine ourselves to the basics. We do not consider the future effects of the policy and we do not consider how such effects may influence the current behaviour of agents. When we told the story of the bonds market, we used it to make sense of the market for liquid assets and not the other way round. We have not proposed an analysis of complex notions of assets and we should therefore confine ourselves to those things which we have clearly defined. We said that the demand for

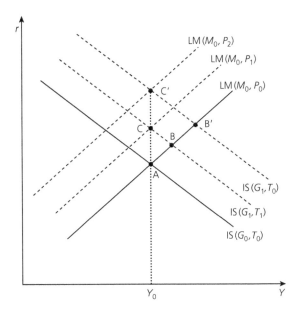

Figure 12.8 A debt-financed increase in government expenditure.

liquid assets is a function of the price of present consumption (interest rates) and income and that interest rates are determined by the equilibrium condition in the market for liquid assets. The way we formulated the problem means that selling government bonds to the public will have no real effect of its own on the system.

Nevertheless, there is one thing which is quite clear about the difference between tax financing and borrowing from the public. The former funds public spending mainly from consumption, while the latter funds it mainly by redirecting resources away from investment. As investment is detrimental to our ability to increase the stock of means of production which facilitates growth, one can say that, in tax financing we pay immediately, while, by lending money to the government, we postpone the payment.

Borrowing from the central bank (printing money)

The last option to finance the increase in government expenditure is through borrowing from the central bank. As we noted in Chapter 11, the central bank is the banker of the government. When the government asks the bank for a loan, the bank provides the government with money which will be 'new' in the economy. Put differently, the increase in government spending means that the government needs money with which to pay suppliers of goods and services. When this money comes from the central bank it means an increase in the quantity of money which circulates in the economy. Naturally, the bank can act to reduce the supply of money by other means, but we do not consider this case now.

Therefore, when the government increases its spending while borrowing from the central bank, Figure 12.9 results. The increase in G will shift the aggregate demand for goods and services up. This means that at any level of income the total demand for goods

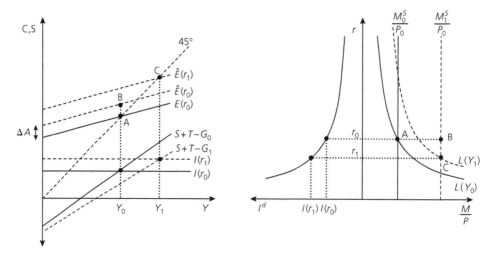

Figure 12.9 Increased government expenditure, financed by an increase in the money supply.

and services is now greater than it used to be. At the same time, the supply of liquid assets will increase by the money which had been passed on from the central bank to the government and from the government into the economy. The two simultaneous moves are denoted by the moves from A to B. We now have excess demand for goods and services and excess supply of liquid assets. What we have here is a combined **fiscal and monetary expansion**.

The Keynesian view

According to the Keynesian view, there will now be an increase in output to fill the gap in the goods market. At the same time, excess supply of liquid assets means that people will want to buy bonds (future consumption), and as they compete for them the price of bonds will rise through the fall in the price of current consumption (i.e. a fall in interest rate). This, in turn, will trigger an increase in the demand for investment, which will push the aggregate expenditure function further up. However, as income begins to grow to satisfy the excess demand for goods and services, demand for liquid assets will increase, also. As this happens, the demand for investment will fall back and the pressure on domestic product will be reduced. The final outcome (point C in the above figure) will definitely mean an increase in output but what will happen to interest rates remains unclear.

The Classical view

As adjustments come mainly through price changed, the effect of the double-push to aggregate demand, by G and I, will result in a large increase in prices. At first we move from A to B which contains the combined effects of ΔG and the initial ΔI which resulted from the increase in money supply (Figure 12.10). However, as price begin to rise, the supply of real balances will fall and interest rates will rise until investment falls sufficiently to completely offset the increase in demand due to the increase in government spending. We end up with another case of full crowding out.

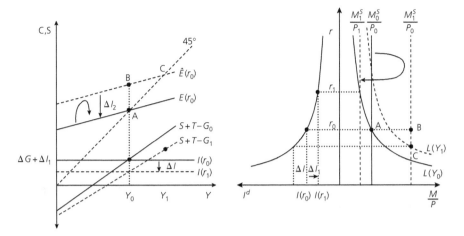

Figure 12.10 Increased government expenditure, financed by an increase in the money supply: the classical view.

View from IS–LM

Again, as before, this whole story is easily told by simply using the IS–LM (Figure 12.11).

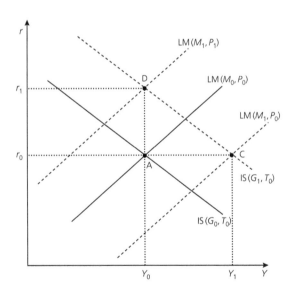

Figure 12.11 Increased governmental expenditure, financed by an increase in the money supply, in the IS–LM framework.

The initial increase in both G and M will manifest itself by a shift to the right of the IS (suggesting that at any level of interest rate, due to a greater demand for goods, equilibrium will only be obtained at a higher level of income) and the LM (suggesting that at any level of output, as the supply of liquid assets increased, equilibrium will be obtained at a lower level of interest rate). Point C is where the Keynesian story will end. As far as the classical story goes, there will be an increase in prices such that the LM will have to shift back up to point D where interest rate has risen and output returned to its original level.

12.4.2 The paradox of thrift reconsidered

Recall, from the Chapter 10, the paradox of thrift (Figure 12.12). An increase in savings (due, say, to a fall in the marginal propensity to consume) will cause output to fall (due to demand deficiency). The fall in output (income) will reduce the level of savings, completely offsetting the initial increase in savings. Therefore, in spite of the increase in the wish to save, savings will return to their original level (or even fall, had the demand for investment been rising with income).

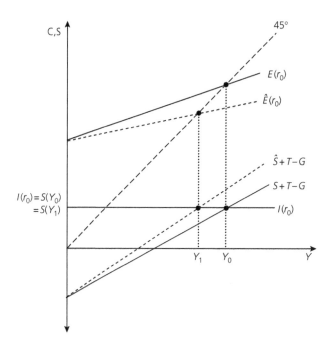

Figure 12.12 The paradox of thrift.

In the context of the complete model this is much less of a paradox (see Figure 12.13). An increase in savings (a fall in consumption) means that at any given level of interest rate there will now be smaller demand for goods and services. The level of income required to sustain an equilibrium in the market is, thus, reduced. The IS schedule will shift to the left. At A we now have excess supply, and, within the Keynesian view, this will lead to a fall in output and subsequently, a fall in demand for liquid assets which will reduce interest rates. This, in turn, will increase investment. We will end up at point B. The outcome of increased savings, therefore, will be to reduce output but to increase investment. While this is clearly no longer a paradox, and savings will increase investment which, in turn,

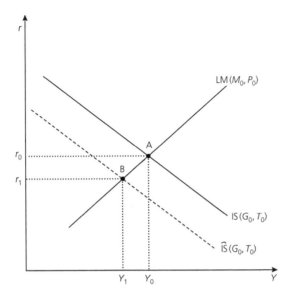

Figure 12.13 The paradox of thrift in the IS–LM framework: the Keynesian view.

will increase the stock of capital and facilitate growth, there will be an immediate fall in output.

In the classical version of events even the last bit will not happen (see Figure 12.14). The effect of increased savings will lead the economy from A to C. As the fall in consumption generates excess supply, prices will now fall. This will cause an increase in the supply

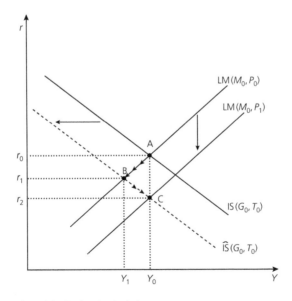

Figure 12.14 The paradox of thrift: the classical view.

of liquid assets and subsequently, a fall in interest rate which will induce investment. Investment will rise until the excess supply at the initial level of income has been eliminated. There is not much left of the paradox here.

Self-assessment and applications

▥ QUESTION 1

A government wishes to demonstrate prudence in its management of the economy by committing itself to a constant surplus (S). There is a proportional tax system and there are no transfers. This is a closed economy.

(a) What will be the economy's multiplier?

(b) Analyse the effects of an increase in taxation on the economy when prices and wages are fixed.

(c) What will happen to investment if the government raises the level of the surplus to which it is committed?

Answer

The particular features of this problem are:

(i) The government is committed to a constant surplus.

(ii) There is a proportional tax system.

(iii) There are no transfer payments.

The first thing we must explore is the meaning of committing the government to a constant surplus. In simple terms, this should mean that:

$$S = tY - G$$

where S is the pre-committed surplus, t is the proportional tax, and G is government spending. By implication, this suggests that government spending is, in fact, a function of income:

$$G(Y) = tY - S.$$

(a) What will be the multiplier? As you can imagine, as the government tax revenues depend on income, its spending will now fluctuate with income. When income goes up there will be greater tax revenues. This means that, in order to stick to the pre-committed surplus, the government would have to increase its spending. This means that an increase in income will push up the aggregate demand from two sources: consumption and public spending; instead of just one source, as in the standard formulation of the model. Hence, it means that any exogenous increase in aggregate demand will generate a greater snow-ball effect on demand and therefore, the multiplier will be greater.

We begin by setting all the behavioural functions of the economy:

$$C(Y) = c_0 + c_1(1 - t)Y$$

$$I(r) = I(r_0)$$

$$G(Y) = tY - S$$

$$AE(Y, r) = A + (c_1(1 - t) + t)Y$$

where

$$A = c_0 + I(r_0) - S.$$

Hence,

$$Y^* = A(r_0)\frac{1}{1 - c_1(1 - t) - t}$$

and the multiplier:

$$\frac{1}{1 - [c_1(1 - t) + t]}.$$

(b) An increase in taxation: normally, we expect increase in taxation to have a negative effect on aggregate demand. Increase in taxation usually spells a fall in consumption due to the fall in disposable income. However, we noticed already that when there is a balanced budget policy, an increase in tax means transfer of more resources from the low marginal propensity to consume of individuals to the high marginal propensity to spend of the government. Hence, the effect is expansionary. The case we have here, where government spending is positively dependent on output, is a very similar case. The first thing we must identify is how will an increase in t affect the aggregate expenditure function. We look at how an increase in t will change AE:

$$\frac{\partial AE}{\partial t} = (1 - c_1)Y > 0.$$

Note also that an increase in t will increase the expression in brackets in the denominator of the multiplier (notice that it will raise the expression in the brackets by $(1-c)$). Therefore, as the expression in the bracket is bigger, the whole expression in the denominator becomes smaller and the multiplier, bigger. This is also intuitively clear as government spending joins consumption in their residual push of aggregate demand when income increases. This means that the IS becomes flatter. Every fall in interest rate will raise demand for investment. When the output increases to satisfy the excess demand, the generated income will cause further increases in demand by consumption and government spending. Thus, the impact on output will be greater than in the case when only consumption responds to increases in income, see Figure 12.15. As the autonomous component is unchanged but the multiplier is greater, the IS shifts to the right and becomes flatter. The outcome of the policy will be to increase the output as well as equilibrium level of interest rate (we move from A to B).

(c) An increase in the level of pre-committed surplus will mean a fall in the autonomous component (A), see Figure 12.16. As the multiplier remains unchanged the IS will shift to the left. From national accounts, we know that $I = S_p + T - G = S_p + S$. In equilibrium, $I(r_1) = S_p(Y_1) - S$. As S is greater and interest rate is lower, overall investment will increase in spite of the fall in private savings.

How would the analysis change had we followed the classical view?

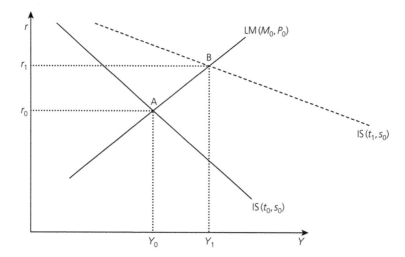

Figure 12.15

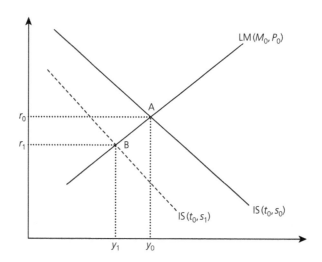

Figure 12.16

▦ QUESTION 2

An economy is in a long recession. To fight idleness, the government proposes to move from a universal system of benefits to a welfare-to-work system, together with a cut in taxation. Accordingly, benefits will be paid out as a tax credit. Assume, to begin with, an economy with a proportional tax system. Analyse the effects of the policy on a closed economy. Are the two components of the policy consistent?

Answer

The initial state of affairs is that the government uses a universal system of benefits (lump sum) as a means of income redistribution. We are also told that there exist a system of proportional tax in this economy. Thus, before the change we had the following set of functions:

$$C = C_0 + c_1 Y_d$$

$$Y_d = -T$$

$$T = ty - B$$

$$C = C_0 + c_1(1 - t)y + c_1 B$$

$$\Rightarrow y = [c_0 + I(r_0) + G_0 + c_1 B]\frac{1}{1 - [c_1(1 - t)]}.$$

Naturally, the multiplier is $1/(1 - M)$ where $M^B = c_1(1 - t)$.

We now move to a system with benefits are no longer universal, in the sense that you get them irrespective of what you do. From now on, you must earn and be liable to pay tax in order to get the benefit. The benefit you get is measured in terms of a tax credit (you pay less tax). Hence, the benefits are proportional to the level of tax revenues:

$$C = C_0 + c_1 Y_d$$

$$Y_d = Y - T$$

$$T = ty - B = ty - b(ty) = ty(1 - b)$$

$$C = C_0 + c_1[1 - t(1 - b)]y$$

$$\Rightarrow y = [c_0 + I(r_0) + G_0]\frac{1}{1 - [c_1(1 - t(1 - b))]}.$$

Now $M^b = c_1[1 - t(1 - b)]$ which is clearly greater than M^B:

$$c_1[(1 - t(1 - b)] = c(1 - t) + ctb > c_1(1 - t).$$

Thus the new multiplier will become greater. However, at the same time, the autonomous components become smaller (as the element cB is no longer in it). So which of the two forces will be more dominant? See Figure 12.17.

To examine the collective effects of the change we must ask what would happen to output when interest rate remains at its original level. Will it move to B or to C?

$$y_1 - y_0 = [c_0 + I(r_0) + G_0]\frac{1}{1 - [c_1(1 - t) + c_1 tb]} - [c_0 + I(r_0) + G_0 + c_1 B]\frac{1}{1 - [c_1(1 - t)]}$$

$$= [c_0 + I(r_0) + G_0]\left[\frac{1}{1 - [c_1(1 - t) + c_1 tb]} - \frac{1}{1 - [c_1(1 - t)]}\right] - c_1 B\frac{1}{1 - [c_1(1 - t)]}.$$

As the multiplier after the change is greater than the one before the change, the expression on the left is clearly positive. However, whether or not $y_1 > y_0$ depends on the magnitude of B. Given the

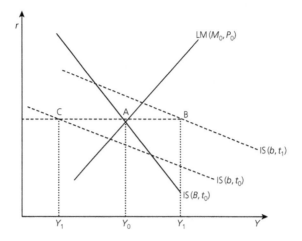

Figure 12.17

relative size of G and I, it is more likely that indeed $y_1 > y_0$. Moreover, if we add the additional element of the policy (i.e., tax cuts) we shall find that the multiplier after the change is even bigger.

$$\frac{1}{1 - [c_1(1 - t) + c_1 tb]} = \frac{1}{1 - M}$$

$$\frac{\partial M}{\partial t} = c_1 b - c_1 = c_1(b - 1) < 0.$$

The inverse relationship between the change in t and the size of M means that a fall in t would increase M. Any increase in M increases the multiplier. Hence, we may conclude that the IS will indeed shift to the right and become flatter.

Both move to a tax credit system and the cut in tax rate leads to increases in the multiplier. In this respect the two component of the policy are perfectly consistent. The effect of the economy will therefore be as shown in Figure 12.18. The change in the benefit system accompanied by a cut in

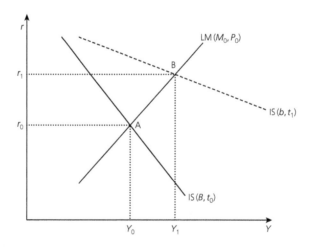

Figure 12.18

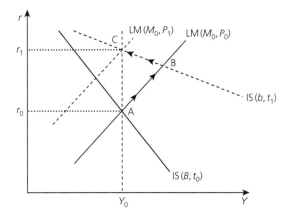

Figure 12.19

tax rates will increase aggregate demand at the given level of interest rate. This, in turn, will cause an increase in output. As income increases, the demand for liquid assets will increase, and this will cause interest rate to rise. This increase in interest rate will offset some of the increases in demand by reducing the demand for consumption. We move from A to B.

If we followed the classical view, shown in Figure 12.19, the increase in demand would not have been matched by an increase in output as demand does not determine output. Hence, the increase in demand would have caused an increase in prices. This, in turn, would have reduced the supply of liquid assets and created excess demand for them. The selling of bonds would have brought their price down through an increase in interest rate which would have offset the increase in demand by reducing the demand for investment. The economy would have moved from A to C.

QUESTION 3

Consider a closed economy. The profits of private corporations constitute a fraction α of national income. These profits are subject to corporate tax and a fraction β of the net profits is distributed to owners. The remaining profits are invested in the economy. To encourage investment, the government proposes to cut the corporation tax. The corporation tax is proportional to profits and so is the regular tax but the rates are not necessarily the same.

(a) Analyse the effects of the government proposal assuming that wages and prices are fixed.

Answer

This is a continuation of a question from Chapter 10. To bring it all together I repeat the part we had already answered.

We begin by noting the information given in the question. We consider a closed economy where:

(i) Profits constitute the fraction α of national income (i.e. αY),

(ii) There is a corporate tax (which is proportional, t_c), which means that after tax profits are $(1 - t_c)\alpha Y$,

(iii) A fraction β of net profits is distributed to shareholders,

(iv) The remaining profits are invested,

(v) There is a regular tax rate t.

The issue: The government considers cutting corporation tax to encourage investment. The initial set-up is therefore as follows:

$$C(y) = C_0 + c_1(1 - t)[Y(1 - \alpha) + \beta(1 - t_c)\alpha y]$$

$$I(r) = I_0 - I_1 r + (1 - \beta)(1 - t_c)\alpha Y$$

$$G = G_0$$

$$\Rightarrow [C_0 + I(r) + G_0] + [c_1(1 - t)((1 - \alpha) + \beta(1 - t_c)\alpha) + (1 - \beta)(1 - t_c)\alpha]Y = Y$$

$$Y = A(r)\frac{1}{1 - [c_1(1 - t)((1 - \alpha) + \beta(1 - t_c)\alpha) + (1 - \beta)(1 - t_c)\alpha]} = A(r)\frac{1}{1 - [M]}.$$

Note that we can now look at M to see how the multiplier might change. An increase in M would mean an increase in the multiplier.

(a) The government considers a reduction in the corporate tax. Clearly this will have a positive effect on the aggregate demand as both demand for investment and demand for consumption will increase. To see this more explicitly we would like to establish how would a change in corporate tax affect M (which is the only place in the aggregate demand function where it is present). We do this by using the concept of 'derivative' which is a formal way of investigating how a value of a function changes with small changes in one of its elements. Here the value we investigate is that of $M(t_c)$. To find out how a change in the value of corporate tax would affect M, assume that you increase t_c by 1. If you look carefully at M you will see that if you increase t_c by 1 (simply replace t_c by $t_c + 1$) and look at the difference between $M(t_c)$ and $M(t_c + 1)$, the answer will be as follows:

$$\frac{\partial M}{\partial t_c} = -c_1(1 - t)\alpha\beta - (1 - \beta)\alpha < 0.$$

This means that there is an inverse relationship between changes in corporate tax and the values of M (and the multiplier). In our case, a fall in corporate tax would increase M and the multiplier and that for any given level of interest rate, there will be equilibrium in the goods market at a higher level of income (IS shifts to the right AND it becomes flatter). The consequences of this policy in a closed economy with fixed wages and prices will be as in Figure 12.20. A cut in the corporate tax would shift the IS to the right and make it flatter. The output will increase and so will the rate of interest. We know that at B: $I = S + T - G$. As T falls, $T - G$ falls. However, the cut in the tax rate would increase disposable income and thus, increase savings at each level of output. As income increased in the move from A to B, savings must have increased further. Thus, at B, private savings increased while government surplus fell. We cannot conclude that investment will either rise or fall.

How would your answer change had the government been committed to a balanced budget where public spending are adjusted to the tax revenues?

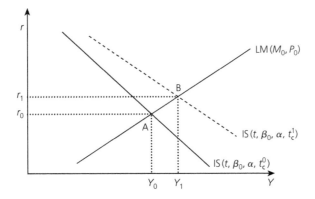

Figure 12.20

The model needs to be adjusted as follows:

$$C(Y) = C_0 + c_1(1 - t)[Y(1 - \alpha) + \beta(1 - t_c)\alpha Y]$$

$$I(r) = I_0 - I_1 r + (1 - \beta)(1 - t_c)\alpha Y$$

$$G(Y) = t(1 - \alpha)Y + t_c\alpha Y$$

$$\Rightarrow [C_0 + I(r)] + [c_1(1 - t)((1 - \alpha) + \beta(1 - t_c)\alpha) + (1 - \beta)(1 - t_c)\alpha + t(1 - \alpha) + t_c\alpha]Y = Y$$

$$Y = A(r)\frac{1}{1 - [c_1(1 - t)((1 - \alpha) + \beta(1 - t_c)\alpha) + (1 - \beta)(1 - t_c)\alpha + t(1 - \alpha) + t_c\alpha]}$$

$$= A(r)\frac{1}{1 - [M]}.$$

Note that, now, the government spending is a function of income as well.

The government proposes a cut in the corporation tax, will this increase investment? As before, we must examine how the change in the corporate tax rate will affect the aggregate demand. Evidently, it is only present in the multiplier so we must again investigate the effects of the change on M:

$$\frac{\partial M}{\partial t_c} = -c_1(1 - t)\alpha\beta - (1 - \beta)\alpha + \alpha$$

$$\frac{\partial M}{\partial t_c} > 0 \quad \text{if} \quad 1 > c_1(1 - t) + (1 - \beta).$$

This means that the effect of the change in corporate tax is independent of the share of profits in national income but very much dependent on how much of it has been distributed, the regular rate of tax and the marginal propensity to consume. The greater is the distributed share (β) the more likely it becomes that the cut in corporate tax will reduce M and thus reduce the multiplier. This is exactly the opposite result to the one we had when government did not commit itself to a balanced budget. For low level of dividend distribution (β), there will be an inverse relationship between the change in corporate tax and the multiplier. In such a case, the effect of cutting corporate tax would be the same as in the case without a balanced budget.

QUESTION 4

In a closed economy, the poor earn the fraction α of national income. Their marginal propensity to consume is greater than that of the rich, but only the rich pay the proportional tax (t). The government, which is committed to a non-interventionist policy, claims that redistribution occurs naturally through the sympathy of the rich who donate, annually, the fraction β of their income to the poor. In addition, the government has a strict balanced budget policy where government spending depend on the amount of tax raised.

(a) Compare the multiplier of the economy with and without donations;

(b) What will be the impact on the economy, of an increase in donations to the poor? Consider the implications for the economy when prices and wages are fixed.

Answer

Again a continuation of a question from Chapter 10. In this question we ask you to try to investigate one element in the complex debate about redistribution. We have an economy where a fraction α of national income is earned by the poor. The government has a balanced budget which is anchored onto tax revenues. The question does not specify whether or not everyone is paying tax or only the rich. You could choose either option. We shall normally assume that only the rich pay tax but occasionally examine the other case also.

For simplicity's sake, we assume that the decision on how much to donate is made on the basis of gross income. We shall also assume that this is a closed economy.

(a) Multiplier with and without donation. The poor's disposable income in this model (including potential donations) is clearly: $\alpha Y + \beta(1 - \alpha)Y$ where the first element is their share in national income while the second element is the proportion β of the income of the rich which is donated to the poor.

The disposable income of the rich is given by: $[(1 - \alpha)Y](1 - t) - \beta(1 - \alpha)Y$ where the first element is the net income after tax while the second element is the donation which they transfer directly to the poor.

We thus begin by setting all the behavioural functions of the entire economy:

$$C(Y) = c_0 + c_1^P(\alpha + \beta(1 - \alpha))Y + c_1^R((1 - t)(1 - \alpha) - \beta(1 - \alpha))Y$$

$$I(r, Y) = I(r_0)$$

$$G(Y) = t(1 - \alpha)Y$$

$$AE(Y, r) = A + c_1^P(\alpha + \beta(1 - \alpha)) + c_1^R((1 - t)(1 - \alpha) - \beta(1 - \alpha) + t(1 - \alpha)]Y.$$

Hence, the multiplier

$$Y^* = A(r_0)\frac{1}{1 - \{c_1^P[\alpha + \beta(1-\alpha)] + c_1^R[(1-t)(1-\alpha) - \beta(1-\alpha)] + t(1-\alpha)\}} = A\frac{1}{1-M},$$

where, again, αY is the poor's income, $\beta(1-\alpha)Y$ is the donation made by the rich and t is the tax rate. We call the expression within the double brackets, M.

Without donation ($\beta = 0$) the multiplier will become

$$\frac{1}{1 - [c_1^P(\alpha) + c_1^R(1-\alpha)(1-t) + t(1-\alpha)]}.$$ It is quite easy to see that

$$M = [c_1^P(\alpha) + c_1^R(1-\alpha)(1-t) + t(1-\alpha)] + \beta(1-\alpha)(c_1^P - c_1^R),$$

where the first square bracket is in the denominator of the multiplier without donation. As the marginal propensity to consume of the poor is greater than the rich, it is clear that M is greater than its equivalent in the no-donation multiplier. Hence, the multiplier with donation is greater than the one without it. The intuitive reason for this is that a transfer from a lower MPC to a higher one will increase demand for consumption.

(b) Here you are expected to conduct an analysis of the overall effects on a closed economy of an increase in voluntary donations. To answer this we must examine the general effect of donation on the multiplier. We must simply observe what will happen to M as β increases:

$$\frac{\partial M}{\partial \beta} = c_1^P(1-\alpha) - c_1^R(1-\alpha) = (1-\alpha)(c_1^P - c_1^R) > 0,$$

which means that as long as the marginal propensity to consume of the poor is greater than that of the rich, M will monotonically increase with β. Note that as M increases so does the multiplier. Hence, in (a) this means that the multiplier with $\beta = 0$ is going to be smaller than the multiplier with $\beta > 0$ and now we have a more general statement that the multiplier will increase as voluntary donations increase. The intuition remains the same: a transfer of income from a lower MPC to a

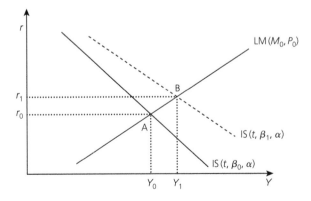

Figure 12.21

higher one increases overall demand. The increase in consumption will therefore signal a shift to the right of the IS while its slope becomes flatter (a greater multiplier), see Figure 12.21. The increase in demand will yield an overall increase in national income and interest rates. This means that the increase in the consumption of the poor was partly funded by increases in income and partly through the fall in investment.

13 Prices, inflation, and unemployment

▨ **MAJOR POINTS IN SUMMARY**

- Deriving aggregate demand (AD) in the price output plane
- The problems with deriving aggregate supply (AS)
- The Keynesian and the classical AS
- The problems with explaining stagflation
- The Phillips curve and the theory of inflation
- The augmented Phillips curve and the role of expectations in explaining stagflation
- Price levels and unemployment: the determinant of the short run aggregate supply.

13.1 Prices and output

So far, very little has been said about the relationship between output and prices. It is not so much because the models we have used have nothing to tell us about this relationship. Rather, it reflects the more interactive nature of macroeconomics. That is, macroeconomics, to a great extent, developed in response to some burning issues.

Towards the end of the nineteenth century and the beginning of the twentieth century, one of the most troubling questions was that of unemployment. This is somewhat para-doxical, as this was also the period of great advancement in production and the spread of the industrial revolutions to many continental countries. But if you think about it, it is not really surprising; since a process of industrialization is a period of enormous structural changes. In fact, some scholars, like Schumpeter, think that the whole period between 1873 and 1898 should be called the Great Depression.[1]

The classical view of output, as manifested in Say's law, suggested that it is supply which determines the level of national product, and hence, employment. It meant that the only role for governments in helping alleviate unemployment is to make life easier for business; to create a conducive environment for businesses (production) to expand.

The Keynesian revolution was to suggest that it is aggregate demand which determ-ines output (hence, employment). The implication of this was that it is **demand**

management (i.e. active and direct government policies) which can alleviate the problem of unemployment. The difficulties with both approaches and the different definitions of unemployment have already been discussed in Chapter 9, so I will not repeat them here.

Later on, economists became increasingly aware of the significance of inflation. The initial and immediate question which followed was, notwithstanding the problem of what determines what, how do prices relate to the models we have portrayed so far? Although inflation—the rate of change in prices—is not exactly the same as price levels, it does sound reasonable to begin the investigation by establishing what it is that determines the latter before we can say much about the former.

The first step, therefore, is to identify the relationship between price levels and output in the existing models; notably, the IS–LM model.

13.2 The aggregate demand: yet another representation

When we began modelling the world of aggregate goods, we formulated a very basic demand schedule which was based on an extremely basic assertion. That the aggregate demand for goods and services in an economy will be a function of national income. The greater is the latter, the more will be the demand for goods and services. In Chapter 10 we saw that this 'simple' principle may be seriously questioned when income distribution is taken into consideration. Altogether, however, we had to start from somewhere and we were, therefore, willing to make all these assumptions. We are not about to make any changes in them but it is good to be frequently reminded about the nature of our investigation, so that we do not get overexcited about the, sometimes surprising, outcomes of our analysis.

Our first presentation of the aggregate demand for goods and services was therefore in the space of demand for goods (AE) and output (Y). At the same time, it became clear that a major component in that demand is the interest rate which is determined in the liquid assets market. We therefore adjusted the presentation to examine the relationship between interest rate and equilibrium levels of output by using the IS tool of analysis. We repeated a similar transformation in the liquid assets market by using the LM tool. We have reestablished the notion of macroeconomic general equilibrium as the point where the two schedules meet.

As price is a component in the supply of liquid assets, we can have an initial insight into its relationship with equilibrium level of income and interest rate. The intuition is simple enough: an increase in the price reduces the supply of real balances. This, in turn, will increase the interest rate and reduce demand for investment and subsequently, aggregate demand. Hence, the level of output needed to supply the new aggregate demand is bound to become smaller (see Figure 13.1).

Beginning at point A we observe that when the price level is P_0 the equilibrium level of output will be Y_0. We now ask ourselves what will happen to the level of output for which the system will be in equilibrium in both the goods and the liquid assets markets, if prices increase to P_1. In the liquid assets market (LM) it means that the supply of real

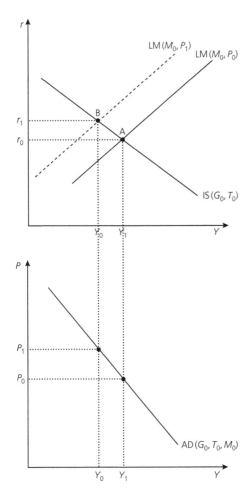

Figure 13.1 Prices, output, and aggregate demand.

balances will fall from (M_0/P_0) to (M_0/P_1). This means that at each level of output, and a given demand for liquid assets, equilibrium can only be achieved at a higher interest rate. In particular, at Y_0, the demand for liquid assets is given. The fall in supply of real balances means that there is now excess demand for liquid assets (at the initial interest rate). People will want to convert some of their less liquid assets (say, bonds) to money. They will want, therefore, to sell their bonds and thus create excess supply of bonds. The price of bonds, which is inversely related to the interest rate, will have to come down through an increase in the interest rate. Hence, the LM will shift upwards to allow for higher interest rates to correspond to each level of income. This, in turn, will cause a fall in demand for investment and a fall in overall aggregate demand. In a model of quantity adjustments this would reduce output and we move along the IS from A to B.

Consequently, the entire system reaches a new equilibrium at Y_1 which corresponds to the higher level of prices (point B). We have thus established an inverse relation between prices and **equilibrium levels** of output in our system. We draw this relationship in the lower diagram in Figure 13.1 and we name the function depicting it as AD (aggregate demand) once more.

All these repetitions of aggregate demand seem to be getting a bit confusing so let us try to put some order in it. As we said before, the first expression (and in fact, the only one which really corresponds to the notion of aggregate demand) was the aggregate expenditure AE. The $AE(Y, r)$ is a genuine behavioural function, as it tells us what would be the level of demand for domestic output at any given level of income (which is derived from this output) and interest rates (which influence the demand for investment).

We then looked at the equilibrium condition in the goods market and chose to define a new function (IS) which, unlike AE, depicts the correspondence between values of income (Y) and interest rate (r) for which there would be equilibrium in the goods market. Therefore IS is not a demand function:

$$IS(y, r, G, T): \quad AE(y, r, G, T) = y$$

Following our initial model we can write it explicitly:

$$C(y) = c_0 + c_1(y - T)$$

$$I(r) = I_0 - I_1 r$$

$$G = G_0$$

$$\Rightarrow [c_0 + I_0 - I_1 r + G_0 - c_1 T] + c_1 y = y$$

$$IS: [c_0 + I_0 + G_0 - c_1 T] + y(c_1 - 1) = I_1 r$$

$$IS: r = \frac{1}{I_1}[c_0 + I_0 + G_0 - c_1 T] + \frac{c_1 - 1}{I_1}y.$$

So what, then, is the AD schedule? Well, as you can see from the Figure 13.1, what typifies points A and B is that both represent general equilibrium. Namely, at A and B both the goods market and the liquid asset market are in equilibrium. So the AD schedule is perhaps the least demand function in the usual sense of the word.

In the case of the liquid assets, the equilibrium between demand and supply of liquid assets is captured by the LM schedule:

$$LM: \left(\frac{M}{P}\right)^d = L(r, y) = \left(\frac{M}{P}\right)^s.$$

The AD schedule is thus a system of two equations with two unknown quantities:

$$LM: L(r, y) = \left(\frac{M}{P}\right)^s$$

$$IS: AE(y, r, G, T) = y.$$

Naturally, the unknowns (the endogenous variables) are y and r. What we do with the AD is to examine some kind of comparative statics. We isolate the price level from these equations and we look at the values of y for which the two equations hold when we change the value of p. This is exactly what we did, earlier, diagrammatically. We looked at what would happen to the equilibrium level of y when we change (exogenously) the price level p.

As AD depicts the equilibrium conditions in both the goods market (IS) and the liquid assets market (LM) its position depends on the values of all other exogenous parameters. They are, of course, the instruments of fiscal policy (*G* and *T*) in the goods market and the instruments of monetary policy (*M*) in the liquid assets market. Thus, AD is a very powerful instrument as it captures in one the general equilibrium condition of the entire economy as subjected to the values of all relevant policy instruments.

This, of course, is very exciting but if prices are exogenous it is not very interesting to construct a special schedule to examine the relationship between it and the equilibrium values of income. Obviously, we know that prices are not exogenous and the whole purpose of this exercise is to try to establish what determines the price level.

Microeconomics tells us that prices are determined in the markets. As the price level (*p*) is nothing but a weighted sum of these prices, you may wonder why we bother to ask the question. Well, the reason this question may be of interest to us here is because we want to see the conditions under which all markets are affected in a similar way. So there is clearly a good reason why we may want to ask how do the macro variables (like *G*, *T*, and *M*) may affect all prices. However, it is far from obvious that what determines the aggregate price level is also a 'market'. After all, there is really no 'market' for the national product.

So, if it is not necessarily a market where aggregate price is determined, why should we be concerned with demand and supply as the mechanisms which determine price level? I suppose that a possible answer to this would be that, in doing so, we emulate in one what might be happening in all markets simultaneously. The AD, as it were, represents the quantity of output that would be required for an equilibrium to emerge. If the actual level of output does not correspond to it, assuming that this shortage is spread across all markets, this may explain why the price level may rise.

13.3 The problem with aggregate supply

While it should be perfectly clear to you why the supply of a single firm will be rising with the increase in price, this is by no means evident at the aggregate level. It is enough to consider the fact that an increase in the general price level may also suggest an increase in the cost of inputs (interest rates, for one, will increase with the increase in the price levels). Therefore, as prices increase, whether or not supply increases depends on the relationship between the change in the prices of final goods and the prices of intermediate goods. We have no particular reason to believe that there exists a particular relationship between these changes. Consequently, we cannot deduce with certainty that aggregate supply increases with prices.

For similar reasons, as we observed above, one should not confuse the downward sloping AD with the demand schedule in microeconomics. While the latter represents the considerations of rational individuals, the former represents the cumulative outcome of their actions and the various institutional arrangements within which they operate.

So what can we say about the aggregate supply? We did manage to discuss some issues pertaining to it in Chapter 9, but now we must have something more concrete. Recall that in Chapter 9, we said that it is not clear what it is that determines output. The classical view has been that output is being determined by the circumstances of industry. This does not tell us anything explicit about the relationship between output and prices and we therefore choose to assume that there is no relationship between prices and output. The Keynesian view, however, suggests that output is demand driven. What would that mean to the price output relationship of the aggregate supply?

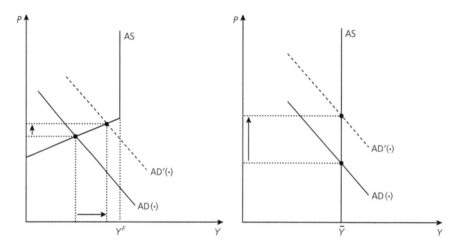

Figure 13.2 Aggregate output: the Keynesian and classical views.

On the one hand, on the right-hand side of Figure 13.2 we have the 'classical view' of aggregate supply representing the notion that as it is the circumstances of industry which determines output, there is no clear relationship between prices and the level of aggregate output.

In the left-hand side of the figure, we depict the Keynesian view of aggregate supply. It has this shape to accommodate the view that whenever there is unemployment, which implies that output can be expanded, the main mechanism of adjustment would be that of quantity. Namely, an increase or decrease in demand will cause output to increase (or decrease) rather than prices. Whenever we reach the point of full employment, the only feasible mechanism of adjustment is that of prices. Therefore, at full employment, the Keynesian supply will have the same relationship with prices as the classical aggregate supply but the question which remains is whether the Keynesian and the classical notions of full employment are the same.

All this has significant implications. The flexibility of prices and the reliance on prices as the major mechanism of adjusting both excess demand and excess supply suggests that demand management will be futile. Any increase in aggregate demand will only result in a subsequent increase in prices without bringing about any *real* change. In the Keynesian context, demand management will be effective as long as the economy is in unemployment. In particular, it will be an effective instrument to resolve the problems of unemployment.

13.4 Inflation and the Phillips curve

Apart from the more methodological debate concerning the validity of the Keynesian and classical approaches, there is a more practical twist to the tale. I said earlier that unlike microeconomics, macro analysis seems much more sensitive to the problems of the hour. We started with the problem of unemployment, and we then examined the relationship between prices and output as implied by the model which we have already constructed. If we accept that the overall level of prices in the economy is determined by the relationship between aggregate demand and aggregate supply, the implication for inflation would be that we expect prices to rise whenever there is excess demand for goods. This anticipation was very much consistent with the experiences of the growing economies of the 1950s and 1960s. In the 1970s, however, another phenomenon developed: **stagflation**. As a result of oil price shocks, many of the industrialized economies experienced the strange occurrence of increase in prices and unemployment. Neither of the above models tell us much about inflation as a process or, for that matter, can accommodate the phenomenon of rising prices and unemployment. However, some help can be drawn from the Phillips curve.

The first thing to note about the Phillips curve is that it is not, in itself, a model. It does not explain anything. It only shows an interesting empirical correlation between the rate of change of nominal wages and the level of unemployment (see Figure 13.3).

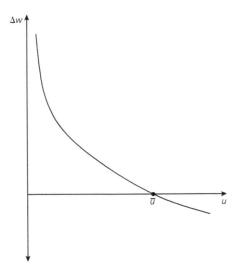

Figure 13.3 The Phillips curve.

Writing down this relationship we will get something of the following form:

$$\Delta w_t = \frac{w_t - w_{t-1}}{w_{t-1}} = -\varepsilon(u - \bar{u})$$

Δ represents what we call the **rate of change**. If wages at period t were 150 and at the previous period $(t-1)$, 100, this means that wages increased at a rate of 50%. Let u—the level of unemployment for which wages remain unchanged—correspond to the potential output, that which is determined by the circumstances of industry. The unemployment which corresponds to the potential output represents, in principle, structural unemployment. Namely, when output is at its potential level, the assumption is that all those who wish to find work will find it (all markets clear). Naturally, some people will be between jobs or would not want to work at the going wage rate. These people constitute, in principle, the 'natural rate' of unemployment. Thus, the Phillips curve suggests that when unemployment exceeds the level of its 'natural rate' wages will be falling, while wages will be increasing whenever $(u - \bar{u}) < 0$.

We can now rewrite the above relation in the following way. We are going to decompose the rate of change until we can express the wage level at a specific period as a function of unemployment:

$$\Delta w_t = \frac{w_t - w_{t-1}}{w_{t-1}} = -\varepsilon(u - \bar{u})$$

rearrange:

$$\frac{w_t}{w_{t-1}} - 1 = -\varepsilon(u - \bar{u})$$

hence:

$$w_t - w_{t-1} = -w_{t-1}\varepsilon(u - \bar{u})$$

and

$$w_t = w_{t-1}[1 - \varepsilon(u - \bar{u})] \qquad (1)$$

which now can read as follows: when labourers come to the negotiation table they will want to keep their wages at least at the level of past years. Whether or not they succeed depends on their bargaining power, which is captured here by the degree of unemployment $(u - \bar{u})$.

We now need a **pricing theory** to translate these findings into a theory of inflation. Recall that in microeconomics we have established that competitive firms will price at marginal cost. This means that

$$P = \text{MC} = \frac{w}{\text{MP}_L}.$$

Across the entire economy pricing might be more complex. First of all not all markets are necessarily competitive and we have to allow to the fact that there might be some industries where prices are above their marginal cost. Second, in the absence of complete perfect competition productivity may vary across industries. Hence we follow a pricing principle which is based on an **average productivity** (a) and allows for the fact that some prices are above marginal cost by using a **mark up** (z). We get then:

$$P_t = (1 + z)\frac{w_t}{a}$$

$$P_t = \frac{(1 + z)}{a}w_t \qquad (2)$$

Substituting equation (1) into (2),

$$P_t = \frac{(1+z)}{a} w_{t-1}[1 - \varepsilon(u - \bar{u})] \quad \text{as} \quad \frac{(1+z)}{a} w_{t-1} = P_{t-1} \tag{3}$$

$$P_t = P_{t-1}[1 - \varepsilon(u - \bar{u})]. \tag{4}$$

Applying now the reversed procedure to the one which led us to equation (1) we shall get,

$$P_t = P_{t-1}[1 - \varepsilon(u - \bar{u})]$$

rearrange:

$$\frac{P_t}{P_{t-1}} = 1 - \varepsilon(u - \bar{u})$$

or:

$$\frac{P_t}{P_{t-1}} - 1 = -\varepsilon(u - \bar{u})$$

which can be written as:

$$\frac{P_t - P_{t-1}}{P_{t-1}} = -\varepsilon(u - \bar{u})$$

which is nothing other than:

$$\Delta P = -\varepsilon(u - \bar{u}) \tag{5}$$

which produces the famous trade-off idea between inflation and unemployment (Figure 13.4).

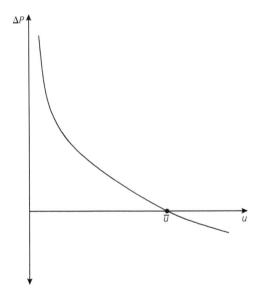

Figure 13.4 Implications of the Phillips curve: the trade-off between inflation and unemployment.

Suppose now that unemployment and output are closely related. This, it must be borne in mind is by no means straightforward. Output may vary even when employment does not change given that there are other means of production too. Still, we shall assume without elaboration that unemployment and output are the two sides of the same coin. This means that the unemployment Phillips curve is the mirror of the supply function shown in Figure 13.5. with the corresponding equation:

$$\Delta P = -\varepsilon(u - \bar{u}) = \phi(Y - \bar{Y}). \tag{5'}$$

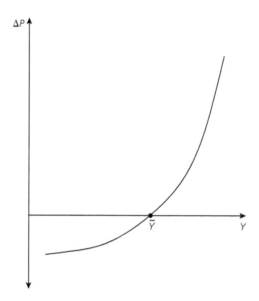

Figure 13.5 Implications of the Phillips curve: inflation and output.

Although this is a theory which suggests a positive relationship between output and inflation, it seems to lend some support to the idea of an upward sloping aggregate supply in the output–price levels plane.

However, this is not where our story ends. Friedman and Phelps argued that the explanation in equation (1) is lacking. In the end, labourers worry about the **real wage** (W/P). If, at the negotiating table, they only make demands which are based on their previous nominal wages while knowing that an increase in their nominal wages will increase prices (and thus reduce their real wages), they will not be behaving in a rational way.

If labourers expect an increase in prices in the coming period they know that their real wages will fall. It will only be natural for them to ask for nominal compensation for the expected price increases. If at time 0 the real wages is (W_0/P_0) and labourers expect prices to increase by ΔP it means that without an increase in their nominal wages, their real wages will fall to the level of $\{W_0/[P_0(1 + \Delta P)]\}$. They will therefore demand an increase in nominal wages such that the level of real wages is at least unchanged. Namely, they will want to get an increase of at least $\Delta W = \Delta P$ which would leave their real wages unchanged:

$$\frac{W(1+\Delta W)}{P(1+\Delta P)} = \frac{W}{P}.$$

We must, therefore, rewrite equation (1) in the following way:

$$w_t = w_{t-1}[1 + \Delta P^e - \varepsilon(u - \bar{u})] \tag{6}$$

where ΔP^e represents the expectations labourers have with regard to increases in price levels. Repeating the entire exercise which led us from equation (1) to equation (5) we will get the following Phillips curve (converting on our way from unemployment to output):

$$P_t = \frac{(1+z)}{a} w_t = \frac{(1+z)}{a} w_{t-1}[1 + \Delta P^e - \varepsilon(u - \bar{u})] \tag{7}$$

$$P_t = P_{t-1}[1 + \Delta P^e - \varepsilon(u - \bar{u})]$$

$$\Delta P = \Delta P^e - \varepsilon(u - \bar{u}) \tag{8}$$

$$\Delta P = \Delta P^e + \phi(Y - \bar{Y}). \tag{8'}$$

This suggests that for each level of expectations there is a Phillips curve and that the original trade-off between inflation and unemployment reflected a zero expectation of price increases (see Figure 13.6).

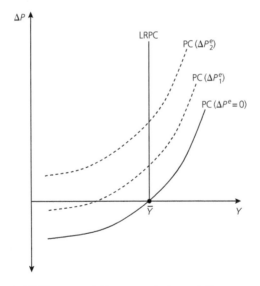

Figure 13.6 The augmented Phillips curve: taking account of expectations.

Now, the question which remains is how do people form those expectations? Being, as it is, a huge topic on its own we shall not really deal with this question. The only thing we want to say here is that, according to some, if people get to know, or understand, the way the economy is operating they are bound to make, in the end, the correct expectations. This means that if one follows this line of argument, in the long run expectations will be correct. That is:

$$\triangle P^e = \triangle P.$$

If that is the case, one can easily see from equation (8′) that in the long run:

$$Y = Y$$

which implies that in the long run supply is, after all, vertical.

Stagflation

Let us examine now what all this means in terms of the ability of the theory to deal with the problem, say, of stagflation. As this is a dynamic model describing how aggregate supply is determined when prices are constantly changing, we must try and imagine an equivalent story of a dynamic demand. To make life easy, let us go back to think of the IS–LM equilibrium condition (from which we derived the AD function in the previous sections). The equilibrium level of demand is a function, among other things, of the interest rate which, in turn, is determined in the liquid assets market. For any given quantity of money (M) and price level (P) there is an equilibrium rate of interest.

Inflation means that prices increase. In other words, for any given stock of money (M) inflation means a depletion of the stock of real balances. From the initial model, we know that a fall in M/P means an increase in interest rate per each level of output. This, in turn, reduces investment and equilibrium level of demand.[2] Naturally, if the government increases the supply of money at the same rate at which inflation increases prices, the supply of real balances will remain unaffected. Thus, without further complication, let us assume that dynamic aggregate demand is inversely related to the rate of inflation. When there is a constant depletion of the stock of real balances, it means that we are, most of the time, in a state of insufficient liquid assets. This means that people will be constantly selling bonds which, in principle, should cause the interest rates to rise. This, in turn, will reduce the demand for investment.

Suppose that initially, there is no inflation and we begin at point A in Figure 13.7. The corresponding Phillips curve is upward sloping and is based on expectations for prices to remain unchanged. Imagine now that due to external shock, there was an increase in the rate of inflation. This means that unless anything else changes, the depletion of the stock of real balances will push up the interest rate and decrease the demand for investment. We end up at point B where we have inflation and unemployment, that is, **stagflation**.

Another way in which we can get from A to B is if people develop expectations for an increase in prices. This means that at A workers will be able to demand compensation for the pending decrease in their real wages. They will thus cause an increase in price which will trigger the inflation they were anticipating and move the economy from A to B through a shift upwards of the Phillips curve.

Naturally, the subject of inflation requires full development. However, at this stage this will only distract us from setting the foundation for the language used within the traditional macro modelling. We have made this detour merely to demonstrate that there is plenty of scope for developing the theory further to deal with new developments in the world. Obviously, the fact that we may be able to offer explanations and predictions

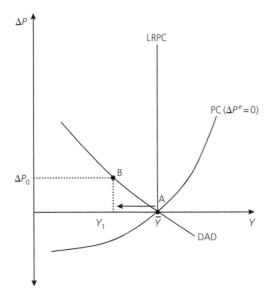

Figure 13.7 The Phillips curve and dynamic aggregate demand.

using these models does not in itself mean that they are empirically true. None of what we have said in this book should be read as a confirmation for the validity of these models.

13.5 A price level interpretation

What will be the implication of the above to our analysis up to here which was entirely conducted in terms of price levels? Here is a possible interpretation, see Figure 13.8. First, the vertical (classical) aggregate supply is seen as a long run supply. Assuming this means that classical economists admit that demand management could be effective in the short run, while Keynesians will have to admit that, in the long run, demand management is not effective. Whether or not this is a reasonable way of settling the methodological dispute is a difficult and complicated question. I shall not even attempt to address it here but I wish to draw your attention to the fact that for such an interpretation to work, the notions of long run and short run must be very well-defined. I fear that this is far from being the case at the microeconomics level. It certainly is far from being the case in macroeconomics. Still, for what it is worth, it allows us to analyse the policy recommendations that will follow the adoption of both classical and Keynesian points of view.

We start at point A which is a long run equilibrium. Among other things, it is assumed that in the labour market, the real wage paid out to workers is w_0/P_0. An expansionary fiscal policy will shift the aggregate demand (AD) to the right as at each level of prices, there will be greater demand for goods and services and together with liquid market considerations, equilibrium will be at a higher level of output.

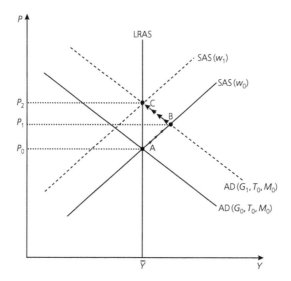

Figure 13.8 Introducing dynamic prices in *AD/AS*.

A shift to the right of the aggregate demand will mean that at the price level of P_0 there is now excess demand for goods. Initially prices will begin to rise which, in turn, will reduce the real wages paid to workers although the nominal wage rate remains unchanged:

$$w_0/P_0 > w_0/P_1.$$

If you recall from Chapter 5 the demand for labour which represents the profit maximizing principle then you must remember that when employers need to pay less (in terms of goods) to their employee, they will be willing to employ more of them. Therefore, the initial increase in price will allow producers to increase their output in response to increased orders. In other words, the economy will move to point B where a combination of quantity and price adjustments took place.

However, for such a thing to be possible, nominal wages must remain at their initial level. This may be possible in what one may consider the short run. If workers have contracts which give them a certain nominal wage (and there is no reason to expect indexation in the contract as we do not have inflation in our case), before the contract will be renegotiated, real wages may indeed fall. We call the line depicting output for any given level of nominal wages the **short run aggregate supply**. As prices increase, real wages fall and the supply of output will be greater.

When these contracts are renegotiated, workers will want to be compensated for their fall in real income. They also know that the employers are likely to pass on to the price the increase in their nominal wages. If they calculate these changes correctly, the economy will move to point C where nominal wages have risen sufficiently to compensate for both the initial increase from P_0 to P_1 but also for the additional increase from P_1 to P_2. Thus real wages at C and at A are the same:

$$w_0/P_0 > w_1/P_2$$

and so will be the outputs at A and C.

Self-assessment and applications

▨ QUESTION 1

In a closed economy with flexible prices and wages, expansionary monetary policy will not have any real effect and will only cause a rise in nominal wages. True or false? Explain.

Answer

The first thing to do is to choose the right framework of analysis. The question asks you about the effects of an expansionary monetary policy on output and nominal wages. Therefore, the right framework of analysis is the IS–LM and AD–AS. Normally, when there is no reference to wages or prices, there is no need to use the AD–AS framework.

The issue at hand is an expansionary monetary policy (see Figure 13.9).

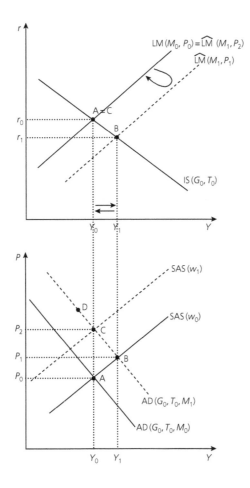

Figure 13.9

An expansionary monetary policy means an increase in M or the supply of real balances. This means that at any given level of income Y, there will be equilibrium in the liquid assets market at a lower level of interest rates. The LM, therefore, shifts downwards. However, before you move the LM curve, note that LM is also dependent on the value of P. As the AD curve responds to all moves in the IS–LM framework, it suggests that price will change too. To prevent your drawing from being clogged up with lines, think before you move the LM. We know that an increase in M will also shift the AD to the right as at a lower interest rates, there will be greater demand for goods and services at any given price level. This implies that a new equilibrium can only be obtained at a higher level of output. As AD moves to the right, prices, in the short run will rise to P_1 and output to Y_1 (point B in the AD–AS framework). An increase in P will slightly reduce the supply of real balances and this, in turn, will shift the LM slightly back. Notice that in the AD model, the effects of a change in price on the IS–LM equilibrium is depicted as movement along the curve. In other words, the initial increase in M will push us to point C (at the initial price level). However, as the excess demand in the goods market means that there will also be an increase in price, we move up, along the curve, to point B. In the IS–LM framework, this means that the LM has gone further out than its current position (at B) before it moved back a bit due to the price effect. Note that at B, the parameters of the LM schedule are M_1, which is the new quantity of money, and P_1, which is the new price level (at B).

Had wages and prices been fixed, this is where the story would have ended. Again, it would mean that in a world where prices and wages are not the main mechanism of adjustment, demand management will be effective in bringing about a change. Note also that, even within the Keynesian interpretation, the fact that some of the adjustment will come through prices does not alter the ultimate effectiveness of demand management.

According to the question, we live in a world of flexible prices and wages. This means that B is only the short run outcome. At B, real wages fell as nominal wages are unchanged but prices are higher. While employers will be happy to employ more people at a lower real wage, workers are unlikely to be happy with the fall of the real income. When wage negotiation open, they will demand a compensation for the increase in prices from P_0 to P_1. They will also want to be compensated for the increase in price that will follow the increase in their nominal wages. Thus, the economy will move to point C with a higher level of nominal wages but the same level of real wages (prices are higher). There will, therefore, be no real effect on the economy when prices and wages are flexible and demand management will have no real impact on the economy. Note that incorrect workers' expectations with regard the change in prices that will follow the increase in their nominal wages may create recession as the SAS (short run aggregate supply) moves too far to the left (point D in the above diagram).

■ QUESTION 2

There is no 'paradox of thrift' in a closed economy when wages and prices are flexible. Explain.

Answer

Recall our earlier discussions of the 'paradox of thrift'. We will now repeat it in the context of our extended framework (see Figure 13.10).

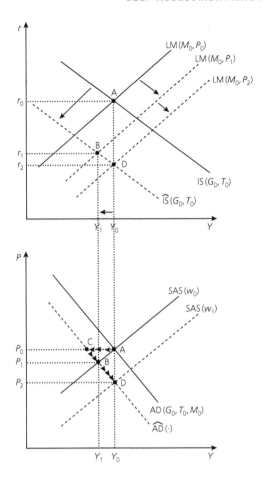

Figure 13.10

An increase in the will to save will cause a decrease in consumption. The IS curve shifts to the left. Here, again, we must remember that a shift of the IS is also a shift in the AD schedule (as the point of general equilibrium between IS and LM changes) and subsequently, a change in P which will change the position of the LM which, in turn, will change the position of the AD schedule.

To take care of it all in a simple manner, it is best to move AD first. A fall in consumption means that at any price level there will now be less demand and the required level of output for which there is general equilibrium will be lower (A to C in the bottom diagram). As there is full wage and price flexibility, this means that prices will fall to P_1 which is a move along the AD curve to point B where we have the SAS. As prices fall, real wages increase and therefore, employers will wish to employ less people at the given level of nominal wages.

A fall in prices also means an increase in the supply of real balances (M/P). At any level of output there will now be excess supply of liquid assets and a subsequent fall in interest rate (why?). This amounts to a shift downwards of the LM schedule. Thus, the initial effect of the fall in consumption is the move from A to B in both diagrams shown in Figure 13.10.

In the long run, employers will wish to reduce nominal wages and workers, who face unemployment, are likely to agree. The correct anticipation of the changes in prices means that we will now move to point D where output remains at its initial level, real wages are unchanged but interest rate has fallen. There is no paradox, whatsoever, as the wish to save more will materialize through higher levels of investment and no fall in output.

QUESTION 3

In an election year, the government increased its spending by borrowing from the public. To prevent an increase in the interest rate, the government convinced the central bank to reduce the reserve ratio for commercial banks. The opposition accused the government of sowing the seeds of recession while mortgaging the future (reducing investment).

(a) Discuss the accusations of the opposition in a closed economy with fixed wages and flexible prices.

(b) Discuss the accusations of the opposition in a closed economy with flexible wages.

Answer

The two changes in the economy proposed by this question are:

(i) An increase in the government's spending (G) financed by borrowing from the public.

(ii) An increase in money supply due to a fall of the reserve ratio.

(a) A closed economy with fixed wages (Figure 13.11). An increase in government spending will shift the IS to the right, as there will now be greater demand for local goods and equilibrium could only be reached at a higher level of output for any given level of interest rate. The fall in reserve ratio will allow banks to lend more. As the supply of liquid assets (in our definition of it) $= R(DM)$ where R is the total amount of money deposited in the banks and DM is the **deposit multiplier**, a fall in the reserve ratio will increase the deposit multiplier and thus, increase the supply of liquid assets. This means that for any level of income, there will be equilibrium at a lower level of interest and the LM shifts downwards.

IS and LM shift to a new equilibrium at a higher level of income and, more or less, the same interest rates. If you use the IS–LM without the AD–AS, namely, assuming fixed prices and wages, this is fine in this section. In such a case, the shift downwards of the LM will be smaller. There is no need to use this framework when wages are fixed. However, if you do use the complete framework, you are expected to demonstrate that you take note of the relevant changes in price levels and their influence on the IS–LM model. Either way, the opposition was wrong.

(b) Closed economy with flexible wages (Figure 13.12). IS and LM shift from equilibrium at A to a short run equilibrium at B (which already includes a change in prices from P_0 to P_1 and a slight shift back by the LM). In the long run, as real wages fell, there will be a nominal compensation which, if correctly anticipating the effects of greater cost on future prices, will bring the economy to point C. As prices increase, the LM will shift to the left until it reaches point C (in the IS–LM framework)

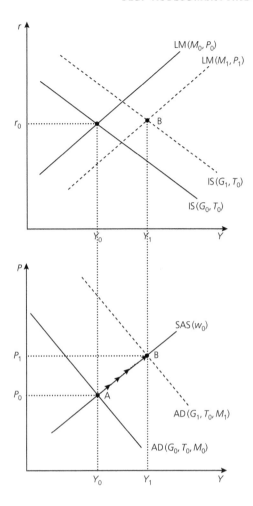

Figure 13.11

where the economy will return to long run equilibrium. The opposition was wrong about recession but right about the future (increase in interest rates will reduce demand for investment).

■ **QUESTION 4**

In order to attract high-flyers and invigorate the economy, the government decides to reduce the highest marginal tax rate and to increase the lower marginal tax rate. The change has been designed in such a way as to keep the overall level of tax receipts unchanged. Some argued that favouring the high-flyers will only bring about a recession and a fall in investment.

(a) Examine the argument in the context of a closed economy with fixed wages.

(b) Would your answer be different had wages been flexible?

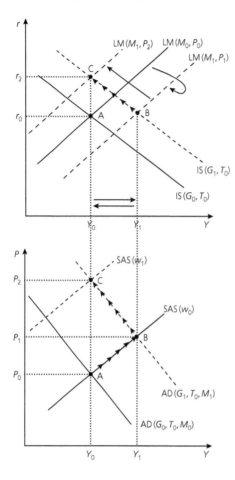

Figure 13.12

Answer

The main problem in this question is to identify the change. To translate, as it were, the question into the language of the model it is clear here that we must distinguish between two groups of consumers: higher earners and low earners. By now, you should have had the feel that the issue at hand is the difference in marginal propensities to consume. As overall tax receipts have not changed, this is really a transfer of income from the poor to the rich. As such, if the poor have a greater marginal propensity to consume than the rich, every pound transferred will yield a net fall in consumption. Alternatively, we can write down the following consumption function:

$$C(Y) = C_0 + c_1^H(1 - t_H)Y_H + c_1^L(1 - t_L)Y_L$$

$$\Delta C = -c_1^H \Delta t_H Y_H - c_1^L \Delta t_L Y_L; \quad \text{as } \Delta t_H < 0 \quad \Delta t_L > 0 \quad \Delta t_H < \Delta t_L$$

$$\Delta C < 0.$$

This means a fall in consumption at any level of income. In principle, this is sufficient to analyse the proposed change. Moreover, as we can see that the changes in consumption are all through the effective marginal propensity to consume (taking tax rates into account) we can deduce that the fall in consumption (at any level of interest rate) must come from the multiplier. Namely, the effect of the change would be to reduce the multiplier and thus shift the IS to the left and make it steeper.

To see how exactly this comes about I develop below the full story, but you may skip it and go straight to section (a) below.

Assume that the share of the rich in income is α and the share of the poor is $(1 - \alpha)$. We now want to see how changing the tax rate for both groups would alter the total amount of tax. Naturally, we would want that total change to be zero, reflecting the assumption that the changes kept the tax receipts in tact. To do this, we ask ourselves how would the overall tax change: this means that

$$\text{as } T(y) = t_h \alpha y + t_L (1 - \alpha)y$$

$$dT = dt_h \frac{\partial T}{\partial t_h} + dt_L \frac{\partial T}{\partial t_L}$$

hence

$$dT = dt_h \alpha y + dt_L (1 - \alpha)y.$$

But we know that the change was such as to leave the total tax revenue unchanged

$$dT = dt_h \alpha y + dt_L (1 - \alpha)y = 0$$

$$\Rightarrow -dt_h = dt_L \frac{1 - \alpha}{\alpha}.$$

Assuming that government spending is fixed at G and that the demand for investment is only a function of interest rate we can conclude that the multiplier of the economy would be:

$$\frac{1}{1 - \left[c_1{}^h (1 - t_h)\alpha + c_1{}^L (1 - t_L)(1 - \alpha) - m_1 \right]} = \frac{1}{1 - M}.$$

We can now investigate what would happen to the multiplier by examining the effect of the proposed change on M. As M increases, so does the multiplier.

$$dM = dt_h \frac{\partial M}{\partial t_h} + dt_L \frac{\partial M}{\partial t_L}$$

$$\frac{\partial M}{\partial t_h} = -c_1^h \alpha, \qquad \frac{\partial M}{\partial t_L} = -c_1^l (1 - \alpha)$$

$$\Rightarrow dM = -c_1^h \alpha dt_h - c_1^l (1 - \alpha)dt_L$$

$$\text{as } -dt_h = dt_L \frac{(1 - \alpha)}{\alpha}$$

$$dM = +c_1^h dt_L (1 - \alpha) - c_1^l (1 - \alpha)dt_L$$

$$= dt_L (1 - \alpha) \left[c_1^h - c_1{}^L \right] < 0.$$

Hence, the effect of the change is really coming through the multiplier. Increasing the rate of tax of the poor while decreasing the one on the rich would cause the multiplier to fall and, thus, cause the slope of the IS to become steeper. Naturally, had this not been accompanied by fixed tax revenues, the answer would have depended on the magnitude of the changes.

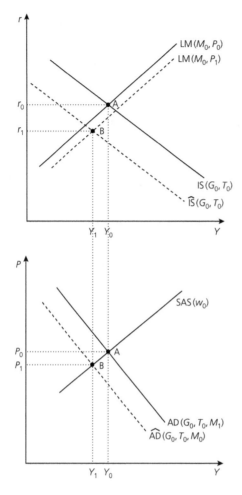

Figure 13.13

(a) Closed economy with fixed wages (Figure 13.13). As there is a fall in consumption the IS will shift to the left (and become steeper). If some of the change came through prices, this would cause a fall in prices and an increase the supply of liquid assets. The LM would therefore, shift downwards. We move from A to B where output fell but demand for investment increased. The opposition was right about recession but wrong about investment.

(b) Closed economy with flexible wages (Figure 13.14). The IS shifts to the left and becomes steeper. This will also shift the AD as general equilibrium would now be reached at a lower level of income for a given level of interest rate. Excess supply for goods will both reduce prices and (through increase in real wages) reduce output. As prices fall, the supply of liquid assets increase and equilibrium interest rate for any given level of income would be at a lower level. The LM shifts downwards. We thus move from A to B. In the long run, nominal wages would be renegotiated and the economy would move from B to C. At a lower level of interest there will be greater demand for investment. The logic of this is as income was transferred from people with high marginal propensity to consume (and a low marginal propensity to save) to those with a low marginal

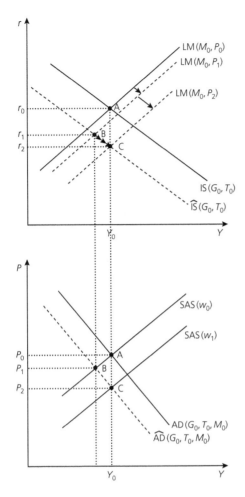

Figure 13.14

propensity to consume (and a high marginal propensity to save), there will be more savings at any level of national income. Hence, investment will increase. The opposition was wrong.

QUESTION 5

The increasing costs of higher education prompted the government to introduce tuition fees. Assume that higher education is productive (i.e. it affects the productivity of workers) and that the number of students in higher education depends on the level of fees.
(a) Analyse the effects of introducing tuition fees on a closed economy with:

(i) fixed prices;

(ii) flexible prices.

(b) How will the introduction of grants for the poor affect the outcomes in (a)?

Answer

This is a question with a sting in its tail. The problem at hand is the funding of higher education. The sting in the tail is the reference to its productivity. Thus, when tuition fees increase, the number of students fall and the overall productivity of the labour force decreases. Of course, this is normally a dynamic question as the effects on the actions in one period will only be felt in later periods but for the sake of simplicity, we shall analyse it all as if it happens contemporaneously.

(a) We assume that higher education is provided by the government. The introduction of tuition fees means that some of the funding is now moved from savings (i.e. borrowing) to consumption. Tuition fees also mean that sending one's offspring to higher education will lower disposable income. We can capture both these features by translating tuition fees into an increase in tax (i.e. an increase in T).

(i) The effects in the case of fixed prices are fairly trivial.

(ii) The effects in the case of flexible prices and wages are somewhat more complex.

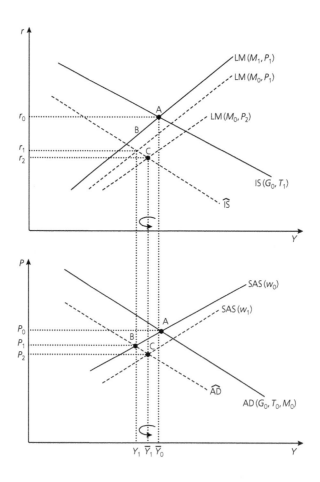

Figure 13.15

As education is productive, an increase in the tuition fees will reduce the number of students and subsequently cause a fall in the labour force's productivity. This means that the potential output of the economy will shift to the left. Consequently, introduction of tuition fees (or their increase) will reduce output but at the same time may increase demand for investment. This, in the long run, may offset some of these failures, see Figure 13.15.

(b) The introduction of grants complicates things a bit. First we must draw a distinction between the rich and the poor. Let us suppose that a proportion α of national income goes to the poor. The cumulative consumption function before the introduction of tuition fees will be (assuming no other taxes):

$$C(y) = \bar{c}_0 + c_1^P \alpha Y + c_1^R (1 - \alpha) y.$$

After the introduction of tuition fees where T_p and T_R denote the tuition fees levied on the poor and on the rich respectively:

$$C(y) = \bar{c}_0 + c_1^P (\alpha Y - T_p) + c_1^R [(1 - \alpha)y - T_R]$$

Thus

$$dC = -c_1^P T_p - c_1^R T_R < 0$$

which, as we said before, means an unequivocal fall in demand for consumption.

But when we introduce grants we get a somewhat different story:

$$C(y) = \bar{c}_0 + c_1^P (\alpha Y - T_p + g) + c_1^R [(1 - \alpha)y - T_R]$$

Thus,

$$dC = (g - T_p)c_1^P - c_1^R T_R.$$

Hence,

$$dC = (g - T_p)c_1^P - c_1^R T_R > 0$$

means

$$\frac{g - T_p}{T_R} > \frac{c_1^R}{c_1^P}.$$

The expression on the right-hand side is always less than unity as the marginal propensity to consume to the rich is smaller than that of the poor. If $(g - T_p) > T_R$ which implies that $g > T_p + T_R$, then it means that the poor are net recipients of government money. This means a transfer from the rich to the poor and, consequently, an increase in consumption. Naturally, whether or not this brings about an increase in T or a fall in it depends on the number of poor who go to university in relation to the number of rich. If the condition is satisfied (and assuming that as a result T fell), there will be an increase in overall demand and the IS will shift to the right. While this policy will yield an increase in the number of poor people attending higher education, the number of rich people will fall. Depending on the relevant elasticities it is possible that the number of students may rise or fall. Let us assume that the number falls. This, as before, will shift potential output to the left. This suggests a stagflationary process, which accompanied with an increase in interest rate will also lead to a fall in demand for investment, see Figure 13.16. As we said before, the validity of these conclusions depends on the magnitude of the grants, the elasticities of learning as a function of disposable income of the different groups and the collective effects that this will have on the net tax revenues.

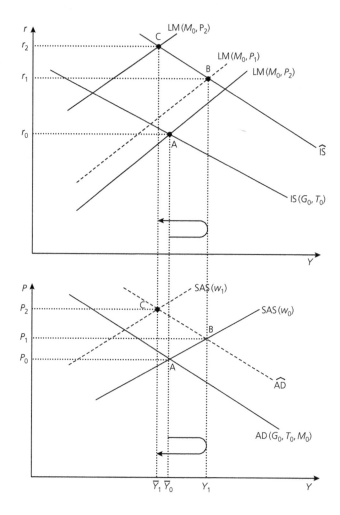

Figure 13.16

QUESTION 6

In a closed economy, the poor get their income from the state alone. They do not work and their income depends entirely on transfer payments. The poor's marginal propensity to consume is distinctly greater than that of the rest of society who pay taxes. Suppose that there is a proportional tax system.

(a) Analyse the consequences of an increase in the tax rate when prices and wages are flexible.

(b) Analyse the consequences of an increase in the tax rate when prices and wages are fixed.

(c) What are the likely consequences of such an increase to the number of poor (who are out of work) and to the extent of their poverty?

(d) How would your answer to (a)–(c) change had the marginal propensity to consume of the poor been exactly the same as the marginal propensity to consume of those at work?

Answer

This is a question about the possible macro effects of a primitive redistribution policy. The following assumptions are made in the text:

(a) the marginal propensity of the poor (c_1^p) is greater than that of the rest of the population;

(b) the poor's income comes only from transfer payments which are a fraction (α) of the total tax revenues (with a proportional tax system): $Y^p = \alpha(tY)$;

The model:

$$C(Y) = c_0 + c_1^p \alpha(tY) + c_1(1-t)Y$$

$$I(r) = I(r_0)$$

$$G = G_0$$

$$\Rightarrow AE(Y, r) = A(r_0) + [c_1^p \alpha t + c_1(1-t)]Y$$

$$\Rightarrow Y^* = A(r_0)\frac{1}{1 - [c_1^p \alpha t + c_1(1-t)]} = A(r_0)\frac{1}{1 - \bar{c}}.$$

Sections (a) and (b) deal with the effects of an increase in the tax rate t. Before we analyse the circumstances of the fixed and flexible prices and wages, we have to establish the immediate effect of such a change on the model. Intuitively, this is quite clear. When the tax rate increases, more income is transferred from the rich to the poor. However, as the poor get only a fraction of the money transferred, the question is whether their effective marginal propensity to consume would be greater or smaller than that of the rich:

$$\frac{\partial \bar{c}}{\partial t} = \alpha c_1^p - c_1.$$

Namely, the effect of the change depends on the magnitude of α. If $\alpha > (c_1/c_1^p)$, which means that the effective marginal propensity to consume of the poor is greater than that of the rich a transfer of income from the rich to the poor would increase consumption. The multiplier becomes bigger and for any given interest rate, equilibrium in the goods' market will be obtained at a higher level of income (a shift to the right of the IS). There is no particular reason to assume this. In fact, assuming that the fraction of tax revenues devoted to redistribution is relatively small—as it is unlikely to be greater than the ratio of marginal propensity to consume—the opposite is a more likely outcome. The analysis here will be based on the presumption that the increase in t will have a greater impact through the fall in consumption of the tax payer than the increase in the consumption of the poor who only get a small fraction of it.

(a) and (b) A closed economy with flexible prices and wages (left-hand diagram of Figure 13.17) and fixed prices and wages (right-hand diagram of Figure 13.17) (note that the changes come through the multiplier and will thus affect the slope of the IS).

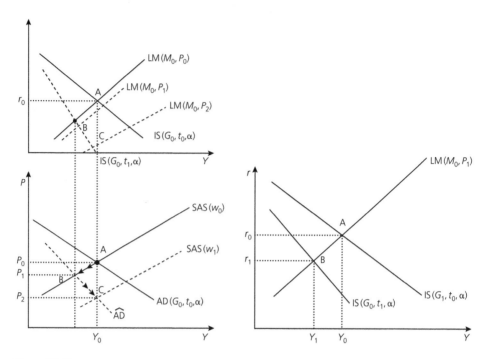

Figure 13.17

In the case of (a) the fall in aggregate demand brings about a fall in income as well as prices. This will cause the downward shift of the LM as the supply of real balances increased. We move from A to B. The fall in prices will raise real wages and instigate the fall in output as employers wish to hire fewer people. When wages are negotiated again, the extent of the unemployment gives the bargaining power to employers who will push nominal wages down until we end up at point C. Output remains unchanged and interest rate will fall (replacing demand for consumption by demand for investment).

In the case of (b) the only effect of the fall in aggregate demand would be to bring about a fall in orders (and output). We move from A to B in the right-hand diagram of Figure 13.17.

(c) The effects on the poor:

(i) In case (a): output has not changed and therefore there is no change in the number of poor (which are presumably part of the 'natural rate'). As t increases, overall consumption will fall but the consumption of the poor $c_1^p \alpha t Y$ will increase. Hence, the poor will be better off and there will be an overall increase in investment.

(ii) In case (b): output falls and this means that the number of people who can draw their income from employment falls too. While t has increased, Y falls by more and this means that the total amount of tax revenues available for the poor is smaller. Thus, in this case the number of the poor increases and they are worse off.

(d) Had the marginal propensity of the poor been the same as that of the tax payers:

$$\frac{\partial \bar{c}}{\partial t} = \alpha c_1 - c_1 = c_1(\alpha - 1) < 0$$

the answers would not have changed unless $\alpha = 1$. In such a case, there will be no change at all.

■ QUESTION 7

In a closed economy, a government sees its role growing with the economy ($G(y) = g_0 + g_1 y$). At the same time, the government is committed to a balanced budget.

(a) Derive the multiplier of the economy.

(b) Analyse the effects of an increase in the autonomous component of public spending on a closed economy where prices and wages are fixed. What will happen to the total amount of public spending, the total amount of private savings, and actual investment?

(c) Analyse the effects of an increase in the autonomous component of public spending on a closed economy where prices and wages are flexible. Will the implication of this for public spending, private savings, and actual investment be different than in (b)?

Answer

This is a closed economy where the government has a policy to increase its spending as the economy grows but, at the same time, it is committed to a balanced budget. In this case, it is easier to think of the case where taxes are adjusted to the level of government spending. Hence, $T(y) = G(Y)$.

(a) The model and the multiplier are therefore:

$$C(Y) = c_0 + c_1(Y - T) = c_0 + c_1(Y - g_0 - g_1 Y) = c_0 - c_1 g_0 + c_1(1 - g_1)Y$$

$$I(r) = I(r_0)$$

$$G(y) = g_0 + g_1 Y$$

$$\Rightarrow Y = [c_0 + I(r_0) + g_0(1 - c_1)]\frac{1}{1 - c_1(1 - g_1) - g_1} = A\frac{1}{(1 - c_1)(1 - g_1)}.$$

(b) An increase in the autonomous component of public spending:

This means that $dg_0 > 0$. The initial effect on Y will be:

$$dA = dg_0(1 - c_1)$$

$$dY = dA\frac{1}{(1 - c_1)(1 - g_1)} = \frac{dg_0(1 - c_1)}{(1 - c_1)(1 - g_1)} = dg_0\frac{1}{1 - g_1}.$$

Assuming that prices and wages are fixed, the following will happen, as described in Figure 13.18. To see the overall effect of the change it is easier to break the change into two stages: the move from A to B where output increases and interest rate remains unchanged. The question is what will happen to total public spending, private savings, and investment at this stage?

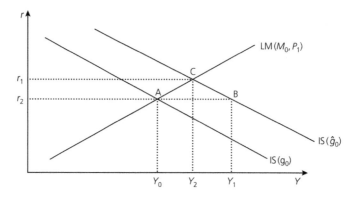

Figure 13.18

The effect on public spending is quite clear:

$$dG = dg_0 + g_1 dY = dg_0 + g_1 \left(dg_0 \frac{1}{1-g_1} \right), = dg_0 \left[1 + \frac{g_1}{1-g_1} \right] > 0.$$

The effects on consumption are,

$$dC = c_1(1-g_1)dY - c_1 dg_0 = c_1(1-g_1)dg_0 \frac{1}{(1-g_1)} - c_1 dg_0 = 0.$$

Therefore, private savings also (dS = dY − dT − dC = 0)[3] have not changed. So what will happen to actual investment?

We know that $I = S + (T - G)$. As neither $T - G$ nor $S(Y)$ have changed, nor will the actual level of domestic investment.

We now consider the effects of the subsequent rise in interest rate. Increased income will increase demand for liquid assets, which will push up the equilibrium level of interest rate. We move along the LM towards point C.

What will now happen to public spending, consumption, savings, and investment? As we move from B to C, the only change is a fall in income. Hence, public spending will fall relative to its level at B but will still be higher than its level at A. T, also, will rise relative to point A. In any case, $T - G$ will remain zero.

As consumption remained unchanged after the initial change (at point B), when income falls, consumption will clearly fall (relative to B and hence, to A). Equally, as private savings, also, remained unchanged by the move from A to B, the fall in income will reduce private savings:

$$dS = dY - dT - dC$$

$$dT = dG = g_1 dY$$

$$dC = c_1(1-g_1)dY$$

hence

$$dS = dY[(1 - g_1)(1 - c_1)]$$

as $dY < 0$ (move from B to C), $dS < 0$ relative to point B where it is the same as in A.

The above discussion completes the answer a more enthusiastic student can go on to discuss further what is given below.

For those who wish to calculate the move from A to C in one move, they must express the equilibrium condition in one equation.

IS: from section (a) above we know that:

IS:

$$Y = [c_0 + I_0 + g_0(1 - c_1)]\frac{-I_1 r}{1 - c_1(1 - g_1) - g_1} = (A - I_1 r)\frac{1}{(1 - c_1)(1 - g_1)}$$

but this time we write an explicit demand for investment function. As for the LM there are some complications as it is more difficult to expect a linear relationship here but for the sake of exposition, we shall make this simplifying assumption:

$$\text{LM}: \frac{M}{P} = L(y, r) = \phi y - \lambda r$$

or $r = (\phi/\lambda)y - (1/\lambda)((M/P)) = \xi y - \lambda^{-1}(M/P)$.

Plugging r into the IS equation we get:

$$Y = (A - I_1 r)\frac{1}{(1 - c_1)(1 - g_1)} = \frac{A}{(1 - c_1)(1 - g_1)} - r\frac{I_1}{(1 - c_1)(1 - g_1)}$$

$$Y = \frac{1}{(1 - c_1)(1 - g_1) + I_1\xi}\left[A + I_1\frac{M}{P}\right].$$

Analysing the complete changes,

$$dY = dA\frac{1}{(1 - c_1)(1 - g_1) + I_1\xi} = dg_0(1 - c_1)\frac{1}{(1 - c_1)(1 - g_1) + I_1\xi}$$

$$dG = dg_0 + dg_1 dY = dg_0\left[1 + \frac{g_1(1 - c_1)}{(1 - c_1)(1 - g_1) + I_1\xi}\right] > 0 \quad (dG = dT)$$

$$dC = c_1(1 - g_1)dY - c_1 dg_0 = dg_0\left[\frac{c_1(1 - g_1)(1 - c_1)}{(1 - c_1)(1 - g_1) + I_1\xi} - c_1\right] < 0$$

$$dS = dY - dT - dC = dg_0\left[c_1 - 1 + \frac{(1 - c_1)(1 - g_1)(1 - c_1)}{(1 - c_1)(1 - g_1) + I_1\xi}\right] < 0.$$

I will leave out the proofs for why the signs are as they are, but we can clearly see that this is consistent with our previous analysis.

Thus, the move from A to C means an increase in public spending, a decrease in consumption, and savings. Consequently, actual domestic investment will fall.

(c) The same increase in public spending, but this time, in a closed economy where prices and wages are flexible, see Figure 13.19. In this case, the outcome of the increase in public spending will be an increase in prices and wages. As in the long run, output has not changed. Hence,

$$dG = dg_0 > 0 \cdots dT = dg_0 \cdots dC = -c_1 dg_0 < 0 \cdots dS = -(1 - c_1)dg_0 < 0.$$

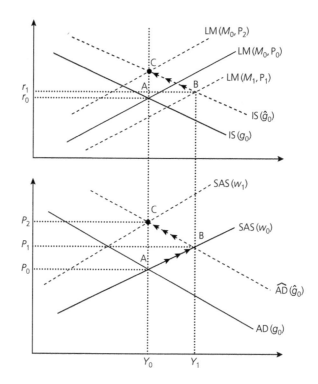

Figure 13.19

This means that in the capital formation equation $I = S + (T - G)$, S is smaller and $T - G$ remains zero. Thus, investment will fall. Note, however, that there is no full crowding out of investment by public spending as the government is committed to a balanced budget. The difference between the effects on spending of an increase in the autonomous component and the marginal propensity to consume of the public explains the residual crowding out.

▨ NOTES

1. See in Schumpeter, J. A. (1954), *History of Economic Analysis*, Oxford University Press, pp 759–760. If you wish to read a more detailed study of the effects of technological progress, you may consult Landes, D. S. (2003), *The Unbound Prometheus*, 2nd edition, Cambridge University Press.

2. Evidently, in a state of inflation (with expectations) we must adjust our theory of demand and distinguish between nominal and real interest rate. This is something that we shall leave out from our current study, as we wish to consolidate the basics.

3.

$$dy = dg_0 \frac{1}{1-g_1}; T = G \Rightarrow dT = dg_0 + g_1 dy = dg_0 \left[1 + \frac{g_1}{1-g_1} \right]$$

$$dS = dy - dT - dC = dg_0 \left[\frac{1}{1-g_1} - 1 - \frac{g_1}{1-g_1} \right] = 0$$

14 The open economy

■ MAJOR POINTS IN SUMMARY

- National accounts of an open economy
- Demand for export and import and their effect on aggregate demand, the net-export function, the multiplier of an open economy
- The balance of payment, foreign currency market: the determinant of demand and supply of foreign currency, capital mobility, the rate of interest, and the price of foreign currency; the difference in the impact on the system under different exchange rate regimes
- Income determination in an open economy and exchange rate policies when there are no capital movements
- Income determination when there is perfect capital mobility, the effects of fiscal and monetary policies under (i) fixed exchange rate and no capital mobility; (ii) flexible exchange rate and no capital mobility; (iii) when there is perfect capital mobility.

14.1 The national accounts for the open economy

Until now we focused our attention on the relationship between aggregate variables in a closed economy. Naturally, almost all the economies in the world are open economies in the sense that they trade with other economies. For some economies, the trade is mainly in goods and services while for others, there are also exchanges at the assets levels.

From an analytical point of view, there is nothing really new in the analysis contained in this chapter. It is mainly the question of adding variables and functions rather than a conceptual change in the analysis. Recall our analysis in Chapter 8.

Having defined national output as the sum of value added, we have established that this means that national product and national income (i.e. generated income) are the two sides of the same coin:

$$NNP = Y.$$

In a closed economy without a government, the use to which we could put our product had been confined to consumption (C) and investment (I). Hence:

$$\text{NNP} = C + I.$$

With a government, there was an additional claim to possible usages of the national product: public consumption (G). Therefore:

$$\text{NNP} = C + I + G.$$

In a world without a government, we would use our income for either consumption or savings. That is to say, $Y = C + S$. With a government, it became:

$$Y = C + S + T.$$

Bearing in mind that NNP $= Y$ we got

$$C + I = C + S$$

or,

$$I = S$$

in the case of an economy without a government and

$$C + I + G = C + S + T$$

or,

$$I = S + T - G$$

which means that actual investment always equals actual savings. Without a government these were private savings (S). With the government these were private savings (S) + government savings ($T - G$) or government surplus.

The fundamental relationship between NNP and Y still holds in an open economy but the resources which are now available to the economy include imports (IM). The usage of these resources is extended also to include export (X).

Hence,

$$\text{IM} + \text{NNP} = C + I + G + X.$$

What people do with their income remains unchanged. They now have to pay taxes (T) before they decide how much to consume and how much to save.

Therefore:

$$Y = C + S + T.$$

Bearing in mind that NNP $= Y$ we have to isolate NNP:

$$\text{NNP} = C + I + G + X - \text{IM}$$

hence:

$$C + I + G + X - \text{IM} = C + S + T$$

or,

$$I = S + (T - G) + (\text{IM} - X)$$

or,

$$I = S + (T - G) - (X - \text{IM}) = S + (T - G) - \text{NX}$$

where $(\text{IM} - X)$ is a negative **net-export** (NX) or, in simple words, a deficit in the current account.

14.2 The goods market

The original aggregate demand was based on the different proposed usages of the national product. We now have to add the demand for the use of our national product for the purpose of net-export. Or, in other words, with international trade we have an additional use for our product and that is to sell it abroad (export). However, as we are also buying from abroad, we can assume that the resources which go into purchasing goods from abroad are, first and foremost, those which we buy from abroad. We need our own national income to use for that part of our export which cannot be generated by imports.

Before we go ahead, however, it is important to clarify an important concept which characterizes international exchanges: the **real exchange rate**. Let E denote the nominal exchange rate. This measures the amount of foreign currency that can be bought with one unit of domestic currency or, conversely, the amount of domestic currency which is required to buy one unit of foreign currency.

There is some confusion with regard to whether E should reflect the former or the latter. To a great extent it is a matter of convention, but most textbooks and articles in academic journals treat the exchange rate in the latter way. Namely, E measures the amount of domestic currency which buys a unit of foreign currency. If, in the United Kingdom we think of exchange rate as £1 = \$1.60, this means that we think in terms of the former definition. E, in this case, will be 1.6. However, the convention tends to be the latter case so we must simply say that \$1 = £0.62. E, therefore, is £0.62. In other words,

E = amount of domestic currency per unit of foreign currency.[1]

Whichever way we choose to think of the exchange rate, the person who buys imported goods as well as the exporter of goods do not think in nominal terms but, rather, they think in real terms. Namely, they think of what they pay, or get, from abroad in terms of what it can buy them at home. Therefore, what really matters is the following concept of exchange rate:

$$\frac{(E P^*)}{P}$$

which is the **real exchange rate**.

E is the nominal exchange rate; P^* is the price level abroad, and P is the domestic price level. If you sell a good abroad and its price is P^*, its value in domestic currency will be EP^*. However, if you want to know something about its purchasing power you will want to know how many units of the domestic product you can buy with it. You find this number by simply dividing what you get in terms of the domestic currency with the domestic prices level: EP^*/P. So, if a shirt in Antarctica costs P\$2 (i.e. two penguins dollars) and the exchange rate is £4 to the P\$ (they had a good fishing year) and you import one shirt, how much does it cost you? The cost of the shirt in money would be P\$2 × £4 = £8. What does it mean to you? Although you may not explicitly do the calculation, you think of it in terms of how many steak and kidney pies you could have bought with it. If the most important thing for you is a steak and kidney pie which costs, say, £2, you would say that the shirt from Antarctica costs you 4 steak and kidney pies. Naturally, we think of a host of things we could buy, and for this the general price level is a good enough index. It is quite useful to think of the exchange rate in this way because we can account for more cases by simply looking at this fairly simple variable.

An increase in E will have a similar effect as an increase in P^*. In both cases exported goods fetch a higher price (in domestic currency terms) while imported goods are more expensive (in domestic terms). Conversely, an increase in the domestic price level (P) means that, in real terms, the return to the exporter is much reduced, while the price of imported goods, also, are much reduced.

We can now describe the demand for export and import.

The demand for export is simply a function of the real exchange rate. Exporters will want to export more as long as their return in terms of domestic product increases:

$$X(EP^*/P) = X_0(EP^*/P)$$

where export is increasing when the real exchange rate increases and decreases when the real exchange rate—the return to the exporter—diminishes.

Demand for imports, on the other hand, depends not only on the real exchange rate but on income too. Naturally, as the real exchange rate increases it means that in real terms we pay more per unit of imported goods and that would reduce the quantity which we wish to import. Whenever income increases, however, our demand for imports, like that of any other kinds of economic goods, will increase. We can therefore write the demand for import in the following way:

$$IM(EP^*/P, Y) = IM_0(EP^*/P) + mY.$$

We have,

$$C(Y) = c_0 + c_1(Y - T)$$
$$I(r) = I_0 - I_1 r$$
$$G = G_0$$
$$X(EP^*/P) = X_0(EP^*/P)$$

and

$$-IM(EP^*/P, Y) = IM_0(EP^*/P) + mY.$$

Hence,

$$E(Y,r) = C(Y,T) + I(r) + G + X(EP^*/P) - IM(EP^*/P, Y)$$

can be written in a more explicit form as

$$E(Y,r) = c_0 - c_1 T_0 + c_1 Y + I_0 - I_1 r + G_0 + (X_0 - IM_0)(EP^*/P) - mY$$
$$= [c_0 - c_1 T_0 + G_0 + I_0 - I_1 r + (X_0 - IM_0)(EP^*/P)] + (c_1 - m)Y$$

We can now draw the extended model adding the NX function while bearing in mind that we assume a **fixed exchange rate**. Note that the NX function has the following property (see Figure 14.1).

$$NX(EP^*/P, Y) = X(EP^*/P) - IM(EP^*/P, Y) = (X_0 - IM_0)(EP^*/P) - mY$$

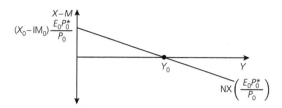

Figure 14.1 The net export function NX with a fixed exchange rate.

When the exchange rate is fixed, the only way to balance an initial surplus is by increasing the income which, in turn, will increase the demand for imports.

The complete market will now have the form as shown in Figure 14.2.

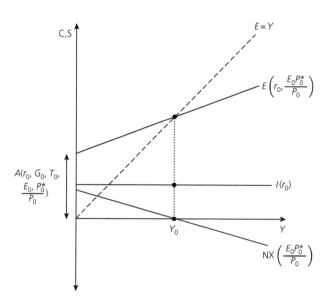

Figure 14.2 Excess demand with net exports.

At equilibrium, again,

$$E(Y_0, r_0, E_0 P_0^*/P_0) = Y_0$$

this means that:

$$E\left(Y_0, r_0, \frac{E_0 P_0^*}{P_0}\right) = A\left(r_0, \frac{E_0 P_0^*}{P_0}\right) + (c_1 - m)\, Y_0 = Y_0$$

hence

$$Y_0 = A\left(r_0, \frac{E_0 P_0^*}{P_0}\right) \frac{1}{1 - (c_1 - m)}$$

which is the new multiplier.

The multiplier of the open economy will inevitably be smaller than that of a closed economy with similar parameters. The reason for it is that the multiplier represents the pressure created on domestic product through the roll-on effect of an initial increase in demand. However, in an open economy, some of these increases in demand can be satisfied through imported goods. Consequently, the pressure on the domestic output will be reduced.

14.3 Exchange rate determination and the money sector

So far we assumed that the real exchange rate is fixed. While there may not be a problem assuming P^* or P as given, the question of the nominal exchange rate (E) is more complex.

To see what it is that determines the nominal exchange rate we must form a picture of the demand and supply of foreign currency for which the nominal exchange rate is the price. The source for this information is the **balance of payment** which is nothing but a report on the sources of foreign currency on the one hand, and the use of foreign currency on the other.

There are basically three major accounts in the balance of payment which account for the source and usage of foreign currency. These are:

(a) The **current account**;

(b) The **Capital Account**;

(c) **Change in reserves**.

The current account is closely associated with the trade balance. Within the current account, the source of foreign currency is export while the use of it is for the purpose of imports.

In the capital account the source of foreign currency are foreigners who wish to hold domestic assets. To do that they will have to buy domestic currency and, therefore, offer (i.e. supply) foreign currency. The use of foreign currency in this account is by locals who wish to hold foreign assets. To do that they will have to buy (i.e. demand) foreign currency.

Change in reserves is the category which ensures that the balance of payment is indeed balanced. It is possible that the current account will be in deficit which is entirely covered by the surplus in the capital account. But if, say, both accounts are in surplus, it means that more foreign currency is offered than is required. In such a case, the residual will be accumulated in the central bank in the form of increased reserves. That is, an increase in reserves is a use of foreign currency. What is important to note is that in such a case, there will always be an effect on the money supply.

When reserves are increased, it means that the central bank bought foreign currency for which it paid in domestic currency. This, evidently, increased the supply of money in the economy. Similarly, whenever there is a deficit in both accounts, it means that the demand for foreign currency exceeds its supply. When, subsequently, reserves are reduced, the quantity of money in the economy will fall too.

On the whole, therefore, we have the following picture:

	Sources of foreign currency	Use of foreign currency
Current account	Export (X)	Import (IM)
Capital account	Foreigners buying domestic assets	Locals buying foreign assets
Reserves	Reduction in reserves (M decreases)	Increase in reserves (M increases)

Whether or not a change in reserves becomes operative depends on the exchange rate regime that exists in the economy. Whenever there is a flexible exchange rate regime it means that demand which is generated by both the current and capital accounts will be equated to supply which is generated by the same accounts. There will be no need for the central bank either to buy or sell foreign currency. An excess demand will cause E to rise (thus reducing demand which is generated, say, by import while increasing supply which is generated, say, by export (why?).

If, on the other hand, the central bank wishes to keep the exchange rate at a certain level we call it a fixed exchange rate regime. In such a case, whenever the demand which is generated by the current and capital account exceeds the generated supply, the bank will sell foreign currency and, thus, bring about a reduction in reserves as well as money supply.

Foreign currency markets are really much more complicated than is implied by all the above. At this stage, however, we are less concerned with the accurate depiction of those markets. Instead we are concerned with the effects of various regimes in the foreign currency markets on the goods and liquid assets markets. Perhaps it would be useful if you thought about the market in terms of demand and supply. In particular, if we exclude the capital account, this notional market will be less of an outrage.

In the absence of capital movements, the demand for foreign currency will come mainly from the demand for imports. We will want foreign currency so that we can buy that which we wish to buy abroad:

$$Q_\$^d = P^* \times \text{IM}(EP^*/P, Y) = D_\$(E, P^*, P, Y).$$

The quantity of foreign currency demanded is the product between the prices abroad and the quantity of goods we wish to buy there. Therefore, demand for foreign currency is the function of all those things which determine the value of this product. Consider, for instance, a demand for imported goods (IM) (see Figure 14.3).

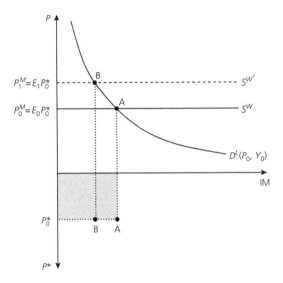

Figure 14.3 The demand for foreign currency: an increase in the nominal exchange rate.

Assuming that the economy is sufficiently small and (for brevity's sake) that there is no domestic production of the imported goods, it will be able to find, at any given price, whichever quantity it wishes. The international supply of IM is, thus, perfectly elastic. The price on the vertical axis is the price in domestic currency. Therefore, a perfectly elastic international supply suggests that we can buy any quantity at the price of $E_0 P_0^*$.

The demand for imported goods, we shall assume, somewhat emulates our usual micro models.[2] Therefore, it will be falling as price increases and it will also be subject to income (Y) and the price of other goods (P).

Equilibrium will initially be at point A. The bottom part of the diagram has quantity of imported goods (IM) on the horizontal axis and international prices P^* on the vertical axis (in absolute terms). This means that point A in the lower part of the diagram which depicts the quantity of IM bought at international price P_0^* created the shaded rectangular region which is really $P_0^* \mathrm{IM}_0 = Q_{\$0}^d$.

You can clearly see that an increase in E will shift up the price of the imported good for which there is an elastic international supply. Thus, at point B we buy less of the good at the same international price. Therefore, there is an inverse relationship between the nominal exchange rate E and the demand for foreign currency.

Equally, an increase in either income Y or in the general domestic price levels (P) will shift the demand for imported goods up (see Figure 14.4).

As national income increases people would want to buy more of all goods including imported goods. When the domestic price level increases, the demand for imported goods increases. This is so because domestic goods and imported goods are also gross substitutes. When the price of one increases, the demand for the other increases as well. In any event,

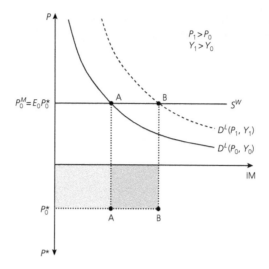

Figure 14.4 The demand for foreign currency: an increase in domestic income or prices.

the new equilibrium will now be at point B where we buy more of the imported good at the same international price. The rectangular region in Figure 14.4 depicting the quantity of foreign currency demanded at B is greater than the one at A.

When international prices change, the situation becomes slightly more complicated (Figure 14.5). When international price P^* rises to P_1^*, the domestic price of the imported

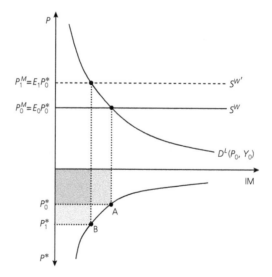

Figure 14.5 The demand for foreign currency: an increase in the foreign exchange rate.

goods rises too ($E_0P_1^* > E_0P_0^*$). Now, there will be equilibrium at point B. However, although we buy fewer imported goods at the higher price, we pay more per unit. The rectangular shape created at A and the one created at B have no clear relationship between them. If the area at B is greater than the area at A, the quantity of foreign currency demanded will increase. If the area at A is greater than the one at B then the quantity of foreign currency demanded will fall.

The move from A to B is clearly dominated by the price elasticity of the demand for imported goods. When this is greater than unity, the area in B will be smaller than the area in A and the demand for foreign currency will fall whenever there is an increase in international price level. Had it been less than unity, the demand for foreign currency will rise whenever there is an increase in international price level.

So we know now that

$$Q_\$^d = P^* \times \mathrm{IM}(EP^*/P, Y) = D_\$(E, P^*, P, Y)$$

and the nature of these relationships (Figure 14.6) are as follows: the supply of foreign currency in the absence of capital movement is mainly determined by the export:

$$Q_\$^s = P^* \times X(EP^*/P) = S_\$(E, P^*, P).$$

This means that when the real exchange rate increases, the quantity of foreign currency demanded would increase too. The real exchange rate would increase whenever E or P^* increase and P decreases.

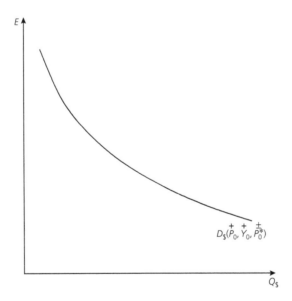

Figure 14.6 Demand function for foreign currency.

If we draw the notional market for export with international prices on the vertical axis and the quantity exported on the horizontal axis as shown in Figure 14.7, we see the following. As we assumed the economy to be a small economy it will behave like a

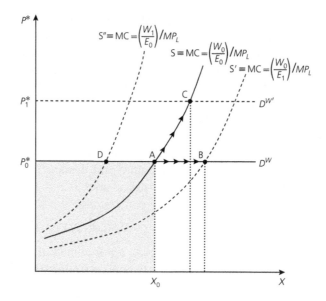

Figure 14.7 The market for exports.

competitive firm and be a price taker in the international market. International demand is, therefore, perfectly elastic at the given international price. Marginal costs are rising (reflecting the diminishing marginal product)[3] but in order to translate them into foreign currency we must divide wages by the nominal exchange rate.

At A, the initial equilibrium, the quantity of foreign currency supplied will be the shaded area. You can now clearly see that an increase in either E (which will lead to point B) or P^* (which will lead to C) will increase the supply of foreign currency. An increase in domestic prices which are represented here by w, will bring about a fall in the supply of foreign currency. Therefore,

$$Q_\$^S = P^* \times X(EP^*/P) = S_\$(E, P^*, P)$$

produces the following supply schedule which we combine with our previous demand for foreign currency (see Figure 14.8). To summarize: in the absence of capital movement, the demand for foreign currency—generated by the demand for imports—will be inversely related to the nominal exchange rate. Also, we can see among the parameters of the demand schedule the domestic price level (P) an increase in which will increase the demand for imports as well as national income (Y). The change in international prices will affect demand for foreign currency according to the price elasticity of the demand for imported goods.

On the supply side—generated by export—we have an increase in the quantity supplied when the nominal exchange rate increases. An increase in domestic prices (P) means that costs of production are now higher. At any level of E, the quantity supplied will, therefore, be reduced. Assuming that international demand to domestic goods is elastic (i.e. greater than 1) the quantity of foreign currency supplied will decrease. An increase in international demand which can present itself by an increase in international prices

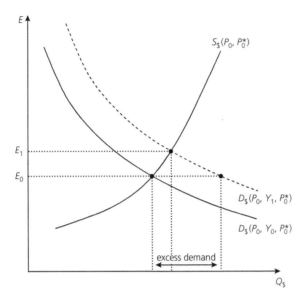

Figure 14.8 Demand and supply of foreign currency.

(P^*) will bring about an increase in export and, consequently, an increase in the quantity of foreign currency supplied at each level of nominal exchange rate (E).

It can now be seen that an increase in, say, income (Y) will increase demand for imports and, at given international and domestic prices, the quantity of foreign currency demanded will increase, also. This will shift the demand schedule to the right. At the initial exchange rate (E_0) there is now excess demand for foreign currency which represents a deficit in the current account. Had the exchange rate regime been that of flexible exchange rate, market forces will push the nominal exchange rate up (a **devaluation** of the local currency), making import more expensive and export more rewarding until equilibrium is restored at E_1. This means that there has been no change in the amount of reserves in the central bank.

If, however, there was a **fixed exchange rate** regime, the excess demand will have to be satisfied from other sources; namely, a *reduction in reserves*. This, in turn, will reduce the quantity of money which is circulating in the economy.

Adding a capital market to all this will complicate the story and, inevitably, will make the above description somewhat 'innocent'. Nevertheless, as demand and supply are perhaps the more familiar tools of analysis, I feel that you will find it easier to think about the balance of payment along these lines. You must only bear in mind that this is far from a proper description of the foreign currency market.

14.4 General equilibrium in an open economy

What is basically left to do is to put all the above together and analyse its effects on the consequences of various policies and circumstances.

The first step should be the translation of the above into the IS–LM framework of analysis. While there is no real change in the LM apart from bearing in mind that the quantity of money supplied depends on the exchange rate regime. The mere construction of the LM remains unchanged. In the goods market, however, we have introduced a new component which is called the net-export function.

14.4.1 No capital movements

For exposition purposes let us begin by assuming that we have an economy where there are *no capital movements* (i.e. no capital account) and there is a fixed exchange rate regime.

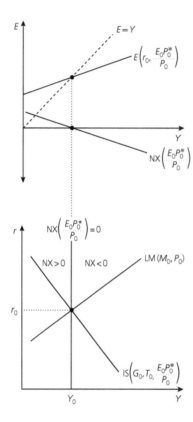

Figure 14.9 Constructing the IS–LM model with no capital mobility and a fixed exchange rate.

The complete market will now have the form as shown in Figure 14.9. As the exchange rate is fixed, there will be only one level of Y for which the current account will be balanced. The position of that point depends on the real exchange rate which affects the autonomous component of the NX function.

$$NX(EP^*/P, Y) = X(EP^*/P) - IM(EP^*/P, Y) = (X_0 - IM_0)(EP^*/P) - mY = 0$$

This is why the NX line in the IS–LM framework is vertical (it is unaffected by interest rate) but its position depends on real exchange rate. If real exchange rate increases, it means that the autonomous component of NX—$(X_0 - IM_0)(EP^*/P)$—will increase (more export less import). This will require a much higher level of Y (and the imports which it generates) to balance the current account.

Anywhere to the left of the point where the current account is balanced there is a lower level of income and, thus, a lower level of imports. In such circumstances, the current account will be in surplus. This means, under the fixed exchange rate regime, that there is now excess supply of foreign currency which, in order to balance the balance of payments, will be used to increase reserves. This, in turn, will increase the supply of money and affect the LM. What will happen at $Y > Y_0$?

Note that the IS itself is a function of the real exchange rate as it represents the demand for the use of domestic output. Whenever the real exchange rate increases, there will be an increase—in real terms—of demand for NX and, therefore, for domestic output. This means a shift in the IS. In turn, this creates some difficulties as both IS and NX shift to the right. Which of these shifts further? This is an important issue as it would affect the outcome in terms of the level of investment.

Suppose that there was an increase in the international price level. How will this affect an economy which is open, with a fixed exchange rate regime, and no capital mobility?

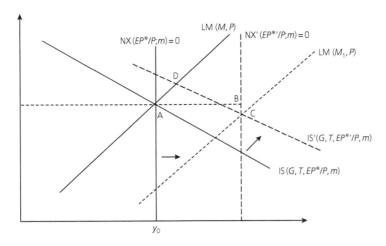

Figure 14.10

We begin by setting the initial scene at point A, see Figure 14.10. The increase in international prices makes the real return for export greater while making imports more expensive. This will cause an increase in demand for net-export at any given level of income. This means an increase in the level of income for which there will be equilibrium in the goods market (the shift of IS to the right) as well as at the level of income which is needed to offset the increased autonomous component of the $NX = 0$:

$$NX\left(\frac{EP^*}{P}, y\right) = \left[X_0\left(\frac{EP^*}{P}\right) - IM_0\left(\frac{EP^*}{P}\right)\right] - m_1 y$$

$$= NX_0\left(\frac{EP^*}{P}\right) - m_1 y = 0$$

$$\Rightarrow y^{NX=0} = \frac{NX_0(EP^*/P)}{m_1}.$$

Clearly, an increase in foreign prices will raise the numerator and thus the level of y for which there NX = 0.

For the given level of interest, the IS moves all the way to point B. The question is whether, or not, NX = 0 moves further to the right. Let us consider point B. As interest is the same as before, assuming that demand for investment is independent of income, the demand for investment would remain unchanged. As at B there is equilibrium in the goods market it also means that the demand for investment is equal to planned savings and the surplus in government budget:

$$I(r_0) = S(y_1) + T - G - NX(y_1).$$

However, clearly $S(y_1) > S(y_0)$ and $T - G$ is unchanged. Thus, for the demand for investment to be the same at B as in A the next export must be positive (NX > 0). If NX > 0 it means that at the level of income at B, there is a surplus in the current account. Namely, the level of income at B is not sufficient to generate enough demand for imports to offset the initial, autonomous, demand for net-export. Hence, the point where it is offset (NX = 0) must be at a higher level of income. The NX must move further to the right than the IS.

At first, the increase in net-export will cause the output to increase and we move along the LM curve (as increased income means a higher level of interest for which there is equilibrium in the goods market) to the new equilibrium (point D). Here, there is still surplus in the current account, which means there is excess supply of foreign currency. As the bank wishes to keep the nominal exchange rate intact, the bank will buy the excess supply in return for an increase in the money supply (increase in reserves). This, in turn, will increase the supply of liquid assets which would suggest that for each level of income, equilibrium will be obtained at a lower level of interest rate. The LM shifts downwards until we get to point C. At point C, interest rates have gone down and this means a greater demand for investment. This increase in investment will be fully financed by an increase in savings as $T - G$ remain unchanged and at C, NX = 0.

Suppose now that instead, there was: an increase in the marginal propensity to import. This will clearly reduce demand for NX which means both a shift to the left for the IS and a lower level of income to offset the initial NX (NX = 0 shifts to the left too). When the change goes through the marginal propensity to import, the IS will also become steeper. Check that, by now, you know why this will happen: see Figure 14.11. As both IS and NX will shift to the left and the question is whether one would shift further to the left than the other. The move to the left of the IS, for a given level of interest rate, would be smaller than the corresponding move by the NX. Recall that at A, by nature of being on the IS, equilibrium conditions in the good markets prevail. This means, among other things, that the capital formation equation holds both *ex ante* and *ex post*. We know that the capital formation always holds but what typifies equilibrium is that the planned investment = planned savings + government surplus – net-export. Therefore, this holds at A:

$$I(r_0) = S(y_0) + T - G - NX(y_0).$$

As a result of an increase in the marginal propensity to import (or due to another change in the autonomous component of the NX function) there will be less demand for domestic

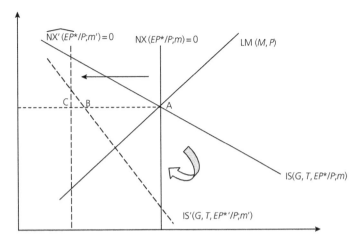

Figure 14.11

output at any given interest rate. IS shifts to the left (point B) where output has adjusted to fit the new aggregate demand. At B, there is a new equilibrium in the goods market and therefore:

$$I(r_0) = S(y_1) + T - G - \widehat{NX}(y_1)$$

where $\widehat{NX}$ represents the new NX function with the higher marginal propensity to import. The demand for investment at B is the same as it was in A (we assume that the demand for investment is independent of income). As $y_1 < y_0$ private savings (S) fell. In equilibrium in the goods market, the demand for domestic investment is equal to the demands for private savings + public savings + net imports ($-NX$). If $I(r)$ were unchanged and S fell, given that $T - G$ are constant, only a negative NX can restore the balance. In other words:

$$\text{if } S(y_1) < S(y_0) \Rightarrow \widehat{NX}(y_1) < 0.$$

But if NX is negative at the new equilibrium at the goods market (for a given interest rate) it means that the point where NX $= 0$ occurs at a lower level of y. In other words, to offset the initial net-export, we need much less income than we have at equilibrium in the goods market (point C). The story would end with a higher interest rate and lower investment which would be due to the fall in savings.

The case of an open economy where there are no capital movements but the exchange rate is flexible will be like the one in Figure 14.12. Here there is no NX constraint as the flexible exchange rate guarantees that at any level of output, nominal exchange rate will adjust to balance the current account without resorting to any change in reserves. This also means that there will be no indirect effects through the money market (the LM). Still, the IS is a function of the real exchange rate because an increase in the real exchange rate means that in real terms people will want to export more and import less.

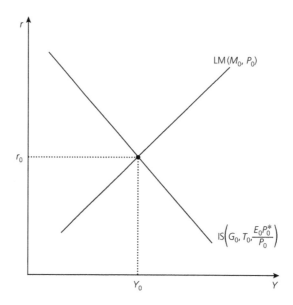

Figure 14.12 Open economy with no capital mobility and flexible exchange rates.

14.4.2 Perfect capital mobility

The introduction of capital mobility means that we now have to take into account the capital account in the balance of payment. At this stage of your study we shall only deal with the simple case where capital mobility is entirely unrestricted. What it is that we are concerned with, as was said before, is not so much the study of the capital market as the analysis of its influences on the goods and liquid assets market.

In the case of a fixed exchange rate, the current account became a constraint to our model. It was evident that unless the economy reaches the level of output where the current account is balanced the economy will not be in equilibrium. However, under a flexible regime, the current account does not impose any restrictions on which level of output can become the equilibrium outcome.

Similarly, perfect capital mobility mainly concerns us as it forms a constraint on our system. Unlike the previous case, this time the constraint is on the domestic interest rate.

Ignoring all other reasons why foreigners may wish to hold domestic assets or locals might wish to hold foreign assets, we concentrate on the role of interest rate. Evidently, whatever is the reason why someone may want to hold domestic assets, he is bound to be affected by the return he gets on his money. Whenever domestic interest rates are higher than those abroad it means that individuals will get a higher return on money which is invested in domestic assets. Everyone, really, will want to move to those assets for which the return is higher.

This means that whenever domestic interest rate (r) is higher than international interest rates (r^*), there will be an almost infinite demand for domestic assets. But to buy domestic assets one must use domestic currency. Therefore, an almost infinite demand for local assets means an almost infinite supply of foreign currency. As the quantity of currency supplied by people wishing to buy local assets (and this may include locals who have until now held foreign assets) is greater than the quantity of foreign currency demanded by those who wish to buy foreign assets (which have a lower rate of return), there would be a surplus in the capital account. This surplus in the capital account will naturally override any conceivable deficit in the current account. This will mean that whenever $r > r^*$ we will be in a chronicle surplus in the balance of payments. Being, as it were, a contradiction in terms, the balance of payments will either be balanced by a continuous decrease in the nominal exchange rate, that is, evaluation (in the case of the flexible regime) or by a continuous increase in reserves. A continuous increase in reserves means that people keep coming to the central bank and bring foreign currency with them. In return for this currency, they will receive domestic currency with which they will be able to fulfil their objective of buying domestic assets. Hence, the quantity of money in the economy will rise.

The meaning of this is that the economy will never reach equilibrium unless the discrepancy between domestic and foreign interest rates is eliminated. International interest rates, therefore, become the constraint of our system (Figure 14.13).

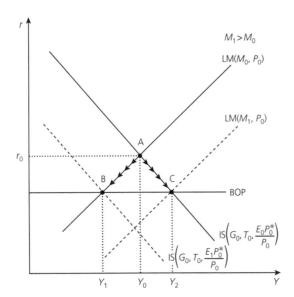

Figure 14.13 Perfect capital mobility.

Suppose that initially there were no capital movements and equilibrium was at r_1. This means that the economy allowed trade in goods but did not allow the free transfers of capital. Now, as a result of liberalization, capital is allowed to move freely. Will this be beneficial or harmful to the economy (naturally, we ignore all dynamic and long-term implications which such reform might imply)?

The answer is: it depends. Once capital markets have been opened, we have to see where the local interest rate is in relation to the international interest rate? When $r_1 > r_0^*$ the opening of the markets will cause what we call an inflow of capital. People from all over the world, preferably, will want to buy local assets for which the rate of return r_1 is greater than that on foreign assets. They will want to buy domestic assets and this would mean that they will bring foreign currency which they will want to convert into domestic currency. This, as we said before would cause excess supply of foreign currency. One of the following scenarios would now unfold.

Flexible exchange rate. In the case of a flexible exchange rate, the excess supply of foreign currency would imply an evaluation of the local currency. E will fall (or rise if we think of $1/E$) and this will imply that the real exchange rate would fall also. If E falls, so does EP^*/P.

In such a case, the cost of imports (in terms of domestic goods) would fall and the return to export would fall. There will therefore be less exports and more imports or, in short, a fall in demand for net-export (NX). As the demand for net-export is the demand for local output, this means that for the same level of interest rate, there will now be less demand for local output. IS, therefore, shifts to the left. As output, and subsequently, income, falls (quantity adjustment), there will now be less demand for liquid assets. As this means that there is an excess supply of liquid assets, there will be an increase in the demand for bonds. This, in turn, will create an excess demand for bonds, which would push bond prices up. The only way this can happen across the market would be for the interest rate to fall. The fall in the interest rate would offset some of the fall in the aggregate demand by raising the demand for investment. All in all, the economy is slowly moving from point A to B. The consequence of liberalization here was a fall in national income (or a recession).

Fixed exchange rate. In the case of fixed exchange rate, the excess supply of foreign currency would mean that the central bank is buying the difference and exchanging it for the local currency (an increase in reserves). As the stock of foreign currency (liquid assets) increases, there will now be excess supply of liquid assets in the liquid assets market. At the given rate of interest and income, people want to hold less liquid assets than are supplied. They will turn to the bonds market to turn the unwanted part of their liquid assets into something a bit less liquid. This means an increase in the demand for bonds which, as we said before, would create excess demand for bonds and a subsequent increase in the bonds' prices. This will happen when interest rates fall. As interest rates fall, the demand for investment will increase and there will now be excess demand in the goods market which will cause an increase in output (quantity adjustment). An increase in output and, subsequently, income would then cause an increase in demand for liquid assets which will offset the initial excess supply. All in all, we move from A to C. In this case, the result of liberalization was an increase in national income.

The outcome of this liberalization in terms of employment is significantly different under the two different exchange rate regimes. If one believes that it is in the nature of such liberalization to allow for a flexible exchange rate, the consequences on the economy would be much less favourable had the government limited the liberalization to the movement of capital alone. But, before you jump to conclusions and make sweeping generalizations, note what would have happened at the initial domestic interest rate been lower than the international returns on assets (see Figure 14.14).

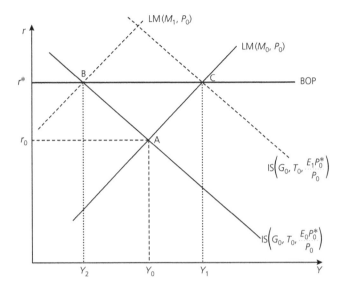

Figure 14.14

We start at A:

Flexible Exchange Rate. As the international interest rate is higher than the domestic one, the return on foreign assets is much greater than the return on domestic assets. This means that people who hold domestic assets (including foreigners) would want to switch to foreign assets. We call this an outflow of capital. But to buy foreign assets one would need to buy foreign currency first. This means that there will now be an increased demand for foreign currency which will generate an excess demand. When the exchange rate is flexible, this means that the nominal exchange rate will rise (devaluation of the local currency). As E increases so does the real exchange rate (EP^*/P). This means that imports would become more expensive in real terms while the return on export would increase. Hence, the demand for net-export (NX) would rise and the aggregate demand for local output would increase too. IS will shift to the right. As output and, subsequently income increase, the demand for liquid assets would increase too. This will create, at the going interest rate, excess demand for liquid assets which would increase the supply of bonds (people are trying to convert less liquid assets into liquid assets). The price of bonds would fall through an increase in the domestic interest rate. This, in turn, would reduce demand for domestic investment and offset some of the increase in demand for local output. All in all we move from A to B where the outcome of liberalization accompanied by flexible exchange rate seems beneficial.

Fixed Exchange Rate. The excess demand for foreign currency would be directed at the central bank who would sell foreign currency to try to keep the exchange rate at its current rate. As the bank sells foreign currency it removes from circulation the domestic currency used to pay for its reserves. As the quantity of liquid assets diminishes, at the same rate of interest and income, the public's demand for liquid assets is greater than the supply. For any given level of income, the equilibrium in the liquid assets market would occur at a higher interest rate. This is a shift upwards of the LM. At the current rate of interest the excess demand would translate into an excess supply of bonds which would decrease their price through an increase in the interest rate. As the interest rate increases, demand for domestic output would fall as demand for investment would fall. All in all, we move from A to C along the IS. The result of liberalization accompanied by a fixed exchange rate would be recessionary.

Therefore, one should not approach macroeconomic analysis with any preconceptions. Unlike microeconomics there are not many results which do not depend on circumstances. In macro, as, in fact, in any analytical examination, one must be conscious of the many factors which may influence the results. The model which we have developed here is genuinely a tool. We must apply it with care and remember that it is very easy to overturn many results. This, of course, does not mean that the model is useless. After all, its purpose was not to instil ideas in your head about what should governments do. Instead, we have drawn up a set of tools with which, I hope, you should be able to form an opinion about what might be the consequences of any macro action and how might relevant institutions influence the outcome.

Self-assessment and applications

In this section, I have collected a few questions which are of a more comprehensive nature. Some of these questions are difficult but you should not lose confidence. I am sure that if you seriously try to deal with these questions, your knowledge—in the sense of using the models—will be considerably enhanced.

▩ QUESTION 1

In an election year, the government increased its spending by borrowing from the public. To prevent an increase in the interest rate, the government convinced the central bank to reduce the reserve ratio for commercial banks. The opposition accused the government of sowing the seeds of recession while mortgaging the future (reducing investment).

(a) Discuss the opposition accusations in an open economy without any capital movements and a fixed exchange rate policy.

(b) Discuss the opposition accusations in an open economy with perfect capital mobility.

Answer

The two changes in the economy proposed by this question are:

(i) an increase in government's spending (G) financed by borrowing from the public;

(ii) an increase in money supply due to a fall of the reserve ratio.

In Chapter 13 we analysed the same case in a closed economy. We now extend the analysis to the open economy:

(a) Open economy without capital mobility and a fixed exchange rate (Figure 14.15).

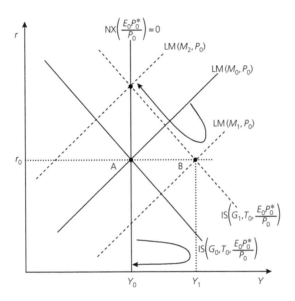

Figure 14.15

IS shifts to the right and LM shifts downwards. The IS–LM equilibrium shifts from A to the equilibrium at B. Greater income will increase demand for imported goods. This will cause excess demand for foreign currency which will be supplied by the central bank through a decrease in the money supply. LM shifts upwards as at each level of income there is now equilibrium at a higher level of interest. Interest rate will rise. The adjustment will last until LM cuts the new IS at a point where $NX = 0$. This means that the effects of increasing government spending would be to cause an increase in the interest rate which would reduce demand for investment. As output remains at its original level, the increase in G was entirely financed (in real terms) by a fall in interest rate. This is what we called crowding out. This is a similar outcome to the one we got for a closed economy with flexible wages.

(b) Open economy with perfect capital mobility (Figure 14.16).

The initial change is the same as in the previous case. IS–LM shift from equilibrium at A to a new equilibrium at B. If the policy mix achieved its aim (no change in interest rates) this is where the economy will remain under both fixed and flexible exchange rate regimes.

▒ QUESTION 2

A government with a budget deficit decides to reduce the size of its army by providing early retirement to a third of its staff. The retired cohort, being, still, relatively young, seeks to

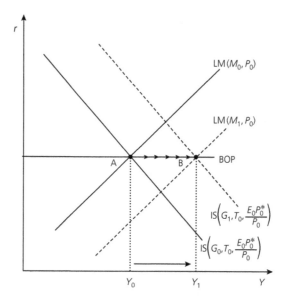

Figure 14.16

compensate themselves for their hard years of service by an ongoing spending spree with a particular taste for imported goods.

(a) Analyse the effects of the government policy in an open economy without capital mobility and with a fixed exchange rate regime.

(b) What will happen to investment in the economy in the case of (a)? Would your answer be different had the exchange rate been flexible?

Answer

The effects of reducing the size of the army by providing early retirement are complex. You must conduct your analysis with greater care.

Direct effect
The immediate effect of reducing the army size is a fall in G. The early retirement means that those ex-servicemen are getting a pension which, in turn, reduces T (net transfers). As the aim of the policy was to tackle a deficit in the government's budget, it is assumed that $|G_1 - T_1| < |G_0 - T_0|$. Namely, the fall in G (which equals to the spending on the servicemen while in the army) is greater than the fall in T.

Influence on aggregate expenditures
Assuming for simplicity's sake, a system of lump sum taxes, this will bring about a fall in the autonomous component of aggregate expenditures:

$$\Delta A = \Delta G - c_1^S \Delta T < 0$$

as

$$\Delta G < 0 \qquad \Delta T < 0$$

and

$$|\Delta G| > |\Delta T|,$$

where c_1^s is the marginal propensity to consume of the ex-servicemen.

At the same time, we know that the ex-servicemen will direct their spending at imported goods. This means that there will be an increase in the marginal propensity to import. This, in turn, will reduce the multiplier as greater part of extra demand would be directed abroad thus reducing the pressure on domestic output. It will also mean that the level of output for which NX will be balanced is lower.

(a) The framework of analysis is obviously the IS–LM with the vertical NX (reflecting the fixed exchange rate regime). As there is no reference to prices or wages, one does not need to deal with the AD–AS model (Figure 14.17).

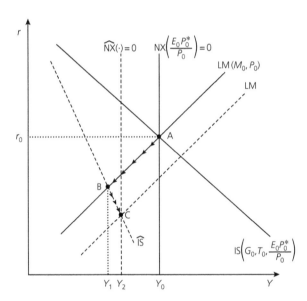

Figure 14.17

We start at point A where there is general equilibrium. The fall in government deficit means that a greater part of public spending is financed by taxes (and thus, by consumption). This means a fall in the autonomous component. As $dA < 0$, then at any level of interest rate, there will be a smaller demand for domestic output. The IS should shift to the left. However, as at the same time there was an increase in the marginal propensity to import, the multiplier: $1/1 - c_1 + m$ would fall too. This, in turn, suggests that the IS will shift further to the left and it becomes steeper. Namely, whenever interest rate falls and there is an increase in demand for investment, a greater share of this increase would be directed to imports (and a smaller to local output). At the same time, the NX line should shift to the left reflecting the fact that with a higher marginal propensity to import, for any given exchange rate and initial net-export, less income would be required to balance export. Recall that $NX = 0$ is really

$$NX\left(\frac{EP^*}{P}, y\right) = \left[X_0\left(\frac{EP^*}{P}\right) - IM_0\left(\frac{EP^*}{P}\right)\right] - m_1 y = NX_0\left(\frac{EP^*}{P}\right) - m_1 y = 0$$

$$\Rightarrow y^{NX=0} = \frac{NX_0(EP^*/P)}{m_1}.$$

It is easy to see that when the marginal propensity to import (m) increases, the level of income for which $NX = 0$ will fall.

Note, however, that while we clearly demonstrated that when the marginal propensity to imports increases the shift of the IS to the left is going to be smaller than the shift in the $NX = 0$, in our case, this is no longer necessarily true. The reason for this is that, here, the IS is affected by two changes and not only by the increase in the marginal propensity to import. In addition to this, the IS also shifts to the left due to a fall in government deficit. Hence, it is quite possible in this case for the IS to shift further to the left than the $NX = 0$ which is only affected by the increase in the marginal propensity to import.

We assume that NX will shift from Y_0 to Y_2. We also assume that the IS will shift further to the left to bring about an equilibrium at Y_1.

Due to the cut in government spending, the economy moves from A to B where there is now a fall in demand for imports which triggers excess demand for export. This will prompt excess supply of foreign currency and as the exchange rate is fixed, this will be absorbed by the central bank which will, in return, increase the supply of liquid assets. LM will shift downwards until equilibrium is restored at C. The reduction in government's deficit has brought about a recession but lower interest rates (hence, greater demand for investment).

(b) This is a question on national accounts:

$$I = S + (T - G) + (Im - X).$$

$(T - G)$ increased; S fell (due to lower income) $(Im - X) = 0$ (the increase in demand for imports by ex-servicemen had been offset by the fall in income). If the demand for investment is a function of the interest rate alone, this would mean that the increase in government savings was greater than the fall in private savings.

Flexible exchange rate

In such a case, the initial move from A to B would have brought about excess supply of foreign currency which would have caused an appreciation of the real exchange rate. NX would fall further and the IS will shift further to the left. The recession will be greater and the increase in demand for investment much more moderate. The new equilibrium would then be at the same level of interest as at point C. This is so because in the end, the increase in I will have to equal to the increase in $T - G$ which has not been affected by the exchange rate regime.

QUESTION 3

In order to attract high-flyers and invigorate the economy, the government decides to reduce the highest marginal tax rate and to increase the lower marginal tax rate. The change has been designed in such a way as to keep the overall level of tax receipts unchanged. Some argued that favouring the high-flyers will only bring about a recession and a fall in investment.

(a) Examine the argument in the context of an open economy with perfect capital mobility and a fixed exchange rate.

(b) Would your answer be different had exchange rate been flexible?

(c) Examine the argument in the context of an open economy without capital mobility and with a fixed exchange rate regime.

Answer

Again, this is a question with which we dealt in Chapter 13 as far as a closed economy is concerned. Here we extend the analysis to the open economy.

To remind you, the main problem in this question is to identify the change. To translate, as it were, the question into the language of the model. It is clear here that we must distinguish between two groups of consumers: higher wage earners and low wage earners. As overall tax receipts have not changed, this is really a transfer of income from the poor to the rich. As such, if the poor have a greater marginal propensity to consume than the rich, every pound transferred will yield a net fall in consumption. Alternatively, we can write down the following consumption function:

$$C(Y) = C_0 + c_1^H (1 - t_H) Y_H + c_1^L (1 - t_L) Y_L$$

$$\Delta C = -c_1^H \Delta t_H Y_H - c_1^L \Delta t_L Y_L, \text{ as } \Delta t_H < 0 \qquad \Delta t_L > 0 \qquad \Delta t_H < \Delta t_L$$

$$\Delta C < 0$$

which means a fall in consumption at any level of income. The logic of this is quite clear as this is a transfer from the poor with a higher marginal propensity to consume to the rich with a lower marginal propensity to consume. We also know that as the tax is dependent on income, that the effect of the change will come through a reduced multiplier. This means that the IS will shift to the left and become steeper. If you are interested in the full exposition of this, please look at the question in Chapter 13.

(a) Open economy with perfect capital mobility and a fixed exchange rate (Figure 14.18). The IS shifts to the left and becomes steeper. There is excess supply for goods at point A output falls. This, in turn, reduces the level of interest rate for which there is equilibrium in the liquid assets market and we move along the LM to the new equilibrium at a lower level of income and a lower level of interest rate (and a greater demand for investment): (A to B). As domestic interest rate is now below the international rate, the return on foreign assets is greater than the return on domestic assets. People will want to buy foreign assets and will, therefore, instigate excess demand for foreign currency (outflow of capital) which, with a fixed exchange rate, will bring to a fall in money supply. The LM will shift upwards and the recession will deepen at point C.

(b) Open economy with perfect capital mobility and a flexible exchange rate (Figure 14.19).

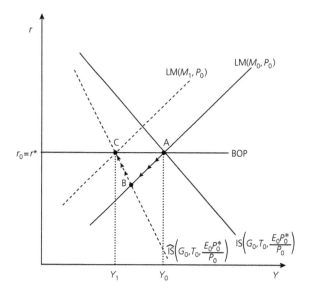

Figure 14.18

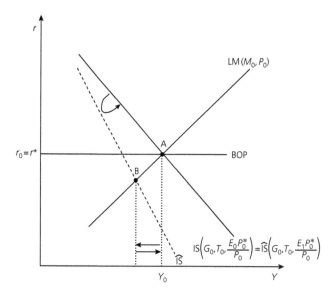

Figure 14.19

The same initial change takes place: IS becomes steeper and we shift from equilibrium at A to equilibrium at B. Domestic interest rate falls and there is an outflow of capital. This means excess demand for foreign currency which, with a flexible exchange rate, will bring to a depreciation (increase in E) that will increase demand for NX. The IS will shift to the right and the economy will return to its original position.

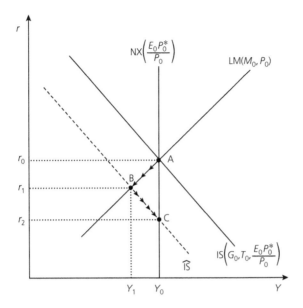

Figure 14.20

(c) Open economy without capital mobility and a fixed exchange rate (Figure 14.20). The same initial change. IS shifts from equilibrium at A to equilibrium at B. Less income will reduce demand for imported goods. There will now be a surplus in the current account. This will cause excess supply of foreign currency which will be absorbed by the central bank through an increase in the money supply. LM shifts downwards and interest rates will fall further (B to C).

QUESTION 4

The government decides to switch from an income tax to an expenditure tax. This means that from now on people will pay tax only on that part of their income which they used for consumption. The tax system remained proportional and the rate of tax has not changed:

(a) What will be the closed economy multiplier after the change and will it be greater or smaller than the previous multiplier?

(b) Analyse the effects of the change on an open economy without capital mobility and with a fixed exchange rate regime.

(c) Analyse the effects of the change on an open economy with perfect capital mobility and with a fixed exchange rate.

(d) Analyse the effects of the change on an open economy with perfect capital mobility and with a flexible exchange rate.

Answer

Again, this is a continuation of a question which we started in Chapter 10 (question 7). I shall repeat here the main initial change.

The government proposes an expenditure tax. This means that now, instead of a tax function of the following nature:

$$T(Y) = tY$$

we will have a tax system of this nature:

$$T(Y) = tC(Y).$$

(a) The multiplier of a closed economy:

We begin by describing the new consumption function:

$$C(Y) = C_0 + c_1(Y - T(Y)) = C_0 + c_1 Y - c_1 tC(Y)$$

$$C(Y)(1 + c_1 t) = C_0 + c_1 Y$$

$$C(Y) = \frac{C_0 + c_1 Y}{(1 + c_1 t)}$$

$$C(Y) = \frac{C_0}{(1 + c_1 t)} + \frac{c_1}{(1 + c_1 t)} Y.$$

This means that now, the AE function will have the following structure and subsequent multiplier:

$$AE(Y, r) = A(r, t) + \frac{c_1}{(1 + c_1 t)} Y.$$

Equilibrium means

$$AE(Y, r) = Y$$

$$A(r, t) + \frac{c_1}{(1 + c_1 t)} Y = Y$$

$$Y = A(r, t) \frac{1}{1 - (c_1/(1 + c_1 t))}.$$

We must now examine the relationship between this multiplier and the normal proportional tax multiplier:

$$\frac{1}{1 - (c_1/(1 + c_1 t))} > \frac{1}{1 - c_1(1 - t)} \tag{1}$$

$$1 - c_1(1 - t) > 1 - \frac{c_1}{(1 + c_1 t)}$$

$$\frac{c_1}{(1 + c_1 t)} > c_1(1 - t)$$

$$1 > (1 - t)(1 + c_1 t)$$

$$1 > 1 - t + c_1 t - c_1 t^2$$

$$t > t[c_1(1 - t)]$$

$$1 > c_1(1 - t). \tag{2}$$

As equation (2) is always true, so must equation (1).

(b) The framework of analysis is obviously the IS–LM with the vertical NX (reflecting the fixed exchange rate regime). As there is no reference to prices or wages, one does not need to deal with the AD–AS model (Figure 14.21).

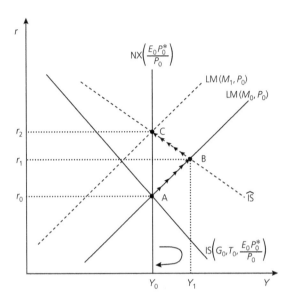

Figure 14.21

We start at point A where there is general equilibrium. The immediate effect of the change will be a reduction in the autonomous component of the AE as we have substituted C_0 with $C_0/(1 + c_1 t)$ the latter being a smaller expression. However, as the multiplier is now greater, at any given level of interest rate there will now be greater demand for consumption and an equilibrium at a higher level of y. Let A be the autonomous component which is common to the AE function before and after the change. Let Y_1 and Y_0 be the equilibrium levels of output in the goods market after and before the change, respectively. Within the framework of the closed economy we will then find:

$$Y_1 - Y_0 = \left[A(r_0) + C_0 \left(\frac{1}{1 + c_1 t} \right) \right] \frac{1}{1 - (c_1/1 + c_1{}^t)} - [A(r_0) + C_0] \frac{1}{1 - c_1(1 - t)}$$

$$= A \left[\frac{1}{1 - (c_1/1 + c_1{}^t)} - \frac{1}{1 - c_1(1 - t)} \right] + C_0 \left[\frac{1}{1 - c_1(1 - t)} - \frac{1}{1 - c_1(1 - t)} \right]$$

$$> 0.$$

This means that at any given rate of interest the overall effect will be an increase in the equilibrium level of income. IS, thus, shifts to the right and becomes flatter. This will also be true in the open economy where the increase in output will bring about a rise in interest rate. As a result, demand for imports rises too and there is now excess demand for foreign currency which will be supplied by the central bank through a decrease in the money supply. The LM will shift upwards and equilibrium will be restored at the initial level of output and a higher interest rate.

(c) and **(d)** Open economy with perfect capital mobility.

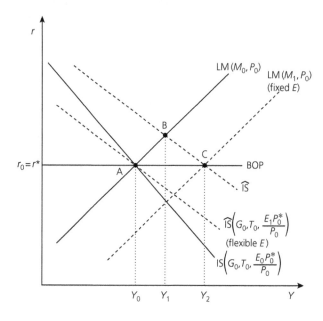

Figure 14.22

We start at point A where there is general equilibrium (see Figure 14.22). As in (b) the change will be a shift to the right of the IS with a slightly flatter slope. This will cause a rise in the level of output and in the domestic interest rate (A to B).

The higher domestic interest rate means that the return on domestic assets is greater than the return on foreign assets. This will cause capital inflows and an excess supply of foreign currency.

Fixed exchange rate.
As the exchange rate is fixed, the excess supply will be absorbed by the central bank through an increase in money supply. This will shift the LM downwards and bring about a further increase in output (from B to C).

Flexible exchange rate.
The excess supply of foreign currency will cause an appreciation that will decrease demand for NX. Hence, the IS will shift to the left and the economy will return to its initial point.

■ **QUESTION 5**

The public in an economy have lost confidence in the safety of the domestic production of a certain product.

(a) What effect might this have on the economy's multiplier?

(b) Analyse the consequences of such a loss of confidence on an open economy without capital mobility with a fixed exchange rate?

(c) Would the outcome be similar if this had been an open economy with perfect capital mobility and a fixed exchange rate?

(d) Critics of government policy argue that only by removing all barriers to the adjustment of the exchange rate will the problem be resolved. Discuss this argument.

Answer

When the public loses confidence in the safety of domestic production they will want to consume less of it and turn to imports if available.

(a) The effect on the multiplier: It is not obvious from the question whether the lack of confidence will manifest itself through a fall in the autonomous component of consumption (and an equivalent rise in the autonomous component of demand for imports), or a fall in the marginal propensity to consume (and an increase in the marginal propensity to import). Had the change been in the marginal propensities rather than the autonomous component of aggregate demand, then:

$$\frac{1}{1-c_1+m_1} > \frac{1}{1-c_1+m_1+dc_1+dm_1}$$

where $dc_1 < 0$ and $dm_1 > 0$ denote the fall and increase in marginal propensity to consume and to import.

Whichever way we formulate the question both changes work in the same direction. The fall in demand for consumption and the increase in demand for imports point at an overall fall in aggregate demand.

(b) Open economy without capital mobility and a fixed exchange rate:

(i) A change in the autonomous components of consumption and import (see Figure 14.23): had the change been in terms of the autonomous components then the diagrams below depict two possible outcomes. As we do not know a priori whether the fall in consumption was greater or smaller than the increase in the autonomous component of import, the economy may move to the equilibrium depicted in point B above. Naturally, the move would not be at once to B. Note that here again we cannot apply the rule regarding the simultaneous shifts of IS and NX=0. This is so because while the change in the marginal propensity to import affects both NX and IS; IS is also affected by a fall in the marginal propensity to consume.

If NX=0 moved to the left of point B (left-hand diagram of Figure 14.23) then at B there would be a deficit in the current account. This means excess demand for imports and, hence, for foreign currency. Given the fixed exchange rate policy, the central bank would sell the difference between the quantity of foreign currency demanded by importers and the quantity supply by the exporters, and in so doing, reduce the supply of liquid assets (as the bank gives foreign currency from its reserves). This would shift the LM upwards to the point where IS, LM, and NX=0 all meet.

Had the NX=0 been to the right of point B (right-hand diagram of Figure 14.23) then at B there would be a surplus in the current account and as a result, excess supply of foreign currency. The bank would buy the difference in order to prevent the nominal exchange rate from depreciating and, in doing so, increase the quantity of liquid assets in the economy (this is so because whenever

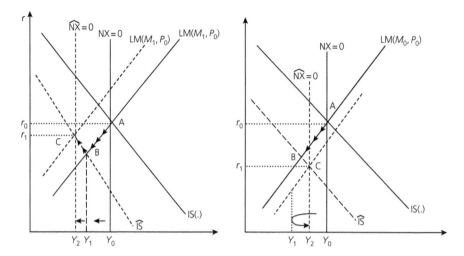

Figure 14.23

there is an increase in the reserve, it means that the bank took foreign currency from an exporter who, say, came back from abroad, and gave him local currency which has not been in circulation; now, it will be). This will shift the LM downward until again, IS,LM, and NX=0 meet. There is, of course, the possibility that the NX would shift further to the left than the IS. In both cases, the investment would rise (if it is independent of income). As $I = S(y) + T - G - NX$ and NX=0, the fact that $T - G$ remains unchanged means that the increase in investment came from the increase in savings triggered by the fall in demand for consumption.

(ii) The change through the marginal propensities to consume and import: As before, as there are changes in both consumption and income, it is difficult to establish which of the curves (IS or NX=0) would move further to the left. However, unlike the previous case, here the slope of the IS will become steeper as a result of the fall in marginal propensity to consume and the rise in marginal propensity to import. To cover more possibilities I shall assume that here the shift of the IS was smaller than the shift in the NX=0. This does not follow from the fact that this time we analyse marginal propensities. I could have, equally well, done so in the previous case.

Here, the shift to the left of the NX=0 is greater than the shift to the left of the IS (Figure 14.24). The economy would move slowly from A to B as there is a fall in demand for local output. As income falls, the demand for liquid assets would fall too and this would bring about a fall in the interest rate. In turn this will slightly offset the initial falls in demand. As the economy reaches a partial equilibrium at B, there is still excess demand for imports (NX< 0). It means that the bank would interfere and sell importers foreign currency from the reserves and thus, decrease the quantity of liquid assets. As this happens, LM shifts upwards until the new equilibrium is obtained at point C. Here, at C, investment fell. This means that as NX=0 and $T - G$ is unchanged, the fall in income more than offsets the increase in savings which resulted from the fall in demand for consumption.

(c) Open economy with perfect capital mobility and a fixed exchange rate (Figure 14.25). The initial shift in the IS is subject to the same qualifications as in (b). At the same time, there is the initial shift in the demand for foreign currency. We start at A and there is a fall in demand for domestic output. As the income falls interest rates will come down and the domestic interest rate

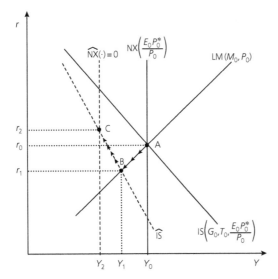

Figure 14.24

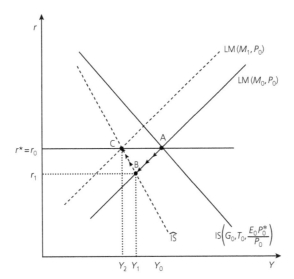

Figure 14.25

will be lower than the international interest rate. Whether or not the fall in income was sufficient to offset the exogenous increase in demand for foreign currency is immaterial, as there will be capital outflow at this lower domestic interest rate. This means further increase in the demand for foreign currency. With a fixed exchange rate, the central bank will be selling foreign currency and reducing the supply of real balances. LM will shift upwards and equilibrium will be restored at point C.

(d) What would have happened had exchange rates been flexible? In case (b), when there are no capital flows, having a flexible exchange rate would have only mattered if the speed of the exchange rate adjustment was faster than the output adjustment. In principle, we said that the exogenous increase in demand for foreign currency could be offset by a fall in output. If nominal exchange rate were allowed to depreciate, it would have brought an increase in demand for net-export. This would have shifted IS to the right and the recession would not have been a serious as in case (b).

With perfect capital mobility (Figure 14.26).

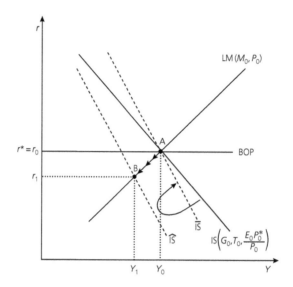

Figure 14.26

After the initial fall in IS and the subsequent outflow of capital, the increased demand for foreign currency would have brought about a depreciation of domestic currency (increase in E) and an increase in demand for NX. IS would have moved back to its initial position and the loss in confidence would have been compensated by exports (not necessarily of the products under suspicion). Note that if the changes affected the slope of the IS, there will be a new IS cutting through point A.

▨ QUESTION 6

A government decides to privatize a branch of its activities through out-tendering. Assuming that the private agency which gains the tender can provide the service for less than it had cost the government, what will be the effects of this policy on:

(a) A closed economy with fixed wages?

(b) A closed economy with flexible wages?

(c) An open economy with perfect capital mobility and a fixed exchange rate?

(d) How would your answers to (a)–(c) change had the policy been accompanied by a decrease in taxes?

Answer

When the government decides to privatize part of its activities through out-tendering, this is not the case of assets sales. Instead, the only effect that this will have is that the spending on the provision of some services will now be lower. The government is substituting salaries with purchases from other firms. This will reduce the size of G. Hence, the question requires an analysis of a contractory fiscal policy.

(a) Closed economy with fixed wages. IS shifts to the left and there is a new equilibrium at a lower level of income and a lower level of interest rate (and a greater demand for investment) (Figure 14.27).

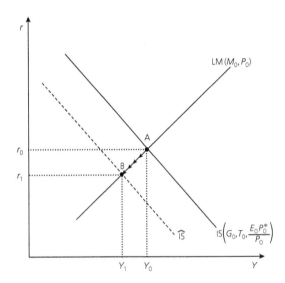

Figure 14.27

(b) Closed economy with flexible wages: (see Figure 14.28). IS shifts to the left and so does AD. Prices fall from P_0 to P_1 which reduces the supply of real balances. At any level of income there will now be equilibrium in this market at a lower level of interest: a shift downwards of the LM. In the long run, as real wages increase, there will be a nominal fall in their value which, if correctly anticipating the effects of lesser cost on future prices, will bring the economy to point C. As prices decrease further, the LM will shift further down until it reaches point C (in the IS–LM) where the economy will return to long run equilibrium.

(c) Open economy with perfect capital mobility and a fixed exchange rate (Figure 14.29): The same initial change. IS shifts to the left from equilibrium at A to equilibrium at B. Domestic interest rate falls and there is an outflow of capital. This means excess demand for foreign currency which, with a fixed exchange rate, will bring to a fall in money supply. The LM will shift upwards and the recession will deepen at point C.

(d) A decrease in taxes suggests an expansionary fiscal policy. A fall in T will increase consumption. If T fell by exactly the same amount as did G (from out-tendering) and the government's marginal propensity to spend is unity, consumption will increase by less than the fall in G. The overall change as a result of both fall in G and a fall in T would be to affect the autonomous component by $dA = dG - c_1 dT$, where $dG < 0$ and $dT < 0$.

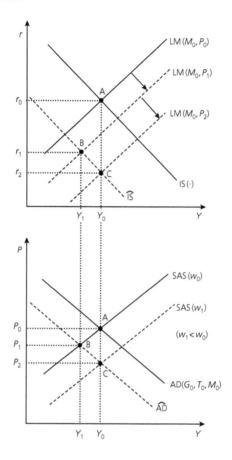

Figure 14.28

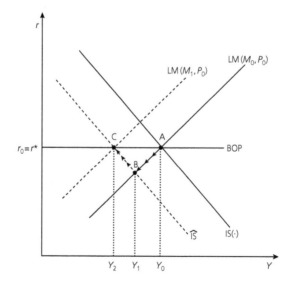

Figure 14.29

Case 1: If the increase in consumption as a result of the fall in T is less than the fall in G, $(|dG| > |c_1 dT|$ then $dA < 0$ and the analysis in (a)–(c) will be basically the same. The only difference will be that the fall in IS (and AD) will be much smaller.

Case 2: If the increase in consumption as a result of the fall in T is exactly the same as the fall in G, there will be no change and the analysis in (a)–(c) will not be relevant.

Case 3: If the increase in consumption as a result of the fall in T is greater than the fall in G, then we will have to analyse an expansionary fiscal policy.

In case (a) this will mean an increase in output and interest rates.

In case (b) this will mean a short run increase in output and interest rates and a fall in real wages. In the long run, it will mean higher prices, the same real wages as before the change, higher interest rates which suggests a crowding out of investment to finance (in real terms) the increase in consumption.

In case (c) as IS increases and domestic interest rates exceed the international rates, there will be an inflow of capital and an excess supply of foreign currency. With the intervention of the central bank, the excess supply of foreign currency will cause an increase in real balances (LM shifts downwards) and as a result, output will increase.

▨ QUESTION 7

Two economies are the main trading partners of each other. Both have similar institutions of perfect capital mobility and a flexible exchange rate. Taxes are proportional in both economies. Economy A has a large deficit in the government's budget while economy B's budget is balanced. The central bank of economy A raises concern for domestic investment and pursues an expansionary monetary policy.

(a) Analyse the effects of the policy on the output, the budget deficit, interest rates, and investment in both economies (bear in mind that there is a single exchange rate in both economies, when there is a depreciation in economy A's currency it means an appreciation in economy B's currency).

(b) Would the central bank of economy B wish to respond? If so, what could it do and how will it affect the two economies?

(c) Would your answer to (a) have been different had the two economies had the same currency and a single central Bank?

Answer

This is a very complicated question so please make sure that you understand every step of the way.

   (a) We have two trading partners with perfect capital mobility and flexible exchange rates. Economy A has a large budget deficit while economy B has a balanced budget. For simplicity's sake, we may assume that NX of country A (which is −NX of country B) is balanced at the initial point. You should first explain the concerns of the central bank in economy A and set out the capital formation equation:

$$I = S_p + (T - G) - NX$$

and see that with NX=0, a deficit means less domestic investment.

Before we launch into the analysis of the effect of the monetary policy in economy A we must note that in the question there is no information regarding to whether the two economies have flexible or fixed wages. Normally, when no information is given with regard to wages and prices you should know to assume fixed prices and wages. We shall therefore conduct the analysis from this point of view.

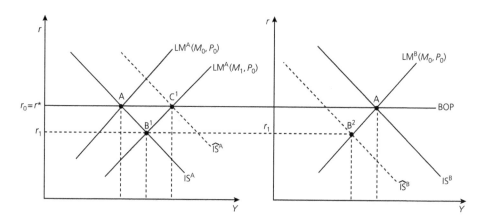

Figure 14.30

We start at point A in both economies (Figure 14.30). An expansionary monetary policy in economy A will shift the LM downwards. We move to point B^1.

As the interest rate in economy A is now lower than international (and economy B's) interest rates, there will be capital outflow from economy A. This will cause an increase in demand for economy B's currency which, in turn, will cause a depreciation of A's currency (excess demand for foreign currency in A) and a corresponding appreciation in B's currency (excess supply of foreign currency). This means that the demand for NX by country A will increase and IS will shift to the right to point C^1. This also means that demand for NX in economy B will fall. IS (in the right hand diagram) will shift to the left and we end up at point B^2. At this first instance, economy A will be producing more, increase tax revenues (as we have a proportional tax system) as well as savings but offsetting (from the point of view of domestic investment) these increases by an increase in NX. There is no reason to believe that in this first instance, the aim of the bank would not have been achieved. However, the system is not in equilibrium (see Figure 14.31).

Economy A is at C^1 and economy B is at B^2. Now, the interest rate in B is lower than the international (and A's) interest rate and there will be capital outflow. This, in turn, will reverse the outcome. There will be excess demand for foreign currency in B which will cause a depreciation (and an appreciation in A). This will increase demand for NX in B and reduce the demand for it at A. IS in A will shift back while IS in B will shift back towards its original position at C^2.

So we now have an unstable situation. The economies are constantly moving along the bold lines connecting points B to C. When A is at C, economy B will be at B and vice versa. Nevertheless, the

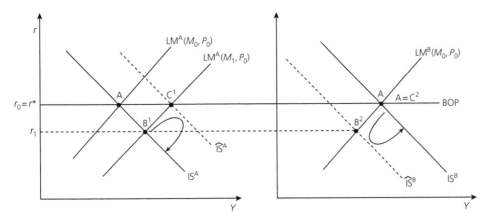

Figure 14.31

position of economy A is slightly better. Economy A enjoys greater output even when at point B, while economy B is fluctuating between recession and no change. When at B, domestic investment at A is increased by the higher level of income (increasing private savings and tax revenues) as well as relatively low level of NX. When at C, NX is offsetting some of these changes but this might be compensated by the further increases in income. Economy B, however, is fluctuating between the initial position and a much reduced level of domestic investment (caused by lower income and the subsequent fall in savings and tax revenues) which is slightly offset by the fall in NX.

(b) The central bank in economy B may intervene in two different ways (Figure 14.32).

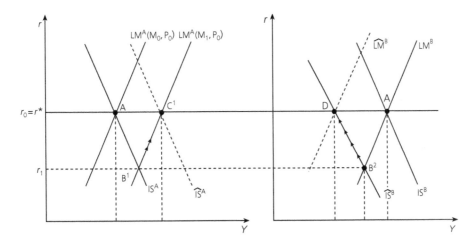

Figure 14.32

It may either choose to stop the fluctuation which can only be achieved if the bank pursues a contractory monetary policy. This will shift the LM in the right-hand diagram of the figure from above upwards and restore equilibrium at a lower level of output as well as domestic investment in economy B. This is a very unlikely policy aim for the central bank of economy B.

The alternative is to choose a fluctuating relationship but on better terms for B (Figure 14.33).

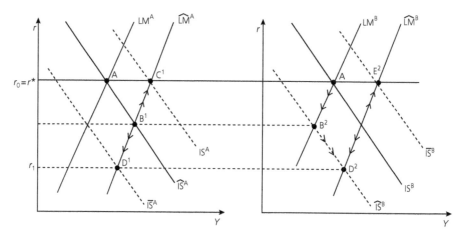

Figure 14.33

This could be done by pursuing its own monetary expansion. By so doing, we move from B^2 to D^2 which will increase the capital outflow from B and produce a much more pronounced depreciation of its own currency. This will lead economy B to point E^2 which, in turn, will make the downturn of economy A worse (point D^1). Now both economies may be fluctuating between different levels of output which are greater everywhere than the original level of output, and both will experience higher levels of domestic investment.

(c) If the two economies had a single currency and a single central bank then an expansionary monetary policy would have shifted the LM downwards in both economies (Figure 14.34).

This would have caused a fall in the interest rate which, in turn, would have invoked an outflow of capital outside the area within the single currency. As a result, there will be a depreciation of the

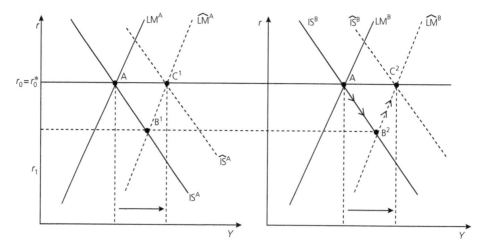

Figure 14.34

single currency. There will be an increase in demand for NX to the world outside the 'fortress' and both economies will enjoy an expansion in output, an increase in tax revenues and private savings which will be slightly offset by the increase in their combined NX.

▓ QUESTION 8

In an election year, three parties are competing for power. The 'extremely helpful party' (EHP) claims that there is an element of government activity which is independent of how well the economy is doing. In addition, the government's activities should expand whenever income is rising. The 'let them pay party' (LTPP) agrees that there is an element of government activity which is independent of how well the economy is doing. However, in their view, some of the government activities should be withdrawn as income increases. The 'do not care party' (DNCP) argues that the government's activities should be confined to maintaining the institutional framework of the economy. This, they claim, is independent of how well the economy is doing. The current party in power is the DNCP.

Analyse the effects of all possible election outcomes on the following items.

(a) The economy's multiplier;

(b) A closed economy with fixed wages? Will your answer be different had wages been flexible?

(c) An open economy with a fixed exchange rate and without capital mobility;

(d) An open economy with a fixed exchange rate and with perfect capital mobility;

(e) An open economy with a flexible exchange rate and perfect capital mobility.

Answer

This is a very simple question. Each of the political parties represent a different form of demand for public consumption.

$$\text{Extremely Helpful Party}: \quad G(Y) = g_0 + g_1 Y,$$
$$\text{Let them Pay Party}: \quad G(Y) = g_0 - g_1 Y,$$
$$\text{Do not Care Party}: \quad G = g_0.$$

At present that DNC party is in power.
(a) The effects on the multiplier:

$$\text{With EHP}: \quad G(Y) = g_0 + g_1 Y \quad \text{hence} \quad M_{EHP} = \frac{1}{1 - c_1 - g_1}$$

$$\text{With LTPP}: \quad G(Y) = g_0 - g_1 Y \quad \text{hence} \quad M_{LTPP} = \frac{1}{1 - c_1 + g_1}$$

$$\text{With DNCP}: \quad G = g_0 \quad \text{hence} \quad M_{DNCP} = \frac{1}{1 - c_1}$$

$$M_{EHP} = \frac{1}{1 - c_1 - g_1} > M_{DNCP} = \frac{1}{1 - c_1} > M_{LTPP} = \frac{1}{1 - c_1 + g_1}$$

(b) A closed economy with fixed wages (Figure 14.35):

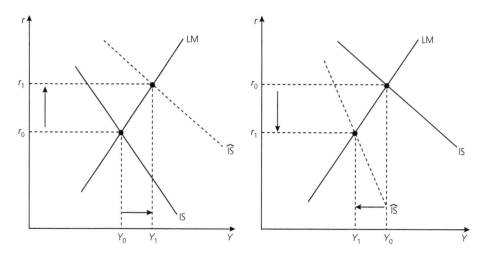

Figure 14.35

If the DNCP wins the election there will be no effect on the economy as everything stays as it was until the election. Hence, we must concentrate on the case of EHP or LTPP winning the election.

The left-hand diagram depicts the effects of EHP's win. At any given level of income there will now be greater demand for domestic product generated by the extra component in the $G(Y)$ function. Hence, IS shifts to the right. In addition, as the multiplier increases, the IS will become flatter.

The right-hand diagram depicts the case of LTPP's win. Here, there will be a smaller demand for domestic product at each level of income. The IS will shift to the left. In addition, as the new multiplier is now smaller IS will become steeper.

In the case of EHP winning the election there will be an increase in output and a rise in interest rate. If LTPP wins the election, output will fall and so will the interest rate.

Had wages and prices been flexible, they will increase in the case of EHP's win (Figure 14.36). The output will remain unchanged in the long run but interest rates will be high. This means a crowding out of investment in favour of public consumption (A, to B and C in the left-hand diagram of the figure).

In the right-hand diagram we have the case of the LTPP which will cause a fall in prices and wages leading to a fall in interest rates. In the long run, the output will remain unchanged and the investment will increase.

(c) Open economy with fixed exchange rate and no capital mobility: EHP's win will shift the IS to the right (left-hand diagram of Figure 14.37). Increase in income will increase demand for imports. This will lead to an excess demand for foreign currency. With fixed exchange rate, the central bank will sell foreign currency and reduce real balances. LM shifts upwards and there will be a crowding out of investment.

LTPP's win is depicted by a shift to the left of the IS. A fall in income will create excess supply of foreign currency which, in turn, will bring about an increase in real balances. LM shifts downwards and we end up at the original level of output with much lower interest rate.

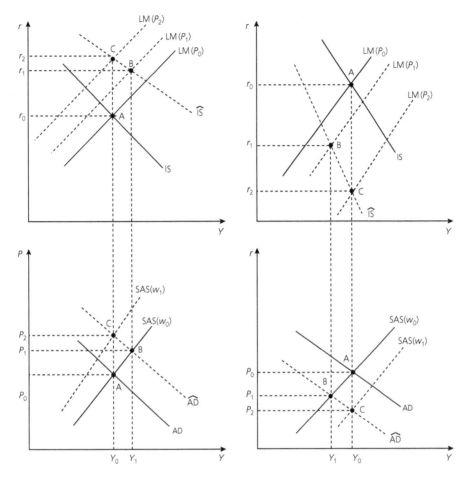

Figure 14.36

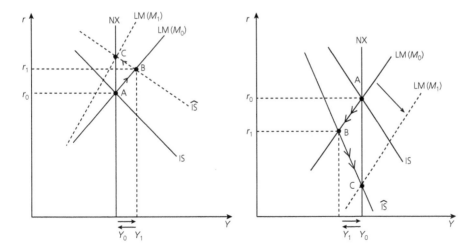

Figure 14.37

(d) Open economy with perfect capital mobility and a fixed exchange rate:

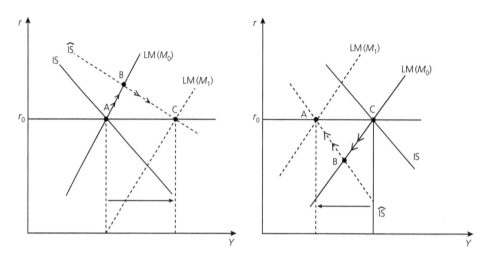

Figure 14.38

EHP (left-hand diagram in Figure 14.38): increase in IS causes interest rate to rise above international level. This will instigate an inflow of capital and an excess supply of foreign currency. The Bank's intervention will cause an increase in real balances. LM shifts downwards. There will be an expansion of output. LTPP: fall in IS causes interest rate to fall below international level. This will create a capital outflow and an excess demand for foreign currency. The bank's interference will cause the supply of real balances to fall. LM shifts upwards and we end up in deep recession.

(e) Open economy with flexible exchange rate (see Figure 14.39):

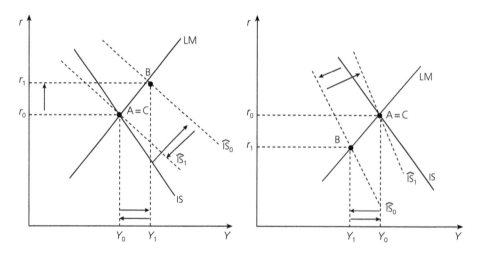

Figure 14.39

EHP (on the left): increase in IS causes interest rates to rise above the international level. Excess supply of foreign currency and an appreciation. This will reduce the demand for NX and the IS will shift back to its original position. LTPP: the fall in demand (shift of the IS to the left) will cause a fall of interest rate below the international level. Outflow of capital cause excess demand of foreign currency and a depreciation of the local currency. This will make imports more expensive and export more attractive. The increase in demand for NX will shift IS back to its original position.

▨ QUESTION 9

In an open economy, the government commits itself to a balanced budget. Equally, it commits a known fraction of its spending for purchases abroad. Suppose that the tax system is based on proportional tax and that the tax is adjusted to spending. Analyse the effects of an increase in the tax rate for the following:

(a) In an open economy without capital mobility and a fixed exchange rate;

(b) In an open economy with perfect capital mobility and a fixed exchange rate;

(c) In an open economy with perfect capital mobility and a flexible exchange rate;

(d) How would your answer to (a) change had the tax system been based on a lump sum tax.

Answer

The conditions in this case are clearly stipulated.

(i) Balanced budget with a proportional tax system: $G = tY$;

(ii) A known fraction, α, of government spending is purchased abroad.

Before we can analyse the effects of an increase in the tax rate, we must examine the complete model. Note that, by implication, an increase in the tax rate means an increase in government spending.

The complete model is thus as follows:

$$C(Y) = C_0 + c_1(1 - t)Y$$

$$I(r) = I_0 - I_1 r$$

$$G = tY$$

$$X\left(\frac{E \cdot P^*}{P}\right) = X_0\left(\frac{E_0 P^*_0}{P_0}\right)$$

$$IM\left(\frac{EP^*}{P}, Y\right) = IM_0\left(\frac{E_0 P^*_0}{P_0}\right) + m_1 Y + \alpha(tY)$$

$$\Rightarrow AE\left(Y, r, \frac{EP^*}{P}\right) = \left[C_0 + I(r) + (X_0 - IM_0)\left(\frac{E_0 P^*_0}{P_0}\right)\right] + [c_1(1 - t) + t - \alpha t - m_1]Y = Y$$

$$Y = A\left(r, \frac{EP^*}{P}\right)\frac{1}{1 - [c_1(1 - t) + t(1 - \alpha) - m_1]} = A\left(r, \frac{EP^*}{P}\right)\frac{1}{1 - M}.$$

In the equilibrium condition, t is an element of M. Thus, to analyse the effects of a change in t we must examine its influence on M (and the multiplier). Clearly, an increase in M corresponds to an increase in the multiplier.

$$\frac{\partial M}{\partial t} = 1 - \alpha - c_1.$$

Hence, if $1 - \alpha > c_1$, an increase in t will cause a greater increase in government demand for local output than the loss of demand from the fall in consumption. In other words, $1 - \alpha$ is the government's marginal propensity to spend locally. If it is greater than the marginal propensity to consume, a transfer from consumers to the government will raise the multiplier and aggregate demand. We shall assume this to be the case but the alternative conclusion is equally acceptable.

(a) An open economy without capital mobility and a fixed exchange rate (Figure 14.40):

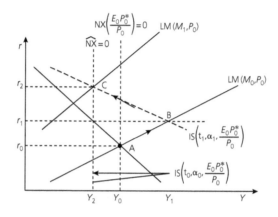

Figure 14.40

Assuming that the effect of the increase in tax was expansionary, this means that for any given level of interest rate, there would now be equilibrium at a higher level of income. As the change is due to the increase in the multiplier, this means a shift to the right of the IS and a flatter slope. However, an increase in the rate of tax would generate an increase in demand for imported goods at any level of income. This means that the level of income in which the initial demand for net export would be offset, is now lower. In other words, the NX=0 line shifts to the left. This is easy to conclude by simply looking at the NX=0 function but if you are interested in the full argument, here it is:

$$NX\left(\frac{E_0 P^*_0}{P_0}, Y\right) = (X_0 - IM_0)\left(\frac{E_0 P^*_0}{P_0}\right) - (m_1 + \alpha t)Y = 0$$

$$Y^{NX=0} = \frac{(X_0 - IM_0)\left(\frac{E_0 P^*_0}{P_0}\right)}{m_1 + \alpha t} \Rightarrow \frac{dY^{NX=0}}{dt} = -\frac{\alpha(X_0 - IM_0)(\bullet)}{(m_1 + \alpha t)^2} < 0.$$

If we start at A we can see that there will now be excess demand for local goods and a deficit in the current account. The economy will start moving towards point B which will exacerbate the deficit in the current account. The excess demand for foreign currency will be met by decline in the central bank's reserves which will lead to a fall in the supply of liquid assets. The LM will thus shift upwards (for any given level of income there will be equilibrium at a higher interest rate). This will carry on until we reach equilibrium at point C where output falls below its original level and the interest rate increases.

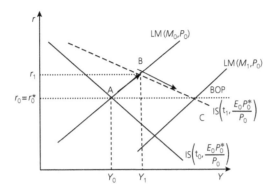

Figure 14.41

(b) and (c) Perfect capital mobility (Figure 14.41): the initial change in this case is simply the shift of the IS to the right and flatter (A to B). This will raise local interest rates above the international level of return rates on assets and subsequently, cause an inflow of capital (foreigners wishing to hold local assets). This, in turn, will cause excess supply of foreign currency. In the case of a flexible exchange rate, E will decrease (appreciation) and the demand for net export will diminish. The IS will shift back to its original position at A. where the increase in government spending has crowded out export.

In the case of a fixed exchange rate, the excess supply of foreign currency will be absorbed by the central bank and cause an increase in the supply of liquid assets. LM will shift downwards and the new equilibrium will be at point C.

(d) We must now reexamine the effect of the increase in tax (in the case of (a)) when the tax system is based on a lump sum tax. We must first rewrite the model:

$$C(Y) = C_0 + c_1(Y - T)$$

$$I(r) = I_0 - I_1 r$$

$$G = T$$

$$X\left(\frac{E \cdot P^*}{P}\right) = X_0\left(\frac{E_0 P^*_0}{P_0}\right)$$

$$IM\left(\frac{EP^*}{P}, Y\right) = IM_0\left(\frac{E_0 P^*_0}{P_0}\right) + m_1 Y + \alpha T$$

$$\Rightarrow \hat{AE}\left(Y, r, \frac{EP^*}{P}\right) = [C_0 + I(r) + (X_0 - IM_0)\left(\frac{E_0 P^*_0}{P_0}\right) + T(1 - \alpha) - c_1 T] + [c_1 - m_1]Y = Y$$

$$Y = \hat{A}\left(r, \frac{EP^*}{P}\right)\frac{1}{1 - [c_1 - m_1]} = A\left(r, \frac{EP^*}{P}\right)\frac{1}{1 - M^T}.$$

In this case, an increase in taxes (T) (driven by the desire to increase G) will not affect the multiplier. Instead, it will change the autonomous component:

$$\frac{\partial \hat{A}}{\partial T} = 1 - \alpha - c_1.$$

Namely, under the same conditions that an increase in proportional tax would cause an increase in aggregate demand for domestic output (shift of the IS to the right), an increase in a lump sum tax will cause a shift to the right of the IS. Equally, an increase in T will cause an increase in demand for imports at any given level of income and therefore, shift the NX$=0$ constraint to the left. Thus, the answer at (a) remains unchanged under a lump sum tax system.

▓ QUESTION 10

Some people envisage a sharp increase in the proportion of old age pensioners in the population. Assuming that pensions are paid out by the government and that old age pensioners tend to spend more time abroad than the young, what will be the effects of the increase in their number on the economy:

(a) When there is no capital mobility and the exchange rate is fixed?

(b) When there is capital mobility and the exchange rate is fixed?

(c) When there is capital mobility and the exchange rate is flexible?

Answer

There are two elements to the information given in this question. First, an increase in the number of old age pensioners means a fiscal expansion (the increase in transfer payments reduces tax revenues, T). The second element is the fact that old age pensioners tend to travel abroad more than the young. This means that there are offsetting effects to this change as the increase in transfers shifts IS to the right while the increase in demand for imports shifts it to the left. To examine the effects we shall assume that old age pensioners only derive their income from the government transfers. We shall also assume a proportional tax and the fraction which is transferred to old age pensioners is β:

$$C(Y) = C_0 + c_1^Y (1 - t)Y + c_1^{OAP} \beta t Y$$

$$I(r) = I_0 - l_1 r$$

$$G = G_0$$

$$X \left(\frac{E \cdot P^*}{P} \right) = X_0 \left(\frac{E_0 P^*_0}{P_0} \right)$$

$$IM \left(\frac{EP^*}{P}, Y \right) = IM_0 \left(\frac{E_0 P^*_0}{P_0} \right) + m_1^Y Y + m_1^{OAP} \beta t Y$$

$$\Rightarrow AE \left(Y, r, \frac{EP^*}{P} \right) = \left[C_0 + I(r) + (X_0 - IM_0) \left(\frac{E_0 P^*_0}{P_0} \right) \right]$$

$$+ \left[c_1^Y (1 - t) + c_1^{OAP} \beta t - m_1^Y - m_1^{OAP} \beta t \right] Y = Y$$

$$Y = A\left(r, \frac{EP^*}{P}\right) \frac{1}{1 - [c_1^Y(1 - t) + t\beta(c_1^{OAP} - m_1^{OAP}) - m_1^Y]} = A\left(r, \frac{EP^*}{P}\right) \frac{1}{1 - M}.$$

Clearly, an increase in the number of old age pensioners means an increase in β which is only an argument of the multiplier:

$$\frac{\partial M}{\partial \beta} = t(c_1^{OAP} - m_1^{OAP}).$$

Hence, if the marginal propensity to spend locally by the old age pensioners is greater than their marginal propensity to spend abroad, the multiplier will increase and the overall effect of the change will be expansionary.

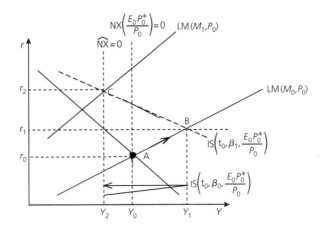

Figure 14.42

(a) An open economy without capital mobility and a fixed exchange rate (figure 14.42): assuming that the effect of the increase in β was expansionary, this means that for any given level of interest rate, there would now be equilibrium at a higher level of income. This is a shift to the right of the IS and it becomes flatter. However, an increase in β would generate an increase in demand for imported goods at any level of income. This means that the level of income in which the initial demand for net export would be offset, is now lower. In other words, the NX=0 line shifts to the left.

If we start at A we can see that there will now be excess demand for local goods and a deficit in the current account. The economy will start moving towards point B which will exacerbate the deficit in the current account. The excess demand for foreign currency will be met by decline in the central bank's reserves which will lead to a fall in the supply of liquid assets. The LM will thus shift upwards (for any given level of income there will be equilibrium at a higher interest rate). This will carry on until we reach equilibrium at point C where output falls below its original level and the interest rate increases.

(b) and (c) Perfect capital mobility (Figure 14.43): the initial change in this case is simply the shift of the IS to the right. (A to B). This will raise local interest rates above the international level of return rates on assets and, subsequently, cause an inflow of capital (foreigners wishing to hold local assets). This, in turn, will cause excess supply of foreign currency. In the case of a flexible exchange

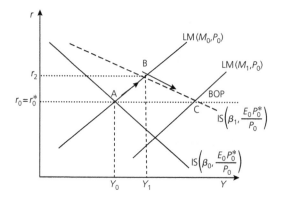

Figure 14.43

rate E will decrease (appreciation) and the demand for net export will diminish. The IS will shift back to its original position at A where the increase in government spending has crowded out export.

In the case of a fixed exchange rate, the excess supply of foreign currency will be absorbed by the central bank and cause an increase in the supply of liquid assets. LM will shift downwards and the new equilibrium will be at point C.

■ QUESTION 11

Both the rise in recurring epidemics and the deterioration of security around the world have considerably increased the number of people who choose to holiday in their home countries rather than travel abroad.

(a) What will happen to an economy's multiplier?

(b) Analyse the effects of the changes on the economy when there are is no capital mobility and a fixed exchange rate.

(c) Analyse the effects of the changes on the economy when there is perfect capital mobility and a flexible exchange rate regime.

(d) How will your answer to (c) change had there been a flexible exchange rate regime?

Answer

Due to the deterioration in security around the world and the rise in recurring epidemics, the public chooses to holiday at home rather than travel abroad. This is basically a very simply story. In terms of the model it simply means a fall in the marginal propensity to import which could be accompanied by a rise in the marginal propensity to consume locally. Either way the effects are unambiguous. This means an increase in the multiplier and thus a shift of the IS to the right and it should also become flatter.

(a) The multiplier. Before the change:

$$C(Y) = C_0 + c_1(1 - t)Y$$

$$I(r) = I_0 - I_1 r$$

$$G = G_0$$

$$X\left(\frac{E \cdot P^*}{P}\right) = X_0\left(\frac{E_0 P_0^*}{P_0}\right)$$

$$IM\left(\frac{EP^*}{P}, Y\right) = IM_0\left(\frac{E_0 P_0^*}{P_0}\right) + m_1 Y$$

$$\Rightarrow AE\left(Y, r, \frac{EP^*}{P}\right) = \left[C_0 + I(r) + (X_0 - IM_0)\left(\frac{E_0 P_0^*}{P_0}\right)\right] + (c_1(1 - t) - m_1)Y = Y$$

$$Y = A\left(r, \frac{EP^*}{P}\right)\frac{1}{1 - [c_1(1 - t) - m_1]} = A\left(r, \frac{EP^*}{P}\right)\frac{1}{1 - M}.$$

Clearly $\partial M/\partial m_1 < 0$ means that a decrease in the marginal propensity to import will increase the multiplier.

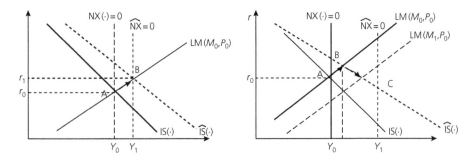

Figure 14.44

(b) An open economy without capital mobility and a fixed exchange rate (Figure 14.44): note that in this case we cannot say a priori whether there would be a single effect of a decrease in the marginal propensity to import or, that in addition, there would also be an increase in the marginal propensity to consume. In the right-hand diagram we depict the inevitable case had the change been confined to a decrease in the marginal propensity to import. Here, the effect on NX=0 would be greater than on IS for a given interest rate.

If, however, there is an additional increase in demand for consumption then it is quite possible that as IS shifts further to the right, we may end up with the case depicted in the left-hand diagram. That the effect on the NX=0 will be to shift to the right is intuitively clear but can also be seen explicitly:

$$NX\left(\frac{E_0 P_0^*}{P_0}, Y\right) = (X_0 - IM_0)\left(\frac{E_0 P_0^*}{P_0}\right) - m_1 Y = 0$$

$$Y^{NX=0} = \frac{(X_0 - IM_0)(E_0 P_0^*/P_0)}{m_1} \Rightarrow \frac{dY^{NX=0}}{dm_1} = -\frac{(X_0 - IM_0)(\bullet)}{m_1^2} < 0.$$

If you chose to analyse the case in the right-hand diagram you should also provide an explanation as to how the process unfolds. Namely, that the initial move is to equilibrium at B where output increased to accommodate the increase in demand for home holidays. However, at this level there will still be a surplus in the current account and as a result, there will be excess supply of foreign currency. Given the exchange rate policy, the central bank will buy the excess supply and cause an increase in the supply of liquid assets. This, in turn, will shift the LM downwards and the economy will expand further until a new equilibrium at point C.

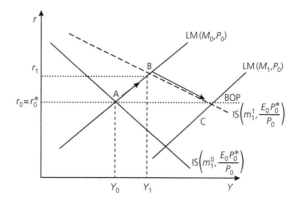

Figure 14.45

(c) and (d) This is the case of perfect capital mobility (Figure 14.45): the initial change in this case is simply the shift of the IS to the right. (A to B). This will raise local interest rates above the international level of return rates on assets and subsequently, cause an inflow of capital (foreigners wishing to hold local assets). This, in turn, will cause excess supply of foreign currency. In the case of a flexible exchange rate E will decrease (appreciation) and the demand for net export will diminish. The IS will shift back to its original position at A where the increase in government spending has crowded out export.

In the case of a fixed exchange rate, the excess supply of foreign currency will be absorbed by the central bank and cause an increase in the supply of liquid assets. LM will shift downwards and the new equilibrium will be at point C.

QUESTION 12

There are two trading economies (A and B). Economy A has perfect capital mobility (with other economies) and a fixed exchange rate policy. Economy B, although the main trading partner of economy A, does not allow any capital mobility. Economy B only imports consumer goods from economy A and its tax system is proportional.

(a) What will the multiplier of economy B?

(b) The government increases the rate of tax in economy B. Analyse the implications that this will have on both economies if:

(i) The marginal propensity to consume is greater than the marginal propensity to import.

(ii) The marginal propensity to consume is smaller than the marginal propensity to import.

Answer

This question deals with the general problem of policy transmission through international trade. It requires a proper understanding of all major components of the macro models you have studied throughout the years. You will learn a great deal if you try to answer this question by yourself. It is not that we are trying to establish the truth about transmission here. What you will learn here is to better understand how the model works and where exactly do inputs from the real world matter. We have two economies here. A and B and main trading partners. In spite of this, there is a fundamental institutional difference between them: economy A allows perfect capital mobility while economy B does not. In addition, economy B only imports consumer goods from economy A. There is a fixed exchange rate between the two countries.

(a) The first step in any analysis is to identify the appropriate theoretical set-up. In our case this is fairly straightforward (Figure 14.46):

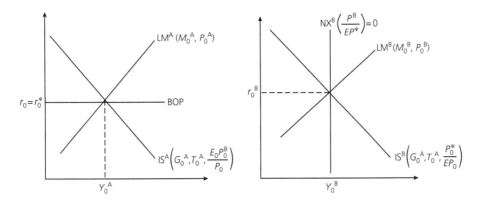

Figure 14.46

The parameters of economy A are standard but they contain the output level of the other economy. Notice, however, that while the economies are major trading partners, as far as A is concerned, B is by no means the sole partner. Economy A exports to B but it may also export elsewhere. The structural equations of economy A are therefore: A has a proportional tax system, its multiplier.

$$C^A(Y) = c_0^A + c_1^A(1 - t^A)Y^A$$

$$I^A(r) = I^A(r_0^*)$$

$$G^A = G_0^A$$

$$X^A\left(\frac{E, p^*}{p^A}, Y^B\right) = X^A\left(\frac{E_0, p_0^*}{p_0^A}, Y_0^B\right)$$

$$IM^A\left(\frac{E, p^*}{p^A}, Y^A\right) = IM_0^A\left(\frac{E_0, p_0^*}{p_0^A}\right) + m_1^A Y^A$$

Hence

$$Y^A = A^A(Y^B)\frac{1}{1 - c_1^A(1 - t^A) + m_1^A}.$$

Note that the demand for investment is determined by the international interest rate.

Economy B, however, has a specific feature which makes its story unique: the demand for imports is a demand for consumer goods from economy A. This means that the demand for imports in economy B is driven by consumers and dependent on their disposable income:

$$C^B(Y) = c_0^B + c_1^B(1 - t^B)Y^B$$

$$I^B(r) = I^A(r_0)$$

$$G^B = G_0^B$$

$$X^B\left(\frac{p^A}{E, p^*}, Y^A\right) = X^B\left(\frac{p_0^A}{E_0, p_0^*}, Y_0^A\right)$$

$$IM^B\left(\frac{p^A}{E, p^*}, Y^B\right) = IM_0^A\left(\frac{p_0^A}{E_0, p_0^*}\right) + m_1^B\left(1 - t^B\right)Y^B$$

Hence

$$Y^B = A^B(Y^A)\frac{1}{1 - (c_1^B - m_1^B)(1 - t^B)}.$$

Here, the demand for investment is determined by the domestic interest rate which is not governed (directly) by the international rate. The particular feature of economy B's demand for import generates this very specific multiplier.

(b) We now move to the problem of policy transmission. We begin when both economies are in equilibrium (point A in the diagrams below). The only policy to be considered is an increase in the tax rate in economy B. Let us first consider the immediate effects that this will have on economy B before any actual change takes place (i.e. the economies are still at A).

The increase in tax rate will clearly reduce both demand for consumption and demand for imports. The effect that this will have on economy B must be studied through two different instruments: the multiplier and the NX=0 constraint.

The multiplier: it is easy to see that an increase in t^B will affect the multiplier according to whether $(c_1^B - m_1^B)$ is greater or smaller than zero. If $c_1^B > m_1^B$ then an increase in the tax will raise the denominator and reduce the multiplier. Alternatively:

$$Y^B = A^B(Y^A)\frac{1}{1 - (c_1^B - m_1^B)(1 - t^B)}$$

$$\frac{\partial Y^B}{\partial t^B} = -\frac{(c_1^B - m_1^B)A^B}{[1 - (c_1^B - m_1^B)(1 - t^B)]^2}$$

If $c_1^B > m_1^B$ then $\dfrac{\partial Y^B}{\partial t^B} < 0$

If $c_1^B < m_1^B$ then $\dfrac{\partial Y^B}{\partial t^B} > 0$

for any given level of Y^A.

This means that the initial effect will be a shift to the left of the IS in case (i) and a shift to the right of the IS in case (ii). The logic too, is fairly clear. When the marginal propensity to consume is greater, the effect of the increase in tax on consumption is greater. Thus the increase in NX as a result of a fall in demand for imports will be offset by the fall in consumption. The opposite will be true in case (ii).

What will happen to the NX constraint?

$$NX^B \left(\frac{p^A}{E, p^*}, Y^A, Y^B \right) = X^B \left(\frac{p_0^A}{E_0, p_0^*}, Y_0^A \right) - IM_0^A \left(\frac{p_0^A}{E_0, p_0^*} \right) - m_1^B (1 - t^B) Y^B = 0$$

Hence

$$\widehat{Y}^B = \frac{X^B (p_0^A / E_0, p_0^*, Y_0^A) - IM_0^A (p_0^A / E_0, p_0^*)}{m_1^B (1 - t^B)}$$

$$\frac{\partial \widehat{Y}^B}{\partial t^B} = \frac{m_1^B (X^B (p_0^A / E_0, p_0^*, Y_0^A) - IM_0^A (p_0^A / E_0, p_0^*))}{[m_1^B (1 - t^B)]^2} > 0$$

for any given level of Y^A.

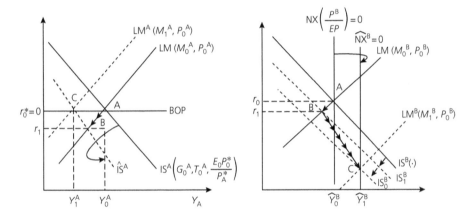

Figure 14.47

We may now conduct the full analysis: case (i) $c_1^B > m_1^B$ (Figure 14.47). We begin at A. The increase in the rate of tax in economy B will cause the IS to shift to the left (the effect on consumption offsets the increase in NX) while the NX=0 constraint shifts to the right. The economy is now in a state of excess supply in the goods market and excess supply of foreign currency. The economy will move from A via B towards C.

At the same time, in economy A, either due to the immediate decrease in export (as the demand from economy B falls even at the initial level of income) or through the combined effect (fall in income of economy B as it begins moving from A to B), IS of economy A will shift to the left (fall in NX). Given that capital flows freely, the fall in domestic interest rate will cause excess demand for foreign currency (the return on foreign assets is greater than the return on local assets). As exchange rate is fixed, the central bank will sell foreign currency and thus, reduce the quantity of money in the economy. This will shift the LM upwards until equilibrium is restored at point C. Here, economy A has lower level of national income which, in turn, means a lower demand for the export of economy B.

Looking back at economy B (as the forces affecting the outcome in economy A are stronger) we can see that the fall in A's national income will reduce their demand for imports (in part, economy B's export). This will shift the NX slightly back while the IS will shift further to the left while the LM moves further downwards. The question is whether point C is at a higher or lower level of national income. If we examine the capital formation equation (which reflects the materialization of the equilibrium conditions) we can see that as NX=0 (unlike economy A where the balance of payment is comprised of two accounts), $I = S + T - G$. We shall call the behavioural function of $S(Y) + T(Y) - G = \Psi(Y)$. In terms of our own model this becomes:

$$\Psi(Y) = S(Y) + T(Y) - G = Y - tY - C(Y)$$

$$\Psi(Y) = -c_0 + (1 - t)(1 - c_1)Y$$

clearly

$$\frac{\partial \Psi}{\partial t} = -Y(1 - c_1) + Y = Y(1 - 1 + c_1) = c_1 Y > 0$$

$$\frac{\partial \Psi}{\partial Y} = (1 - t)(1 - c_1) + t > 0$$

This means that when t increased, the amount of resources available for investment (savings) grew. As the pressure from both IS and LM is for interest rate to fall, the demand for investment will rise to utilize the increase in the supply of resources for investment. It is quite possible that as both IS and LM pull down the interest rate, the fall may be so great as to increase demand for investment beyond that which has become available at the initial level of income. To reach equilibrium, the output will have to increase to generate more resources to satisfy the increase in the demand for investment. We may therefore conclude that point C will be at a level of national income which is higher from the original.

Case (ii) $c_1^B < m_1^B$. Here, the effects of the fall in imports (i.e. increase in NX) are greater than the effects on demand for consumption. Thus, both IS and NX=0 shift to the right as in Figure 14.48.

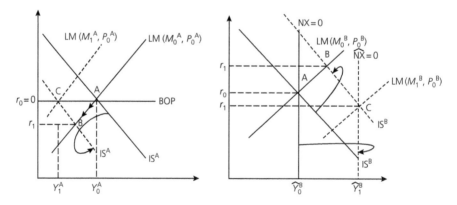

Figure 14.48

The story for A, here, is similar to the one we had before with a different magnitude of change. As the impact of the increase in tax on NX of B is greater, so will it have a greater negative effect on economy A. The increase in demand for NX in B means a sharp decrease in the NX of A. This will shift the IS of A further to the left than in the previous story. The same mechanism will then come into operation and the economy will end at a point like C where the IS will move further with the changes in the output of economy B.

The fall in economy A's output will cause a fall in the NX of economy B which will shift both NX=0 and IS back to the left. In addition, the presence of a surplus in the current account will cause the LM to shift downwards. We face again the question where will the process end.

Looking at the same $\Psi(Y)$ function from before, we can see that at A, there was an increase in the available resources for investment (when t increased). If interest rate were to rise, the only way an equilibrium can be restored (if we assume the demand for investment is independent of income) is by a fall in national income that will reduce the amount of resources available for investment. This means that as we move from A to C in economy B, we must be to the left of A. Namely, the effects of the fall in A's income should completely offset the shift of the NX=0 to the right. It is, of course, possible that the story will end at a level of interest which is below the original level. This will indicate an increase in investment which could be explained by the increase in tax + the increase in savings due to the rise in national income.

NOTES

1. If you prefer to carry of thinking of the nominal rate of exchange as the amount of foreign currency per unit of domestic currency, simply write $1/E$ whenever I write E.

2. A word of caution is needed here. We must be careful here as the market for IM is not a market for a single commodity but a market for an aggregated good. As such, it cannot be subject to the same rules as in micro analysis. Nevertheless, for expositional purposes, I feel that the supply and demand for foreign currency can be better explained on the back of your micro intuition. However, you must be aware that the markets for imports and exports are aggregated markets which need further clarifications before we can apply to them micro considerations.

3. The same qualifications as those raised with regard to the micro presentation of imported goods market apply to the exported goods market.

▪ TECHNICAL NOTES

If you are not familiar with the language of economics, work through these short notes before beginning the main part of the book. Make sure you thoroughly understand what is being said, and how it is expressed in economics terms. It will be particularly useful in helping you understand the numerous formulae and figures that we use in this book. In these notes we will explain

- Sets (and specifications of sets);
- Numbers (natural numbers, integers, real numbers, rational numbers);
- Points in planes;
- Functions and graphs (including slopes).

Introduction

When we look around ourselves we see many individual things—often more than we can make sense of or communicate clearly to others. We need to find effective ways to think about and describe all these things.

Listen to the scream of a hungry Neanderthal husband to his 'wife' in the cave. 'Dinner, dear!'

For his wife to understand what he wants, they must both know exactly what 'dinner' means. She is unlikely to offer him a tree or a stone to eat. She knows, as well as he does, that 'dinner' refers to the kinds of things that we eat at a certain time of the day. So, instead of the poor wife offering him a random selection of objects from sticks to dung, using the word 'dinner' brings the number of objects under consideration down to a manageable number.

'Dinner' defines a certain group of objects within the complex world that surrounds us. Of course, this group of objects varies across cultures, but in all of them there will be one word to identify the *set* of objects from which the meal is likely to be prepared.

Suppose now that 'dinner' or, 'things we eat at this time of the day' includes only two objects: bread and eggs. Would the Neanderthal and his wife consider 100 eggs as 'dinner'? Probably not. She is more likely to consider 'two slices of bread and one egg' as an example of 'dinner'. So it is not enough just to group those things in the world to which we want to relate. We must also be able to *count*, or *enumerate*, them. The two fundamentals here are sets and numbers.

Sets and specifications

Sets

A **set** is a collection of well-defined objects, which are called its **elements** (or members).

- *What is the set, and what are the elements in the dinner example we have just used?*

In economics, if X is an element, or member, of a set S, we write

$$X \in S$$

The negation of this is:

$$X \notin S$$

which says 'X is *not* part of the set S'.

In slightly different terms, we could write the broadest definition of our 'dinner' set like this

$$D = \{X | X \text{ is edible}\}$$

Put into words, this reads: the 'dinner set' contains all 'things' which are edible (the vertical line in expressions like these means 'where' or 'such that' or 'conditional on'). This therefore says

dinner is all X such that X is edible.

But do we eat all things which are edible, or is our taste refined by custom and culture?

Specifying a set

We can specify a set in two ways: either by enumeration (listing what is in the set) or by description.

Example of enumeration

$$A = \{1, 2, 4\}$$

or

$$B = \{\text{Romeo}, \text{Juliet}\}$$

Here A is the set containing the numbers 1, 2, and 4 and B is the set containing Romeo and Juliet. We have **enumerated** all the members.

In our dinner example, the set called 'dinner' (D) may be enumerated like this:

$$D = \{\text{Eggs}, \text{Bread}\}$$

This does not tell us *how many* eggs, or bread, constitute a meal. However, the wife not only knows what 'things' might constitute the 'dinner' set, she also knows her husband's capacity.

Description. Suppose that to eat more than 5 eggs in a meal is considered dangerously unhealthy. To eat more than 10 slices of bread is also inappropriate. The 'meal' set—those meals that a good wife will offer her Neanderthal husband—will only contain those meals that are healthy. Hence, the 'meal' set, to which both husband and wife are *implicitly* referring, is a subset of D, where D is the set of all *possible* meals (including unhealthy meals). It is given by the expression

$$M = \{(E, B)|0 \le E \le 5, 0 \le B \le 10\}.$$

- *Can you see what the letters M, B, and E stand for in this expression?*

Here (E, B) is a typical member of the meal set comprising eggs (E) and bread (B). Put into words, M is the set of healthy combinations of E and B such that there are between 0 and 5 eggs and between 0 and 10 slices of bread. Clearly the set M is itself contained in, or is a subset of, the set D (we denote this by $M \subseteq D$).

- *Practise writing down some similar expressions for sets, for example: what will be the set describing the guest list for your dinner party?*

Here are some other examples of a **descriptive** way of writing a set, this time a set of solutions to a mathematical problem:

$$C = \{X|X^2 - 25 = 0\}.$$

C is the set of all the values of X that solve the equation $X^2 - 25 = 0$. If we add $+25$ to each side of the equation, the equation becomes: $X^2 - 25 + 25 = +25$, which can be reduced to $X^2 = 25$.

The solution of this equation is the square root of 25 (which is either $+5$ or -5). In this case, we could have enumerated to se like this:

$$C = \{+5, -5\}.$$

Now consider that set L:

$$L = \{Y|Y \text{ loves Romeo}\}$$

L here is the set of 'all things that love Romeo'. On enumeration, the set may look like this:

$$L = \{\text{Juliet, Romeo, Romeo's mother, Romeo's dog, the girl next door}, \ldots\}$$

For the description of a set to be meaningful, we must have an idea about the **range** of the objects which might be included in the set. In our earlier examples, we must known the possible values of the variables X and Y:

- In C, the range of X is the set of all real numbers;
- In L, the range of Y may be all the characters in Shakespeare's play, *Romeo and Juliet*.
- In our meal set M, the range of E consists of all real numbers between 0 and 5, and of B, all real numbers between 0 and 10.

Numbers

Natural numbers

Numbers are one of the means of describing a set. The most natural way of using numbers is the process of **counting**. The numbers we use for counting (two slices of bread, one egg and so on) are called **natural numbers**.

The set of natural numbers is defined as

$$\mathbb{N} = \{1, 2, 3, 4, \ldots\}$$

Natural numbers are therefore *positive whole numbers*. But how will you count how much money you have in your bank if you are £200 overdrawn? Well, you are obviously the proud owner of a negative sum: −£200. But while 200 is a natural number, −200 is not: it is whole, but not positive. Perhaps you will dismiss your overdraft as being an unreal number and a capitalist conspiracy.

Integers

To allow for circumstances where we want to consider negative numbers we define a new group of numbers called **integers**. These are all the natural numbers and *also* their negative values. It also includes the number zero, but we will not discuss this here.

The set of integers is defined as

$$\mathbb{Z} = \{\ldots, -3, -2, -1, 0, 1, 2, 3, \ldots\}.$$

However, the world around us is too complex to be depicted by *integers* (whole numbers, positive or negative) alone. Rather, the world seems to be continuous. Suppose that the distance between two points (say A and B) is an integer (say one mile). Suppose that you live at A and your college is at B. If there is a fast-food outlet half-way, does this mean that you cannot ever have lunch simply because there is no way of describing the distance between your home, or college, and the fast-food outlet? Of course not, there is a distance: it is real, and you can imagine yourself stopping at the fast-food outlet. However, we cannot account for it in a world of integers. We, therefore, need to define yet another group of numbers, which can help us to depict the world better. These are called the **rational numbers**.

Rational numbers

The set of rational numbers is defined as:

$$\mathbb{Q} = \{X/Y | X \in \mathbb{Z} \wedge Y \in \mathbb{N}\}.$$

Put into words, this equation says that $\mathbb{Q}$ is the set of *fractions* X/Y such that X is an integer (which can be a negative number) *and* ($\wedge$ = and) Y is a natural number. Thus the set of rational numbers could include any such numbers as $1/2$, $-1/15$, $-125/6000$ or their decimal equivalents.

If the set $\mathbb{Q}$ contained all possible numbers which we might come across in real life, we could stop here. However, in reality there are also numbers that are *not rational*—the number π for example. We know that the area of a circle with radius r is $A = r^2\pi$, and that when $r = 1$, the area of the circle will be π. This is real, but cannot be expressed as a rational number, Similarly, $\sqrt{2}$ and Euler's constant e are not rational numbers.

Real numbers

To say that a number is not rational means that we cannot obtain the number as a fraction of (or ratio between) integers and natural numbers. All **real numbers** have a **decimal** expression (for example, $12/15 = 0.8$, and $15/11 = 1.363\,636\,36\ldots$). Rational numbers can be defined as real numbers whose decimal expression *terminates* (as in $12/15$) or else *repeats itself* over and over again (as with $15/11$).

For instance, $5/2$ terminates (it is equal to decimal 2.5) and $22/7$ repeats itself (it is equal to decimal $3.142\,857\,142\,857\,142\,857\ldots$). π, however, neither terminates nor repeats itself:

$$\pi = 3.141\,592\,653\,589\,793\ldots.$$

The set of all real numbers, $\mathbb{R}$, can be represented geometrically, by a straight line, as in Figure 1.

$-\infty \qquad\qquad\qquad\qquad +\infty$

Figure 1 The real number line.

We call this line the real number line, and it stretches from negative infinity to positive infinity. However, we can also express sets in a geonetrical way.

A point in a plane

Sometimes, we define sets of objects across multiple dimensions. For instance, our 'dinner' from before contains more than one object. We said that it contains both bread and eggs. If we can count bread and eggs in terms of real numbers then the line which depicts the real numbers will not be sufficient to describe the object called 'dinner'. We will need two lines: one to count bread, and another to count eggs. The set 'dinner' can therefore be written like this, with $\mathbb{Q}$ standing for 'rational numbers':

$$D = \{(X, Y) | X \in \mathbb{Q} \wedge Y \in \mathbb{Q}\}.$$

- *Write out in words exactly what this expression means.*

In words, dinner is a set comprising X (the name for bread) which can be counted by real numbers *and* Y (the name for eggs), which can be counted by real numbers as well.

'Dinner', therefore, is defined by *two* real number lines, as Figure 2 shows.

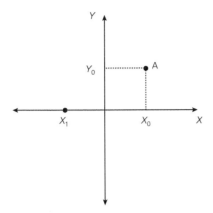

Figure 2 The (X, Y) plane.

The intersecting axes X (horizontal) and Y (vertical) are the names of the variables that are enumerated by real numbers. In our 'dinner' case, X stands for 'silces of bread' and Y stands for 'eggs'. To distinguish between the name of the variable and a particular quantity of it, we use an index number, denoted by a subscript. Hence,

- X_0 denotes a certain quantity of X;
- X_0 units of X may mean '10 slices of bread';
- X_1 will denote another quantity of X, which may or may not be the same as X_0.

We may add further quantities, called X_2, X_3, and so on.

But remember that, in these expressions, the subscripts $0, 1, 2, 3$ and so on do not describe the *magnitude* of these quantities. They only identify them: it may be better to think of them as the initial, 1st, 2nd, and 3rd quantities, respectively.

The two lines of real numbers define what we call a 'plane'. This plane (of real numbers) is often denoted by $\mathbb{R}^2$ (meaning 'two sets of real numbers'). A typical point in this plane, say A in Figure 2, is defined as:

$$A = (X_0, Y_0).$$

This means that A is a combination of X_0 units of X and Y_0 units of Y.

Each point in the plane of real numbers has two coordinates. The first one refers to variable X, the second refers to variable Y. This, in turn, divides the plane into four quadrants. The upper right hand quadrant contains elements like A where the coordinates of both variables are positive numbers (including zero, which is both positive and negative at the same time). The bottom right quadrant is where an element in the plane has a positive X coordinate but a negative Y coordinate. The third quadrant on the bottom left contains those elements for which both variables are assigned a negative number. In the fourth quadrant, X has negative values while Y has positive values. In Figure 2, X_1 is a negative number, which is not very meaningful if X denotes slices of bread.

Coordinates: *these are always written in the form (X,Y), so that when you see a form such as $(5, 3)$ you know that 5 is the value of X, and 3 is the value of Y.*

As far as our 'dinner' is concerned we can rule out any negative consumption. We must, therefore, redefine the 'dinner' set to accounts for positive (including zero) consumption of both bread (X) and eggs (Y):

$$D = \{(X, Y)|(X, Y) \in \mathbb{R}^2_+\}$$

where $\mathbb{R}^2_+$ depicts the positive quadrant in the real numbers plane.

So when our male chauvinist Neanderthal comes to the cave an yells 'Dinner, dear', both he and his wife know that he is asking for positive quantities of bread and eggs (the positive quadrant). However, while both of them know what the components of a meal are, the actual composition can vary considerably across cultures and fashions. In other words, what exactly the meal is depends on where and when the Neanderthal story takes place. At this stage, let us consider only the capacity limitations (which are almost universal). To eat more than 10 slices of bread or more than 5 eggs is considered dangerously unhealthy.

The subset called 'meal' which is a set contained in the set of all possible 'dinners', contains the point (0,0) but cannot go beyond point A because of the limits set by reasons of health. Thus a meal cannot include more than 10 slices of bread ($X \leq 10$) or 5 eggs ($Y \leq 5$). The set M, therefore, is contained in the shaded area of Figure 3, including the edges:

$$M = \{(X, Y)|0 \leq X \leq 10, 0 \leq Y \leq 5\}.$$

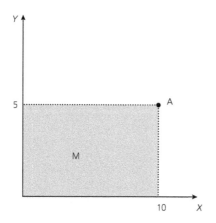

Figure 3 The set of possible meals depicted in the (X, Y) plane.

Functions and graphs

So far, we have been dealing with how to conceptualize the world around us. We examined some categories through the use of sets and we also used the figures to show that sets can have geometrical representation. We have not begun, however, to introduce any kind of order to the world. We have not, for example, discussed issues like causality.

'Causality' is a very difficult concept, and here we shall only deal with the question of how to represent a *causal relationship*.

Graphs

Consider the development of baby. There are many variables which determine its development. How can we tell whether the baby is developing properly? We can think about the two related variables, the length (height) and weight of the baby. The baby may be growing taller but not putting on enough weight at the same time. Conversely, a baby may be gaining too much weight given that it is not simultaneously growing in length.

To have a balanced picture, we must observe how well the baby is doing in *both* important dimensions of its growth. A total that can help us do so is the **graph**.

Both length and weight are enumerated by real numbers. Therefore, the development of these two variables will have to be analysed in the real numbers plane, $\mathbb{R}^2$. Since we know that a negative value of weight, or length, is meaningless, we can concentrate on the positive quadrant of the real numbers plane, as in Figure 4.

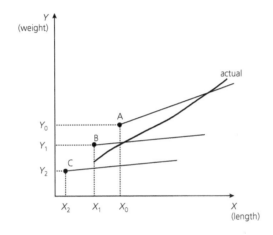

Figure 4 A depiction of babies' weight–length combinations.

Here X and Y denote the length and weight of a baby, respectively. We have drawn three lines in the plane to represent th expected growth rates of babies that are relatively large (A), average (B), and relatively small (C) at birth. Each line consists of a set of points in the positive quadrant which have two coordinates each: one for the length X and one for the weight Y. The graph lines define sets. In other words, the lines connect a large number (actually an infinite number) of points with different values of X, Y.

From each of the initial points A, B, and C we may now move along the relevant graph. As we do so, we observe a systematic increase in the values of *both* variables. This suggests a connection between the weight and length for which we believe the development of a baby is normal given different conditions at birth. (We have omitted the important dimension of time, which would have complicated our story. We shall assume that at least in one dimension the baby develops over time.)

The actual progress of any particular baby may not follow any of these lines. We shall have to create a special graph for it. We can then relate the actual development graph to the desired paths and determine how well the baby is developing. The thick line labelled 'Actual' is an example of such a line.

The *graph line*, therefore, provides us with a set of points which represent a certain relationship. This does not mean it is a *causal* relationship. That is to say, it does not mean that the values of X (length) determine, or explain, the values of Y (weight) nor that the values of Y explain, or determine, the values of X. We simply use the graph to depict the combination of length and weight which constitute our accepted view of balanced growth.

In a similar way we could draw a line within the meal set M that would depict what one may consider a balanced diet (Figure 5).

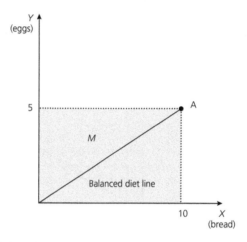

Figure 5 A graph of all balanced diets.

Meals-that-do-not-kill (no more than 5 eggs and 10 slices of bread) are captured by the shaded area in this figure, which represents the set

$$M = \{(X, Y)|0 \leq X \leq 10, 0 \leq Y \leq 5\}.$$

A balanced diet means a balanced consumption of portein (coming from eggs) and carbohydrates (coming from bread). It implies a certain correspondence between the amount of eggs and bread that one eats. The heavy line in this figure depicts such a diet. Again, there is no causal relationship, and the graph simply defines a certain set, the elements of which consist of eggs and slices of bread.

Slopes and functions
Slopes
Consider the subset of balanced diet depicted by the line in Figure 6. Here, the balanced diet is described by the straight line going from the origin, the point ($X = 0$, $Y = 0$) or simply (0,0), to point F where $X = 10$, $Y = 5$ (that is (10,5)). What can we learn from this line, apart from a detailed list of combinations of bread and eggs that are considered to form a balanced diet? We can find the value of one thing in terms of its desired relation to another (The desired outcome is a balanced diet).

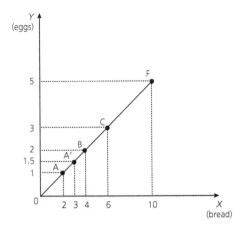

Figure 6 Balanced diets again.

Table 1 A balanced diet

Slices of Bread (X)	Eggs (Y)	As a point in the plane
2	1	$A = (2, 1)$
4	2	$B = (4, 2)$
6	3	$C = (6, 3)$

Notice that according to the line, the following combinations of X and Y (among others) constitute a balanced diet (Table 1). Suppose that we are consuming 2 slices of bread and 1 egg (point (2,1)), and we now wish to increase our consumption of bread to 3 slices. Worried about unbalancing our diets with the extra carbohydrate, we would immediately want to compensate for it with some protein (and cholesterol) so that our diets remain balanced. How many more eggs should we consume?

We could easily take a ruler and set it vertically against the point $X = 3$ and find the corresponding coordinate of Y which will yield a point on the balanced diet line. This will tell us how many eggs we can consume with 3 slices of bread without breaking our diets. The answer will obviously be to consume 1/2 an egg more (point A' in the above diagram).

What if we were consuming 4 slices of bread and 2 eggs (point (4,2)) and we now want 1/2 a slice more of bread? We could repeat the exercise with the ruler. But even without using the ruler I can tell you that we would need to consume a 1/4 of an egg more.

If we repeat the exercise for any conceivable increase in the consumption of bread from any conceivable point of consumption, we will be able to derive a rule. Doing it in this way means following the logic of **induction** (from the particular to the general). But we may also be able to establish the rule by **deduction** (from the general to the particular). What you want to find is how the *change* in the value (the number) of one variable, say 'slices of bread', relates to the change in the value of the other so that we are still in the set of 'balanced diets'.

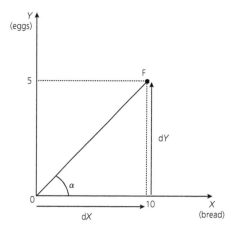

Figure 7 The definition of a slope.

Notation: *We usually use the letter 'd' (or its Greek equivalents δ and ∆), to denote change. Hence, dX means the change in the value of X. Between points A and B in the above diagram, the value of X changed from 2 to 4. Hence, dX = 2.*

Let us consider for a moment the two extremes of the 'balanced diet line'. At one end there is the point (0,0) which I shall call point O and at the other end there is point F (for Full), where F = (10, 5). Between O and F, the value of X changed by 10 and the value of Y changed by 5. Hence, dX = 10; dY = 5. The definition of the **slope** of a graph is:

$$\text{slope} = \frac{dY}{dX}$$

which is, in fact, the tangent of the angle α, tan α, (see Figure 7). It tells us by how much Y has changed for a given change of X.

In our case, the slope of the 'balanced diet line', (which is the tangent of angle α) is

$$\frac{dy}{dx} = \frac{5}{10} = \frac{1}{2}.$$

In maths we may not be interested in the *meaning* of the number 1/2. In economics, however, we give meaning to mathematics by assigning significance to the various variables. In turn, this assigns meanings to concepts like the slope. If you think carefully, the slope suggests 5 eggs *per* 10 slices of bread. Or 1/2 an egg per slice of bread, which is the same thing. It gives us some kind of an equivalence scale which is represented by the special line of our 'balanced diet'. One egg is equivalent, in our 'balanced diet', to 2 slices of bread. The operational implications are that if you wish to increase your consumption by 1 slice of bread, you must add 1/2 an egg to your consumption of eggs in order not to deviate from your 'balanced diet'. If you want 2 eggs, you must add 4 slices of bread. If you want 2.5 eggs, you will have to add 5 slices of bread and so on and so forth.

If you look at points A, B, and C in Figure 6, you will find that this general rule (just like the rule of 1/2 an egg per slice of bread) applies everywhere on the quadrant. The reason for this is simply that the 'balanced diet' line is a straight line. The property of a straight line is that it has the same slope everywhere. If you now choose any two points along this line you will find that the changes ratio of the variables values always agrees with what we have found: half an egg as an equivalent to one slice of bread.

Functions

Having established a general rule which relates slices of bread X to eggs Y, we may want to write this rule in a more explicit fashion. In other words, we want to find a form that will provide a brief, and comprehensive, description of the 'balanced diet' line in the above diagram. That is to say, we are searching for a function.

A **function** is a rule which assigns to each element in one set to a *unique* element in another set. In our case we have two sets. Set B denotes the set containing various quantities of bread:

$$B = \{X|0 \le X \le 10\}.$$

E denotes the set containing the various quantities of eggs allowed:

$$E = \{Y|0 \le Y \le 5\}.$$

The 'balanced diet Function' f (f stands for function, of course) is a *rule* which assigns a value in E to each value in B (generally denoted by $f:B \to E$). In our case, both E and B contain real numbers so that f is a 'real numbers' function and we can say that $f:R \to R$. So f is a 'mapping' from real numbers to real numbers. It tells us how many eggs we can consume with any possible quantity of bread. We know that with 0 bread slices we may consume 0 eggs. But we also know that for every extra slice of bread we must consume an addition of 1/2 egg. Hence we write

$$Y = f(X) = \frac{1}{2}X.$$

You can now check this function by setting values for X and finding whether or not the function yields a value of Y which corresponds to what you would find if you had used a ruler. We can easily see now what role the slope plays in this function. We know that for every change in X (dX) we will need a change in the consuption of eggs (Y) to maintain a balanced diet. We can therefore write

$$dy = \frac{1}{2}dx.$$

This means that if we increase the consumption of bread by 1 slice ($dX = 1$), the consumption of eggs (Y) will have to change by the addition of 1/2 an egg ($dy = \frac{1}{2}$). Divide both sides by dX and we get:

$$\frac{dY}{dX} = \frac{1}{2}$$

which is exactly the slope of the line (the function).

The interpretation which we gave to the slope (as an equivalent scale) is influenced by the nature of the variables as well as by the direction, or sign, of the slope.

Our 'balanced diet' concentrated on the balanced intake of carbohydrates and proteins. Increased consumption of food (in the dinner set M) required a simultaneous *increase* in both variables. It is the fact that the consumption of both bread and eggs had to be increased in order to maintain a balanced diet that forced on us the interpretation whereby 1/2 an egg and 1 slice of bread are equivalent in some way. Equivalence here is an expression of **dependency**. Whether we stay on our balanced diet when we increase the consumption of one good *depends* on an equivalent increase in the consumption of the other.

We say that a line has a positive slope whenever the signs of both changes are the same. Here, staying within the boundaries of a balanced diet meant an increase in both X and Y. As $dx > 0$ and $dy > 0$,

$$\frac{dY}{dX} > 0.$$

If instead, we thought of 'balanced diet' in terms of calories, the picture would be different. Let X and Y represent the same variables (that is, slices of bread and eggs, respectively) and suppose that there are 50 kilocalories in a slice of bread and 80 kilocalories in an egg. Suppose also that a 'healthy diet' means a meal of 400 kilocalories. This is not the same as a balanced diet: this time we are going to set a 'constraint' of a maximum of 400 kilocalories in total. The set H of healthy meals will be a subset of our original 'dinner' set D. Remember that we defined D like this:

$$D = \{(X, Y)|X \in \mathbb{Q} \wedge Y \in \mathbb{Q}\}.$$

Constraints

The new 'healthy meal' set obviously contains positive amounts of food and is confined to the positive quadrant. However, it now has an additional constraint, since the amount of calories derived from the consumption of bread (50 kilocalories per slice times the number of slices, namely, $50X$), and that derived from consuming eggs ($80Y$), should not exceed 400:

$$H = \{(X, Y)|(X, Y) \in D : 50X + 80Y \leq 400\}.$$

In words, the set of healthy meals contains all combinations of slices of bread and eggs which are in the dinner set (i.e. the positive values of X and Y), provided that the sum of their calories does not exceed 400.

Let us examine first where the constraint is binding. We want to find the points where the number of calories allowed has been exhausted. That is, to find the combinations of X and Y for which

$$50X + 80Y = 400.$$

We are trying to find a rule which will describe the combinations of X and Y for which we consumed the entire quantity of calories which is allowed. The way we have written the constraint automatically reminds us of the idea of a **function**. But this is a very strange function. To turn it into something more familiar, we simply rearrange it:

$$50X + 80Y = 400$$

take $50X$ from both sides

$$80Y = 400 - 50X$$

divide both sides by 80

$$Y = f(X) = 5 - \frac{5}{8}X.$$

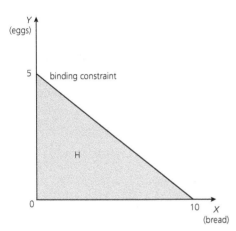

Figure 8 A constraint.

To draw the function, we must know at least two of the following three things: the intercept with the X-axis, the intercept with the Y-axis and the slope. The **intercept** with the X-axis denotes the value of X when $Y = 0$, and the intercept with the Y-axis denotes the value of Y when $X = 0$. It is easy to establish that if $X = 0$, $Y = 5$ (0,5) and that the slope of this function is $-(5/8)$. Note that this is a negative number. Before coming back to the slope let us first draw the line using the two intercepts. We know that (0,5) is one point on the graph. We can also easily establish the value of X when $Y = 0$:

$$Y = 5 - \frac{5}{8}X$$

set $Y = 0$

$$0 = 5 - \frac{5}{8}$$

$$-\frac{5}{8}X = -5$$

$$X = 8$$

What, then, is the slope of the *healthy diet constraint*? Since the healthy diet constraint is a straight line, the slope can easily be deduced from the tangent of the angle β in Figure 8, which is clearly $-5/8$.

Suppose that we increase the consumption of bread by 1 slice ($dX = 1$). This means that we have added 50 calories to our consumption. To remain on a healthy diet, we must *reduce* the consumption of eggs (Y). Given that each egg has 80 calories, we will need to reduce this consumption by 5/8 of an egg. If we change $X(dX)$, we change the value of Y by the coefficient in front of X. In the above equation it is $-(5/8)$:

$$Y = f(X) = 5 - \frac{5}{8}X$$

$$dY = -\frac{5}{8}dX$$

Hence,

$$\frac{dY}{dX} = -\frac{5}{8}.$$

Once again, in economics we must think of the meaning of these concepts. Here, the sign of the slope is negative. This means that the equivalence scale suggests **substitution**. If we want more of one good (bread) we must give up some of the other good (eggs) so that we stay within the constraint of the healthy diet. In our case, the slope means that we must give up 5/8 of an egg (Y) for every extra slice of bread (X).

One could say that the 'health' price of a slice of bread is 5/8 of an egg!

Self-assessment

Before leaving this chapter, check that you can define the following correctly, and give an example of the appropriate form:

1. description of a set (for example, your immediate family: parents, brothers and sisters)
2. enumeration of a set (using the same example)
3. natural numbers
4. integers
5. rational numbers
6. a plane
7. X, Y coordinates
8. a slope
9. a function
10. a binding constraint.

EPILOGUE

By now you must be exhausted. If you worked your way through this book properly, you should be in a position where you not only understand the fundamentals of economic analysis but you can also relate them to problems in the real world. You should have tasted the power of economics as a conceptual framework within which many social issues could be discussed but you must have also recognized its limitation. Evidently, to fully appreciate the significance of economic analysis to the real world and to questions of social and economic organization one must reexamine the main conclusions from this study in the light of uncertainty, strategic behaviour and the spread of information. These are normally the subject matter of intermediate studies.

The purpose of this book was to introduce you to the language of economic analysis and I hope that you have gained enough confidence to be able to articulate the underlying principles which govern the economic perspective on social organization. Equally, however, I hope that I have made you sufficiently aware of the fact that economics is a social discipline although this may not yet have been appropriately reflected in the tools of analysis which you have come across. Indeed, as I said above, you must further refine these tools to take into account the more realistic scene economists confront but you may also wish to think whether these tools may need further refinements in terms of the social context within which the economic system operates.

I have tried to introduce you to the core elements of economic investigation without pretending that it is either all encompassing or even empirically true. The social scene is very complex and does not lend itself easily to generalization. Whether or not it can be meaningfully isolated as a separate subject of investigation has been a source of great controversies over many years. In the past, many fields of human inquiry were part of the general study of philosophy. As knowledge accumulated, many fields of study developed their own agenda, methodology and technique to become independent. People would like to think that the same has happened in economics. The popular view is that Adam Smith marks the birth of the independent discipline called economics. It is so mainly because he published a book—the *Wealth of Nations*—which seemed to be entirely devoted to economic analysis. However, this is a serious misinterpretation of the history of economics. First of all, in terms of methods, there was nothing unique about the method Smith used to analyse economics. He used the same method in his examination of moral sentiments and their role in the process of socialization and the emergence of social norms. Secondly, Adam Smith was quite explicit about the significance of other areas of social studies to the understanding of economics. Irrespective of whether Smith's theory was right or wrong, it is impossible to understand it outside the context of his writings on ethics and jurisprudence. Later, at the height of the classical era, John Stuart Mill contemplated at length the logic of the independent study of economics. While he was sure that from a methodological point of view this is quite reasonable, he was also convinced that the dynamics of the subject is such that it cannot be understood outside the broader context of social examination.

There can be little doubt about the success of economics in developing a language with which a whole host of social issues could be discussed. However, some interpret this success as a great scientific achievement. Namely, they believe that economics has been successful in capturing and understanding the social world to a degree in which we could both explain it and form predictions about it. I am sure that to some extent this may indeed be true. But in any case, this would be very limited and narrow.

The apparent success of economics has driven other social disciplines to adopt many principles of economic investigation. This provoked others to accuse economics of imperialism. There is, of course, some truth in it as economists have recently begun to write papers on politics, international relations and history. I am sure that there is more to these subjects than the re-naming of actors or re-labelling of axes.

Still, I believe, it is not such a bad idea for other social sciences to adopt the discipline of economics—literally speaking—in the sense of properly developing a logically coherent language in order to study any area within the social science. However, it would have been perhaps better if other disciplines helped in better developing the language of economics so as to better capture the complex social environment within which we all live.

■ INDEX